Macroeconometric Modeling of Japan

ECONOMETRICS IN THE INFORMATION AGE: THEORY AND PRACTICE OF MEASUREMENT

Series Editors: Lawrence R Klein *(Univ. of Pennsylvania)*
Kanta Marwah *(Carleton Univ.)*

ISSN: 2010-1236

Published

Vol. 1 Selected Papers of Lawrence R Klein: Theoretical Reflections and Econometric Applications
edited by Kanta Marwah

Vol. 2 Interregional Input-output Analysis of the Chinese Economy
edited by Shinichi Ichimura & Hui-Jiong Wang

Vol. 3 Econometric Modeling of China
edited by Lawrence R Klein & Shinichi Ichimura

Vol. 4 Macroeconometric Modeling of Japan
edited by Shinichi Ichimura & Lawrence R Klein

Econometrics in the Information Age:
Theory and Practice of Measurement – Vol. 4

Series Editors: Lawrence Klein & Kanta Marwah

MACROECONOMETRIC MODELING OF JAPAN

Editors

Shinichi Ichimura
Kyoto University

Lawrence R. Klein
University of Pennsylvania, USA

World Scientific

NEW JERSEY • LONDON • SINGAPORE • BEIJING • SHANGHAI • HONG KONG • TAIPEI • CHENNAI

Published by

World Scientific Publishing Co. Pte. Ltd.
5 Toh Tuck Link, Singapore 596224
USA office: 27 Warren Street, Suite 401-402, Hackensack, NJ 07601
UK office: 57 Shelton Street, Covent Garden, London WC2H 9HE

British Library Cataloguing-in-Publication Data
A catalogue record for this book is available from the British Library.

MACROECONOMETRIC MODELING OF JAPAN
Econometrics in the Information Age: Theory and Practice of Measurement — Vol. 4

ISBN-13 978-981-283-461-4
ISBN-10 981-283-461-3

Typeset by Stallion Press
Email: enquiries@stallionpress.com

Printed in Singapore by B & Jo Enterprise Pte Ltd

Preface

This book is a collection of macroeconometric models and analyses of the Japanese economy in the broad sense. Macroeconometric models are interpreted to include not only the standard econometric models developed by L. R. Klein and his followers but also other simpler social accounting approaches, Leontief's Input-Output analyses, CGE models or various types of quantitative analyses. They are not mutually exclusive methods but may be used appropriately in combination for various problems. This book purports to be a useful guide for the quantitative studies of the development of the Japanese economy from her emergence as a modern state up to the present time, as well as the policy implications associated with extrapolation of the course of the contemporary Japanese economy into the future.

The progress of econometric methods, the cumulating experiences of model-building, and the technical progress in computers and software have been so remarkable since the post-World War II years that one may be amazed not only by the past achievements of macroeconometric studies in Japan and other countries but also by the future expectation of great contributions to human welfare.

In recent years, however, trust in macroeconometric studies seems to have declined in the private and the public sectors. This worrisome issue may have been due to the careless formality in the applications of routine methods to complicated real economic issues on the part of many econometricians. Simple applications of routine or established models and methods cannot substitute the careful observations of reality and efforts to find new approaches to achieve better analyses. But failures are the start of successes. This critical time of the world crisis in 2008 to 2009 may be a good time to reflect upon the macroeconometric models and analyses of the Japanese or the US as well as the European economies.

In selecting the models in this book, we have relied first of all on several excellent surveys and readings of Japanese econometric models that have been published. They are all carefully surveyed in the Introduction of this book: A Historic Survey of Macroeconometric Models in Japan. In particular, Kazuo Sato's survey: "Econometric Models of the Japanese Economy" in *A History of Macroeconometric Model-Building*, edited by Ronald G. Bodkin, L. R. Klein, and Kanta Marwah, 1991 covers ordinary econometric models up to 1988 very well. Secondly, as for the models missed by Sato and the works after 1988, we relied heavily on the advices of many old and young friends. Though it is impossible to list them all, we must express our deep gratitude for the generous help given by Professors Takahiro Akita, Akihiro Amano, Kanemi Ban, Hidekazu Eguchi, Michio Hatanaka, Yoshihisa Inada, Satoshi Inomata, Masahiro Kuroda, Chikashi Moriguchi, Etsuo Oizumi, Hiroshi Sadamichi, Mitsuo Saito, Shuntaro Shishido, and many others.

We dedicate this volume to Sonia and Yukiko as a token of our gratitude with nice memories from over half a century.

May 27, 2009

Lawrence R. Klein
Professor Emeritus
University of Pennsylvania

Shinichi Ichimura
Professor Emeritus
Kyoto University

Honorary Counselor
ICSEAD

List of Editors and Authors

Editors

Lawrence R. Klein
Professor Emeritus, University of Pennsylvania
Nobel Laureate
lrk@ssc.upenn.edu

Shinichi Ichimura
Professor Emeritus, Kyoto University
Honorary Counselor, ICSEAD
s-ichimura@mub.biglobe.ne.jp

Authors

(Chapter 1)
Shinichi Ichimura
Afore-mentioned

(Chapter 2)
Hyun Suk
Institute for Monetary and Economic Research
Bank of Korea, Korea
hyun@bok.or.kr

(Chapter 3)
Yuji Shimanaka
Chief Economist, Business Cycle Research
Councilor, Mitsubishi UFJ Securities
Guest Professor, Waseda University
shimanaka-jyuuji@sc.mufg.jp

Tatsushi Shikano
Senior Economist, Business Cycle Research
Mitsubishi UFJ Securities
Shikano-tatsushi@sc.mufg.jp

(Chapter 4)
Masahiro Tatemoto (1924–1997)
Professor Emeritus, Osaka University

Shinichi Ichimura
Afore-mentioned

(Chapter 5)
Takahiro Akita
Professor, International University of Japan
akita@iuj.ac.jp

(Chapter 6)
Mitsuo Ezaki
Professor Emeritus, Nagoya University
Professor, Faculty of Economics
Oita University
ezaki@gsid.nagoya-u.ac.jp

Shoichi Ito
Professor, Kwansei Gakuin University
sito@kwansei.ac.jp

(Chapter 7)
Kazuhisa Tsujimura
Professor, Faculty of Economics
Keio University
sito@kwansei.ac.jp

Masako Tsujimura
Research Economist, Keio Economic Observatory
Keio University

(Chapter 8)
Lawrence R. Klein
Afore-mentioned

(Chapter 9)
Lawrence R. Klein
Afore-mentioned

Yoichi Shinkai
Professor Emeritus, Osaka University

(Chapter 10)
Lawrence R. Klein and Shinichi Ichimura
Afore-mentioned

Susumu Koizumi
Professor Emeritus, Osaka University

Kazuo Sato (1927–2004)
Professor, Faculty of Economics
Rutgers University

(Chapter 11)
Kanemi Ban
Professor, Faculty of Economics
Osaka University
ban@econ.osaka-u.ac.jp

(Chapter 12)
Mitsuo Saito
Professor Emeritus, Kobe University
mitsuosaito@mtd.biglobe.ne.jp

(Chapter 13)
Yoshihisa Inada
Professor, Konan University
inada@konan-u.ac.jp

(Chapter 14)
Shuntaro Shishido
Professor Emeritus, Tsukuba University
International University of Japan
Director of Research Institute of Econometric
World Modeling and Analysis (RIEWMA)
Mq9eTie1@aol.com

Akira Kawakami
Chief Technical Official, University of Tsukuba

Kiyoshi Tamashiro
Director, Tamashiro Research Institute

Contents

List of Tables and Figures

Introduction: A Historic Survery of Macroeconometric Models in Japan

Part I. Social Accounting and Survey Analysis

Chapter 1: Factors for Rapid Growth of the Japanese Economy: A Social Accounting Approach

Chapter 2: Social Accounting Analysis of Japan's Lost 90s

Chapter 3: Business Indexes and Survey Data for Forecast

Part II. Input Output Analyses and CGE Models

Chapter 4: Factor Proportions and Foreign Trade: The Case of Japan

Chapter 5: Interregional Interdependence and Regional Economic Growth in Japan

Chapter 6: The Flying-Geese Pattern of East Asian Development: A Computable General Equilibrium Approach

Chapter 10: OSAKA ISER Model

Chapter 11: The Japan Model for World Project LINK

Chapter 12: The Saito Model of the Japanese Economy

Chapter 13: High Frequency Model vs. Consensus Forecast

Chapter 14: Policy Alternatives for Japan Toward 2020

Introduction

A Historic Survey of Macroeconometric Models in Japan

Shinichi Ichimura

1. Available Statistics in Japan

1.1. *Rich historic statistics*

Japan has very rich statistical data historically as well as now. Before emerging as a modern state in 1868, she had many reliable statistical data such that various economic activities could be traced back at least to the 16th century. Suffice it to show three examples. (1) In 1582–1591 the acreage and productivity of cultivated land were estimated almost nationwide by *Taiko Kenchi* (land-surveying by Toyotomi, Hideyoshi) by standardized measures and methods, and ever since then.[1] (2) Her foreign trade statistics with the Netherlands, China and Korea since the 16th century have been recorded, including the Edo period (1603–1867) when the country was closed to migration and trade, except for trade with those three countries.[2] (3) Wages and prices are known almost throughout the Edo period.[3]

1.2. *Long term economic statistics*

This archive-minded tradition was carried over to the new government in the Meiji era (1868–1912). It produced and kept many statistical data, covering prices, wages, various industries' amounts of production, consumption, foreign trade figures *etc*. These sources made it possible for the

---

[1] See Naotaro Sekiyama (1952), Hiroshi Kito (2000). They go back to the 8th century or even earlier. Data became more reliable in the mid-Edo period. On *Taiko Kenichi*, see Mitsuru Miyagawa (1957–1963).

[2] As for Japan-Netherlands trade, see Yoko Nagazumi (1987) and Yasuko Suzuki (2004).

[3] Nobuo Koyanagitsu (2006).

Hitotsubashi University group to produce the long-term economic statistics from about 1875 to 1940 in an impressive 14-volume *Japanese Long-Term Economic Statistics*, edited by Kazushi Ohkawa, Miyohei Shinohara and Mataji Umemura, Toyokeizai Shimpo-sha, 1965–1985.[4]

The Bureau of Statistics, Ministry of General Affairs, produces the post-World War II data for the long-term. These data are linked to the Hitotsubashi series and compiled as the continuous series. They are available in the home page of the Bureau of Statistics. They cover the main items in the areas: 1. Land, 2. Population, 3. Economy, 4. Society, 5. Culture. Economic statistics for the period from 1868 to 2002 include:

1. GDP statistics (personal consumption, wages, housing statistics, fixed investment, mining and manufacturing productions, their indices, tertiary industrial activities),
2. Enterprise statistics (enterprises' profits, employment, population, working hours),
3. Prices,
4. Exports and Imports,
5. Balance of payments,
6. Money and banking.

   They are annually updated and made available.

On these bases the two leading economists at Hitotsubashi University: Kazushi Ohkawa, and Miyohei Shinohara published and edited with many others[5] a number of books and articles. The representative ones are listed below.[6]

1.3. *Japanese national income statistics*

The national income statistics were the core of those long-term economic statistics (often abbreviated as LTES). Long before then, however, even earlier than the works of Richard Stone and Simon Kuznets established the conception of national income and its social accounting, some economists in pre-war Japan tried to estimate the Japanese incomes and national product.

---

[4]They are presented in Japanese but the statistical tables have English terms.

[5]Their contributions were very significant too: Tsuyoshi Noda, Koichi Emi, Hiromitsu Ishi.

[6]Ohkawa-Rosowsky (1973); Ohkawa-Shinohara-Meissner (1979); Ohkawa-Ranis-Meissner (1985). Among many important contributions of M. Shinohara only two are quoted: one mainly for the pre-war development, and another for post-war development. Shinohara (1982, 1994).

In 1933, Shigemi Hijikata (U. of Tokyo) estimated the Japanese national incomes from 1900 to 1930. In the next year, the government Bureau of Statistics officially estimated and published the Japanese National Income for 1925.[7] This work was extended backward to 1887 and forward to 1928. Even during World War II, the Ministry of Finance estimated the National Income for 1939 and extended it backward to 1919.

International interest in the Japanese national income statistics increased, and some economists like Colin Clark began estimating it himself. However, the national income widely used abroad then was the one presented by Kazuki Mori at the International Statistical Conference held in Tokyo in 1930. It was the preliminary figure of the Cabinet Bureau of Statistics mentioned above.

Immediately before World War II, it was mainly Richard Stone who established the solid accounting system of national income. Post-war Japanese scholars and government statistical offices quickly adopted that system of national income accounts.[8] In 1952, they began supplying annually the solid national economic calculation report as an official work by the Institute of Economic Research (IEP) at the Economic Planning Agency (EPA). After 2001, the National Income Division, the Economic and Social Research Institute (ESRI) at the Cabinet Office took over this work.

Government statistical offices have maintained other ordinary statistics listed in connection with LTES above with occasional revisions and offered very rich sources of data even for compiling the input-output table for the year of 1951. *The Japan Statistical Yearbook* publishes annually almost all important statistics, but there are many other statistical data published by the statistical bureaus of many ministries and prefecture governments. Particularly for manufacturing industries, *the Census of Manufacturers* is conducted every year. No other advanced economies conduct it annually. Japan had the *Industrial Census* even before the war. *The Census of Commerce* has been conducted every three years since 1950, every five years after 1997.

1.4. *Interindustrial relations tables*

The first Japanese Interindustrial Relations Table (IO Table) was produced for the year of 1951 with the cooperation of various government statistical agencies around the Department of Research and Statistics, Ministry of

[7] Shigemi Hijikata (1933); Cabinet Bureau of Statistics (1934).

[8] A pioneering but somewhat deficient estimate of national income was provided by Yuzo Yamada (1951).

Trade and Industry (MITI) with some advice of S. Ichimura. The estimation methods followed closely to the ones used for the production of the US Table for 1947, but with many original devices.[9] The outcome was more detailed and reliable. The voluminous MITI report (1957) gave the methods and findings of the Japanese experiences in detail.[10] As soon as the table was completed, Ichimura (1957): *The Structure of the Japanese Economy* applied it to the analysis of the issues facing Japan then — dilemma between unemployment and unfavorable balance of trade.[11]

Soon it became fashionable to produce the IO table in each prefecture. It spread fast all over the country, and soon all 47 prefectures had their own prefecture IO tables.[12] Some go as far as to produce an interregional table within each prefecture and use it for regional designing for the prefecture. In 1958, the first 1951 interregional IO table for the *Kinki* Region and the rest of Japan was produced by Kansai Economic Federation's secretariat under the guidance of S. Ichimura, using the data of each prefecture in the *Kinki region*.[13] Soon it spread to other regions as well as to the central government. They integrated these regional IO tables to produce the Interregional IO Table, dividing Japan into several regions. Soon the MITI began producing the Interregional and Interindustrial Relations Table for nine regions every five years. Akita (1994) uses them for Interregional Analysis of the Japanese economy.

Thus, Japan became a paradise for IO specialists. The news spread worldwide and attracted the attention of statisticians in other Asian countries. The Philippines was the first to have taken up the project of producing its own IO table and then Indonesia.[14] Just when other countries

---

[9]During the WWII the Japanese government made use of partial input-output relations table for economic control. The experiences were used to fill in some input-output relations. Practical difficulties had to be overcome by young statisticians like Yoshizo Tonoki, Etsuo Oizumi, Kiyoshi Kamoshita and others.

[10]MITI (ed.) (1957) contains the methods and sources to construct the IO Table for 1951 and simple applications. In this project the key person was Nagase Shinetsu, director of Research and Statistics Department.

[11]Ichimura (1960) applied the table for predictive purposes by endogenizing household consumption.

[12]Ministry of General Affairs (2000).

[13]Secretariat of Kansai Economic Federation (1960). The interregionl tables were available in English, too.

[14]Bantegi, head of Statistical Bureau in Manila, asked Ichimura to train his staff to compile IO tables and produced the first IO table in 1967. In Indonesia, Takao Kaneko produced in 1972 the first preliminary IO table for 1969 for LEKNAS-Kyoto U. Project by using the Philippine input coefficients.

were about to follow, the Institute of Developing Economies (IDE) in Japan stepped into this area. A little earlier, R. J. Wonnacott had constructed an international IO table for Canada and the US in 1964. IDE was attracted by a proposal of T. Watanabe to use international IO models for the North-South issues and during 1965 to 1971 tried to compile some international IO tables covering six regions (North America, Europe, Oceania, Latin America, Asia and Japan) or ten Asian countries. These experimental attempts gave the staff good opportunities to evaluate the reliability of statistical materials in those developing countries. In 1973, IDE launched a proper project to compile a comprehensive international IO table among East and Southeast Asian countries *plus* the US. They began the work by sending some experts to the countries like Indonesia, Thailand and Singapore, which had no reliable IO tables, to construct them and also to study the bilateral trade relations in IO tables with the countries which already had the national IO tables. The IDE experts, in collaboration with national statistical offices and research institutes, completed three national IO tables (Indonesia for 1971, Singapore for 1973, and Thailand for 1975) and three bilateral IO tables for 1970 (Korea-Japan, the US-Japan, and the Philippines-Japan). This laid the foundation of their subsequent works.

In 1978, IDE re-started the project to construct the 1975 multilateral IO table among ASEAN countries, Japan, Korea and the US. First, existing tables had to be updated to the year 1975 for Malaysia, the Philippines, Singapore, and the US. Second, the 1975 bilateral IO tables were constructed for Indonesia-Japan, Thailand-Japan, and for Korea-Japan. Third, they were linked together as a single multilateral IO table. It was completed in 1983 and became the prototype of the subsequent projects. After 1988 the major task was to include China and some Asia-Pacific countries. Thus, the 1985 multilateral table covered both China and Taiwan. Since then, IDE has successfully completed the multilateral tables for every five years.[15] The latest development is the release of "Transnational Interregional IO Table between China and Japan 2000", which linked the interregional table of China and that of Japan to present cross-border transactions on a region-to-region basis.[16] The tables available now are listed in Table 1, together with Table 2 which gives a list of World Trade Matrices including important trade partners of Japan.

---

[15]S. Inomata and H. Kuwamori (2008).

[16]The 2005 Asian International IO Table, and the 2005 BRICs International IO Table will be published soon. This is the first international IO table incorporating the BRICs (Brazil, Russia, India, China) with the major three: the US, Japan and the EU.

Table 1. IDE Input-Output Tables.

A: National Input-Output Tables		B. International IO Tables	
Country	**Years**	**Countries**	**Years**
Indonesia	1971, 75, 85, 90	Japan-Korea	1970, 75, 85, 90
Singapore	1972, 75, 85, 90	Japan-Philippines	1970, 85, 90
Thailand, basic	1975	Japan-USA	1970
Thailand, analytical	1975	Japan-Indonesia	1975, 85, 90
Malaysia, peninsula	1975, 85, 90	Japan-Thailand	1975, 85, 90
The Philippines	1975, 90	ASEAN	1975
China	1985, 90, (2000)	Japan-China	1985, 90
Taiwan	1985, (90), 90	Japan-Singapore	1985, 90
		Japan-Malaysia	1985, 90
USA	(1975), (05)	Japan-Taiwan	1985, 90
Multi-regional for China	2000	Asian	1985, 90, 95
		Asian (I: notes, II data)	2000, 05
		Transna'l & Interre'l China-Japan*	2000
		BRICs (I: notes, II data)	2005

*Those in ( ) are updated ones.
**IO between regions in China and regions in Japan are recorded.
Note: Most tables are available from: (English) http://www.ide.go.jp/English/Publish/Books/Sds/material.html, (Japanese) http://www.ide.go.jp/Japanese/Publish/Books/Tokei/material.html.

Table 2. IDE Trade Matrix List.

1. World Trade Matrix, 1964 — Total Value of All Commodities
2. World Trade Matrix, 1966 — Total Value of All Commodities
3. World Trade Matrix, 1968 — Total Value of All Commodities
4. World Trade Matrix, 1964–1976
5. International Trade Matrix for Asia and Pacific Region, by Industry: 1965–1983
6. International Trade Matrix for USSR and Eastern Europe: 1980–1984
7. International Trade Matrix for Asia-Pacific Region by Industrial Group, 1975–1992: I: Export; II: Import; III: Analytical Tables
8. World Trade Matrix: By Asian International Input-Output Table 24 Sectors
9. Trade Matrix for Asia-Pacific Region, 2000

1.5. *Survey data*

Similarly to other major industrialized countries, Japan has been using various business indexes and survey data for the purpose of capturing and forecasting economic trends. The *Diffusion Index* (DI), the *Consumer*

Confidence Survey, the Bank of Japan (BOJ) *Short-Term Economic Survey on Enterprises* (abbreviated as *Tankan*) as well as the Nikkei Index at the stock market are widely reported in the newspapers and used for forecasting business trends. There have been few comparative studies, however, on the relationship between these survey findings and the other short-term forecasts using econometric models. Shimanaka-Shikano (2010): "Business Indexes and Survey Data for Forecast" is a new contribution to Ichimura-Klein (2010) and gives an exposition of availability and the use of those indices for forecast.

1.6. *Flow of funds table*

The last important source of data for macroeconometric modeling is the statistics of financial activities. Availability of the *Flow of Funds Tables* and the *Assets and Liabilities Tables a la* IMF format shows the quality and the standard of various financial statistics in Japan. They are prepared by the BOJ and are very reliable. Tsujimura (2003) gives an exposition and use of those tables for modeling. It is adopted as "A Flow-of-Funds Analysis of Quantitative Monetary Policy" in Ichimura-Klein (2010).

2. Social Accounting Approaches and Use of Survey Data

2.1. *Great ratios in national income accounts*

The first economic survey of the Japanese economy was issued in 1947. Since then, the government has published the survey annually, up to the present time. It is popularly called the *Economic White Paper* and has been a best seller, since it has been regarded as the government economists' best analysis of the current conditions of the Japanese economy. Its concise quantitative analysis has almost been a textbook for university students and businessmen. Its standard style has settled: first to rely on the national income accounts for macroeconomic analysis of the national economy and then dig into the problems of the sectors where some urgent issues have arose. The White Paper improved in quality year after year and offered the major topics for policy discussions among government, business and academic circles.

The most straightforward way to use the national income accounts was suggested by Klein-Kosobud (1961); as *great ratios*: saving ratio, capital-output ratio (or incremental capital output ratio), and money to real GDP ratio in combination with some information of labor force and population. The Japanese Economic Survey has not strictly followed any specific conceptual framework but adopted more or less the similar social accounting formats and combined them with sectoral or industrial analyses. As examples of such social accounting approaches, Ichimura-Klein (2010) adopted two articles: (1) Ichimura (1968): "Rapid Growth of the Japanese Economy — A Social Accounting Approach for the Early Reconstruction Stage of the Japanese Economy", and (2) Hyun Suk (2010): "Social Accounting Analysis of Japan's Lost 90s" for its mature stage. Ichimura tries to identify the specific factors of rapid recovery and development by subdividing the Japanese economy into several industrial sectors and large and small scale enterprises with careful attention to technological changes. Suk tries to see if the over-all general or formal approach can depict some characteristics of the lost 1990s without any specific hypotheses. Interpretation of the Japanese economy in the 1990s, however, requires a deeper understanding of the financial sectors so that Tsujimura (2003) mentioned above must be considered.[17]

2.2. *Identification of post-war Japanese business cycles*

The Japanese government has regarded the business cycles as an important factor for policy decisions and identified mainly with reference to the Diffusion Index published by the EPA (or ESRI after 2002). As the knowledge of post-war business circles is needed for understanding the discussions on the Japanese economy, the government's identification of business cycles is reproduced as Table 3.[18] Shimanaka-Shikano (2010) explains how the phases of cycles are identified and interpreted according to Burns-Mitchell or Schumpeter.

3. Input-Output Analysis and CGE Models

3.1. *Structural analysis with IO tables*

Since the first application of Ichimura (1957) already quoted, there have been mushrooming studies of interindustrial analyses. The earliest noteworthy one was the application of the first IO table and some supplementary

[17] As for the arguments on the lost 1990s, the most comprehensive is Fumio Hayashi (2008).
[18] Among academic economists, Shozaburo Fujino (Hitotsubashi U.) was known as a pioneer of business cycle studies (Fujino, 1965). Fujino (2008) examines the cycles before the Meiji reform on scanty data.

Table 3. Reference Business Cycles in the Japanese Economy, 1951–2008.

No.	Trough	Peak	Trough	Boom	Recession
1		1951/6	1951/10	Special Procurement boom	
2	1951/10	1954/1	1954/11	Investment boom	
3	1954/11	1957/6	1958/6	"Jinmu" boom	Flat pan recession
4	1958/6	1961/12	1962/10	"Iwato" boom	
5	1962/10	1964/10	1965/10	Olympic boom	Security slump
6	1965/10	1970/7	1971/12	"Izanagi" boom	Nixon slump
7	1971/12	1973/11	1975/3	Archipelago reform boom	First oil crisis
8	1975/3	1977/1	1977/10		Mini recession (Yen revalued)
9	1977/10	1980/2	1983/2		Global recession (second oil crisis)
10	1983/2	1985/6	1986/11	High-Tech boom	Yen revaluation recession
11	1986/11	1991/2	1993/10	Bubble boom	First Heisei recession
12	1993/10	1997/5	1999/1	Camphor boom	Second Heisei recession
13	1999/1	2000/11	2002/2	IT bubble	Third Heisei deflationary recession
14	2002/2	2007/10	2008/10	"Izanami" boom	
15	2008/10			Global financial crisis	

Notes: Jinmu is the name of the first emperor in Japanese history. "Jinmu" boom means the unprecedented boom since Jinmu's reign. Similarly for Iwato (an event in Japanese myth times), Izanagi (a mythical male figure) and Izanami (a mythical female figure). Heisei is the yearly calendar for the present emperor.

data of sectoral capital coefficients to the so-called Leontief Paradox: Tatemoto-Ichimura (1959): "Factor Proportions and Foreign Trade — the case of Japan", *The Review of Economics and Statistics,* which is in Ichimura-Klein (2010). The second important contribution was Chenery-Watanabe-Shishido (1962): "The Patterns of Japanese Growth, 1914–1954". By constructing even the pre-war IO tables, they proposed the way of identifying the factors for economic growth with changes of final demand, technology and industrial composition.[19] T. Watanabe pursued the applications to economic policy-making and compiled his publications

[19]This work had a significant impact on the studies at the World Bank in analyzing the factors of growth for developing countries when H. Chenery was its Vice President.

in Watanabe (1970).[20] S. Shishido made a significant contribution in the historical and prospective analyses of industrial composition and technical progress in the Japanese economy. Only three works among many are quoted below.[21] There are many other applications of various kinds by many authors. In 1999 those economists as well as business and government circles organized the Pan-Asian and Pacific Association for Input-Output Studies (PAPAIOS[22]) and published the organ quarterly, three times in Japanese and once in English (*Journal of Applied Input-Output Studies*). A list of articles published in them includes the main works in the field, though contributions elsewhere are also important.

3.2. *Applications to regional analyses and CGE models*

Most applications of IO analysis in Japan have been to regional analyses, especially within a prefecture or some sub-national region. As Section 1.4 mentioned, the MITI has produced the nation-wide interregional IO tables every five years since 1960. Their practical applications are, however, very rare, such that Akita (1994) is precious. Section 1.4 also referred to the IO tables of other Asian economies. The IDE helped them and completed International IO tables. On those bases IDE attempted to analyze the international, interindustrial or interregional linkages. A list of important works are given in Inomata-Kuwamori (2008).

Another application of IO tables is constructing computable general equilibrium (CGE) models. IO analysis itself is the simplest CGE model.[23] When the statistical data are scanty or just for one or a few years, it is an unavoidable choice. Sometimes it is useful for analysis of taxation or environmental issues. In Japan Ezaki (1986): "A Computable General Equilibrium Model of the Japanese Economy", *Kobe Economic and Business Review* was perhaps a forerunner in this field. Then followed some works by others. Ezaki-Ito (1995): "A CGE Model of Flying Geese Pattern of

[20] It contains some important contributions of his IO analyses. For example, Chapters II. The Pattern of Japanese Industrialization; IV. Technical Progress and Economic Growth; VIII. Stabilization Policies and Business Cycles. His concern was also an international comparison of IO analyses.

[21] Shishido (1990); Shishido (1991); Shishido, with Kiyo Harada and Yuh Matsumura (1991). Shishido's contribution to macroeconometric models incorporating IO tables are quoted in Section 4.

[22] Its home page: http://www.sanken.keio.ac.jp/papaios/index-jp.html.

[23] A useful up-to-date collection of papers in the field of applications of CGE models to regional analyses is Masaru Doi (ed.) (2006). It gives a useful list of past works as well.

Development in East Asia", is a precious piece combining Japanese and Asian IO tables to analyze the development pattern among Japan, Asian NIEs and Southeast Asian countries in succession. That is why it is accepted in Ichimura-Klein (2010).

3.3. *Flow of funds tables and its applications*

IO tables are concerned primarily with the transactions of goods and services. Some CGE models cover financial or monetary transactions but not very extensively. The Flow of Funds (FOF) accounts, however, systematically compile the financial transactions and the financial assets and liabilities. Tsujimura (2003)[24] presented the procedure to produce the Asset-Liability-Matrix (ALM) from the FOF accounts, so as to be able to use the tools and experiences of IO analysis. It applied ALM to examine the quantitative monetary policy introduced by the BOJ in March 2001 and concluded that there was a tactical error in the BOJ's policies in money market operations. Thus, it proved to be a powerful device for such an examination. Tsujimura (2004) collected more articles applying the information of FOF tables, including an important contribution by Ogawa-Saito-Tokutsu (2004). Their paper integrated the FOF analysis with standard econometric models and methods.

4. Macroeconometric Models

4.1. *Kazuo Sato's survey and other readings of Japanese models*

The most comprehensive and relatively up-to-date excellent survey of Japanese macroeconometric models is K. Sato's "Econometric Models of the Japanese Economy", in Bodkin-Klein-Marwah (1991) and covers macroeconometric models up to 1988. Yet it missed some important works during the period. The reason was that although Sato read an outstanding survey of macroeconometric models: Saito-Moriguchi (1985), he missed three particularly important readings of econometric models[25]: Tatemoto-Ichimura (1970), Morishima-Murata-Nosse-Saito (1972), and

[24]Kazusuke Tsujimura and Masako Tsujimura compiled their contributions in their new book (2008).

[25]It is the best survey in Japanese of the models up to 1985, based on a questionnaire survey to the authors of major models. It comparatively examines the parameter values of main behavior equations and estimation methods for many models. Some parts are reproduced in Sato (1991).

Kosobud-Minami (1977) and also overlooked the valuable proceedings of an international conference at the BOJ: Ando-Eguchi-Farmer-Suzuki (1985). As a result many outstanding works were not on his list. They are listed in the references below. Tatemoto-Ichimura (1970) collected the 20 best models up to 1970. Morishima *et al.* (1972) collected some works around the important Saito model. Kosobud-Minami (1977) translated some models in Tatemaoto-Ichimura (1970) into English and assembled some more by selecting later excellent models. Ando *et al.* (1986): *Monetary Policies in Our Times* is a valuable record of the international conference at the BOJ mainly on the monetary policies against stagflation. It contains a model by Amano (1985) and discussions on monetarist *vs* Keynesian policies, including the empirical examination by Ando (1985).

Basically, I support Sato's observations,[26] identifying the three stages of development of model-building in Japan: first, learning in the late 1950s to the early 1960s; second, practice in the late 1960s, and third, maturation in the 1970s to the present. Pioneering groups were concentrated in Tokyo, Osaka-Kyoto, and Nagoya. Since the early 1960s, hundreds of econometric models have been constructed. Among them, we take up in this historic survey only the models of the Japanese economy as a whole. For instance, Kosobud-Minami (1977) selected 15 models in 5 parts: 1. consumption and investment, 2. production and factors of production, 3. market clearing and price formation, 4. international trade, 5. growth models. According to this classification, our historic survey covers only Parts 3 and 5.[27] Many outstanding sectoral models are not covered.

In Tokyo, T. Uchida, T. Watanabe, K. Mori and others tried to construct relatively small models first at the Tokyo Center for Economic Research

---

[26] Apart from model-building, I would add one critical note on his remarks about the state of modern economics in pre-war and war-time Japan. Sato underestimates the influence of J. M. Keynes' *General Theory* (1936) and J. R. Hicks, *Value and Capital* (1936) in Japan. During the war both books were re-printed in Japan and used as text-books for reading seminars in many universities. Although Marxian economics and German historical school were more influential in most universities, there were some outstanding economists who not only read them but also published outstanding original articles on the themes of the books before and even during the WW II. Examples are: Nisaburo Kito (Hitotsubashi University), Takuma Yasui (Tohoku University), Yasuma Takata, Masazo Sono, Hideo Aoyama (Kyoto University) and others.

[27] Similarly Sato (1991) took up only the national economy models, classifing them into 5 groups: 1. general equilibrium and projection model, 2. special purpose models, 3. internationally linked models, 4. short-term forecast models, 5. monetarist models. We do not classify them but similarly characterize each model.

(TCER). Soon some government economists like Shuntaro Shishido at the IER of the EPA joined. At Osaka University a group of economists like S. Ichimura, S. Koizumi, K. Sato, Y. Shinkai, and others at the Institute of Social and Economic Research (ISER) began to construct a large model in 1959 endeavoring under the guidance of L. R. Klein, depicting the characteristics of the developing Japanese economy. Soon, M. Saito and A. Amano joined.[28] Both groups began producing some practical models in the early 1960s.

4.2. *Long-term modeling and quantitative economic history*

While most economists in Osaka were working on data preparation and parts of a large econometric model, L. R. Klein spent part of his time with his colleagues to produce small long-term Japanese models by making use of the Hitotsubashi LTES. They were Klein (1961), Klein-Shinkai (1963), and Ueno (1961; 1963; 1968; 1977). The earliest by Klein covered the pre-war period only: 1878–1938, whereas Klein-Shinkai covered 1930–1950 — both in Ichimura-Klein (2010), and Ueno (1977) 1906–1968. All these models used the same LTES for pre-war period, so that their findings are comparable with the Hitotsubashi group's analyses. These are also comparable with the contributions by quantitative economic historians like Takafusa Nakamura.[29]

4.3. *Standard macroeconometric models in early stages*

As far as the macroeconometric models *a la* Klein-Goldberger (1955) are concerned, in the 1960s, the Tokyo group began producing a few practical models of medium size such as Uchida-Mori (1960), Uchida-Kuribayashi-Yajima-Watanabe (1966), and its peak was Tatemoto-Uchida-Watanabe (1967). In the late 1960s and the 1970s to the 1980s, the EPA Institute of Economic Research played an important role in producing excellent macroeconometric models themselves as well as mobilizing the best econometricians in Tokyo, Osaka-Kyoto and Nagoya. Examples are Shishido-Kohno-Nagaya-Tanaka (1968) and Shishido-Ichikawa-Noda-Furuya-Oshizaka-Nishi kawa (1970).

---

[28] Ueno participated in the group's seminar from Nagoya U. as a pioneering econometrician in Nagoya.

[29] Representative works are: Nakamura (1968); (1971), (1979, 3rd ed. 1993); (1985); (1995); and (2004).

In Osaka ISER, on the other hand, we independently worked on the construction of a large Japanese model comparable with the US Brookings Model,[30] primarily to depict the characteristics of Japanese economic growth at that stage. What we had in mind then were: (1) its high dependence on foreign trade, particularly imports of food and energy, (2) the dual structure of industries (large and small size enterprises), and (3) deliberate monetary policy to keep the interest rate low. We encountered two difficulties in conducting the work: first, the data problem, and second, computation limits.

First, we began constructing a model for the manufacturing sectors, subdividing them into five industries: Primary, Heavy, Light, Energy, and Tertiary Industries. Heavy and Light Industries were further divided into large and small sizes. This subdivision into large and small enterprises of production, labor, capital, and wages was most time-consuming and hard work. *The Census of Manufacturers* data made it possible to subdivide the enterprises, but *the Census of Commerce* was only available every five years so that the Tertiary Industry could not be subdivided. The demand side for the industrial output was based on the principles of effective demand for sectoral basis similar to input-output analysis. The production functions were used to determine the factor incomes and demand for labor. Export and import functions were divided more in details than the industrial sectors, and the demand for and the supply of money were analyzed, distinguishing cash and deposit money to trace the Bank of Japan's policies in determining its money supply and official discount rate of interest. This ISER model is adopted as a chapter in Ichimura-Klein (2010).

The second difficulty was the limitations in computer facilities. Not only in Japan, but also in the US in 1960 to 1961, the best IBM computers could provide the estimated results of behavior equations every three days or so due to the need of punching in the specification. This condition did not improve much at UC Berkeley and U of Pennsylvania even around 1965 to 1967 when I was working to complete and simulate the model. For example, the available computers could not solve a simultaneous system of about 500 non-linear (in variables) equations without linearization.[31] As

[30]In 1960–1961 when we were working on the ISER model in Osaka with L.R. Klein, we had no knowledge of the Brookings model being constructed in the US which was later published as Duesenberry *et al.* (1965).

[31]To overcome the difficulty, I had to linearize the variables at the point of last year of observations and obtain the coefficients of all the variables in the form of matrix about 500×500 to calculate its inverse matrix. Then the impact and other multipliers presented in ISER model book were obtained.

for the appropriate computer programs for large, multi-country models, see the Appendix.

Anyhow, the whole ISER model and its simulation were completed in 1967, and the findings were made available as discussion papers of Osaka University ISER and reported at the International Symposium in Novosibirisk in 1969. The entire results were not widely known, however, until a mimeographed monograph: *An Econometric Analysis of the Japanese Economy* (Ichimura-Klein-Koizumi-Sato, 1977) was distributed at the 1977 LINK meeting in Kyoto. This extensive model was simulated for fiscal expenditure, taxation and monetary policies, and its findings were compared with the results of a medium size Evans-Klein model in the US (Evans-Klein, 1968), because the Brookings model was not simulated for any policies. It was significant, therefore, that such a large ISER model proved to be workable with sufficient care.[32] This model would be still useful to see the characteristics of Japanese growth process in the early stage and to learn the way of building and simulating econometric models for developing countries.

4.4. *Models integrated with IO analysis and internationally linked*

Soon, however, the honeymoon period for model-builders in the late 1960s came to a sudden end in the early 1970s. Two major events in the world hit Japan as well: the first oil shock and the Nixon devaluation of US dollars accompanied by flexible exchange rates. These changes forced model-builders to reconsider the structure of their models in many aspects. Moreover, the National Income statistics of Japan were completely revised in the 1970s according to the UN Standard of National Accounts, and the revised time-series did not become available until early 1979. The 1970s were, therefore, a rather futile decade to build new models. Simultaneously, however, two favorable developments occurred for model-builders in the 1970s. One is that construction of IO tables and their applications and macroeconometric model-building spread to other Asian countries. The former was already explained. The latter was undertaken at central banks' research departments (Korea, the Philippines, and Thailand) or planning agencies (Taiwan, Indonesia) or universities (Hong Kong, Singapore, Malaysia).

[32]Osaka ISER model had about 500 equations including identities. Asian LINK model: (Ichimura-Ezaki, 1985) was also about the same size. However, in the 1980s, an improvement of computer capacity and the application of the Gauss-Seidel method resolved the problem to solve a system of many non-linear equations.

Those models were assembled with their later improvements in Ichimura-Matsumoto (1993). Another was that the growing Japanese economy became more integrated with the East Asian neighbors. These two facts necessitated and made it possible to construct the Japanese models internationally linked with Asian economies.

Under these circumstances, Japanese model-builders made some important steps forward even in the 1970s, more in the 1980s and later, offering several new models.[33] One of the common characteristics was to integrate IO tables, as the Osaka ISER model was designed from the very beginning. The Japanese models had to deal with the changing industrial composition of the manufacturing sector and international trade. Important works were: Saito (1971), Tsujimura-Kuroda (1974), and Moriguchi (1979). In particular, Saito (1971): "An Interindustry Study of Price Formation", *Review of Economics and Statistics* was the econometric model that integrated IO analysis more extensively than the Osaka ISER model. Despite the title, it was an ordinary econometric model and analyzed the changes in output, employment and prices of industrial sectors.[34] It marked a start of his outstanding works and resulted in some more works by his colleagues in Morishima *et al.* (1972). Tsujimura-Kuroda (1974): *General Equilibrium Analysis of the Japanese Economy* (J) was also a multi-sectoral standard model combined with IO analysis and established a base of the Keio group.[35] There quickly followed a similar work by Tsujimura-Kuroda-Shimada (1981). At Kyoto U., Moriguchi (later Osaka U.) initiated model-building and produced his KQ75 model after several earlier models (Moriguchi, 1979). Leading a group of academic and business economists at the Kansai Economic Research Center (now Kansai Institute of Social and Economic Research: KISER), he produced a medium annual model emphasizing the public finance sector: KERC (1978).[36]

---

[33]It was most regrettable that Sato's survey almost completely missed Saito's outstanding contributions. Sato missed also one important individual work: Seiji Hirai (1982). He performed a stochastic simulation of his Japan model. It is the first and genuine experiment of that type in Japan.

[34]In this sense it differed from many CGE models that handled the same issues.

[35]In Tokyo, Hitotsubashi U., U. of Tokyo and Keio U. led econometric studies; a little later was Tsukuba U.

[36]Moriguchi offered his forecast at KERC for many years, and his forecast was reported in the Nikkei newspapers and provided the business circles with economic forecasts independent of the government. After 1988 he was a leading econometrician of the PEO (Pacific Economic Outlook) conference sponsored by the PECC (Pacific Economic Cooperation Conference) annually held in Osaka with the participants from the APEC member countries.

Macroeconometric model-building developed not only in Asia but earlier in Europe. L. R. Klein initiated to organize an international project called Project LINK and construct the world-wide model linking multiple national models together. In this project[37] the Japan model has always been an important part. Moriguchi contributed his quarterly model from the beginning to the mid-1990s, when Kanemi Ban (Osaka U.) took over. The latest version of Ban model is taken as the Japan model for LINK in Ichimura-Klein (2010). Besides Project LINK, however, a number of internationally linked econometric models and interindustrial trade relations models were developed in Japan in the 1980s and continued into the 1990s. Sato's survey referred appropriately to the models of (1) Kyoto U. Center for Southeast Asian Studies, (2) the IDE group, (3) Shishido groups at Tsukuba U. and the International U. of Japan, (4) Kinoshita group at Nagoya U., and, (5) the EPA world model and other groups.

Representative reports of each group were: (1) Ichimura-Ezaki (1985): (2) IDE (1984: 1984a); (3) Shishido (1988); (4) Kinoshita *et al.* (1983); (5) EPA world model (1983; 1989). Among these, the global models that closed the system for the world as a whole with the rest of the world were only Ichimura-Ezaki (1985), Shishido (1988) and the EPA world model. Along with the world model at EPA, Soshichi Kinoshita (Nagoya U.) also cooperated with the EPA and produced with others an international trade model: Kinoshita *et al.* (1983). It was accidental that they all started about the same time and completed at nearly the same time, except for the EPA world model which lasted longer. Unfortunately those model-builders had no good opportunities for comparative examination of their models.

The most ambitious of all was the EPA World Model: a global quarterly model consisting of Japan, France, UK, Germany, Italy, Canada, US, Australia, Korea and the rest of the world. The project was led by Akihiro Amano on the academic side and Masaru Yoshitomi on the EPA side in cooperation with many capable government economists. The first version was published in October, 1982, and the fifth version was presented at the Sixth International conference at the EPA, Tokyo in February, 1989 and at many other international conferences. Its structure, simulation analyses,

An annual report of the forecasts of APEC member economies based on participants' econometric models has been published by KISER every year. In 2004 the role of chief economist from Japan was succeeded by Yoshihisa Inada (Konan U.).

[37]Project LINK held its annual meeting twice at the UN and another country for many years, but their proceedings are not published, except for one for 1991 and 1992 in Moscow and Ankara: Hickman-Klein (1998). It includes two contributions by S. Shishido and Mitsuru Toida from Japan.

multipliers are made available in the project's Discussion Papers (1989).[38] The Japan model in the World Model was originally the Master model in Shishido *et al.* (1970) and has been carried over, after termination of the world model project, as the present ESRI short-term quarterly model and has been updated ever since.

This World Model squarely dealt with the issues of flexible Yen/dollar exchange rate after 1973–1974. It was a significant contribution of A. Amano as an international economics expert. Amano (1983; 1985; 1988) was the first to construct an econometric model with flexible exchange rates. He applied his approach to Project LINK models with their experts Amano-Holtham-Hooper-Pauly (1986) and Amano (1986).

4.5. *Macroeconometric models after 1988*

None of the Japanese or Asian models covered by Sato's survey integrated any model of China nor trade with China. Although Ichimura-Ezaki (1985) had a model of China by Haruki Niwa, it could not include China in Asian LINK mainly due to the data problem. But after 1979, China adopted Den Xiaoping's *reform and open* policies and achieved enormous development, so that in the late 1980s it became non-negligible for any model-builders. Besides, the statistical data similar to Western countries became available.[39] Then, many Japanese econometricians specialized in Asia began working on Asian models including China.

Besides those included in Ichimura-Klein (2000): *Econometric Modeling of China*, S. Kinoshita (1993) at Nagoya U. and later Sugiyama U. constructed his own East Asian model including China. His group pursued to construct the global model and produced Ozaki (1999) and Yamada-Kinoshita (2006).[40] S. Shishido continued his world model (1988) and shifted his interest to Northeast Asia including China (1999, 2007). Yoshihisa Inada (Konan U.) as an adjoined professor at ICSEAD (International Center for the Study of the East Asian Development) led a project of East Asian model including China. His China model is available in Ichimura-Klein (2000) and his entire Asian model as discussion papers of

---

[38] They can be seen in the home page of ESRI.

[39] On these matters and China model as such, see Ichimiura-Klein (2000).

[40] Their Japan models contained forward-looking variables for expectation so that they adopted the "Fair method" for solving the system and simulation. See Appendix, Fair (1984, pp. 371–375, and http://fairmodel.econ.yale.edu/fp/fp.htm.

ICSEAD. The Japan models in the internationally linked models were of standard Klein-Goldberger size. The elaborate EPA world model was not revised to take account of the Chinese economy.[41]

M. Saito has been a persistent macroeconometric model-builder of the Japanese economy at Osaka U. and later Kobe U., working almost independently of the groups mentioned above. Even after Saito (1971), a characteristic of his models has been to incorporate the IO tables both in real IO relations and the formation of industrial prices. The same is true with the latest version of his Japan model: Saito (2000). A core system of equations of his model is included in Ichimura-Klein (2010) with some new notes responding to L. R. Klein's queries. This is probably the best model for beginners to learn about macroeconometric modeling of the Japanese economy now.

As for the financial side of the Japanese economy, Saito and his colleagues produced Ogawa-Saito-Tokutsu (2003) by making use of the flow of funds information but simultaneously relying on all the other statistics about the financial transactions of Panel data. It is an outstanding piece of work following the general equilibrium model of Tobin-Brainard type and strictly follows the standard econometric methods to avoid the multi-collinearity prevalent among the financial variables. The conclusions derived from this model combined with his real side model gave a plausible ex-post forecast for the bubble economy in the 1990s.[42]

Saito's and Keio group's multi-sectoral models were applied to the energy and environmental issues in Japan, as Saito (1982) and Kuroda (1998; 2000). There are many models applied to energy and environmental problems, but they are not taken up here unless they have unique characteristics as macroeconometric models.

The Japanese government has had several models for the public use besides the world model. One is the ESRI quarterly short-term model already referred to previously. It is updated every year by the ESRI economists, and its simulation results like multipliers are used for government policy-making and made available in the ESRI homepage. Despite its importance, it was not adopted in Ichimura-Klein (2010) because of

---

[41]The ESRI maintained its efforts to analyze the feedback between the world economy and Japan. A significant contribution was made by K. Ban *et al.* (2002).

[42]His simulation showed that the 5 trillion Yen increased demand for land for two years, supported by the sufficient increase of money supply, causes land price to rise by 2.15%–3.15%, cpi to increase by 0.33%–0.77% and a decline of real GNP rate of growth by 0.14%–0.21% during the period.

the difficulties for ordinary econometricians to understand the specifications.[43] Another model currently in use and available in ESRI home page is an annual model for the medium-term programming. It consists of a core part of about 280 equations and identities *plus* a few thousand equations in the sub-models. It is too difficult for outsiders to dig into without detailed exposition. The ESRI not only uses these two models for official purposes but also organizes a consensus forecast group, asking the selected research groups to offer their quarterly forecasts. It is explained in Inada (2010).

The Bank of Japan used to have an internationally known econometric model like Eguchi (1972). See, for instance, Eguchi (1976) in Federal Reserve Bank of SF (1976). K. Sato (1991) reports that the BOJ used some monetarist models for forecast and analysis in the mid-1970s, but no specific articles seem to have been available to outsiders. Some economists inside the BOJ say that it still uses some econometric models, but no published articles contain empirical equations.

The Nihon Keizai Newspaper's subsidiary, Nikkei Digital Media, Inc. offers NEEDS data bank and their own econometric model services. Their models are made available only to their customers.[44] Its other subsidiary Japan Center for Economic Research kindly organizes an annual meeting of academic and business econometricians for exchange of information and runs a course to train econometricians.[45]

4.6. *High frequency short-term forecasting model and medium-term model*

Fortunately, however, there are two most up-to-date macroeconometric models that are intensively used and offer their findings in the public domain. They are comparable with the government official forecasts and analyses. One is Yoshihisa Inada's High Frequency Model, and another is Shishido's multi-sectoral model called DEMIOS. Both are adopted in Ichimura-Klein (2010). Inada Model is the Japanese version of similar models in the US, utilizing daily, weekly or monthly data to improve the short-term forecast more often than quarterly. He is following closely the

---

[43]One difficulty is complex notations, and another is many complicated identities. Unless further explained in detail, outsiders could not understand the system.

[44]Saito-Moriguchi (1985) offers some information of NEEDS models in the past.

[45]Many other private business corporations or their think-tanks run their own econometric models, but most of them are not published, as the Central Institute of Electric Power Industry used to do.

methods explored by L. R. Klein's group at the U. of Pennsylvania. Every month he announces his forecast at the KISER a few quarterlies ahead and for next year, and every week at his own Konan U. to his clients as well as through the home page of Project LINK. His model is constantly tested against the real outcomes every month. Inada (2010) compares his findings with the Consensus Forecast announced by the Economic Planning Association, affiliated with the EPA.

The Shishido model is one of the medium term models in use for many years, constantly updated and improved. It has been giving the forecasts 4 to 5 years ahead with some prescribed policy alternatives. His prognosis has been rather different from the government's, often more optimistic, and his policy recommendations have been bolder than the government's. The government has been rather concerned with the cumulating public debt, whereas he seems to be more optimistic in assuming the high elasticity for income multipliers and tax revenues. The interested reader may compare his findings with another optimism of Klein-Adams-Kumasaka-Shinozaki (2007): *Accelerating Japan's Economic Growth: Resolving Japan's Growth Controversy*.

Appendix: On Computer Programs for Large Multi-County Econometric Models

The computer limitations were briefly sketched in the text, as I have experienced them. After solving the Osaka ISER model, the computer facilities at Japanese universities quickly improved year after year. Yet the standard programs available around 1970 like SPSS etc. or later TSP. SPSS, SAS, Eviews and RAT7 were not adequate enough to solve the large econometric models with nonlinear variables and equations. It was highly desirable to have some devices for checking the human errors in inputting the data or specifications. Many expert econometricians and computer scientists or informatics cooperated to produce convenient programs for multi-country dynamic system. The central figure of the group was Ippei Sugiura (1925–2009). Similar issues have been handled in the US by Ray Fair, Yale U. The representative contributions are as follows.

1. Ezaki, Mitsuo, M. Shibayama, and S. Ichimura (1984). An Econometric Link System for the East and Southeast Asian Countries, Japan and the United States. *Southeast Asian Studies*, 22(3) 260–283.
2. Fair, Ray (1984). *Specification, Estimation, and Analysis of Macroeconometric Models*. Harvard University Press.

3. Fair, Ray (1994). *Testing Macroeconometric Models*. Harvard University Press.
4. Fair, Ray (2004). *Estimating How the Macroeconomy Works*. Harvard University Press.
5. Ichimura, S., Ippei Sugiura and Hans Tjian (1966). A Simulation System Program for Large Econometric Models, Working Paper No. 198, Center for Research in Management Science, U. of California, Berkeley.
6. Sadamichi, H. and Y. Nunokami (1993). International Use of the Econometric Models and Data Base Via Bulletin Board Systems. In *the Proceedings of the International Conference of OA & International Management*, Beijing, October. In *Office Automation*, 14(3, 4) 128–130.
7. Sadamichi, H. and Y. Nunokami (1982). A Database System of Economic Time Series. *Kobe Economic & Business Review*, 28, 43–47.
8. Shibayama, M. *et al.* (1989). Research Report to Scientific Grant (B): An Integrated Computer Network for Econometric System of Japan, US and Asian Countries (Japanese).
9. Sugiura, Ippei (1973). *ASTRO-FOIL — Program System for Planning and Prediction*. Nihon Hyoronsha, Tokyo (Japanese).
10. Sugiura, Ippei H. Sadamichi and Y. Nunokami (1981). *STEPS — Econometric Analysis by Computers*. Toyokeizai Shimposha, Tokyo (Japanese).
11. Yasuda, Satoshi (1985). Sekai Model Bunseki System (An Analytical system for the World Model). Annual Report of Economic and Management Research, Kobe University Institute of Economic and Management Research (Japanese).
12. Yasuda, Satoshi (1986). A system of Solving LINK World Models — for the case of CSEAS. *News Letters of Special Research Project for Development of Programs for Multi-Purpose Statistical Data Bank*, 13(4) (Japanese).
13. Yasuda, Satoshi (1986). Virtual Computers and System of Computer Languages — Analytical Systems for World Econometric Model. Monograph Series of Kobe University Institute of Economics and Management (Japanese).
14. Yasuda, Satoshi (1999). *Structures of Econometric Models and Solution Methods — Ordering and Sparsing*. The Japanese Institute of Management Science (Japanese).

References

Akita, Takahiro (1994). Interregional Interdependence and Regional Economic Growth in Japan. *International Regional Science Review*, 16(3).

Amano, Akihiro, K. Ban and C. Moriguchi (1976). A Quarterly Forecasting Econometric Model of Japan: KYQ 75 Discuss. Paper 095, KIER, Kyoto U (Japanese).

Amano, Akihiro (1977). Japan's Balance of Payments and its Adjustment: Quarterly Econometric Model, 1961–1967. In Kosobud-Minami (1977).

Amano, Akihiro (1983). Exchange Rate Modeling in the EPA World Econometric Model. In de Grauwe-Peters (1983).

Amano, Akihiro (1985). Alternative Approaches to Exchange-Rate Determination and Some Implications of Structural Balance of Payments Approach for International Macroeconomic Interdependence. In Ando *et al.* (1985).

Amano, Akihiro, Gerald Holtham, Peter Hooper and Peter Pauly (1986). Comparative Exchange Rate Simulations. *The European Economic Review*, 30(1).

Amano, Akihiro (1986). Exchange Rate Simulation — A Comparative Study. *EER, ibid.*

Amano, Akihiro (1988). Comment on Simulation Properties of Three Internationally Linked Models. In EPA (1988).

Amano, Akihiro (1988). Japan's External Imbalance and Exchange Rates. In Uno-Shishido (1988).

Ando, Albert, H. Eguchi, Roger Farmer and Yoshio Suzuki (eds.) (1985). *Monetary Policy in Our Times*. Cambridge, MIT Press.

Ando, Albert (1985). Coordination of Monetary and Fiscal Policies. In Ando *et al.*

Ban, Kanemi and Kiyomi Watanabe *et al.* (2002). An East Asian macroeconometric LINK model — Structure and simulation properties. *The Economic Analysis*, 164. Esri.

Bodkin, R. G., L. R. Klein and K. Marwah (1991). *A History of Macroeconometric Model-Building*. Brookfield, Vermont: Edward Elgar.

Cabinet Bureau of Statistics (1934). Study report of National Income in 1925.

Chenery, Hollis, T. Watanabe and S. Shishido (1962). The Patterns of Japanese Growth, 1914–1954. *Econometrica*, January.

De Grauwe, Paul and Thoo Peters (eds.) (1983). *Exchange Rates in Multi-Country Econometric Models*. London: Macmillan.

Dietzenbacher, Erik and Michael L. Lahr (eds.) (2004). *Wassily Leontief and Input-Output Economics*. Cambridge University Press.

Doi, Masaru (ed.). (2006). *Computable General Equilibrium Approaches in Urban and Regional Policy Studies*. WSPC.

Dusenberry, M. J., G. From, L. R. Klein and E. Kuh (eds.) (1965). *The Brookings Quarterly Econometric Model of the U. S. Economy*. Chicago: Rand McNally.

Eguchi, Hidekazu (1972). The Bank of Japan Econometric Model of Japan. *Chosa Geppoh*, Bank of Japan (Japanese).

Eguchi, Hidekazu (1976). Econometric Modeling at the Bank of Japan. In *Fed. Reserve Bank, San Francisco Proceedings*, 1976.

EPA world model team (1982). EPA Sekai Keizai Model no Kozo (The Structure of EPC World Model). *Keizai Bunseki*, 87 (Japanese).

EPA world model team (1982). The EPA World Econometric Model: Overview. (Japanese).

EPA (ed.) (1988). *Papers and Proceedings of the Fourth EPA International Symposium, 1988*. EPA.

EPA world model team (1989/2). Analyses of Model derived from IS-LM, Aggregate Demand-Aggregate Supply, and BP Curves, World Econ. Model Disc. Pap. no. 29 presented at the 6th Intern'l Conf. at EPA.

Evans, M. K. and L. R. Klein (1968). *The Wharton Econometric Forecasting Model. 2d ed. Philadelphia*. The Wharton School, University of Pennsylvania.

Ezaki, Mitsuo (1986). A Computable General Equilibrium Model of the Japanese Economy. *Kobe Economic and Business Review, 32 annual.*

Ezaki, M. and S. Ito (1995). The Flying-Geese Pattern of Development in East Asia: a computable general equilibrium approach. Discussion Paper No. 31, GSID Nagoya U., July.

Federal Reserve Bank of San Francisco (1976). *Proceedings of the First Pacific Basin Central Bank Conference on Econometric Modeling*, Held May 27–29, 1975.

Fujino, Seizaburo (1965). *Business Cycles in Japan*. Keiso Shobo (Japanese).

Fujino, Shozaburo (2008). *Japanese Growth and Cycles*. Keiso Shobo (Japanese).

Furukawa, S. and S. Inomata (1993). Significance of Construction and Analysis of International IO Tables of Asia-Pacific Region. In Sano-Tanamura (1993).

Hayashi, Fumio (ed.) (2008). *Keizai Seido no Jissho-Bunseki to Sekkei (Positive Anaysis and Design of Economic Institutions. I. Causes for Long Stagnation and Institutions; II. Functional Disorder of Finance; III. Designing Economic Institutions*. Keiso Shobo (Japanese).

Hickman, B. G. and L. R. Klein (ed.) (1998). *LINK 1991–1992 Proceedings*. WSPC.

Hijikata, Shigemi (1933). *Kokuminshotoku no Kosei (Composition of National Income)*. Nihon Hyoron Sha, Tokyo (Japanese).

Hirai, Seiji (1982). *Simulation Analysis of the Japanese Economy*. Sobunsha (Japanese).

Ichimura, Shinichi (1957). *The Structure of the Japanese Economy*. Sobunsha (Japanese).

Ichimura, Shinichi (ed.) (1960). *The Future of the Japanese Economy*. Yuhikaku (Japanese).

Ichimura, Shinichi (1968). Factors for Rapid Economic Growth — A Social Accounting Approach. In Ohkawa-Klein (1968).

Ichimura, Shinichi (1977). An Econometric Analysis of Japanese Exports and Imports. In Kosobud-Minami (1997).

Ichimura, S., L. R. Klein, S. Koizumi and K. Sato (1977). *An Econometric Analysis of the Japanese Economy*. The Japanese Association for Asian Studies.

Ichimura, S. and M. Ezaki (ed.) (1985). *Econometric Models of Asian LINK*. Springer-Verlag.

Ichimura, S. and Yasumi Matsumoto (ed.) (1993). *Econometric Models of Asia-Pacific Countries*. Springer-Verlag.

Ichimura, S. and L. R. Klein (ed.) (2000). *Econometric Modeling of China*. WSPC.

Ichimura, S. and L. R. Klein (ed.) (2010). *Macroeconometric Modeling of Japan*. WSPC.

IDE (1984). *Econometric LINK system for ASEAN: Overview*. IDE.

IDE (1984). *Econometric LINK system for ASEAN: Vol I and II*. IDE.

Inada, Yoshihisa (2010). High Frequency Model vs. Consensus Forecast. In Ichimura-Klein (2010).

Inomata, S. and H. Kuwamori (2008). *Compilation of the International Input-Output Table for the BRICs — A Feasibility Study*. Asian International IO Series, No. 71, IDE, March.

Kansai Economic Federation (1960). *Nihon Keizai to Chiiki Keizai (The Japanese Economy and the Regional Economy)*. Sobunsha, Tokyo (Japanese).

Kansai Economic Research Center (1978). *Econometric Analysis of the Japanese Economy and its Public Finance*. KERC.

Kinoshita, Soshichi (1993). A Linked International Model for the Pacific Basic Economy. In Ichimura-Matsumoto (1993).

Kinoshita, Soshichi, Y. Kajino, M. Saito, Y. Shiina and M. Yamada (1983). Development and application of a world industry and trade model for the analysis of international industry and trade structure focusing on Japan. ERI, EPA mono. series no. 38 (Japanese).

Kinoshita, Soshichi and Mitsuo Yamada (1989). The Impacts of Robotization on Macro and Sectoral Economies within a World Econometric Model. *Technological Forecasting and Social Change*, April, 211–230.

Kito, Hiroshi (2000). *Jinko kara Yomu Nihon no Rekishi (Japanese History seen from Population)*. Kodan-sha (Japanese).

Klein, L. R. and Arthur. S. Goldberger (1955). *An Econometric Model of the United States, 1929–1952*. Amsterdam: North-Holland.

Klein, L. R. and Richard F. Kosobud, (1961). Some Econometrics of Growth: Great Ratios in Economics. *QJ E*, 12(2), 139–150.

Klein, L. R., F. G. Adams, Y. Kumasaka and A. Shinozaki (2007). *Accelerating Japan's Economic Growth: Resolving Japan's Growth Controversy*. Routledge.

Kosubud, R. F. and Ryoshin Minami (eds.) (1977). *Econometric Studies of Japan*. Urbana, U. of Illinois Press.

Koyanagitsu, Nobuo (2006). *Kinsei Chingin Bukka Shi Shiryo: revised (Sources for History of Wages and Prices in the Edo period)*. Seiko-sha (Japanese).

Kuroda, Masahiro (1998). Multisectoral general equilibrium model and its simulation for environmental preservation policies, KEO Dis. Pap.-.15. (Japanese).

Kuroda, Masahiro (2000). Forecasting Baseline CO_2 Emissions in Japan. In Ching-Cheng Chang, Robert Mendelsohn, and Daigee Shaw (eds.), *Global Warming and Asian Pacific*.

MITI Department of Research and Statistics (ed.) (1957). *Nihon Keizai no Sanngyo Renkanhyo (Interindustrial Analysis of the Japanese Economy)*. Toyokeizai Shipo-sha (Japanese).

MITI Statistical Association and Institute of Industries (ed.) (1979). *Tsusan Tokei-Shi (History of MITI Statistics)*, Volume IV: Statistical Analysis; Chap. 3: Interindustrial Analysis (Japanese).

Ministry of General Affairs (2000). *Report of Interindustrial Relations Tables in All Prefectures* (Japanese).

Miyagawa, Mitsuru (1957–1963). *Taiko Kenchi Ron (On the Taiko land Survey)*, Vol. 1–3. Ochanomizu-Shobo, Tokyo (Japanese).

Moriguchi, Chikashi (1979). The Structural Change of the Japanese Economy in the recent decade from a Macroeconometric viewpoint. *Keizai Kenkyu*, January, 20–29 (Japanese).

Moriguchi, C., M. Aoki and T. Sawa (1983). *Nihon Keizai no Kozo Bunseki (Structural Analysis of the Japanese Economy)*. Sobunsha (Japanese).

Morishima, M., Y. Murata, T. Nosse and M. Saito (1972). *The working of econometric models*. Cambridge Univ. Press.

Morishima, M., M. Shinohara and T. Uchida (1960). *Atarashii Keizai Bunseki (New Economic Analysis)*. Sobunsha, Tokyo (Japanese).

Nagazumi, Yoko (ed.) (1987). *Exports and Imports Items and Commodities by Chinese Ships: 1637–1833*. Sobunsha (Japanese).

Nakamura, Takafusa (1968). *Sengo Nihon Keizai — seicho to Junkan (Postwar Japanese Economy — Growth and Cycles)*. Iwanami-shoten.

Nakamura, Takafusa (1971). *Senzenki Nihon Keizai Seicho no Bunseki (Analysis of Prewar Japanese Economy)*. Iwanami-shoten (Japanese).

Nakamura, Takafusa (1979; 1993). *Nihon Keizai — Seicho to Kozo (The Japanese Economy — Growth and Structure)*. University of Tokyo Press (Japanese).

Nakamura, Takafusa (1985). *Meiji Taisho Ki no Keizai (The Japanese Economy in the Meiji-Taisho Era)*. University of Tokyo Press (Japanese).

Nakamura, Takafusa (1995). *Showa Keizai-shi (Economic History of Showa)*. Iwanami- shoten (Japanese).

Nakamura, Takafusa (2004). *A History of Showa Japan*.

Ogawa, K., M. Saito and I. Tokutsu (2004). Land Prices and Share Prices in Japan: An Econometric Approach. In Tsujimura (2004), pp. 177–210.

Ohkawa K. and L. R. Klein (ed.) (1968). *Economic Growth: Japanese Experiences since the Meiji Era*. Ill. Irwin: Homewood.

Ohkawa, Kazushi and Henry Rosowsky (eds.) (1973). *Japanese Economic Growth; Trend Acceleration in the Twentieth Century*. Stanford University Press.

Ohkawa, Kazushi, M. Shinohara and M. Umemura (ed.) (1965–1985). *Nihon Choki Keizai Tokei (Japanese Long-Term Economic Statistics)*. Toyokeizai Shimposha (Japanese).

Ohkawa, Kazushi, G. Ranis and Larry Meissner (ed.) (1985). *Japan and the developing countries: a comparative analysis*. Basil Blackwell.

Ohkawa, Kazushi, M. Shinohara and Larry Meissner (ed.) (1979). *Patterns of Japanese Economic Development—A Quantitative Appraisal*. Yale University Press.

Ozaki, Taiyo (1999). *Sekai Keizai no Macro Keiryo Model Bunseki (Macroeconometric Analysis of the World Economy)*. Koyoshobo.

Peterson, William (ed.) (1991). *Advances in Input- Output Analysis*. Oxford Univ. Press.

Saito, Mitsuo (1971). An Interindustry Study of Price Formation. *Review of Econ. and Stat.*, Feb. 11–25, in Morishima *et al.* (1972).

Saito, M. and T. Oono (1982). An Energy Model of the Japanese Economy, 1961–1979. In *Research Report on Energy to M. of Education*, 1–51 (Japanese).

Saito, M. and C. Moriguchi (1985). A Survey of Econometric Models of Japan. Discussion Papers 8503 Kyoto Institute of Economic Research, October (Japanese).

Saito, Mitsuo (2000). *The Japanese Economy*. WSPC.

Sato, Kazuo (1991). Econometric Models of the Japanese Economy. In Bodkin *et al.* (1991).

Sano, T. and C. Tamamura (eds.) (1993). *International Industrial Linkages and Economic Interdependency in Asia-Pacific Region*. IDE.

Sekiyama, Naotaro (1952). *Nihon no Jinko* (*Japanese Population*). Shibundo (Japanese).

Shimanaka and Shikano (2010). Business indexes and survey data for forecast. In Ichimura-Klein (2010).

Shinohara, Miyohei, (1982). *Industrial Growth, Trade, and Dynamic Patterns in the Japanese Economy*. University of Tokyo Press.

Shinohara, Miyohei (1994). *Postwar Business Cycles for 50 Years*. Nihon Keizai Shimbun (Japanese).

Shishido, S., A. Kohno, S. Nagaya and S. Tanaka (1968). Use of national accounts for short-term econometric model, 1954–1966. *Review of Income and Wealth*, Sept., 267–309.

Shishido, S., Y. Ichikawa, T. Noda, K. Furuya, A. Oshizaka and S. Nishikawa (1970). A Master Model for Short-Term Economic Predictions. Monograph No. 21, IEP, EPA. Government printing office (Japanese).

Shishido, Shuntaro (1988). The Japanese growth alternatives and the world economy simulations with Tsukuba-FAIS world econometric model. In Uno-shishido (1988).

Shishido, Shuntaro (1990). Technical Innovations and IO Analysis. *PAPAIOS-Business Journal*, 1(1) (Japanese).

Shishido, Shuntaro (1991). Prediction Methods for Input Coefficients — V. RAS Algorithm. *PAPAIOS-Business Journal*, 1(2) (Japanese).

Shishido, S., K. Harada and Y. Matsumura (1991). Technical Progress in an IO Framework with special reference to Japan's High Technology Industries. In Peterson, W. (1991).

Shishido, S., S. Itoh, M. Hamada, K. Kawamura, O. Kwon and T. Nakajima (1999). Multi-regional Econometric Model for Northeast Asia. *Journal of Econometric Study of Northeast Asia (JESNA)*, March.

Shishido, Shuntaro (2004). Japan's economic growth and policy-making in the context of IO models. In Dietzenbacher, E. and M. Lahr (2004).

Shishido, S, A. Kawakami, M, Kuroka- wa, A, Movshuk and K, Tamashiro (2007). Policy Simulation with an Integrated Model for Japan and Northeast Asia. *JESNA*, November.

Shishido, S. Akira Kawakami and Kiyoshi Tamashiro (2010). Policy Alternatives for Japan Toward 2020. In Ichimura-Klein (2010).

Suk, Hyun (2010). Social Accounting Analysis of Japan's Lost 90s. In Ichimura-Klein (2010).

Suzuki, Yasuko (2004). *Kinsei Nichi-Ran Boeki no Kenkyu (A Study of the Japan-Netherlands Trade in the Edo Period)*. Shibunkaku (Japanese).

Tatemoto, Masahiro and Shinichi Ichimura (1959). Factor Proportions and Foreign Trade — The Case of Japan. *The Review of Economics and Statistics*, 41(4), 442–446.

Tatemoto, Masahiro and Shinichi Ichimura (eds.) (1970). *Nihon Keizai no Keiryo-Bunseki (Econometric Analyses of the Japanese Economy)*. Toyokeizai Shimposha (Japanese).

Tatemoto, M., T. Uchida and T. Watanabe (1967). A Stabilization Model of the postwar Japanese Economy. 1954–1962. *International Economic Review, February*. In Kosobud-Minami (1977).

Tsujimura, Kotaro and Masahiro Kuroda (1974). *Nihon Keizai no Ippan Kinko bunseki (General Equilibrium Analysis of the Japanse Economy)*, Kogakusha, Tokyo (Japanese).

Tsujimura, Kotaro, Masahiro Kuroda and Haruo Shimada (1981). *Economic Policy and General Interdependence*. Kogakusha (Japanese).

Tsujimura, Kazusuke and Masako Tsujimura (2003). Asset Liability Matrix Analysis derived from the Flow of Funds Accounts: the Bank of Japan's Quantitative Monetary Policy Examined. *Economic Systems Research*, 15(1).

Tsujimura, Kazusuke (ed.) (2004). *Shikin Junkan Bunseki no Kiseki to Tenbo (Traces and Prospects of Flow of Funds Analysis)*. Keio U. Press (Japanese).

Tsujimura, Kazusuke and Masako Tsujimura (2008). *Kokusai Shikin Junnkan Bunseki (International of Flow of Funds Analysis — Techniques and Applications)*. Keio Univ. Press (Japanese).

Uchida, Tadao and Kei Mori (1960). A Simulation Analysis of the Japanese Economy. In *Atarashii Keizai Bunseki (New Economic Analysis)*. Sobunsha (Japanese).

Uchida, T., S. Kuribayashi, A. Yajima and T. Watanabe (1966). *Economic Forecasting and Macroeconometric Models*. Nihonkeizai Shinbunsha (Japanese).

Ueno, Hiroya (1977). A Long-term Model of Japanese Economic Growth. In Kosobud-Minami (1977).

Uno, Kimio and S. Shishido (1988). *Statistical Data Bank Systems: Socio-Economic Database and Model-Building in Japan*. Northholland-Elsevier.

Watanabe, Tsunehiko (1970). *Quantitative Economic Analysis*. Sobunsha, Tokyo (Japanese).

Yamada, Mitsuo and Soshichi Kinoshita (eds.) (2006). Macroeconometric Analysis of East Asian Development). Chukyo U. Institute of Econ. Res. Monograph no. 12 (Japanese).

Yamada, Yuzo (ed.) (1951). *Nihon Kokumin Shotoku Suikei Shiryo (Materials for Estimating Japanese National Income)*. Toyokeizai Shimposha (Japanese).

Part I

Social Accounting and Survey Analysis

Chapter 1

Factors for Rapid Growth of the Japanese Economy: A Social Accounting Approach*,†

Shinichi Ichimura

1. Introduction

This chapter deals with the development of the Japanese economy from 1951 to 1961, a period during which per capita national income grew from \$179 to \$525. The annual average rate of growth in real national income over these eleven years was about 9.5% and was considerably faster than that of West Germany or the Soviet Union. Since, however, it is only in 1955 or 1956 that Japanese per capita income reached the pre-war maximum, the beginning half of the period under investigation covers the years of predominantly post-war recovery, and only the latter half significantly shows the true development of Japanese economic life beyond the pre-war standard. This paper, therefore, deals with an interesting transitional period from recovery to development.

This chapter offers an anatomical analysis of rapid Japanese economic growth in terms of social accounting of national income and related statistical aggregates. The social accounting scheme we adopt here is the one that we have constructed for the Osaka Econometric Model of Post-war Japan. It is basically the national income accounts supplemented by simplified input-output tables and accounts of labor force, capital stock by industrial sectors and the money flow table. As we immediately explain, it is essential for the

*This paper was published as "Factors for Rapid Economic Growth," in K. Ohkawa and L.R. Klein (eds.) (1968). *Economic Growth: Japanese Experiences since the Meiji Era*. Ill. Irwin: Homewood.

†The research was done during the author's visit at the U. of California, Berkeley in 1965–1966, supported by a grant from the Ford Foundation. I thank Mr. Hans Tjian who carried out the time-consuming computation.

analysis of a national economy not only to have a consistent overall social accounting system for economic time-series in current value but also to define price indices and wage rates appropriately so that the basic identities hold, even in real terms.

After constructing consistent time-series in real terms within the framework of social accounting or in a way that satisfy basic identities, we take selected ratios of important variables and use them to test simple but important hypotheses used in explaining the rapid Japanese economic growth. This kind of simple anatomy of social accounts is admittedly inferior to an elaborate econometric model analysis but, if it is wisely done, it can effectively reveal some important aspects of economic growth and supplement or check more high-powered analysis of econometric models or equations. It can draw attention to a few important points of interest so that it can be free from rigid hypotheses. It is the method which Simon Kuznets often adopts in his international comparison of long time-series of different countries' national incomes or similar to the model which Lawrence R. Klein constructed to describe the long-term growth of the U.S. economy in terms of "great ratios" of economic growth. (See Kuznets (1966) and Klein, 1962, pp. 180–207). In Japan, too, a number of economists including Dr. Osamu Shimomura, Miyohei Shinohara and Government's *White Papers* have skillfully made use of a few crucial ratios like *marginal capital coefficient* or *incremental capital-output ratio* and have given very sensible analyses and even predictions of post-war economic growth.

It does not seem appropriate to lump these analyses together under what R. Stone called "casual empiricism" (Stone *et al.*, 1954) but more properly they are parts of social accounting analysis of a national economy. What we attempt here is nothing but an anatomy of the social accounts of the Japanese Economy from 1951 to 1961.[1] Section 2 gives an exposition of the use of this method and its limitations. Section 3 explains a system of social accounts adopted in this chapter. Section 4 discusses the sectoral breakdowns or Japanese economic growth and sectoral characteristics of technological progress. Section 5 takes up the problems of supply of labor and capital. Section 6 discusses their allocations among sectors through the market mechanism of free enterprise. The appraisal of Japanese growth under free enterprise is examined to some extent. Section 7 analyzes the characteristic composition of National Expenditure in Japan.

---

[1] As for anatomical analyses of social accounts, see for instance Stuvel (1965) and Yanousky (1967). R. Stone's Transaction Model and its applications in Stone (1966) are also similar studies.

2. Exposition of a Simple Social Accounting Model

Suppose that a simple system of social accounts is given for a closed economy as in Table 1. The notations are given below the table.

The symbols with primes denote money-values, and those without primes denote values in constant Yen. It should be obvious that the following identities hold:

$$X' = M' + C' + I' \tag{2.1}$$
$$X' = M' + W' + P' \tag{2.2}$$
$$Y' = W' + P' \tag{2.3}$$
$$W' = \omega N \tag{2.4}$$
$$P' = \pi K \tag{2.5}$$
$$X' = p_x X \tag{2.6}$$
$$I' = p_k I \tag{2.7}$$
$$C' = p_c C \tag{2.8}$$
$$M = X - C - I \tag{2.9}$$
$$Y = C + I \tag{2.10}$$
$$Y' = pY \tag{2.11}$$
$$M' = p_m M \tag{2.12}$$

Table 1. Basic Social Accounting.

	Industry	Investment	Consumption	Output
Industry	M	I	C	X
Wages	W			
Profit	P			Y
Expenditure	X	I	C	$X + Y$

C = Consumption
I = Investment
M = Material input
X = Total National Production
Y = National Income
N = Labor employed
K = Capital Stock
W = Wage Payments
P = Profit
pc = consumers' price-index
p_k = investment price-index
p_m = materials price-index
p_x = output price-index
p = national income deflator
ω = wage rate
π = profit rate

Here p and p_m are implicit deflators defined for given values of p_x, p_c and p_k, and two equations hold for real wage incomes and its:

$$W = W'/p = w/p \times N, \tag{2.13}$$

$$P = P'/p = \pi/p \times K. \tag{2.14}$$

Three basic identities for National Income hold also in real terms:

$$Y = X - M, \tag{2.15}$$

$$Y = C + I, \tag{2.16}$$

$$Y = W + P. \tag{2.17}$$

They represent production, expenditure and distribution sides of national product and offer the bases for analyzing various factors in economic growth. They can be rewritten in terms of growth rates:

$$\frac{\Delta Y}{Y} = \frac{\Delta(1 - M/X)}{(1 - M/X)} + \frac{\Delta X}{X} \tag{2.18}$$

$$\frac{\Delta Y}{Y} = \frac{\Delta C}{C}\frac{C}{Y} + \frac{\Delta I}{I}\frac{I}{Y} \tag{2.19}$$

$$\frac{\Delta Y}{Y} = \frac{\Delta(W/P)}{(W/P)}\frac{W}{Y} + \frac{\Delta P}{P}, \tag{2.20}$$

where ΔY denotes the increase of Y in one period, and the same interpretation holds for other similar magnitudes. (2.18) breaks down the growth rate of national product into the change in the ratio of value added to output and the change in total output. If, therefore, M/X becomes smaller, the growth rate of national product can exceed that of total industrial output.

It would not be unusual to associate X with labor and capital so that we may define:

$$X = \rho N, \tag{2.21}$$

$$X = \sigma K, \tag{2.22}$$

where ρ and σ stand for the observed average productivities of labor and capital. Needless to say,

$$\frac{\Delta X}{X} = \frac{\Delta \rho}{\rho} + \frac{\Delta N}{N}, \tag{2.23}$$

$$\frac{\Delta X}{X} = \frac{\Delta \sigma}{\sigma} + \frac{\Delta K}{K}. \tag{2.24}$$

We have, always, $\Delta\rho > 0$, but $\Delta\sigma$ may be positive or negative. Since

$$\frac{\Delta\rho}{\rho} = \frac{\Delta\sigma}{\sigma} + \frac{\Delta(K/N)}{K/N}, \tag{2.25}$$

$\Delta\rho/\rho$ can exceed $\Delta\sigma/\sigma$ by the growth rate of the capital-labor ratio. If $\Delta\sigma = 0$, $\Delta\rho/\rho$ is precisely equal to the rate of growth in K/N. They are nothing but the identities that give the relations among related variables. No simple rules of causation can be deduced from them. But careful observation of these variables often reveals interesting aspects of economic growth.

The changes of ρ and σ in (2.23) to (2.25) may or may not be related to a change in production function. It is not possible to make any inference about technical progress without explicit introduction of hypotheses on production function. Let us assume that production in this system is of the Cobb-Douglass type, and that the theory of marginal productivity of labor holds approximately. Then,

$$X = AN^{\alpha}K^{\beta}, \tag{2.26}$$

$$\alpha\frac{X}{N} = \gamma\frac{w}{p_x}, \tag{2.27}$$

where γ is an index that shows the degree of approximation of marginal productivity of labor to real wage. Then,

$$\frac{\Delta\alpha}{\alpha} = \frac{\Delta\gamma}{\gamma} = \frac{\Delta\,(w/p_x)}{w/p_x} - \frac{\Delta\rho}{\rho} = \frac{\Delta(W'/Y')}{W'/Y'} + \frac{\Delta(Y'/X')}{Y'/X'}, \tag{2.28}$$

where α and γ are not observables. By comparing the growth rate of ρ with that of w/p_X, we can make an inference about the change of α, provided that we could tell something about $\Delta\gamma/\gamma$. If, for instance, it is safe to assume that the degree of competition in the Japanese economy did not increase so that $\Delta\gamma/\gamma < 0$, and the growth rate of labor productivity exceeds that of real-wage, then we may infer that $\Delta\alpha/\alpha < 0$; namely, technical progress was of the labor-saving type in the Hicksian sense.[2]

Similar inferences can be made from the conditions for the marginal productivity of capital. From (2.26), we obtain

$$\beta\frac{X}{K} = \delta\frac{\pi}{p_x}, \tag{2.29}$$

[2]Technical progress with respect to M/X will be analyzed analogously below.

where δ is an index that shows the degree of approximation of marginal productivity of capital to real rate of it, π / p_X. This and (2.27) give

$$\frac{\alpha}{\beta}\frac{K}{N} = \frac{\gamma}{\delta}\frac{w}{\pi}, \tag{2.30}$$

and (2.29) and (2.30) give

$$\frac{\Delta\beta}{\beta} - \frac{\Delta\delta}{\delta} = \frac{\Delta(\pi/p_X)}{\pi/p_X} - \frac{\Delta\sigma}{\sigma} = \frac{\Delta(P'/Y')}{P'/Y'} + \frac{\Delta(Y'/X')}{Y'/X'}, \tag{2.31}$$

$$\begin{aligned}\left(\frac{\Delta\alpha}{\alpha} - \frac{\Delta\beta}{\beta}\right) - \left(\frac{\Delta\gamma}{\gamma} - \frac{\Delta\sigma}{\sigma}\right) &= \left(\frac{\delta w}{w} - \frac{\delta\pi}{\pi}\right) - \frac{\Delta\,(K/N)}{K/N} \\ &= \frac{\Delta\left(W'/P'\right)}{W'/P'}.\end{aligned} \tag{2.32}$$

If $\Delta\gamma/\gamma = \Delta\delta/\delta$, then the sign of the right-hand terms in (2.32) can determine the bias of technical progress; namely, if $\Delta\alpha/\alpha - \Delta\beta/\beta < 0$, $= 0$ or > 0, then technical progress is respectively *labor-saving*, *neutral* or *capital-saving*. If, however, the sign of $\Delta\gamma/\gamma - \Delta\delta/\delta$ is not known, it is desirable to pay attention to all of (2.28), (2.31) and (2.32) and make our inference.

It is of some use to summarize the supply side of national product by the following equation to be derived from the equations above:

$$\frac{\Delta Y}{Y} = \frac{\Delta A}{A} + \frac{\Delta(Y/X)}{Y/X} + \alpha\frac{\Delta N}{N} + \beta\frac{\Delta K}{K} + \Delta\alpha \log N + \Delta\beta \log K. \tag{2.33}$$

Especially if $\alpha + \beta = 1$, then

$$\frac{\Delta Y}{Y} = \frac{\Delta A}{A} + \frac{\Delta(Y/X)}{Y/X} + \frac{\Delta N}{N} + \beta\left(\frac{\Delta K}{K} - \frac{\Delta N}{N}\right) + \Delta\beta \log\frac{K}{N}, \tag{2.34}$$

where each term on the right hand side shows a different factor which contributes to the growth rate of national product. $\Delta A/A$ is the growth rate of overall efficiency; $\Delta(Y/X)/(Y/X)$ is the growth rate of the value-added to output ratio; $\Delta N/N$ is the growth rate of employment; $\Delta(K/N)/(K/N)$ is the growth rate of the capital-labor ratio; and the last term is the contribution of biased technical progress. If $\Delta\beta > 0$, labor-saving technical progress contributes to $\Delta Y/Y$ more as K/N increases.

Now we turn to National Expenditure represented by (2.16) and (2.19). Rapid economic growth requires not only that the various factors on the supply side, like those in (2.33) or (2.34), be large but also that the level and growth rate of Effective Demand remain large. Moreover, the composition of National Expenditure must be consistent with requirements from the supply side. This is particularly important with respect to investment. Take the simplest case in which C is proportional to Y:

$$C = (1 - s)Y, \tag{2.35}$$

and we know from (2.19) that

$$\Delta Y/Y' = \Delta I/I. \tag{2.36}$$

Given I, and comparing it with K and assuming also that all the other terms in (2.34) are given, we can obtain the growth rate of supply of Y. If supply should be equal to demand, this would have to equal (2.36). Hence, we can establish

$$\frac{\Delta I}{I} - \frac{\Delta K}{K} = \frac{\Delta A}{A} + \frac{\Delta(Y/X)}{Y/X} + \Delta\beta \log\frac{K}{N} - \alpha\frac{\Delta(K/N)}{K/N}. \qquad (2.36)$$

Unless this equality holds from one period to another, Effective Demand is not equal to the supply of National Product.

Finally (2.20) shows the relation between $\Delta Y/Y$ and the functional distribution of income. From this and (2.32) we know that if technical progress is labor-saving and $\Delta\gamma/\gamma - \Delta\delta/\delta = 0$, then labor's share of national income must decline so that ΔP/P must be larger than $\Delta Y/Y$.

Furthermore it, is of some interest to notice that we can derive from (2.16) and (2.17) the following identity:

$$\frac{W}{P} = \left(\frac{l}{l - C/Y}\right)\frac{I}{P} - l. \tag{2.37}$$

This implies that if the average propensity to consume does not change, W/P must change in the same direction as I/P (see Kaldor, 1960). Hence, under the same assumptions above, $\Delta I/I < \Delta P/P > \Delta Y/Y > \Delta W/W$. If, therefore, $\Delta I/I$ exceeds $\Delta P/P$ when W/P is falling, C/Y must be declining.

3. Our Social Accounting System and Statistical Data

The basic scheme of social accounts for our system is given in Table 2. [See Ichimura *et al.* (1964a) or Chap. 10]. It contains five industrial sectors: (1) Agriculture, (2) Heavy Industry, (3) Textile Industry, (4) Other

Table 2. Social Accounts and Interindustrial Relations Table in the Osaka ISER Model

	Current Materiap Input						Inventory Investment						Private capital formation							Gov ex		Cons.					
	A	**hL**	**hS**	**ML**	**MS**	**E**	**A**	**H**	**M**	**d**	**m**	**p**	**A**	**hL**	**hS**	**ML**	**MS**	**E**	**R**	**Ca**	**Oth**	**f**	**t**	**oth**	**Ex**	**Im**	**Total**
A	∩	∩	∩	∩	∩	∩	J_A															+			E_a	$-B_f$	X_A
hL	+	+	+	+	+	+		J_{fh}		+	+	+	+	+	+	+	+	+	+	+	+			+	E_h	$\cap -B_h$	X_{hL}
hS	M_A	M	M	M	M	M		+		J_d	J_m	J_p	I_A	I_{hL}	I_{hS}	I_{ML}	I_{MS}	I_E	I_R	G_I	G_o			+	+	$-B_m +$	X_{hS}
ML	+	+	+	+	+	+			J_{fM}	+	+	+	+	+	+	+	+	+	+	+	+	+	+	+	E_M	$+ -B_c$	X_{ML}
MS	+	+	+	+	+	+			+	+	+	+	+	+	+	+	+	+	+	+	+	C_f	C_t	C_o	+	∪+	X_{MS}
E	∪	∪	∪	∪	∪	∪								+	+	+	+	+	+	+	+	+	+	+			X_E
T	Ta	T_{hL}	T_{hS}	T_{ML}	T_{MS}	T_E	Adj item																				
W		W_{hL}	W_{hS}	W_{ML}	W_{MS}	W_E	Yg	ξ													Wg						+
P	Y_A	P_{hL}	P_{hS}	P_{ML}	P_{MS}	P_E																					Yg
D	D_A	D_{hL}	D_{hS}	D_{ML}	D_{MS}	D_E	Dr	Dg																			+
																											+
Total Exp.							(	+	+	J	+	)	(	+	+	I_p	+	+	)	G	+	C	+	+	E	$-B$	

Manufacturing Industry, and (5) Tertiary Industry. (2), (3) and (4) are further divided into large and small-scale enterprise. The dividing line between the two is corporate paid-in capital of 50 million Yen. The notations are:

X_{ij} = Total Production of Industry i of Scale, j, where $i = a, h, M, E$; $j = L, S$; a denotes agriculture, h heavy, M other manufacturing and E tertiary; L large scale and S small scale
M_{ij} = Materials input for Industry i of Scale j
T_{ij} = Indirect Tax *minus* Subsidies for Industry i or scale j
W_{ij} = Wage Payments by Industry i of Scale j
D_{ij} = Depreciation in Industry i of Scale j
P_{ij} = Profits in Industry i of Scale j
Y_o = Rental Income
D_r = Depreciation of residential houses
D_g = Depreciation of government-owned buildings
I_{ij} = Fixed Capital Formation in Industry i of Scale j
I_R = Residential Capital Formation
G_I = Government Capital Formation
J_a = Inventory Investment of Agriculture
J_d = Dealers' Inventory Investment
J_m = Producers' Inventory Investment of Raw Materials
J_P = Producers' Inventory Investment of Goods in Process
J_{fi} = Industry i's Inventory Investment of Finished Products
C_f = Consumption of Food
C_t = Consumption of Textiles
C_O = Consumption of Other Goods
W_g = Government Wage Payments
G_c = Govern. Non-wage Consumption
E_a = Exports of Agricultural Products
E_h = Exp. of Heavy Industry Products
E_M = Exp. of Other Manuf. Products
B_m = Imports of Raw Materials
B_f = Imports of Food
B_h = Imports of Heavy Ind. Products
B_c = Imports of Consumption Goods
Y_G = Gross National Product
ξ, η, d_s = Some statistical adjustments

Here it is to be noted that Heavy Industry includes Mining besides Metal, Machinery and Armament Industries. The M Sector covers all the rest of the Manufacturing Industries. Agriculture includes Forestry and Fishery. All other industries are included in the E sector.

The following identities must hold in money values:

$$Y'_G = Y'_a + Y'_{hL} + Y'_{hS} + Y'_{ML} + Y'_{MS} + Y'_E + Y'_O + W'_g + \xi' \quad (3.1)$$

$$Y'_G = C' + I' + J' + G' + E' - B' + \eta' \quad (3.2)$$

$$Y'_G = W' + P' + Y'_a + Y'_O + T' + D' + d'_s \quad (3.3)$$

$$C' = C'_f + C'_t + C'_O \quad (3.4)$$

$$I' = I'_{hL} + I'_{hS} + I'_{ML} + I'_{MS} + I'_E + I'_a \quad (3.5)$$

$$J' = J'_a + J'_d + J'_p + J'_m + J'_{fh} + J'_{fM} \quad (3.6)$$

$$G' = G'_c + G'_I + W'_g \quad (3.7)$$

$$D' = D'_{hL} + D'_{hS} + D'_{ML} + D'_{MS} + D'_E + D'_R + D'_g \quad (3.8)$$

$$T' = T'_{hL} + T'_{hS} + T'_{ML} + T'_{MS} + T'_E + T'_a \quad (3.9)$$

$$E' = E'_a + E'_h + E'_M \quad (3.10)$$

$$B' = B'_m + B'_h + B'_c + B'_f \quad (3.11)$$

$$W' = W'_{hL} + W'_{hs} + W'_{ML} + W'_{MS} + W'_E \quad (3.12)$$

$$P' = P'_{hL} + P'_{hS} + P'_{ML} + P'_{MS} + P'_E \quad (3.13)$$

$$P'_{ij} = X'_{ij} - M'_{ij} - W'_{ij} - D'_{ij} - T'_{ij}(i = h, M, E;\ j = L, S) \quad (3.14)$$

As we discussed in the preceding section, we can define similar identities in real terms by appropriate use of price indices. Real GNP (Y_G) can be defined as:

$$Y_G = C + I + J + G + E - B + \eta, \quad (3.15)$$

where

$$C = C'_f/p^c_f + C'_t/p^c_t + C'_o/p^c_o$$

$$I = I'/p_k$$

$$J = J'_d/p^J_d + J'_m/p^J_m + J'_p/p^J_p + J'_{fh}/p_h + J'_{fM}/p_M$$

$$G = G'_c/p^c + W'_g/p^g_w + G'_I/p_k$$

$$E = E'_a/p^e_a + E'_h/p^e_h + E'_M/p^e_M$$

$$B = B'_m/p^b_m + B'_h/p^b_h + B'_c/p^b_c + B'_f/p^b_f,$$

and the new notations denote:

p_f^c = consumers' price-index of food,
p_t^c = consumers' price-index of textiles,
p_o^c = consumers' price-index of other goods,
p_k = Price-index of investment goods,
p_a = Price-index for dealers inventory investment,
p_m^J = Price-index for raw materials,
p_p^J = Price-index for goods in process,
p_h = Price-index of Heavy Industry products,
p_M = Price-index of Other Manufacturing products,
$p^c = C'/C$ = Implicit deflator for total consumption,
p_w^g = index of wages,
p_a^e = export price-index for agricultural products,
p_h^e = export price-index for heavy industry products,
p_M^e = export price-index for other manufacturing products,
p_m^b = import price-index for raw materials,
p_h^b = import price-index for heavy industry products,
p_c^b = import price-index for consumption goods,
p_f^b = import price-index for food.

Needless to say, the implicit deflator for GNP can be obtained by

$$Y'_G/Y_G = p \tag{3.16}$$

It is easy to see that the value added of each sector, say, Y_{ij} in real terms can be obtained by

$$Y_{ij} = (X'_{ij} - M'_{ij})/p = \frac{p_i}{p}\left(l - \frac{p_i^m}{p_i}\frac{M'_{ij}/p_i^m}{X'_{ij}/p_i}\right)\frac{X'ij}{p_i}, \tag{3.17}$$

where

$$p_i^m = \text{price-index of raw materials for Industry } i.$$

From (3.14) and (3.17) it can be seen that

$$Y_{ij} = \frac{w_{ij}}{p}N_{ij} + \frac{\pi_{ij}}{p}K_{ij} + \frac{T_{ij}}{p} + \frac{D_{ij}}{p}, \tag{3.18}$$

where w_{ij}, π_{ij}, N_{ij} and K_{ij} are defined for each sector in the same way as w, π, N, K are for the entire system. Thus identities similar to (3.1),

(3.2) and (3.3) can be established, and they can be used to analyze various aspects of economic growth in the same way as in the preceding section.

The statistical data are compiled according to the scheme of Table 2 for 44 quarters from the beginning of 1951 to the end of 1961. The time-series used are published in Ichimura *et al.* (1946), except for some additional data prepared for this paper and listed in the Appendix. Price indices are mostly components of the wholesale price index published by the Bank of Japan. The detailed explanation of statistical data will be made available later.

4. Rapid Industrialization, Dual Structure and Technical Progress

Let us observe first the industries that grew most rapidly. The rate of growth in, say, X_{hL} is computed by estimating

$$\log X_{hL}(t) = \log A_{hL} + \alpha_{hL}t + \log U_t. \tag{4.1}$$

We then compare α's in different sectors. The same method is used to compute the growth rates in any other variables or their ratios. If those growth rates for X, Y, Z, are α, β, γ, and $Z = XY$, then $\alpha + \beta = \gamma$.

To simplify the presentation, $\Delta X/X$ will be denoted by $g(X)$. Table 3 shows the annual growth rates in total production of sectors, 1951–1961 and the growth rates of raw material input coefficients M/X.[3]

Table 3. Growth Rates of Industrial Production and Raw Material Input Coefficients.

	$G(X)$	$G(M/X)$
Heavy : Large	18.5	0.6
Other : Large	15.7	0.9
Heavy: Small	14.1	0.3
Other : Small	11.0	−1.2
Tertiary	6.4	−0.6
Agriculture	4.8	1.4

[3]Here and in the following discussion we do not consider the so-called "vertical integration" of firms, particularly among different scales of firms, but treat large and small scales of industries as if they were producing the same industrial product-mix, only in different scales. To the extent that this is inadequate, our discussion must be reconsidered.

Since the raw materials input coefficients did not change significantly, except for Agriculture and Tertiary Industries, and also the relative prices of raw materials and outputs changed very little, we can compute the contribution of each sector to the growth rate of GNP according to (3.1) (3.17). It is clear that the leading industry was Heavy Industry in simple classification.

There is no doubt that there was an avalanche of new technologies in post-war Japan and that this was one of the major factors in its rapid growth. In order to assess their importance, we follow the method explained in Section 2. Table 4 shows the means and the growth rates of capital coefficients and labor productivities in six sectors; Table 5 shows the rates of change in factor and output prices and factor shares.

These tables reveal, first of all, the surprisingly large differentials in productivities among different scales of same industry as well as among different industries. For instance, labor productivity in the *ML* sector is three times as large as that in the *MS* sector, and almost 1.5 times as big as that in the *HL* sector. Since there is no significant difference in M/X; for instance, $M_{hL}/X_{hL} = 0.68$, $M_{ML}/X_{ML} = 0.68$, these differentials can

Table 4. Capital Coefficient, Labor Productivity, Capital-Labor Ratio and Their Rates of Growth.

	K/X	X/N	K/N	$g(X/K)$	$G(X/N)$	$g(K/N)$
HL	1.73	4.46	7.10	5.6	11.8	6.2
ML	1.40	6.50	8.55	4.0	10.1	6.1
HS	0.75	2.44	1.78	3.1	7.1	4.0
MS	0.80	2.14	1.56	9.1	6.4	−3.1
E	1.62	1.77	2.87	−3.0	0.4	3.4
A	1.08	1.15	1.22	7.3	5.6	2.5

Table 5. The Growth Rates of Output, Labor and Capital, and Their Prices.

	$g(X)$	$g(N)$	$g(K)$	$g(p)$	$G(w)$	$g(\pi)$
HL	18.5	6.7	12.9	0.5	8.9	6.9
ML	15.7	5.6	11.7	−0.4	8.7	2.6
HS	14.1	6.9	10.9	0.5	7.3	8.0
MS	11.0	5.0	1.9	−0.4	7.2	10.9
E	6.4	6.0	9.3	4.2	8.4	1.6
A	4.1	−1.5	0.4	0.8	(7.0)	

be compensated only by the differentials in factor prices. This is nothing but the problem of what is referred to as the *dual structure* of the Japanese Economy. By observing the growth rates of the productivities we can see also that the productivity differentials widened rather than narrowed among industries as well as between scales throughout the period. These sectoral differences in observed technical relations and their changes must be related to the differences in technical progress among sectors. By an argument similar to those explained in connection with (2.28), (2.31) and (2.32) we seem to be able to infer the types of technical progress that prevailed in different sectors during this period. Since it does not seem that there was any noticeable change in the degree of competition in the *hL*, *hS* and *ML* sectors, the rates of change in the indices of the degree of competition can safely be suppressed for these sectors. The *hL* sector shows in Table 6 that its technical progress was *labor-saving* and in Table 3 slightly *material-using*. The *ML* sector shows that its change was *neutral* and slightly *material-saving*. In the case of the *MS* sector, the same sign for wN/pX and $\pi K/pX$ does not permit the straight-forward classification of this sector's technical progress. If, however, the degree of competition in the capital market may be assumed to have increased in this sector, then $g(\delta) < 0$ so that 2.2% may very well have been negative. Hence we seem to be able to infer that this sector's technical progress was *capital-saving* and *material-saving*.[4]

Table 6. Factor Shares and Biases of Technical Progress.

	$g\left(\frac{wN}{pX}\right)$	$g\left(\frac{\pi K}{pX}\right)$	$g\left(\frac{wN}{\pi K}\right)$	$g\left(\frac{M}{X}\right)$	**Class. I**	**Class. II**
HL	−3.4	0.8	−4.2	0.6	Labor-saving	Material-using
ML	−1.0	−1.0	0	0.9	Neutral	Material-using
HS	−0.4	4.3	−4.7	0.3	Labor-saving	Material-using
MS	1.6	2.2	−0.6	−1.2	Capital-saving	Material-saving
E	3.8	0.3	3.5	−0.6	Capital-saving	Material-saving
A	(−0.6)			1.4	Labor-saving	Material-using
	$g(\alpha)-g(\gamma)$	$g(\beta)-g(\delta)$	$g(\alpha/\beta)-g(\gamma/\delta)$			

[4]For classification of technical change, see for instance, Fei and Ranis (1964). It seems important to keep in mind that rapid technical progress tends to be concentrated in some leading firms in the industry and thereby increase the degree of imperfect competition. Hence, one should always suspect that $\Delta\gamma$ or $\Delta\delta$ may be positive rather than negative in a fast-growing economy.

Similar arguments seem to hold for Tertiary Industry as well, because this is the sector dominated by small-scale unincorporated firms. Thus it may be assumed that $g(\delta) < 0$ in this sector, and that technical progress was *capital-saving* as well as *material-saving*. Technical progress in Agriculture requires similar but converse arguments. Assume that $g(w)$ in Agriculture is equal to the average of $g(w)$ in the industrial sectors. It is well known that the price of rice is not a competitive price but is fixed by political as well as economic considerations. If $p^o \alpha X/N = \gamma w$ holds, as Table 6 shows, $g(\alpha) - g(\gamma) = -0.7$. Since the logic in determining w here involves determination of p_A first and then of farmer's mixed income, and since there is no reason to believe that the supply price of farmers' labor does not increase nearly as fast as the industrial wage, $g(p_A) = 0.8$, $g(w) = 7.0$ can be explained by the decline of the bargaining power of farm relative to industrial labor. This implies $g(\gamma) < 0$, and $g(\alpha) < -0.7$. Thus we may conclude that Agricultural technical progress is "labor-saving." Unlike the other sector $g(p_A^m)$ and $g(p_A)$ showed different rates: $g(p_A^m) = 1.7$ and $g(p_A) = 0.8$; therefore we need to compare them with $g(M/X)$. But we know from Table 3, Table 6 and these figures that $g(p_A^m M_A/p_A X_A) = 1.7 - 0.8 + 1.4 = 3.3$ and $g(p_A^m M_A/w_A N_A) = 1.7 - 7.0 + 6.2 + 2.1 = 3.0$, we can conclude that Agriculture's technical change is not only *labor-saving* but also *material-saving*. The post-war introduction of chemical weeding and fertilizers must have been the major source of increase in agricultural productivity.

These various types of technical progress in six sectors may be summarized by a triangle in Figure 1. The relative position of each point marked by sectoral designation to the central point in the triangle indicates the change of factor proportions per unit of output according to the distance to each corner. If, for instance, a point A is located as it is in the following triangle, it shows that the amounts of three factors per unit of output in 1961 compared with those in 1951 for the same set of relative prices are less labor, more capital, and more materials. On the whole it is quite clear that technical progress was primarily *labor-saving*. This is very significant in view of the high rate of unemployment prevailing during this period. According to (2.33) or (2.34), this type of technical progress was an additional factor given rise to rapid growth on the supply side along with additional factors represented by other terms in (2.33) or (2.34).

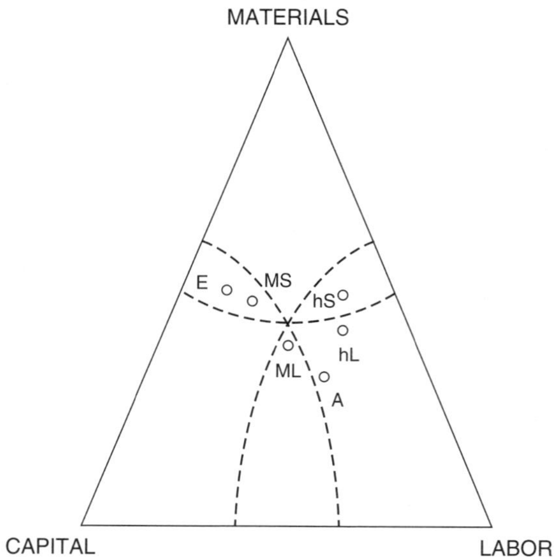

Figure 1. Types of Technical Progress.

5. Supply of Productive Factors and Technical Progress

Let us proceed further in showing how the various productive factors contributed to Japanese economic growth on the supply side. Table 5 gives an unusually high rate of growth in non-agricultural employment, which accounts for a very high percentage of growth in industrial production of each sector, as the first column of Table 7 shows. Since the following identity must hold for the employment of Industrial Labor:

$$N_f = N_I + N_a \div U + N_{s+g}, \tag{5.1}$$

where N_f: labor force, N_a: agricultural employment, N_I: industrial employment and N_{s+g}: employers and government employees; we can write

$$g(N_I)\frac{N_I}{N_f} = g(N_f) - g(N_a)\frac{N_a}{N_f} - g(U)\frac{U}{N_f} - g(N_{s+g})\frac{N_{s+g}}{N_f}. \tag{5.2}$$

A high rate of increase in employment in the industrial sector is possible only by the matching high rates of increase (or decrease) in the terms on the right-hand side of (5.2). In the period from 1951 to 1961, $g(N_{s+g}) \fallingdotseq 0$

Table 7. Factors Contributing to Industrial Growth of GNP.

	$G(Y)$	$g(N)$	$\beta g(K/N)$	$\Delta\beta \log K/N$	$g(Y/X)$	$g(A)-g(Y/X)$
HL	17.6	6.7	2.4	2.0	−0.9	7.4
ML	15.8	5.6	2.8	0	0.1	7.3
HS	13.7	6.9	1.2	0.6	−0.4	5.4
MS	12.2	5.0	−0.9	0.1	1.2	6.8
E	7.1	6.0	1.5	−0.9	0.7	−0.2
A	3.8	−1.5	(2.3)	0	−0.3	(4.0)

so that this term may be ignored. In 1956, $N_I/N_f = 0.38$, $N_a/N_f = 0.32$, $U/N_f = 0.19$, $N_{s+g}/N_f = 0.11$. It is important, however, to divide the whole period into two parts; from 1951 to 1956 and from 1956 to 1961. Throughout the entire period, the high rate of increase in labor force: $g(N_f) = 2.0\%$, is the main factor making a high value of $g(N_I) = 6.0$ possible. But during the period up to 1956 it was particularly rapid as a result of the high birth rate just before the war; whereas after 1957, $g(N_f)$ slowed down reflecting the fall in birth rate during the war. The absolute increase from 1951 to 1956 was about 6 million and the annual average was 1.2 million, whereas from 1956 to 1961, the absolute increase suddenly dropped to about 3 millions with annual average of 0.6 million. In spite of rapid growth of employment, from 1951 to 1956, N_I increased by about 4 million and the Industrial sector as a whole failed to employ all the new labor force. As a result N_a and U increased during the first half period. Employment in the industrial sector, however, kept increasing at a faster pace in the second half period. The absolute increase in N_I was about 6 million in this period with the annual average 1.2 million. This sharp rate of increase was matched not only by the high, though falling, rate of increase in N_f but also by the rapid rate of decrease in N_a and U. $g(N_a)$ in this period was about −3.0% (the absolute number was 2.1 million), and g(U) was −4.0% (the absolute number was 1.5 million). Indeed, 60% of new industrial workers were absorbed from the reserve army of labor in unemployment and agriculture, which awaited the opportunities of industrial employment since they had received improved training and education, particularly during the first period. This reserve army must still have contained a considerable number of demobilized soldiers and returning emigrants. These troops numbered 5 million and more than compensated for the loss of 2 million vigorous youth and civilians during the war. Thus, the most important factor in rapid Japanese economic growth was this ample supply of good quality labor during a limited span of time.

The contribution of this increase of labor to the growth of industrial production can be seen by an identity similar to (2.34). Assume that

$$Y_{ij} = A_{ij} N_{ij}^{l-\beta} K_{ij}^{\beta} \tag{5.3}$$

then, omitting the subscripts for simplicity,

$$\frac{\Delta Y}{Y} = \frac{\Delta A}{A} + \frac{\Delta N}{N} + \beta \frac{\Delta (K/N)}{K/N} + \Delta \beta \log \frac{K}{N}. \tag{5.4}$$

This expression partitions the factors contributing to the growth of Y into four parts; the growth of employment $\Delta N/N$, the part attributed to the growth of the capital-labor ratio for given β, the part due to biased technical progress, and the overall increase of efficiency. Notice that if technical progress is "labor-saving", $\Delta\beta > 0$ so that the last term is positive. Note also that (5.4) relates Y to N and K only, but since Y may increase for the same N and K if M/X decreases, this aspect needs some consideration. If M/X decreases or Y/X increases, the growth rate of Y exceeds that of X. The change in the overall efficiency not related to "material-saving" technical progress can be seen by $g(A) - g(Y/X)$.

Table 7 shows the percentage contribution of each factor to the total growth rate in each sector. Clearly the dominant factor is, as we said above, the very rapid growth of employment in the industrial sector.

The second important factor is capital accumulation. In order to exceed the rapid growth of employment and achieve an ever-increasing capital-labor ratio, capital must be accumulated very rapidly. Except for the MS sector a significant part of industrial growth can be attributed to the high rate of capital accumulation shown in the third column of Table 5. Such an unusually high rate of capital accumulation is surely an important factor in rapid economic growth, as we shall see in details later.

The assumed values of β's are: 0.39, 0.45, 0.30, 0.30, 0.44 and 0.5 in the order of sectors listed in the table. They are computed by the ratios of the arithmetic mean of P_{ij} to that of $P_{ij} + W_{ij}$ over the sample period except for agriculture. 0.5 was simply assumed for agriculture for lack of better information. $\Delta\beta$ was computed by multiplying $g(\pi K/pX)$ (Table 6) for each industry group by the corresponding β estimate for that industry group. Since $g(\pi K/pX) = g(\beta) - g(\delta)$, this is only an approximation.

The third factor, bias in technical progress, seems to have been important in Heavy Industry in particular, but not so important in Other

Manufacturing. It had an inverse effect in Tertiary Industry. The remaining part of growth rate may be attributed to the overall efficiency. This part appears to be as important as the growth rate of employment. The only exception was Tertiary Industry, in which 85% of $g(Y)$ was due to $g(N)$. The increase in overall efficiency in all the manufacturing industries is very significant, but this is not too surprising. The first half of the period was still a phase of post-war recovery. Not only were there well-trained workers and administrators but also much unused complementary capital equipment and social capital which must have made the marginal productivities of labor and capital, as a result of post-war investment, unusually high. The following chart of capital-output ratios clearly demonstrates a sharp decline in *capital-output ratios* from 1951 to 1956 in most sectors. This may be taken as a manifestation of post-war recovery phenomena. Since this favorable condition gradually disappeared after 1956, $g(A)$ must have receded in the latter half of the period. In fact there was an extremely high rate of capital accumulation in all the sectors after 1956 to compensate for the declining trend in $g(A)$. Indeed, $g(K)$ was considerably larger in all sectors after 1956 than it was before.

6. Resource Allocation and Market Mechanism

The Japanese economy is often cited as a showcase of free enterprise achievement of rapid economic growth. Nobody doubts that labor and capital were utilized more efficiently and allocated more optimally in Japan than in the Soviet Union, but this does not imply that resource allocation in Japan was actually optimal. Through simple use of ratios of relevant variables we shall try to analyze this problem.

Observe the third column of Table 6. If we could assume that $g(\gamma/\delta)$ is the same for hL and hS sectors, then it implies that technical progress in the hS sector was more *labor-saving* than in the hL sector. This is hard to believe. In fact, the first column of the same table seems to imply the reverse. Comparison of the first with the second columns leads to suspicion that $g(\delta)$ was larger in the hL sector than in the SL sector; i.e. the degree of competition in the capital market declined for large scale heavy industry corporations. To the extent that π/p and w/p deviated more from the marginal productivities of capital, allocation of capital was less than optimal. Similar observations are difficult to make for the other manufacturing industry, because of the difference in technical progress in large and small-scale firms.

Table 8. Sectoral Allocation of Capital.

	π	K/X (average)	K/X (1961)	$\Delta K/\Delta X$	$g(K)\%$	I (bil.Yen)	$g(I)\%$
HL	8.5	1.73	1.31	2.25	12.9	0.57	27.1
HS	11.6	0.75	0.63	0.92	10.9	0.17	16.6
ML	8.6	1.40	1.16	1.42	11.7	0.53	15.3
MS	9.7	0.80	0.49	0.90	1.9	0.50	12.2
E	13.6	1.62	1.88	0.86	9.3	1.34	13.7
A		1.08	0.91	1.92	0.4	0.39	8.9

* $\Delta K/\Delta X$ was computed by $K/X(1+g(X/K)/g(X))$. The second column is the arithmetic mean of K/X in the period.

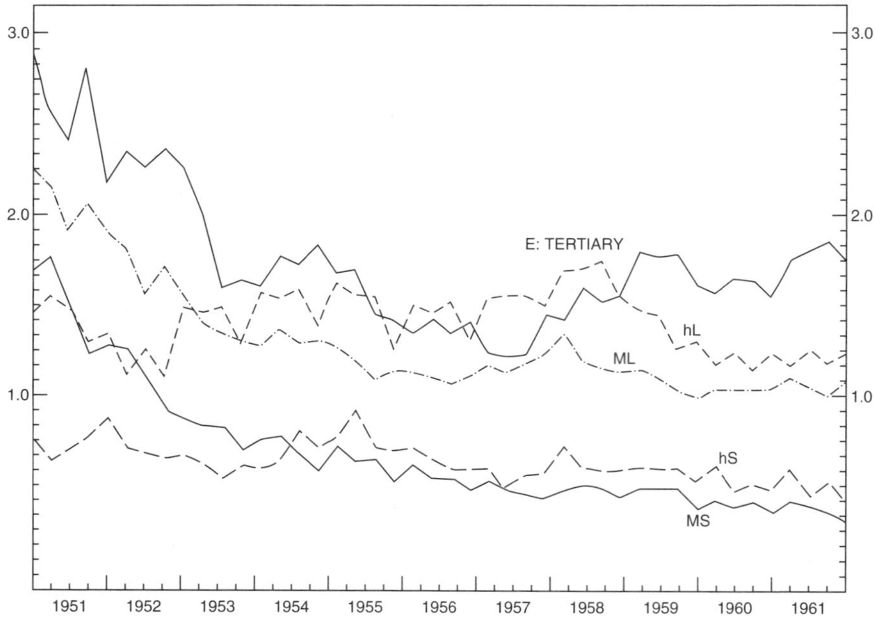

Figure 2. Capital-Output Ratios in Five Sections.

If, however, it can be assumed that large and small firms produce similar products, then something may be said about the market force in allocating resources among different scales of firms in the same industry. Table 8 and Figure 2 shows that π is higher for small firms, and that capital coefficients, both average and marginal, are consistently lower for smaller firms. Yet there is no indication in the absolute value of investment or in the growth rates of capital and investment that increasingly more capital is attracted to the hS sector rather than the hL sector. This seems to imply that capital was misallocated toward large corporations. This is consistent with the direction of change in the degree of competition or monopoly in heavy industry mentioned above.

The same proposition holds for other manufacturing industry. Despite the higher π and lower capital coefficients, capital was not allocated enough to smaller firms in this industry. Tertiary industry consists predominantly of smaller corporations and private businesses in Japan. In this industry $g(K)$ and $g(I)$ are below the values in the hL and *ML* sectors, not to mention agriculture in this connection. Thus it seems conclusive that the capital market was not sufficiently competitive to allocate capital optimally by the market mechanism.

The arguments concerning the allocation of capital among industries are more involved, because demand conditions must be taken into consideration. It seems possible, however, to judge demand and supply conditions in the market by observing $g(p)$ in Table 5. In particular, the high rate of price rise in tertiary industry and agriculture seems to indicate that there was a need to increase productivity in these two sectors. In the case of tertiary industry π is very high, and the marginal capital coefficient is very low. Nevertheless $g(K)$ and $g(I)$ do not show any significant rise compared with other industries.[5] In the case of agriculture the marginal capital coefficient is higher than in any other sector, except for the hL sector, which is after all a very capital-intensive industry. But extremely low rates of growth in capital and investment seems to require a careful inquiry into the underlying causes of difficulties in agricultural investment.[6] Thus, even among industries there seems to have been some misallocation of capital during this period.

[5] This must have something to do with the topic often discussed in Japan that the service and distribution industries are especially inefficient. However, as Table 12 in the next Section shows, post-war Japan inherited an excess capacity of overhead capital. This fact must have made it possible for some industries like transportation or communication to be satisfied with low rates of capital accumulation. The ratio of overhead capital to tertiary industry output has declined up to 1957 and then began to rise. Hence, the low rate of capital accumulation was not so unusual in the first half of the period as in the latter half.

[6] If we assume the existence of a Cobb-Douglas production function and the β's equal to those in Table 7, then the marginal productivity of capital can be computed as $\beta X/K$. They are hL, 0.23; hS, 0.60; *ML*, 0.26; *MS*, 0.61; E, 0.22; A, 0.46. The argument on capital allocation needs no change, except for agriculture. But β is probably less than 0.5 so that 0.46 is an overestimate. If $\beta = 0.4$, in place of 0.46 we have 0.37.

Table 9. Sectoral Allocation of Labor.

	W	X/N	$X/N(61)$	$(1-\beta)X/N$	$G(N)$	ΔN (thousand)
HL	0.83	4.46	7.8	2.7	6.7	8.1
HS	0.43	2.44	3.7	1.3	5.6	7.4
ML	0.69	6.50	11.8	4.6	6.9	7.1
MS	0.29	2.14	2.7	1.5	5.0	16.3
E	0.46	1.77	1.9	1.0	6.0	60.3
A	(0.21)	1.55	1.6	1.1	−1.5	−20.0

* w in A is computed as 70% of *per capita* income in A. β is assumed to be the same as Table 7.

The allocation of labor can similarly be analyzed. Table 9 shows the same kinds of related variables for six sectors. The higher rate of money wages and the higher marginal productivity of labor in heavy industry attracted more labor into large corporations. This desirable direction of allocation of labor among large and small businesses holds also for other manufacturing industry. The small difference in $g(N)$ between the two scales of industries seems to reflect the non-optimal allocation of capital just discussed. If more capital had been allocated to small businesses, $g(N)$ would have been significantly less in smaller scale enterprise.[7]

The same argument seems to hold for tertiary industry. Since this sector had a high rate of w and π combined with low productivity of labor and yet absorbed only labor, but not capital, the substitution of capital for labor would have made it possible to reduce price inflation in this industry by not bidding up wages so much, particularly in the latter period. The domestic migration of labor out of agriculture is a necessary consequence of the income differential and productivity gap between agriculture and industry, as Table 9 shows. Thus, we conclude that there is some evidence for capital to have been misallocated among different scales of business as well as among industries, but ample supply of labor alleviated the serious consequences that might have resulted from this faulty allocation.

[7] Hugh Patrick cast some doubt in his comment on the reliability of capital stocks data for the *MS* sector. Since, however, K_{MS} is computed by adding to the base year's value I_{MS} which is obtained by subtracting I_{ML} from the investment of the whole Industry and I_{ML} is reliable, his conjecture can only concern under estimation of industrial investment. It may be that small-scale firms often purchase inexpensive used capital equipment, which would make our price deflator too high for I_{MS}. The author does not believe that these factors can be decisive in upsetting the reasoning in the text.

7. The Growth of National Expenditure and Its Composition

Now we turn to the demand side of GNP. We already discussed the high rate of capital accumulation as an important factor in rapid economic growth. This is possible only when the rest of the items in National Expenditure do not occupy an unusually large proportion.

Table 10 shows the average composition over the period and the growth rate of each item in National Expenditure. Fixed Capital Formation occupied 24.8%, of which 59% was Private Fixed Capital Formation. Moreover, the percentage of Fixed Capital Formation kept on increasing toward the end of this period, and in 1961 it was above 30%. It is of interest to note that some components of inventory investment grew at a slower pace than GNP, but that the predominant part of inventory investment, particularly goods in process and dealers' inventories, grew significantly faster than 15%. It is a reflection of inefficiency of the Tertiary Industry in the Japanese economy, which we discussed earlier.

Table 10. Composition of National Expenditure And Growth Rates in its Components.

	Composition %	Growth Rate %		Composition %	Growth Rate%
C_f	32.1	4.9	I_R	2.0	11.1
C_t	5.3	9.0			
C_o	24.3	9.1	G_I	8.2	11.3
sub	61.7	6.9	$G_c + W_g$	10.8	9.7
J_{fh}	0.3	15.5			
J_{fM}	0.5	4.0	E_a	0.7	11.1
J_m	0.8	6.3	E_h	3.8	19.4
J_p	1.7	20.1	E_M	6.1	15.8
J_d	1.7	15.2	sub	10.6	16.8
J_A	−0.3	2.0	B_m	−9.0	15.3
sub	4.7	15.1	B_f	−1.4	3.1
I_{HL}	2.6	27.1	B_h	−0.9	15.5
I_{ML}	2.4	16.6	B_c	−0.8	14.9
I_{HS}	0.8	15.3	sub	−12.1	13.9
I_{MS}	0.9	12.2	Y_G		9.6
I_E	6.1	13.7			
I_A	1.8	8.9			
sub	14.6	16			

Table 11. Gross Capital Formation's Ratio to GNP and Share of Residential I in Total I, 1962.

	I (bill. $)	I/Y_G (%)	I_R/I (%)
Japan	17.4	35.3	7.2
West Germany	19.5	25.1	23.3
Italy	8.2	23.1	23.6
Sweden	3.0	22.2	23.1
Canada	7.7	21.8	18.3
France	11.2	17.8	22.3
U.K.	12.6	16.9	18.1
U.S.A.	82.4	15.8	27.7

Source: U.N.; World Statistical Yearbook (1963).

Table 11 shows the ratio of Gross Capital Formation to GNP and the ratio of residential investment to gross investment in some countries in 1962. Japan's high investment ratio can be readily seen. Such a high rate of capital accumulation was made possible by the items growing less proportionately than national expenditure in Japan. The average growth rate of GNP in real terms was about 9.6%, whereas consumption increased at the rate of only 6.9%. This is undoubtedly the most important factor in the high rate of capital accumulation. Most of the rest of components grew faster than GNP itself. Particularly significant are private capital formation and exports. They led to rapid growth.

Another reason for the high ratio of investment to GNP is the fact that the balance of trade could almost always remain negative in this period. On average the propensity to import (12.1%) exceeded the ratio of exports to GNP (10.6%). This was possible only because of the inflow of foreign capital, which amounted to 1.5 times of GNP on average over this period. Were it not for an offsetting reduction in capital formation to match this amount of capital import, the growth rate would have been correspondingly lower. If the ratio of private industrial capital formation to the increment of GNP remained stable, then the decline in growth rate would be computed as approximately 0.9%: $1.5 \times (9.6/16/0) = 0.9$. One could say that it was rather surprising for the Japanese economy with so few natural resources to have become less dependent on imports despite such an unusually high rate of industrial growth. Having lost 45% of its former territory, including two main rice-supplying areas, Taiwan and Korea, Japan could afford to be almost self-sufficient in food up to the end of this period, thanks to the great achievement of Japanese agriculture discussed in Section 4. Imported raw materials, however, have become an increasingly important part of industrial materials. The ratio B_m/M_M has risen at the annual rate of 1.3%. On the other hand, the development of new capital goods industry made it possible for the proportion of imported capital equipment to total domestic fixed capital formation B_h/I_p to decline at the rate of 1.2% a year.[8]

The most remarkable characteristics of capital accumulation in Japan are, however, the composition of investment itself. First we note that residential investment occupies a small proportion (say, 8.1%) of total capital formation. This has been a characteristic of Japanese capital formation, even in pre-war years,[9] and the construction cost of simple houses in Japan might have been much cheaper. The proportion is astonishingly small if one remembers that most of the big cities were bombed during the war, and that nearly half a million people moved from rural to metropolitan areas every year during this period. The second characteristic is that government investment occupies also a relatively small proportion, 33.0% of total gross capital formation or only 56.2% of private industrial capital formation. This may, however, not be so surprising, because the overhead capital inherited from the pre-war economy must have saved the post-war government investment particularly during the first half of the period.

In this connection, Table 12 supplements the argument we presented before with reference to the chart of sectoral capital-output ratios and the investment in tertiary industry. The high overhead capital to GNP ratio in the post-war years shows a gradual decline toward the pre-war level. This fact is particularly noticeable if we take the ratio of K_g to the level of output in Tertiary Industry, which includes some industries heavily dependent on overhead capital.

The last factor contributing to low G_I/Y_G is the extremely low expenditure for defense. As Table 13 shows, government expenditure on national accounting basis occupied 19% of GNP, of which defense expenditure occupied only 6.8%. Since GNP is 1.23 times as much as National Income for this period, the ratio of defense expenditure to national income is 1.6%, which should be compared, for example, with Germany's 5.0%, Italy's 4.1%, France's 8.1%, England's 8.3% or USA's 12.5% all in 1958. The effect on Japanese economic growth of more expenditure for defense can

[8]The Japanese balance of trade was helped by the general fall in import prices. $g(p_f^b) = -3.5$, $g(p_h^b) = 3.0$, $g(p_m^b) = -2.9$, $g(p_c^b) = -2.7$. On average, the annual rate of fall in the import price index is 2.5%.

[9]The percentage of residential investment in gross capital formation in Japan was 9.5% in 1934–1936; 13.5% in 1930.

Table 12. Overhead Capital, GNP and Output of Tertiary Industry.

	K'_g	Y'_G	K_g/Y_G	K_g	X_E	K_g/X_E	K_E/X_E
1926	3,917	4,446	.88				
1930	4,922	4,589	1.07				
1935	6,132	6,248	.98				
1940	7,151						
1945	6,804						
1948	8,031						
1951	8,861	6,386	1.39	8,843	364.8	24.2	5.2
1952	9,188	7,146	1.29	9,196	645.8	14.2	3.2
1953	9,637	7,830	1.23	9,692	759.2	12.8	3.0
1954	10,100	7,993	1.26	10,245	953.4	10.7	2.5
1955	10,518	8,895	1.18	10,770	1,078.0	10.0	2.3
1956	10,996	9,615	1.14	11,277	1,243.3	9.1	2.2
1957	11,532	10,495	1.10	11,853	1,499.9	7.9	2.1
1958	12,991	10,448	1.24	12,525	1,214.5	10.3	2.8
1959	13,923	12,356	1.13	13,369	1,612.2	8.3	2.4
1960	15,086	14,065	1.07	14,265	2,040.1	7.0	2.1
1961	16,614	16,231	1.02	15,507	2,066.4	7.5	2.3

Source: K'_g, Y'_G are taken from data prepared at the Economic Planning Agency; others from Ichimura *et al.* (1964b).

be computed if we can accept some assumptions. Suppose, for instance, that the Japanese government had to spend as much as Italy; i.e., 3.3% of GNP; the new resource required for defense were realized by decreasing the components of GNP like consumption, inventory investment, private capital formation and imports; and that the ratio of the increment of GNP to private capital formation (0.6) remain unchanged. Then the percentage decline of I_p/Y_G is $3.3\% \times 0.20 = 0.66\%$, and the fall of $g(Y_G)$ is $0.66 \times 0.6 = 0.4\%$. This gives some idea of how much the Japanese growth was promoted by saving defense expenditure.

For all these reasons, the Japanese Economy could devote an unusually high proportion of Gross National Product to productive fixed capital formation and allocate them intensively in export industries or capital goods industries and succeed in achieving a high rate of economic growth.

Appendix: Statistical Data

Almost all the statistics used this article are available in Ichimura *et al.* (1964b). The following are some additional data compiled for this chapter.

Table A.1. Annual Data for Agriculture.

	K_A	I_{Aa}	X_{Aa}	$K_{A,-1}/X_{Aa}$	X_{Aa}/N_{Aa}	K_{Aa}/N_{Aa0}	$I_{Aa}/K_{A,-1}$
1950	15,612						
1951	15,771	158.6	13,757	1.13	1.00	1.15	1.01
1952	15,914	143.1	14,293	1.10	1.04	1.16	0.91
1953	16,088	174.0	13,011	1.22	0.93	1.15	1.09
1954	16,175	87.1	12,380	1.30	0.89	1.16	0.54
1955	16,278	102.7	14,934	1.08	1.07	1.16	0.63
1956	16,350	71.8	14,641	1.11	1.07	1.19	0.44
1957	16,330	−20.0	15,180	1.08	1.12	1.20	−0.12
1958	16,344	14.3	15,944	1.02	1.21	1.24	0.09
1959	16,394	49.8	17,085	0.96	1.35	1.30	0.30
1960	16,572	177.6	17,307	0.95	1.41	1.35	1.08
1961	16,789	217.1	18,215	0.91	1.56	1.44	1.31

*K_A: Capital stocks at the beginning of the year; taken from the unpublished data at the Economic Planning Agency; units billion Yen. I_{Aa}: Net investment in Agriculture. X_{Aa}, N_{Aa} are taken from Ichimura *et al.* (1964b).

Table A.2. Quarterly Data for Agriculture, Tertiary Industry and Government Sector.

	I_A	M_A	M_E	P_E^m	I_g	K_G
1951.1	14.9	793	3,676	0.865	77.2	8,634
2	77.6	561	3,760	0.961	59.0	8,693
3	28.9	832	3,919	0.957	71.8	8,765
4	37.2	1,290	4,597	0.973	78.2	8,843
1952.1	44.5	907	5,004	1.003	95.6	8,939
2	114.1	675	5,758	0.970	71.1	9,010
3	68.6	898	5,560	0.970	88.4	9,098
4	−84.1	1,585	6,432	0.970	97.5	9,196
1953.1	115.3	864	5,288	0.990	120.4	9,316
2	114.3	723	5,425	0.980	107.8	9,424
3	65.8	981	5,659	1.000	128.0	9,552
4	−151.4	1,681	6,924	1.02	139.5	9,692

(*Continued*)

Table A.2. (*Continued*)

	I_A	M_A	M_E	P_E^m	I_g	K_G
1954.1	101.2	962	5,931	1.03	173.4	9,865
2	162.2	771	6,031	1.01	104.0	9,969
3	53.0	1,071	5,920	0.99	133.5	10,103
4	−299.3	1,867	7,103	1.004	141.5	10,245
1955.1	142.6	960	6,230	1.015	172.3	10,412
2	158.7	841	6,222	0.989	101.0	10,518
3	27.1	1,386	6,397	0.994	121.0	10,639
4	−225.7	2,087	7,921	1.001	130.5	10,770
1956.1	97.4	1,052	6,951	1.017	150.0	10,920
2	154.2	900	7,380	1.035	114.7	11,035
3	4.3	1,333	7,377	1.060	118.8	11,154
4	−184.1	1,952	9,057	1.088	123.1	11,277
1957.1	84.4	1,053	7,828	1.087	139.3	11,416
2	169.9	893	8,162	1.100	115.5	11,532
3	0.8	1,474	8,416	1.086	144.9	11,677
4	−275.1	2,226	9,283	1.087	176.0	11,853
1958.1	135.0	1,128	8,040	1.048	190.6	12,044
2	222.2	880	8,290	1.045	137.5	12,182
3	1.9	1,509	8,498	1.044	159.4	12,341
4	−344.8	2,362	9,905	1.053	183.8	12,525
1959.1	102.4	1,226	8,643	1.048	272.4	12,797
2	237.6	1,027	9,279	1.071	150.6	12,948
3	−34.1	1,522	9,574	1.082	191.7	13,140
4	−253.1	2,577	11,324	1.109	228.9	13,369
1960.1	182.5	1,231	10,120	1.084	294.2	13,663
2	280.1	1,029	11,946	1.106	181.3	13,844
3	−24.2	1,908	11,859	1.104	238.0	14,082
4	−260.8	2,778	13,809	1.135	282.6	14,265
1961.1	236.8	1,370	11,361	1.102	349.8	14,615
2	345.7	1,178	12,235	1.143	251.0	14,866
3	31.9	2,163	12,872	1.162	288.8	15,155
4	−397.3	3,302	16,073	1.196	352.4	15,507

*K_g: Social Overhead Capital, taken from the unpublished data at the Economic Planning Agency; units billion Yen; I_g: Net Government Investment.

References

Fei, J. and G. Ranis (1964). *Development of the Labor Surplus Economy: Theory and Policy*. Irwin.

Ichimura, S., L. R. Klein, S. Koizumi, K. Sato and Y. Shinkai (1964a). A Quarterly Econometric Model Of Japan, 1952–1959. *Osaka Economic Papers*, March.

Ichimura, S., L. R. Klein, S. Koizumi, K Sato and Y. Sinkai (1964b) A Quarterly Econometric Model Of Japan, 1952–1959: Data Appendix. *Osaka Economic Papers*, July.

Ichimura, S. (1996). *Japanese Economy in the World*. Tokyo: Chuokoron-Sha (Japanese).

Kaldor, N. (1960). Alternative Theories of Distribution. *The Review of Economic Studies*, February.

Klein, L. R. (1962). *An Introduction to Econometrics*. Prentice Hall.

Kuznets, S. (1966). *Modern Economic Growth*. Yale University Press.

Shimomura, O. (1958). *To Accomplish Economic Growth*. Tokyo: Kochikai (Japanese).

Shinohara, M. (1954). *The Structure of Economic Growth*. Tokyo: Kunimoto Shobo (Japanese).

Stone, R. (1966). *Mathematics in the Social Sciences and Other Essays*. Chapman & Hall.

Stone, R. *et al.* (1954). *The Measurement of Consumers' Expenditure and Behaviour in the United Kingdom, 1920–1938, vol. I*. Cambridge University Press.

Stuvel, G. (1965). *System of Social Accounts*. Oxford University Press.

Yanovsky, M. (1967). *Anatomy of Social Accounting Systems*. Chapman & Hall.

Chapter 2

Social Accounting Analysis of Japan's Lost 90s

Hyun Suk

1. Introduction

This chapter aims at applying the Social Accounting Matrix (SAM) framework to the analysis of the lost 90s of the Japanese economy. The SAM collects in a coherent square matrix system[1] the statistical data on the production and income generation in Input-Output (IO) table and Systems of National Accounts (SNA), the incomes received by different institutions, and their expenditures. Unlike the ordinary IO table and the SNA system, the SAM framework in this chapter covers the interrelations between the real and financial sectors and the savings-investment balance to analyze the long recession in the 90s (Defourne and Thorbecke, 1984).

As for its causes, economists explored both from the demand-side and the supply-side. The demand-siders attributed the gap between real and potential GDP to the insufficient stimulus of fiscal and monetary policies, whereas the supply-siders did so to the slowing growth in total factor productivity (TFP).[2] The third view, however, focused on the inadequate financial intermediation as a cause of misallocation of resources. This credit misallocation took two forms: credit crunch (*kashi-shiburi*)[3] and

[1]SAM was proposed by R. Stone and elaborated by Pyatt and Thorbecke (1976) and Pyatt and Round (1985). For the data used in a SAM, various kinds of consistency checks have to be carried out in order to assure full consistency between the different data sources.

[2]Hayashi and Prescott (2003) argued with a stochastic growth model that the lost decade was caused by two factors, a fall in TFP growth and a reduction in the length of work week. Since then, low TFP growth has become one of the accepted factors for the long recession.

[3]It means that banks suffering from non-performing loans reduce their lending to firms, forcing them to cut down their investment and other activities.

ever-greening of the loans (*oikashi*).[4] Under the circumstances, the optimistic entrepreneurs heavily dependent on bank loans during the bubble period encountered difficulties in repaying their debt, despite their good performance, because of sudden financial disintermediation and turmoil in the 1990s. Malfunction of financial intermediation aggravated the negative effects of slower economic growth.

Thus, it is necessary to study the interaction between the real sector and the financial sector under the depressed and unstable financial conditions. For this purpose, this chapter first constructs a macroeconomic social accounting matrix (MSAM).[5] Second, it calculates both the supply-driven multipliers and the demand-driven multipliers. The former are based on the supply-driven IO approach,[6] whereas the latter are obtained from the standard IO approach. Lastly, MSAM multipliers are decomposed into M_2 considering savings-investment balance.

2. Construction and Applications of MSAM

2.1. *Macroeconomic SAM*

Table 1 shows the MSAM to be used in our analysis. Its rows and columns record the activities of firms (production), households, government and the foreign sector. The principle of double-entry accounting requires that for each account the total revenue (row sum) should equal the total expenditure (column sum). In our analysis, production, households and capital transactions (savings) are treated as endogenous and the government and the rest of world (ROW) as exogenous.

A basic macroeconomic model may be constructed, consisting of equations (2.1)–(2.5).

$$Y = C + Z + G + E - M - T1 \tag{2.1}$$

$$Y = C + S^h + T2 \tag{2.2}$$

$$Z = S^h + S^g + S^f \tag{2.3}$$

[4]It means that banks extend the loans to insolvent firms in order to deflect their failures. Ogawa (2007) summarizes the related literatures on these two banking policies.

[5]SAM is useful not only for data compilation but also economic analysis and policy preparation. It is usually the database for CGE models. It is Macro SAM, because it does not extensively disaggregate the industrial sectors and the economic institutions.

[6]The supply-driven IO approach is suggested by Ghosh (1958) and Augustinovics (1970).

Table 1. Japanese Macroeconomic SAM (MSAM).

	Endogenous			Exogenous	
	Sec 1 ... Sec n	**HH**	**INV**	**GOV**	**ROW**
Sec 1 ... Sec n	Input–Output A	Consumption C	Investment Z	Gov. Expen. G	Export E
HH	Factor Payment Y				
SAV		Household Saving S^h		Gov. Savings S^g	Foreg. savings S^f
GOV	Indirect Taxes T_1	Income Tax T_2			
ROW	Import M				

*HH: households, INV: investment, GOV: government, ROW: the rest of the world, SAV: savings.
Note: For the details of constructing the Japanese MSAM, see Hosoe *et al.* (2004).

$$S^g = T(\equiv T_1 + T_2) - G \tag{2.4}$$

$$F = M - E \tag{2.5}$$

where Y: GNP, C: Consumption, Z: Investment, G: Government Expenditure, E: Exports, M: Imports, S^h: Household Savings, $S^f(M - E)$: the Balance of Trade, T: Total Taxes, T_1: Production Tax + Tariff, T_2: Income Tax, A: Intermediate goods. It is assumed that $C = cY$ and $S^i = s^i Y$, so that c is the marginal propensity to consume, and s^i: is the marginal propensity to save of sector i (the government or households, or the rest of the world).[7]

2.2. *The MSAM multipliers*

MSAM multipliers are calculated to analyze the interindustrial effects in the real side and the interactions between the real side and the financial side in the simplified loanable funds market. For this purpose, the MSAM is divided

[7]Japanese MSAM was constructed mainly from the data of IO table and SNA. Sectoral intermediate goods are taken from the IO table. Factor income consisting of compensation of employees (labor income) and operating surplus (capital income) are regarded as household income. The sum of private and public gross domestic fixed capital formation becomes investment. Government savings is taken from SNA, and foreign savings is calculated from the difference between the import and the export. Finally household savings and income tax are calculated from the SAM property. Such MSAM's are shown for 1985 and 2000 as examples here.

into the real and financial sectors. The multiplier analysis is implemented by partitioning the accounts into endogenous and exogenous accounts. It takes into account all the interactions in each step of the process of linkages among incomes, expenditures, and production. It is not a single multiplier but a matrix of multipliers representing the effects of addition to one cell in the original SAM on the rest of the cells and traces the complicated interactions inherent in the circular process.

The first step of the SAM multiplier model is to compute column shares divided by the total amount of each column S to obtain a coefficients matrix. It represents the structure of the economy which is analogous to Leontief input coefficients matrix. This multiplier matrix captures the interdependence of the endogenous variables given exogenous shocks. Following the IO analysis (demand-driven approach), a linear multiplier model is constructed on the assumption that all the expenditure coefficients in the SAM are constant. In most applications, it is customary to regard the government and the rest of the world as exogenous, while sectoral government revenue and imports remain endogenous but are leaked from the multiplier analysis. The coefficient matrix S^* including endogenous account is constructed by eliminating the exogenous account. In addition, this chapter calculates another type of linear multiplier on the assumption that all the revenue (row) coefficients in the SAM are constant (supply-driven approach).[8] This approach treats savings and government revenue accounts as exogenous. Both supply-driven multipliers (SM) and demand-driven multipliers (DM) are calculated to grope for the cause of the long recession in the 1990s from both supply and demand sides.

$$Y^d = (I - S^*)^{-1} X_1 = M \cdot X_1, \tag{2.6}$$

$$Y^s = X_2 (I - R)^{-1} = X_2 G, \tag{2.7}$$

[8] Supply-driven approach in IO analysis is still controversial. The author does not side with it but simply compares the responses to shocks in both approaches as a way to search for the causes of the long recession. As for the interindustrial linkage multiplier effect of SM and DM, construction industry's effect is not larger than others despite its larger investment multiplier. Interestingly, the total interindustrial linkage multiplier effect of DM is larger than that of SM only in 1985 during the bubble period, whereas in the other period, SM is larger than DM. As equations (2.6) and (2.7) show, the government expenditure or exports is the exogenous driving force in demand-driven multiplier, whereas the government revenue or imports is the exogenous driving force in the supply-driven multiplier. One could interpret this that the public policy on the demand side was effective only in 1985, while the policy on the supply side was effective in the other years. The economic policy packages to stimulate the depressed economy through the public construction in the 1990s were not so effective, while they increased the fiscal burdens.

where Y^d, X_1 and M denote total expenditure of SAM (column total), the exogenous accounts (government expenditure and export), and the demand-driven multiplier matrix, respectively. I is the identity matrix, and S^* is the endogenous share coefficient matrix. Similarly, supply-driven SAM multiplier matrix G is calculated. Y^s, X_2, R and G denote the total income of SAM (row total), exogenous accounts (government revenue and import), the share coefficient matrix and the supply-driven multiplier matrix, respectively.

Unlike other general models, the capital account is also endogenized, following Robinson *et al.* (1988), to capture the role of the savings-investment balance to determine national income. Thus, endogenous accounts are lumped into two groups. The first includes the factor and production markets in the real side and consists of activities (a) and household accounts (c, y). The second incorporates the financial flows consisting of capital accounts that summarize the loanable funds market. S^* is decomposed further into two groups to capture the interaction between the real side and the financial side. The upper right in S_1^* stands for the demand for investment and the lower left in S_2^* stands for savings.

$$S^* = S_1^* + S_2^* = \begin{pmatrix} a & c & 0 \\ y & 0 & 0 \\ 0 & 0 & 0 \end{pmatrix} + \begin{pmatrix} 0 & 0 & z \\ 0 & 0 & 0 \\ 0 & s^h & 0 \end{pmatrix} \tag{2.8}$$

This grouped SAM multiplier matrix could be decomposed into three multiplicative components (Pyatt and Round, 1979) to elucidate the routine of complex transmission linkages in the macro economy.

$$Y^d = (I - S^*)^{-1}X = (I - S_1^* - S_2^*)X \tag{2.9}$$

$$Y^d = (I - D^2)^{-1}(I + D)(I - S_1)^{-1}X = M_3M_2M_1X \tag{2.10}$$

$$D = (I - S_1^*)^{-1}S_2^*.$$ [9]

M_1 stands for the "within accounts (intra-group or transfer) effect", that is, the multipliers of an exogenous injection into one set of accounts will have on the same set of accounts. M_2 represents the "cross (open-loop or extra-group) effect", i.e., an injection of an exogenous shock into one set of accounts has on the other set of accounts with no reversal

[9] To derive multiplicative SAM multipliers $(I - S^*)y = xS^*$ is partitioned into S_1^* and S_2^* then $(I - S_1^* - S_2^*)y = xy = (I - S_1^*)^{-1}S_2^*y + (I - S_1)^{-1}x[I - (I - S_1^*)^{-1}S_2^*]y = (I - S_1^*)^{-1}xy = [I - (I - S_1^*)^{-1}S_2^*]^{-1}(I - S_1^*)^{-1}x$ set $D = (I - S_1^*)^{-1}S_2^*$ and using $(I - D)^{-1} = (I - D^2)^{-1}(I + D)$; $y = (I - D^2)^{-1}(I + D)(I - S_1^*)^{-1}x$.

effects. M_3 captures the multiplier effect of the full circular flow, so-called "between-accounts (inter-group or closed-loop) effect." It measures the full circular effects resulting from an exogenous injection into the system after returning to the original account. This analysis focuses only the cross effect M_2 of investment on the real sectors operating through the savings-investment balance when exogenous shock is given to the government expenditure.[10]

$$M_1 = \begin{pmatrix} [I-(a+cy)]^{-1} & c[I-(a+cy)]^{-1} & 0 \\ y[I-(a+cy)]^{-1} & (I-a)[I-(a+cy)]^{-1} & 0 \\ 0 & 0 & I \end{pmatrix}$$

$$M_2 = \begin{pmatrix} I & 0 & [I-(a+cy)]^{-1}z \\ 0 & I & y[I-(a+cy)]^{-1}z \\ 0 & s^h & I \end{pmatrix}$$

$$M_3 = \begin{pmatrix} I & [I-(a+cy)]^{-1}z \cdot s^h[I-y[I-(a+cy)]^{-1}z \cdot s^h]^{-1} & 0 \\ 0 & [I-y[I-(a+cy)]^{-1}z \cdot s^h]^{-1} & 0 \\ 0 & 0 & [I-s^h y[I-(a+cy)]^{-1}z]^{-1} \end{pmatrix}$$

3. SAM Multiplier Analysis

To decipher the Japanese economy, first the total multipliers are calculated and then decomposed into M_2 considering savings-investment balance to analyze the cross effect of investments on the real sector. M calculates all the effects such as intra-group, cross and circular effects for given shocks to exogenous accounts. This multiplier M could not discern the path of exogenous shocks in the loanable funds markets. MSAM is divided into real SAM S_1^* and financial SAM S_2^*, and M_2 multipliers are calculated by decomposing further the total to discern the multiplier path of investment. M_2 indicates the degree of effect that an exogenous shock to the government investment can exert on the real sector, and low M_2 multipliers indirectly mean a deterioration of financial intermediation due to credit crunch or ever-greening of the loans.

---

[10] M_3 adds no information of the trajectory of the exogenous injection (Round, 1999).

Table 2. Multipliers (M and M_2) of Investments.

	M				M_2			
	1985	**1990**	**1995**	**2000**	**1985**	**1990**	**1995**	**2000**
Sec01	0.23	0.15	0.15	0.12	0.12	0.08	0.07	0.06
Sec02	0.17	0.08	0.07	0.08	0.09	0.05	0.03	0.04
Sec03	0.38	0.30	0.33	0.30	0.20	0.17	0.16	0.15
Sec04	0.14	0.12	0.11	0.07	0.07	0.06	0.05	0.04
Sec05	0.21	0.18	0.19	0.15	0.11	0.10	0.09	0.08
Sec06	0.18	0.14	0.15	0.13	0.10	0.08	0.07	0.07
Sec07	0.19	0.09	0.09	0.11	0.10	0.05	0.04	0.06
Sec08	0.13	0.10	0.11	0.09	0.07	0.06	0.05	0.05
Sec09	0.29	0.22	0.18	0.14	0.15	0.12	0.09	0.07
Sec10	0.09	0.08	0.07	0.06	0.05	0.04	0.03	0.03
Sec11	0.17	0.17	0.18	0.15	0.09	0.09	0.09	0.08
Sec12	0.33	0.30	0.30	0.29	0.17	0.17	0.14	0.15
Sec13	0.43	0.38	0.43	0.45	0.22	0.21	0.21	0.23
Sec14	0.26	0.27	0.29	0.25	0.14	0.15	0.14	0.13
Sec15	0.04	0.04	0.04	0.04	0.02	0.02	0.02	0.02
Sec16	0.26	0.24	0.27	0.24	0.14	0.13	0.13	0.12
Sec17	**1.12**	**1.07**	**1.21**	**1.08**	**0.59**	**0.60**	**0.59**	**0.56**
Sec18	0.16	0.11	0.14	0.13	0.09	0.06	0.07	0.07
Sec19	0.04	0.03	0.04	0.04	0.02	0.02	0.02	0.02
Sec20	**0.69**	**0.65**	**0.87**	**0.76**	**0.36**	**0.36**	**0.43**	**0.39**
Sec21	0.28	0.26	0.30	0.28	0.14	0.14	0.15	0.14
Sec22	0.38	0.34	0.50	0.46	0.20	0.19	0.25	0.24
Sec23	0.28	0.24	0.42	0.27	0.15	0.14	0.20	0.14
Sec24	0.09	0.08	0.12	0.16	0.05	0.04	0.06	0.08
Sec25	0.01	0.01	0.01	0.01	0.00	0.00	0.00	0.01
Sec26	0.10	0.10	0.13	0.13	0.05	0.06	0.07	0.07
Sec27	0.04	0.04	0.07	0.08	0.02	0.02	0.04	0.04
Sec28	0.05	0.03	0.04	0.03	0.03	0.02	0.02	0.02
Sec29	0.40	0.43	0.58	0.65	0.21	0.24	0.29	0.33
Sec30	0.37	0.35	0.44	0.42	0.19	0.20	0.22	0.22
Sec31	0.02	0.01	0.02	0.01	0.01	0.01	0.01	0.01
Sec32	0.07	0.06	0.05	0.03	0.04	0.03	0.02	0.02

Source: Author's calculation.

Table 2 shows the total multiplier effect of investment in each industry in 1985 and 2000. The investment multiplier in the construction sector (sector 17) is the largest of all and peaked in the bubble period as a result of public construction in the 1990s through the stimulating policy packages. The values of the multiplier for this industry were: 1.12 → 1.07 → 1.21 → 1.08.

Furthermore, commerce, electrical machinery, food, personal services, and real estate have large multipliers, while the public service sector such as other public services, water supply and waste management services, and public administration have small multiplier effects as expected. Interestingly, R&D and service industries in 2000, such as business services, personal services sector, communication and broadcasting, and education and research have higher multiplier effects than during the economic bubble in 1985 while the total multipliers of primary industries (sector 1 to 10) and construction, iron and steel, foods, etc., declined.

It is not necessarily true that the movements of the M multipliers have the same direction as M_2 multipliers, indicating the financial impact of investments on the real sector. The major difference between M multiplier and M_2 multiplier is that the former indicates the response of investment when shocks are given to the government expenditure, whereas the latter indicates the financial impact of investment on the real sector.

For the construction industry, M multiplier declined ($1.12 \rightarrow 1.07$) but M_2 multiplier increased ($0.59 \rightarrow 0.6$) in 1990 when the industry's share increased ($7.8\% \rightarrow 9.7\%$). Maybe the financial impact of investment on the industry increased in 1990, and that bank loans allocated to it had a positive financial intermediary effect. In 1995, however, M multiplier ($1.07 \rightarrow 1.21$) increased but M_2 multiplier ($0.6 \rightarrow 0.59$) decreased, although M multiplier increased substantially but financial impact of investment on the real side declined when the share of construction industry declined from 9.7% to 9%. In 1995, financial misallocation to this industry might have happened because the loan to the industry kept increasing (Figure 1).

In the case of the real estate industry, M and M_2 declined after the bubble burst in 1990 but increased in 1995 and declined in 2000. The share of the industry kept increasing ($5.1\% \rightarrow 5.2\% \rightarrow 6.5\% \rightarrow 6.6\%$). The amount of bank loan to the industry shows a sharp increase up to 1998 and then starts declining. These multipliers of the above two industries seems to allow an inference that the real estate industry could promptly clear of its non-performing loans or that it was actually not affected directly by falling land price, whereas construction industry was affected severely and directly by the same factor. This multiplier analysis indicates which industry gets larger impacts of investment and which policies exert more effects, demand-driven or supply-driven. Figure 2 shows the M_2 effects of investments on the real sector. Most M multipliers and M_2 multipliers of primary sector declined because the share of these industries and their financial impact

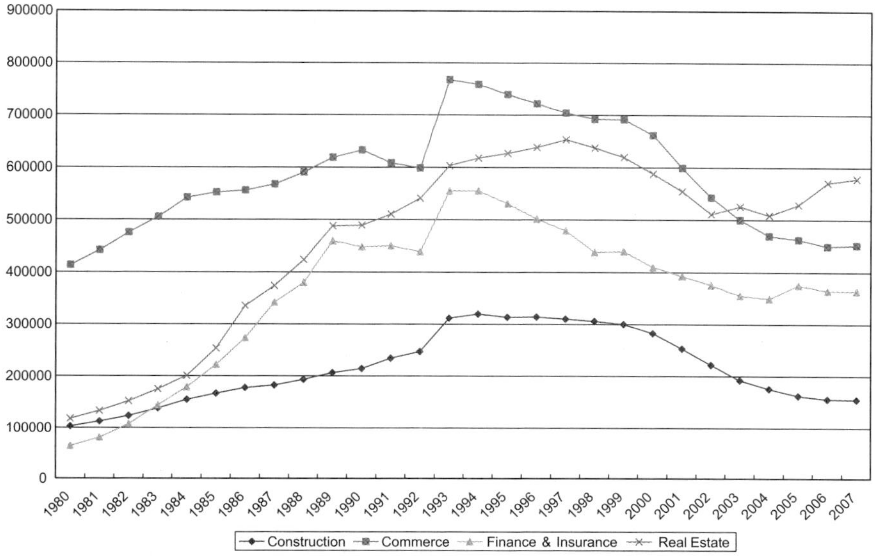

Figure 1. Bank Loan Allocation (Outstanding, Hundred Million Yen).

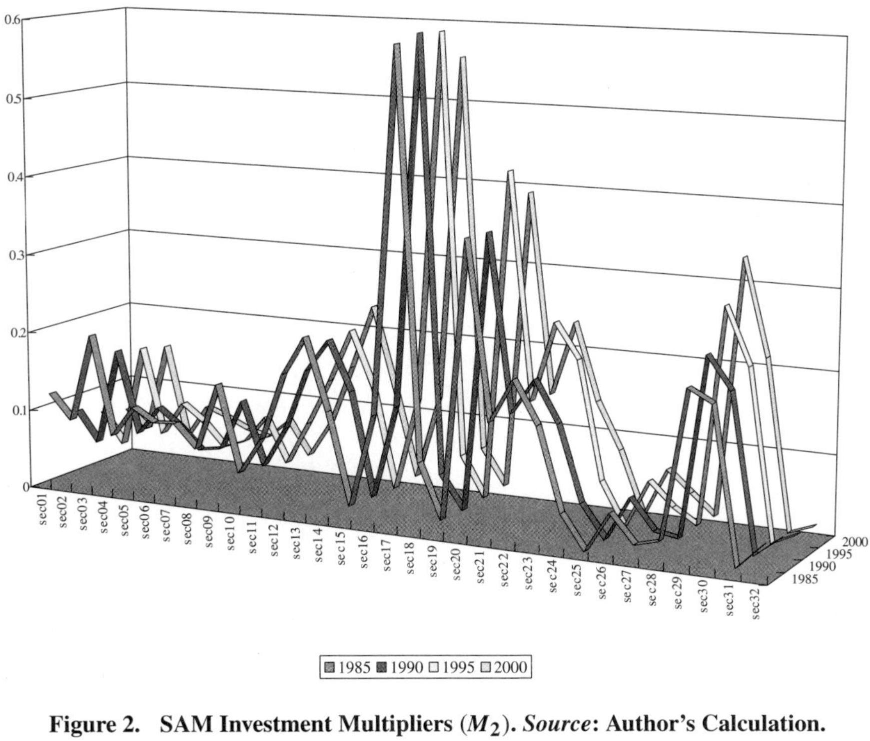

Figure 2. SAM Investment Multipliers (M_2). *Source*: Author's Calculation.

Table 3. Structural Change of Japanese Industry 1985–2000.

No	Sectors	1985	1990	1995	2000
sec01	Agriculture, forestry & fishery	3.0%	2.3%	1.9%	1.6%
sec02	Mining	2.1%	1.2%	0.8%	1.0%
sec03	Foods	5.3%	4.8%	4.4%	4.4%
sec04	Textile products	2.0%	1.8%	1.4%	1.0%
sec05	Pulp, paper & wooden products	2.3%	2.2%	2.0%	1.7%
sec06	Chemical products	3.5%	3.1%	2.9%	2.9%
sec07	Petroleum & coal products	2.6%	1.4%	1.2%	1.5%
sec08	Ceramic, stone & clay products	1.2%	1.2%	1.0%	0.9%
sec09	Iron & steel	3.9%	3.0%	2.1%	1.8%
sec10	Non-ferrous metals	1.1%	1.1%	0.8%	0.8%
sec11	Metal products	1.6%	1.9%	1.6%	1.4%
sec12	General machinery	3.3%	3.6%	3.0%	3.0%
sec13	Electrical machinery	5.5%	5.8%	5.6%	6.2%
sec14	Transportation equipment	4.9%	5.2%	4.4%	4.4%
sec15	Precision instruments	0.6%	0.6%	0.5%	0.5%
sec16	Miscellaneous manuf. products	3.6%	3.8%	3.5%	3.4%
sec17	Construction	7.8%	9.7%	9.0%	7.7%
sec18	Electricity, gas & heat supply	2.3%	1.7%	1.9%	1.9%
sec19	Water supply & waste management services	0.7%	0.6%	0.8%	0.8%
sec20	Commerce	8.7%	9.1%	10.4%	9.8%
sec21	Financial & insurance	3.6%	3.8%	3.8%	3.8%
sec22	Real estate	5.1%	5.2%	6.5%	6.6%
sec23	Transport	4.1%	4.0%	5.4%	4.1%
sec24	Communication & broadcasting	1.2%	1.2%	1.5%	2.2%
sec25	Public administration	2.3%	2.6%	2.7%	3.6%
sec26	Education & research	2.9%	3.1%	3.4%	3.6%
sec27	Medical service, health & social security and nursing care	2.9%	2.9%	3.7%	4.4%
sec28	Other public services	0.7%	0.4%	0.5%	0.4%
sec29	Business services	4.8%	5.9%	6.6%	7.8%
sec30	Personal services	5.1%	5.5%	5.8%	6.1%
sec31	Office supplies	0.2%	0.2%	0.2%	0.2%
sec32	Activities not elsewhere classified	1.0%	0.8%	0.6%	0.4%

Source: Input-Output Table.

of investment on the real sector declined, but those in communication and broadcasting, business service, and personal services have increased. Their growth reflects the structural changes of the Japanese industry over time, as Table 3 shows above.

4. Summary

This paper attempted to analyze the interindustrial linkage between the real sector and the financial sector. The method was to construct the MSAM from 1985 to 2000, calculate DM and SM, decompose the multipliers, and then estimate the impacts of investment on each industry through savings-investment balance. It discerned the multiplier path of exogenous shocks and enabled M_2 multiplier to indicate the financial impact of investment on the real sector. These results seem to show whether the credit allocation and resource mobilization to one industry is efficient or not. The next step would be to use the same database and extend this multi-sectoral analysis to the computable general equilibrium model incorporating the behaviors of the various economic agents involved.

Table A.1. Japanese MSAM for 1985 and 2000

	Aggregated Japanese Macroeconomic SAM for 1985 (Million Yen)							
	IND1	**IND2**	**IND3**	**HH**	**INV**	**GOV**	**ROW**	**Total**
IND1	2,091,725	25,094,674	4,803,476	4,137,344	482,311	0	95,439	36,704,969
IND2	3,852,908	116,810,260	54,544,996	50,830,919	30,732,951	556,777	38,371,057	295,699,868
IND3	2,933,011	51,830,017	83,152,025	130,700,613	59,343,195	45,206,778	8,440,293	381,605,932
HH	10,539,738	75,342,597	226,028,993	0	0	0	0	311,911,328
SAV	0	0	0	87,754,882	0	13,751,300	−10,947,725	90,558,457
GOV	774,260	12,024,470	8,228,555	38,487,570	0	0	0	59,514,855
ROW	16,513,327	14,597,850	4,847,887	0	0	0	0	35,959,064
Total	36,704,969	295,699,868	381,605,932	311,911,328	90,558,457	59,514,855	35,959,064	

Industry 1 (IND1) consists of sector 1 and sector 2, industry 2 (IND2) consists of sector 3 to sector 16, and industry 3 (IND3) consists of the rest of the sectors (17–32).

Table A.1. (*Continued*)

	Aggregated Japanese Macroeconomic SAM for 2000 (Million Yen)							
	IND1	**IND2**	**IND3**	**HH**	**INV**	**GOV**	**ROW**	**Total**
IND1	1,562,691	15,771,500	4,219,022	3,958,821	951,413	0	88,912	26,552,359
IND2	2,755,139	120,208,446	65,135,612	64,913,971	39,086,367	459,179	46,455,421	339,014,135
IND3	2,705,110	62,529,262	154,082,781	231,288,605	89,645,939	85,262,687	10,942,384	636,456,768
HH	8,132,415	91,879,380	384,032,949	0	0	0	0	484,044,744
SAV	0	0	0	136,190,995	0	654,200	−7,161,476	129,683,719
GOV	1,709,748	17,084,297	19,889,669	47,692,352	0	0	0	86,376,066
ROW	9,687,256	31,541,250	9,096,735	0	0	0	0	50,325,241
Total	26,552,359	339,014,135	636,456,768	484,044,744	129,683,719	86,376,066	50,325,241	

References

Augustinovics, M. (1970). Methods of International and Intertemporal Comparison of Structure. In *Contributions to Input-Output Analysis,* A. P. Carter, A. Brody (eds.), pp. 249–269.

Alarcon, J., J. van Heemst, S. Keuning, W. de Ruijter and R. Vos (1991). *The Social Accounting Frame work for Development: Concepts, Construction and Applications*. Avebury: Institute of Social Studies.

Caballero, R., T. Hoshi and A. Kashyap (2004). Zombie Lending and Depressed Restructuring in Japan. mimeo.

Defourny, J. and E. Thorbecke (1984). Structural Path Analysis and Multiplier Decomposition within a Social Accounting Matrix Framework. *The Economic Journal*, 94, 111–136.

Ghosh, A. (1958). Input-output Approach in an Allocation System. *Economica*, 25, 58–64.

Hayashi, F. and E. Prescott (2002). The 1990s in Japan: A Lost Decade. *Review of Economic Dynamics*, 5, 206–235.

Hoshi, T. (2000). Naze Nihon wa Ryudosei no Wana kara Nogarerarenainoka (Why couldn't the Japanese economy get out of a liquidity trap?). In *Zero Kinri to Nihon Keizai* (*Zero Interest Rate and the Japanese Economy*), Fukao, M. and H. Yoshikawa (eds.). Nihon Keizai Shimbunsha, pp. 233–266.

Hosoe, N., H. Hashimoto and K. Gasawa (2004). *Textbook of Applied General Equilibrium Modeling*. Tokyo University Press.

Iwata, K. and T. Miyakawa (eds.) (2004). *What is the True Cause of the Lost Decade?* Toyo Keizai Shinposha.

Kawai, M. (2005). Reform of the Japanese Banking System. Hi-Stat Discussion Paper Series No. 102, June 2005.

Klein, L.R. (2003). Some Potential Linkages for Input-output Analysis with Flow of Funds. *Economic Systems Research*, 15(3), 269–277.

Nakamura, Y. (2005). Multiplier Analysis of Social Accounting Matrix. *Economia*, 51, 11–25, Yokohama National University.

Ogawa, K. (2007). Credit Allocation of Japanese Banks in the 1990s: Evidence from the Short-term Economic Survey of Enterprises. The Institute of Social and Economic Research, Osaka University. Discussion Paper No. 680.

Otake, H. and N. Ryukawa (eds.) (2004). *The Issue of Heisei Depression: The Verification of the Lost Decade*. Toyo Keizai Shinposha.

Peek, J. and E. Rosengren (2003). Unnatural Selection; Perverse Incentive and the Misallocation of Credit in Japan. NBER Working Paper Series No. 9643.

Pyatt, G. and E. Thorbecke (1976). *Planning Techniques for a Better Future: A Summary of a Research Project on Planning for Growth, Redistribution, and Employment*. Geneva: International Labour Office.

Pyatt, G. and J. Round (1985). *Social Accounting Matrices: A Basis for Planning*. World Bank.

Robinson, S. and D. Roland-Holst (1988). Macroeconomic Structure and Computable General Equilibrium Models. *Journal of Policy Modeling*, 10(3), 353–375.

Robinson, S. (2003). Macro Models and Multipliers: Leontief, Stone, Keynes and CGE Models. International Food Policy Research Institute (IFPRI) Working Paper.

Sakuragawa, M. (2002). *Kin-yu Kiki no Keizai Bunseki* (*Economic Analysis of Financial Crisis*). University of Tokyo Press.

Websites

Input-Output Table, Statistics Bureau, Ministry of Internal Affairs and Communications, http://www.stat.go.jp/data/io/.

Systems of National Accounts (SNA), Cabinet Office Economic and Social Research Institute, http://www.esri.cao.go.jp/jp/sna/menu.html.

Japan Industry Productivity (JIP) Database 2008, METI, http://www.rieti.go.jp/jp/database/JIP2008/index.html.

Chapter 3

Business Indexes and Survey Data for Forecast

Yuji Shimanaka and Tatsushi Shikano*

1. Introduction

In major industrialized countries, it has become very common to use various business indexes and survey data for the purpose of capturing and forecasting the economic trends. In Japan, information such as the Diffusion Index (DI), the Consumer Confidence Survey, and the Bank of Japan (BOJ) Short-Term Economic Survey on Enterprises (abbreviated as *Tankan*) are widely used for the same purposes. This chapter provides an introduction to their practical use as well as the recent debates on the success or failures of the forecasts based on them. It will also give the reader a certain portrayal of the Japanese economy in recent decades and the predictions based on them. These findings have been hardly compared with other short-term forecasts using econometric models. The chapter also attempts to compare these methods with other quantitative models.[1]

2. The Criteria to Recognize Economic Conditions

2.1. *The business indexes, GDP statistics, and the BOJ Tankan*

In describing economic conditions, how they are to divided them into different phases is very important. Each phase is identified with the various

*We express our gratitude to the editors for giving us the opportunity to contribute to this volume and introduce the works closely related to our daily obligations. Y. Shimanaka is the chief economist of Business Cycle Research and Councilor, Mitsubishi UFJ Securities, and Guest Professor, Waseda University. T. Shikano is the senior economist of Business Cycle Research, Mitsubishi UFJ Securities.

[1]This chapter substantially revised the introduction and Chapter 1 of Shimanaka (2003).

criteria using the Indexes of Business Conditions, GDP Statistics, and the BOJ *Tankan*. The three criteria usually referred to are: (1) the direction of change, (2) the rate of change (growth), and (3) the level. They are roughly measured by the following three coincident indicators shown in Figure 1.[2]

1. the Cabinet Office's Indexes of Business Conditions — a DI (see website of the cabinet office: http:// www.esri.cao.go.jp/en/stat/di/di2e.html, http:// www.esri.cao.go.jp/en/stat/hojin/hojin.yosuku_kaisetu-e.html)
2. the growth rate of real GDP, and
3. the BOJ *Tankan's* Business Conditions DI, mainly for large manufacturing enterprises (Bank of Japan, 2008).

If business conditions are divided into four phases: (a) revival, (b) expansion, (c) recession, and (d) contraction, stagnation or bust, the direction of change is upwards for both (a) and (b), and downwards for (c) and (d) at the same levels in both phases. The important point is the one which divides the upward and downward phases. It is the turning point of business cycles emphasized by W. C. Mitchell and A. F. Burns. They identified it as the cross-point where the coincident DI dips below the 50 percent line or as the point where coincident series of the cumulative DI or composite index (CI) literally marks a peak or a trough.

Mitchell-Burns first defined the peak and trough as the turning points, where the direction of change switches from going upward to downward or *vice versa*, and then divided the business cycles into two phases: the periods of upward change: *expansion* and the downward change: *contraction* (Burns and Mitchell, 1947, pp. 3–8). They further divided each of the two phases into two segments: *revival* and *expansionary* for *expansion* as well as *recession* and *contraction* for *contraction*. This is the basis for the well-known four-phase diagram (Figure 2–①): revival(a) → expansion(b)→ recession(c) → contraction(d). Japan's official business cycle phases are designated on the basis of this Mitchell-Burns division.

For the actual assessment, the Economic and Social Research Institute (ESRI) in the Cabinet Office first calculates a special ex-post DI called the Historical Diffusion Index (HDI) based on the 11 individual indexes comprising of the coincident series of the Indexes of Business Conditions. The ESRI mechanically identifies the trough or the peak of the business cycles by the points immediately before the HDI breaks the 50 percent line from

[2]In June 2008, however, the Cabinet Office shifted the emphasis in announcing Indexes of Business Conditions from DI to CI.

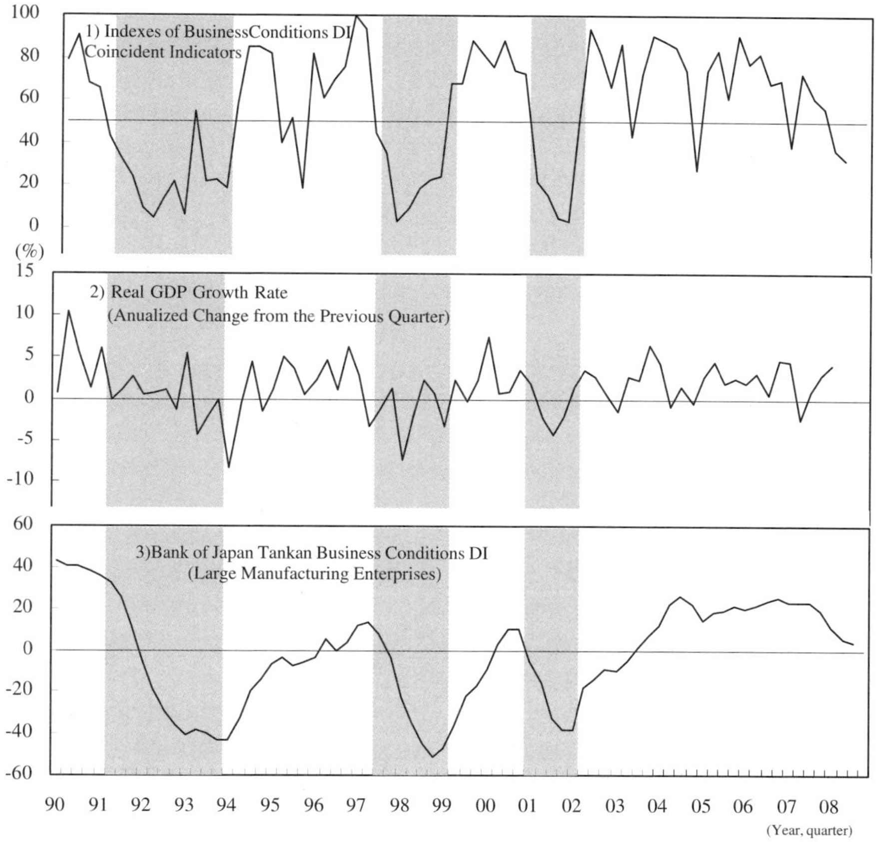

Figure 1. Indexes of Business Conditions, Real GDP, BOJ Tankan.

Notes: The shadowed areas ( ) represent economic recession phases (based on CAO statistics). (1) The latest figures for the Indexes of Business Conditions are for April–May 2008. (2) The latest figures for real GDP Growth are for January–March 2008. (3) The latest figures for the BOJ Tankan Survey are a forecast for July–September 2008.

Source: Cabinet Office (CAO) "Indexes of Business Conditions", "National Accounts", Bank of Japan (BOJ) "Short-term Economic Survey on Enterprises".

above to below or from below to above, respectively. Thus, the "Reference Dates of Business Cycles" (*official Reference Dates*) are determined as the turning points, after taking into consideration the trends in other major economic indexes and the opinions of the experts of the Investigation Committee for Business Cycle Indicators. For instance, in June 2003, the trough

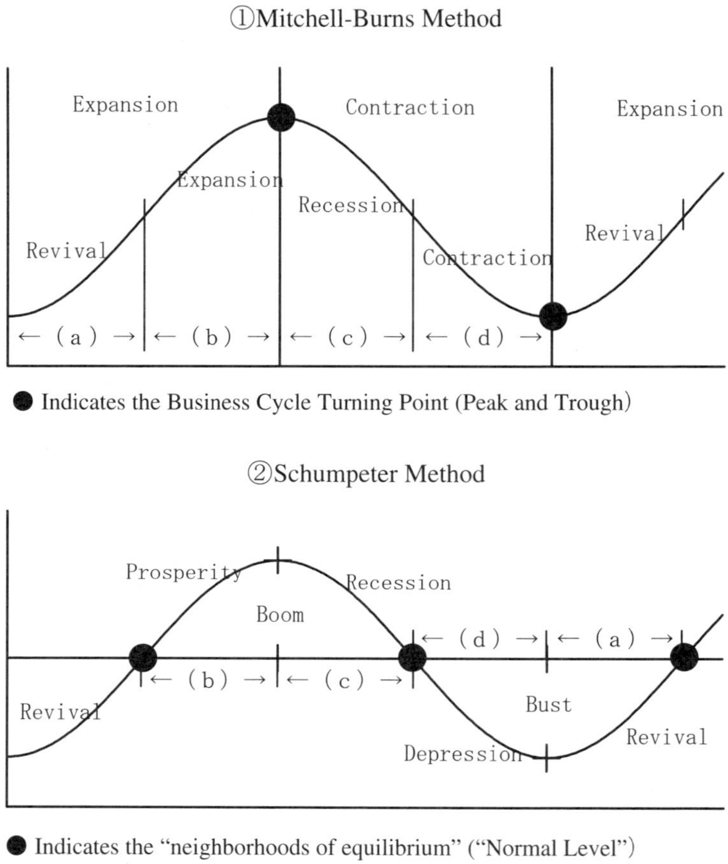

Figure 2. The Two Methods of Dividing Economic Phases.

shown in January 2002 in the 13th post-war business cycle was identified to be a tentative date.[3]

The dates in the past have basically matched the results of calculation of the HDI and do not involve any arbitrary factors. Conversely, the primary mission of the approach using the leading indexes will be a preliminary forecast and projection of business cycle turning points that can be expected to finally match the official Reference Dates.

[3]The Cabinet Office later determined through the Investigation Committee for Business Cycle Indicators held in November 2004 that the peak and the trough of the 13th Business Cycle were in November 2000 and January 2002, respectively.

2.2. *Schumpeter's approach and the BOJ's Tankan*

Another way of dividing the phases of business cycles is to observe the horizontal line between (a) and (b), or (c) and (d). This is what J. A. Schumpeter emphasized as *the neighborhoods of equilibrium* or *the normal point*. He regards this method as relying on the subjective judgment or the practical prospects of entrepreneurs. The quick way to find them is to conduct the questionnaire surveys to business corporations. In Japan, It is usually considered in proximity as the point where the Business Conditions DI is zero in BOJ's *Tankan*, or where the responses for *favorable* and *unfavorable* reach equilibrium (Figure 2-②).

Unlike the peaks and troughs in the Mitchell-Burns method, Schumpeter's two major phases are: *prosperity* or *boom* above the *neighborhoods of equilibrium* and *depression* or *bust* below that level. The former was further segmented into *prosperity* and *recession*, and the latter into *depression* and *revival*. Thus, his approach also has four-phases: prosperity(b) → recession(c) → depression(d) → revival(a). (Schumpeter, 1935, pp. 2–10) Then, the relation between the direction approach *a la* Burns-Mitchell and the level approach *a la* Schumpeter is only whether the two phases are *vertically* divided between (a)–(b) and (c)–(d), or *horizontally* divided between (b)–(c) and (d)–(a). In the Japanese discussions on business cycles, some confusion has occurred due to the misuse of terminologies in this context.

2.3. *Momentary wind velocity and the GDP growth rate*

The rate of change or growth as the second criteria to judge the business conditions is usually indicated by the change from the previous quarter or its annualized growth rate. It is, as it were, the momentary wind velocity of the business cycle. Sometimes, it can be very high and yet the state of economy is below the surface in terms of the level, if the economy has not entered an expansionary phase. In such a case, the economy is growing out of stagnation or reviving out of depression.

It is also possible that the economy is in an expansionary phase but gradually decelerating its growth rate. Following the conceptual framework clarified above, it refers to the condition when: (ii) the rate of change (growth) is declining, (i) the direction of change in the coincident DI continues to be above 50%, and (iii) the level of the Business Conditions DI is also greater than zero.

In other words, if the coincident DI is not below 50% and the Business Conditions DI remains above zero despite a deceleration of the GDP growth rate or the rate of increase of the coincident CI, it would be a prime example for description like "remains in an expansionary phase but is gradually decelerating."

Thus, in Japan, there are most suitable business cycle indicators for each criteria of three: (i) the direction of change, (ii) the rate of change, and (iii) the level. This can be a critique on the debate of business conditions in terms of GDP growth rates for economic outlook.

2.4. *Predicting the economic outlook by the direction of change*

These three criteria are mutually complementary in making a general assessment of the economy. Furthermore, the rate of change precedes the changes in the level of economic activities, so that it can be used to predict the outlook for future levels of economic activities. For example, an interesting prediction can be made by using the BOJ *Tankan* Survey. In Figure 3, the bold line indicates the movements in the level of economic activities, and the dotted line indicates the difference between the current and previous quarters; i.e. quarterly difference in relation to the BOJ *Tankan* Survey's Business Conditions DI — *favorable* minus *unfavorable* — for large manufacturing enterprises.

Figure 3 clearly shows that the dotted line for quarterly differences has consistently preceded the solid bold line for the change in levels. To measure the changes in levels from the previous quarter mathematically means to differentiate and look at the range of marginal changes from the previous level. Since the fact that the curve of the original level (i.e. the Business Conditions DI) forms a relatively smooth pattern like a sigmoid curve, it is considered that the curve for quarterly differences indicates the nature of the time-wise precedence in relation to that of the level of economic activities.

According to the graph in Figure 3 for the Business Conditions DI for large manufacturing enterprises, the average leading period is about 3.3 quarters, especially when taking the average of both the peaks and troughs. For example, the past correlation has been that the curve for the change in levels would peak out about three quarters after the curve for the quarterly difference had peaked out, so the bold solid curve would proceed in the same direction as the dotted curve was following.

A clearer example of the relationship between the direction of change and the level is indicated by comparing the trends between the Business

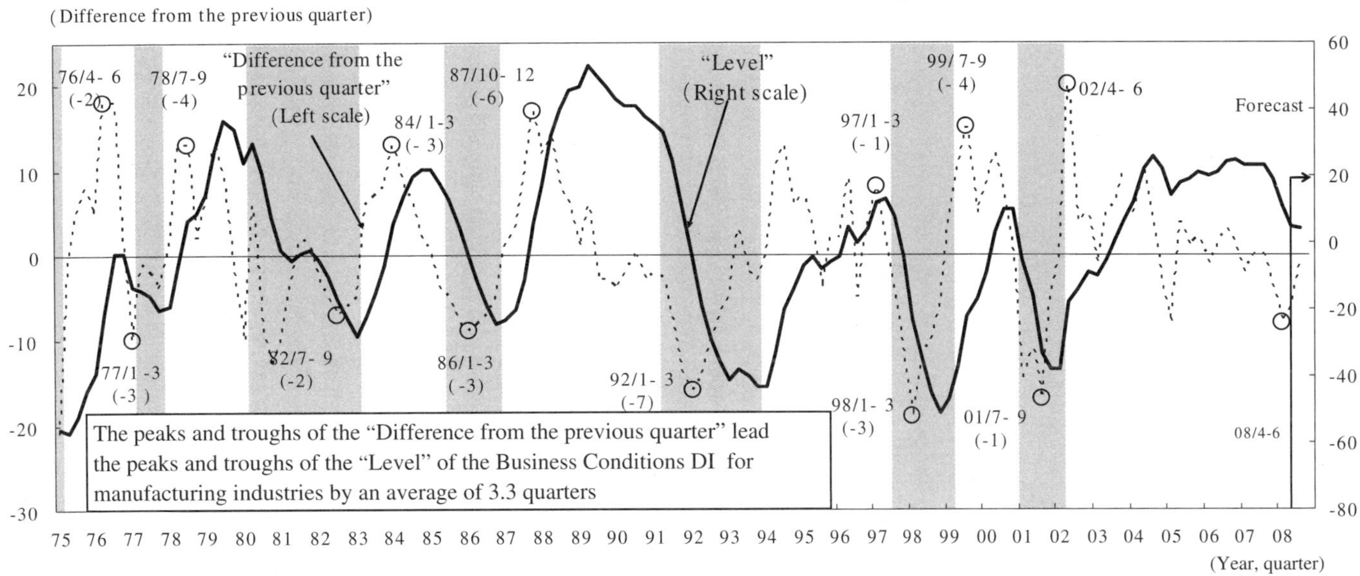

Figure 3. Business Conditions DI (Large Manufacturing Enterprises) ("Difference from the Previous Quarter" and the "Level").
Note: Shadowed areas indicate economic recession phases (based on Cabinet Office statistics). There is a break in statistics between the data before the December 2003 survey and data after the M arch 2004 survey. The latest data for April–June 2008 is based on forecasted figures. The value indicated in parentheses in the graph represents the number of quarters leading the trough of the "Level" curve.
Source: BOJ "Short-term Economic Survey on Enterprises".

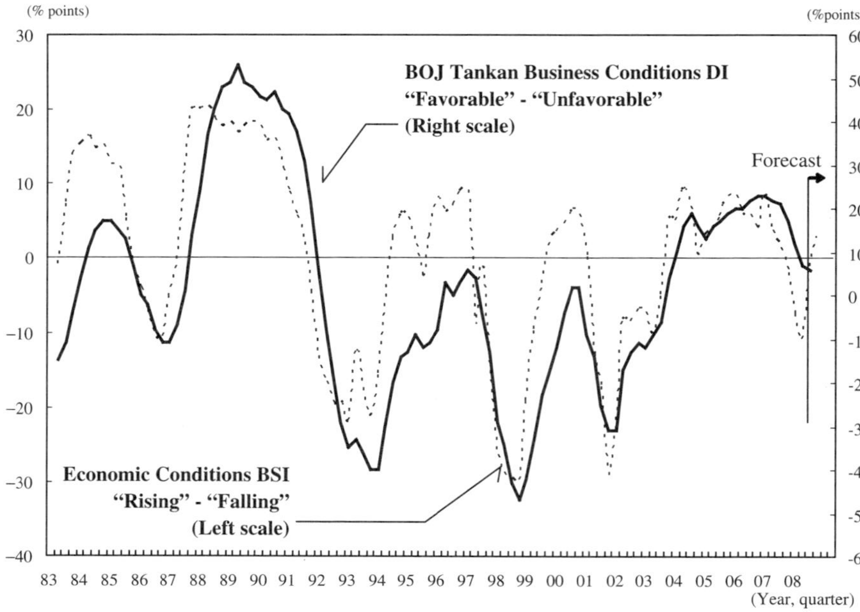

Figure 4. Comparison of the Business Outlook Survey and the BOJ Tankan Business Conditions DI, Economic Conditions BSI (All Manufacturing Enterprises).

Note: "BOJ Tankan" corresponds to the quarter including the survey month. "Economic Conditions BSI" based on the MOF "Business Outlook Survey" until the January–March quarter of 2004, and the CAO "Business Outlook Survey" from the April–June quarter of 2004 onward (Seasonally adjusted based on authors' estimates).

Source: Compiled by the authors based on BOJ "Short-term Economic Survey on Enterprises", Ministry of Finance "Business Outlook Survey", Cabinet Office "Business Outlook Survey".

Survey Index (BSI) in the Business Outlook Survey[4] and the BOJ's *Tankan* (Figure 4). In the graph, the former leads the latter by approximately one to two quarters (i.e. a half year) and this is due to the fact that, setting aside the difference in survey coverage, the Business Outlook Survey is asking about the *direction of change*. Japanese corporations are asked about the direction of change in the business conditions in the Business Outlook Survey. The question is as to whether companies feel that their business conditions are *rising*, *unchanged*, *falling*, or *unknown*. The economic conditions BSI

[4]It is compiled every three months by the Cabinet Office and the Ministry of Finance (refer to website: http://www. esri.cao.go.jp/en/stat/hojin/hojin-yosoku_kaisetu-e.html.).

represents the percentage of corporations answering that economic conditions were "improving" *minus* the percentage of corporations answering "declining". On the other hand, the BOJ *Tankan* Survey asks about the *level* of the economy itself: whether economic conditions are *favorable*, *not so favorable*, or *unfavorable*. As such, it represents the percentage of corporations answering *favorable* minus the percentage of corporations answering *unfavorable*.

For the same *change of direction*, a small deviation always arises between the one based on a macro perspective and the other based on a micro perspective. The Business Outlook Survey includes these two major BSI about corporate sentiments. Note that when the level of the BSI for macro economic conditions is lower than that for micro-based business conditions, that timing often coincides with the one when the overall domestic economy is approaching a recessionary phase.

This phenomenon can be confirmed from the trend in the so-called "Economy Judgment Index". It is calculated by subtracting the BSI for micro conditions from the BSI for macro conditions. If the difference is positive, it may be interpreted, the economy is in a recovery or expansionary phase, whereas if the difference is negative, the economy is in a recessionary phase.[5] The timing when the Economy Judgment Index turned positive or negative since the October–December period of 1988, almost coincided or slightly preceded the official Reference Date for Business Cycles for recovery, expansion, and recession.[6] Around January 2002, when the previous recessionary phase ended, this Index had turned positive right from the January–March period (Figure 5). The fact that this Index itself forms a regular cycle which largely coincides with the actual business cycle may seem peculiar at first glance, but Japanese business management tends to view their business climate differently from the current state of the overall economy, regardless of recovery or recession. These phenomena occur so frequently that such tendency may be considered relatively stable.

[5]The Economic Assessment Index was developed by Masatoshi Moriyama of Mitsubishi UFJ Securities Co., Ltd.

[6]Since the Business Outlook Survey was started only in April–June quarter of 2004, we used the figures of the UFJ *Tankan* Survey for the earlier periods. The UFJ *Tankan* is a corporate survey conducted from the April–June quarter of 2002 to the January–March quarter of 2006 by the UFJ Institute Ltd (now the Mitsubishi UFJ Research and Consulting Co., Ltd). It succeeded the Sanwa Tankan conducted by the former Sanwa Research Institute & Consulting Corporation (refer to website: http://www.murs.jp/shimanaka/tankan.top.html.).

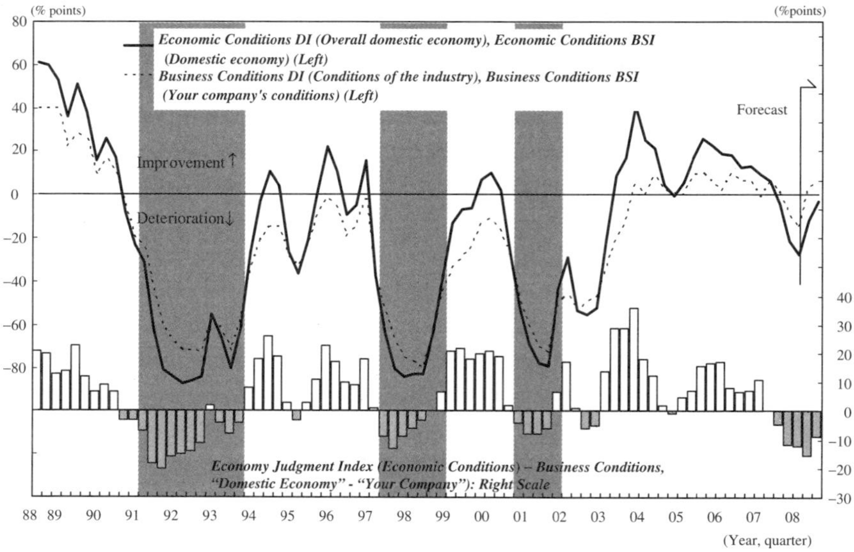

Figure 5. Former UFJ Tankan, Business Outlook Survey Assessment for Economic Conditions and Business Conditions (All Enterprises) "Rising"–"Falling".

Note: The shadowed areas represent economic recession phases (based on Cabinet Office statistics). Former UFJ Tank an until the January–March quarter of 2004, and the Business Outlook Survey from the April–June quarter of 2004 onward.

Source: CAO and MOF "Business Outlook Survey", Mitsubishi UFJ Research & Consulting Co., Ltd. "UFJ Tankan Survey".

2.5. *Monthly surveys — Reuters, economy watchers, and the consumer confidence*

The BOJ's *Tankan* Survey and the Business Outlook Survey have wide survey coverage and have established their reputation on effectively capturing the recent trends. Both are conducted, however, only quarterly so that during three months between two surveys other monthly surveys with narrower coverage must be utilized. Another survey similar to the BOJ *Tankan* is the Reuters Tankan Business Confidence Survey DI. It is conducted to 400 companies with capital of 1 billion yen or more and announced monthly. It largely moves in parallel with the BOJ *Tankan* Survey, so that it can be taken as a guide for the movement of the BOJ *Tankan* during 3 months until the next one.

The Economy Watchers Survey is conducted to slightly over 2,000 businessmen working in industries and looks into the direction of change. It asks them to observe the items of economic activities that sensitively reflect the trends in the household and corporate sectors, or employment conditions. The questions are asked if they are "better or will get better" or "worse or will get worse" on the current conditions and future outlook (refer to website: http://www5.cao.go.jp/keizai3/watcher-e/outline.pdf). The Economy Watchers Survey's DI for future economic conditions in the manufacturing industry leads its own assessment of current conditions and leads the Reuters's assessment on current business conditions for the manufacturing industry by 3 to 6 months (Figure 6).

The Reuters Tankan slightly lags *the Economy Watchers Survey*'s DI for current economic conditions for the manufacturing industry, particularly in *selective expenditures* like durable goods or cultural and leisure activities.

A household survey for consumer sentiment is *the Consumer Confidence Index* in *the Consumer Confidence Survey*. It asks the assessment on items like *Overall livelihood, Income growth, Employment*, and the *Willingness to buy durable goods*, etc., or whether it "will get better or worse", and compiles the consumer sentiment on them into an index. *The Consumer Confidence Index* tends to lead private consumption (refer to website http://www.esri.cao.go.jp/eu/stat/shouhi/zgshohi_kaisetu-e.html.) (Figure 7).

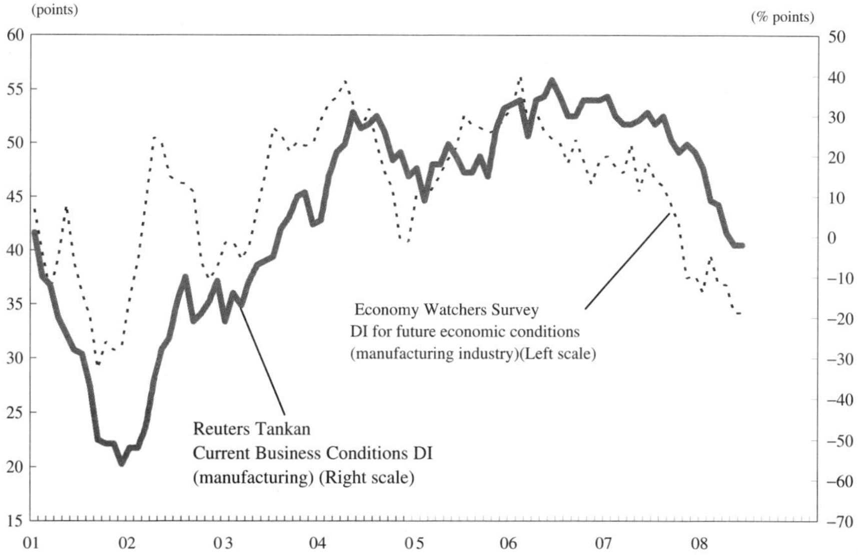

Figure 6. Economy Watchers Survey on Future Business Conditions and Reuters Tankan on Current Business Conditions.

Source: Reuters "Reuters Tankan Survey", Cabinet Office "Economy Watchers Survey".

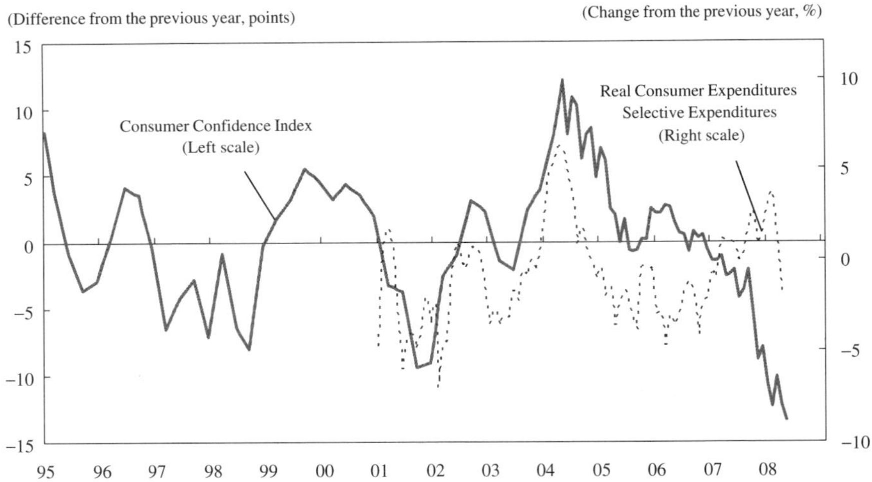

Figure 7. Consumer Confidence Index and Real Consumption.

Note: "Selective expenditures" are compiled by the Ministry of Internal Affairs and Communications (MIC) for specific goods and service expenditures with an elasticity value of 1.00 or greater against the fluctuation of overall expenditures.

Source: Cabinet Office "Consumer Confidence Survey", MIC "Family Income and Expenditure Survey".

The Economy Watchers Survey's DI for future economic conditions, discussed above, also moves in parallel with *the Consumer Confidence Index* (Figure 8).

There are many cases when the trend for items related to the retail; food and services have preceded consumption. This attribute can be used to capture the recent and short-term outlook for private consumption.

3. The Use of Leading Indexes — MUS Leading Index

3.1. *The history of Japan's business indexes*

For economic forecast, the successive approximation method and macroeconometric models are widely used today. For the successive approximation method, economic systems are largely classified into exogenous and endogenous variables. Discussions will be held by a group consisting of members assigned to be responsible for individual variables, and the predictive figures are ultimately determined by the leader of the group. On the other hand, the macroeconometric models are a method, which obtains the

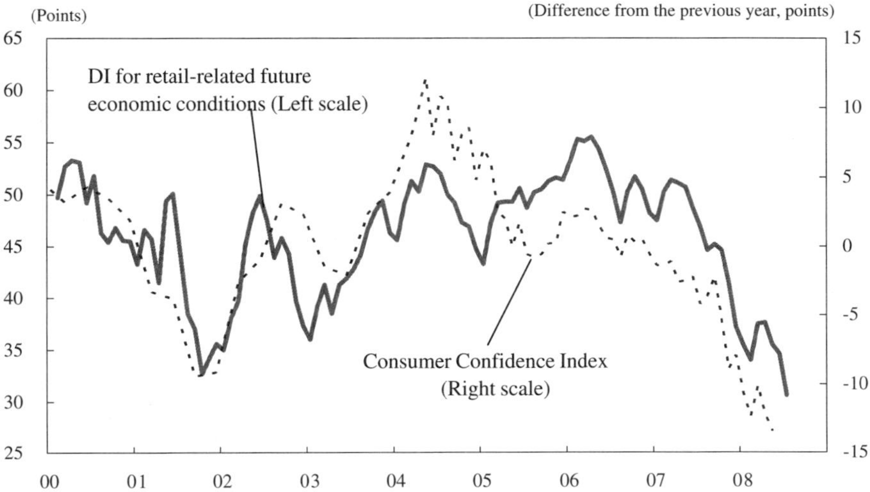

Figure 8. Consumer Confidence Index and Assessment on Future Retail Businesses.
Source: Cabinet Office "Economy Watchers Survey" "Consumer Confidence Survey".

solution of this process by using simultaneous equations. The third method is to use business indexes, or leading indexes or indicators.

Business indexes are based on a number of indexes that sensitively respond to developments in the business cycle, which are selected from various longitudinal economic data. The index is created by processing and compounding these selected indexes using some form of statistical method. Business indexes have two purposes. The first is the academic purpose of measuring and analyzing business cycles. The second is the practical purpose of assessing current economic conditions and predicting the outlook of the economy. This chapter takes up the latter.

The history of business indexes in post-war Japan goes back to 1956, when a DI research project was launched in the former EPA's Research Bureau. It started to release its DI on a monthly basis from 1960. This is what now continues as the "Indexes of Business Conditions". After the CI was developed by the US National Bureau of Economic Research (NBER) in 1968, the EPA announced the CI along with the DI as a reference index. Recently, however, the format of the EPA's announcement was changed in June 2008 and now centers on the CI.

Many unique indexes were developed in addition to the EPA's Indexes of Business Conditions, such as the BOJ's "Business Fluctuation Indicator" (1956), the Diffusion Indexes developed by the former Sumitomo Bank and the Mitsubishi Economic Research Institute (1958–1961), the former EPA's Business Warning Indicator (1968), the former Yamaichi Research Institute's "YRI Business Index" (1979), and the Japan Center for Economic Research's "JCER Business Index" (1990).[7] In general, business indexes consist of three: the leading index, coincident index, and the lagging index, as is the Cabinet Office's Indexes of Business Conditions. The index which is of the most practical use is the leading index.

3.2. *The MUS Leading Index (MUS-LI) for the Japanese economy*

In March 1991, Shimanaka developed the Sanwa Leading Index (SLI) with his colleagues at the Sanwa Research Institute & Consulting Corporation (now Mitsubishi UFJ Research and Consulting Co.). It became the world's first leading index using the DI method for an index which mainly covers the financial market, such as long- and short-term interest rates and the foreign exchange rates. Its name was changed to the UFJ Leading Index (UFJ-LI) in 2002 and to the MUS-Leading Index (MUS- LI) in 2007. Leading indexes for various areas were later added to the MUS-LI such as the MUS-LI for the Japanese Economy. It was introduced in March 1995. The MUS-LI now includes 8 series covering 7 categories. The calculation method takes the same approach as the Cabinet Office's DI, but its main form of representation adopts the cumulative DI. It consists of two indexes: the *composite series* and the long-term leading series. The former is composed of 14 indexes from various sectors including the finance, stock price, commodity market, housing investment, and the US economy, whereas the latter is comprised of 7 indexes, which have been recognized to have a longer leading period (Table 1).

The graph in Figure 9 shows the month-to-month movements of the two series of indicators of the MUS-LI. The average leading time lag to the past 12 business cycle turning points is about 7 months for the composite series and 9 months for the long-term leading series. These turning points mostly coincide with the peaks and troughs of the cumulative coincident

[7]Behind the development of these business indexes and the various debates was a group of economists including Masao Baba, Kazuo Mori, Shoji Tahara, Nobuhiro Nomura, Masahiro Fukuyama. They became the core members of the Japan Association of Business Cycle studies (JABC), established under the chairmanship of Miyohei Shinohara in 1985, currently chaired by Nobuyuki Nakahara.

Table 1. The Trends in Individual Indexes Composing the MUS-LI for the Japanese Economy.

	2007 7–9	2007 10–12	2008 1–3	2008 4–6	2007 6	2007 7	2007 8	2007 9	2007 10	2007 11	2007 12	2008 1	2008 2	2008 3	2008 4	2008 5	2008 6
Indexes of Business Conditions — Cumulative DI (Cabinet Office)	8.740	8.761	8.735	8.696	8.716	8.729	8.743	8.747	8.761	8.756	8.766	8.734	8.747	8.725	8.705	8.688	
MUS-LI (composite series) DI	52	35	36	*32*	57	64	50	43	36	29	39	36	36	36	29	36	
Cumulative DI	↑	↓	↓	↓	↑	↑	→	↓	↓	↓	↓	↓	↓	↓	↓	↓	
	836	789	746	*725*	829	843	843	836	821	800	789	775	761	746	725	711	
MUS-LI (leading long-term series) DI	43	24	33	*29*	57	43	43	43	14	43	14	43	14	43	14	43	
Cumulative DI	↓	↓	↓	↓	↑	↓	↓	↓	↓	↓	↓	↓	↓	↓	↓	↓	
	479	400	350	*314*	500	493	486	479	443	436	400	393	357	350	314	307	
1 Real Money Supply					○	○	○	▲	▲	▲	▲	▲	▲	▲	▲	▲	
Year-on-year (%)	2.0	1.4	1.3	*0.9*	2.0	2.0	2.0	1.9	1.6	1.4	1.4	1.4	1.3	1.0	1.1	0.7	
② Yield Curve (%)					○	○	○	▲	▲	▲	▲	▲	▲	▲	▲	○	○
	1.269	1.112	0.937	*1.159*	1.433	1.433	1.222	1.150	1.204	1.059	1.074	0.969	0.992	0.849	0.960	1.219	1.297
③ TOPIX/Nominal					○	○	▲	▲	▲	▲	▲	▲	▲	▲	▲	○	
Industrial Shipments Index Seasonally adjusted	0.145	0.134	0.112	*0.113*	0.158	0.158	0.139	0.138	0.140	0.131	0.130	0.115	0.112	0.108	0.111	0.114	
4 Nikkei Commodity Price					○	○	○	▲	▲	▲	▲	▲	○	○	○	○	○
Index (17 Items) (End of month) Year-on-year (%)	15.1	10.2	13.7	19.6	15.3	18.5	12.9	13.7	13.5	9.9	7.2	7.9	16.8	16.5	18.7	19.4	20.7
⑤ Condominium Sales					▲	▲	▲	○	▲	○	▲	▲	▲	○	○	○	
Contract Rate, Tokyo Metropolitan Area Seasonally adjusted (%)	68.2	62.4	59.9	*67.4*	65.7	72.2	64.5	67.9	62.7	64.3	59.8	58.7	58.3	62.8	63.9	70.9	

(*Continued*)

Table 1. ***(Continued)***

	2007 7–9	2007 10–12	2008 1–3	2008 4–6	2007 6	2007 7	2007 8	2007 9	2007 10	2007 11	2007 12	2008 1	2008 2	2008 3	2008 4	2008 5	2008 6
⑥ Newly Constructed					○	▲	▲	▲	▲	○	○	○	○	○	▲	▲	
Housing Starts Seasonally adjusted (Thousand units)	67	80	95	*93*	113	80	61	61	71	80	88	99	96	91	96	89	
⑦ Number of New Car					▲	▲	○	○	○	○	▲	○	▲	○	▲	▲	
Registrations (Automobiles) Seasonally adjusted (Thousand units)	360	371	375	*367*	361	343	374	363	384	382	346	388	381	355	381	352	
⑧ Terms of Trade					▲	▲	▲	▲	▲	▲	▲	▲	▲	▲	▲	▲	▲
	0.859	0.813	0.781	0.735	0.865	0.864	0.856	0.856	0.834	0.817	0.789	0.708	0.779	0.777	0.758	0.740	0.708
9 Unit Labor Cost <Inverse					▲	○	▲	○	▲	▲	○	▲	▲	▲	○	○	
cycle> Year-on-year (%)	−3.6	−3.4	−0.7	*−1.8*	0.3	−6.5	−4.3	−0.1	−4.6	−3.5	−2.0	−0.7	−3.5	2.2	−1.3	−2.2	
10 Producers Inventory Ratio					▲	○	▲	▲	○	▲	○	▲	○	▲	▲	▲	
of industrial products <Inverse cycle> Seasonally adjusted (2005 = 100)	100.9	100.5	101.1	*101.1*	100.9	99.9	99.5	103.4	99.51	101.21	101.3	99.7	98.3	105.3	101.2	101.0	
11 Production Ratio of					▲	○	▲	○	○	○	○	▲	▲	○	○	○	
Industrial Production Goods/ Final Demand Goods Seasonally adjusted	1.024	1.053	1.041	*1.042*	1.020	1.027	1.009	1.035	1.048	1.053	1.059	1.035	1.025	1.063	1.053	1.031	
12 Producers Shipment Index					○	○	○	○	○	▲	=	○	○	▲	▲	▲	
of the Non-ferrous Metals Industry Seasonally adjusted (2005 = 100)	105.4	105.0	105.5	*100.8*	103.2	104.4	106.2	105.5	104.8	104.7	105.5	105.2	107.6	103.6	98.6	102.9	

(Continued)

Table 1. (*Continued*)

		2007 7–9	2007 10–12	2008 1–3	2008 4–6	2007 6	2007 7	2007 8	2007 9	2007 10	2007 11	2007 12	2008 1	2008 2	2008 3	2008 4	2008 5	2008 6
13	Balance of Tokyo Electric Power Company's Large Volume Sales Seasonally adjusted					○	▲	○	▲	○	▲	○	○	○	▲	▲	▲	▲
		0.335	0.338	0.340	0.335	0.337	0.325	0.343	0.335	0.338	0.339	0.337	0.338	0.345	0.336	0.338	0.336	0.332
⑭	U.S. Manufacturing Industry Capacity Utilization Seasonally adjusted					○	○	○	○	▲	▲	▲	○	▲	▲	▲	▲	
		81.3	81.0	80.6	*79.5*	81.0	81.4	81.2	81.3	80.8	81.1	81.0	81.0	80.3	80.3	79.6	79.4	

Note: The arrows in the first row of the Cumulative DI each indicate: ↑ — Increase, → — Unchanged, ↓ — Decline from the previous month. The symbols on the upper row of each data (above the numerical figures) indicate: ○ — Increase, = — Unchanged, ▲ — Decline from 3 months ago. However, the symbol means the opposite for data series which are labeled to have <Inverse cycles>. The long-term leading series of the MUS-LI for the Japanese Economy is comprised of the 7 indexes which have a circled number before them (i.e. ② ③ ⑤ ⑥ ⑦ ⑧ ⑭) After the public release of the yield for listed Japanese government bonds ended, the long-term interest rate used to calculate the yield curve has been changed to the newly issued 10-year Japanese government bonds from April 2005. Numerical figures in italics indicate provisional figures.

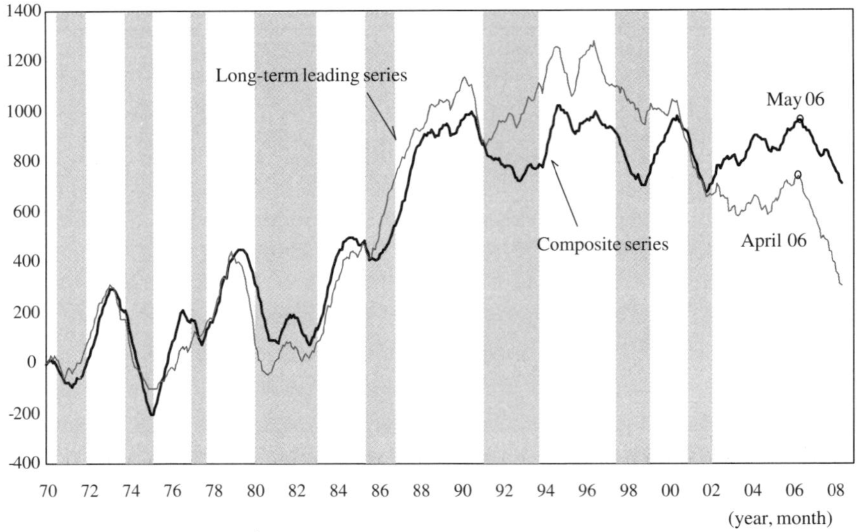

Figure 9. MUS-LI for the Japanese Economy Cumulative DI.

Note: Shadowed areas indicate economic recession phases (based on Cabinet Office statistics). The leading time lag of the cumulative DI of the long-term leading series to the actual economy is average of 9 months, longer than the leading time lag of the composite series (average of 6 months). This can therefore be used as supplementary material for the overall economic assessment. The long-term leading series are comprised of ② ③ ⑤ ⑥ ⑦ ⑧ ⑭ in the table above for individual indexes.

DI. Therefore, assessing the economic outlook using the MUS-LI is a two-step process — first, the long-term leading series and next, the composite series. The prediction of timing of changes in the business cycle is captured by the long-term leading series which generally reaches its turning point earlier and then, can be confirmed in advance by the change in the direction of the composite series.

The MUS-LI comprises of the following 14 items:

1. Real money supply (M_2/Consumer prices, year-to-year)
2. The difference between long- and short-term interest rates (yield of listed Japanese government bonds — call rate)
3. TOPIX/Nominal industrial shipments index
4. Nikkei commodity price index (17 items, at each month-end, year- to year)
5. Condominium sales contract rate,
6. Tokyo metropolitan area newly-constructed housing starts index

7. Number of new car registrations (Automobiles)
8. Terms of trade
9. Unit labor cost (Year-on-year, inverse cycle)
10. Producers inventory ratio of industrial products (Inverse cycle)
11. Production ratio of industrial production goods/final demand goods
12. Producers shipment index of the non-ferrous metals industry
13. Balance of Tokyo Electric Power Company's large volume sales
14. US manufacturing industry capacity utilization

The CI for the respective item is published in addition to DI and the Cumulative DI (Figures 9, 10, Tables 1, 2). One of the characteristics of the components adopted in the MUS-LI is that it includes relevant indexes from the overseas sector like items 8 and 14 above. Furthermore, the lagging indexes such as interest rates are viewed as the "ultimate leading indicators in all leading indicators", and as such, many indictors which respond sensitively to lagging indexes are included. They refer to items 2. The difference between long- and short-term interest rates (Yield curve),

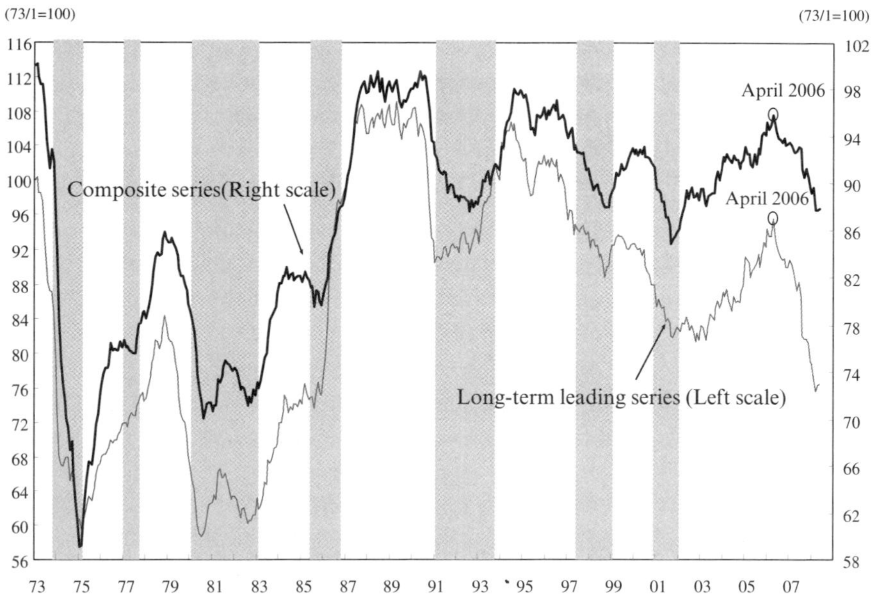

Figure 10. Change in the MUS-LI for Japanese Economy CI.

Note: The shadowed areas indicate economic ression phases (based on Cabinet Office statistics). The leading time lag of the CI to the actual economy is 7 months on average for the composite series and 10 months on average for the long-term leading series.

Table 2. Change in the MUS-LI (Japanese Economy) CI.

CI	06/11	06/12	07/1	07/2	07/3	07/4	07/5	07/6	07/7	07/8	07/9	07/10	07/11	07/12	08/1	08/2	08/3	08/4	08/5
Composite Index Series	93.2	93.4	93.6	93.3	92.8	92.6	92.7	93.1	93.0	91.3	90.6	91.3	90.6	89.5	89.2	89.2	87.7	87.7	87.8
Long-term Index Series	89.9	90.0	90.7	90.3	89.2	88.5	87.3	88.3	86.6	82.0	81.7	81.8	81.1	79.0	78.9	77.2	75.7	76.4	76.5

Note: The shadowed areas indicate previous peaks.
Source: Figures 9, 10 and Tables 1, 2 are based on Mitsubishi UFJ Securities Business Cycle Research Institute "MUS Leading Index for the Japanese Economy".

3. TOPIX/Nominal industrial shipments index, 5. Condominium sales contract rate, Tokyo metropolitan area, 6. Newly-constructed housing starts index, and 7. Number of new car registrations. These seven indicators comprise the "long-term leading series", which is used along with the "composite series" including production-related and other indicators.

3.3. *The performance of the MUS-LI for the Japanese economy*

The key factor for leading indexes would be, first of all, its ability to signal business cycle turning points ahead of their actual occurrence. The performance of MUS-LI in this respect is examined here.

The composite DI of the MUS-LI has shown leading signals for all 15 *turning points* since the trough of the business cycle in December 1971 (Table 3). The average leading time lag was 5.3 months for the troughs and 7.0 months for the peaks. The average leading lag time for both the troughs and peaks was 6.1 months. The long-term leading series gave leading signals to 14 out of 15 turning points (one case was a lagging signal), and led the turning points by 9.1 months on average.

Looking at the CI in the same way, the composite series showed leading signals for 13 out of 14 turning points, and the long-term leading series signaled 12 out of 14 turning points. The average leading period was 7.4 months and 10.5 months, respectively (Table 4).

Another key factor for leading indexes is the reliability of the signals they show. This can be examined by observing the cases where signals from leading indexes did not result in actual turning points. The so-called "three-months rule" is often applied for assessing the Indexes of Business Conditions. Under this rule, the DI is considered to have "given a signal" if the DI falls below 50% for three consecutive months during an expansionary phase, or if the DI exceeds 50% for three consecutive months during a contraction phase. Since the 1970s, only in two cases did the composite series giving a signal under the *three-month rule* not result in actual *turning points*; for an expansionary phase and a contraction phase, respectively. The long-term leading series had only 5 such cases. These may be regarded as a good performance overall.

Since a CI indicates the direction and the volume of the economy, leading indexes can be used as a basis to calculate projections for future growth rates, the BOJ's Business Conditions DI, and so on. The leading indexes are not necessarily the ones targeted at the economic growth rates, but a comparison of the projected values based on the CI of the MUS-LI with

Table 3. The Leading Nature of the MUS-LI for the Japanese Economy (DI).

(Number of months, counts)

Business Cycle Reference Dates		Turning Point of Composite Series		Turning Point of the Long-Term Leading Series	
Trough	Peak	Trough	Peak	Trough	Peak
71.12		−8		−12	
	73.11		−7		−9
75.3		−1		2	
	77.1		−5		−5
77.10		−3		−11	
	80.2		−7		−14
83.2		−4		−9	
	85.6		−8		−2
86.11		−11		−15	
	91.2		−7		−11
93.10		−11		−28	
	97.5		−10		−11
99.1		−2		−2	
	2000.11		−5		−8
2002.1		−2		−2	
Average leading period (months)		−5.3	−7.0	−9.6	−8.6
		−6.1		−9.1	
Number of leading times		8/8	7/7	7/8	7/7
		15/15		14/15	

Note: Negative = leading, positive = lagging.
Source: Cabinet Office "Indexes of Business Conditions", Mitsubishi UFJ Securities Business Cycle Research Institute "MUS Leading Index".

actual growth rates since 1995 shows that the absolute-value of the error for the projected growth rates based on the composite series for two quarters ahead and the projected growth rates based on the long-term leading series for 3 quarters ahead are both just 1.0 percentage point short (Figure 11).

Similar comparisons between the forecasts by private research institutes using quantitative macroeconometric models and the successive approximation method and the actual results have been performed by Yamazawa (2008). His calculation covering 14 institutions reported that the average for the absolute value of error was 1.93 percentage points. Simple comparison of the two projection errors cannot be made, since the latter were for a slightly longer period ahead, ranging from a half year to 1.5 years, than

Table 4. The Leading Nature of the MUS-LI for the Japanese Economy (CI).

(Number of months, counts)

Business Cycle Reference Dates		**Turning Point of Composite Series**		**Turning Point of the Long-Term Leading Series**	
Trough	**Peak**	**Trough**	**Peak**	**Trough**	**Peak**
	73.11		−9		−9
75.3		−2		−1	
	77.1		0		—
77.10		−3		—	
	80.2		−15		−15
83.2		−6		−6	
	85.6		−13		−3
86.11		−11		−15	
	91.2		−9		−1
93.10		−14		−33	
	97.5		−10		−17
99.1		−3		−4	
	2000.11		−5		−19
2002.1		−4		−3	
Average leading period (months)		−6.1	−8.7	−10.3	−10.7
		−7.4		−10.5	
Number of leading times		7/7	6/7	6/7	6/7
		13/14		12/14	

Note: Negative = leading, positive = lagging.
Source: Cabinet Office "Indexes of Business Conditions", Mitsubishi UFJ Securities Business Cycle Research Institute "MUS Leading Index".

the former, but the projections by the MUS-LI for 2 to 3 quarters ahead are not necessarily less reliable than more elaborate model ones.

Recently, projections through the Vector Auto Regression (VAR) model are also used. In the projections by this model[8] based on 6 variables (the real GDP, GDP deflator, unemployment rate, call rate, dollar-yen exchange rate and long-term interest rates) and a time lag of four quarters (from the January to March quarter of 1976 to the January to March quarter of 2008), and calculations of the deviation from the actual results, the average for the absolute value of error was 1.3 percentage points. While this result also

[8] The unit root test of data for projecting the VAR model confirmed them to become stationery in 1 finite difference. The lag was set at 4 terms based on AIC standards.

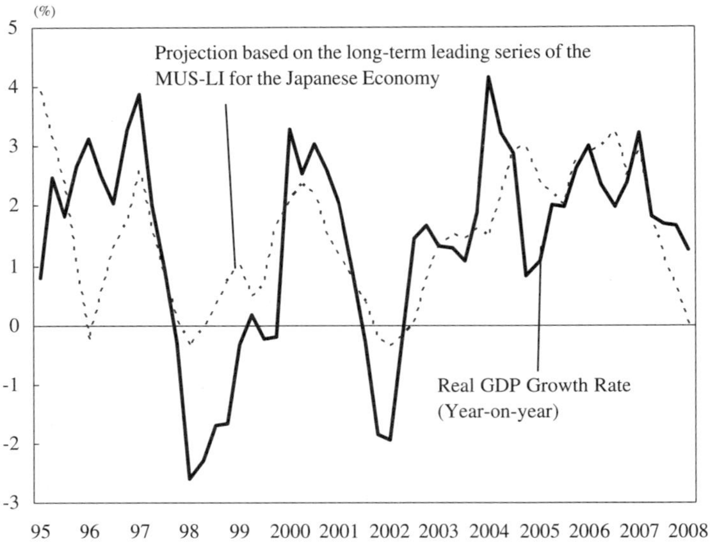

Figure 11. The Real Growth Rate and Projections using the MUS-LI.

Note: The projections were estimated based on the following formula:

$$\text{Real GDP Growth (Year-on-year)} = \underset{(9.0)}{1.64} + \underset{(5.9)}{0.26}*\text{MUS-LI(CI) (from 3 quarters ago)}$$

Projection period was 1995.1Q-2008.1Q. Value in () are t-values, $R*R = 0.40$.

Source: Cabinet Office "Indexes of Business Conditions", Mitsubishi UFJ Securities Business Cycle Research Institute "MUS Leading Index".

cannot be simply compared, the error of the forecasts using the MUS-LI was smaller.

3.4. *The merits and demerits of forecasts using leading indexes*

At the end of 1996, Shimanaka attempted, using the MUS-LI (SLI then), to forecast the end of the expansionary phase of the 12th business cycle (which was later officially determined as May 1997), and the adjustment phase of the economy in the first half of fiscal 1997. Furthermore, the author projected as of July 1997 that the adjustment, i.e. the recession phase of the economy, would continue throughout the year of 1997. Setting aside the degree of strength, the direction of change was on target (Shimanaka, 1996).

The performance of the forecast of the economy in February 1998 using the MUS-LI (former UFJ-LI) for 6 to 9 months ahead was also favorable in retrospect. At the time, the composite series of the MUS-LI dropped in December after November 1997, and the October-December quarter marked the fifth straight decline on a quarterly basis. On the other hand, the long-term leading series also marked a consecutive drop in November and December, showing that the decline was yet to bottom out. As such, Shimanaka suggested that "based on the average time lag indicated, the current recession period is likely to continue at least until the summer of 1998". The results later turned out to be as forecasted, and the economic recession period continued until January 1999 (Shimanaka, 1997).

The most significant feature of forecasting with business indexes including the MUS-LI is its mechanical and visual nature as well as its objectivity. Once calculated, business indexes autonomously show the direction of change regardless of the producers' wish. Its track can be seen on a chart and is self-explanatory. This is the major difference from the forecasts using the successive approximation method or the quantitative model. The former is the product from the judgments and ideas of several people at various stages. In the latter, forecasting the exogenous variables as prerequisites must be done in advance and requires more information for policies to be taken and *craftsmanship*.

Forecasts with business indexes, on the other hand, always involve an inherent risk of making a horrible mistake, such as the failure of the former Harvard Index Chart in anticipating the Great Depression. They have limitations, because this method is not primarily appropriate for quantitative forecasts. In addition, when major structural changes are under way or drastic changes in political matters may occur, this method must be carefully employed by considering their impact on the individual indexes. Furthermore, it is crucial to make constant efforts to revise the index so that the preceding nature is maintained.

Putting things the other way around, however, when structural changes are emphasized, business indexes may serve as an antidote. Despite the popular optimism in the late 1980s that business cycles were dead, the next serious recession was just around the corner. In 1991, the debate on the *demise of inventory cycles* almost led the government statistical offices to reduce the number of inventory-related indexes from the Business Conditions Index. At that time, however, the EPA's leading index was actually declining and signaling the signs of the coming recession.

In April 2000, the New Economy argument became popular in the US, and the significance of business cycles was downplayed again. But the forecast based on the MUS-LI for the Japanese economy turned out to correctly foresee the turning-point of the cycle in 2000. Shimanaka (2000, p. 108) predicted that the business cycle was likely to reach a peak as early as the first half of fiscal-2000 and head for a down-swing during the second half. Actually, the peak came in November 2000, and the economy followed the forecast. In summary, the predictive power of the leading indexes should not be taken lightly, since their concern centers on locating the cycles' turning points. Other quantitative models naturally have many merits as a tool for public investment management — an area of rising global demand. The authors believe that both business leading indexes and other econometric models and methods should play the essential roles in comprehensive assessment and forecast of the national economy.

References

Bank of Japan (2008). Explanation of the Short-term Economic Survey of Enterprises in Japan (TANKAN). http://www.boj.or.jp/en/type/exp/stat/tk/extk.htm.

Burns, A. F. and W. C. Mitchell (1947). *Measuring Business Cycles*. New York: National Bureau of Economic Research.

Cabinet Office (2006), Keikidoukoushisuu no mikata, tsukaikata (Guide for Using Indexes of Business Conditions). http://www.esri.cao.go.jp/jp/stat/di/0610pamph/0610pamph.html.

Cabinet Office. Guide for Using Diffusion Indexes and Composite Indexes. http://www.esri.cao.go.jp/en/ stat/di/di2e.html.

Cabinet Office. Ministry of Finance. Explanation of Business Outlook Survey. http://www.esri.cao.go.jp/en/stat/hojin/ hojin-yosoku_kaisetu-e.html.

Cabinet Office. Explanation of Monthly Consumer Confidence Survey Covering All of Japan. http://www.esri.cao.go.jp/en/stat/ shouhi/zgshohi_kaisetu-e.html.

Cabinet Office. Outline of the Economy Watchers Survey. http://www5.cao.go.jp/keizai3/watcher-e/outline. pdf

Mitsubishi UFJ Research and Consulting. UFJ Tankan Survey. http://www.murc.jp/shimanaka/tankan/ top.html.

Shimanaka, Y. (1991). Sanwa Leading Index. Sanwa Research Institute.

Shimanaka, Y. (1996). Keizai kyoushitsu: Keiki, 97-nendo kamiki wa chousei (The Economy Classroom: Economy to be in Adjustment Phase During the First Half of Fiscal 1997). *Nihon Keizai Shimbun*, December 27, 1.

Shimanaka, Y. (1998). Keizai kyoushitsu: Keiki shisuu bunseki ∼ Junkan no kiseki, ichimoku ryouzen ni (The Economy Classroom: Business Index Analyses — the Track of the Business Cycle will be Clear at a Glance). *Nihon Keizai Shimbun*, February 5.

Shimanaka, Y. (2000). *Nihon keizai no yudan* (*The Carelessness of the Japanese Economy*), Toyo Keizai Inc.

Shimanaka, Y. and UFJ Institute Ltd. Investment Research Division (2003). *Jissen: keiki yosoku nyumon* (*Practical Introduction to Economic Forecasting*). Toyo Keizai Inc.

Schumpeter, J. A. (1935). The Analysis of Economic Change. *Review of Economic Statistics*. xvii, May.

Yamazawa, N. (2008). Keiki ga keizai yosoku ni ataeru eikyou (The Impact of Economic Conditions on Economic Forecasts). JCER Discussion Paper No. 114, May.

Part II

Input-Output Analyses and CGE Models

Chapter 4

Factor Proportions and Foreign Trade: The Case of Japan*

Masahiro Tatemoto and Shinichi Ichimura†

1. The Leontief Paradox?

Professor Leontief's investigations into the structural basis of American foreign trade revealed that "an average million dollars" worth of exports embodies considerably less capital and somewhat more labor than would be required to replace from domestic production an equivalent amount of [American] competitive imports. America's participation in the international division of labor is based on its specialization on labor-intensive, rather than capital-intensive, lines of production."[1] This observation obviously contained a paradox because, according to the factor proportions account of international trade, the United States was expected to export those commodities in whose production its relatively abundant factor, capital, was important, and to import those which required relatively large amounts of its scarce factor, labor. Thus, Professor Leontief objected to the widely held opinion that the United States was a capital abundant (hence labor scarce) country and asserted that the opposite was true. This paradox has now become a highly controversial issue, and a number of papers, all very critical, have appeared

*This chapter was published in the *Review of Economics and Statistics*, 1959 (November, Vol. 41, pp. 442–446). Permission for reprint granted by the MIT Press.

†The authors wish to express their gratitude to Messrs. Hiroshi Atsumi, Tetsuo Fukumura, Yoichi Shinkai, and Takeyuki Okamoto for assistance in computation, and to Dr. Francis Seton, Nuffield College, Oxford, and their colleague Professor Michio Morishima for their valuable criticisms and suggestions. Needless to say, any errors remaining are the authors' responsibility.

[1]Leontief, W. (1953) Domestic Production and Foreign Trade: The American Capital Position Re-Examined. *Proceedings of the American Philosophical Society*, 97, September, reprinted in *Economia Internationale*, VII (1954).

in various journals.[2] Most of them, however, contained only conjectural comments. No further input-output studies have so far been attempted to support or refute Professor Leontief's findings, except for his own second, more comprehensive report[3] which supports the principal conclusions of his earlier work. At the end of the former report, he makes the following remark: "A comprehensive, two-sided explanation of our economic relationship with the rest of the world will not, of course, be possible before the internal economic structure of at least one of the most important of our trading partners has been studied as fully as that of our own."

We believe that Japan may be ranked among the most important of American trading partners, and her internal economic structure has been revealed by the Inter-industry Relations Table, 1951, which was completed in 1956 by the Ministry of International Trade and Industry (MITI) with the cooperation of one of the authors.[4] It is the main purpose of this chapter to present as a first report of our joint work at the Institute of Social and Economic Research, Osaka University, an input-output analysis of Japanese foreign trade and related problems.[5]

2. Computational Procedures and Statistical Data

The usual input-output system can be written as:

$$[I - A](x) = (b)y - (c)z + (r) \ \ldots \ (I)$$

where A = matrix of input coefficients, I = a unit matrix, (x) = a column vector of output in million Yen, (b) = a column vector of export coefficients defined as each sector's exports per million Yen of total exports, (c) = a column vector of competitive import coefficients defined as each sector's imports per million Yen of total competitive imports, y = total value of exports in million Yen, z = total value of competitive imports in million Yen, and (r) = a column vector of residuals of final demands.

[2]Cf. page 386 of the article cited in footnote 3 below.

[3]Leontief, W. (1956). Factor Proportions and the Structure of American Trade: Further Theoretical and Empirical Analysis. *REVIEW*, XXXVIII, November.

[4]The methods and the detailed explanations of the MITI input-output table are given in *Interindustrial Analysis of the Japanese Economy*, Oriental Economist, Tokyo, 1957. The English summary was published in 1958 as *Interindustrial Analysis of the Japanese Economy*, Council for Industry Planning.

[5]The published works by the members of the Institute are: Ichimura, S. (1957). *The Structure of the Japanese Economy*. Tokyo; Sobun-Sha; Ichimura, S. (ed.) (1958). *Applications of Interindustrial Analysis*. Tokyo, Yuhikaku; Kansai Economic Federation (ed.) (1958). *The Japanese Economy and Regional Economies*, Tokyo: Sobun-Sha, all in Japanese.

Solving (i) for x and pre-multiplying that x by the row vectors of capital and labor coefficients (defined as the amounts of capital and labor directly required by each sector per million Yen of its output), we obtain:

$$(k)'(x) = (k)'[I - A]^{-1}\{(b)y - (c)z + (r)\} \tag{2.1}$$

$$(n)'(x) = (n)'[I - A]^{-1}\{(b)y - (c)z + (r)\} \tag{2.2}$$

where (k) and (n) represent capital and labor coefficients, respectively. Here, the expression $(k)'[I - A]^{-1}$ (b) in (2.1) may be interpreted as the amounts of capital directly and indirectly required by increasing exports by one million Yen (without changing their composition), and likewise $(k)'[I - A]^{-1}$ (c) as the amount of capital directly and indirectly required to replace one million Yen's worth of imports by domestic production; $(n)'[I - A]^{-1}$ (b) and $(n)'[I - A]^{-1}(c)$ may be interpreted in a similar way.

The original MITI table contained 187 sectors, but the corresponding input coefficients matrix was not inverted. To our regret, therefore, we had to base our computation on an inverse matrix consisting of only 29 consolidated sectors.[6] We do not believe, however, that this influences our qualitative conclusions. Lately, the capital coefficients were computed by the Council for Industry Planning in cooperation with MITI and the Economic

[6]The inverse matrix used here is the one computed at Stanford University and was offered us by Professor Tsunehiko Watanabe, Peers' College, Tokyo. There are, however, at least five other inverse matrices available in Japan. The first is an inverse of the consolidated 36 sectoral input coefficients matrix for 1951, which is attached to the MITI report, *Interindustrial Analysis of the Japanese Economy*. The second is a similar inverse matrix of input coefficients table for 1954 attached to the same book. The third inverse matrix is appended to S. Ichimura, *The Structure of the Japanese Economy*, 1957. This matrix is computed from the input coefficients table of 38 sectors for 1951, which is different from the one used for the computation of the first inverse matrix in the aggregation. These three inverse matrices were all computed by MITI and are based on the input coefficient tables including the ratios of competitive imports to each sector's total output as diagonal elements; that is, $[I - A + m]$, where m is a diagonal matrix. The fourth inverse matrix was based on the input coefficients table calculated for predicting the total output of each industry in 1962. These input coefficients are adjusted, therefore, for the expected changes in technology. The fifth is an inverse matrix of the interregional input (and trade) coefficients table calculated by the Kansai Economic Federation. This interregional input-output table divided each of the 187 industries into the Kinki area and the rest of Japan, and for the purpose of inverting the input coefficients matrix, it was consolidated to 30 industries and the above-mentioned two regions; namely, the 60×60 matrix was inverted. The last two are available only in the mimeographed forms at the moment.

Planning Board.[7] They are entered in column (i) of Table 1. The labor coefficients computed by MITI (together with the input-output table) mainly from the Labor Force Survey data are entered in column (2). Columns (3) and (4) show the numerical values of $(k)'[I - A] - 1$ and $(n)'[I - A]^{-1}$, respectively. Columns (5) and (6) indicate (b) and (c) calculated from the MITI table.[8] The latter is based on the Customs Statistics of the Ministry of Finance. Then, the values of total capital and labor requirement — i.e. $(k)'[I - A]^{-1}(b)$ and $(n)'[I - A]^{-1}(b)$ — can easily be computed. They are shown in columns (7) and (8). The similar values for competitive imports are entered in columns (9) and (10). These represent the direct and indirect capital and labor requirements of the composite commodities of "1951 Japanese Exports" and the domestic production substituted for "1951 Japanese Competitive Imports."

3. Statistical Results and Implications

Our final results are shown in Table 2 and are compared with Professor Leontief's original findings for the United States in 1947. From these figures, we can immediately determine what Professor Leontief called "an index of comparative capital-labor intensity," that is, the capital-labor input ratio for competitive imports divided by the same ratio for exports. These are entered in the last column (γ) of Table 2. If the value of this index exceeds unity, the country's exports are labor-intensive and its imports capital-intensive. This is the case of the United States. If it is less than unity, the pattern is opposite. This is the case of Japan.

According to our findings, an average million Yen's worth of Japanese exports embodies more capital and less labor than would be required for the domestic replacements of competitive imports of an equivalent amount. This implies, if interpreted in the manner of Leontief, that Japan's specialization in the international division of labor is found in capital-intensive, rather than labor intensive, lines of production. If the intuitive notion that

[7]Cf. Council for Industry Planning (ed.) (1958). *The Capital Structure of the Japanese Economy*, Tokyo. The English edition is available at the Council. This book reports not only the total capital coefficients cited here but also interindustrial capital coefficients, average and marginal, for 32 sectors.

[8]The MITI table considered any imports which have similar domestic products as competitive imports, but here we changed the definition and took as non-competitive imports the following: coffee and other agriculture products, textile materials, crude petroleum, tin and other metals, hides and rubber.

Table 1. Labor and Capital Requirements per Million Yen of Japanese Exports and of Competitive Imports Replacements, 1951.

	Direct Capital Coefficient (¥) Mill, Per ¥ Mill. of Output	Direct Labor Coefficient (Man Year Per ¥ Mill. of Output)	Direct and Indirect Requirement Per Mill. Yen of Final Output		Exports Per Mill. Yen of Total Exports	Competitive Imports Per Mill. Yen of Total Exports	Requirements of Exports		Requirement of Competitive Imports	
			Capital	Labor			Capital	Labor	Capital	Labor
	(1)	(2)	(3)	(4)	(5)	(6)	(7)	(8)	(9)	(10)
1. Apparel	121	918	11,691	6.666	26,343	3,215	31,034	1777	3,759	21
2. Shipbuilding	301	1.731	9,561	3.880	11,402	26,371	10,901	44	25,212	102
3. Leather	60	880	13,762	9.403	1,353	2,722	11,860	13	3,742	26
4. Processed foods	133	687	8,030	4.478	21,565	148,107	17,316	97	118,926	663
5. Fishing	619	3.627	9,449	5.001	11,290	4,142	10,668	56	3,914	21
6. Grain mill products	133	687	17,946	12.700	1,240	6,227	2,225	16	11,175	79
7. Transportation	2.987	2.838	35,390	4.182	112,804	0	399,208	471	0	0
8. Industry n. e. c.	58	1.829	6,618	4.228	28,403	5,114	18,796	120	3,384	22
9. Transport equipment	301	1.731	9,614	4.307	8,979	16,706	8,632	39	16,061	72
10. Rubber	111	929	8,020	3.824	5,673	254	4,550	222	204	1

(Continued)

Table 1. (*Continued*)

	Direct Capital Coefficient (¥) Mill, Per ¥ Mill. of Output	Direct Labor Coefficient (Man Year Per ¥ Mill. of Output)	Direct and Indirect Requirement Per Mill. Yen of Final Output		Exports Per Mill. Yen of Total Exports	Competitive Imports Per Mill. Yen of Total Exports	Requirements of Exports		Requirement of Competitive Imports	
			Capital	Labor			Capital	Labor	Capital	Labor
	(1)	(2)	(3)	(4)	(5)	(6)	(7)	(8)	(9)	(10)
11. Textiles	121	918	13,328	8.041	347,466	9,540	463,085	2.794	12,714	77
12. Math, and elec. equipment	179	1.731	9,230	3.657	41,891	16,861	38,664	153	15,562	62
13. Iron and steel	159	471	8,606	2.285	134,764	9,272	115,979	308	7,980	21
14. Nonmetallic mineral prod.	296	1.900	9,995	4.185	34,470	1,237	34,454	144	1,236	5
15. Lumber and wood	327	2.948	16,670	11.058	14,671	2,063	24,457	162	3,439	23
16. Chemicals	220	651	10,689	3.533	46,944	70,470	50,178	166	75,325	249
17. Printing	104	1.115	8,465	3.464	808	2,425	684	3	2,053	8
18. Agriculture	1.675	13.353	18,787	14.195	13,450	422,976	25,268	191	794,63	6.004
19. Nonmetallic minerals	499	2.504	8,168	3.462	301	10,196	246	1	8,328	35
20. Petroleum products	241	200	6,215	1.137	169	48,857	105	0	30,363	56

(*Continued*)

Table 1. (*Continued*)

	Direct Capital Coefficient (¥) Mill, Per ¥ Mill. of Output	Direct Labor Coefficient (Man Year Per ¥ Mill. of Output)	Direct and Indirect Requirement Per Mill. Yen of Final Output		Exports Per Mill. Yen of Total Exports	Competitive Imports Per Mill. Yen of Total Exports	Requirements of Exports		Requirement of Competitive Imports	
			Capital	Labor			Capital	Labor	Capital	Labor
	(1)	(2)	(3)	(4)	(5)	(6)	(7)	(8)	(9)	(10)
21. Nonferrous metal	159	438	6,238	1.768	34,640	22,549	21,609	61	14,066	40
22. Metal mining	499	2.893	7,791	3.569	376	73,068	293	1	56,924	261
23. Coal products	241	353	11,738	2.997	56	0	66	0	0	0
24. Trade	492	4.155	8,750	4.890	80,494	0	70,431	394	0	0
25. Paper	136	1.115	9,318	4.266	11,609	33,451	10,817	50	31,169	143
26. Electric light and power	4.124	1.147	48,233	3.048	0	0	0	0	0	0
47. Coal	489	2.381	9,668	3.581	131	48,757	127	0	47,138	175
28. Service	2.411	3.114	28,292	4.347	8,528	15,416	24,127	37	43,615	67
29. Crude petroleum	499	1.389	5,848	1.554	0	0	0	0	0	0
					1,000,000	1,000,000	1,385,780	5.520	1,330,926	8.233

Table 2. Capital and Labor Requirements per Million Yen of Exports and of Competitive Import Replacement.

	Capital (α) (1951 Yen) (1947 Dollars)	Labor (β) (Man-Years)	(α/β)	(γ)
Japan, 1951				
Exports	1,385,780	5.520	251,047	0.644
Comp. Imports	1,330,926	8.233	161,657	
U.S., 1947				
Exports	2,550,780	182.313	13,992	1.300
Comp. Imports	3,091,339	170.004	18,184	

Japan is a labor-abundant and hence capital-scarce country is accepted, then our findings seem to offer another instance of the famous Leontief paradox. These paradoxical findings occur at least partly because Japan's place in the world economy is midway between the advanced and underdeveloped countries. In consequence, she may be expected to have a comparative advantage in labor-intensive goods when trading with the former and in capital-intensive goods when trading with the latter. If this conjecture is not too far from reality, there would be a tendency in Japanese foreign trade for labor-intensive exports to go to advanced countries and capital-intensive exports to underdeveloped countries. Since about 25% of Japanese exports went to advanced and 75% to underdeveloped countries in 1951, it is not surprising to find that on balance Japan appears as a "capital-abundant" country in comparison with the rest of the world.

In order to make an empirical test of this conjecture, we have computed the capital-labor ratio of Japanese exports going to the United States in 1951 to be compared with the ratio for her total exports; and the same ratio of the US exports going to Japan to be compared with the ratio for United States total exports. To do this, we consolidated all the exports items (listed in the Foreign Trade Returns, 1951, of the Ministry of Finance) into the 29 sectors of our original breakdown and all the imports items from the United States into the 192 sectors of Professor Leontief. The statistical results are shown in Table 3.[9]

[9]The reader may suspect why we did not compute the same ratio for the domestic replacement of American imports from Japan. This we could not do because of lack of data. At the next opportunity we shall report our more comprehensive investigations which are going on now.

Table 3. Capital-Labor Input Ratio for Japanese-American Trade.

	Capital (α)	Labor (β) (Man-Years)	α/β
Japan's Exports to US	1,026,387 (1951 Yen)	18.8839	54,352
US Exports to Japan	2,741,786 (1947 Dollars)	141.2169	19,415

They indicate that the capital-labor ratio of Japanese exports to the United States is lower than for her total exports. This seems to imply that Japan exported less capital-intensive goods to the United States (in 1951, 15% of Japanese exports was directed to the United States), and relatively labor-intensive goods to countries other than the United States. This may be considered as supporting the generally held opinion that Japan's foreign trade is two-sided.[10] We suspect that American foreign trade might have a similar nature. If data were available on the capital-labor ratios for United States exports broken down by countries, then more conclusive findings might be expected about the position of the United States in the international division of labor.[11]

Another interesting fact is that the capital-labor ratio for United States exports to Japan is not only larger than that for the United States total exports but also exceeds that for competitive imports. This means that United States exports to Japan are more capital-intensive than United States domestic production for replacing its competitive imports from the rest of the world. This would seem also to demand more careful investigation into the so-called Leontief paradox. We would like to refrain from drawing any sweeping conclusions here.

[10] Cf. Economic Planning Board, *Survey of Japanese Economy* (1956–1957).

[11] According to A. Daniere, "relative foreign inefficiency is less in the production of B than in the production of A," where A denotes manufactured goods and B denotes raw materials (ores, oils, rubber, and other important United States imports), due to differences in material resource endowment. Since these raw material products, on the whole, require a high capital-labor ratio, the large raw material component of United States imports suggests, in agreement with the authors' view, that the Leontief capital intensiveness situation holds better in the trade with raw material areas than with industrial countries. See Daniere, A. (1956). American Trade Structure and Comparative Cost Theory. *Economia Internazionale*, IX, 426.

Chapter 5

Interregional Interdependence and Regional Economic Growth in Japan*

Takahiro Akita

1. Introduction

Changes in consumer preferences and economic conditions have differential impacts on a regional economy that correspond to a region's industrial structure and resource endowments. When the national economy makes structural adjustments, some regions reveal higher economic growth than others, which is usually ascribed to differences in regional industrial structure and locational advantages or disadvantages. Shift-share analysis has been widely used as an effective and convenient device for explaining differences between regional and national growth rates (Tervo and Okko, 1983; Barff and Knight, 1988; Markusen *et al.*, 1991). The conventional shift-share method decomposes regional growth, usually in terms of employment, into three components: national growth, industrial mix, and competitive or regional shift. The national growth component measures a region's expected growth if it had grown at the national rate over the period. The industrial mix component measures the proportional shift due to a difference in industrial mix between the region and the nation, and the competitive shift component measures the differential shift due to differences in growth rates of the same industry between a region and the nation. The third component is simply a residual that captures all that remains unexplained, such as local advantages, changes in technology, and effects of regional industrial policies. Shift-share analysis has, however, been subject to a number of criticisms. It is essentially a descriptive method that attempts to investigate the difference between the actual regional growth and the growth that would have

*This chapter was published in *International Regional Science Review*, 1994 (Vol. 16, No. 3). Permission for reprint granted by SAGE Publishing Co.

occurred if the region had grown at the rate of the national average. In other words, the national economy is used as the norm against which regional growth performances are evaluated. Shift-share analysis, therefore, lacks a firm behavior-based theoretical foundation and is unable to identify either demand-side or supply-side growth factors.

Furthermore, it cannot take into account changes in interindustry linkages or in interregional linkages. To avoid some of these problems with shift-share analyses, Akita (1992) employed single-region IO tables to investigate, from the demand side, the sources of regional industrial growth for Hokkaido, the northernmost and second largest of the four main islands of Japan (Figure 1).[1] By applying Chenery and Syrquin's (1979)

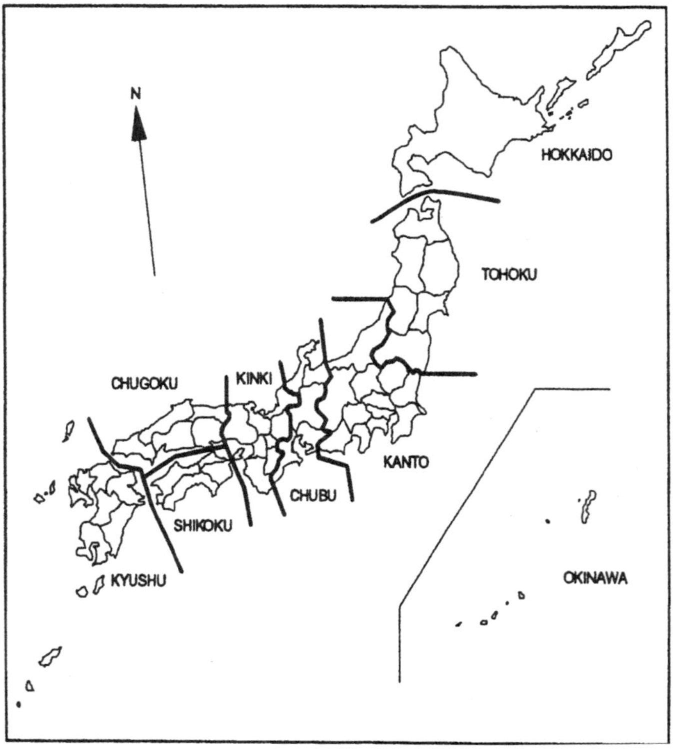

Figure 1. Nine Regions of Japan.

[1] In the articles, the term "single-region IO tables" refers to competitive-import-type regional IO tables, where interregional imports as well as international imports are assumed to compete with locally produced goods. The regional input coefficients matrix is estimated using a set of estimated regional supply proportions and the regional technical coefficients matrix.

growth-factor decomposition methods to single-region IO tables, demand-side regional growth factors could be identified, factors such as changes in regional final demand, expansion of regional exports, and import substitution in a comparative static framework. Although previous applications of Chenery and Syrquin's method have looked at national growth, none have examined regional growth within a country (Chenery and Syrquin, 1979; Chenery, 1980; Chenery, 1986; Kubo *et al.*, 1986; Urata, 1987; Fujita and James, 1987; Akita, 1991). By using regional IO tables, the growth-factor decomposition method could explicitly examine changes in technical coefficients as one of the prominent forces of regional economic growth.

Because it is based on a single-region IO model, however, the formula employed by Akita (1992) views a region as somewhat isolated from other parts of the country and is thus not designed to analyze growth factors originating in other regions. The single-region formula considers the influence of other regions only through regional import substitution and changes in regional exports. Import substitution is measured by changes in estimated regional supply proportions, not by changes in survey-based regional input coefficients, and exports meeting final demands are not differentiated from those for intermediate demands.

Because a region cannot exist in isolation from other parts of the country, and interactions among regions often play a significant role in regional economic growth, this article extends the conventional growth-factor decomposition method by using an interregional IO model, specifically, the one proposed by Island (1951). The extended formula places a region in an interregional context and attempts to examine, from the demand side, the sources of regional growth. In an interregional IO framework, the origins of growth factors can be explicitly identified as coming either from within the specific region or from other regions. Growth factors originating outside a region include the impact of changes in demands in the other regions on the growth of the region in question through interregional multiplier effects, in which survey-based interregional trade coefficients play an important role. The extended formula can also analyze regional growth due to changes in interregional trade coefficients.

One of the main objectives of this study is to evaluate the role of interregional interactions in the growth of a regional economy. As Beyers (1989) noted, analyses of structural changes and industrial growth in an interregional IO system are almost nonexistent, due, in part, to the lack of survey-based interregional IO tables for more than one time period. Japan, however, is an exception. The central government, more specifically, the Ministry of International Trade and Industry of Japan (MITI), has constructed survey-based interregional IO tables every five years since 1965 for the nine regions of Japan (Figure 1).

The 1975, 1980, and 1985 interregional IO tables are used in this study to conduct the growth-factor decomposition analysis for each of these nine regions. The ten-year study period between 1975 and 1985 is divided into two five-year subperiods in order to investigate changes in the pattern of regional economic growth. After the data and method are described, the study's major findings and conclusions will be presented.

2. Data and Method

2.1. *Data*

Although 25-sector interregional IO tables provide the raw data for this study, they have all been converted into 23-sector tables because of a slight difference in sector classification between the table for 1985 and those for 1975 and 1980. The extended growth-factor decomposition method, discussed in detail below, is thus applied to the 23-sector interregional IO tables, but to illuminate the overall picture of regional economic growth, the results are presented in an aggregate form.

While the growth-factor decomposition analysis is performed for each of the nine regions, the analysis is simplified by transforming the nine-region interregional IO tables into two-region IO tables. Analysis of each region is conducted by aggregating the other eight regions into one. Finally, to see the real changes during the period, the 1975 and 1980 interregional IO tables are converted to constant 1985 prices by using national sectoral output inflators (EPA, 1990), because neither sectoral real output figures nor sectoral real gross domestic product figures are available.

2.2. *Method*

The growth-factor decomposition method used here extends the Chenery and Syrquin (1979) method to interregional IO systems and is based on the following balance equations for interregional IO accounts for two regions:

$$X^L = A^{LL}X^L + A^{LR}X^R + F^{LL} + F^{LR} + E^L - M^L \qquad (2.1)$$

$$X^R = A^{RL}X^L + A^{RR}X^R + F^{RL} + F^{RR} + E^R - M^R \qquad (2.2)$$

where the superscript L denotes the region in question and R the rest of the nation, and X^K, E^K, and M^K ($K = L, R$) are vectors of gross regional outputs, international exports, and international imports, respectively. F^{KJ}

is a vector of final demands of region J for goods and services in region K, where $J = L, R$ and $K = L, R$ while A^{KJ} is a matrix of regional input coefficients when $K = J$ and a matrix of interregional trade coefficients when $K \neq J$.

The international import proportion of sector i in region L, m_i^L, is defined as

$$m_i^L = M_i^L \Bigg/ \left(\sum_{j=1}^{n} a_{ij}^{LL} X_i^L + F_i^{LL} \right),$$

where a_{ij}^{LL} is the (i, j)th element of the matrix A^{LL}, and M_i^L, X_i^L, and F_i^{LL} are the ith element of the vectors M^L, X^L, and F^{LL}, respectively. Equation (2.1) is then reduced to

$$X^L = (I - \hat{m}^L)(A^{LL}X^L + F^{LL}) + A^{LR}X^R + F^{LR} + E^L - M^L \quad (2.3)$$

or

$$X^L = \hat{p}^L(A^{LL}X^L + F^{LL}) + A^{LR}X^R + F^{LR} + E^L - M^L, \quad (2.4)$$

where $\hat{m}^L$ is a diagonal matrix of international import proportions for region L and $\hat{p}^L = I - \hat{m}^L$. In (2.3) and (2.4), it is assumed that international imports of goods and services of region L are not exported to region R. The basic balance equations for two-region interregional IO accounts can now be rewritten as

$$\begin{bmatrix} X^L \\ X^R \end{bmatrix} = \begin{bmatrix} \hat{p}^L A^{LL} & A^{LR} \\ A^{RL} & \hat{p}^R A^{RR} \end{bmatrix} \begin{bmatrix} X^L \\ X^R \end{bmatrix} + \begin{bmatrix} \hat{p}^L F^{LL} + F^{LR} \\ F^{RL} + \hat{p}^R F^{RR} \end{bmatrix} + \begin{bmatrix} E^L \\ E^R \end{bmatrix}$$

for which the solution will be given by

$$X = (I - A_D)^{-1}(F_D + E)$$

or

$$X = B(F_D + E), \quad (2.5)$$

where $B = (I - A_D)^{-1}$ is the Leontief inverse net of international imports and

$$X = \begin{bmatrix} X^L \\ X^R \end{bmatrix}, \quad F_D = \begin{bmatrix} \hat{p}^L F^{LL} + F^{LR} \\ F^{RL} + \hat{p}^R F^{RR} \end{bmatrix}, \quad E = \begin{bmatrix} E^L \\ E^R \end{bmatrix}$$

and

$$A_D = \begin{bmatrix} \hat{p}^L A^{LL} & A^{LR} \\ A^{RL} & \hat{p}^R A^{RR} \end{bmatrix}.$$

Equation (2.5) can now be used to decompose a change in regional gross outputs into several factors. Considering that the Leontief inverse matrix, $B = (I - A_D)^{-1}$, is composed of four submatrices,

$$B = \begin{bmatrix} B^{LL} & B^{LR} \\ B^{RL} & B^{RR} \end{bmatrix}$$

so that one can obtain the following growth-factor decomposition equation for region L:

$$\begin{aligned} dX^L &= B_t^{LL}\big[\hat{p}_t^L dF^{LL} + dF^{LR} + dE^L + d\hat{p}^L\big(A_0^{LL}X_0^L + F_0^{LL}\big) \\ &\quad + \hat{p}_t^L dA^{LL}X_0^L + dA^{LR}X_0^R\big] + B_t^{LR}\big[\hat{p}_t^R dF^{RR} + dF^{RL} + dE^R \\ &\quad + d\hat{p}^R\big(A_0^{RR}X_0^R + F_0^{RR}\big) + \hat{p}_t^R dA^{RR}X_0^R + dA^{RL}X_0^L\big], \qquad (2.6) \end{aligned}$$

where subscripts 0 and t designate the base year and the terminal year, respectively, and d denotes a change over the period. For example, dX^L is a vector of changes in regional gross outputs. A detailed derivation of the equation can be found in the Appendix.

The growth-factor decomposition equation (2.6) is obtained by using the terminal-year structural parameters $\hat{p}_t$ and B_t, and the base-year volume weights, X_0 and F_0. A growth-factor decomposition equation can also be derived based on the base-year structural parameters $\hat{p}_0$ and B_0, and the terminal-year volume weights, X_t and F_t, but in this study, a simple average of these two equations was used.

The first square bracket in equation (2.6) shows the sources of output growth that originate within region L, while the second square bracket presents the sources of output growth that originate elsewhere in the nation (region R). Although the terms with dF^{LR} and dA^{LR} can be regarded as factors originating outside the region, they are classified with those originating in the region because they affect the level of region L outputs directly rather than through interregional multiplier effects. Each bracketed expression contains four major growth factors: expansion of domestic final demands (elements 1 and 2), expansion of international exports (element 3), changes in international import proportions (element 4), and changes in regional input and interregional trade coefficients (element 5 and 6).[2]

[2]Since $dA^{LL} = dA^L - dA^{RL}$, where A^L is the matrix of regional technical coefficients, a change in regional input coefficients is the difference between a change in technical coefficients and a change in interregional trade coefficients.

As shown by Round (1985, 1989), the Leontief inverse, B, can be multiplicatively decomposed into three separate components.

$$B = \begin{bmatrix} (I - D^{LR}D^{RL})^{-1} & 0 \\ 0 & (I - D^{RL}D^{LR})^{-1} \end{bmatrix} \begin{bmatrix} I & D^{LR} \\ D^{RL} & I \end{bmatrix} \begin{bmatrix} D^{LL} & 0 \\ 0 & D^{RR} \end{bmatrix}, \tag{2.7}$$

where $D^{LL} = (I - \hat{p}^L A^{LL})^{-1}$, $D^{RR} = (I - \hat{p}^R A^{RR})^{-1}$, $D^{LR} = (I - \hat{p}^L A^{LL})^{-1} A^{LR}$ and $D^{RL} = (I - \hat{p}^R A^{RR})^{-1} A^{RL}$. The first matrix in equation (2.7) is a multiplier matrix accounting for interregional feedback effects and is referred to as an interregional closed-loop multiplier matrix, whereas the second matrix is an interregional open-loop multiplier matrix, since it captures the effect that one region has upon the other region. The last matrix is the intraregional multiplier matrix.

Since the first square bracket in equation (2.6) is pre-multiplied by B^{LL}, the total effect of each growth factor in the bracket on region L outputs includes not only the intraregional multiplier effect for region L but also the intraregional feedback effect. On the other hand, the second square bracket is pre-multiplied by B^{LR}. Therefore, the total effect of each growth factor originating in region R on region L outputs is the product of intraregional multiplier effect for region R, the interregional open-loop multiplier effect that region R has on region L, and the interregional feedback effect.

The growth-factor decomposition equation can now be represented compactly as

$$\begin{aligned} dX^L = {} & (DD1)^{LL} + (DD2)^{LL} + (EE)^{LL} + (IS)^{LL} + (IO1)^{LL} \\ & + (IO2)^{LL} + (DD1)^{LR} + (DD2)^{LR} + (EE)^{LR} + (IS)^{LR} \\ & + (IO1)^{LR} + (IO2)^{LR}, \end{aligned}$$

where the components are arranged to correspond to those in equation (2.6). The components are explained as follows:

Growth factors originating in region L

$(DD1)^{LL}$ is the effect of expansion of final demands in region L for goods and services in region L which are either locally produced or imported internationally;

$(DD2)^{LL}$ is the effect of the expansion of final demands in region R for goods and services produced in region L (i.e. the effect of the expansion of interregional exports from region L to region R to satisfy final demands in region R);

$(EE)^{LL}$ is the effect of the expansion of international exports from region L;

$(IS)^{LL}$ is the effect of increasing the proportion of regional demands in region L that are satisfied by goods and services produced in region L (rather than imported internationally);

$(IO1)^{LL}$ is the effect of increasing regional input coefficients in region L; and

$(IO2)^{LL}$ is the effect of increasing interregional trade coefficients (for the trade flows from region L to region R).

Growth factors originating in the rest of the nation (Region R)

$(DD1)^{LR}$ is the effect of the expansion of final demands in region R for goods and services in region R which are either locally produced or imported internationally;

$(DD2)^{LR}$ is the effect of expansion of final demands in region L for goods and services in region R (i.e. the effect of the expansion of interregional exports from region R to region L to satisfy final demands in region L);

$(EE)^{LR}$ is the effect of the expansion of international exports from region R;

$(IS)^{LR}$ is the effect of increasing the proportion of regional demands in region R that are satisfied by goods and services produced in region R (rather than imported internationally);

$(IO1)^{LR}$ is the effect of increasing regional input coefficients in region R; and

$(IO2)^{LR}$ is the effect of increasing interregional trade coefficients (for the trade flows from region R to region L).

3. Major Findings

Tables 1 and 2 summarize the results obtained from the extended growth-factor decomposition analysis. Each entry in Table 1 is the absolute growth attributed to a specific factor. Table 2 represents the proportional contribution of each factor to total regional output growth. Part 1 of both tables gives the contribution of factors within the region (components with

Table 1. Sources of Regional Economic Growth: Absolute Growth in Region *L* (*LL*)[a].

Region	*DD*1	*DD*2	*EE*	*IS*	*IO*1	*IO*2	Total 1
Hokkaido							
75–80	2,478	167	12	58	552	−321	2,946
80–85	1,422	894	−95	−172	−664	112	1,496
Tohoku							
75–80	3,226	1,081	348	−367	589	634	5,510
80–85	1,835	1,997	1,190	−54	−2,368	1,913	4,512
Kanto							
75–80	26,738	5,414	7,231	−1,834	906	2,294	40,748
80–85	30,404	12,457	12,475	−1,145	−12,018	9,124	51,297
Chubu							
75–80	4,125	1,529	4,191	−824	1,313	1,349	11,683
80–85	2,645	5,969	4,489	−321	−4,027	2,427	11,183
Kinki							
75–80	5,175	2,818	2,627	−823	−1,152	133	8,778
80–85	8,062	6,805	3,054	−565	−8,049	4,202	13,509
Chugoku							
75–80	2,574	1,165	1,418	−496	−168	−1,015	3,479
80–85	886	1,805	7	−168	−2,915	2,289	1,904
Shikoku							
75–80	1,292	490	132	−153	471	−131	2,101
80–85	1,078	744	455	99	−1,351	336	1,360
Kyushu							
75–80	4,459	1,183	594	−490	281	1,008	7,035
80–85	2,723	1,936	471	274	−2,502	1,304	4,205
Okinawa							
75–80	81	60	25	14	231	−224	188
80–85	720	87	40	36	−109	−92	682
JAPAN[b]							
75–80	**77,665**	**−23**	**22,764**	**−5,970**	**10,270**	**−89**	**104,618**
80–85	**95,569**	**206**	**30,108**	**1,979**	**−17,218**	**41**	**110,686**

[a]In billion Yen.
[b]Totals for Japan are exclusive of Okinawa.

superscript *LL*), while part 2 gives the contribution of factors from the rest of the nation (components with superscript *LR*).

Though there is variation among regions, the rest of the nation has played a prominent role in regional economic growth. It has accounted for more than 20% of total output growth in most of the regions (Table 2). This contribution is especially conspicuous for the Chugoku region, where it exceeds 40% for the 1975–1980 period and 50% for the 1980–1985 period.

Table 1. (*Continued*): Region *L*-Region *R* (*LR*)[a].

Region	*DD*1	*DD*2	*EE*	*IS*	*IO*[c]	Total 2	Total	*GR*[d]
Hokkaido								
75–80	561	8	187	−65	91	783	3,729	3.5
80–85	664	11	178	45	−290	608	2,103	1.7
Tohoku								
75–80	939	25	417	−70	182	1,492	7,002	4.5
80–85	1,276	47	581	26	−292	1,637	6,149	3.3
Kanto								
75–80	2,847	731	1,765	−267	937	6,013	46,762	4.9
80–85	2,950	1,449	2,390	170	−133	6,827	58,123	4.8
Chubu								
75–80	2,253	92	949	−164	432	3,563	15,246	5.1
80–85	2,128	249	1,310	13	−384	3,316	14,499	3.9
Kinki								
75–80	3,022	268	1,456	−223	824	5,346	14,124	3.1
80–85	2,585	589	1,903	32	−486	4,624	18,132	3.4
Chugoku								
75–80	1,503	28	657	−141	445	2,492	5,971	3.1
80–85	1,566	74	857	30	−472	2,056	3,960	1.8
Shikoku								
75–80	652	2	277	−65	198	1,064	3,165	4.0
80–85	715	18	277	−14	−300	696	2,056	2.2
Kyushu								
75–80	1,081	43	497	−88	156	1,688	8,723	4.0
80–85	1,259	74	673	12	−363	1,654	5,859	2.3
Okinawa								
75–80	61	0	15	−7	6	75	263	1.8
80–85	66	0	15	5	−3	83	765	4.5
JAPAN[b]								
75–80	**36**	**12**	**5**	**−1**	**53**	**105**	**104,722**	**4.3**
80–85	**189**	**12**	**9**	**19**	**−27**	**202**	**110,888**	**3.7**

[c] $IO = IO1 + IO2$.
[d] *GR* is the annual average growth rate of real gross output for the period.

These high rates are indicative of Chugoku's large industrial base that supplies basic industrial materials for the other regions, especially Kinki. Two other western regions, Kinki and Shikoku, also depend highly on the rest of the nation. The Kanto region, located in the central portion of the country, shows the lowest dependence. Here the contribution from the rest of nation was just a little above 10%, which shows that the regional economy is relatively closed and much of the regional growth was brought about by

Table 2. Sources of Regional Economic Growth: Percentage Share Within Region *L* (*LL*).

Region	*DD*1	*DD*2	*EE*	*IS*	*IO*1	*IO*2	Total 1
Hokkaido							
75–80	66.5	4.5	0.3	1.6	14.8	−8.6	79.0
80–85	67.6	42.5	−4.5	−8.2	−31.6	5.3	71.1
Tohoku							
75–80	46.1	15.4	5.0	−5.2	8.4	9.1	78.7
80–85	29.8	32.5	19.4	−0.9	−38.5	31.1	73.4
Kanto							
75–80	57.2	11.6	15.5	−3.9	1.9	4.9	87.1
80–85	52.3	21.4	21.5	−2.0	−20.7	15.7	88.3
Chubu							
75–80	27.1	10.0	27.5	−5.4	8.6	8.8	76.6
80–85	18.2	41.2	31.0	−2.2	−27.8	16.7	77.1
Kinki							
75–80	36.6	20.0	18.6	−5.8	−8.2	0.9	62.1
80–85	44.5	37.5	16.8	−3.1	−44.4	23.2	74.5
Chugoku							
75–80	43.1	19.5	23.7	−8.3	−2.8	−17.0	58.3
80–85	22.4	45.6	0.2	−4.2	−73.6	57.8	48.1
Shikoku							
75–80	40.8	15.5	4.2	−4.8	14.9	−4.1	66.4
80-85	52.4	36.2	22.1	4.8	−65.7	16.3	66.1
Kyushu							
75–80	51.1	13.6	6.8	−5.6	3.2	11.6	80.7
80–85	46.5	33.0	8.0	4.7	−42.7	22.2	71.8
Okinawa							
75-80	30.9	22.9	9.5	5.2	87.9	−85.1	71.5
80-85	94.1	11.3	5.3	4.7	−14.3	−12.0	89.1
JAPAN[a]							
75–80	74.2	0.0	21.7	−5.7	9.8	−0.1	99.9
80–85	86.2	0.2	27.2	1.8	−15.5	0.0	99.8

[a]Percentages for Japan are exclusive of Okinawa.

factors within the region, especially from the expansion of final demands, $(DD1)^{LL}$. Table 3, which compares the nine regions of Japan in terms of area, population size, and income level, shows that Kanto generated more than 40% of the total gross domestic product in 1985. This indicates that the openness of a regional economy is somewhat related to the income and urbanness of the region.

Table 2. (*Continued*): Region *L*-Region *R* (*LR*).

Region	*DD*1	*DD*2	*EE*	*IS*	*IO*[b]	Total 2	Total	*GR*[c]
Hokkaido								
75–80	15.0	0.2	5.0	−1.7	2.5	21.0	3.5	15.0
80–85	31.6	0.5	8.5	2.1	−13.8	28.9	1.7	31.6
Tohoku								
75–80	13.4	0.4	5.9	−1.0	2.6	21.3	4.5	13.4
80–85	20.7	0.8	9.4	0.4	−4.7	26.6	3.3	20.7
Kanto								
75–80	6.1	1.6	3.8	−0.6	2.0	12.9	4.9	6.1
80–85	5.1	2.5	4.1	0.3	−0.2	11.7	4.8	5.1
Chubu								
75–80	14.8	0.6	6.2	−1.1	2.8	23.4	5.1	14.8
80–85	14.7	1.7	9.0	0.1	−2.6	22.9	3.9	14.7
Kinki								
75–80	21.4	1.9	10.3	−1.6	5.8	37.8	3.1	21.4
80–85	14.3	3.3	10.5	0.2	−2.7	25.6	3.4	14.3
Chugoku								
75–80	25.2	0.5	11.0	−2.4	7.5	41.8	3.1	25.2
80–85	39.5	1.9	21.6	0.8	−11.9	51.9	1.8	39.5
Shikoku								
75–80	20.6	0.1	8.8	−2.0	6.3	33.6	4.0	20.6
80–85	34.8	0.9	13.5	−0.7	−14.6	33.9	2.2	34.8
Kyushu								
75–80	12.4	0.5	5.7	−1.0	1.8	19.4	4.0	12.4
80–85	21.5	1.3	11.5	0.2	−6.2	28.3	2.3	21.5
Okinawa								
75–80	23.3	0.0	5.5	−2.5	2.2	28.5	1.8	23.3
80–85	8.6	0.0	2.0	0.6	−0.4	10.8	4.5	8.6
JAPAN[a]								
75–80	0.0	0.0	0.0	0.0	0.1	0.1	4.3	0.0
80–85	0.2	0.0	0.0	0.0	0.0	0.2	3.7	0.2

[b]$IO = IO1 + IO2$.
[c]*GR* is the annual average growth rate of real gross output for the period.

The pattern of regional economic growth also changed substantially between periods. There was a marked increase in direct effect of the other regions' final demand expansion, $(DD2)^{LL}$, between 1975–1980 and 1980–1985 (Table 1). This factor's proportional contribution to total regional growth jumped from 10–20% to more than 30% for most of the regions (Table 2). There was also an increase in the direct effect of increasing in interregional trade coefficients (for the trade flows to the other regions),

Table 3. Major Economic Indicators in 1985.

	Land Area		Population			Income			GRDP[a]	
Region	km^2	% of Total	People (×1000)	% of Total	Density	Yen (Billion)	% of Total	Per Capita	Yen (Billion)	% of Total
Hokkaido	83,519	22.1	5,679	4.7	68	11,297	4.3	1,989	12,889	4.0
Tohoku	66,911	17.7	9,729	8.0	145	17,002	6.5	1,748	20,550	6.4
Kanto	70,777	18.7	45,808	37.8	647	111,549	42.4	2,435	135,438	42.2
Chubu	29,961	7.9	12,501	10.3	417	27,799	10.6	2,224	36,239	11.3
Kinki	31,483	8.3	20,899	17.3	664	47,061	17.9	2,252	57,348	17.9
Chugoku	31,783	8.4	7,749	6.4	244	15,245	5.8	1,967	19,223	6.0
Shikoku	18,806	5.0	4,228	3.5	225	7,394	2.8	1,749	8,644	2.7
Kyushu	42,150	11.2	13,276	11.0	315	24,146	9.2	1,819	28,763	9.0
Okinawa	2,254	0.6	1,179	1.0	523	1,819	0.7	1,543	2,063	0.6
JAPAN	**377,644**	**100**	**121,048**	**100**	**321**	**263,312**	**100**	**2,175**	**321,157**	**100.0**

[a]GRDP = Gross Regional Domestic Product.
Source: Economic Planning Agency (1988).

$(IO2)^{LL}$. These two effects, $(DD2)^{LL}$ and $(IO2)^{LL}$, seem to have compensated for the reduced effect of increasing the region's input coefficients, $(IO1)^{LL}$, which curtailed the regional economic growth for the 1980–1985 period as it became negative for the period. Finally, except for Kanto, Kinki, and Okinawa, there was a significant decrease in the absolute effect of the region's final demand expansion, $(DD1)^{LL}$ (Table 1). These observations suggest that the regional economies, facing a stagnant regional demand in the 1980–1985 period, tried to maintain their regional growth by becoming more dependent on the other regions.

The reasons for the patterns above can be found in the changing macroeconomic conditions of the 1970s and 1980s. In the 1970s, the Japanese economy was faced with a succession of problems and changes that eventually led to a stable growth after nearly two decades of unprecedented rapid growth (Akita, 1992). The outbreak of the first oil crisis in October 1973 brought about a fourfold increase in the dollar price of crude oil. Combined with an extraordinarily easy money situation, this triggered rampant inflation in the 1973–1974 period. The Japanese economy fell into the so-called "tri-lemma of inflation, recession, and balance of payments deficits." The second oil crisis in 1979 again raised the standard price of crude oil from about $14 per barrel to more than $30. Though the shock was not as severe as the first oil crisis, the Japanese economy could no longer enjoy the cheap imported energy resources that had prevailed in the rapid-growth period.

Japanese fiscal policy was drastically changed in 1975. In the rapid-growth period, tax revenue increases were sufficient to permit balanced budgets. From 1974 onward, however, the government was faced with revenue shortages. While expenditures increased because of inflation, tax revenue remained flat as corporate tax receipts declined due to a sudden drop in corporate profits and indirect taxes stagnated after the first oil crisis. In order to cover the fiscal deficits, the central government decided in 1975 to start issuing a large amount of deficit financing bonds. At the same time, to recover from the recession, the government adopted a radical stimulate policy whereby national construction bonds were issued essentially to meet increased public works expenditures. The total amount of national bonds grew rapidly. By the end of the 1970s, it had reached 10 trillion Yen, more than 30 percent of total government revenue. To cope with this unhealthy situation, the government decided in 1981 to start drastic administrative and fiscal reforms in which public works expenditures were completely frozen.

These problems and changes have had profound and differential impacts on regional economies. Regions which depend highly on the central government's public works expenditures (i.e. Hokkaido, Tohoku, Chubu, Chugoku, Shikoku, and Kyushu) experienced a significant decrease in output growth for the 1980–1985 period as the construction industry, which relies heavily on public works expenditures, recorded a negative growth in the period. There was, in fact, a marked decrease in the effect of the region's final demand expansion, $(DD1)^{LL}$, due in large part to the stagnant construction industry.

Among the six regions that experienced a decrease in output growth, Tohoku and Chubu showed a relatively better performance than the other four, maintaining a growth rate higher than 3% even in the 1980–1985 period. The main factor seems to be a difference in the performance of the manufacturing industry. In Tohoku and Chubu, processing and assembling industries (e.g. electronics and automobile industries) have made remarkable progress, thereby maintaining relatively high growth in the manufacturing industry. In the other four regions, manufacturing has stagnated either because of negative growth in the materials industries or relatively slow progress in the processing and assembling industries, or both.

The Japanese industrial structure underwent a substantial change after the first oil crisis. In the rapid-growth period, heavy and chemical industrialization was the engine of growth, wherein the basic materials industries were developed in tandem with the processing and assembling industries through interindustrial linkages. The sharp rise in energy prices changed this pattern greatly, however. Combined with the stagnation of domestic demand due to the falling growth rate, the development of the basic materials industries, such as aluminum smelting, oil refining, petrochemical, and iron and steel, stagnated further and impaired the profitability of these industries. As a highly energy-intensive manufacturing industry, aluminum smelting lost ground in Japan and was thrown into a process of large-scale structural adjustment. The iron and steel industry also became stagnant in the 1980s due to sluggish demand from the construction industry and increasing imports of steel products from Korea and Taiwan.

Performance of the processing and assembling industries has been quite different. Less dependent on imported raw materials and blessed with further technological improvements, their international competitiveness has strengthened markedly and they have made rapid advances. In other words, a structural change in the manufacturing industry occurred so as to increase the proportion of the processing and assembling industries.

4. Conclusions

This chapter developed an extended growth-factor decomposition formula based on an interregional IO model. It allowed an explicit analysis of the role of interregional and interindustrial linkages in the growth of a regional economy. A region cannot exist in isolation from the other parts of a country. Through interregional trade and migration, a region interacts with other regions. The extended formula proved to be useful in providing a consistent framework in which one can examine interregional interactions and their effects on regional economic growth.

The application to Japanese interregional IO tables between 1975 and 1985 revealed that interregional interdependence had exerted significant effects on regional economic growth, though there are some variations among the regions. There was a significant change in the pattern of regional economic growth between 1975–1980 and 1980–1985, which seems to reflect a shift in the central government's economic policies toward a smaller government (e.g. a reduction in the central government's public works expenditures, deregulations, and privatization). There is an indication that the regions are becoming more interdependent.

This research is not without limitations. First, due to the lack of regional sectoral output inflators, the national sectoral output inflators were used to obtain real interregional IO tables, thus distorting some of the relative magnitude of regional sectoral output. Second, the growth-factor decomposition analysis based on IO tables approaches the issues from the demand side and thus should be supplemented by a supply-side growth-factor decomposition analysis. Third, this research is essentially a comparative static analysis which evaluates the static equilibrium solutions in the base and terminal years and does not take into account the continuous changes over the study period.

Appendix

To derive the extended growth-factor decomposition equation, A_D and F_D are defined as follows:

$$\begin{aligned} A_D &= \begin{bmatrix} \hat{p}^L & 0 \\ 0 & \hat{p}^R \end{bmatrix} \begin{bmatrix} A^{LL} & 0 \\ 0 & A^{RR} \end{bmatrix} + \begin{bmatrix} 0 & A^{LR} \\ A^{RL} & 0 \end{bmatrix} \\ &= \hat{P} A^a + A^b \\ F_D &= \begin{bmatrix} \hat{p}^L & 0 \\ 0 & \hat{p}^R \end{bmatrix} \begin{bmatrix} F^{LL} \\ F^{RR} \end{bmatrix} + \begin{bmatrix} F^{LR} \\ F^{RL} \end{bmatrix} \\ &= \hat{P} F^a + F^b. \end{aligned}$$

Using equation (2.5) and these definitions, changes in gross outputs can be represented as:

$$dX = X_t - X_0 = B_t(\hat{P}_t F_t^a + F_t^b + E_t) - B_0(\hat{P}_0 F_0^a + F_0^b + E_0). \tag{A.1}$$

Next, we define

$$dF^a = F_t^a - F_0^a, dF^b = F_t^b - F_0^b, \quad \text{and} \quad dE = E_t - E_0.$$

Then

$$F_t^a = F_0^a + dF^a, F_t^b = F_0^b + dF^b, \quad \text{and} \quad E_t = E_0 + dE. \tag{A.2}$$

Substituting equation (A.2) into equation (A.1) gives

$$\begin{aligned} dX = B_t \lfloor (\hat{P}_t dF^a + dF^b) + dE \rfloor + B_t(\hat{P}_t - \hat{P}_0)F_0^a \\ + (B_t - B_0)(\hat{P}_0 F_0^a + F_0^b + E_0). \end{aligned} \tag{A.3}$$

Since

$$\begin{aligned} B_t - B_0 &= B_t[(B_0)^{-1} - (B_t)^{-1}]B_0 \\ &= B_t \lfloor (\hat{P}_t - \hat{P}_0)A_0^a + \hat{P}_t(A_t^a - A_0^a) + (A_t^b - A_0^b) \rfloor B_0 \end{aligned}$$

and considering $X_0 = B_0(\hat{P}_0 F_0^a + F_0^b + E_0)$, equation (A.3) is reduced to

$$dX = B_t[(\hat{P}_t dF^a + dF^b) + dE + d\hat{P}(A_0^a X_0 + F_0^a) + (\hat{P}_t dA^a + dA^b)X_0], \quad \text{(A.4)}$$

where $d\hat{P} = \hat{P}_t - \hat{P}_0$, $dA^a = A_t^a - A_0^a$, and $dA^b = A_t^b - A_0^b$.

By expanding equation (A.4), we obtain equation (2.6) in the text, since

$$B_t = \begin{bmatrix} B_t^{LL} & B_t^{LR} \\ B_t^{RL} & B_t^{RR} \end{bmatrix} \quad \text{and} \quad X_0 = \begin{bmatrix} X_0^L \\ X_0^R \end{bmatrix}$$

References

Akita, T. (1991). Industrial Structure and the Sources of Industrial Growth in Indonesia: An IO Analysis between 1971 and 1985. *Asian Economic Journal*, 139–158.

Akita, T. (1992). Sources of Regional Economic Growth in Japan: A Case of Hokkaido between 1970 and 1985. *Journals of Applied IO Analyses*, 1, 88–107

Barff, R. A. and P. L. Knight III (1988). Dynamic Shift-Share Analysis. *Growth and Change*, 19, 1–10.

Beyers, W. B. (1989). Structural Change in Interregional IO Models: Form and Regional Economic Development Implications. In *Frontiers of IO Analysis*, R. E. Miller, K. R. Polenske, and A. Z. Rose (eds.). NY: Oxford University Press.

Chenery, H. B. (1980). Interactions Between Industrialization and Exports. *American Economic Review*, 70, 281–287.

Chenery, H. B. (1986). Growth and Transformation. In *Industrialization and Growth: A Comparative Study*, H. Chenery, S. Robinson, and M. Syrquin (eds.). New York: Oxford University Press.

Chenery, H. B. and M. Syrquin (1979). A Comparative Analysis of Individual Growth. In *Economic Growth and Resources*, R.C.O. Mathews (eds.). NY: Macmillan.

Economic Planning Agency (1988). *Annual Report on Prefectural Accounts*. Tokyo: Economic Planning Agency.

Economic Planning Agency (1990). *Report on Revised National Accounts on the Basis of 1985*. Tokyo: Economic Planning Agency.

Fujita, N. and W. E. James (1987). Exports and Technological Changes in the Adjustment Process of the Japanese Economy in the 1970s. *Hitotsubashi Journal of Economics*, 28, 107–122.

Isard, W. (1951). Interregional and Regional IO Analysis: A Model of a Space Economy. *Review of Economics and Statistics*, 33, 318–328.

Kubo, Y., S. Robinson and M. Syrquin (1986). The Methodology of Multisector Comparative Analysis. In *Industrialization and Growth: A Comparative Study*, H. Chenery, S. Robinson, and M. Syrquin (eds.). NY: Oxford University Press.

Markusen, A. R., H. Noponen and K. Driessen (1991). International Trade, Productivity, and U.S. Regional Job Growth: A Shift-Share Interpretation. *International Regional Science Review*, 14, 15–39.

Ministry of International Trade and Industry (1975, 1980, and 1985). *Interregional IO Tables*. Tokyo: Ministry of International Trade and Industry.

Round, J. I. (1985). Decomposing Multipliers for Economic Systems Involving Regional and World Trade. *Economic Journal*, 95, 383–399.

Round, J. I. (1989). Decomposition of IO and Economy-Wide Multipliers in a Regional Setting. In *Frontiers of IO Analysis*, R. E. Miller, K. R. Polenske, and A. Z. Rose (eds.). New York: Oxford University Press.

Tervo, H. and P. Okko (1983). A Note in Shift-Share Analysis as a Method of Estimating the Employment Effects of Regional Economic Policy. *Journal of Regional Science*, 23, 115–121.

Urata, S. (1987). Sources of Economic Growth and Structural Change in China: 1956–1981. *Journal of Comparative Economics*, 11, 96–115.

Chapter 6

The Flying-Geese Pattern of East Asian Development: A Computable General Equilibrium Approach

Mitsuo Ezaki and Shoichi Ito

1. Introduction

The rapid growth of East Asian economies, particularly in the 1980s, is often described as following a *flying-geese pattern* of development. Leading Japanese economy was caught up by Asian Newly Industrializing Economies (NIEs) like Korea, Taiwan, Hong Kong and Singapore, and Asian NIEs were also followed by ASEAN (Indonesia, Malaysia, Philippines and Thailand) and China. This pattern looks like a flock of geese flying in tiers of the inverted V shape. It was Kaname Akamatsu in mid-1930s (Akamatsu, 1935) who observed such a development pattern of newly industrializing Japan. He attempted first to stylize the development of woolen goods, cotton spinning and weaving, textile machinery, etc. following a path from imports to domestic production, then to exports in accordance with the principle of comparative advantage. Later, Akamatsu and his followers applied the same analysis to the pattern of industrial relocation among East Asian countries (Akamatsu, 1956).[1]

This chapter tries to quantitatively substantiate his argument with a CGE world model including ten East Asian countries on the basis of the linked IO tables of 1985 provided by the I DE (1992).[2] The ten countries are Indonesia, Malaysia, Philippines, Singapore, Thailand, China, Taiwan, Korea, Japan,

[1]Chen (1995) proposes a drastic modification of the flying-geese pattern by emphasizing technological cycle rather than product life cycle and calls it as the Parading Soldiers Pattern or *Aerobatics*. See Ezaki (1994) for the flying-geese pattern and related analyses.

[2]Lee and Roland-Hoist (1995) provide a linked CGE system for the same ten countries on the same basis of linked IO tables, but their framework and purposes differ from ours.

and the United States. The remaining countries in the world, except Hong Kong, are lumped together as the rest of the world (ROW).

Next, Section 2 gives a brief, general explanation of the flying-geese pattern of development. Section 3 presents our link CGE system and analyzes their interdependence by showing elasticity-multiplier. Section 4 investigates the same pattern mainly from the view-point of technology change in terms of both comparative statics and dynamics. Finally, Section 5 sums up our findings. In the interpretation of our findings, we rely on a theoretical exposition by Amano (1994, Ch. 6). Namely, the significant changes in comparative advantages are caused, if by technological changes, mainly by change in efficiency or productivity rather than technological shift from labor-intensive to capital-intensive ones. A crucial factor for growth and structural changes in East Asia has been the total factor productivity (TFP) growth, as Paul Krugman (1994) argued.

2. Flying-Geese Pattern of Development

Akamatsu's argument was elaborated by his followers (Akamatsu, 1962; Kojima, 1973; Yamazawa, 1993). Figure 1 shows its three schemes: a basic type and two variations. The first indicates the process for a certain industry like cotton spinning and weaving to grow, mature, and decline. Variation I shows that this cycle occurs one industry after another within a country and changes its industrial composition. II indicates the international shift of industries; that is, an industry declining in one country moves to another country and prospers there, changing the location of industries in the world. These cycles occur in accordance with changes in comparative advantage — production cost, factor endowment, and relative factor prices.[3] Many Japanese economists interpreted this pattern of Variation II as *multiplex catching-up* process. (Watanabe and Kajiwara, 1983; Watanabe and JETRO, 1989; Watanabe *et al.*, 1991, etc.).

Figure 2 presents typical patterns which show the relation of multiplex catching-up. It measures along the vertical axis each country's revealed comparative advantage (RCA) as defined by Balassa (1965). It indicates

[3]This argument resembles Vernon's theory (1966) of *product cycle* (PC). It begins with production of innovative commodity in a technologically advanced country, then it shifts to the stage of mass production and exports, and finally ends with transplantation of industry by direct investment, whereas Variation II above begins with imports of standard commodity and their substitution by domestic production. In this sense, the flying-geese pattern of development is also called "catching-up product cycle" (CPC).

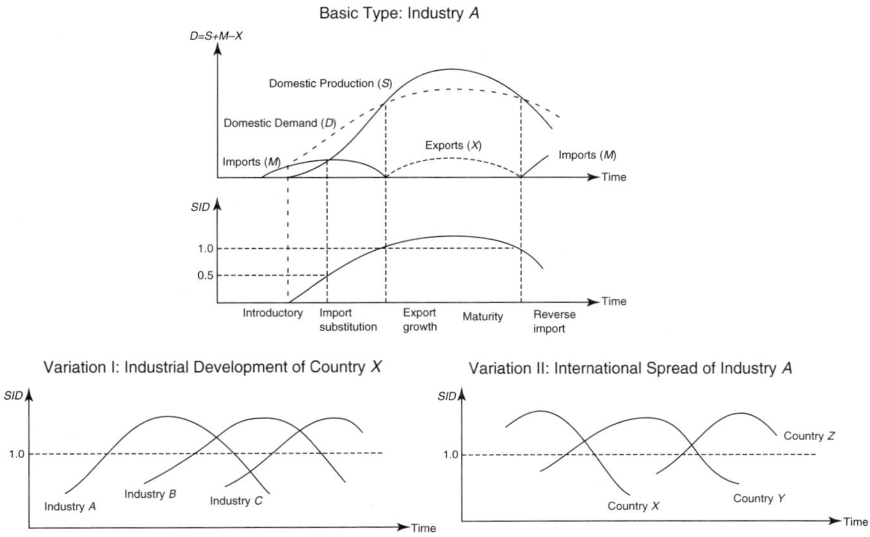

Source: Yamazawa (1984, 1993).

Figure 1. Flying-Geese Pattern of Industrial Development.

changes in international competitiveness of machinery industry (SITC 7) for three regions of East Asian countries. Competitiveness of ASEAN countries is still low (with RCA less than 0.5) but its speed of increase is remarkable. NIEs already has attained competitiveness more than the world average (with RCA higher than 1.0).

Competitiveness of Japan is slowing down steadily. Figure 2, which piles up three regions, beautifully shows the multiplex catch-up process in such an important industry among Japan, Asian NIEs, and ASEAN.

3. Link CGE System and Elasticity-Multipliers

3.1. *Basic framework*

Our link CGE system consists of country models and linkage part. The linkage part consists of the import demand of each country matching export supply of the other countries, so that it is a part of each country model. Each of our ten country models has two special characteristics in common. First, it explicitly introduces financial variables into a multi-sector general equilibrium model to determine absolute price levels endogenously. The

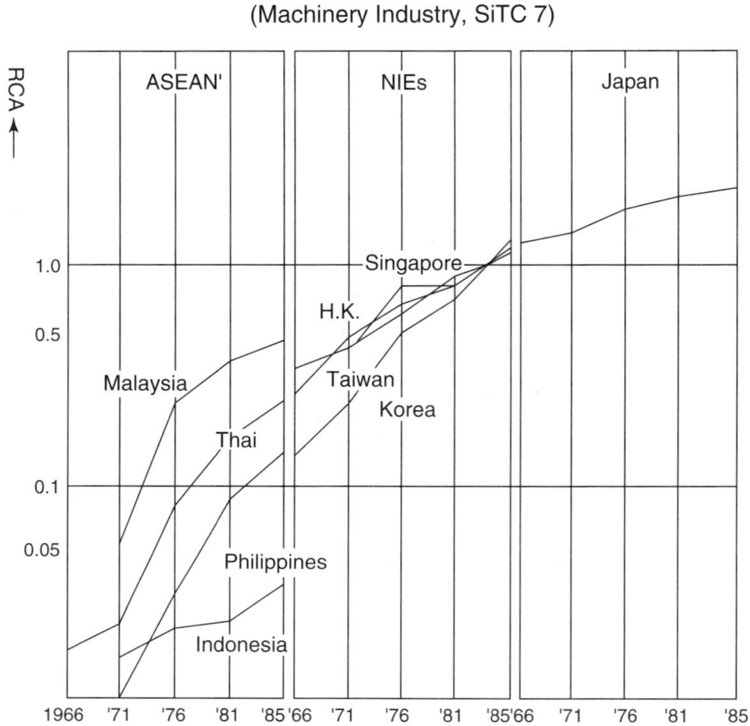

Source: Watanabe and JETRO (1989).

Figure 2. Multiplex Catching-up in East Asian Countries (Machinery Industry, SITC 7).

financial sector is simply treated, however, to avoid unnecessary complexities in this big link system as well as due to the limitation of data on assets and liabilities by institutional sectors.

Second, our country model adopts as a market-clearing mechanism not only price adjustment but also quantity adjustment, depending on the characteristics of each country. In the labor market, for example, price adjustment is assumed for relatively developed countries like Singapore, Taiwan, Korea, Japan, and the United States, whereas quantity adjustment is assumed for relatively less developed countries like Indonesia, Malaysia, Philippines, Thailand, and China. In the former, equilibrium wage is determined to clear the market, but in the latter, wage is given outside of the market and determines demand for labor, to which supply of labor adjusts with excess supply realized as unemployment or underemployment.

Table 1. Classification of Markets.

	Product Market (9 industries):*
XI (AgrFod)	agriculture, forestry and fishery, including food, beverage and tobacco manufacturing (IO code: 1-5,8)
X2 (MinPet)	mining and quarrying, including petroleum and petroleum products (IO code 6,7,13)
X3 (ManLab)	Labor-intensive manufacturing, consisting of textiles, leather, wood, rubber and other miscall. manufacturing products (IO code: 9, 10, 14, 19)
X4 (ManCap)	capital-intensive manufacturing consisting of pulp, paper, printing, chemical, non-metal and metal products (IO code: ll, 12, 15, 16)
X5 (ManTec)	technology-intensive manufacturing, consisting of machinery and transport equipments (IO code: 17,18)
X6 (ElGaWa)	electricity, gas and water supply (IO code: 20)
X7 (Constr)	construction (IO code: 21)
X8 (TraTra)	trade and transport (IO code: 22)
X9 (Servic)	services (IO code: 23,24)
Labor Market (1 type of labor)	
L	total employment, consisting of paid- and self-employment
Financial Market (5 types of assets & liabilities)	
AC: currency; *AD*: deposits; *AL*: loans; *AO*: other domestic assets & liabilities; *AF*: foreign assents & liabilities. As for these symbols, see Table 2	
Exchanges Market (1 type of foreign exchange)	
ROW$: foreign exchanges in terms of ROW (rest of the world) currency unit	

*IO code is based on the 24-sector code in *Asian International Input-Output Table 1985* (IDE, 1992). Industry abbreviation is shown in brackets.

As Table 1 shows, our country model describes the market economy of each country in four major markets: (1) product markets of nine industries, (2) labor market with no distinction between formal and informal and between employed and self-employed, (3) financial markets consisting of five financial assets, of which only currency (*AC*) and foreign assets (*AF*) appear explicitly in the system, and (4) foreign exchanges market in terms of the currency unit of ROW taken as the numeraire region in our link system. Our classification of nine industries follows Yamazawa and Watanabe (1988) who analyzed the changing comparative advantages of Asian countries and Catching-up Product Cycle.

For the outputs of nine industries, price adjustment is assumed to clear the markets in all of ten countries. In the labor market, either price or quantity adjustment is adopted depending on countries. In the

Table 2. Financial Assets and Liabilities: Indonesia.

	Assets			Liabilities		
	Non-banking National Economy	Banking Sector (*B*)	Rest of World (*W*)	Non-banking National Economy	Banking Sector (*B*)	Rest of World (*W*)
(Notation)						
Net assets	—	—	—	AN	AN_B	AN_w
Currency	AC	AC_B	—	—	AC_B^*	—
Deposits	AD	—	—	—	AD_B^*	—
Loans	—	AL_B	—	AL^*	AL_B^*	—
Others	AO	AO_B	—	—	AO_B^*	—
Net foreign	AF	AF_B	AF_w	—	—	—
(IFS code*)						
Net assets	—	—	—	$\sum 77a.d^{\#}$	$0.0^{\#\#}$	$\sum 77a.d^{\#}$
Currency	14, −20	20	—	14	—	—
Deposits	24, 25a, 25b	—	—	—	24, 25a, 25b	—
Loans	—	12a, 12b, 12d 12e, 12f, 22a 22bx, 22d, 22f	—	12, −12e, 22	26g	—

(*Continued*)

Table 2. (*Continued*)

	Assets			Liabilities		
	Non-banking National Economy	Banking Sector (B)	Rest of World (W)	Non-banking National Economy	Banking Sector (B)	Rest of World (W)
Others	15, 16b, 16d 16e, 17a, 17r, 26b 26d, 27a, 27r	—	—	—	15, 16b, 16d, 16e, 17a, 17r, 26b 26d, 27a, 27r	—
Net foreign	$\sum 77a.d$, −11, 16c, 16cl −21, 26c	11, −16c −16cl, 21, −26c	$-\sum 77a.d$	—	—	—
(Data1985, m$)**						
Net assets	—	—	—	−15,496	0	15,496
Currency	3,405	2,647	—	—	6,052	—
Deposits	16,698	—	—	—	16,698	—
Loans		32,141	—	25,803	6,338	—
Others	18,380	0	—	—	18,380	—
Net foreign	−28,178	12,682	15,496	—	—	—

*See International Financial Statistics of IMF. 14a $\neq$ 14–20 for Indonesia. **Data in Rupiah are converted into US$ by the exchange rate 1110.58 Rp/$. # Accumulation of surplus in the current balance of payments. ## Zero by assumption.

financial markets, quantity adjustment is adopted for four financial variables except currency. Thus, the demand for financial assets or liabilities (AD, $AL^* + AL_B^*$, $AO + AO_B$ and $AF + AF_B$) is assumed always to match the corresponding supply of financial assets or liabilities (AD_B^*, AL_B, AO_B^* and $-AF_W$) with exogenously given interest rates, so that they may not explicitly appear in the model except for foreign assets and liabilities which are directly related to the current balance of payments.

Currency, on the other hand, has a special role in our country model. Its equilibrium between demand ($AC + AC_B$) and supply (AC_B^*) is guaranteed by Walras' Law. Our model includes both demand for and supply of currency, which are derived from intra-institutional identities between assets and liabilities (and net worth). Our model, however, omits the equilibrium condition for currency and regards currency as numeraire.

Since the price of currency is unitary in every country, our model will determine all the prices in their absolute levels.[4] Currency is of crucial importance in this sense. In the foreign exchanges market, either price or quantity adjustment can be adopted for each country. If we treat exchange rate (ER) as endogenous, foreign capital inflow ($FW\$ \cdot ER$) will be treated as exogenous. This is the case of price adjustment. If we treat exchange rate as exogenous, foreign capital inflow ($FW\$$) will be determined endogenously as residuals between imports and exports. This is the case of quantity adjustment. Our link system can deal with both cases. Comparative statics in this Section shows the results of both cases. Comparative statics in the next Section is based mainly on the former (i.e. endogenous *ER*). However, comparative dynamics in the same Section depends only on the latter (i.e. exogenous *ER*), since it is computationally difficult to maintain endogenous *ER* for a long period of simulation.

3.2. *Data*

The most important data source for our link CGE system is the link IO table of 1985 provided in IDE (1992). It includes detailed information on sectoral transactions between countries for both intermediate and final demand items, using the framework of inter-regional IO table for the world economy. Such detailed information, however, is not fully utilized in our

[4]This way to determine absolute price levels differs from the standard one that introduces an equation for the average price level. See Adelman and Robinson (1978, p. 225), Dervis *et al.* (1982, p. 150), Lee and Roland-Hoist (1995, p. 26).

model due to the adoption of Armington assumption, and the original IO table is disintegrated into ten country IO tables and nine trade matrices. The country IO tables thus obtained include freight and insurance (*BF*) and import duty and sales tax (*DT*) as additional inputs to intermediate and final demand, so that our country models differ from the standard formulation in the treatment of these two items. Furthermore, the original IO table is unified in terms of US dollars. Ten country IO items, therefore, are all measured in terms of US dollars, and all related local variables such as currency supply must be measured also in terms of US dollars.

Data for labor: paid employment and self-employment for nine industries are obtained either directly or indirectly from ILO's *Yearbook of Labor Statistics* and UN's *Industrial Statistical Yearbook*, except China and Taiwan for which local statistical yearbooks of various kinds are utilized. Guess work is unavoidable in relation to self-employment and wage imputation. Capital stocks for nine industries are estimated, first, the total capital stock for 1985 in each country by using average *ICOR*[5] and GDP, and then allocating it to nine industries by assuming no differences in sectoral rates of return to capital, i.e., by using national average rate of return. Data for financial markets are explained in Table 2, which refers to the case of Indonesia as an example. Concepts and data are all derived from IMF's *International Financial Statistics*. Concepts defined in terms of IFS code differ slightly from country to country. Furthermore, we cannot divide non-banking into, say, three institutional sectors of households, corporate and government as far as we rely solely on IFS. The division in Table 2, however, seems useful enough for our purpose of endogenizing currency or money.

Data for trade matrices are derived from the link IO table as mentioned above. However, there are missing cells in the derived trade matrices in relation to Hong Kong and ROW, which are filled by using UN's *International Trade Statistics Yearbook* only for the first five industries.[6] Missing parts are left unfilled for the remaining four industries. Finally, data for government revenues and direct taxes are obtained from IMF's *Government Finance*

[5]We set ICOR at the following levels: 4.0 (I), 4.0 (M), 5.0 (P), 4.0 (S), 4.0 (T), 2.0 (C), 3.0 (N), 3.0 (K), 7.0 (J), and 6.0 (U). They are roughly 5–6 years averages around 1985.

[6]Five industries are identified by SITC numbers as follows: (1) AgrFod = 0, 1, 44, 22, 29; (2) MinPet- 24, 27, 28, 3; (3) ManLab = 21, 23, 26, 61, 62, 63, 65, 82-89; (4) ManCap = 5, 64, 66, 67, 68, 69, 25; (5) ManTec = 7, 81.

Statistics Yearbook for all countries except Taiwan, for which related local statistical yearbooks are utilized.

3.3. *Structure*

The notations of variables and parameters and the system of equations are listed in Tables 3 and 4. Note that super-bar means exogenous variable, and suffix $i(k)$ means industry i of country k, where 1. Indonesia (I),

Table 3. Notations of Variables in the System.

Price variables			
$PX_{i(k)}$	output price	$PM_{i(k)}$	import price
$PM\$_{i(k)}$	import price in numeraire (ROW)	$PE\$_{i(k)}$	export price in numeraire (ROW)
$P_{i(k)}$	price of composite goods	$PN_{i(k)}$	Price of net output (value added)
$W_{i(k)}$	wage rate	$W_{(k)}$	overall average wage rate
$R_{i(k)}$	rental rate of capital	$R_{(k)}$	overall average rental rate of cap.
$ER_{(k)}$	foreign exchange rate per ROW currency	$ER'_{(k)}$	foreign exchange rate per unit of US dollar
$PC_{(k)}$	deflator for private consum. expend	$PG_{(k)}$	deflator of gov. consum. expend.
$PI_{(k)}$	deflator of fixed investment	$PJ_{(k)}$	deflator of inventory investment
$PO_{(k)}$	deflator of statistical discrepancy	$PE_{(k)}$	deflator of exports
$PM_{(k)}$	deflator of imports	$GDP_{(k)}$	deflator of GDP
Quantity variables			
$X^S_{i(k)}$	supply of gross output	$X^D_{i(k)}$	demand for gross output
$L_{i(k)}$	demand for labor in efficiency unit	$L^s_{(k)}$	$i(k)$ demand for labor in original unit
$K_{i(k)}$	Existing capital or demand for capital	$C_{i(k)}$	private consum. demand for gross output
$G_{i(k)}$	Govern. consum. demand for gross output	$I_{i(k)}$	fixed investment demand for gross output
$J_{i(k)}$	inventory invest. demand for gross output	$O_{i(k)}$	quantity of statistical discrepancy
$Q_{i(k)}$	Quantity of composite goods	$D_{i(k)}$	domestic demand for gross output

(Continued)

Table 3. (*Continued*)

$M_{i(k)}$	total composite import demand of country k	$E_{i(k)}$	foreign countries' total demand for k's export
$E_{i(lk)}$	country k's import demand for l's export	$\bar{L}_K^S$	total supply of labor in efficiency and original units
$K_{(k)}^D$	total demand for labor in efficiency unit	$K_{(k)}^S$	total supply of physical capital
$L_{(k)}^D$	total demand for phys. capital	$C_{(k)}$	real private consum. expenditure
$G_{(k)}$	real gov. cons. expen.	$\bar{I}_{(k)}$	real fixed investment
$l_{(k)}$	real inventory invest.	$\bar{O}_{(k)}$	real statistical discrepancy
$E_{(k)}$	real exports	$M_{(k)}$	real imports
$GDP_{(k)}$	real GDP		
Rate variables			
$D_{i(k)}$	domestic demand ratio of composite goods	$E_{i(lk)}$	import demand ratio for export of country l
$RCA_{i(k)}$	index of revealed comparative advantage	$RCD_{i(k)}$	index of revealed comparative disadvantage
Value variables			
$YP_{(k)}$	personal income	$YFI_{(k)}$	private income of freight and insurance
$YG_{(k)}$	government income	$SP_{(k)}$	personal saving
$SG_{(k)}$	government saving	$GDP_{(k)}^n$	nominal GDP
$FITR_{(k)}$	net factor and transfer income from abroad	$FW\$_{(k)}$	net capital inflow (deficits in current balance of payment)
$AN_{(k)} \ldots AFW_{(k)}$		see Table 2	
Parameters			
$\bar{A}_{i(k)}$	scale factor of Cobb-Douglas production function		
$\bar{a}_{ij(k)}$	labor share of Cobb-Douglas production function		
$\lambda_{i(k)}$	efficiency parameter for labor input ($= W_{i(k)}/W_{(k)}$)		
$\bar{a}_{ij(k)}$	intermediate input coefficient of good j in industry i		
$B_{i(k)}$	scale factor of Cobb-Douglas composite goods function		
$\beta_{i(k)}$	import share of Cobb-Douglas composite goods function		
$\bar{M}_{i(k)}^0$	scale factor of Cobb-Douglas composite import function		
$\varepsilon_{i(k)}$	share factor of Cobb-Douglas composite import function		
$\gamma C_{i(k)}$	share parameter of Cobb-Douglas utility function		

(*Continued*)

Table 3. (*Continued*)

Shares and ratios			
$\bar{b}_{ai(k)}$	quantity ratio to real govern. Consumption	$\bar{b}_{ji(k)}$	quantity ratio to real fixed investment
$\bar{b}_{li(k)}$	quantity ratio to real inventory investment	$\bar{b}_{oi(k)}$	quantity ratio to real statistical discrepancy
$\bar{S}_{p(k)}$	personal saving rate	$\bar{S}_{G(k)}$	government saving rate
$\overline{de}_{i(k)}$	dumping rate in export price	$\bar{f}_{xi(k)}$	freight and insurance portion in production
$\bar{f}_{ci(k)}$	freight and insurance portion in private consum.	$\bar{f}_{Gi(k)}$	freight and insurance portion in gov. Consumption
$\bar{f}_{li(k)}$	freight and insurance portion in fixed investment	$\bar{f}_{ji(k)}$	freight and insurance portion in inventory investment
Tax parameters			
$tm_{i(k)}$	tariff rate in import demand (no data available)	$se_{i(k)}$	subsidy rate in export supply (no data available)
$td_{i(k)}$	indirect (net of subsidy) rate in production	$tm_{xi(k)}$	tariff portion in production
$tm_{ci(k)}$	tariff portion in private consumption	$tm_{ci(k)}$	tariff portion in government consumption
$tm_{li(k)}$	tariff portion in fixed investment	$tm_{ji(k)}$	tariff portion in inventory investment
$ty_{L(k)}$	tax-rate on individual income	$ty_{K(k)}$	tax-rate on corporate income and profits
$ty_{(k)}$	portion of gov. income other than td, tm, ty_L and ty_K.		

Table 4. System of Equations.

$$PM_{t(k)} = PM\$_{t(k)} \cdot (1 + \overline{tm}_{t(k)}) \cdot ER_{(k)} \tag{3.1}$$

$$PE\$_{i(k)} = PX_{i(k)} \cdot (1 + \overline{se}_{i(k)}) - \overline{de}_{i(k)}/ER_{(k)} \tag{3.2}$$

$$P_{i(k)} = (PX_{i(k)} \cdot D_{i(k)} + PM_{i(k)} \cdot M_{i(k)})/Q_{i(k)} \tag{3.3}$$

$$PN_{i(k)} = PX_{i(k)} - \sum P_{j(k)} \cdot \bar{a}_{ij(k)} - PX_{i(k)} \cdot (\bar{f}_{xi(k)} + \overline{tm}_{xi(k)} + \overline{ta'}_{i(k)}) \tag{3.4}$$

$$X^s_{i(k)} = \bar{A}_{i(k)} \cdot L^{ai(k)}_{i(k)} \cdot K^{1-\alpha_{i(k)}}_{i(k)} \tag{3.5}$$

$$L_{i(k)} = \alpha_{i(k)} \cdot PN_{i(k)} \cdot X^S_{i(k)}/W_{(k)} \text{ where } L_{i(k)} = \lambda_{i(k)} \cdot L'_{i(k)} \tag{3.6}$$

$$L^D_{(k)} = \sum L_{i(k)} \tag{3.7}$$

$$L^D_{(k)} = L^S_{(k)} \text{ and } W_{(k)} = W^*_{(k)} \text{ where } W_{(k)} = \text{equilibrium wage} \tag{3.8}$$

$$W_{(k)} = \bar{W}_{(k)} \text{ and } L^D_{(k)} < L^S_{(k)} \text{ where } \bar{W}_{(k)} = \text{exogenous} \tag{3.8'}$$

$$K_{i(k)} = \bar{K}_{i(k)} \tag{3.9}$$

(*Continued*)

Table 4. (*Continued*)

$K_{i(k)} = (1-\alpha_{i(k)}) \cdot PN_{i(k)} \cdot X^S_{i(k)}/R_{(k)}$	(3.9′)
$R_{i(k)} = (1-\alpha_{i(k)}) \cdot PN_{i(k)} \cdot XS_{i(k)}/R_{(k)}$	(3.10)
$K_{i(k)} = \bar{K}_{i(k)}$	(3.10′)
$R_{(k)} = \sum_{Ri(k) \cdot K_{i(k)}/KS_{(k)}} \quad KS_{(k)} = \sum_{Ki(k)}$	(3.11)
$K^D_{(k)} = K^S_{(k)}$ and $R_{(k)} = R^*_{(k)}$, where $R^*_{(k)}$ = equilibrium rate	(3.11′)
$YP_{(k)} = (1-\overline{ty}_{L(k)}-\overline{ty}_{(k)}) \cdot W_{(k)} \cdot L^S_{(k)} + (1-\overline{ty}_{K(k)}-\overline{ty}_{(k)}) \cdot R_{(k)} \cdot K^S_{(k)} + YF_{(k)}$	(3.12)
$YF_{(k)} = \sum \bar{f}_{xi(k)} \cdot PX_{i(k)} \cdot X^S_{i(k)} + (\bar{f}_{s(k)}/(1+\bar{f}_{c(k)}+\overline{tm}_{s(k)})) \cdot PC_{(k)} \cdot C_{(k)}$ $+ (\bar{f}_{G(k)}/(1+\bar{f}_{G(k)}+\overline{tm}_{G(k)})) \cdot PG_{(k)} \cdot G_{(k)}$ $+ (\bar{f}_{l(k)}/(1+\bar{f}_{l(k)}+\overline{tm}_{l(k)})) \cdot Pl_{(k)} \cdot l_{(k)}$ $+ (\bar{f}_{j(k)})/(1+\bar{f}_{j(k)}+\overline{tm}_{j(k)})) \cdot PJ_{(k)} \cdot J_{(k)}$ $- \sum \overline{de}_{i(k)} \cdot PX_{i(k)} \cdot E_{i(k)}$	(3.13)
$YG_{(k)} = (\overline{ty}_{L(k)}+\overline{ty}_{(k)}) \cdot W_{(k)} \cdot L_{(k)} - (\overline{ty}_{K(k)}+\overline{ty}_{(k)}) \cdot R_{(k)} \cdot K^S_{(k)}$ $- \sum \overline{td}_{i(k)} \cdot PX_{i(k)} \cdot PX_{i(k)} \cdot X^S_{i(k)} + \sum \overline{tm}_{xi(k)} \cdot PX_{i(k)} \cdot X^S_{i(k)}$ $+ \sum \overline{tm}_{i(k)}/(1+\overline{tm}_{i(k)}) \cdot PM_{i(k)} \cdot M_{i(k)}$ $+ \sum \overline{tm}_{o(k)}/(1+\bar{f}_{o(k)}-\overline{tm}_{c(k)}) \cdot PC_{(k)} \cdot C_{(k)}$ $+ \sum \overline{tm}_{G(k)}/(1+\bar{f}_{G(k)}+\overline{tm}_{G(k)} \cdot PG_k \cdot G_{(k)}$ $+ \sum \overline{tm}_{t(k)}/(1+\bar{f}_{l(k)}+\overline{tm}_{i(k)}) \cdot PI_{(k)} \cdot \bar{I}_{(k)}$ $+ \sum \overline{tm}_{j(k)}/(1+\bar{f}_{j(k)})+\overline{tm}_{j(k)}) \cdot Fl_{(k)} \cdot J_{(k)}$ $- \sum \overline{se}_{i(k)} \cdot PX_{i(k)} \cdot E_{i(k)}$	(3.14)
$SP_{(k)} = \bar{S}_{P(k)} \cdot YP_{(k)}$	(3.15)
$SG_{(k)} = \bar{S}_{G(k)} \cdot YG_{(k)}$	(3.16)
$C_{i(k)} = \gamma_{Ci(k)} \cdot (1-\bar{S}_{F(k)}) \cdot YP_{(k)}/(1+\bar{f}_{s(k)}+\overline{tm}_{c(k)}/P_{i(k)} \left(\sum \gamma_{Ci(k)} = 1\right)$	(3.17)
$C_{i(k)} = \sum C_{i(k)}(PC_{(k)} \cdot C_{(k)} \equiv (1+\bar{f}_{C(k)}+\overline{tm}_{C(k)}) \cdot \sum P_{i(k)}C_{i(k)})$	(3.18)
$PC_{(k)} = (1-\bar{S}_{P(k)}) \cdot YP_{(k)}/C_{(k)}$	(3.19)
$G_{(k)} = (1-\bar{S}_{G(k)})YG_{(k)}/PG_{(k)}(PG_{(k)} \cdot G_{(k)}$ $\equiv (1+\bar{f}_{G(k)}+\overline{tm}_{G(k)}) \cdot \sum P_{i(k)}G_{i(k)})$	(3.20)
$G_{i(k)} = \bar{b}_{Gi(k)} \cdot G_{(k)}$	(3.21)
$PG_{(k)} = (1+\bar{f}_{G(k)}+\overline{tm}_{G(k)}) \cdot \sum \bar{b}_{Gi(k)} \cdot P_{i(k)}$	(3.22)
$I_{(k)} = \bar{I}_{(k)}(PI_{(k)} \cdot I_{(k)} \equiv (1+\bar{f}_{I(k)}+\overline{tm}_{I(k)}) \cdot \sum P_{i(k)}I_{i(k)})$	(3.23)
$I_{i(k)} = \bar{b}I_{i(k)} \cdot I_{(k)}$	(3.24)

(*Continued*)

Table 4. (*Continued*)

$PI_{(k)} = (1 + \bar{f}_{I(k)} + \overline{tm}_{I(k)}) \cdot \sum \bar{b}_{Ii(k)} \cdot P_{i(k)}$	(3.25)
$J_{i(k)} = \bar{b}_{Ji(k)} \cdot \bar{J}_{(k)}(PJ_{(k)} \cdot J_{(k)} \equiv (1 + \bar{f}_{J(k)} + \overline{tm}_{J(k)}) \cdot \sum P_{i(k)} J_{i(k)})$	(3.26)
$PJ_{(k)} = (1 + \bar{f}_{J(k)} + \overline{tm}_{J(k)}) \cdot \sum \bar{b}_{Ji(k)} \cdot P_{i(k)}$	(3.27)
$O_{i(k)} = \bar{b}_{Oi(k)} \cdot \bar{O}_{(k)}$	(3.28)
$PO_{(k)} = \sum^{\bar{b}}_{Oi(k)} \cdot P_{i(k)}$	(3.29)
$FN_{(k)} = (SP_{(k)} + SG_{(k)}) + \overline{FITR} - (PI_{(k)} \cdot I_{(k)} + PJ_{(k)} \cdot J_{(k)} + PO_{(k)} \cdot O_{(k)})$	(3.30)
$AC_{(k)} = AN_{(k)}, -1 + FN_{(k)}$	(3.31)
$AC_{(k)} = AN_{(k)} + \bar{Z} - AF_{(k)};\ \bar{Z} = (\overline{AL}_{s(k)} - \overline{AL}_{s(k)} - AL'_{s(k)}) - \overline{AD}_{(k)} - \overline{AO}_{(k)}$	(3.32)
$AC'_{s(k)} = \overline{AC}_{s(k)} + \bar{Z} + AF_{s(k)}$	(3.33)
$AC_{(k)} + \overline{AC}_{s(k)} = AC'_{s(k)}$ (Walras' Law)	(3.34)
$AF_{w(k)} = -(AF_{(k)} + AF_B(k))$	(3.35)
$AF_{w(k)} = -(AF_{B(k)} + AF_{w(k)})$ (See equation (3.47′))	(3.35′)
$FW\$_{(k)} \cdot ER_{(k)} = AFW_{(k)} - AFW_{(k)}, -1$	(3.36)
$FW\$_{(k)} \cdot ER_{(k)} = AFW_{(k)} - AFW_{(k)}, -1$	(3.36′)
$O_{i(k)} = \sum \bar{a}_{ij(k)} \cdot X^S_{i(k)} + C_{i(k)} + G_{i(k)} + I_{i(k)} + J_{i(k)} + O_{i(k)}$	(3.37)
$d_{i(k)}(= D_{i(k)}/Q_{i(k)} = 1/\bar{B}_{i(k)} \cdot (\beta_{i(k)}/(1 - \beta_{i(k)}) \cdot PX_{i(k)}/PM_{i(k)})^{\beta_{i(k)}}$ or 1.0 where $Q_{i(k)} = \bar{B}_{i(k)} \cdot M^{\beta_{i(k)}}_{i(k)} \cdot D^{2-\beta_{i(k)}}_{i(k)}$	(3.38)
$D_{i(k)} = d_{i(k)} \cdot Q_{i(k)}$	(3.39)
$M_{i(k)} = (\beta_{i(k)}/(1 - \beta_{i(k)}) \cdot PX_{i(k)}/PM_{i(k)} \cdot D_{i(k)}$ or 0.0	(3.40)
$e_{i(lk)} = \frac{\varepsilon_{i(lk)}/\varepsilon_{i(nk)}) \cdot (PE\$_{i(n)}/PE\$_i(l))}{M^0_{i(k)} \cdot \prod(\varepsilon_{i(lk)})/\varepsilon_{i(nk)})^{\varepsilon i(lk)} \cdot (PE\$_{i(n)}/PE\$_{i(l)})^{\varepsilon}_{i(lk)}}$, where $M_{i(k)} = \bar{M}^0_{i(k)} \cdot E^{\varepsilon_{i(lk)}}_{i(k)} \ldots E^{\varepsilon_{i(k)}}_{i(n\underline{k})} (\sum \epsilon_{i(lk)} = 1)$	(3.41)
$E_{i(k)} = e_{i(lk)} \cdot M_{i(k)}$ or $E_{i(k)} = \bar{b}_{Ei(lk)} \cdot M_{i(k)}$ $(l = l \ldots 5, 8, 9$ excluding $(i = 8, k = l))$ $(t = 6, 7$ and $(l = 8), k = l))$	(3.42)
$PMS_{j(k)} = \sum PE\$_{i(l)} E_{j(lk)}/M_{i(k)}$	(3.43)
$E_{i(k)} = \sum E_{i(kh)}$	(3.44)
$X^D_{i(k)} = D_{i(k)} + E_{i(k)}$	(3.45)
$X^S_{i(k)} = X^D_{i(k)}$ and $PX_{i(k)} = PX^*_{i(k)}$ where PX^*_{ik} = equilibrium price	(3.46)
$\sum PM\$_{i(k)} M_{i(k)} - \sum PE\$_{i(k)} - E_{i(k)} - FITR\$_{(k)} - FW\$_(k) = 0$ and $ER_{(k)} = ER^*_{(k)}$ where $ER^*_{i(k)}$ = equilibrium rate	(3.47)
$E_{i(k)} = \overline{ER}_{(k)}$ and $FW\$_{(k)} = \sum PM_{i(k)} \cdot M_{i(k)} - \sum PE\$_{i(k)} \cdot E_{i(k)} - FITR\$_{(k)}$	(3.47′)
$E_{(k)} = \sum E_{i(k)}$	(3.48)
$PE_{i(k)} = \sum PX_{i(k)} \cdot (1 - \overline{se}_{i(k)} - \overline{de}_{i(k)}) \cdot E_{i(k)}/E_{(k)}$	(3.49)
$M_{(k)} = -\sum M_{i(k)}$	(3.50)

(*Continued*)

Table 4. (*Continued*)

$$PM_{(k)} = \sum(PM_{i(k)}/(1+\overline{tm}_{i(k)}))\cdot M_{i(k)}/M_{(k)} \quad (3.51)$$

$$\begin{aligned} GDP^{n}_{(k)} &= YP_{(k)} + YG_{(k)} = \sum(PX_{i(k)} - \sum P_{j(k)}\cdot\bar{a}_{ji(k)})\cdot X^{S}_{i(k)} \\ &\quad + ((\bar{f}_{C(k)} + \overline{tm}_{C(k)}/(1+\bar{f}_{C(k)}+\overline{tm}_{C(k)}))\cdot PC_{(k)}\cdot C_{(k)} \\ &\quad + ((\bar{f}_{G(k)} + \overline{tm}_{G(k)}/(1+\bar{f}_{G(k)}+\overline{tm}_{G(k)}))\cdot PG_{(k)}\cdot G_{(k)} \\ &\quad + ((\bar{f}_{I(k)} + \overline{tm}_{I(k)}/(1+\bar{f}_{I(k)}+\overline{tm}_{I(k)}))\cdot PI_{(k)}\cdot I_{(k)} \\ &\quad + ((\bar{f}_{J(k)} + \overline{tm}_{J(k)}/(1+\bar{f}_{J(k)}+\overline{tm}_{J(k)}))\cdot PJ_{(k)}\cdot J_{(k)} \\ &\quad + \sum\overline{tm}_{i(k)}/(1+\overline{tm}_{i(k)})\cdot PM_{i(k)}\cdot M_{i(k)} \\ &\quad - \sum(\overline{se}_{i(k)} + \overline{de}_{i(k)})\cdot PX_{i(k)}\cdot E_{i(k)} \\ &= FC_{(k)}C_{(k)} + PG_{(k)}G_{(k)} + PI_{(k)}\bar{I}_{(k)} + PJ_{(k)}\bar{J}_{(k)} \\ &\quad + PO_{(k)}\bar{O}_{(k)} + PE_{(k)}E_{(k)} - PM_{(k)}M_{(k)} \end{aligned} \quad (3.52)$$

$$GDP_{(k)} = C_{(k)} + G_{(k)} + \bar{I}_{(k)} + \bar{J}_{(k)} + \bar{O}_{(k)} + E_{(k)} - M_{(k)} \quad (3.53)$$

$$PGDP_{(k)} = GDP^{n(k)}/GDP_{(k)},\ k = 11 \text{ (Hong Kong)},\ 12(W),\ I = 1,\ldots,9. \quad (3.54)$$

$$M_{i(k)} = \bar{M}_{i(k)},\quad [\propto \textstyle\sum_k M_{i(k)}(k = 1,\ldots,10)] \quad (3.55)$$

$$PE\$_{i(k)} = \overline{PE\$}_{i(k)} \quad (3.56)$$

$$e_{i(lk)} = \frac{\epsilon_{i(lk)}/\epsilon_{i(nk)}\cdot(PE\$_{i(n)}/PE\$_{i(l)})}{M_{i(k)}\cdot\prod(\varepsilon_{i(lk)}/\varepsilon_{i(nk)}^{z_{i(lk)}}\cdot PE\$_{i(n)}/PE\$_{i(l)})^{z}_{i(nk)}} \text{ where} \quad (3.57)$$

$$M_{i(k)} = \bar{M}^{0}_{i(k)}\cdot E^{\varepsilon_{i(ik)}}_{i(lk)}\ldots E^{\varepsilon_{i(nk)}}_{i(nk)}(\textstyle\sum\epsilon_{i(lk)} = 1$$

$$E_{i(k)} = e_{i(lk)}\cdot M_{i(k)}(i = 1\ldots5) \text{ or } E_{i(k)} = \bar{b}_{Ei(lk)}\cdot M_{i(k)}(i = 6\ldots9) \quad (3.58)$$

$$PM\$_{j(k)} = \sum PE\$_{i(l)} - E_{i(lk)}/M_{i(k)} \quad (3.59)$$

$$E_{i(k)} = \sum E_{i(kh)} \quad (3.60)$$

$$FITR\$_{(11)} = 0.0,\ FITR\$_{12} = -\textstyle\sum_{1}^{11} FITR\$_{(k)} \quad (3.61)$$

$$Fw\$_{(11)} = \sum PM\$_{i(k)} - M_{i(k)} - \sum PE\$_{i(k)}\cdot E_{i(k)} - FITR\$_{(11)}(ER_{(11)} = \text{exogenous } FW_{(12)} = -\textstyle\sum_{!}^{11} FW\$_{(k)} \quad (3.62)$$

$$\sum PE\$_{i(12)}\cdot E_{i(12)} - \sum PM\$_{i(12)}M_{i(u)} + FITR\$_{(12)} + FW\$^{12} = 0 \quad (3.63)$$
$$(ER_{(i2)} = \ell, \text{ due to Global Walras' Law})$$

Inter-temporal Change for Time t ($t = 0$ (1985), ..., 10(1995)); Country k ($k = 1\ldots10$), Industry i ($i = 1\ldots9$)

$$KS_{(k),t} = KS_{(k),t-2} + \bar{I}_{(k),t} - \delta_{(k)}\cdot KS_{(k),t-1} \quad (3.64)$$

$$KS_{(k),t+1} = KS_{(k),t} + \bar{I}_{(k),x+2} - \delta_{(k)}\cdot KS_{(k),t} \text{ and} \quad (3.64')$$
$$(K_{i(k)}/K^{S}_{(k)})_{t+2} = (K_{i(k)}/K^{S}_{(k)})_{t}[1+\mu\cdot(R_{i(k),t} - R_{(k),t})/R_{(k),t}]((\mu = 0.1)$$

Identity for Country Walras' Law ($k = 1,\ldots,10$)

$$\begin{aligned} &W(k)\cdot(LD(k) - LS(k)) + R(k)_{o}(\Sigma Ki(k) - KS(k)) + \Sigma PXi(k) \\ &\cdot(XDi(k) - XSi(k)) + (AC)k) + ACB(k) - AC^{*}B(k)) + ER(k) \\ &\cdot(\Sigma PM\$i(k) - Mi(k) - \Sigma PE\$i(k) - Ei(k) - FITR\$(k) - FW\$(k)) \equiv 0, \\ &(= 0 \text{ for } k = I, M, P, T. \text{ and } C) \text{ and } (= 0 \text{ for all } k' \text{ s in static model}) \end{aligned} \quad (3.65)$$

Identity for Global Walras' Law

$$\begin{aligned} &\textstyle\sum_{k=\ell}^{12}[\sum_{i=\ell}^{9} PM\$i(k)\cdot Mi(k) - \sum_{i=\ell}^{9} PE\$i(k)\cdot Ei(k) \\ &\quad - FITR\$(k) - FW\$(k)] = 0 \end{aligned} \quad (3.66)$$

2. Malaysia (M), 3. Philippines (P), 4. Singapore (S), 5. Thailand (T), 6. China (C), 7. Taiwan (N), 8. Korea (K), 9. Japan (J), and 10. USA (U).

Parameter values of the model (shares, ratios, constant terms, elasticity's, etc.) are all derived from the data sources mentioned above either directly or indirectly. This simple procedure for parameter estimation is possible because the model adopts the simplest form for its behavioral and technological equations. Namely, production functions [equation (3.5)], consumption (or utility) functions [equation (3.17)], and aggregation functions [equation (3.38), equations (3.41) and (3.57)] are all of Cobb-Douglas type with constant returns to scale. Savings, and therefore total consumption are assumed to be proportional to income in both private and government sectors [equations (3.15), (3.16)]. The system consists of country models [equations (3.l)–(3.54)] for ten countries (I, M, P, S, T, C, N, K, J and U) and trade models [equations (3.55)–3.63] for Hong Kong (H) and the rest of the world (R).

The system includes two kinds of identities which amount to Walras' Law. First, the identity equation (3.65) is each country's Walras' Law. As already mentioned, equilibrium condition for currency: equation (3.34); i.e. ($AC_{(k)} + AC_{B(k)} = AC^*_{B(k)}$) is dropped by using this identity, and the model determines absolute price levels by setting the price of currency at one (1.0). Demand for currency: equation (3.32) and supply of currency: equation (3.33) are derived from identities between assets and liabilities within the two institutions: non-banking and banking. Second is the identity equation (3.66) which leads to global Walras Law. One of the equilibrium conditions between demand for and supply of foreign exchanges, equations (3.47) and (3.63), becomes redundant by this identity.[7] In our system, the equilibrium condition in ROW: equation (3.63), is dropped, and the currency of ROW is regarded as global *numeraire* by setting the exchange rate for ROW at one (1.0). Our system, therefore, is unified in terms of the ROW currency, not the US dollar.

The system adopts two kinds of adjustment (price or quantity) to attain supply-demand equality in both labor and capital markets. In the case of labor, as already mentioned, price adjustment, equation (3.8), is assumed for countries I, M, P, T and C, whereas quantity adjustment, equation (3.8′), for countries S, N, K, J and U. In the case of capital markets, fixed quantity, equation (3.9), is assumed basically for all countries, but price adjustment, equation (3.11′), is employed for comparative statics and dynamics of

[7]Equations (3.47′) and (3.62) are not equilibrium conditions but identities.

technology changes in order to allow for capital allocation between industries under changing situations. Price adjustment in comparative dynamics, which means instantaneous adjustment within one year period, can be replaced also by gradual adjustment over time, equation (3.64′).[8]

The system allows for composite goods in each industry in two steps. The first is the aggregation of component imports into composite imports in each industry, as equations (3.41) and (3.57). It is assumed that imports from different countries are not perfect substitutes even when they belong to the same industry. The second is the aggregation in the national level of imported and domestically produced goods in each industry, as equation (3.41) shows. It is again assumed that foreign and domestic products are not perfect substitutes even when they belong to the same industry. This treatment of imports is of standard type in CGE modeling known as Armington procedure (Dervis *et al.*, 1982, p. 221).

3.4. *Solution method*

To solve the system of non-linear equations consisting of some 4000 endogenous variables and 5000 parameters, we employ the Gauss-Seidel iteration method, which can be handled by FORTRAN language on personal computer. It requires each of the equations to be expressed by an explicit function with only one dependent variable on the left-hand side. In Table 3, the equilibrium conditions are expressed in the form of implicit functions, so that they are rewritten with the corresponding prices on the left-hand side as follows:

$$W_{(k)} = \Sigma \alpha_{i(k)} \cdot PN_{i(k)} \cdot X^S_{i(k)} / L^S_{(k)} \tag{3.8}$$

$$R_{(k)} = \Sigma (l - \alpha_{i(k)}) \cdot PN_{i(k)} \cdot X^S_{i(k)} / K^S_{(k)} \tag{3.11′}$$

$$PX_{i(k)} = PX_{i(k)}[-1] + 0.1 \cdot \left(X^D_{i(k)} / X^S_{i(k)} - 1 \right) \tag{3.46}$$

$$\begin{aligned} ER_{(k)} &= ER_{(k)}[-1] + 0.1 \\ &\quad \cdot \{ \Sigma PM\$_{i(k)} M_{i(k)} / (\Sigma PE\$_{i(k)} E_{i(k)} + FITR\$_{(k)}) - 1 \} \end{aligned} \tag{3.47}$$

where $[-1]$ means the previous iteration. The last two equations are formulated as adjustment functions, assuming that the equilibrium condition is

[8]Dervis *et al.* (1982) proposed this type of gradual price adjustment.

attained by adjusting the corresponding price ($PX_{i(k)}$ or $ER_{(k)}$) positively when excess demand exists (or negatively when excess supply exists) in each stage of the iteration process.[9]

3.5. *Elasticity-multipliers*

First, we analyze the degree of interdependence (or transmission of economic impulses) among East Asian countries including the United States.[10] For that purpose, a shock is given to real investment ($I_{(k)}$) by the amount of 1% of GDP in each country. Table 5 presents the results of comparative statics in terms of percentage increases in real GDP for two cases (endogenous *ER* and exogenous *ER*) by the name of elasticity-multiplier. Diagonal elements indicate multipliers while off-diagonal elements, elasticities. Case I (endogenous exchange rate) gives larger multipliers and smaller elasticities than Case II (exogenous exchange rate) for most countries, because the increase in effective demand leaks and spreads more in Case II where no restraints are imposed on the current balance of payments through currency depreciation. Big impacts from US on other countries in Case II reflect this situation. Japan is an exception, probably Singapore too. Impacts from Japan are relatively larger in Case I. It means that the increase in internal effective demand, when combined with Yen depreciation, gives larger leakages though not very large. Table 6 shows impacts on domestic variables for Case I. Impacts on GDP are the same as those in Table 5 (Case I). Positive shocks on real investment contribute to real GDP growth mainly through construction industry and cause inflation both at national and industry levels and depreciation in currency. Whether other industries prosper or not depends on the conditions of the labor market. If surplus labor is available as in countries I, M, P, T and C, all the other industries also can grow by absorbing abundant resources, making GDP multipliers higher. If no surplus labor is available as in S, N, K, J and U, increased investment raises wage rate and reallocates scarce labor toward construction and machinery, resulting in smaller multipliers on real GDP. The assumption of labor market is crucial on the results to be obtained, at least in the level of industries.

---

[9]This is the procedure used in his CGE model of Thailand (Ezaki, 1994).

[10]Ichimura and Ezaki (1985, Ch. 13) did a similar analysis with macroeconometric models.

Table 5. Elasticity-Multipliers: Comparative Statics with Investment Increased by 1% of GDP in Each Country Individually.

To/From:	I	M	P	S	T	C	N	K	J	U	ALL
Case I: Endogenous Exchange Rate (ER)											
I	2.56	−0.01	0.00	0.00	−0.0	−0.01	0.00	0.00	0.16	0.05	3.05
M	0.04	1.53	0.02	0.02	0.00	0.03	0.01	0.01	0.42	0.22	2.22
P	0.05	0.04	2.08	0.00	0.03	0.04	0.00	0.01	0.36	0.24	3.78
S	0.00	−0.02	−0.01	0.85	−0.04	−0.06	0.02	0.00	0.10	0.05	−0.38
T	0.10	0.08	0.02	0.01	2.92	0.10	0.01	0.03	0.55	0.34	3.82
C	0.04	0.03	0.01	0.00	0.05	2.42	0.00	0.01	0.26	0.15	3.43
N	−0.07	−0.08	−0.04	0.01	−0.09	−0.09	1.07	−0.03	−0.05	−0.24	0.13
K	−0.01	−0.01	0.00	0.00	−0.03	−0.01	0.01	1.23	0.05	−0.02	0.73
J	0.00	0.00	0.00	0.00	−0.01	−0.01	0.01	0.01	1.12	−0.04	0.99
U	0.00	0.00	0.00	0.00	−0.01	0.00	0.00	0.00	0.06	1.82	1.98
Increase in Real GDP (%), Case II: Exogenous Exchange Rate (ER)											
I	1.73	0.01	0.01	0.01	0.00	0.07	0.01	0.01	0.02	1.14	4.20
M	0.04	0.73	0.03	0.03	0.03	0.10	0.02	0.02	0.07	1.79	4.32
P	0.04	0.06	1.99	0.00	0.01	0.10	0.02	0.01	0.04	2.54	6.94
S	0.06	0.07	0.01	0.87	0.06	0.07	0.02	0.03	0.16	1.91	2.80
T	0.03	0.04	0.01	0.01	1.51	0.13	0.01	0.02	0.07	2.12	5.80
C	0.02	0.01	0.01	0.00	0.00	1.82	0.00	0.00	0.02	1.09	4.21
N	−0.01	−0.01	0.01	0.03	0.02	0.02	0.69	0.02	0.09	1.50	1.95
K	0.01	0.01	0.01	0.01	0.01	0.03	0.01	1.09	0.07	1.32	2.09
J	0.02	0.01	0.00	0.00	0.01	0.06	0.01	0.02	1.44	0.95	1.85
U	0.01	0.00	0.00	0.01	0.00	0.02	0.00	0.01	0.02	1.51	1.67

Note: Column "All" means the case of investment increased in all countries at the same time.

4. Comparative Statics and Dynamics of Technology Changes

4.1. *Theory of flying-geese pattern*

Amano (1994, Ch. 6): "Evolution of Manufacturing Comparative Advantages in Asian NIEs" gave an interesting theoretical explanation to the flying-geese pattern in the case of two factors of production (labor and capital), two kinds of technology (traditional (XX) and modern ($X'X'$) of which the latter is more capital intensive), and several industries which are different in capital intensity (X, Y, Z). The figure below graphically shows this situation in terms of isoquants. The theory describes the flying-geese pattern or the process of evolution in comparative advantages by the following steps: (1) change (or jump) in technology from traditional to

Table 6. Own Elasticities: Comparative Statics with Investment Increased by 1% of GDP in Each Country Individually.

	I	M	P	S	T	C	N	K	J	U
(The Case of Endogenous Exchange Rate)										
GDP	2.56	1.53	2.08	0.85	2.92	2.42	1.07	1.23	1.12	1.82
PGDP	1.13	0.44	0.20	0.02	1.45	0.73	0.06	0.28	5.51	2.96
GDP_n	3.72	1.98	2.29	0.87	4.42	3.16	1.13	1.52	6.70	4.56
C	2.45	0.72	1.65	0.36	1.65	1.87	0.44	0.61	1.16	1.02
PC	0.96	0.84	0.22	0.02	2.03	0.80	0.02	0.21	4.96	2.65
I	4.57	3.45	6.38	2.41	4.57	3.28	5.43	3.49	3.71	6.04
PI	1.89	1.18	0.43	0.04	3.09	1.41	0.06	0.38	5.19	2.99
E	0.72	0.83	0.33	0.01	2.37	1.99	0.01	−0.01	−1.85	1.27
PE	1.58	0.82	0.23	0.01	1.95	0.91	0.03	0.23	5.00	2.71
M	1.89	0.92	1.47	0.32	0.44	0.01	0.52	0.48	3.03	0.82
PM	2.37	1.77	0.66	0.02	5.25	3.36	0.03	0.18	0.85	3.07
L^D	3.44	1.53	1.92	—	3.62	2.59	—	—	—	—
W	—	—	—	0.42	—	—	0.53	0.84	6.28	3.92
K^D	—	—	—	—	—	—	—	—	—	—
R	3.42	1.62	1.79	0.32	3.75	2.89	0.33	0.80	6.00	3.34
ER	2.27	1.69	0.67	0.02	5.14	3.22	0.04	0.17	−0.04	2.47
ER'	2.43	1.79	0.68	0.02	5.32	3.43	0.04	0.19	2.20	—
FW$	−2.22	−1.65	−0.65	−0.02	−4.88	−3.11	−0.03	−0.16	0.03	−5.37
X^S1	2.55	0.72	1.29	−0.12	2.28	1.97	−0.40	−0.41	−0.26	−0.59
X^S2	0.18	0.26	0.32	−0.19	1.01	1.28	−0.11	−0.54	−1.24	−0.57
X^S3	1.95	0.98	1.66	−0.18	1.77	1.29	−0.30	−0.41	−0.37	0.23
X^S4	1.81	0.86	0.89	−0.05	2.38	1.54	−0.15	−0.23	−0.70	−0.40
X^S5	2.38	1.14	1.27	−0.10	2.77	1.63	0.31	0.49	−0.39	1.18
X^S6	1.07	0.27	0.29	−0.08	0.57	1.06	−0.08	−0.13	−0.15	−0.45
X^S7	3.89	2.54	5.00	1.44	3.74	2.95	3.61	2.24	2.78	3.02
X^S8	1.80	0.82	0.93	−0.25	1.35	1.67	−0.11	−0.14	0.00	0.01
X^S9	2.07	0.86	0.84	−0.06	1.70	1.54	−0.19	−0.12	−0.14	−0.37
*PX*1	0.50	0.44	0.15	0.01	1.31	0.45	0.02	0.22	4.99	2.35
*PX*2	1.84	1.02	0.24	0.01	3.63	1.04	0.01	0.11	2.63	1.71
*PX*3	0.93	0.68	0.11	0.02	2.06	0.96	0.02	0.20	4.98	2.81
*PX*4	2.05	0.95	0.41	0.02	2.92	1.48	0.02	0.18	4.58	2.62
*PX*5	2.20	1.18	0.37	0.02	3.22	1.62	0.04	0.30	5.05	2.96
*PX*6	1.67	0.82	0.36	0.01	2.79	1.36	0.01	0.08	4.29	2.12
*PX*7	1.84	0.98	0.51	0.08	2.69	1.26	0.10	0.47	5.36	3.03
*PX*8	1.44	0.60	0.28	0.02	2.11	0.73	0.03	0.23	5.30	2.76
*PX*9	0.84	0.44	0.17	0.02	1.58	0.78	0.02	0.22	5.29	2.69

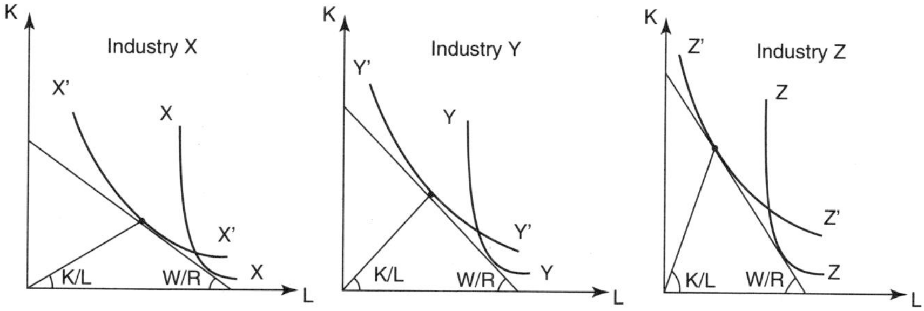

Figure 3. Theoretical Diagram for the Flying-Geese Pattern.

modern in industry X, (2) comparative advantage strengthened in industry X, (3) change in technology from traditional to modern in industry Y, (4) comparative advantage strengthened in industry Y and weakened in industry X, (5) change in technology from traditional to modern in industry Z, and so on. And this evolutionary process, which accompanies steady increase in capital intensity (K/L), is supposed to occur in accordance with steady increase in wage rental ratio (W/R). See Figure 3.

Empirical applications of this theory to Asian NIEs are also made in Amano (1994) by using three key concepts: $RCA(= (E - M)/(E + M)$ where E is exports and M is imports), capital intensity ($= K/L$), and technology intensity ($= T/L$ where T is accumulation of R&D expenditures). Data are of SITC two-digit numbers on the four Asian NIEs and Japan. A interesting finding is that RCA has significantly negative correlations with both capital and technology intensities, of which the latter is bigger in impact.

4.2. *Differences in technology*

The essence of the theory above is the steady change in technology from labor-intensive to capital-intensive within industry as well as between industries in accordance with the steady increase in wage-rental ratio. We will investigate the flying-geese pattern in East Asia or the evolutionary process of comparative advantages in East Asia along the line of this theory based on our link CGE system. For that purpose, we will first of all make clear the technology situation in East Asia in the light of our modeling framework. Our CGE system employs Cobb-Douglas production function of constant returns to scale ($X = A \cdot L^{\alpha} \cdot K^{1-\alpha}$) for all of the nine industries in all of the ten countries. This function has two parameters: scale

(A) and distribution (α). A indicates the overall efficiency in production technology or total factor productivity (TFP). α indicates the degree of labor-intensiveness in production, i.e. whether a certain specific production technology is more labor-intensive than others or not. We can compare overall efficiency and relative labor-intensiveness or capital-intensiveness between countries as well as between industries in Figure 4, which present isoquants for unit level of production ($X = 1.0$) along logarithmic scale:

$$\log K = -\log A/(1-\alpha) - \alpha/(l-\alpha) \cdot \log L$$

In the figures, intercepts indicate overall efficiency (for the same factor share, α), while slopes indicate the degree of labor-intensiveness (for the same relative factor price W/R), so that lower intercept means higher productivity, while steeper slope means stronger labor-intensive- ness. Countries may be identified by the initials in Figure 4. It shows isoquants for 10 countries in four of the 9 industries selected, which shows differences or similarities of production technology between countries. First, differences in efficiency or productivity between countries are relatively large compared with differences in labor- or capital-intensiveness.

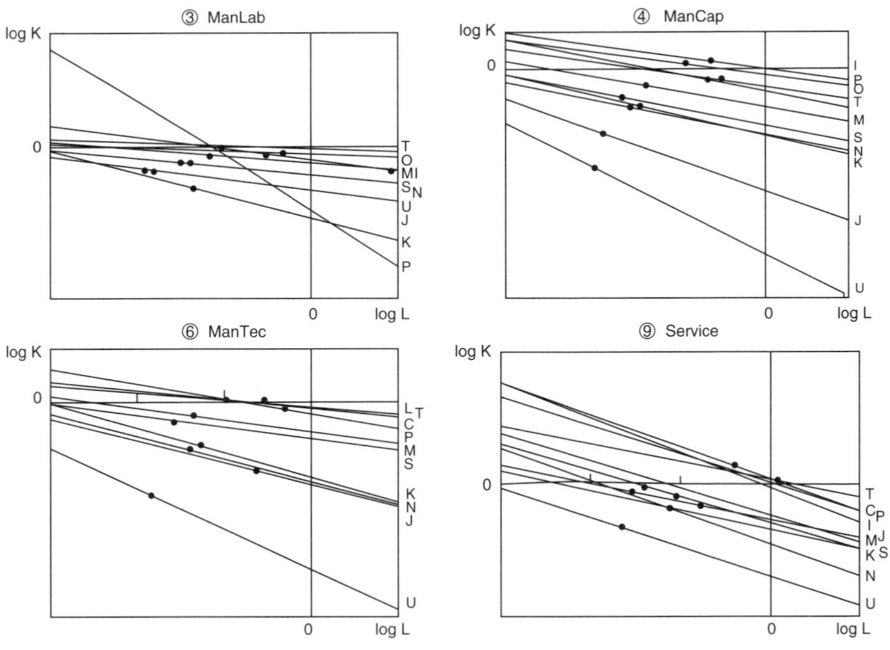

Figure 4. Isoquant of Ten Countries for Selected Industries (1985).

The service industry (9th, Service) is a typical example with only small differences in slope but with fairly large differences in intercept. Second, this is more or less true for manufacturing. However, in the case of labor intensive manufacturing (3rd, ManLab), Philippines shows an exceptionally steep slope probably due to the abnormality of the year 1985.[11] In the case of capital intensive manufacturing (4th, ManCap), on the other hand, the slopes of Japan and the US are steeper than those of other countries without exceptions, meaning the technology of Japan, and the US in this industry to be more labor-intensive, though not very much. This rather unexpected result may be said to be due to our selection of production function of the Cobb-Douglas type. If we adopt production function of the CES type for this industry:

$$X = A \cdot [\delta \cdot L^{-\rho} + (1-\delta) \cdot K^{-\rho}]^{-1/\rho} \quad (\rho = (l-\sigma)/\sigma)$$

then we get the optimal K/L as a function of wage-rental ratio (W/R):

$$K/L = (W/R)^{-\sigma} \cdot a \quad \text{where } a = ((1-\delta)/\delta)^{\sigma}$$

If the elasticity of substitution (σ) is set equal to, say, 0.5, we get $a = 4.3$ for Indonesia, $a = 10.5$ for Japan and $a = 8.8$ for the US, so that production technology in Japan and the US becomes more capital-intensive than in Indonesia unlike the case of Cobb-Douglas type (or other CGE type with $\sigma = 2.0$). In the case of machinery industry (5th, ManTec), the same may be true for US. It is, however, quite interesting to observe the proximity of technology between Japan, Korea and Taiwan in this industry.

4.3. *Comparative statics of technology changes*

Figure 4 indicates that technology does not differ much between Japan, Taiwan and Korea in labor intensive manufacturing (ManLab) and technology-intensive manufacturing (ManTec) but differs in capital-intensive manufacturing (ManCap). It indicates also that Taiwan-Korea differ in technology from ASEAN excluding Singapore and China in the three manufacturing industries.

Based on these observations, we will attempt to do comparative statics of technology changes in order to see what will happen to comparative

[11] 1985 was the third year of the debt crisis in the Philippines; real GDP growth was −7.3% in both 1984 and 1985. Malaysia and Singapore also experienced negative GDP growth in 1985 (−1.1% and −1.3% respectively).

Table 7. Scenarios for Simulation.

	$A_{i(k)}$ to $A_{i(N)}$	or $A_{i(M)}, A_{i(J)}$	$\alpha_{i(k)}$ to $\alpha_{i(N)}$	or $\alpha_{i(M)}, \alpha_{i(J)}$
Case A (ManLab)				
Indonesia	2.37	10.02	.754	.688
Malaysia	4.69	"	.637	"
Philippines	2.99	"	.934	"
Thailand	1.55	"	.469	"
China	2.06	"	.560	"
Case B (ManCap)				
Indonesia	0.98	5.92	.380	.497
Malaysia	2.90	"	.450	"
Philippines	1.17	"	.391	"
Thailand	1.77	"	.467	"
China	1.69	2.90	.473	.450
Taiwan	5.92	11.38	.497	.617
Korea	5.33	"	.517	"
Case C (ManTec)				
Indonesia	1.31	11.15	.380	.678
Malaysia	4.06	"	.516	"
Philippines	1.61	"	.585	"
Thailand	1.54	"	.427	"
China	1.64	4.06	.425	.516

advantages when ASEAN and China catch up in technology with Taiwan in each of the three industries of ManLab, ManCap and ManTec, and also when Taiwan and Korea catch up in technology with Japan in the industry ManCap. For that purpose, shocks are given to scale and distribution parameters (A and α) as follows: see Table 7.

In the shocks given above, efficiency clearly improves in each country but degree of capital intensiveness does not increase in almost all countries except for Indonesia and Philippines of ManLab (Case A). Note that shocks to China in ManCap and ManTec are given by referring to Malaysia.[12] Note also that solution with shocks are obtained by assuming equilibrium in the capital stock market only for the country with shocks in order to allow for capital re-allocation under different technologies.

[12]Shocks referring to Taiwan do not make the system converge. The same is true for comparative dynamics, where China is referred to Malaysia in all the three cases.

Results of comparative statics for Cases A, B and C are presented in Table 8, where E/X and M/X mean export and import ratios to total production in each manufacturing industry, while *RCA* (Revealed Comparative Advantage) and *RCD* (Revealed Comparative Disadvantage) are defined in real terms as:

$$RCA_{i(k)} = (E_{i(k)}/\Sigma_i E_{i(k)})/(\Sigma_k E_{i(k)}/\Sigma_i \Sigma_k E_{i(k)})$$
$$RCD_{i(k)} = (Mi(k)/\Sigma_i M_{i(k)})/(\Sigma_k M_{i(k)}/\Sigma_i \Sigma_k E_{i(k)})$$

From Table 8: Case A, we can see that ASEAN4 and China will increase more or lessen their real GDP catching up with Taiwan in labor intensive manufacturing technology. Big impacts on Thailand and then China may be said to be mainly due to big changes in efficiency parameter rather than distribution parameter. Increases in real GDP are accompanied by proportional increases in labor demand, for which no supply constraint is imposed. In the sectoral level, however, the industry with shocks (ManLab), which realizes big efficiency improvement, drastically decreases its input of labor in all countries irrespective of the direction of change in factor intensity. Output increases drastically while output price decreases drastically due to drastic efficiency improvement.

The impact of technology changes on comparative advantage of the industry is that export ratio (E/X) increases generally with only one exception, while import ratio (M/X) decreases in all countries. Improvement in comparative advantage is far clearer in terms of *RCA* and *RCD* indices. That is to say, *RCA* increases drastically in all countries while *RCD* slightly decreases in all countries. Impacts on comparative advantage of other countries, especially on relatively developed countries (i.e. N, K, J and U), are generally very small though the signs are generally of anticipated direction toward deterioration. Even when shocks are given to five countries (I, M, P, T and C) at the same time, these combined impacts on the remaining countries (N, K, J and U) are still small.

Table 8: Case A, Columns (la) and (lb) provides important results from supplementary experiments on Indonesia, where only scale parameter (A) or only distribution parameter (α) is changed. The first case [Column (la)], which allows for efficiency improvement only, gives almost the same outcome as Column (1), which allows both for efficiency improvement and strengthened capital intensiveness. However, the second case [Column (lb)], which allows for strengthened capital intensity only, gives only negligible results close to zero. Thus, we may say that the actual effect on comparative advantage is caused mainly by efficiency or TFP improvement rather than

Table 8. Impacts of Technology Changes (Comparative Statics) Case A: Labor Intensive Manufacturing Industry (Ma).

Technology Changed to	(1) Indonesia $(\Delta A, \Delta\alpha)$ Taiwan	(2) Malaysia $(\Delta A, \Delta\alpha)$ Taiwan	(3) Philip. $(\Delta A, \Delta\alpha)$ Taiwan	(4) Thailand $(\Delta A, \Delta\alpha)$ Taiwan	(5) China $(\Delta A, \Delta\alpha)$ Taiwan	(1a) Indon. $(\Delta A, -)$ Taiwan	(1b) Indon. $(-, \Delta\alpha)$ Taiwan	(1c) Indon. $(\Delta A, \Delta\alpha)$ $(K_i = K_i)$ Taiwan
(% rate of changes)								
GDP	3.34	3.07	5.31	21.7	9.19	3.5	0.13	3.34
PGDP	0.93	−2.27						
GDPn	4.31	0.73	6.42	20.8	1.63	4.56	0.12	3.69
LD	3.44	0.82	4.87	21.8	3.48	3.78	−0.01	2.42
W								
KD								
ER	6.05	3.28	12.1	48.7	15.4	6.55	0.06	6.76
ER′	6.80	3.39	12.4	50.4	18.9	7.18	0.06	7.26
FW$	−5.72	−3.18	−10.8	−32.7	−13.4	−6.16	−0.06	−6.35
XS3	40.9	28.2	53.9	87.4	35.3	40.1	5.74	46.2
PX3	−33.6	−18.3	−31.6	−31.6	−30.4	−32.9	−1.22	−36.8
LD3	−70.8	−25.6	−73.2	−37.2	−65	−66.2	−9.5	−80.2
KD3	−62.1	−41.4	+57.2	−78.8	−79.8	−68.5	+25.4	—
(level changes)								
E/X3(%)	+3.2	−0.6	+2.1	+4.1	+2.1	+3.2	−1	+3.7
From	22.9	44.2	31.5	23.9	11.2	22.9	22.9	22.9
M/X3(%)	−2.2	−3.8	−6.5	−4.3	−2.2	−2.2	−0.3	−2.4
From	5.3	15.4	15.3	7.5	5.1	5.3	5.3	5.3

(Continued)

Table 8. *(Continued)*

Technology Changed to	(1) Indonesia ($\Delta A, \Delta\alpha$) Taiwan	(2) Malaysia ($\Delta A, \Delta\alpha$) Taiwan	(3) Philip. ($\Delta A, \Delta\alpha$) Taiwan	(4) Thailand ($\Delta A, \Delta\alpha$) Taiwan	(5) China ($\Delta A, \Delta\alpha$) Taiwan	(1a) Indon. ($\Delta A, -$) Taiwan	(1b) Indon. ($-, \Delta\alpha$) Taiwan	(1c) Indon. ($\Delta A, \Delta\alpha$) ($K_i = K_i$) Taiwan
*RCA*3	+0.29	+0.17	+0.47	+0.66	+0.40	+0.28	+0.01	+0.32
From	0.56	0.91	1.25	1.81	2.12	0.56	0.56	0.56
*RCD*3	−0.04	−0.02	−0.07	−0.09	−0.1	−0.04	+0.00	−0.05
From	0.23	0.41	0.61	0.46	0.64	0.23	0.23	0.23
*RCA*3-*N*	−0.01	−0.004	−0.005	−0.02	−0.05			
*RCA*3-*K*	−0.01	−0.004	−0.005	−0.02	−0.04			
*RCA*3-*J*	−0.003	−0.001	−0.001	−0.004	−0.015			
*RCA*3-*U*	−0.002	−0.001	−0.001	−0.004	−0.007			
*RCD*3-*N*	+0.007	+0.003	+0.000	+0.004	−0.008			
*RCD*3-*K*	+0.001	+0.001	−0.001	−0.001	−0.005			
*RCD*3-*J*	+0.004	+0.001	0.000	+0.013	+0.020			
*RCD*3-*U*	−0.001	−0.001	+0.002	−0.002	+0.000			

by the change in the nature of technology from labor intensive to capital intensive one. We must confirm this by comparative dynamics since wage-rental ratio (W/R) declines in the comparative statics of Table 8: Case A. Studies of Case B and Case C are omitted in this presentation. We simply report that they show more or less the same results on capital intensive manufacturing (ManCap).

4.4. *Comparative dynamics of technology changes*

Our next study is on the dynamic impact of technology changes over a long time. Since it is very difficult to get a stable converged solution for such a large system of non-linear equations as ours for a long period, we adopt a convenient method. We first obtain a baseline solution and compare it with the solutions after shocks. We first decide target or probable growth rate of real *GDP* exogenously for ten countries, i.e. I: 6%, M: 6%, P: 5%, S: 5%, T: 7%, C: 7%, N: 5%, K: 5%, J: 3%, U: 3%. Then, making real *GDP* grow exogenously at the rates above, we simulate a modified link system [with equation (3.53) in Table 3 changed as $I = GDP - C - G - J - 0 - E + M$) for 10 periods from 1985 to 1995, and calculate real investment of each country which is consistent with exogenous *GDP* growth (by using *GDP* identity above) for the same period. Finally, treating as exogenous the real investment thus obtained, we simulate our original link system with real *GDP* now as endogenous for the same period. We must note that dynamic solution is different from static one on two scores. First, exchange rate (*ER*) is treated as exogenous, so that foreign capital inflow (*FW$*) becomes endogenous.[13]

Second, each country's capital market is assumed to be cleared instantaneously in each period [equation (3.64) but not (3.64′) in Table 3). Tables 8 and 9 present baseline solution in terms of average growth rates (1985–1995) and levels in terminal year 1995. Table 9 shows that average growth rates of *GDP* are more or less the same, though not exactly, as assigned target rates. We give the same technology shocks to our dynamic system and comparative statics to see what happens to comparative advantages when ASEAN-4 catches up in technology with Taiwan, and China with Malaysia

[13]The system converges only for the first several years when *ER* is endogenous. It seems to be too burdensome for exchange rate to play the role of adjustment factor under a rapidly changing dynamic environment.

Table 9. Impacts of Technology Changes (Comparative Dynamics): 1985–1995.

Average Growth %	Base No Change	ManLab			ManCap		MamTec	
		ΔA, $\Delta\alpha$	ΔA	$\Delta\alpha$	ΔA, $\Delta\alpha$	Δ	ΔA, $\Delta\alpha$	$\Delta\alpha$
GDP I	6.2	6.8	6.8	6.6	6.9	7.0	6.2	7.1
GDP M	6.3	7.2	7.2	6.9	7.1	7.2	6.0	7.5
GDP P	7.3	5.8	5.8	5.3	6.0	6.4	5.1	6.5
GDP S	7.2	5.2	5.2	5.2	5.1	5.2	4.9	5.2
GDP T	4.9	8.8	8.8	7.5	7.9	8.0	7.1	8.2
GDP C	5.0	7.9	7.9	7.4	7.8	7.8	7.3	7.8
GDP N	3.0	4.6	4.6	4.5	4.7	5.0	5.1	4.4
GDP K	3.0	4.9	4.9	4.9	5.1	5.2	5.0	4.9
GDP J	3.0	3.0	3.0	3.1	3.0	3.0	3.0	3.0
GDP U	3.0	2.9	2.9	2.9	2.9	2.9	3.0	2.9
PGDP I	0.4	0.3	0.3	1.2	0.2	0.1	−0.1	0.1
PGDP M	0.2	0.1	0.0	1.1	0.2	0.1	0.0	0.0
PGDP P	2.7	4.5	4.3	5.8	3.6	3.2	1.1	4.3
PGDP S	2.6	5.9	5.9	6.5	5.9	5.8	1.1	7.0
PGDP T	1.3	0.4	0.4	3.1	1.9	1.7	0.3	1.4
PGDP C	1.0	0.5	0.5	2.0	0.5	0.5	0.1	0.2
PGDP N	3.4	6.2	6.1	6.9	6.0	5.5	1.6	7.3
PGDP K	2.9	5.6	5.6	6.3	5.3	5.0	1.2	6.7
PGDP J	2.0	3.9	3.9	4.5	4.0	4.0	0.8	4.7
PGDP U	2.6	5.0	5.0	5.7	5.1	5.1	1.1	6.0
LD I	6.5	6.9	6.9	6.7	7.2	7.1	6.5	7.2
LD M	6.1	6.9	6.8	6.9	6.9	6.8	6.2	7.1
LD P	6.3	6.6	6.7	5.3	6.4	8.0	4.6	8.3
LD T	7.4	8.7	8.5	7.8	7.8	8.5	6.9	8.6
LD C	7.2	7.9	7.8	7.3	7.9	7.8	7.5	7.7
LD S, N, K, J, U → 1.0								
W S	6.0	9.7	9.7	10.4	9.7	9.6	4.3	11.0
W N	6.5	9.2	9.2	10.0	9.5	9.2	4.6	10.3
W K	6.1	8.9	8.9	9.7	9.1	8.8	4.3	10.1
W J	3.3	5.4	5.4	6.0	5.5	5.4	2.1	6.1
W U	4.0	6.4	6.4	7.1	6.5	6.5	2.5	7.4
W I, M, P, T, → PGDP								
R I	0.8	1.5	1.5	2.0	1.3	1.2	0.5	1.4
R M	0.1	0.7	0.8	1.4	0.8	0.7	−0.2	0.8
R P	7.3	9.8	9.6	10.4	8.5	8.8	5.0	10.3
R S	1.0	4.4	4.4	5.1	4.4	4.3	−0.5	5.6
R T	2.5	3.0	3.1	3.9	3.7	3.7	1.4	3.5
R C	2.1	2.3	2.4	3.1	2.1	2.1	1.4	1.8
R N	1.4	3.9	3.9	4.6	3.5	3.6	−0.3	4.9

(*Continued*)

Table 9. (*Continued*)

Average Growth %	Base No Change		ManLab			ManCap		MamTec	
			ΔA, $\Delta\alpha$	ΔA	$\Delta\alpha$	ΔA, $\Delta\alpha$	Δ	ΔA, $\Delta\alpha$	$\Delta\alpha$
R K	−0.5		2.1	2.0	2.8	1.7	1.6	−2.0	3.1
R J	1.9		3.9	3.9	4.5	4.0	3.9	0.7	4.6
R U	3.0		5.4	5.4	6.0	5.5	5.4	1.5	6.3
Level %	'85	'95	'95	'95	'95	'95	'95	'95	'95
FW$/GDP I	2.1	4.8	3.5	3.5	2.9	2.5	2.3	5.2	1.7
FW$/GDP M	1.9	15.4	13.6	13.6	12.4	13.2	12.7	18.0	12.4
FW$/GDP P	0.1	0.5	−1.1	0.0	−2.3	−1.8	−0.8	0.3	−1.4
FW$/GDP S	0.0	−8.6	−13.0	−13.0	−13.5	−12.9	−13.0	−6.0	−14.4
FW$/GDP T	4.1	9.4	9.3	9.4	6.6	6.9	7.4	10.4	6.7
FW$/GDP C	3.8	6.6	6.0	6.0	5.6	5.3	5.2	7.3	4.8
FW$/GDP N	−15.2	−10.6	−11.1	−11.1	−11.5	−11.3	−11.5	−10.5	−11.3
FW$/GDP K	0.9	−0.2	−1.4	−1.4	−1.7	−1.5	−1.5	0.8	−1.8
FW$/GDP J	−3.7	−7.4	−7.8	−7.8	−7.9	−7.7	−7.7	−7.0	−7.8
FW$/GDP U	2.8	2.1	1.9	1.9	1.9	2.0	2.0	2.1	1.9

in each of the three manufacturing industries (ManLab, ManCap and ManTec), and also when Taiwan and Korea catch up with Japan in the industry of ManCap. In the dynamic context, however, we will show only the case of lump sum shocks divided and smoothed over 10 years of the simulation period. In other words, shocks are given to each industry annually by the following amounts (and accumulated) given to all countries in question for each industry but with total shocks.

<ManLab, ManTec>

$0.1 \times (A_{3(N)} - A_{3(k)})$ and $0.1 \times (\alpha_{3(N)} - \alpha_{3(k)})$ for $k =$ I,M,P,T

$0.1 \times (A_{3(M)} - A_{3(k)})$ and $0.1 \times (\alpha_{3(M)} \sim \alpha_{3(k)})$ for $k =$ C

<ManCap> $0.1 \times (A_{4(N)} - A_{4(k)})$ and $0.1 \times (\alpha_{4(N)} - \alpha_{4(k)})$ for $k =$ I,M,P,T

$0.1 \times (A_{4(M)} - A_{4(k)})$ and $0.1 \times (\alpha_{4(M)} - \alpha_{4(M)})$ for $k =$ C

$0.1 \times (A_{4(J)} - A_{4(k)})$ and $0.1 \times (\alpha_{4(J)} - \alpha_{4(k)})$ for $k =$ N,K

Dynamic solutions with these shocks are presented in terms of growth rates and levels in Tables 9 and 10 (columns of ΔA, $\Delta\alpha$). The two tables also include solutions with shocks given either to scale parameters only (columns of ΔA) or to distribution parameters only (columns of $\Delta\alpha$).

Table 10. Impacts of Technology Changes (Comparative Dynamics): 1985–1995.

	Base	ManLab					Base	ManCap				Base	ManTec		
	No Changes	ΔA	$\Delta\alpha$	ΔA	$\Delta\alpha$		No Changes	ΔA	$\Delta\alpha$	ΔA		No Changes	ΔA	$\Delta\alpha$	ΔA
	1985	1995	1995	1995	1995		1985	1995	1995	1995		1985	1995	1995	1995
E/X3% I	22.9	20.1	25.1	25.0	22.6	*E/X4* I	11.3	8.8	11.1	11.3	*E/X5* I	2.9	2.6	2.6	3.5
E/X3% M	44.2	38.8	42.3	42.6	40.9	*E/X4* M	34.5	28.0	29.2	29.7	*E/X5* M	58.4	46.8	42.9	48.9
E/X3% P	31.5	26.2	29.0	28.8	28.2	*E/X4* P	15.5	12.4	14.8	14.0	*E/X5* P	43.0	42.8	45.3	47.4
E/X3% S	65.3	69.2	69.1	69.1	68.6	*E/X4* S	44.7	51.1	49.8	49.8	*E/X5* S	78.6	86.5	85.3	88.0
E/X3% T	23.9	19.2	21.7	21.9	19.8	*E/X4* T	15.0	11.3	12.7	12.4	*E/X4* T	15.9	11.7	12.2	14.6
E/X3% C	11.2	9.1	10.8	10.8	10.3	*E/X4* C	3.1	2.3	2.7	2.7	*E/X4* C	3.2	2.7	2.5	3.7
E/X3% N	57.1	60.9	59.9	59.9	60.0	*E/X4* N	16.4	17.8	17.2	18.0	*E/X4* N	51.8	49.4	49.7	48.4
E/X3% K	44.0	46.0	45.0	45.0	45.0	*E/X4* K	13.6	14.7	14.7	15.3	*E/X4* K	32.6	32.1	31.8	31.2
E/X3% J	11.4	13.5	13.3	13.3	13.5	*E/X4* J	7.8	10.4	9.7	9.7	*E/X4* J	25.8	31.9	31.4	31.1
E/X3% U	5.5	6.0	5.7	5.7	5.7	*E/X4* U	5.2	6.3	5.7	5.7	*E/X4* U	11.5	13.3	13.5	12.3
RCA3 I	0.56	0.71	1.03	1.02	0.76	*RCA4* I	0.23	0.27	0.45	0.47	*RCA5* I	0.03	0.05	0.07	0.08
RCA3 M	0.91	0.97	1.14	1.17	0.94	*RCA4* M	0.64	0.65	0.73	0.75	*RCA5* M	0.58	0.59	0.66	0.71
RCA3 P	1.25	1.32	1.72	1.69	1.38	*RCA4* P	0.85	0.76	1.02	1.02	*RCA5* P	0.66	0.72	1.04	1.08
RCA3 S	0.49	0.45	0.42	0.42	0.43	*RCA4* S	0.56	0.58	0.52	0.52	*RCA5* S	1.06	1.05	1.04	1.04
RCA3 T	1.81	1.83	2.48	2.55	1.59	*RCA4* T	0.45	0.46	0.59	0.58	*RCA5* T	0.25	0.27	0.37	0.39
RCA3 C	2.12	2.22	2.47	2.48	2.22	*RCA4* C	0.59	0.60	0.68	0.68	*RCA5* C	0.25	0.27	0.33	0.34
RCA3 N	2.71	2.63	2.54	2.54	2.58	*RCA4* N	0.72	0.74	0.76	0.86	*RCA5* N	0.91	0.89	0.88	0.92
RCA3 K	2.59	2.46	2.38	2.38	2.42	*RCA4* K	0.93	0.95	1.04	1.13	*RCA5* K	0.89	0.90	0.89	0.92
RCA3 J	0.65	0.59	0.57	0.57	0.59	*RCA4* J	0.95	0.91	0.88	0.87	*RCA5* J	2.10	1.94	1.93	2.00
RCA3 U	0.60	0.56	0.55	0.55	0.55	*RCA4* U	1.00	0.94	0.92	0.92	*RCA5* U	1.49	1.46	1.45	1.49

(*Continued*)

Table 10. *(Continued)*

	Base	ManLab					Base	ManCap				Base	ManTec		
	No Changes	ΔA	$\Delta \alpha$	ΔA	$\Delta \alpha$		No Changes	ΔA	$\Delta \alpha$	ΔA		No Changes	ΔA	$\Delta \alpha$	ΔA
	1985	1995	1995	1995	1995		1985	1995	1995	1995		1985	1995	1995	1995
*RCD*3 I	0.23	0.21	0.16	0.16	0.18	*RCD*4 I	1.79	1.79	1.57	1.56	*RCD*5 I	1.23	1.16	1.02	1.01
RCD3 M	0.41	0.35	0.33	0.33	0.35	*RCD*4 M	1.21	1.12	1.12	1.11	*RCD*5 M	1.25	1.38	1.39	1.42
*RCD*3 P	0.61	0.65	0.59	0.60	0.63	*RCD*4 P	1.03	1.08	0.95	0.95	*RCD*5 P	0.81	0.79	0.76	0.69
*RCD*3 S	0.62	0.69	0.76	0.76	0.72	*RCD*4 S	0.76	0.78	0.82	0.82	*RCD*5 S	0.82	0.83	0.85	0.83
*RCD*3 T	0.46	0.44	0.37	0.37	0.46	*RCD*4 T	1.42	1.39	1.29	1.29	*RCD*5 T	0.79	0.80	0.73	0.68
*RCD*3 C	0.65	0.63	0.58	0.58	0.64	*RCD*4 C	2.01	2.02	1.98	1.98	*RCD*5 C	1.23	1.09	1.01	0.98
*RCD*3 N	0.51	0.50	0.52	0.52	0.51	*RCD*4 N	1.30	1.19	1.19	1.12	*RCD*5 N	0.79	0.90	0.92	0.89
*RCD*3 K	0.47	0.47	0.47	0.47	0.47	*RCD*4 K	1.11	1.02	0.99	0.95	*RCD*5 K	0.82	0.88	0.90	0.89
*RCD*3 J	0.53	0.57	0.61	0.61	0.58	*RCD*4 J	0.79	0.80	0.87	0.87	*RCD*5 J	0.26	0.25	0.26	0.25
*RCD*3 U	1.11	1.11	1.09	1.09	1.08	*RCD*4 U	0.84	0.79	0.83	0.84	*RCD*5 U	1.28	1.24	1.27	1.24

Note: (1) Technology change is (I, M, P, T) → N and C → M for ManLab, (I, M, P, T) → N, V → M and (N, K) → J for ManCap, (I, M, P, T) → N and C → M for Mantec. (2) Technology change is assumed to occur gradually by 1/10 ev(3) $CA = (E_{i(k)}/\Sigma Ei_{(k)})/(\Sigma_i E_{i(k)}/(\Sigma_i \Sigma E_{i(k)})$. $RCD_{i(k)} = (M_{i(k)}/\Sigma_i M_{i(k)})/(\Sigma_k M_{i(k)}/\Sigma_i \Sigma_k M_{i(k)})$.

Let us concentrate on the case of labor intensive manufacturing industry (ManLab) as before. Technology catching up of ASEAN-4 and China accelerates *GDP* and employment growth of these countries, causing improvement in inflation (*PGDP*) and the balance of payments deficit (*FW$/GDP*). It prevents export ratios of the industry (E/X) from declining and import ratios of the industry (M/X) from rising. It improves comparative advantages of the industry drastically in terms of *RCA* while comparative disadvantages of the industry moderately in terms of *RCD*. In relation with other countries such as NIEs, Japan and the United States, it decelerates *GDP* growth of these countries only slightly, causing inflation (*PGDP*), wage hike (W) and capital outflow (*FW$/GDP*). As to the comparative advantage position of these countries, it deteriorates their position in the negative direction though only slightly.

In what way will this situation change, if technology shocks are given only to efficiency parameter A but not to both A and α? In Tables 9 and 10, ManLab, we can see almost no differences between "both A and α" and "only A" in growth performance, employment, inflation, balance of payments deficit, export and import ratios, and *RCA* and *RCD* indices. On the other hand, we get fairly different results if technology shocks are given only to distribution parameter α. That is to say, growth and employment performance in this case is rather closer to baseline results with no shocks or in-between at most.

The same is true for export and import ratios and *RCD*, and definitely true for *RCA*. Especially for Indonesia, a high *RCA* level achieved by "both A and α" is achieved also by "only A", while the level of *RCA* achieved by "only α" is almost the same as baseline level with no shocks. And in Indonesia, this improvement in *RCA* under technology change is accompanied by the increase in wage rental ratio (W/R). We can say also from the comparative dynamics point of view that actual change in comparative advantage, if it is caused by technology changes, will be caused mainly by efficiency or TFP improvement rather than by the change in the nature of technology from labor intensive to capital intensive one. We may be able to get more or less similar observations from comparative dynamics on the remaining two industries of ManCap and ManTec.

5. Concluding Remarks

The flying-geese pattern of development of Akamatsu has been widely applied to the development of East Asian countries, and Amano (1994) gave an interesting theoretical argument to such an evolutionary process of comparative advantages. The process accompanies shifts in technology and industries from labor-intensive to capital-intensive in accordance with steady rise in wage-rental ratio. We have attempted to substantiate this kind of arguments by using a link CGE system consisting of ten East Asian countries and the rest of the world and obtained the following findings by comparative static and dynamic analyses.

If actual and significant changes in comparative advantages take place by technology changes, they are caused not by the changed types of technology such as labor-intensive to capital-intensive but rather efficiency or productivity closely related to growth in total factor productivity (TFP). Our conclusion is that as Krugman (1994)[14] provocatively said, TFP growth is a crucial factor for the East Asian miracle.

Our finding above is based on the link CGE modeling, but we must add some reservations. First, production, consumption and aggregation functions are all of Cobb-Douglas type. They are better replaced by more sophisticated ones such as CES, and parameter values in dynamic simulations must be changed over time. Second, computation method needs to be improved especially to lessen errors and discrepancies in the identities leading to Walras' Law. Third, since foreign direct investment (FDI) is of crucial importance to technology in contemporary East Asia, FDI must be introduced into our system. These are some of our important technical problems to be tackled in the next stage of our link study.

References

Adelraan, I. and S. Robinson (1978). *Income Distribution Policy in Developing Countries: A Case Study of Korea.* Oxford University Press.

Akamatsu, K. (1935). Trade of Woolen Products in Japan. *Studies of Commerce and Economy*, July (Japanese).

Akamatsu, K. (1956). Flying-Geese Pattern of Industrial Development in Japan — On Machinery Industry. Hitotsubashi University Studies, November.

Akamatsu, K. (1962). A Historical Pattern of Economic Growth in Developing Countries. *The Developing Economies*, March–August.

Amano, A. (1994). *Study of World Economy-Development and Interdependence.* Tokyo: Yuhi-kaku (Japanese).

Balassa, B. (1965). Trade Liberalization and "Revealed" Comparative Advantage. *The Manchester School of Economic and Social Studies*, May, 99–124.

[14]See also Young (1994) and Kim and Lau (1994).

Chen, E. K. Y. (1995). Foreign Direct Investment and Technology Transfer in East Asia. Paper presented at the Symposium East Asian Economic Development held at MITI, Tokyo, on April 6–7.

Dervis, K. J. De Melo and S. Robinson (1982). *General Equilibrium Models for Development Policy*. Cambridge University Press.

Ezaki, M. (1994). A Computable General Equilibrium (CGE) Analysis of the Thai Economy. In H. Motamen-Scobie (ed.), *Economic Progress and Growth*. Chapman and Hall, pp. 177–220.

Ezaki, M. (1995). Growth and Structural Changes in Asian Countries. *Asian Economic Journal*, 9(2), July, 113–136.

Ichimura, S. (ed.) (1988). *Challenge of Asian Developing Countries: Issues and Analysis*. Asian Productivity Organization.

Ichimura, S. and M. Ezaki (eds.) (1985). *Econometric Models of Asian Link*. Tokyo: Springer-Verlag.

Institute of Developing Economies (1992). Asian International Input-Output Table 1985. IDE. Statistical Data Series No. 65, IDE, Tokyo, September.

Kim, J. and L. J. Lau (1994). The Sources of Economic Growth of the East Asian Newly Industrializing Countries. *Journal of the Japanese and International Economies*, 8(3), September, 235–271.

Kojima, K. (1973). Re-organization of North-South Trade: Japan's Foreign Economic Policy for the 1970s. *Hitotsubashi Journal of Economics*, 13(2), February, 1–28.

Krugman, P. (1994). The Myth of the Asia's Miracle. *Foreign Affairs*, November/December.

Lee, H. and D. Roland-Hoist (1995). CGE modeling of Trade and Employment in Pacific Rim Countries. Irvine Economic Paper No. 94–95-11, Department of Economics, University of California, Irvine, January.

Vernon, R. (1966). International Investment and International Trade in Product Cycle. *Quarterly Journal of Economics*, 80, May.

Watanabe, T. and H. Kajiwara (1983). *Era of Horizontal Trade in Asia*. JETRO, (Japanese).

Watanabe, T. and JETRO (1989). *Era of Industrial Revolution in Asia*. JETRO, (Japanese).

Watanabe, T., H. Kajiwara and K. Takanaka (1991). *Era of Interdependence in Asia*. Yuhi-Kaku (Japanese).

Yamazawa, I. (1984). *Japan's Economic Development and International Trade*. Toyo Keizai Shinpo-sha (Japanese).

Yamazawa, I. and T. Watanabe (1988). Industrial Restructuring and Technology Transfer. In S. Ichimura, Ch. 6, pp. 203–226.

Yamazawa I. *et al.* (1993). Dynamic Interdependence among the Asia-Pacific Economies. *Keizai Bunseki*, No. 129, March.

Young, A. (1994). The Tyranny of Numbers: Confronting the Statistical Realities of the East Asian Growth Experience. Working Paper No. 4680, National Bureau of Economic Research, March.

Chapter 7

A Flow-of-Funds Analysis of Quantitative Monetary Policy*

Kazusuke Tsujimura and Masako Tsujimura

1. Introduction

Flow-of-funds (FOF) analysis stems from Copeland (1947, 1949). Since then, it has developed as an accounting system describing the intersectoral financial transactions between the institutional sectors. FOF accounts were included in the System of National Accounts in 1968, along with National Income Accounts, National Balance Sheets, Balance of International Payments Accounts and IO Tables. FOF accounts consist of balance sheets of the institutional sectors, in their traditional tabulation practice. This FOF format is widely employed because of the ease of compilation based on the corporate accounting system.

To bring FOF accounts into practical economic analysis, several attempts have been made since the early days of FOF development. It is possible to classify the analytical framework of FOF into three large groups. First, Powelson (1960) and Mathews (1962) extended the idea by making full use of the quadruple-entry system originally proposed by Copeland (1952). Alford (1986) brought this accounting-oriented technique to completion. The disadvantage of this technique for policy examination, however, is the existence of multiple (i.e. non-unique) solutions. Second, Dawson (1958), Cohen (1963), Hamada (1969), Tobin (1969) and Alho (1991) developed

*This is taken, after a slight modification, from "Asset-Liability-Matrix Analysis Derived from Flow-of-Funds Accounts: The Bank of Japan's Quantitative Monetary Policy Examined," *Economic Systems Research*, 2003 (Vol. 15, No. 1, pp. 51–67), copyright © International Input-Output Association (IIOA), reprinted by permission of Taylor & Francis Ltd (http://www.tandf.co.uk/journals) on behalf of the International Input-Output Association (IIOA).

general equilibrium models based on FOF accounts. Later, these studies expanded into SAM-CGE models, using traditional FOF as part of them. The problem is that this kind of model tries to include all economic activities at once, which makes it rather difficult to examine the effects of detailed changes in a particular policy. Third, Stone (1966) and Klein (1983) proposed converting balance sheets of FOF accounts into a square matrix, called the asset-liability matrix (ALM), by means of the supply-and-use method that is widely employed in the compilation of the System of National Accounts (see United Nations, 1999). The merit of the square matrix is that we can apply the affluent assets of IO analysis to the FOF data. That is, ALM makes it possible to examine the effects of a certain policy on each separate institutional sector from the perspective of inter-sectoral financial transactions.

The first purpose of this chapter is to present the compilation procedure of ALM in order to study the ideas of Stone and Klein. The second purpose is to demonstrate an application of ALM in the examination of the quantitative monetary policy that the Bank of Japan (BOJ) introduced in March 2001 then, after the terrorist attacks on 11 September 2001, revised accordingly in line with other central banks.

The use of ALM in FOF analysis enables us to utilize one of the most valuable assets of IO analysis originated in Leontief (1941). There are several fundamental differences, however, between the ALM and IO analyses. In the $\boldsymbol{Y}$-table of the ALM, which is the sector-by-sector matrix, the column denotes the portfolio of fund-raising, while the row indicates the portfolio of fund-employment of a particular institutional sector. In this sense, the ALM is an IO matrix that describes the flow of funds. However, it is also possible to construct an IO matrix that gives an account of the flow of financial instruments instead of the flow of funds. The column of this type of ALM ($\boldsymbol{Y}^*$-table) denotes the portfolio of fund-employment, while the row indicates the portfolio of fund-raising. In this context, the matrix $\boldsymbol{Y}^*$ is a transposition of matrix $\boldsymbol{Y}$. This two-sided nature of ALM gives a significant theoretical importance to the FOF analysis. The simultaneous equations symbolised by the $\boldsymbol{Y}$-tables portray the relations between the excess liabilities and the control total, while those represented by the $\boldsymbol{Y}^*$-table depict the correspondence between the excess financial assets and the control total. The coexistence of these two systems of equations gives two alternative Leontief inverses to the structure of ALM. This distinctive feature of ALM is best demonstrated in the investigation of the quantitative monetary policy adopted by the BOJ.

In the spring of 2001, the BOJ announced that it would shift the target of money market operation from the interbank interest rate to the balance of current accounts held by the financial institutions at the central bank. Simultaneously, the BOJ proclaimed it was to increase the balance of current accounts by one trillion Yen, while adding the same amount of Japanese Government Bonds (JGB) on its assets. There is an asymmetry in the propagation of the supply and demand of the funds in the financial system. The demand for funds should be eventually financed by the "gross induced savings" (GIS), while the supply of funds brings "gross induced investments" (GII) in due course. The quantitative monetary policy requires the central bank to choose two items simultaneously, one in assets and another in liabilities. The aforementioned action changes GII on the one hand and GIS on the other. The asymmetry in the propagation process gives "net induced investments" (NII) as a difference between GII and GIS. The sign and the amount of the NII is nothing but an indicator of the effect of the monetary policy made on the real economy. A policy that induces a positive NII gives an expansion in the economy, so that it will be welcomed, especially in the course of a recession. In contrast, a money market operation that yields a negative NII, i.e. net induced savings (NIS), weakens the economy so that this should be avoided at any cost while the depression prevails. We conclude the chapter with an evaluation of the BOJ's quantitative monetary policy in terms of the ALM analysis.

2. Asset Liability Matrix

2.1. *E- and R-tables*

Japanese Flow-of-Funds Accounts are based on the 1993 IMF Manual and compiled by the BOJ every three months (for details, see IMF, 2000; BOJ, 1999, 2000). The ALM used in this chapter has been compiled from the Financial Assets and Liabilities tables of the FOF in the first quarter of 2001. The first step to draw up an ALM is to pick out the assets and liabilities vectors separately from the balance sheets of the FOF in order to construct two matrices $\boldsymbol{E}$ and $\boldsymbol{R}$. $\boldsymbol{E}$ is a matrix that shows the portfolio of fund-employment of each institutional sector, $\boldsymbol{\varepsilon}$ and $\boldsymbol{t}^E$ are vectors that represent, respectively, excess liabilities and the sum of each row. Likewise, $\boldsymbol{R}$ is a matrix that shows the portfolio of fund-raising of each institutional sector, and $\boldsymbol{\rho}$ and $\boldsymbol{t}^R$ are vectors that represent excess assets and the sum of each row, respectively. $\boldsymbol{t}$ is the vector that consists of either the sum of assets or liabilities, whichever is greater. n and m denote the number of financial instruments and the number of institutional sectors. The structure of the $\boldsymbol{E}$- and $\boldsymbol{R}$-tables in terms of their components is depicted in Figures 1 and 2.

e_{11}	e_{12}	$\cdots$	e_{1m}	t_1^E
e_{21}	e_{22}	$\cdots$	e_{2m}	t_2^E
$\vdots$	$\vdots$	$\ddots$	$\vdots$	$\vdots$
e_{n1}	e_{n2}	$\cdots$	e_{nm}	t_n^E
ε_1	ε_2	$\cdots$	ε_m	
t_1	t_2	$\cdots$	t_m	

Figure 1. E-Table.

r_{11}	r_{12}	$\cdots$	r_{1m}	t_1^R
r_{21}	r_{22}	$\cdots$	r_{2m}	t_2^R
$\vdots$	$\vdots$	$\ddots$	$\vdots$	$\vdots$
r_{n1}	r_{n2}	$\cdots$	r_{nm}	t_n^R
ρ_1	ρ_2	$\cdots$	ρ_m	
t_1	t_2	$\cdots$	t_m	

Figure 2. R-Table.

2.2. *Y- and Y*-tables*

The ALM based on the fund-raising portfolio is denoted by $\boldsymbol{Y}$, while the one based on fund-employment is symbolized by $\boldsymbol{Y}^*$. We use superscript * in the case of the fund-employment assumption. To compile the $\boldsymbol{Y}$-table in accordance with the fund-raising portfolio, first matrix $\boldsymbol{R}$ is substituted for matrix $\boldsymbol{U}$ (commodity by sector) and the transposed matrix $\boldsymbol{E}'$ is substituted for $\boldsymbol{V}$ (sector by commodity). That is

$$\boldsymbol{U} \equiv \boldsymbol{R}, \tag{2.1}$$

$$\boldsymbol{V} \equiv \boldsymbol{E}'. \tag{2.2}$$

In the case of the $\boldsymbol{Y}^*$-table that represents the fund-employment portfolio, we take matrix $\boldsymbol{E}$ as $\boldsymbol{U}^*$ and $\boldsymbol{R}'$ as $\boldsymbol{V}^*$.

$$\boldsymbol{U}^* \equiv \boldsymbol{E}, \tag{2.3}$$

$$\boldsymbol{V}^* \equiv \boldsymbol{R}'. \tag{2.4}$$

The coefficient matrices $\boldsymbol{B}$ and $\boldsymbol{B}^*$ are constructed by dividing the cells in each column of $\boldsymbol{U}$ and $\boldsymbol{U}^*$ by the column sums $\boldsymbol{t}$.

$$b_{ij} = \frac{u_{ij}}{t_j}, \tag{2.5}$$

$$b^*_{ij} = \frac{u^*_{ij}}{t_j}. \tag{2.6}$$

In the same manner, coefficient matrices $\boldsymbol{D}$ and $\boldsymbol{D}^*$ corresponding to $\boldsymbol{V}$ and $\boldsymbol{V}^*$ are defined as

$$d_{ij} = \frac{v_{ij}}{t^E_j}, \tag{2.7}$$

$$d^*_{ij} = \frac{v^*_{ij}}{t^R_j}, \tag{2.8}$$

where t^E_j is the sum of assets and t^R_j is the sum of liabilities for financial instrument j. Hence, d_{ij} is regarded as institutional sector i's share of assets for financial instrument j, while d^*_{ij} is institutional sector i's share of liabilities for financial instrument j. The $m \times m$ coefficient matrices $\boldsymbol{C}$ and $\boldsymbol{C}^*$ corresponding to $\boldsymbol{Y}$ and $\boldsymbol{Y}^*$ are estimated using the institutional sector portfolio assumption: an equivalent of the industry technology assumption in the scheme of IO analysis.

$$\boldsymbol{C} = \boldsymbol{DB}, \tag{2.9}$$

$$\boldsymbol{C}^* = \boldsymbol{D}^*\boldsymbol{B}^*. \tag{2.10}$$

Using these matrices $\boldsymbol{C}$ and $\boldsymbol{C}^*$, transaction quantity matrices $\boldsymbol{Y}$ and $\boldsymbol{Y}^*$ are obtained in the following manner:

$$y_{ij} = c_{ij}t_j, \tag{2.11}$$

$$y^*_{ij} = c^*_{ij}t_j, \tag{2.12}$$

where y_{ij} is the amount of funds provided from institutional sector i to institutional sector j, and y^*_{ij} is the amount of financial instruments supplied from institutional sector i to institutional sector j. These tables are shown in Figures 3 and 4.

When we compare the $\boldsymbol{Y}^*$-table with the $\boldsymbol{Y}$-table, the vectors $\boldsymbol{\varepsilon}^Y$ and $\boldsymbol{\rho}^Y$ are situated symmetrically. Moreover, matrix $\boldsymbol{Y}^*$ is obtained by interchanging matrix $\boldsymbol{Y}$'s rows and columns. As demonstrated in the Appendix, whether we adapt the fund-raising assumption or the fund-employment assumption, only one transaction quantity matrix is derived from a pair of

y_{11}	y_{12}	$\cdots$	y_{1m}	ε_1^Y	t_1^Y
y_{21}	y_{22}	$\cdots$	y_{2m}	ε_2^Y	t_2^Y
$\vdots$	$\vdots$	$\ddots$	$\vdots$	$\vdots$	$\vdots$
y_{m1}	y_{m2}	$\cdots$	y_{mm}	ε_m^Y	t_m^Y
ρ_1^Y	ρ_2^Y	$\cdots$	ρ_m^Y		
t_1^Y	t_2^Y	$\cdots$	t_m^Y		

Figure 3. Y-Table.

y_{11}^*	y_{12}^*	$\cdots$	y_{1m}^*	ρ_1^Y	t_1^Y
y_{21}^*	y_{22}^*	$\cdots$	y_{2m}^*	ρ_2^Y	t_2^Y
$\vdots$	$\vdots$	$\ddots$	$\vdots$	$\vdots$	$\vdots$
y_{m1}^*	y_{m2}^*	$\cdots$	y_{mm}^*	ρ_m^Y	t_m^Y
ε_1^Y	ε_2^Y	$\cdots$	ε_m^Y		
t_1^Y	t_2^Y	$\cdots$	t_m^Y		

Figure 4. Y^*-Table.

matching $\boldsymbol{E}$ and $\boldsymbol{R}$. In that sense, the matrices $\boldsymbol{Y}$ and $\boldsymbol{Y}^*$ are just like two sides of the same coin.

3. Methodologies

3.1. *ALM with BOJ as exogenous institutional sector*

The objective of this paper is to analyze the effect of monetary policy by estimating the induced amount of demand and supply of funds through the intersectoral financial transactions represented by the Leontief inverse. It is, therefore, necessary to deal with BOJ as an exogenous institutional sector. We define the vectors $\boldsymbol{\varepsilon}_J^Y$ and $\boldsymbol{\rho}_J^Y$ as follows:

$$\boldsymbol{\varepsilon}_J^Y = \begin{bmatrix} \varepsilon_{BOJ,1}^Y + \varepsilon_1^Y \\ \varepsilon_{BOJ,2}^Y + \varepsilon_2^Y \\ \vdots \\ \varepsilon_{BOJ,m}^Y + \varepsilon_m^Y \end{bmatrix}, \quad \boldsymbol{\rho}_J^Y = \begin{bmatrix} \rho_{BOJ,1}^Y + \rho_1^Y \\ \rho_{BOJ,2}^Y + \rho_2^Y \\ \vdots \\ \rho_{BOJ,m}^Y + \rho_m^Y \end{bmatrix}.$$

$\boldsymbol{C}_{BOJ}$ is the matrix obtained from matrix $\boldsymbol{C}$ by removing the row and column containing elements concerning the BOJ. Likewise $\boldsymbol{C}^*_{BOJ}$ is the matrix obtained from matrix $\boldsymbol{C}^*$ by removing the row and column containing BOJ elements.

The fundamental equations with respect to the $\boldsymbol{Y}$- and $\boldsymbol{Y}^*$-tables are expressed as follows:

$$\boldsymbol{C}_{BOJ}\boldsymbol{t}^Y + \boldsymbol{\varepsilon}_J^Y = \boldsymbol{t}^Y, \tag{3.1}$$

$$\boldsymbol{C}^*_{BOJ}\boldsymbol{t}^Y + \boldsymbol{\rho}_J^Y = \boldsymbol{t}^Y. \tag{3.2}$$

Solving each equation for $\boldsymbol{t}^Y$ yields

$$\boldsymbol{t}^Y = (\boldsymbol{I} - \boldsymbol{C}_{BOJ})^{-1}\boldsymbol{\varepsilon}_J^Y, \tag{3.3}$$

$$\boldsymbol{t}^Y = (\boldsymbol{I} - \boldsymbol{C}^*_{BOJ})^{-1}\boldsymbol{\rho}_J^Y, \tag{3.4}$$

where $\boldsymbol{I}$ denotes the $(m-1) \times (m-1)$ unit matrix, $(\boldsymbol{I} - \boldsymbol{C}_{BOJ})^{-1}$ is the $(m-1) \times (m-1)$ Leontief inverse matrix, which gives the demand for funds as induced by each institutional sector, and $(\boldsymbol{I} - \boldsymbol{C}^*_{BOJ})^{-1}$ is the $(m-1) \times (m-1)$ Leontief inverse matrix, by which we can calculate the amount of the ultimately induced supply of funds. From the viewpoint of the real economy, the induced demand for funds is the gross induced savings (GIS), the amount of new savings required, while the induced supply of funds refers to the gross induced investments (GII) that enables us to make still more investments.

3.2. *Evaluation of quantitative monetary policy*

It is possible to calculate the effect of quantitative monetary policy carried out by BOJ using the Leontief inverse in the same framework described above. $\boldsymbol{\varepsilon}_{BOJ}$ is the $n \times 1$ vector of liabilities held by BOJ in the form of financial instrument i, i.e. $\varepsilon_{BOJ,i}$. The $n \times 1$ vector $\boldsymbol{\rho}_{BOJ}$ is the assets vector where element $\rho_{BOJ,i}$ denotes the financial instrument i held by BOJ. Vectors $\boldsymbol{\varepsilon}_{BOJ}$ and $\boldsymbol{\rho}_{BOJ}$ then should be transformed into $(m-1) \times 1$ vectors $\boldsymbol{\varepsilon}^Y_{BOJ}$ and $\boldsymbol{\rho}^Y_{BOJ}$, each of which is classified by the institutional sector in order to make it possible to use the Leontief inverse. $\boldsymbol{\varepsilon}^Y_{BOJ}$ is the $(m-1)\times 1$ vector of liabilities held by BOJ owing to each of the $m-1$ institutional sectors. The $(m-1) \times 1$ vector $\boldsymbol{\rho}^Y_{BOJ}$ is the assets vector where an element $\rho^Y_{BOJ,i}$ denotes the claims of BOJ on each institutional sector. The method of transformation here is as follows:

$$\boldsymbol{\varepsilon}^{Y}_{BOJ} = \boldsymbol{D}_{BOJ}\boldsymbol{\varepsilon}_{BOJ}, \tag{3.5}$$

$$\boldsymbol{\rho}^{Y}_{BOJ} = \boldsymbol{D}^{*}_{BOJ}\boldsymbol{\rho}_{BOJ}. \tag{3.6}$$

$\boldsymbol{D}_{BOJ}$ is the matrix obtained from matrix $\boldsymbol{D}$ by removing the row containing elements concerning the BOJ. Likewise $\boldsymbol{D}^{*}_{BOJ}$ is the matrix obtained from matrix $\boldsymbol{D}^{*}$ by removing the row containing BOJ elements.

Given $\boldsymbol{\varepsilon}_{BOJ}$ and $\boldsymbol{\rho}_{BOJ}$ exogenously, the induced savings and the induced investments are calculated using the model in Section 3.1:

$$\boldsymbol{\eta}_{S} = (\boldsymbol{I} - \boldsymbol{C}_{BOJ})^{-1}\boldsymbol{\varepsilon}^{Y}_{BOJ}, \tag{3.7}$$

$$\boldsymbol{\eta}_{I} = (\boldsymbol{I} - \boldsymbol{C}^{*}_{BOJ})^{-1}\boldsymbol{\rho}^{Y}_{BOJ}. \tag{3.8}$$

$\boldsymbol{\eta}_{S}$ is the $(m-1)\times 1$ vector of induced savings, where element η_{S_i} denotes the induced saving generated in institutional sector i. $\boldsymbol{\eta}_{I}$ is the $(m-1)\times 1$ vector of induced investments, where element η_{I_i} indicates induced investment generated in institutional sector i. Note that GIS (i.e. $H_S = \sum_i \eta_{S_i}$) is the sum of $\boldsymbol{\eta}_{S}$, and GII (i.e. $H_I = \sum_i \eta_{I_i}$) is the sum of $\boldsymbol{\eta}_{I}$. By subtracting GIS from GII, we obtain NII as follows:

$$H_{I-S} = H_I - H_S. \tag{3.9}$$

We present the development in $\boldsymbol{\varepsilon}_{BOJ}$ and $\boldsymbol{\rho}_{BOJ}$ from December 2000 through September 2001 in Table 1.

3.3. *Contributing factors to fluctuations in NII*

Next we must answer what the financial instrument might contribute to NII. Let $\boldsymbol{\varepsilon}^{u}_{BOJ,k}$ be a $(n \times 1)$ vector of liabilities of BOJ with its kth element only $= 1$ and all others $= 0$. Similarly $\boldsymbol{\rho}^{u}_{BOJ,h}$ is a $(n \times 1)$ vector of assets of BOJ with only the hth element $=$ 1 and 0 elsewhere, i.e. $\boldsymbol{\varepsilon}^{u}_{BOJ,k} = [0\cdots 0\ 1\ 0\cdots 0]'$ and $\boldsymbol{\rho}^{u}_{BOJ,h} = [0\cdots 0\ 1\ 0\cdots 0]'$.

Let us define the vector $\boldsymbol{\varepsilon}^{uY}_{BOJ,k}$ and the vector $\boldsymbol{\rho}^{uY}_{BOJ,h}$ which are $(m-1)\times 1$ vectors transformed from $\boldsymbol{\varepsilon}^{u}_{BOJ,k}$ and $\boldsymbol{\rho}^{u}_{BOJ,h}$, respectively.

$$\boldsymbol{\varepsilon}^{uY}_{BOJ,k} = \boldsymbol{D}_{BOJ}\boldsymbol{\varepsilon}^{u}_{BOJ,k}, \tag{3.10}$$

$$\boldsymbol{\rho}^{uY}_{BOJ,h} = \boldsymbol{D}^{*}_{BOJ}\boldsymbol{\rho}^{u}_{BOJ,h}. \tag{3.11}$$

By multiplying the vectors by the Leontief inverse, we can estimate the amount of GIS ($\boldsymbol{\eta}^{u}_{Sk}$) generated by a unit increase in the kth item of the

Table 1. Balance Sheets of the BOJ (100 Million Yen).

	Dec. 2000		Jan. 2001		Feb. 2001		Mar. 2001		Apr. 2001	
	Assets	Liabil.	Assets	Liabil.	Assets	Liabil.	Assets	Liabil.	Assets	Liabil.
Currency		676197		617202		614007		628296		642257
Dep. with the BOJ		68270		50909		46790		58142		50671
Gov. deposits		93827		171222		195998		220725		122732
BOJ loans	8274		11808		19560		14086		5837	
Bills purch. and sold	40093	28069	56092	34326	101261	38024	98200	43863	87073	37104
Repur. agr. & s.l. transa.*	183777		184316		186119		184978		182607	
Gov. financing bills	160953		148091		152231		178726		92867	
Central gov. sec.	401990		409788		380991		398593		548775	
Share & other equities	1202	1	1202	1	1202	1	1202	1	1202	1
Deposits money	1445	235	4047	235	3957	235	34359	235	12423	235
Outward inv. in securities	36856		36936		35663		32523		32778	
Gold and SDRs etc.	4445		4445		4445		4445		4445	
Others	42225		41937		41642		41551		41867	
Finan. surplus or deficit		14661		24770		32016		37401		156874
Total	881260	881260	898665	898665	927071	927071	988663	988663	1009874	1009874

(**Continued**)

Table 1. (Continued)

	May 2001		Jun. 2001		Jul. 2001		Aug. 2001		Sep. 2001	
	Assets	**Liabil.**	**Assets**	**Liabil.**	**Assets**	**Liabil.**	**Assets**	**Liabil.**	**Assets**	**Liabil.**
Currency		620285		652395		638342		632388		639081
Dep. with the BOJ		50260		57058		50537		59293		124794
Gov. deposits		115504		123690		166514		167547		154796
BOJ loans	6111		5299		5651		5952		6323	
Bills purch. and sold	128711	39130	148621	65017	143034	40033	155910	57019	173078	4800
Repur. agr. & sec. len. transa.*	181046		163394		152245		102904		124208	
Gov. financing bills	41357		95413		132845		122950		93284	
Central gov. sec.	561798		602525		636554		656788		671205	
Share & other equities	1202	1	1202	1	1202	1	1202	1	1202	1
Deposits money	7083	235	9382	235	2755	235	2802	235	4429	235
Outward inv. in securities	33191		33684		34058		34534		37225	
Gold and SDRs etc.	4463		4463		4463		4463		4463	
Others	41745		41616		41765		41829		41787	
Finan. surplus or deficit		181292		207203		250910		212851		233497
Total	1006707	1006707	1105599	1105599	1154572	1154572	1129334	1129334	1157204	1157204

*Full exposition: Repurchase agreement and securities lending transactions.
Source: The Bank of Japan.

financial assets of BOJ. Likewise, we can calculate the amount of GII ($\boldsymbol{\eta}^u_{Ih}$) generated by a unit increase in the hth item of the liabilities of BOJ.

$$\boldsymbol{\eta}^u_{Sk} = (\boldsymbol{I} - \boldsymbol{C}_{BOJ})^{-1}\boldsymbol{\varepsilon}^{uY}_{BOJ,k}, \tag{3.12}$$

$$\boldsymbol{\eta}^u_{Ih} = (\boldsymbol{I} - \boldsymbol{C}^*_{BOJ})^{-1}\boldsymbol{\rho}^{uY}_{BOJ,h}. \tag{3.13}$$

The incremental GIS, GII and NII are obtained as follows:

$$H^u_{Sk} = \sum_{i=1}^{m-1} \eta^u_{Sk,i}, \tag{3.14}$$

$$H^u_{Ih} = \sum_{i=1}^{m-1} \eta^u_{Ih,i}, \tag{3.15}$$

$$H^u_{I-S,hk} = H^u_{Ih} - H^u_{Sk}. \tag{3.16}$$

The estimated results are presented in Section 4.2. The relations between GII, GIS and NII are presented as follows using the above formulae.

$$\begin{aligned} H_{I-S} &= H_I - H_S \\ &= \sum_{k=1}^{n} H^u_{Ik}\rho_{BOJ,k} - \sum_{k=1}^{n} H^u_{Sk}\varepsilon_{BOJ,k} \\ &= \sum_{k=1}^{n}(H^u_{Ik}\rho_{BOJ,k} - H^u_{Sk}\varepsilon_{BOJ,k}). \end{aligned} \tag{3.17}$$

In the equations above, each term in parenthesis identifies which financial instrument causes what amount of NII. This relationship leads us to a new indicator of measurement of contribution κ_k.

$$\kappa_k = H^u_{Ik}\rho_{BOJ,k} - H^u_{Sk}\varepsilon_{BOJ,k}. \tag{3.18}$$

The decomposition of the changes in NII (ΔH_{I-S}) over a period and the decomposition of changes in κ_k ($\Delta\kappa_k$) over time can be calculated as the difference between the present value and the value in the preceding period. The indicator $\Delta\kappa_k$ is the degree of contribution.

4. Estimation Results

4.1. *Monthly fluctuations and the degree of contribution to NII*

The fluctuations in the three indices namely GII (H_I), GIS (H_S) and NII (H_{I-S}) between December 2000 and September 2001 are depicted

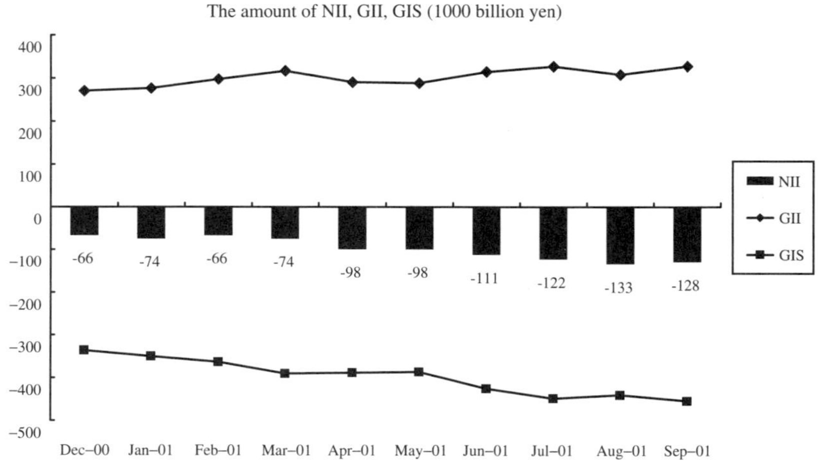

Figure 5. Monthly Change in NII.

in Figure 5. During this period, before and after the introduction by the BOJ of the quantitative monetary policy in March, the NII not only stayed in the negative region (despite Japan suffering from a severe depression for the first time in more than 40 years), but the magnitude was increasing. This suggests that, in this period, the money market operation around the newly adopted quantitative monetary policy was a total failure.

The monthly change in the NII and the degrees of contribution are shown in Figure 6. NII is decreasing in every month except for February, May and September. In March, during which the alteration of the target of the BOJ monetary policy took place, the balance of the current account held by commercial banks and other institutions increased by 1.1 trillion Yen, while the central bank added more than 1.7 trillion Yen of JGB to its asset portfolio. As a consequence of this shift in the monetary target, the NII decreased by almost 10 trillion Yen. While the increment of JGB as an asset pushed up the NII by 2.8 trillion Yen, the increase in the balance of the current account slashed the figure by as much as 5.4 trillion Yen. As far as the degree of contribution is concerned, the combined effect of the two was not significant. The main positive contributing factors in this month were BOJ accounts at the agent commercial banks and the increment of the government financing bills held by the central bank. Two prime elements that made excess negative contributions were the increase in government deposits with BOJ and the addition in the banknotes issued. In conclusion, the installation of the quantitative monetary target failed to give favorable

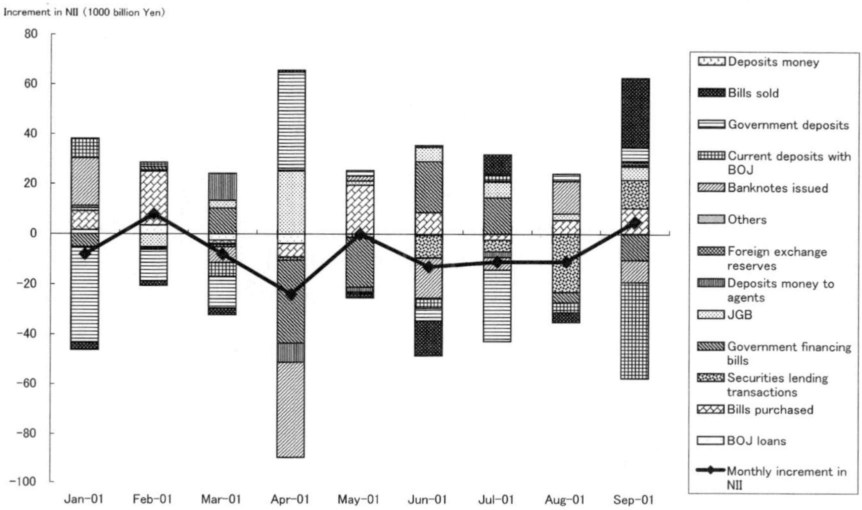

Figure 6. Degree of Contribution to Monthly Increment in NII.

effects to the exhausted Japanese economy then. In August 2001, the BOJ announced that the outstanding balance of current accounts held at the central bank should be raised from around 5 to 6 trillion Yen. However, the net induced investment kept declining even further. Although the decline in the amount of the banknotes issued made a positive contribution of 13 trillion Yen to the NII, security-lending transactions gave a negative effect of 23 trillion Yen. Meanwhile, the commercial financial institutions added 0.9 trillion Yen to their balance of current accounts with BOJ to make it 5.9 trillion Yen, implying a degree of contribution to the NII of −4 trillion Yen. JGB holdings by BOJ grew 2 trillion Yen to 65 trillion Yen and the degree of contribution was +2 trillion Yen. The net contribution of these two items combined was negative, setting aside its small size.

On 18 September, the BOJ announced a further relaxation package of its monetary policy after the terrorist attack in the US on 11 September. In cooperation with fellow central banks, the BOJ promised to keep the balance of the current account held by the commercial banks and other institutions well above the previous level. Actually, the balance doubled within a month to reach 12.5 trillion Yen by the end of September. The fundamental difference of this package from the previous ones was that the BOJ carefully avoided specifying what kind of asset allocation to take to match the increment in its liabilities. Actually, the 6.5 trillion Yen increase in the current accounts, which was partially offset by the decrease in the bills sold to the open market by BOJ, produced 1.8 trillion Yen of bills bought from the commercial banks and 2.2 trillion Yen of securities under repurchase agreement, while the JGB held by BOJ increased by 1.5 trillion Yen. The result of this revision in the policy was favorable as the NII improved from −133 at the end of August to −128 by the close of September. The negative contribution of the increase in the current accounts with BOJ was almost completely offset by the decrease in the bills sold by the central bank, so that the increase in the bills purchased through the open market operation and in the securities under repurchase agreement could give a significant boost in the NII.

In conclusion, it can be said that the shift in the target for money market operations from the current uncollateralized overnight call rate to the outstanding balance of the current accounts at BOJ has so far had only limited significance. The fact that the NII was hovering in the negative region throughout this period suggests that the newly introduced quantitative monetary policy was a total failure. However, a detailed examination of the degree of contribution gives a clue to a successful quantitative monetary policy. For example, in those months in which improvements in NII took place, the contribution of bills purchased was apparent. In the next section, a further study in this direction will be performed.

4.2. *Examination of money market operation methods*

Since the objective of monetary policy is to adjust the amount of funds to the trend of market economy, the daily money market operation must vary according to business fluctuations. This chapter examines what monetary policies should be taken when the market is dull or brisk. It takes NII as an indicator to review the policy to evaluate the effects of monetary policy on the real economy. We have estimated the monthly alterations in NII caused by the changes of BOJ's balance sheet from December 2000 to September 2001 (see Section 3.2 above). But this information is not sufficient to learn which monetary policy is desirable in response to fluctuations in the real economy, so we have taken up combinations of assets and liabilities within the scope of money market operations and evaluated the effects in terms of NII (see Section 3.3). Table 2 gives the results according to the size. Combinations in the upper part of the table have positive effects on the real economy. They are the kind of policies to be adopted in time of depression. Conversely, combinations listed in the lower part of the table are suitable for the overheating economy.

Table 2. Monetary Operation Options and Induced Effects* (100 Million Yen).

Assets	Liabilities	GII	GIS	NII
Bills purchased	Banknotes issued	48102	35931	12171
Securities lending transactions	Banknotes issued	47089	35931	11158
BOJ loans	Banknotes issued	45878	35931	9947
Bills purchased	Bills sold	48102	43820	4282
Securities lending transactions	Bills sold	47089	43820	3269
Gov. financing bills	Banknotes issued	38778	35931	2847
BOJ loans	Bills sold	45878	43820	2058
Bills purchased	Current deposits with BOJ	48102	46324	1778
Bills purchased	Gov. deposits	48102	47177	925
Securities lending transactions	Current deposits with BOJ	47089	46324	765
Securities lending transactions	Gov. deposits	47089	47177	−88
BOJ loans	Current deposits with BOJ	45878	46324	−446
BOJ loans	Gov. deposits	45878	47177	−1299
Foreign exch. reserves	Banknotes issued	32538	35931	−3393
Gov. financing bills	Bills sold	38778	43820	−5042
Gov. financing bills	Current deposits with BOJ	38778	46324	−7546
Gov. financing bills	Gov. deposits	38778	47177	−8399
Foreign exch. reserves	Bills sold	32538	43820	−11282
Foreign exch. reserves	Current deposits with BOJ	32538	46324	−13786
Foreign exch. reserves	Gov. deposits	32538	47177	−14639
JGB	Banknotes issued	16986	35931	−18945
JGB	Bills sold	16986	43820	−26834
JGB	Current deposits with BOJ	16986	46324	−29338
JGB	Gov. deposits	16986	47177	−30191

*The amount of GII, GIS and NII due to 1 trillion Yen increase in asset and liability items.

This analysis shows that the best combination of liability and asset to stimulate the real economy is to raise funds by means of banknote issuing and to employ funds in the bill-purchasing operation. It is confirmed that the method of monetary control traditionally adopted by the central banks in the western countries has a marvelous effect on expanding the economy in terms of NII. A combination of banknote issuing and securities lending transactions is in second place, while that of banknote issuing and BOJ loan facilities is third. These money market operations have been universally adopted by central banks worldwide. Judged in terms of NII, as mentioned above, raising funds by banknote issuing and employing funds by purchasing bills, lending securities against cash or tendering BOJ loans, are good for getting over the recession. As neutral monetary operations, where NII is nearly zero, there are combinations of government deposits and securities lending transactions; deposits with BOJ and BOJ loans and so on. The option of money market operation actually taken by the BOJ — to raise funds by means of current deposits held by commercial banks etc, and to employ it as JGB, which poses a negative NII — is ranked second from the bottom. Clearly the increased purchase of JGB leads to less GII than any other monetary operations. Thus, we could assert that the policy of holding more long-term government bonds is an effective method for cooling a boom but not at all suitable in a depression.

5. Policy Implications

As a conclusion, it can be said that there was a tactical error in the quantitative monetary policy adopted by the BOJ in 2001. In particular, the combination of fund raising through the current account held by commercial banks etc., and fund employment in JGB, could be disastrous. However, this does not mean that the BOJ should abandon the quantitative monetary policy altogether. The exploration above suggests that a good combination of fund raising and employment produces a positive NII so that it is an effective remedy in a recession, particularly when other policy options are not readily available. The best mixture of money market operation is to raise funds through banknotes and employ these funds in the form of bill buying operations. This is the procedure the world central banks have followed from the very early stages of their history. It is easy to depart from this tradition, but it is rather difficult to find an alternative money market operation practice that gives equally good performance.

There is no doubt that the best policy the BOJ should take is to return to the good old days and concentrate upon the bill buying operation. However, it is rather difficult to return to the old way of life because, nowadays, Japanese companies do not issue as many bills as they used to. The amount of bills exchanged at the Tokyo Clearing House has decreased from 2600 trillion Yen in 1993 to 700 trillion yen in 2000 because of the prolonged recession and changing business practice. Nevertheless, there are several alternative combinations of money market operations that give a positive NII regardless of the magnitude. Table 2 shows that some form of fund employment, such as securities under repurchase agreement and BOJ loans to commercial banks, gives a relatively large amount of NII. The repurchase transactions of securities, known as securities lending against cash in Japan, have flourished since its introduction in the mid 1990s. The balance of this kind of transaction is more than 50 trillion Yen, while that with BOJ is only 18 trillion Yen, so that there is ample room for increased money market operation in this field. Although the balance of BOJ loans to commercial banks has been kept at a minimum in recent years, the establishment in February 2001 of a Lombard-rate-like complementary lending facility makes it possible for the central bank lending to expand. As for the fund raising, it is difficult to control the balance of banknotes issued, though the central bank can still rely on the bill selling operation to adjust the total balance as it wishes. It is more or less commonplace for the BOJ to sell and buy bills on its balance sheet simultaneously. Table 2 confirms that even this straddling operation would let NII be positive.

It was a constructive step for the BOJ to have taken the decision to shift the target of the monetary policy from the interbank interest rate to the balance of current accounts held by commercial banks and other financial institutions. Unlike the interbank rate, which is supposed to be determined in the market, the central bank can adjust its balance sheet as it wishes through various means of money market operations. The outcome of adopting the new policy is not promising so far. A combination of money market operations, like the one the BOJ has practiced which brings negative NII, is ruinous when the economy is under recession. In contrast, an operation that creates positive NII is a welcome remedy to cure an economy suffering from a slump. The most important thing in exercising this kind of policy is to make a quantitative analysis of the scheme in advance in order to find the best available combination of money market operations. The authors believe that the ALM framework of FOF analysis is a powerful and practical device to fulfill this kind of examination.

Appendix

This appendix shows the relation between $\boldsymbol{Y}$- and $\boldsymbol{Y}^*$-tables.

A.1. *Y and Y* matrices*

Matrix $\boldsymbol{C}$ is the coefficient matrix of $\boldsymbol{Y}$, so that each element can be written as follows:

$$c_{ij} = \sum_{k=1}^{n} d_{ik} b_{kj} = \sum_{k=1}^{n} \frac{v_{ik}}{t_k^E} \frac{u_{kj}}{t_j}. \tag{A.1}$$

Since, $u_{ij} = r_{ij}$ and $v_{ij} = e_{ji}$, it follows that

$$c_{ij} = \sum_{k=1}^{n} \frac{e_{ki}}{t_k^E} \frac{r_{kj}}{t_j}. \tag{A.2}$$

Thus each element of matrix $\boldsymbol{Y}$ is expressed as follows:

$$y_{ij} = t_j c_{ij} = t_j \sum_{k=1}^{n} \frac{e_{ki}}{t_k^E} \frac{r_{kj}}{t_j} = \sum_{k=1}^{n} \frac{e_{ki} r_{kj}}{t_k^E}. \tag{A.3}$$

On the other hand, matrix $\boldsymbol{C}^*$ is a coefficient matrix of $\boldsymbol{Y}^*$.

$$c_{ij}^* = \sum_{k=1}^{n} d_{ik}^* b_{kj}^* = \sum_{k=1}^{n} \frac{v_{ik}^*}{t_k^R} \frac{u_{kj}^*}{t_j}. \tag{A.4}$$

Considering that $u_{ij}^* = e_{ij}$ and $v_{ij}^* = r_{ji}$, it follows that

$$c_{ij}^* = \sum_{k=1}^{n} \frac{r_{ki}}{t_k^R} \frac{e_{kj}}{t_j}. \tag{A.5}$$

Thus each element of matrix $\boldsymbol{Y}^*$ is expressed as follows:

$$y_{ij}^* = t_j c_{ij}^* = t_j \sum_{k=1}^{n} \frac{r_{ki}}{t_k^R} \frac{e_{kj}}{t_j} = \sum_{k=1}^{n} \frac{r_{ki} e_{kj}}{t_k^R}, \tag{A.6}$$

where $t_i^R = t_i^E$ is satisfied, thus

$$y_{ij} = y_{ji}^* \tag{A.7}$$

or, in matrix terms

$$\boldsymbol{Y}' = \boldsymbol{Y}^*. \tag{A.8}$$

Hence, matrix $\boldsymbol{Y}^*$ is the transposed matrix of $\boldsymbol{Y}$.

A.2. $\boldsymbol{\varepsilon}^Y$ *and* $\boldsymbol{\rho}^Y$ *in the Y-table*

First, let us denote the difference between the total of assets or liabilities (whichever is greater) t_j^Y and the column sum of y_j^Y of matrix $\boldsymbol{Y}$ as ρ_j^Y; that is the typical element of vector $\boldsymbol{\rho}^Y$. We denote the column sum of matrix $\boldsymbol{C}$ as c_j, then ρ_j^Y is given as

$$\rho_j^Y = t_j^Y - y_j^Y = t_j^Y - c_j t_j^Y = t_j^Y - t_j^Y \sum_{i=1}^{m} \sum_{k=1}^{n} d_{ik} b_{kj}, \tag{A.9}$$

where $\sum_i d_{ik} = 1$, thus

$$\rho_j^Y = t_j^Y - t_j^Y \sum_{k=1}^{n} b_{kj}. \tag{A.10}$$

Considering that $t_j = t_j^Y$, $b_{ij} = u_{ij}/t_j$ and $u_{ij} = r_{ij}$, it follows that

$$\rho_j^Y = t_j - \sum_{i=1}^{n} u_{ij} = t_j - \sum_{i=1}^{n} r_{ij} = \rho_j. \tag{A.11}$$

Since $\rho_j^Y = \rho_j$ for all the elements, $\boldsymbol{\rho}^Y = \boldsymbol{\rho}$ is proved.

Second, let us denote the difference between the total of assets or liabilities (whichever is greater) t_i^Y and the row sum y_i^Y of matrix $\boldsymbol{Y}$ as ε_i^Y; that is the typical element of vector $\boldsymbol{\varepsilon}^Y$. ε_i^Y is given as follows:

$$\begin{aligned}\varepsilon_i^Y &= t_i^Y - y_i^Y = t_i^Y - \sum_{j=1}^{m} t_j^Y c_{ij} = t_i^Y - \sum_{j=1}^{m} t_j^Y \left(\sum_{k=1}^{n} d_{ik} b_{kj}\right) \\ &= t_i^Y - \sum_{k=1}^{n} d_{ik} \left(\sum_{j=1}^{m} b_{kj} t_j^Y\right).\end{aligned} \tag{A.12}$$

Considering $b_{ij} = u_{ij}/t_j$, $t_j = t_j^Y$ and $t_i^E = t_i^R$, it follows that

$$\varepsilon_i^Y = t_i - \sum_{k=1}^{n} d_{ik} \left(\sum_{j=1}^{m} u_{kj}\right) = t_i - \sum_{k=1}^{n} d_{ik} t_k^R = t_i - \sum_{k=1}^{n} d_{ik} t_k^E, \tag{A.13}$$

where $d_{ij} = v_{ij}/t_j^E$ and $v_{ij} = e_{ji}$, thus

$$\varepsilon_i^Y = t_i - \sum_{k=1}^{n} v_{ik} = t_i - \sum_{k=1}^{n} e_{ki} = \varepsilon_i. \tag{A.14}$$

Since $\varepsilon_i^Y = \varepsilon_i$, for all the elements, $\boldsymbol{\varepsilon}^Y = \boldsymbol{\varepsilon}$ is proved.

A.3. $\boldsymbol{\varepsilon}^Y$ *and* $\boldsymbol{\rho}^Y$ *in the* Y^**-table*

First, let us denote the difference between the total of assets or liabilities (whichever is greater) t_j^Y and the column sum y_j^{Y*} of matrix $\boldsymbol{Y}^*$ as ε_j^{Y*}; that is the typical element of vector $\boldsymbol{\varepsilon}^{Y*}$. We denote column sum of $\boldsymbol{C}^*$ matrix as c_j^*, then ε_j^{Y*} is given as follows:

$$\varepsilon_j^{Y*} = t_j^Y - y_j^{Y*} = t_j^Y - c_j^* t_j^Y = t_j^Y - t_j^Y \sum_{i=1}^{n} b_{ij}^*. \tag{A.15}$$

Considering that $t_j = t_j^Y$, $b_{ij}^* = u_{ij}^*/t_j$ and $u_{ij}^* = e_{ij}$, it follows that

$$\varepsilon_j^{Y*} = t_j - \sum_{i=1}^{n} u_{ij}^* = t_j - \sum_{i=1}^{n} e_{ij} = \varepsilon_j. \tag{A.16}$$

Since $\varepsilon_j^{Y*} = \varepsilon_j$ for all the elements, $\boldsymbol{\varepsilon}^{Y*} = \boldsymbol{\varepsilon}$ is proved.

Second, let us define vector $\boldsymbol{\rho}^{Y*}$ with typical element ρ_i^{Y*} as the difference between the total of assets or liabilities t_i^Y and the row sum y_i^{Y*} of $\boldsymbol{Y}^*$ matrix, then ρ_i^{Y*} is expressed as follows:

$$\begin{aligned}\rho_i^{Y*} &= t_i^Y - y_i^{Y*} = t_i^Y - \sum_{j=1}^{m} t_j^Y c_{ij}^* = t_i^Y - \sum_{j=1}^{m} t_j^Y \left(\sum_{k=1}^{n} d_{ik}^* b_{kj}^* \right) \\ &= t_i^Y - \sum_{k=1}^{n} d_{ik}^* \left(\sum_{j=1}^{m} b_{kj}^* t_j^Y \right).\end{aligned} \tag{A.17}$$

Considering that $b_{ij}^* = u_{ij}^*/t_j$, $t_j = t_j^Y$ and $t_i^E = t_i^R$, it follows that

$$\rho_i^{Y*} = t_i - \sum_{k=1}^{n} d_{ik}^* \left(\sum_{j=1}^{m} u_{kj}^* \right) = t_i - \sum_{k=1}^{n} d_{ik}^* t_k^E = t_i - \sum_{k=1}^{n} d_{ik}^* t_k^R, \tag{A.18}$$

where $d_{ij}^* = v_{ij}^*/t_j^R$ and $v_{ij}^* = r_{ji}$, thus

$$\rho_i^{Y*} = t_i - \sum_{k=1}^{n} v_{ik}^* = t_i - \sum_{k=1}^{n} r_{ki} = \rho_i. \tag{A.19}$$

Since $\rho_i^{Y*} = \rho_i$ for all the elements, $\boldsymbol{\rho}^{Y*} = \boldsymbol{\rho}$ is proved.

References

Alford, R. F. G. (1986). *Flow of Funds*. Aldershot: Gower.

Alho, K. (1991). *Financial Markets and Macroeconomic Policy in the Flow-of-Funds Framework*. Aldershot: Avebury.

Bank of Japan (1999). *Guide to Japan's Flow of Funds Accounts*. Tokyo: Bank of Japan.

Bank of Japan (2000). *Compilation Method of Japan's Flow of Funds Accounts*. Tokyo: Bank of Japan.

Cohen, J. (1963). Circular Flow Models in the Flow of Funds. *International Economic Review*, 4, 153–170.

Copeland, M. A. (1947). Tracing Money Flows through the United States Economy. *American Economic Review*, 37(2), 31–49.

Copeland, M. A. (1949). Social Accounting for Money Flows. *The Accounting Review*, 24, 254–264.

Copeland, M. A. (1952). *A Study of Moneyflows in the United States*. New York: National Bureau of Economic Research.

Dawson, J. C. (1958). A Cyclical Model for Postwar U.S. Financial Markets. *American Economic Review*, 48, 145–157.

Hamada, F. (1969). An Econometric Model of Flow-of-Funds. *Keio Economic Studies*, 6, 64–115.

International Monetary Fund (2000). *Monetary and Financial Statistics Manual*. Washington, DC: International Monetary Fund.

Klein, L. R. (1983). *Lectures in Econometrics*. Amsterdam: North-Holland.

Leontief, W. (1941). *The Structure of American Economy, 1919–1939*. New York: Oxford University Press.

Mathews, R. (1962). The Australian Flow-of-Funds Accounts. *Economic Record*, 38, 94–107.

Powelson, J. P. (1960). *National Income and Flow-of-Funds Analysis*. New York: McGraw-Hill.

Stone, R. (1966). The Social Accounts from a Consumer's Point of View. *Review of Income and Wealth*, 12, 1–33.

Tobin, J. (1969). A General Equilibrium Approach to Monetary Theory. *Journal of Money, Credit and Banking*, 1, 15–29.

United Nations (1999). *Handbook of Input–Output Table Compilation and Analysis*. New York: United Nations.

Part III

Macroeconometric Models

Chapter 8

An Econometric Model of Japanese Economic Growth, 1878–1937

Lawrence R. Klein[1]

1. Introduction

One of the economic marvels of the capitalist era has been the growth of Japan. It is an outstanding case among Asiatic nations of the Far East, and much historical research has been devoted to the interpretation of this development. Undoubtedly this research will continue for some time to come. The problem of Japanese growth is so important and interesting, however, that diverse methods of research that throw light on it from many angles should be used. Parallel to the striking developments in econometric model building now taking place in Japan for current business-cycle analysis, I propose in this chapter to take up long-run growth analysis by using the model-building technique. Fortunately, a rich body of statistics on long-run development has recently been made available in Japan by Professor Ohkawa.[2] His data on national income and employment for the period since 1878 form the basic sample on which the model of this chapter is based. The present period, i.e. since World War II, is well documented statistically; therefore it is possible to extend the sample well beyond Ohkawa's terminal data of 1942. Data are widely available, although significant gaps

[1]This was published in *Econometrica*, 29(3), July, 1961. Permission granted by the Econometric Society. Much of the work was done in residence at the Institute of Social & Economic Research, Osaka University. The author depended heavily on contributions of colleagues there who guided him and tutored him on the understanding of the Japanese economy. Dr. Jung-Chao Liu of Tunghai University, Taiwan, rendered invaluable statistical assistance. Later statistical help came from Mr. Motoo Abe, at the Wharton School of the University of Pennsylvania.

[2]K. Ohkawa (1957). *The Growth Rate of the Japanese Economy Since 1878*. Kinokuniya.

exist, for the 1930s; thus there is comparatively little problem in preparing samples of statistical information for use in models of recent development. It is a fairly long sweep of history, however, that I am trying to interpret statistically in this study.

Although the Japanese development problem is of great importance in historical perspective, the decade of the 1950s and future prospects are possibly even of greater importance. The recovery of Japan from her great defeat in World War II is no less remarkable than that of West Germany. Her prospective growth rate apparently equals that of the Soviet Union. At a time when many American economists are seriously worried about the prospective growth rate[3] of the United States, growth models of the rapidly developing economies are interesting devices that merit our attention. It is not difficult to see how I was led into this type of study.

2. The Nature of the Model

If I were given free scope in the preparation of a Japanese growth model, knowing that I would be able to find data for the variables explicitly treated in the system, I would have proceeded in quite a different manner from that actually adopted. The customary models in the theory of growth are formulated in terms of savings, investment, capital, the real wage, aggregate output, aggregate employment, the interest rate, foreign trade, and similar variables. The relationships connecting these variables enable us to discuss growth with reference to savings propensities, marginal productivities, accelerators, import propensities, and the like. At these meetings, just a year ago, I presented together with my associate, R. S. Kosobud, a paper on a statistical model of American growth in just these terms.

The Japanese model was, however, constructed within the confines of a more limited scope. I posed this problem: What is the best econometric model of growth that can be prepared from Professor Ohkawa's body of data, supplementing it perhaps with standard trade and demographic statistics that are available in most countries of the world? This would not be an interesting question unless I knew at the outset that some of the main qualitative and institutional characteristics of the Japanese economy, thrown up

[3]The paper, Some Econometrics of Growth: Great Ratios of Economics, has been published 1961 in the *Quarterly Journal of Economics*, LXXV, 173–198. A previous model of the more familiar type had been prepared by my former student, the late Stefan Valavanis-Vail (1955). An Econometric Model of Growth: U.S.A. 1869–1953. *American Economic Review, Papers and Proceedings*, XLV, 208–221.

by prior historical observation, could be revealed in a model so restricted in scope. From questioning my Japanese colleagues I determined that some of the main aspects of Japanese growth in the past 100 years can be treated under the following headings:

1. Food. It is a primary problem of production economics to feed the large island population from limited domestic resources. Food imports to supplement domestic rice and other agricultural production have been essential. Over the years, however, Japan has moved steadily towards a high degree of agricultural self sufficiency in food products.

2. Trade. Japan has relatively few of the raw materials necessary to sustain a developing manufacturing production. These raw materials, some food, and capital equipment must be imported. In order to pay for these imports, Japan had the choice of exporting or attracting foreign investment. She chose to pay for imports almost entirely by exporting and maintained a relatively small net balance either positive or negative. Basically, Japan paid her own way in international trade and did not import capital to a significant extent.

3. Population. An abundance of highly skilled and well educated cheap labor made the Japanese economy extremely productive and competitive in world markets. Population, as a whole, grew as a result of the interaction of a normal birth-death process. Net emigration was not a significant factor. The internal population shift from rural to urban areas accompanied the ascendancy of manufacturing production and made possible inexpensive output.

4. Savings and investment. An unequal distribution of income, an oligopolistic alliance between industry and finance (*Zaibatsu*), and a reluctance to draw upon foreign capital gave rise to a high rate of savings to provide funds for fixed capital expansion. The model presented below attempts to reflect the first three of these major characteristics of the Japanese economy. In Professor Ohkawa's study there were no historical statistics of savings and investment. He simply developed series on national income and numbers gainfully occupied in each of three main sectors of the economy-primary, secondary, and tertiary industry. Professor Rosowsky has recently developed series on fixed capital formation, and these might eventually be integrated in an expanded growth model, but complementary statistics on savings have not yet been developed. Similarly, there are no comparable statistics on income distribution by factor shares. In Ohkawa's industrial classification, the primary sector consists of agriculture, forestry, and fishing. The secondary sector consists of manufacturing and mining. Construction and government are placed in the tertiary sector together with trade,

services, and finance. The long term trends in output per gainfully occupied person, which are central relationships in the present model, are so similar in the secondary and tertiary sectors that these two are lumped together. Thus, the model has only two sectors; one consisting of agriculture, forestry, and fishing and the other consisting of the rest of the domestic economy. The first assumption in building the model is that technological advance will lead to a steady growth of productivity in each of the two sectors of the economy:

$$x_{1t}/n_{1t} = A_1(1+\rho_1)^t u_{1t} \tag{2.1}$$

$$x_{2t}/n_{2t} = A_2(1+\rho_2)^t u_{2t}, \tag{2.2}$$

where x_{1t} is real net output of the primary sector, x_{2t} is real net output of the secondary and tertiary sectors, n_{1t} is the number of persons engaged in the primary sector, n_{2t} is the number of persons engaged in the secondary and tertiary sectors, and U_{it} is a random disturbance.

Each of these equations says that productivity grows at the compound interest rate p in the respective sector. Ai and ou are parameters to be estimated from the sample data. If logarithms are formed on each side of (2.1) and (2.2), the equations become semi-logarithmic trend regressions,

$$\log x_i/n_{lit} = \log A_i + t\log(1+\rho_i) + \log U_{it}, \quad \text{or}$$

$$\log x_{it}/n_{nt} = A_i' + \rho_i' t + v_{it}.$$

These productivity equations deal with "persons engaged," and in order to relate such variables to total population an equation on labor force participation is introduced. It too is based on a trend with compound interest growth.

$$(n_{1t}+n_{2t})/n_t = A(1+\rho)^t u_{3t}. \tag{2.3}$$

In this equation n_t is population. Having brought a population variable into the model, I must give it endogenous explanation. Frequently, in short run business cycle models population is regarded as exogenous, although recent experience would indicate that this is far from adequate. In a long run model population is an important endogenous variable. The treatment used here follows closely that of Valavanis-Vail in his earlier American growth model.

First, there is a non-statistical equation

$$n_t = n_{t-1}(1+b_t-d_t-e_t) \tag{2.4}$$

where b_t is the birth rate, d_t is the death rate, and e_t is the net emigration rate. This equation merely states that population of the present period equals population of the previous period increased by births, decreased by deaths, increased by immigration, and decreased by emigration. Net emigration has been quite small and will be neglected in the subsequent argument. The birth rate and death rate are new endogenous variables brought into the system in (2.4). They must be explained. In the early stages of industrialization both birth and death rates increased. Birth rates increased because of the rising living standards which made it possible for families to support more children. Against this trend was the effect of the rural-urban shift, but the former tendency outweighed the latter effect. After reaching a peak in the period just before World War II the Japanese birth rate began to fall; the effects of urbanization became more dominant. Since the end of the War, the birth rate has continued to fall and appears to have leveled in recent years. The level to which the birth rate has settled or will eventually settle is substantially above zero; therefore I have placed an asymptotic level in the equation, towards which the birth rate falls as per capita output rises. The pattern of the death rate is similar but less pronounced. It rises less and falls less; moreover, there is no reason to introduce a positive asymptotic level towards which the death rate falls. It could possibly approach zero in the natural course of events. The equations expressed in logarithmic form are

$$\log(b_t - \beta) = \alpha_0 + \alpha_1 \log(x/n)_{t-1} + \alpha_2[\log(x/n)_{t-1}]^2 + u_{5t}, \quad (2.5)$$

and

$$\log d_t = \delta_0 + \delta_1 \log(x/n)_{t-1} + \delta_2[\log(x/n)_{t-1}]^2 + u_{6t}, \quad (2.6)$$

where x/n is real per capita output. The birth and death rates of each time period are multiplied in (2.4) by the population of the preceding time period. These rates are assumed to depend on per capita incomes of this preceding time period.

Japan has imported food to supplement domestic production. It is well known that in the case of rice, the strategic food component, imported varieties are considered inferior to domestic. As domestic production of food rises, imports should be curtailed. This is the usual pattern suggested, but I have not been able to discern direct evidence of this type of relationship. I have instead posited a global form of "Engel's Law" for Japan. As per capita income rises the percentage represented by food declines. All domestic primary output is added to food imports. This is assumed to represent total domestic outlay on food. This procedure is not strictly correct as a statistical measure since some primary production may be exported and some is not in the food category. The version of "Engel's Law" is

$$(x_{1t} + I_{it})/x_t = B_1(x_t/n_t)^{\beta_1} u_{7t}, \tag{2.7}$$

where I_{it} is real food imports and x_t is real output. The statement of "Engel's Law" requires $-1 < \beta_1 < 0$.

The remaining imports, $I - I_1$, include the raw materials and capital equipment so vital to Japan's productive system. The equation relating output to input is

$$x_{2t} = B_2 10^{\beta_2(I_t - I_{1t})} u_{8t} \tag{2.8}$$

By making this function semi-logarithmic (after forming logarithms of both sides), I implicitly make the marginal productivity of imports steeply progressive ($\beta_2 > 0$).

Two non-statistical equations close this system. One states that primary and all other net output make up total net output-all in real terms. The other equation is one of trade balance. Import value equals export value in a common price system.

$$x_{1t} + x_{2t} = x_t, \tag{2.9}$$

$$I_t = (p_t/p_{it})/E_t, \tag{2.10}$$

where E_t is real exports, p_{et} is export price in Yen, and p_{it} is import price in Yen. For purposes of this study E is considered to be exogenous. It is assumed to depend on conditions in overseas markets. In the newer business cycle models of Japan covering the recent period, this overseas dependence is made explicit, but it would be difficult to find suitable data on the entire trading world outside Japan for the whole sample period. The only price variables in this real system are p_e and p_i. The latter, like exports, depends on foreign conditions. Export prices, p_e, are a reflection of domestic production conditions. The assumption here is that public authorities will choose an exchange policy to keep p_e/p_i at a competitive level in world markets. This has often been cited as the type of policy followed by Japan in her "double devaluation" of the 1930s, a policy which does appear to have maintained exports effectively. I shall regard p_e/p_i as an exogenous variable.

The ten endogenous variables in this ten-equation system are $x_1, x_2, n_1, n_2, x, n, I, I_1, b$, and d. The process of algebraic solution is of some interest in pointing out some of the lines of causation. Using lagged values of x/n, values of b and d can be computed from (2.5) and (2.6). Substitution in (2.4) determines n. Equation (2.3), therefore, gives a simple relation between n_1 and n_2. Exports and exchange policy determine total imports in (2.10). It remains to determine x_1, x_2, n_1, n_2, x, and I_1. The derived relation between n_1 and n_2 together with (2.1), (2.2), (2.7), (2.8), and (2.9) gives six equations to determine the six remaining unknowns. Since t is fixed for each solution point, all except (2.7) and (2.8) are linear equations in the six unknown variables. Equations (2.1) and (2.2) express x_1 and x_2 as linear functions of n_1 and n_2 respectively for given t. But a linear relation has already been deduced between n_1 and n_2; therefore both x_1 and x_2 can be expressed as linear functions of n_1. Equation (2.9) states that x is the sum of x_1 and x_2; hence x is easily expressed as a linear function of n_1. The two nonlinear equations, (2.7) and (2.8), involve x_1, I_1, and x; and x_2 and I as unknowns. (n and I are already known and can be substituted.) All the unknowns except I_i can thus be replaced by linear functions of n_1, and the final result is two nonlinear equations in n_1 and I_1. These can be solved quickly by well-known approximation methods. Of course, in this substitution and elimination process, the disturbances, u_i, have been neglected.

3. The Sample and Estimates

Ohkawa's statistical record of Japanese growth forms the basic sample for estimating our model. The modern era of capitalist development in Japan is often put at the time of the Meiji restoration in 1868, but the underlying movement towards capitalism began much earlier. Ohkawa's statistics begin with the year 1878. His estimates of output and the gainfully occupied are carried forward by five year periods, quinquennia, to 1942. Extrapolation of these series during the post-war period can be made on an approximate basis from the wealth of data that are now becoming available for many sectors of the economy.

The last of Ohkawa's quinquennia, covering the years 1938–1942, is essentially a war period. Before Pearl Harbor, the Japanese economy had gone over to a war footing; therefore our sample consists of 12 quinquennia, beginning with 1878–1882 and ending with 1933–1937. This is not unlike the sample used by Valavanis-Vail in estimating his model. Kuznets' series, on which he relied, were for overlapping decades, beginning with 1869. In both cases, the averaging over time tends to smooth out short-run cycles. The series of disjoint quinquennia, in the present sample, has an advantage compared with overlapping decades in that serial correlation is not necessarily introduced by the method of data presentation.

The equations with unknown coefficients among the set of 10 comprising the system could easily be estimated as least-squares regressions from 12 observations. The ordinary methods of least-squares regression (multiple and simple correlation) have been used in the equations where the explanatory variables are pure time trends or lagged variables. These are equations (2.1), (2.2), (2.3), (2.5), and (2.6). Equations (2.7) and (2.8), the remaining two requiring parameter estimation, were not estimated by the simple correlation technique because this would, as is well known, give rise to bias. Both variables in each of the equations are endogenous. In each case, the equations were estimated by the method of subgroup averages.[4]

The numerical values of output are expressed in millions of 1928–1932 Yen. Population and work force are in millions of persons. Birth and death rates are quinquennial figures. Time trend is measured 1 to 12 beginning with the first quinquennium, 1878–1982, and increasing by one for each successive five-year period. The estimated system is (in common logarithms)

$$\log x_{1t}/n_{1t} = \underset{}{1.7053} + \underset{(0.0026)}{0.05159t}, \quad R^2 = 0.97; \tag{3.1.e}$$

$$\log x_{2t}/n_{2t} - 2.0938 + \underset{(0.0037)}{0.0609t}, \quad R^2 = 0.95; \tag{3.2.e}$$

$$\log n_{1t} + n_{2t}/n_t = -0.2295 - \underset{(0.0016)}{0.0089t}, \quad R^2 - 0.73 \tag{3.3.e}$$

$$n_t = n_{t-1}(1 + b_t - d_t - e_t); \tag{3.4}$$

$$\log(b_t - 0.09) = -7.2920 + \underset{(0.623)}{6.0120} \log(x/n)_{t-1}. - \underset{(0.158)}{1.4523}, [\log(x/n)_{t-1}]^2, \quad R^2 = 0.93 \tag{3.5.e}$$

$$\log d_t = -3.1882 + \underset{(0.495)}{2.298} \log(x/n)_{t-1} - \underset{(0.125)}{0.590}[\log(x/n)_{t-1}]^2, \quad R^2 = 0.65 \tag{3.6.e}$$

[4]Consider the linear equation $x_t = \alpha + \beta y_t + u_t$ $(t = 1, 2, \ldots, T)$. Assume T to be an even number. Order the observations by size of y_t and divide the sample into two groups according as y_t falls in the first half of ordered values or in the second half. Compute the mean values of each variable, x_t and y_t, in the two groups. Call the subgroup averages (x_{1t}, y_{1t}) and (x_{2t}, y_{2t}). Estimates of α and β denoted by a and b are solutions of $\bar{x}_{1t} = a + by_{1t}$, $x_{2t} = a + by_{2t}$. Such estimates are consistent, under mathematical conditions on x_t and y_t.

$$(\log x_{1t} + I_{1t})/x_t = -0.758 - \underset{(0.281)}{0.573} \log x_t/n_t, \quad R^2 = 0.90; \tag{3.7.e}$$

$$\log X_{2t} = 2.92 + \underset{(0.000231)}{0.000427}(I_t - I_{1t}), \quad R^2 = 0.89; \tag{3.8.e}$$

$$x_{1t} + x_{2t} = x_t \tag{3.9}$$

$$I_t = (p_{et}/p_{it})E_t, \quad R^2 = 0.98. \tag{3.10}$$

These estimates imply a quinquennial growth rate of approximately 12.6% in productivity in the primary sector. In the secondary and tertiary sectors the rate is about 15%. The participation rate estimated in (3.3.e) is nearly constant at an average of approximately 50%. The quinquennial rate of decline is only 2%.

The birth rate rises and later falls with the growth of per capita national income. The minimum rate which is reached asymptotically is 9% per quinquennium. The rate has fallen as low as 10.2% in the post-war period. Both the positive and negative coefficients of $\log(x/n)_{-1}$ and $[\log(x/n)_{-1}]^2$ are smaller in the death rate than in the birth rate equation. The death rate rises and falls more gently than does the birth rate.

The Engel coefficient in (3.7.e) when transformed,

$$\log x_t + -0.758 + 0.427 \log t$$

is small compared with the international average of roughly 0.6 determined by Houthakker.[5] His estimate, however, is more strictly confined to family food consumption and is based on cross section samples of individual budgets. The dependent variable in the present model includes more than family food consumption, and the independent variable covers the whole of national income. In some past years exports have exceeded imports in current Yen valuation. In the majority of cases, however, imports cost more than was earned from the sale of exports; therefore Japan has been a small scale capital importer. The equation of trade balance is only approximate. It is not a bad fit to the data, but in application of the statistical model, it is important to recognize that it is perhaps too restrictive to limit imports only to the value of exports.

[5] H. S. Houthakker (1957). "An International Comparison of Household Expenditure Patterns, Commemorating the Centenary of Engel's Law," *Ecoxnometrica*, XXV, 532–551.

4. Extrapolation and the Rate of Growth of the Japanese Economy

This model provides an interpretation of Japanese economic history. It shows how exports affect the economy, the need for food imports, the need for other imports, the growth of population, and the growth of productivity. All these factors are interrelated in the system. Apart from this type of analysis the model can be used in the study of growth, which is an extremely important question for Japan.

As an extrapolating device, the model can be used to estimate the endogenous variables given the level of exports and terms of trade. In the post-war quinquennia that have already been observed, it is possible to check the model to see how well it explains recent facts or whether the Japanese economy has yet recovered to an evolution implied by the pre-war system. There was an enormous disruption of economic life in the war, and post-war development was, at first, chaotic. A turning point occurred just after the Korean war, when Japan developed into a major supply base for the United Nations and American forces. From this point onwards, economic progress has been rapid but orderly. Much of the more traditional capitalist scheme of development reappeared. The first quinquennium that squares well with our established system of ordering is 1953–1957. Subsequent quinquennia bring us into the era of ex ante extrapolation (forecasting). This first quinquennium is considered from the point of view of ex post extrapolation.

For extrapolation it is necessary to know the volume of exports and terms of trade. These determine, by equation (3.10), the volume of imports. In the first extrapolation, i.e. to 1953–1957, imports are set at the observed level. Chronologically, t should be fixed at 16 for 1953–1957. In the trend equations if this value of t were to be substituted, it would be assumed that normal trend developments had been taking place during the war years. It is undoubtedly wrong to assume that this is the case, yet it would not be wholly correct to set t at 14 for 1953–1957 and assume that post-war developments began at the point where the pre-war era finished.[6] When

[6] In the selection of sample values, I stopped at $t = 12$ for 1933–1937 since 1938–1942 was assumed to be a period of war economy. The great period of destruction and dislocation came during the next two quinquennia 1943–1947 and 1948–1952. These two are skipped in the numbering of t for extrapolation, and $t = 14$ is selected for 1953–1957, on the assumption that post-war trends were resumed from the last pre-war position. This position is assumed to be 1938–1942 even though this quinquennium was not used in the sample.

Table 1. Extrapolation of the model to 1953–1957 (million 1928–32 yen and million persons)

		Computed value	
Variable	Actual Value	$t = 14$	$t = 16$
X_1	4,227	4,619	5,486
X_2	15,951	19,550	25,350
X	20,178	24,169	30,836
n_1	15.29	17.26	16.16
n_2	25.09	22.11	21.67
n	89.17	89.09	89.09
I_1	843	967	703
$1 + b - d$	1.0559	1.06	1.06

the economy resumed a more normal pace of development after 1950 it was able to capitalize on much of the technological "know-how" that had become accepted knowledge throughout the world by that time. Therefore, two sets of extrapolation are given, one for $t = 14$ in 1953–1957 and one for $t = 16$ in 1953–1957. These are shown in Table 1. The associated level of real exports in this table is that value which, together with the prevailing terms of trade, would bring imports to the actual levels of 1953–1957. In subsequent tables we assume arbitrary growth rates for real exports and imports with fixed terms of trade.

Both extrapolations give an overestimate of output in each sector. This could be the fault of the model, or it could be a reflection of the fact that the Japanese economy had not recovered to its normal expansion path by 1953–1957 (assuming the actual development in foreign trade). If it is assumed that t is 16 in 1953–1957, both outputs are overestimated by a larger extent than for the case in which $t = 14$. On the side of employment, n_2 is underestimated, and n_i is somewhat overestimated. Post-war developments in productivity were more favorable in the primary than in the other sectors. Generally, it appears that by setting $t = 16$, too much technical progress is attributed to the economy as a whole.

For the future, there is considerable debate over the prospective rate of growth of the Japanese economy. Will it continue to grow during the 1960s as it has during the 1950s? If so, this would make its long run growth rate considerably higher than the long run figure for 1878–1937. As can be seen in Table 1, total output is by 1953–1957 not up to the level indicated by extrapolation of the present model. It is of some interest to examine the next three quinquennia of growth implied by the model to see where the Japanese economy might be in the decade of the 1960s. The present political administration of Japan has as its program the doubling of real national income in the decade 1960–1970. How realistic is this goal in terms of the model?

To extrapolate the model, some assumptions must be made about export growth and the consequent ability to import. Four possible annual growth rates of real exports are assumed: 4%, 5%, 6%, and 7%. The terms of trade are kept fixed. This implies equal percentage growth rates in real exports and imports. For the calculations, real imports are put at the actual levels for 1953–1957 and expanded by 4%, 5%, 6%, and 7%, respectively, for the possible paths of economic development.

In all three cases, there is a shift in the work force away from primary industry. With larger export volume, imports are correspondingly larger and more food imports are relied upon to supplement a declining domestic agriculture. The shift of the work force away from primary industry outruns the rate of technical improvement; therefore the total of primary output falls. This is probably a false implication of the model. The total of $x_i + A_1$, however, grows. There is a great expansion in all four cases of secondary and tertiary industry. This expansion is larger, the higher is the growth rate in exports. In none of the cases, though, does national income double between 1960 and 1970. These are the mid years of quinquennia corresponding to $t = 15$ and $t = 17$. At the most the expansion is by about three-quarters (5–3/4% per annum) instead of 100%. The four growth rates of exports are associated with different rates of expansion of total output, but historically exports have grown at roughly 6%. In the 1953–1957 quinquennium, output had not yet reached the trend expansion of the model. Output would have had to have been about 30% larger to meet the trend value. Between the period $t = 14$ and $t = 15$ for an export expansion of 6%, output must grow by 70% to meet the trend value. The mid year for $t = 15$ is 1960. The required rate of growth to have an increase of 70% in five years is 11.2% per annum. The annual rate of growth of the Japanese economy during the post-war period has been put at 9.9%; therefore, it is quite possible that recovery to the long run trend is about to be reached, provided that technical progress of the war period is neglected. If trend growths are extrapolated right through the war period, it might be concluded that the economy is still far below the long run level of performance.Assuming that the economy is now near the long run growth curve, will it continue to grow henceforth along the historical path, in the neighborhood of 4.5% annually, or will it continue to grow at the very high rate it has exhibited since the period of recovery starting in the early 1950s? The optimists have a target that comes to 7.2% per annum. The post-war rate may have averaged above 9%. The trend figure is significantly lower. Which rate will prevail? This is an unsettled question.

The econometric contribution to this problem has been the formulation of a system for exhibiting the numerical trend development of the historical past. If the future has the structure of the past, the model gives a basis for numerical extrapolation of the future trend growth subject to uncertainty about exports. In conclusion, I should like to make some non-econometric observations on possible structural changes in the Japanese economy that have taken place since World War II. These changes appear to be large and important to people looking at them in today's perspective. Possibly, in a model interpreting trends since 1878, they are not so significant. They are (a) land reform, (b) breaking up of monopolies, (c) growth of trade unions, (d) loss of dependent territories, (e) reduction in military establishment, and (f) physical destruction of World War II.

The rapid technological development in agriculture and especially in industry, accompanied by an urban-rural population shift, have been notable features of the post-war period contributing to the high rate of growth of the 1950s. Nevertheless, there has, for a long time, been rapid technical progress in all sectors of the economy. Land reform in agriculture after World War II and the establishment of a market economy in the countryside may now enable people to shift more rapidly from rural to urban areas without endangering necessary agricultural production for meeting the food problem. This is a structural change making for a higher rate of growth now than historically, but it must be offset by the knowledge that there has always been a high degree of technical progress in both agriculture and industry. Agricultural policy now calls for government support of the rice price. An artificially high domestic price discourages some migration from the primary to other sectors and makes for less reliance on imported rice. The figures in Table 2 suggest a marked population shift away from agriculture during the 1960s and large increases in food imports. The model, from which these extrapolations are deduced, is not based on a structural policy of price supports and undoubtedly over-emphasizes the magnitude of the rural-urban shift.

The *Zaibatsu* were broken up in the reforms after World War II, but it is not altogether clear that competition will be more fruitful than monopoly, particularly in finance and heavy industry, where much of the *Zaibatsu* strength has been concentrated. This structural change, however, appears to be transient. Many observers of the Japanese economy feel that the *Zaibatsu*

Table 2. Extrapolation of the Model to 1968–72.

Variable	1958–62 $t = 15$	1963–67 $t = 16$	1968–72 $t = 17$
	Export Growth of 4 per cent		
x_1	4,786	4,844	4,773
x_2	25,620	33,260	42,920
x	30,406	38,104	47,693
n_1	15.88	14.27	12.49
n_2	25.19	28.43	31.89
n	94.72	100.56	106.65
I_I	1,593	2,426	3,501
$1 + b - d$	1.0633	1.0617	1.0606
	Export Growth of 5 Per cent		
x_1	4,605	4,354	3,844
x_2	26,260	34,950	46,180
x	30,865	39,304	50,024
n_1	15.27	12.83	10.05
n_2	25.82	29.87	34.31
n	94.72	100.54	106.62
I_I	1,822	3,006	4,606
$1 + b - d$	1.0633	1.0615	1.0607
	Export Growth of 6 Per cent		
x_1	4,406	3,835	2,795
x_2	26,900	36,750	49,870
x	31,306	40,585	52,665
n_1	14.62	11.30	7.31
n_2	26.45	31.41	37.05
n	94.72	100.54	106.61
I_I	2,049	3,618	5,834
$1 + b - d$	1.0633	1.0614	1.0604
	Export Growth of 7 Per cent		
x_1	4,199	3,264	1,584
x_2	27,600	38,700	54,150
x	31,799	41,964	55,734
n_1	13.93	9.62	4.14
n_2	27.14	33.07	40.26
n	94.72	100.53	106.59
I_I	2,293	4,304	7,264
$1 + b - d$	1.063	1.061	1.060

are again forming and reasserting their positions of power. It would be a weak argument to depend on the establishment of more competition for accelerating growth. Concurrent with the break-up of the major industrial combines, trade unions grew in strength in post-war Japan. They are now a significant political and economic force, whereas they were impotent and small before the war. The existence of strong trade unions may affect entry into the secondary and tertiary sectors of the economy. The overall result will probably be to restrain the rural-urban shift, and be another structural change making for overestimation of the extent of the shift in extrapolations of the model.

The holdings in Manchuria, Korea, and Formosa are now lost to Japan. In the statistical model, trade with these areas is regarded as external trade; therefore a structural change is not to be expected as a result of the changing status of these territories. Although Japanese exports have recovered markedly in recent years, there is econometric evidence to doubt that a structural change has occurred that would place the propensity to export above the historical pattern and make for more rapid growth. In an intermediate range model fitted jointly to the years 1930–1936 and 1951–1958, I find a significant negative shift of the propensity to export, post-war as compared with pre-war.[7]

Manchuria provided valuable raw materials for Japanese industry and a ready market for homeland exports. Korea and Formosa similarly aided the Japanese economy. These supports are now gone, except for some standard trading on a commercial basis. The imperial and general external position of Japan is not one that makes for especially rapid growth. Japanese trade has, in the 1950s, shifted largely towards North America. Rapid gains were made in this market during the latter part of the decade, but America's external position is now such that rapid gains are no longer to be expected. Unless Japan discovers some fresh trading possibilities (Latin America, Africa, Southeast Asia, Communist nations?) it is wise and prudent to use intermediate range growth rates for exports rather than high rates for extrapolation. I should prefer to concentrate on the use of an export growth rate of 6%, which is close to historical fact. In countries with large excess capacity, military expenditures provide a stimulus towards the achievement of full employment. Such expenditures do not contribute much to future productivity and growth. The Japanese military economy of the late 1930s led to a form of economic expansion, but its contribution to growth has probably

[7]This model has been prepared with the collaboration of Y. Shinkai of Osaka University.

been much less than has the peacetime nature of the economy of the 1950s.[8] The best manpower has been made available to agriculture and industry. Resources have been put into fixed civilian capital that laid the groundwork for future production. In the Japanese case low military expenditures, like high imports, have contributed to growth. The conventional type of multiplier analysis applied to the case of the United States generally leads to an opposite conclusion.

But will the military sector of the Japanese economy remain insignificant? The breaking up of monopolies appears to be a transitory event, and the elimination of the military factor in Japanese life may similarly turn out to be temporary. For the short run, however, the present size of the military establishment will enhance a high growth rate. Professor Milton Friedman has recently stated in a public address that he knows of a sure formula for promoting rapid growth. Destroy the greater part of a nation's fixed capital in war activity and dislocate the whole economic structure. Eventual recovery from this chaotic state of affairs will be rapid, giving a growth rate of 8–10% annually. West Germany, Japan, and the Soviet Union are striking examples of this type of growth. Perhaps there are structural changes in each case, allowing the countries concerned to grow at rates far above their secular paths for a long time. Reconstruction of war damage is, however, now fairly complete. There is little doubt that the experience of the 1950s reflects reconstruction growth. This is a factor that will be absent in the 1960s. Professor Shinohara has argued that Japanese growth rates have, for many years, shown a long cycle of about 20–25 years in duration. The decade of the 1950s provide a half-cycle of experience above the long run average growth rate. Naive interpretation of his results would suggest that the 1960s will approximately give a half-cycle below average. This would be somewhat consistent with extrapolation of the present long run model into the decade ahead. In Table 2, with export growth set at 6%, total output expands at an annual rate of 5.3% between 1958–1962 and 1968–1972. This rate is still above the long run average, which is 4.3% but considerably below the post-war average. Considering the possible structural changes listed above and their future impact, I should conclude that the model's results, slightly above the long run average, are reasonable and provide a better framework for future planning than does the official program with the target of doubling real national income in ten years.

[8]In 1934–1936, just before the war Japan spent about 7.1% of her national income on military goods and services. In 1957, the corresponding figure was 1.9%.

Chapter 9

An Econometric Model of Japan, 1930–1959*

Lawrence R. Klein and Yoichi Shinkai[1]

1. Introduction

There are probably more econometric models (in existence or far along in the process of construction) of Japan than of any other country in the world. The reason for proposing the present scheme therefore needs explanation. A very major model construction project that may have practical use in suggesting the lines of economic policy has been under way among the Osaka group for some time. This is perhaps the largest and most ambitious econometric project ever undertaken. It is a detailed quarterly model covering the post-war period. A model of the scope being considered cannot be estimated, tested, revised, and successfully applied in a short period of time. There is even some uncertainty as to its ultimate workability since it is such a massive scheme and nothing of comparable size or detail is known to exist in use elsewhere.

We thus thought it useful to have a companion model, in parallel, that is more aggregative over the dimensions of time and commodities. Our model in this chapter is an aggregative annual model. It is not unlike similar annual models of the USA, Canada, UK, and Holland that have been in use for some time. It is meant to serve as a companion piece and checking device for the larger system. After a relatively short period of time (about six months), it

*This chapter was published in *International Economic Review*, January, 1963 (Vol. 4, No. 1). Permission granted by the editor.

[1]The research upon which this study was based was initiated during the visit of L. R. Klein to the Institute of Social and Economic Research of Osaka University. Thanks are due to the Rockefeller Foundation for support of this visit under their grant to Osaka University and to the staff members of the Institute who patiently gave their guidance and advice to the development of this project.

has become available for trial applications. It is also informative, at this early stage, on some structural characteristics of the Japanese economy. While it belongs to the same general class of models as its foreign predecessors, it bears many distinctive characteristics of the Japanese economy apart from the numerical values of its estimated parameters.

The detailed quarterly model must of necessity be limited to a sample period of the era after World War II. Actually, the Japanese economy is not suitable for the types of study that we propose in this period until after the start of the Korean War and the end of the Occupation. Quarterly data are not available in large measure before the post-war period. Annual data do exist, however, for a period beginning in 1930. This makes possible the investigation of a problem that is avoided in work on the post-war quarterly model, namely, the study of structural change between the 1930s and 1950s. To many observers it may appear self-evident that behavior and technology have radically changed as a result of the impact of World War II. There is often much that is basic in economic structure, transcending even the disruptive effects of a major catastrophe such as war. We shall attempt to isolate some of the changing and the stable characteristics of the Japanese structure in the period 1930–1958.

We do not, however, include the years 1937–1950 in our sample.[2] It would be possible to extend some of our related annual series beyond 1930, say to the end of World War I, but we have decided to rely on the efforts of Professor Ueno of Nagoya University for a model extending back to 1919.

2. Rationale of the Model

Essentially, the system is the Keynesian type model of effective demand for an open economy. There are consumption and investment equations, with the national income-national product accounting identities. There are export and import propensity equations, production functions, and wage- price determination equations. A main feature of the Japanese economy is the relation between the primary or agricultural sector and the rest of the economy. This is brought out in our model by two separate production functions, a relationship between food imports and domestic agricultural production,

[2]The normality of economic life during the period 1951–1955 is certainly questionable. We might have given special treatment to these years, by means of a dummy variable, but treating them as we did, on an equal footing with other observation periods, we did not obtain unusual residuals for these years. See Table A.2.

and an equation on the shift of labor between the two sectors. There is a birth and death population process as well as a liquidity preference equation.

Features of many preceding models have naturally affected our choice of other equations in the system, but the open economies of Holland and the UK provided some of the closest analogies. To account for possible structural change, we introduced additive dummy variables (0,1), which assumed zero values for pre-war years and unit values for post-war years. In cases where scatter diagrams showed changes in slope as well as level of relationships, we introduced dummy variables in products with variables with respect to which the slope changed.

Consumption: We made use of the ordinary aggregate consumption function in our model, but we explicitly took into account the effects of population size, taxes, lags, and income distribution. Since the equation is expressed in real terms, we might say that we also took into account the price level. As can be seen in equation (2.1), our income and consumption variables are measured per capita; this brings population into the equation. The income variable is disposable income; therefore, taxes and transfer payments are introduced. By writing current consumption as a function of last year's consumption we have lag effects, and it is well known that this form is a transformation of a distributed lag of the Koyck type.[3] Income distribution is represented through our use of a factor share ratio-property income divided by wage income.

Investment: The propensity to invest, as expressed in our model, resembles similar relationships used in many mathematical models of the trade cycle.[4] Investment, capital stock, property income, and interest rate are the familiar variables used. We relate the percentage rate of expansion of fixed capital (investment divided by the stock of capital) to the rate of return on capital (property income as a percentage of fixed capital). The rate of interest as a cost factor deterring investment has been unsuccessfully explored in many econometric models. In principle, this is an important variable in the investment process linking the real and monetary sectors. For the Japanese economy the principle may turn out to be significant in practice because rates are relatively high and fluctuate by a wide margin. There is much bank

[3]L. M. Koyck (1954). *Distributed Lags and Investment Analysis*. Amsterdam: North-Holland Publishing Co.

[4]The well known models of Kalecki and Kaldor are the best examples of systems with such investment relationships. M. Kalecki (1935). A Macrodynamic Theory of Business Cycles. *Econometrica*, III, 327–344. N. Kaldor (1940). A Model of the Trade Cycle. *Economic Journal*, L, 78–92.

borrowing and comparatively less internal financing for investment than in the US and other countries. In this aggregative model we have not separated working and fixed capital investment.

Exports: Japanese sales abroad are made to depend on two main variables, world activity and relative prices. The activity variable could be an index of world production — an index of world income — or an index of world trade. We have chosen world trade for our variable. It is probably more accurately measured over the span of our sample than are the other possible variables. We assume implicitly that Japan enjoys some marginal share of the world market. Exports could also be affected by relative price which we measure by the ratio of an index of world export prices to an index of Japanese export prices. Both indexes are expressed in gold, to take devaluations into account automatically.

Imports: Three categories of imports are distinguished. They are food, materials, and all other. Food imports are singled out for separate study because they are, in Japan, related to domestic food production as a supplement. When domestic agricultural output is high, food imports tend to be low and vice versa. This is particularly true for rice, the dominant food crop. Our equation posits an inverse relation between real per capita food imports and real per capita agricultural output. Another relevant variable is the relative rice price, the ratio between the domestic and imported price of rice. Not only the physical production situation, but also the economic advantage of foreign compared with domestic rice will affect imports. This allows for the fact that foreign rice may be considered to be of inferior quality, for the strength of reaction to the relative rice price depends on Japanese tastes. Materials are, for the most part, imported to be used in manufacturing. We, therefore, related material imports to the level of non-agricultural output. Other imports are used throughout the economy, and we related these to the level of aggregate national product. In all the import equations, real magritudes and relative prices are used. Relative price variables were considered in all import equations, but the only significant effect of prices was found in the case of food imports. These equations complete the endogenous components in the make up of national product. We now turn to the group of equations dealing with supply, market prices and population.

Production: Nonagricultural output is, as usual, made to depend on labor and capital as input factors. Technological trends were also considered but later dropped in the statistical estimation of coefficients. In agriculture, we do not have separate capital input data. We related output per agricultural worker to important factors that affect farm production. One of these is natural conditions, expressed in the form of a regularly published series on damaged crop area as a result of adverse growing conditions. Such conditions may cover weather, pestilence and other natural phenomena. A negative association is to be expected between output and this variable. A positive association is introduced through the use of a variable showing the quantity of fertilizer input. A final factor to consider is an upward technological trend. Significant technical progress is, in fact, found in this case.

Prices and wages: In the UK and Dutch models, price mark-up equations for the open economy have been used.[5] These equations show the mark-up of final price over prime unit costs. The main prime costs are wages and import prices. The US and Canadian models differ by using equations for labor's share.[6] These might be interpreted as marginal productivity conditions if the production relations can be approximated by equations of the Cobb-Douglas type. The literature of theoretical economics also has these distinctions, for the case of full-cost pricing, or mark-up over costs, is considered to be a practical alternative to marginalist pricing theory. The equation of labor's share may be transformed from $wN_e = \alpha pY$ to $p = 1/\alpha \cdot wN_e/Y$ in which $p =$ price of output, $Y =$ volume of output, $w =$ wage rate, $Ne =$ employment. Our mark-up equation is a slight generalization of this form since p is made to be a linear combination of wN_e/Y, and $p_i M/Y$, where $p_i =$ price of imports, $M =$ import volume.

We can interpret this equation as saying that price is marked up over prime unit costs, w and p_i, but that the mark-up is modified by productivities of labor and imports. As these inputs become more productive, there is need for only a smaller margin of mark-up to reach a given level of profit. The equation of wage determination states that wages adjust to changes in final prices but that labor's bargaining position is affected by the state of demand in the labor market. The latter variable is represented by unemployment. All variables in this relation are expressed in percentage terms-percent change in wage rates, percent change in price level, and percent of labor force unemployed. Similar equations have been estimated for the US and UK models.[7]

---

[5]L. R. Klein *et al.* (1961). *An Econometric Model of the UK*. Oxford: Blackwell. Central Planning Bureau (1956). *Scope and Methods of the Central Planning Bureau*. The Hague.
[6]L. R. Klein and A. S. Goldberger (1955). *An Econometric Model of the United States, 1929–1952*. Amsterdam: North-Holland Publishing Co.
[7]L. R. Klein and A. S. Goldberger, *op cit.*; L R. Klein, *et al.*, *op cit.*

Liquidity preference: The Keynesian theory of demand for cash is a generalization over the classical quantity theory in that velocity (or its reciprocal) is not assumed to be constant. It is assumed to be variable and dependent on the rate of interest. In its most general form, this theory expresses the nominal amount of cash as a joint function of money income and interest rate. This theory is based on the assumption that assets may be held in two forms, cash or securities (bonds). We have broadened the scope of possible asset forms to include goods, or, in a sense, equity investments. The desirability of holding goods or equities against either money or bonds is indicated by prospective price changes, which show the extent to which capital gains can be made. We follow A. J. Brown, who pioneered in statistical research on liquidity preference, by including a price change and an interest rate variable in our explanation of cash holdings.[8] We have transformed the dependent variable to the reciprocal of the velocity ratio rather than the level of cash holding itself.

Population: In most econometric models, population is considered to be exogenous. An important exception is the work of Valavanis-Vail on an American growth model.[9] He starts from the identity

$$N_t = N_{t-1}(1 + b_t - d_t - e_t),$$

which states that population (N_t) of period t is equal to population of period $(t - 1)$ augmented by births and decreased by deaths and net emigration. The rates of birth, death, and emigration for the basic time unit considered are b, d and e. We have used this identity and attempted to find explanatory equations for b and d. Net emigration is regarded as negligible, as far as Japan is concerned. The birth rate is assumed to depend on per capita income and the death rate to be a declining trend function of time.

Labor Supply: Two aspects of labor supply are given explicit treatment in the model. Both are significant in the Japanese scene. Following our prior explanation of population development, we want an expression to show how many of the population are available for productive effort. We have a labor force participation rate — the ratio of labor force to population — which is a simple function of time. The rate of participation is slowly growing, apart from a wartime setback. The other important aspect of Japanese labor supply is its distribution between agriculture and industry, emphasized by

[8]A. J. Brown (1939). Interest, Prices and the Demand Schedule for Idle Monery. *Oxford Economic Papers*, II, 46–69.

[9]S. Valavanis-Vail (1955). An Econometric Model of Growth: USA, 1869–1953. *American Economic Review, Papers and Proceedings,* XLV, 208–221.

the modern shift from rural to urban areas. We make the ratio of employment in the two sectors depend on the level of the real wage rate. This is essentially the wage rate paid in the nonagricultural sector, and this equation shows the pull of workers from agriculture, the attraction being high income rates in industry.

Identities and restrictions: We have completed the analysis of the content of our model in terms of behavior or technological equations. The system is not closed, however, without some identities. We have the equality between national product and national income, or, what is the same thing, total output expressed as a sum of expenditures and also as a sum of income flows, adjusted for indirect taxes and subsidies. Unemployment is the difference between labor force and employment. Net investment is the rate of change of capital stock, and the aggregate wage bill is the product of wage rate and employment. Both indirect and direct taxes are used in the model as separate variables. Under conditions of existing tax laws they could be approximately expressed as functions of total income or product. Such equations would act as restrictions on the system. We have not explicitly shown such restrictions in this writing of the model.

2.1. *The variables*

$^*C$ = consumption in billions of 1934–1936 Yen.
$^*N$ = population in million persons.
$^*Y - T_d$ = deflated disposable income, billions of 1934–1936 Yen.
$^*P$ = deflated non-wage income, billions of 1934–1936 Yen.
$^*W$ = deflated wage income, billions of 1934–1936 Yen.
$^*I$ = net investment in billions of 1934–1936 Yen.
$^*K$ = year end capital stock in billions of 1934–1936 Yen.
i = interest rate.
$^*F_e$ = exports in billions of 1934–1936 Yen.
T_w = index of world trade.
p_w = index of world export prices.
p_j = index of Japanese export prices.
$^*F_{if}$ = food imports in billions of 1934–1936 Yen.
$^*Y_f$ = domestic food production in billions of 1934–1936 Yen.
P_d = domestic rice price.
P_m = imported rice price.
$^*F_{im}$ = material imports in billions of 1934–1936 Yen.
$^*Y$ = net national product in billions of 1934–1936 Yen.
$^*F$ = “other” imports in billions of 1934–1936 Yen.

$^*N$ = nonagricultural employment in million persons.
$^*N_J$ = agricultural employment in million persons.
F = index of fertilizer input.
H = damaged area of cultivated land in ten million cho.
t = trend, in years, beginning with unity in 1930 ($\times$ 1/10).
$^*p$ = index of price level, 1934–1936: 1.00.
P_i = index of import prices.
$^*w$ = wage rate in thousands of current Yen.
$^*M$ = total imports in billions of 1934–1936 Yen.
$^*U$ = unemployment rate.
$^*L$ = cash balances in billions of current Yen.
$^*b$ = birth rate.
d = death rate.
e = net emigration rate.
$^*N_L$ = labor force in million persons.
G = government current expenditures in billions of 1934–1936 Yen.
T_i = indirect taxes less subsidies in billions of 1934–1936 Yen.
D = pre-war-post-war shift (0 in pre-war and 1 in post-war period).

Endogenous variables in this list are marked with an asterisk (*). For purposes of statistical estimation, taxes are not treated as endogenous. Disposable income in the above list is marked endogenous, but Y is regarded as endogenous, while T_d is not; thus one must take account of this fact in counting equations and variables. We have denoted L as endogenous and i as predetermined. The usual practice in business cycle theory is the opposite, but our procedure appears to be more realistic. We have provided no explanation of Japanese rice, or total export prices; hence these are not treated as endogenous. Considering the role of government agricultural policy it is not unrealistic to treat the rice price as predetermined.

2.2. *The estimated equations*

Our sample consists of yearly observations for the period 1930–1936 and 1951–1958. The method of estimation is Theil's *two-stage-least- squares.*[10]

$$\begin{array}{llll} C/N = 0.055 + 0.230(Y - T_d)/N & + 0.576(C/N)_{t-1} & + 0.0191(P/W) & \\ R^2 = 0.96 \qquad (0.072) & (0.069) & (0.0049) & (2.1) \end{array}$$

[10]Predetermined variables used in the first stage of the two-stage-least-squares estimation procedure were $(C/N)_{t-1}$, D, P_d/P_m, P_w/P_j, F, H, p_i, T_w, G and T_d.

$$I/K = -0.005 + 0.478(P/K) - 0.678\,i + 0.0561D$$
$$R^2 = 0.94 \quad (0.140) \quad (0.244) \quad (0.0108) \qquad (2.2)$$

$$F_e = -2.92 + 3.917T_w + 2.457(p_w/p_j) - 3.37D$$
$$R^2 = 0.85 \quad (0.731) \quad (0.417) \quad (0.40) \qquad (2.3)$$

$$F_f/N = 0.00396 - 0.0618Y_f/N + 0.000463p_d/p_m - 0.00405D$$
$$R^2 = 0.88 \quad (0.0473) \quad (0.00032) \quad (0.00067) \qquad (2.4)$$

$$F_{im} = -1.27 + 0.260(Y - Y_f) - 1.163D$$
$$R^2 = 0.87 \quad (0.029) \quad (0.231) \qquad (2.5)$$

$$F_{io} = 0.96F + 0.0563Y - 1.713D$$
$$R^2 = 0.97 \quad (0.0132) \quad (0.122) \qquad (2.6)$$

$$Y - Y_f = 6.46 + 0.770N_e + 0.106K$$
$$R^2 = 20.89 \quad (0.083) \quad (0.048) \qquad (2.7)$$

$$Y_f/N_f = 0.114 + 0.0590F - 0.0986H + 0.0269t$$
$$R^2 = 0.90 \quad (0.0224) \quad (0.0387) \quad (0.0102) \qquad (2.8)$$

$$p = 0.370 + 0.995wN_e/(Y - Y_f) + 0.73p_iM/Y + 124.4D$$
$$R^2 = 0.99 \quad (0.083) \quad (0.25) \quad (13.2) \qquad (2.9)$$

$$(w - w_{-1})/w_{-1} = -0.260 + 0.746(p - p_{-1})/p_{-1} - 16.98U$$
$$R^2 = 0.64 \quad (0.183) \quad (10.8) \qquad (2.10)$$

$$L/pY = -0.229 - 0.000867(p - p_{-1}) - 0.214D_i$$
$$R^2 = 0.59 \quad (0.000368) \quad (0.104) \qquad (2.11)$$

$$log_{10}(b - 0.015) = -0.414 - 6.491\,Y/N - 0.3045D$$
$$R^2 = 0.98 \quad (0.565) \quad (0.0332) \qquad (2.12)$$

$$log_{10}(d - 0.005) = -1.775 - 0.277t$$
$$R^2 = 0.99 \quad (0.004) \qquad (2.13)$$

$$N_e/N_J = -0.241 + 3.799w/p + 0.191D$$
$$R^2 = 0.92 \quad (0.59) \quad (0.049) \qquad (2.14)$$

$$N_L/N = 0.442 + 0.0398t - 0.0822D$$
$$R^2 = 0.30 \quad (0.0143) \quad (0.0314) \qquad (2.15)$$

$$C + I + G + Fe - M = Y$$
$$P + W = Y - T,$$
$$F_{if} + F_{im} + F_{io} = M$$
$$K - K_{t-1} = I$$
$$w/p(N) = W$$
$$U = (N_L - N_e - N_f)/N_L$$
$$N = N_{t-1}(1 + b - d - e)$$

3. Some Properties of the System

In this section we shall discuss some of the interesting properties of our system from the point of view of each equation.

Consumption: Our consumption function can be rewritten in the form

$$C = 0.055N + 0.230Y_d + 0.576(C/N)_{-1}N - 0.0191(P/W)N,$$

where $Y_d = Y - T_d$ stands for disposable income. It is seen immediately that the short run marginal propensity to consume is 0.23. This value may be compared with findings by other economists: 0.346 by H. Ueno; 0.313 by T. Uchida and K. Mori; 0.373 by H. Eguchi.[11] Our value appears to be low. This may be due to the fact (1) that our function is estimated in per capita terms while the other functions are not, (2) that our sample periods extend to the pre-war years, in some of which $\delta C/\delta Y_d$ assumes negative values. If we put $C/N = (C/N)_{-1}$ in the above equation, we get a sort of long run marginal propensity to consume, which turns out to be 0.542.

The comparable findings by other economists are: 0.749 by H. Ueno; 0.616 by T. Uchida and K. Mori; 0.777 by H. Eguchi. The average propensity to consume at the point of sample means is 0.899, which is calculated simply as $\Sigma_t C_t / \Sigma_t (Y_d)_t$. The Japanese people as individual consumers have been saving about 10% of their income in real terms.

The reader will notice that the share of non-wage income in the total national income has a negative effect on consumption, as would be expected.

[11] H. Ueno (1961). *Econometric Analysis of the Japanese Economy*. Tokyo: Toyokeizai, p. 167; T. Uchida and K. Mori (1960). A Simulation Analysis of the Japanese Economy. In M. Morishima, M. Shinohara and T. Uchida, (eds.) *New Economic Analysis*. Tokyo: Sobunsha, p. 214; H. Eguchi (1959). An Econometric Model of the Japanese Economy. Mimeograph, November.

The magnitude of this effect may be expressed by means of an "elasticity" coefficient which assumes the value -0.0877 in the year 1958.[12] This means that a 10% rise in the ratio of non-wage to wage income reduces real consumption by roughly 1%. As regards our remark above that $\delta C/\delta Y_d$ assumes negative values in some of the pre-war years, it must be noted that in our estimated equation (2.1) the contribution of Y_d in the explanation of C/N is rather small, and that the lagged per capita consumption $(C/N)_{-1}$ has a coefficient which is more than twice as large. (This may be the reason why the pre-post-war shift variable turned out insignificant here.) Thus the total correlation coefficient is high in spite of the bad fit between Yd/N and C/N in the pre-war years.

Investment: The investment function can be rewritten as

$$I = -0.005K + 0.478P - 0.678\,iK \quad \text{for pre-war years,}$$

$$I = 0.051K + 0.478P - 0.678\,iK \quad \text{for post-war years.}$$

If we regard i as "the" rate of interest, and assume that it is roughly equal to the rate of profit, then $P = iK$. In that case net investment becomes negative in the pre-war equation; this means that when excess profits $(P - iK)$ are zero, entrepreneurs will not only stop net investment, but let the existing stock of capital decumulate. This is what would have happened in the pre-war years.

In the post-war period, on the other hand, if we put $P = iK$ and substitute the average value of post-war i, the investment function becomes $I/K = 0.0341$. After the war we have observed a very high rate of growth in the Japanese economy. The above finding suggests that capital in the Japanese economy would have been growing at an annual rate of 3.4% even if excess profits had been zero. One is tempted to attribute this to an optimistic and spirited outlook on the part of Japanese entrepreneurs.

The contribution of interest rate is fairly large in explaining the variable I/K. Our finding that the rate of interest has a significant effect on investment behavior is to be expected because in the Japanese economy the financing of capital is said to draw heavily on the money market, financing by accumulated profits being much less important than in Western countries.

Exports: It is noted that the coefficient of the shift variable is negative, and its magnitude 3.37 is rather large as compared with the average value of

[12]By elasticity we mean $[\delta C/\delta(P/W)](P/W)/C$. For the sake of brevity we shall refer throughout this section to the magnitude $(\delta y/\delta x)x/y$ as the elasticity of y with respect to x.

exports, which is 3.30. This means that with same levels of world trade and the relative price of world and Japanese exports, Japanese exports would have been much larger in the pre-war years than in the post-war years. It is commonly believed that the abnormally high level of Japanese exports in the pre-war period was due, in part at least, to her effort for political reasons to increase exports to her colonies, especially to Manchuria.[13] Some attribute it to the fact that in these periods Japan was depreciating her rate of exchange very rapidly.[14] This was of course true. However, since we have accounted for changes in the rate of exchange in our data processing, the explanation of the negative coefficient on the shift variable must be found elsewhere. The elasticities of exports with respect to the two independent variables, T_w and $p_w p_{ji}$, are 1.068 and 1.360. They are evaluated at the average level of each variable. It is to be noted that both elasticities exceed unity, implying that a 1% rise in the volume of world trade or in relative prices would increase Japanese exports by more than 1%.

Imports: As for the import function of foods, the coefficient of the shift variable is rather big because the average level of the explained variable is 0.00477. An explanation of this large positive shift may be as follows: In the post-war period, the price of rice has been under control so that the observed values of P_d have been smaller than they would have been in the absence of price control. The portion of the post-war imports of rice that should have been explained by higher P_d/P_m must therefore be explained by something else. Hence a positive coefficient on the shift variable.

A referee has pointed out that our series on food imports may show too much of an increase between pre-and post-war periods. Some estimates indicate that the food share in total imports fell from 1934–1936 to 1957. Our figures are based on aggregation of individual food imports. Lacking more definitive data on revised estimates of imports by type, we cannot decide whether our series are incorrect.

A remarkable thing in the import function of materials and of other things is that neither relative prices nor the holdings of gold and foreign currencies turned out to be significant. It is also noticeable that the shift variables have negative coefficients. In the case of material imports this may be explained by a technological improvement that led to material savings in

[13]Note that our series on exports includes exports of goods and services from the Japanese Mainland to the colonies.

[14]W. W. Lockwood (1954). *The Economic Development of Japan*. Princeton: Princeton University Press, pp. 64–77.

the production of nonfood goods. In the case of other imports an explanation is found in the increased supply potential of final products in post-war Japan. Combining the three import functions, we get total imports as a function of domestic production

$$M = 0.3167\,Y - 0.3222\,Y_f + (\text{a function of } p_d/p_m,\ N,\ \text{and } D).$$

As the average level of Y_f/Y is 0.167, this function may be rewritten as

$$M = 0.2629\,Y + \text{something}.$$

The marginal propensity to import is thus about 0.26 in real terms.

Non-agricultural production: The production elasticities are calculated as 1.006 (with respect to labor) and 0.418 (with respect to capital). They add to 1.424, a value significantly larger than unity. Thus the production of nonfood goods takes place under increasing returns to scale. This might be due to fairly remarkable improvements in the technique of production. It also indicates the industrial youth of Japan. That there have been steady technological improvements can be seen from the fact that both output per man and the output-capital ratio have been rising. On the other hand, the contribution of labor in equation (2.7) is larger and that of capital is smaller in the post-war periods than in the pre-war periods. It may be that destruction of capital stock during the war made it necessary to produce a given output with less capital and more labor than before the war. But the dislocation in

Table 1. ***Ex-post*** **Extrapolation to 1959.**

Variable	Observed value	Estimated value	Percentage error
F_{im}	4.11	3.50	14.8
F_{if}	0.588	0.57	13.0
C	19.6	19.1	2.4
I	7.43	5.26	29.2
F_{io}	0.882	0.773	12.4
Y	29.7	27.1	8.7
Y_f	4.03	4.34	−7.7
N_e	28.3	26.7	5.8
N	15.4	17.1	−10.8
W	174.7	170.8	2.2
U	0.0130	0.0133	−2.3
P	12.9	11.4	11.2
W	13.6	12.4	8.3
E	4.89	4.69	4.0

the modes of production during and after the war was not serious enough to make the shift variable statistically significant in this equation.

Agricultural production: The trend variable, t, expresses the effect of technological improvements on agricultural' productivity. To assess, in some way, the relative importance of this factor and of fertilizer input, we have calculated the "elasticities"; 0.322 with respect to F and 0.215 with respect to t. Interpreting this equation, it should be noted that the pre-war H series refers to damages by weather, but the post-war H includes damages due to other causes.

Price: The general price level in our model, the implicit GNP deflator, is made a function of the two main components of prime costs, the value productivity of nonagricultural labor and that of imports. Those indices are not directly comparable; so we have calculated the "elasticities" with respect to the two variables in order to assess mark-up coefficients of the general price over prime costs. The result is 0.514 with respect to labor productivity and 0.873 with respect to import productivity. These figures can be compared with corresponding findings in the UK and Dutch models: 0.421 and 0.216 in the UK and 0.48 and 0.16 in the Dutch model.[15]

In the UK and Dutch models, general price is a function of wage rate and import price, not of productivities. It should also be noted that there are included other explanatory variables that may affect the values of the mark-up coefficients. Nevertheless, we remain convinced from the results cited above that in Japan the mark-up coefficients are significantly higher, the contribution of import productivity being especially larger. This may sustain the commonly held view that a strong inflationary tendency is inherent in the Japanese economy and that the movement of the price level is very sensitive to that of import prices.

Wage: Our wage rate determination equation shows that a 10% rise in the general price level induces a 7.5% increase in the wage rate within the same year. Can it be said that a three-quarters adjustment of wages to prices within the same year is fairly rapid? If this is so, and if we consider the large mark-up coefficients of prices over costs discussed in the preceding paragraph, we must conclude that our findings testify to a strong inflationary tendency in the Japanese economy.

---

[15]L. R. Klein and R. J. Ball (1959). Some Econometrics of the Determination of Absolute Prices and Wages. *Economic Journal,* LXIX, 465–482, and J. Tinbergen (1956). *Economic Policy: Principles and Design*. Amsterdam: North-Holland Publishing Co., p. 110.

Putting $4w = 0$ and $ap = 0$ in equation (2.10), we find the level of unemployment consistent with stable wages and prices. The calculation shows that this value is about 0.0153; that is to say, we have to accept 1.53 percent unemployment if we are to have wage and price stability. Since the average level of unemployment in the sample period is 1.18% and the highest level is 1.69 (in 1932), it can be argued that the level of unemployment required for stable growth is fairly high. In this connection, the reader may question the plausibility of our unemployment figures, for the average level of 1.18% is abnormally low on Western standards. This is due to the fact that the unemployment data we used excludes all those who were employed part-time or in "disguised" employment. It is sometimes said that 1% unemployment according to these data corresponds to 4% or 5% in Western countries.

Liquidity: In the liquidity function, as it stands, the sampling errors are tolerable although the total correlation coefficient is low. If the pre-war series of interest rates were taken into account, the sampling error for the coefficient of interest rate would become intolerably large. It must be recalled in this connection that in equation (2.2) the rate of interest as a cost element in investment decisions is found significant in the pre-war as well as post-war periods. This may be explained by referring to the "low interest policy" of the Government and Monetary Authorities in the pre-war years that kept the rate of interest lower than it would otherwise have been, thus invalidating the liquidity function. On the other hand, investment decisions are made according to the given rate of interest, whatever it may be, so that our pre-war investment is explained significantly by interest rate fluctuations.

Birth and death rates: Although birth and death rates will be affected by various factors, economic and non-economic, we have found simple equations that fit well for our sample period. In the case of birth rate, per capita income and a shift variable explain most of the observed variations. A negative coefficient for the shift variable means that there was a once-for-all decrease in the birth rate after the war. This was apparently due to a change in the attitude of people towards birth control, which had been regarded as "unpatriotic" before the war but is now encouraged. The decrease in the death rate reflects progress in medical science. Birth and death rates in the post sample years deviate from past trends; both rates seem to show upward trends, or they are not falling as fast as in the past. Improvements in the standard of living may have changed the minds of people for more children; or rapid industrial expansion has increased occupational diseases and accidents. Anyway, we did not think that our equations (2.12) and (2.13) would do well for forecasting purposes, and decided to treat population as a predetermined variable for forecasting.

Labor supply: The ratio of nonagricultural to agricultural labor shows an upward trend in the post-war period. This trend may have started during the war partly because of the accelerated increase in industrial production and partly because of a rise in agricultural productivity. This may explain a positive coefficient for the shift variable. As to the sensitivity of the N_e/N_J ratio to the real wage rate, calculations show that a 1% increase in the real wage rate brings about a 1% rise in the N_C/N_f ratio. In the case of total labor supply, a 10% increase in the trend variable induces a 1.3% increase in the labor force participation ratio.

4. Extrapolation to 1959

As explained in Sec. 2, the model was fit to sample data terminating with the year 1958. Subsequently, data became available for 1959, and we extrapolated the model to that year, given approximately current values of predetermined variables at the time of the extrapolation. These were not forecasts, prepared in advance of the event. A much simpler problem than extrapolation of the entire system, is the computation of residuals for the fitted equations in 1959. This is a prior step to extrapolation of the whole model since it may show where individual components of the system are malfunctioning. Most of the equations fit well in 1959 except the investment

Table 2. Predetermined Variables used in the Extrapolations.

Variables	1959	1960	1961
$(C/N)_{-1}$	0.200	0.211	0.212
T_w	1.39	1.54	1.61
p_w/p_j	2.09	2.07	2.07
P_d/P_m	2.09	2.09	2.09
F	.80	1.85	1.90
H	0.469	0.455	0.455
N	93.0	93.9	94.8
T_i	3.25	3.56	4.35
G	3.34	3.50	4.12
I	0.0790	0.0790	0.0750
P	365.08	371.25	384.24
N_L	44.3	Endogenous	Endogenous

function, the industrial production function, the cost mark-up equation, the wage determination equation, the birth rate equation and the death rate equation. Investment and production are underestimated in their respective equations. The results are symptomatic of the investment boom and technical changes that are going on in present-day Japan. The equations of the model dealing with price and wage formation have similarly underestimated the inflationary pressure generated by this expansionary boom. Birth rates are underestimated and death rates overestimated, giving rise to a faster population growth than our equations suggest. Birth rates have been low in post-war Japan, but we may have exaggerated that tendency. There is no sign yet of a basic reversal in this trend of the birth rate. Residuals were computed for the last sample years, since 1956, as well as for 1959, to see if there are systematic biases in the equations (one-signed residuals, year after year), but we found no cause for revising our equations on this account. Residuals for the whole sample period are given in Table A.2.

The model is nonlinear, and this makes the simultaneous solution for extrapolation algebraically complicated. If we fix some of the variables that are associated with the large residuals noted above, for 1959, we can enormously simplify the system by nearly reducing it to a set of linear equations. We might fix the value for population on the assumption that we can extrapolate directly from past trends more accurately than by using our birth and death rate equations that are in error for 1959. We similarly fixed the value for the price level on the basis of our judgment of continued inflationary pressures. For 1959, this judgment did not have to be exercised, but for 1960 and 1961 it did. The interest rate is also fixed in advance for the extrapolation period.

The factorial income distribution ratio, P/W, is a nonlinear element in the consumption equation, but this term was fixed at its 1959 value. Nonlinear expressions, wN_e and N_e/N_f, were approximated by a Taylor's expansion, with linear terms only, about the previous year's values. The relationship between disposable and total income was approximated by the linear equation

$$Y_d = -3.56 + 0.92Y.$$

The following variables were assigned their observed levels in 1959[16]: $(C/N)_{-1}, T_w, p_w/p_i, p_d/p_m, F, H, N_L, N, T_i, G, K_{-1}, i, p$. In Table 1

[16]In 1959, N_L was assigned its observed value for the solution. In later extrapolations this variable was treated as endogenous.

we give the results of the extrapolation, and in Table 2 we present values of the predetermined variables used in the extrapolation. The largest error is in the estimation of investment as we might have guessed on the basis of fit of the individual equations.

The error in total production is considerably smaller, in percentage terms, because investment is not the largest component of national product. Material imports are poorly estimated and these are large in the total import bill; therefore total imports are estimated with almost as large a percentage error as materials; however, total imports are estimated more accurately than is investment.

The wage rate and unemployment variables are very near the actual levels. Absolute standards of precision cannot be set, but if all variables could be estimated within 5% of the true value we would undoubtedly be pleased. In most cases we have been within 10% of the true value. This leaves much room for improvement. Nevertheless, we do find that the model is functioning in the general neighborhood of the true values of the endogenous variables. This is our principal conclusion from the extrapolation to 1959.

Some consequences of the error in estimation of investment can be seen in further calculations. We reduced the system to two linear equations relating I and Y. One of these two equations is a direct transformation of the investment equation, and the other is a "partially reduced form" derived from algebraic substitution and elimination of all the other equations of the system. We then shifted each of these two linear equations by a constant amount so that they intersected at the actual values for I and Y in 1959. This necessitated a large adjustment to the investment equation and a small adjustment to the "partially reduced form". An important result follows from this adjustment. The adjusted calculation gives a higher rate of growth for output (the actual growth rate, in fact) for 1958–1959 and in doing so generates a balance of trade deficit. Before adjustment, our calculations show $F_e - F_{im} - F_{if} - F_{io} = +275$ billion Yen, calculated at current prices. In real terms, our extrapolation had underestimated total imports. After adjustment for higher investment and more rapid growth, we get

$$F_e - F_{im} - F_{if} - F_{io} = -26 \text{ billion Yen},$$

calculated at current prices. Our model suggests that the cost of rapid growth is a strain on the balance of trade.

5. Prospects for Japanese Development in the Light of the Model

Two genuine (or *ex ante*) forecasts have been made for 1960 and 1961. The calculations were started in the latter part of 1960, and statistics for the year were not yet known, although we knew, in a general way, how the economy was functioning in months just preceding the work on the predictions. For 1961, there was no advance indication of the actual statistics. Even though the model did not extrapolate well in all departments to 1959, we felt that it could be used to show internal (within model) changes from 1959 to 1960 and from 1960 to 1961. We compare values computed for 1960 with those computed for 1959 and those computed for 1961 with those computed for 1960. Lagged values of variables used in the 1960 extrapolations were taken to be actual and not computed values for 1959. The values of predetermined variables used in the extrapolation are shown in Table 2.

From these, we can see the *a priori* presumptions that are built into the calculations. These values must be taken into account in evaluating our appraisal of the near term prospects for Japanese development. Steady growth in population, world trade, fertilizer input, the price level and government spending are projected. Interest rates are expected to fall by a small amount between 1960 and 1961. The estimated values for major variables in 1960 and 1961 show a steady rate of economic growth over the 1959

Table 3. Predictions of Endogenous Variables, 1960 and 1961.

Variables	Estimate 1960	Percentage Increase 1959–1960	Estimate 1961	Percentage Increase 1960–1961
C	19.9	5.2	20.7	3.0
I	5.48	4.2	6.08	10.9
F_{im}	3.80	8.6	4.25	11.8
F_{if}	0.677	18.6	0.567	−16.2
F_{io}	0.848	9.7	0.950	12.0
Y	28.4	4.7	30.2	6.5
Y_f	4.51	3.9	4.59	1.8
N_e	27.4	2.6	28.8	5.1
N_f	17.3	1.2	17.2	−0.6
W	175	22.6	212.6	21.3
U	0.0146	9.8	0.0043	−70.5
N_L	45.3	2.3	46.2	2.0
P	12.0	5.3	12.4	3.3
W	12.9	4.0	13.5	4.7
F_e	4.83	2.9	5.10	5.6

estimates. The 1959–1960 growth in total output is approximately known from preliminary estimates, and our 1960 extrapolations understate both the level and rate of growth. Again investment appears to be underestimated. Consumption in 1960 is estimated fairly close to a preliminary value of the actual figure, 19.9 as compared with 20.1.

The estimated growth rates in real output are 4.7% and 6.5% for 1959–1960 and 1960–1961, respectively. These are low figures compared with 12.9 for 1958–1959 and with a presumption that the rate did not fall between 1960 and 1961. Our estimated growth rates in total output and the associated components of the national product indicate a balance-of-trade surplus in 1960 and in 1961. The figures are 212 billion Yen and 188 billion Yen at current prices.

In the 1959 extrapolations, as explained above, we adjusted the model so that the investment equation and the residual relation between I and Y intersected at the observed values of these two variables. We did not make a new adjustment for 1960 or 1961 values, but we did use the 1959 adjustments to the constant terms of the two equations in extrapolating the model to 1960 and 1961. This adjustment increases the 1959–1960 estimated growth rate (6.2%) but not the 1960–1961 estimated rate (3.6%). The level of investment is raised in 1960 and in 1961 with this adjustment, but apparently not enough to make the model estimates grow as fast as the economy actually did grow. These adjustments for higher levels of investment and output turn the estimated balance-of-trade surpluses into deficits, −129 billion Yen in 1960 and −84 billion Yen in 1961.

Our model suggests that the ambitious plan of growth for Japan — doubling of real national product between 1960 and 1970, implying a rate of growth of 7.2% per annum — is faster than the pattern that would evolve from historical relationships. The main features of disagreement between our model and the rapid growth of the first years of this decade are in capital formation and foreign trade. We obtain lower values for investment and a balance-of-trade surplus. If the economy grows much faster through a greater investment program, the trade balance appears to suffer. Unless large amounts of foreign capital can be obtained, it would appear that actual growth rate — in excess of those suggested by our model — will generate a balance-of-payments disequlibrium. Most of the 1960–1970 decade lies in the future, and the experience of the first years has not assured that the 7.2% rate can be maintained as a decade average. Our model serves as a device to emphasize clearly and quantitatively the areas of expansion and stress in this development program.

Appendix

The basic time series and general comments: *The National Income White Paper*[17] published yearly by the Economic Planning Agency (EPA) presents consistent figures of the national income and product flows. On the product side, our series of consumption, gross investment, government current expenditures, exports and total imports are taken bodily from the constant price national product series listed in the *White Paper*. For the classification of imports into foods, materials, and other imports we had to use different sources, as specified below.

On the income side, constant price series are not prepared by the EPA. We first construct wage income, nonwage income, primary industry income, and personal disposable income from the *White Paper*. We then use the implicit price deflator of the national product to obtain deflated series for the income flows. Indirect taxes and subsidy figures, and book value depreciation figures are also corrected by the implicit price deflator. Our net investment series are obtained simply by deducting the book value depreciation in constant prices from the gross investment series. Our figures on food production are real incomes in primary industry. The currently published EPA series are available from 1930.[18] The 1929 values of income and product variables which enter the model as initial lags are derived from tables prepared by Dr. K. Ohkawa.[19] The basic time series and specific comments: our series on the stock of capital is obtained by cumulating net investment. For the benchmarks of the pre-war and the post-war series, respectively, we use the *National Wealth Statistics* figures for 1930 and 1955, deflated by the EPA index of producer-good prices. Thus we assume that the increase or decrease in capital stock during the war period is explained by the difference between the two national wealth estimates.

The indices of the volume of world trade and world import prices are taken from the *Review of World Trade* (League of Nations) for the pre-war years, and from the *Statistical Yearbook* (United Nations) for the post-war years. In order to make the pre-war and post-war series comparable, we adjusted the League of Nations figures by the ratio of the 1938 UN figure to the 1938 LN figure.

---

[17]Referred to here as the *White Paper*.

[18]As of February, 1961.

[19]K. Ohkawa (ed.) (1960). *National Income*. Tokyo: Shunjusha.

The pre-war series of Japanese export prices is the gold-dollar price of the Japanese exports listed in the *Review of World Trade*. The post-war series is the unit price of exports prepared by EPA. It is not easy to link the two series in this case; so we left the gap between them to be explained by a shift variable in the export function (after making a rough adjustment parallel to one in the world trade series).

We constructed series on the values of food imports and material imports from the Ministry of Finance *Trade Statistics*. Price indices of imported foods and of imported materials are constructed by calculating the weighted average of the unit prices of principal import commodities. Our series of food imports and material imports in constant prices are obtained from the value and price series. Our series of the remaining import items is obtained as a residual by deducting the above two import series in constant prices from total import figures listed in the *White Paper*. The series on fertilizer inputs is constructed by calculating the weighted averages of chemical fertilizer inputs, the weights being the relative prices of fertilizers.

A post-war series on the rate of unemployment is taken from the *Labor Force Survey* by the Prime Minister's office. A pre-war series is calculated from the monthly reports by the Ministry of Home Affairs. To make the two series comparable, we adjusted the pre-war series so that the average level of pre-war unemployment is equal to that of post-war unemployment.

Sources of data

$C, Y - T_d, P, W, I, F_e, Y_f, Y, M, G, T_i, K$: Economic Planning Agency, *National Income White Paper*

i: Bank of Japan, *Economic Statistics of Japan*

T_w, p_w: League of Nations, *Review of World Trade*
United Nations, *Statistical Yearbook*

p_j: League of Nations, *Review of World Trade*
Economic Planning Agency, *National Income White Paper*

F_{if}, F_{im}, F_{io}: Ministry of Finance, *Trade Statistics*

p_d, p_w: H. Ohuchi (ed.) (1958). *Collection of Japanese Economic Statistics*. Tokyo: Nippon Hyoron.

N: Bank of Japan, *Economic Statistics of Japan*

N_L, N_e, N_f Y: Yamada (ed) (1957). *Estimates of the Japanese National Income*.
Tokyo: Toyokeizai.
Prime Minister's Office, *Labor Force Survey*

U: Ministry of Home Affairs, *Monthly Report*
Prime Minister's Office, *Labor Force Survey*
F, H: Ministry of Agriculture and Fishery, *Yearly Statistical Tables*
p_w, w, p_i: Economic Planning Agency, *National Income White Paper*
L: Bank of Japan, *Economic Statistics of Japan*
b, d, e: Bank of Japan, *Economic Statistics of Japan*

Sources of data for extrapolation and forecasting

In this section we will briefly indicate the general nature of the material used in making estimates of the values of exogenous variables and of lagged endogenous variables for the forecast period. The government current expenditure and indirect taxes, including central and local government items, are estimated from fiscal budget figures of the central government by assuming that the share of the central government in the total expenditure and tax absorption is constant or is changing "smoothly". Variables in the export function are estimated from the UN *Monthly Bulletin of Statistics* and Bank of Japan *Statistical Monthly*. For 1961 values, the volume of world trade is extrapolated from the post-war trends, while the relative price of world and Japanese goods is assumed to remain unchanged. The average yield on private long term bonds is taken from Bank of Japan *Statistical*

Table A.1. Sample Data.

	Y	*Ca*	*I*	*G*	*Pb*	*Fe*	*M*
1930	12.8	10.9	0.79	1.67	1.03	2.52	3.13
1931	13.1	10.8	0.81	2.31	0.90	2.89	3.72
1932	13.1	10.8	0.64	2.52	0.93	2.87	3.70
1933	13.5	10.8	0.63	2.62	0.98	2.98	3.59
1934	15.1	11.1	1.78	2.52	0.97	3.48	3.78
1935	15.4	10.7	1.91	2.61	1.01	4.21	4.05
1936	15.9	11.0	2.09	2.62	1.04	4.47	4.34
1951	16.8	10.6	4.09	1.73	288.00	2.15	1.79
1952	18.5	12.5	3.53	2.27	300.00	2.30	2.08
1953	20.1	13.9	4.17	2.26	319.00	2.67	2.92
1954	20.7	14.5	3.69	2.56	331.00	3.00	3.06
1955	22.9	15.4	4.53	2.72	329.00	3.48	3.24
1956	24.2	16.5	5.24	2.71	340.00	3.92	4.18
1957	26.0	17.4	6.50	2.85	350.00	4.27	5.05
1958	26.3	18.4	4.63	3.29	344.00	4.32	4.34

(*Continued*)

Table A.1. Sample Data.

	Finm	*FW*	*Io*	*W*	*P*	Y_f	*Ta*
1930	1.46	0.21	1.46	4.83	6.59	1.78	1.85
1931	1.66	0.27	1.80	4.98	6.68	1.86	1.95
1932	1.65	0.21	1.84	4.92	7.28	2.19	1.62
1933	1.80	0.18	1.62	4.93	7.77	2.53	2.75
1934	1.87	0.19	1.72	5.48	8.13	2.30	2.79
1935	1.98	0.20	1.87	5.46	8.88	2.61	2.48
1936	2.17	0.20	1.96	5.76	9.22	2.89	2.40
1951	1.23	0.41	0.14	6.31	8.78	3.44	4.60
1952	1.37	0.50	0.21	7.41	9.29	3.72	4.26
1953	1.95	0.52	0.45	8.40	9.49	3.46	5.14
1954	1.84	0.63	0.58	9.01	9.29	3.50	4.79
1955	2.01	0.62	0.62	9.58	10.40	4.16	5.38
1956	3.16	0.57	0.45	10.58	11.19	3.82	5.73
1957	3.87	0.55	0.63	11.57	11.93	3.80	6.31
1958	2.99	0.59	0.76	12.73	11.68	3.96	5.18

*1929 values: a 11.5; b 1.25

	T_i	K	W^c	T_w	p_w/p_j	p_d/p_m	p_i
1930	1.35	57.4	0.33	0.75	1.12	2.28	0.8
1931	1.46	58.2	0.32	0.69	1.16	3.28	0.6
1932	0.90	58.9	0.32	0.60	1.58	2.70	0.7
1933	0.77	59.5	0.32	0.59	1.58	2.54	0.9
1934	1.44	61.3	0.33	0.62	1.68	1.82	1.0
1935	1.05	63.2	0.33	0.65	1.68	3.84	1.0
1936	0.86	65.3	0.38	0.68	1.74	3.34	1.0
1951	1.74	44.7	90.70	0.95	1.84	1.46	399.0
1952	1.77	48.2	100.62	0.94	1.94	1.24	347.0
1953	2.22	52.3	120.20	1.00	2.07	1.28	299.0
1954	2.36	56.0	128.60	1.05	2.13	1.63	289.0
1955	2.89	60.6	130.60	1.14	2.26	1.82	281.0
1956	2.46	65.8	141.60	1.24	2.21	2.01	289.0
1957	2.49	72.3	150.90	1.31	2.22	2.13	307.0
1958	1.92	76.9	157.80	1.29	2.20	2.21	265.0

	N^d	N_L	N_e	N_f	U	B	D
1930	63.9	30.0	14.9	14.7	0.0129	0.0324	0.0189
1931	64.9	29.4	14.2	14.8	0.0146	0.0322	0.0190
1932	65.9	29.7	14.4	14.8	0.0169	0.0329	0.0177
1933	66.9	30.2	15.0	14.8	0.0140	0.0315	0.0177
1934	67.7	31.2	16.0	14.8	0.0123	0.0300	0.0181
1935	68.7	31.8	16.7	14.7	0.0115	0.0317	0.0168

(Continued)

Table A.1. (***Continued***)

1936	69.6	31.2	16.3	14.5	0.0107	0.0300	0.0175
1951	84.5	36.6	20.1	16.2	0.0108	0.0253	0.0099
1952	85.8	37.8	20.9	16.4	0.0126	0.0234	0.0089
1953	87.0	39.9	22.3	17.2	0.0114	0.0215	0.0089
1954	88.2	40.6	23.2	16.8	0.0148	0.0200	0.0082
1955	89.3	42.0	24.1	17.2	0.0165	0.0194	0.0078
1956	90.3	42.7	25.4	16.8	0.0152	0.0185	0.0080
1957	91.1	43.7	26.9	16.3	0.0123	0.0172	0.0083
1958	92.0	44.0	27.7	15.7	0.0131	0.0179	0.0074

*1929 values: C: 0.40; d: 62.9

	I	*L*	*F*	*H*	*T*
1930	0.0636	2.96	0.46	0.021	0.1
1931	0.0624	2.73	0.47	0.077	0.2
1932	0.0649	2.91	0.55	0.041	0.3
1933	0.0512	3.13	0.62	0.031	0.4
1934	0.0460	3.33	0.66	0.215	0.5
1935	0.0441	3.36	0.85	0.136	0.6
1936	0.0438	3.66	1.01	0.030	0.7
1951	0.0901	867.00	1.29	0.253	2.2
1952	0.0902	1116.00	1.01	0.170	2.3
1953	0.0898	1201.00	1.21	0.418	2.4

	I	*L*	*F*	*H*	*T*
1954	0.0904	1198.00	1.26	0.554	2.5
1955	0.0882	1392.00	1.55	0.327	2.6
1956	0.0738	1809.00	1.65	0.477	2.7
1957	0.0791	2003.00	1.70	0.450	2.8
1958	0.0788	2149.00	1.56	0.469	2.9

Monthly, and its 1961 value is assumed to fall by 1%, as indicated by the monetary authorities. The deflators are estimated from the same source, and in the absence of reasons to make changes, we have assumed that there will be no change. Fertilizer input is extrapolated from its past trend, and estimates of the damaged area of cultivated land are put at the average of the past five years. Estimates of population published by the Institute of Population Study are fairly reliable, and we have used them in estimating lagged per capita consumption for 1959 and 1960. As for the lagged endogenous variables for 1961, we used the values of endogenous variables estimated by extrapolations to 1959 and 1960.

Table A.2. Residuals from Structural Equations.

Year	Equation No.				
	(2.1)	**(2.2)**	**(2.3)**	**(2.4)**	**(2.5)**
1930	−0.003	0.0069	−0.25	−0.00004	−0.13
1931	0.000	0.0062	0.26	0.00038	−0.01
1932	0.001	0.0006	−0.44	0.00006	0.08
1933	0.006	−0.0124	−0.29	−0.00011	0.23
1934	0.001	0.0016	−0.16	0.00012	−0.17
1935	−0.005	−0.0023	0.46	−0.00043	−0.08
1936	−0.001	−0.0006	0.45	−0.00002	0.05
1951	−0.004	0.0073	0.20	−0.00128	0.17
1952	0.003	−0.0090	0.14	−0.00011	−0.03
1953	0.003	0.0030	−0.04	−0.00015	0.06
1954	−0.005	−0.0032	−0.06	0.00086	−0.21
1955	−0.002	0.0013	−0.25	0.00095	−0.43
1956	0.002	−0.0027	−0.08	0.00003	0.38
1957	0.001	0.0135	−0.03	−0.00038	0.52
1958	0.000	−0.0102	0.15	0.00004	−0.41
	(2.6)	**(2.7)**	**(2.8)**	**(2.9)**	**(2.10)**
1930	−0.22	−0.1	−0.021	0	−0.082
1931	0.10	0.7	−0.013	0	0.041
1932	0.14	0.1	−0.002	0	0.009
1933	−0.10	−0.5	0.013	0	−0.051
1934	−0.09	0.4	0.011	0	−0.031
1935	0.04	−0.3	0.010	0	−0.095
1936	0.11	0.0	0.010	0	0.001
1951	−0.05	−0.3	−0.011	−3	0.003
1952	−0.08	0.0	0.008	−3	0.070
1953	0.07	0.4	−0.008	2	0.005
1954	0.17	−0.1	0.007	3	0.029
1955	0.08	0.1	−0.001	8	0.039
1956	−0.16	0.3	−0.009	4	0.052
1957	−0.08	0.3	−0.012	0	−0.011
1958	0.03	−0.5	0.014	−8	0.019
	(2.11)	**(2.12)**	**(2.13)**	**(2.14)**	**(2.15)**
1930	−0.005	−0.047	−0.054	0.03	0.023
1931	0.002	−0.039	−0.024	−0.13	0.003
1932	0.010	−0.041	−0.041	−0.09	−0.003
1933	0.009	−0.065	−0.010	0.01	−0.007
1934	0.000	0.031	0.031	0.03	−0.001

(Continued)

Table A.2. (***Continued***)

Year	**Equation No.**				
	(2.11)	**(2.12)**	**(2.13)**	**(2.14)**	**(2.15)**
1935	−0.012	0.091	0.013	0.12	−0.003
1936	−0.007	0.070	0.069	0.02	−0.022
1951	0.003	0.024	0.074	0.09	−0.015
1952	0.002	0.038	0.003	−0.02	−0.011
1953	−0.007	0.031	0.031	−0.08	0.004
1954	−0.025	−0.063	−0.027	−0.05	0.001
1955	−0.027	0.023	−0.058	−0.06	0.007
1956	0.017	0.002	−0.030	−0.02	0.006
1957	0.017	−0.089	0.070	0.05	0.009
1958	0.020	0.037	−0.042	0.08	0.003

Chapter 10

Osaka ISER Model

I. An Outline of the Model

Lawrence R. Klein and Shinichi Ichimura

1. The ISER Model in Contemporary Macroeconomic Theory

The dominant model in macroeconomics is some version of the Keynesian scheme of income determination. A simplified account of the Keynesian system would decompose total production into a few expenditure components such as consumer expenditures, outlays for residential construction, fixed business capital formation, inventory investment, net exports, and government expenditures. Each component would then be related to overall GNP, each having some functional relationship to GNP. Equilibrium GNP is the solution of this simple equation.

This kind of model is useful for explaining some key principles of income determination. It is inadequate, however, as a reliable forecasting or analysis device, and it is quite uninformative on behavior in many parts of the economy. It says nothing explicit about the price level, the wage rate, the level of unemployment, the interest rate, the money supply, the terms of trade, or many other interesting economic phenomena. The Keynesian model can be extended to include these other kinds of variables if a production function, marginal productivity equation, labor supply function, price determination equation, money demand, and money supply function are added to the system. This is a more complete model that becomes an aggregative or one-sector version of the Walrasian-type system.

In many respects, but not completely, our model is an applied version of the more complete Keynesian system in which price, output, employment, wage rate, interest rate, money supply, and terms of trade are all determined within the system, but it is a multi-sector model and differs in this respect from the one-sector aggregative Keynesian system. We have several price levels, several output values, several wage rates, etc. within our system. The complete Keynesian model determines *the* wage rate and employment. It, therefore, gives, indirectly factor shares of wage and non-wage income. Our model gives several types of wage income and also other factor shares. Regarding the national income accounts from two sides, the totality of factor payments and the totality of expenditures, we find a high degree of decomposition of both sides within our model.

Ours is also meant to be a practical system, describing reality as closely as possible. We, therefore, introduce many specific lags and institutional constraints that are not found in purely theoretical models. Our system would not perform well unless we introduce these practical aspects of behavior. Some peculiar aspects of the Japanese economy that are not found in many theoretical models are: dualism, the food problem, and foreign trade. Parallel functioning of large and small-scale enterprise in manufacturing has much institutional significance for Japan but is rarely found in general macro models. It is often found in developing economies. England has a food problem but not as acute as the Japanese. While the Japanese situation is under control and stable, it is not without special consequences for economic organization and deserves special treatment.

The simplest macro models have been extended to cover exporting and importing (foreign trade multiplier analysis). These extensions are the particular versions of macroeconomics used in our model, where trade is of extreme importance. The dependence on imported materials and some forms of capital goods have significant consequences for the Japanese economy. Attention must be paid, as well, to the form and area of exports.

The other model used in macroeconomics is the input-output (IO) or interindustrial model of Leontief. It might be classified as microeconomic since it contains many equations, possibly as many as 200–500. Yet we prefer to call it a macro model because it aggregates over households and producing plants. It is multi-sectoral and consequently much more disaggregated than Keynesian models, but it is not microeconomics in the sense that Orcutt's models are micro models.[1]

IO models, by themselves, do not determine all the variables in which we are interested, such as prices, profits, wage rates, interest rates, or even the aggregate level of activity. They mainly give detail on inter-industry flows

[1] Orcutt, G. H. *et al.* (1961). *Microanalysis of Socio-Economic Systems: A Simulation Study*. New York: Harper.

of intermediate goods. If equations of final demand, and others are added to the system, they become complete but very large. IO systems are available in Japan; therefore, we have a choice between using this framework with added equations to determine the final demand, or developing an Keynesian aggregative model with less sector detail.

Three research strategies appear to be feasible. First, we could estimate a number of final demands and related equations for each of the sectors of the Japanese input-output table. Second, we could build an aggregative model of income determination (Keynesian type) with a few sectors — far more than in most aggregative models of this type but not of the order of magnitude of IO analysis. Finally, we could establish a compromise between the two approaches and build one joint system based on a *collapsed* number of IO sectors, say 25–50.

The first approach has the drawback that there are so many sectors to be dealt with that a careful treatment of each final demand equation is not possible. Some simplified, unified form must be chosen for each equation. For example, final consumer demand might be represented by a series of simple Engel curves, leaving out many special variables associated with each separate demand. In addition, the data preparation task is enormous, and hardly feasible on a quarterly basis. The job would require the preparation of time series of final demand by industry and by type of demand.

We have selected the second type of model, with the economy divided into five producing sectors 1. heavy manufacturing, 2. textile manufacturing, 3. other manufacturing, 4. non-manufacturing tertiary industry, and 5. agriculture. There are also equations dealing with foreign trade, finance, and some aspects of distribution. Using this subdivision, we are able to study large and small-scale enterprise separately. This is something that has not yet been done for IO analysis. For the moderate number of sectors we chose, the data collection problem has been very serious and the number of equations has grown as large as 150 excluding identities. Our problem has been to fill in the detail of many economic variables.

It would be possible to condense an IO system into 5×5 sectors of detail and fully integrate the two approaches. At this level of aggregation, we might find the table too concentrated, with heavy manufacturing producing largely for itself. This seems to be too much condensation to bring out the best qualities of IO analysis. It would seem wiser to try to build an integrated model with an intermediate number of sectors, at least 25. In the United States, a large model is being constructed that combines input-output with the analysis of income determination, on a quarterly basis. The data collection problem has proved to be very large, but not insuperable for this size. As a first step, an integrated modal of the two approaches, using a 7-sector condensation of an IO table has been constructed. This is not without its merits, but better results are expected when the sector detail is enlarged by a factor of 4 or 5. Meanwhile, we ignored in a formal sense IO methods in the construction of our model, yet there are some equations that are similar to those that have been used in the American 7-sector model to bridge the gap between models of IO and income determination.

2. The Model and Data Availability

Lack of available data would constrain our work in the direction of integrating IO and income determination models. Our data collection problem has been significant for this type of macro income determination model. We have split production by five sectors, but we do not have the corresponding consumer expenditure data to match these sectors. Production and related statistics come from the *Censuses of Manufacturers* and the statistics of corporations, while the data on consumption expenditures come from the national income accounts. Consumer expenditures are subdivided into textiles to correspond with the textile-producing sector; into food to correspond with the agricultural sector: but not into other categories to correspond with the other sectors. Even textile and food consumption do not match perfectly the final consumer demand of the associated producing sectors. Following data we must subdivide in one way on the side of production and in another way on the side of final demand.

Some variables can readily be split by producing sector or industry scale but some cannot. Production, employment, fixed capital formation, wage rate, and some other variables are known for each of the three manufacturing sectors, separately for large and for small scale firms. Price level and unfinished inventories are known for different manufacturing sectors but not for large and small firms, respectively. To cope with these limitations, we must introduce some proxy equations or approximation modifications of the system to keep it fully determined. The foreign trade, demographic, and monetary statistics are generally available on a broad scale and in great detail. The form of the model is not seriously limited by data availability in these cases, but domestic trade and distribution statistics are not complete enough to permit extensions of the contemplated model.

3. The General Framework

The principal idea underlying our model is illustrated in the following scheme: production — factor income payment — demand for goods and services — production — factor income payment — and so on.[2]

Entrepreneurs in a capitalist economy initiate production. They make payments to labor and other factors. Households (and firms), wherein these factors reside, demand goods with their payments. Entrepreneurs are then induced by this demand to produce more goods and pay out more factor incomes. Demand arises again, and the process goes on and on. This is the outline of the working of our dynamic economy, and the equations of our model illustrate this scheme.

The precise structure of our model will become clear when all the numerically estimated equations are completely listed below. At this stage we consider only the broad or general layout of the model. First, let us consider the producing sectors. In manufacturing these are all treated alike, giving equations in parallel, but parameter differences are indicative of structural difference. The sectors are *heavy*, *textile*, and *other*, manufacturing. Textiles were very important in an earlier industrialization era of Japan. Recent years have seen rise of importance of steel, shipbuilding, motor vehicles, machinery (all in the *heavy* category) and chemicals, drugs, plastics, electronics, instruments optics (all in the *other* category). This manufacturing decomposition is not unique, but it is significant, of historical interest, and convenient.

In each sector, there is a distinction between large-scale enterprise (capital greater than ¥50 million) and small-scale enterprise. This distinction is an important institutional characteristic of the Japanese economy and is not a theoretical distinction. The equations of each sector are

1. production decisions
2. production functions
3. wage determination
4. price determination
5. material inputs
6. material price determination
7. fixed capital formation

---

[2]This idea was emphasized by J. Duesenberry in connection with US model-building: Duesenberry, J. G. Fromm, L. R. Klein and E. Kuh (1965). *The Brookings Quarterly Econometric Model of the US Economy*. Chicago: Rand McNally.

The production determination equations may be looked upon as a form of inventory adjustment relating final demand in the economy as a whole (GNP components) to industry output or sales. Since separate equations are made for large and small scale enterprise, while final demand variables are economy-wide, they might also be called market-sharing equations, showing how firms of different scale share in total demand for an industry's product. Similar equations were used in the UK model, but no distinction was made as to scale of enterprise. In that model such equations were used in lieu of inventory equations, lacking the necessary data on stocks. We too lack the data on stocks by scale of enterprise, but it is possible to have equations both for inventory demand and for adjustment of production to *excessive* or *deficient* demand in a consistent system.

The production functions are standard Cobb-Douglas equations homogeneous of degree one in labor and capital, apart from a technical trend and constant term. Capital inputs are roughly adjusted for degree of utilization. Wage rates within an industry and scale size are related to productivity, and possibly other variables. These equations should reflect both conditions within the industrial sector and in the general labor market for the economy as a whole.

While wage rates are separated by scale size, prices are not, as a result of data limitations. Prices are determined for a sector as a mark-up over prime costs — the price of materials to the sector and unit labor costs to the sector. The latter variable combines wage rate and productivity variables. These price equations are not pure mark-up equations, however, for they reflect inventory positions within the industry. These, in turn, depend on market demand for the industry's product. The stock-sales ratio for finished goods inventory is used as a variable in equation.

Substitution in production is assumed for labor and capital, but material inputs are better considered to be in fixed proportion to output. We have separate equations relating material inputs to production for large and small-scale enterprises respectively. These are part of the representation of technology for the sector.

Associated with material inputs are material prices, and these are determined in much the same way as sector output prices, i.e. as mark-ups over prime costs. In this case the prime costs are wage rate (for the economy as whole and not for the sector in which the materials are used) and the price of *imported* materials. Thus imports and labor costs are the prime costs involved in these mark-up equations. In the case of the other (residual) manufacturing sector, domestic agricultural materials as well as imported materials are used; therefore the price of agricultural products is used as a third prime cost variable.

The material input equation is a technical relation between a factor input and production. The material price determination equation, viewed as a mark-up equation, serves as a factor demand equation suitable for a non-competitive market. Industry technology in each sector is fully described when we add the production functions to the material input functions. The production function contains two factor input variables — labor and capital. The demand for the labor factor, like the demand for the material factor, is covered by the equation for output price determination. The wage determination equations are also related to demand for the labor factor, but they should, in principle at least, contain labor supply conditions. In any event, the wage and price determination equations together play the role that marginal-productivity of labor equations play in labor demand in theoretical macro models.[3] This leaves us with the need for one more type of equation in each sector to determine the demand for the other factor — capital. In the Keynesian macro models, this equation takes the form of the marginal efficiency of capital schedule. In effective demand models, this schedule appears explicitly as the propensity to invest, or the investment function. Our investment functions associated with each producing sector cover fixed investment and use output, capacity output, business cash flow, and interest rate as explanatory variables. These functions are separately developed for large and small-scale enterprise.

Summing up, we find that our manufacturing sector models include all the kinds of relationships that are needed to extend the usual kind of macro models of income determination to a full explanation of employment level, wage rate, and price level. These include technical functions for production, factor demand or price mark-up equations, and inventory adjustment. Below, we shall consider some additional equations of inventory investment demand, but they will not be as finely disaggregated as fixed investment demand.

The sector equations that we have described so far refer to manufacturing only — heavy, textiles, and other. There are two remaining sectors of production — agriculture and tertiary industry. The latter includes transportation, trade, services, public utilities, communication, finance, and other

---

[3]In a multi-sector model with many separate price levels, we need equations to determine sector labor input and price. In an aggregative model with one sector and one price, the interpretation of the roles of wage and price determination equations is slightly different.

residual activities. The equations for this sector are like those for manufacturing, except there are no explicit material inputs or material prices, either as dependent or independent variables. Also, there is no distinction between large and small-scale enterprise.

Agriculture receives somewhat different treatment. In the first place, annual crops in farming make quarterly analysis difficult and, in some cases, unrealistic. In the second place, entrepreneurial decision-making follows along different lines in agriculture than in industry. We have an annual production function for agriculture, but capital measurements are not available. The factor inputs are employment and fertilizer. We have a variable to represent crop damage due to natural causes. Nevertheless, there is a large unexplained element, which we classify as random error. Annual output is distributed quarterly by a numerical regression on dummy seasonal variables. Completing the sector, we have an equation of price determination in a mark-up form adjusted for changes in agricultural productivity, and an employment equation to show how decisions are made in choosing between agricultural and non-agricultural work. Relevant variables are relative sector wages and the state of labor market. Agriculture as in many countries receives the benefit of special government support programs. The government's buying price of rice is an exogenous variable in the price determination equation. In the manufacturing sectors, material input prices were determined by separate mark-up equations. In agriculture, material input prices are treated as exogenous.

The consuming or household sector of the model is dominated by the well-known propensity to consume equations or consumption functions. The household sector is not, strictly speaking, a pure consumption sector. In this sector housing services are produced so that we need a consumer investment equation for residential construction. This is part of investment but more appropriately grouped with the household sector.

The consumption functions are estimated separately for food, textiles, and all other consumer expenditures. These classifications do not match those for production since we are not able to find data that would show the amount of final household consumption arising out of heavy, other manufacturing, and tertiary industry respectively. Each of the three consumption functions is similarly constructed, to depend on disposable income, income distribution, and lagged consumption. Each type of consumption has a different implicit price deflator associated with it in the national income accounts. Since disposable income is separately deflated by each of these for the three equations estimated, we must have equations to determine consumer price deflators. These deflators are essentially marked up prices, over the basic prices of output in the producing sectors and over wage rates in the tertiary sector. These mark-ups cover the cost of distribution in the economy, i.e. the costs of transferring goods and services in the producing sectors to the final consuming sector.

Finally, residential investment is made a function of real disposable income and the relative costs of renting an existing structure vs. building a new structure for occupancy.

Total effective demand in the *private domestic sector* is completed with an overall set of equations for inventory investment. These are not split between large and small-scale enterprise, but they are split, where possible, by producing sector. Within the inventory process itself, they are split by stage of fabrication into raw materials, goods in process, and finished inventories. Raw material inventories depend, in our model, on the order position of industry (heavy manufacturing). Goods in process depend on the output flow of each sector, in technical relationships. At the final stage of the manufacturing process, finished goods inventories depend on sales and speculative price changes. In each case, we have generalized the inventory–output relationship beyond the pure accelerator theory to flexible accelerator or stock adjustment mechanism. In these cases, inventory investment depends positively on output or sales and negatively on beginning-of-quarter stocks. Besides inventory investment of manufactures, we have inventory investment of dealers. Inventory demand here depends on sales, imports, and price changes.

Adding exogenous government expenditures for goods and services to consumption, residential investment, business fixed investment, and inventory investment completes Domestic Final Demand. Japan, however, is very much an open economy; so that our model must cover the foreign component of final demand. This will appear as exports *less* imports of goods and services. We develop separate equations for each and also disaggregate within the totals of exports and imports.

There are four import equations — rice and barley, other food, machinery, and materials and other products. Rice imports depend on domestic food consumption, domestic agricultural production, and the rural-urban population distribution. Other food imports depend on food consumption and the relative price of domestic vs. imported food. The comparative importance of rice and other foods in the Japanese diet is changing, and our import functions should reflect this. Machinery imports depend on domestic capital formation, and material imports depend largely on manufacturing output.

Exports are split into two kinds of groups. One group is by type of product, and another is by export area. The area classification is particularly important for certain commodities where there are regional quotas for Japanese exports, regional discrimination against Japanese exports or regional preference for Japanese exports. The product classification is fourfold — heavy industry, textiles, food and other. The residual category corresponds closely with *other* manufacturing in the producing sectors.

Heavy industry exports are further subdivided into ships, machinery, and steel and other metal products. Shipbuilding for export depends upon orders for ships, which, in turn, depend on world tonnage requirements and relative prices — Japanese vs. the rest of the world in heavy industry products. Machinery exports are a function of world production of machinery, reparation payments to Asian countries, the foreign exchange reserve position of Asian countries, and relative price. These same variables, applying specifically to external steel trade and prices, determine the demand for Japanese steel exports.

Textile exports to the United States depend on the quota limitation for such exports, in addition to US consumption and relative textile prices (Japanese vs. US). Textile exports to Europe, Canada and to the rest of the world depends on the same kind of activity and relative price variables, with appropriate adjustment for the region involved. In the case of textiles, export price is regarded as a separate endogenous variable, depending on the domestic and the world textile prices. In all the export equations, overseas activity and price variables are regarded as exogenous.

Food exports are also divided by regions, but Canada is grouped with the US instead of with Europe. This natural regional grouping was not used for textiles because of the importance of the US quota. Food exports to Europe and to the Rest of the World are separately determined as functions of income levels and relative prices in each of the two areas, respectively. In the case of textiles there was an equation of export price determination, but agricultural export prices are not endogenously generated within the model.

A residual group of exports, all commodities except heavy industry products, textiles, and food are determined by two separate equations. One covers US, Canada, and Europe. The other covers the rest of the world. As in the other export equations, overseas activity and relative prices are the explanatory variables. An equation relating the export price of this residual group to the domestic price of *other* manufacturing and the world price of such goods is also included.

A series of equations dealing with the income side of the national income accounts are needed in order to maintain the completeness of the system. Disposable income, in the consumption functions, for example, is computed after the subtraction of corporate savings from the total of other forms of income. It is not considered to be disposable by persons, apart from the corporations who control this income total. Corporate savings are related to corporate income (and lagged dividends) in a savings function, but we must then explain the distribution between corporate and other forms of business income. This is done in a separate distributional equation, but in order to make the relationship firm, we must define business income separately from *rentier* income (property income). *Rentier* income is explained separately in terms of real estate and deposit capital, together with their rates of return.

In the investment functions, the internal cash flow variable used is gross operating profit. Disposable income is computed after subtraction of depreciation and business interest payments, while both these variables are included in business gross operating profit.[4] Real depreciation for each sector is related, by coefficients based on service lives in individual sectors, to capital stocks. For national income purposes we need an equation to convert real depreciation into current-value accounting measures. Business interest payments are simply related to corporate income.

A group of equations dealing with foreign trade covers only commodity trade in imported and exported merchandise. For national income accounting purposes, the figure on the commodity balance must be supplemented by invisibles. To get an important variable foreign exchange reserves, we must account for capital transactions. We have not done this explicitly but included an empirical equation relating the change in foreign exchange reserves to the commodity balance of trade.

The focus of attention in macro models is the determination of income, output, and employment. To a large extent this amounts to an analysis of the *real* economy, as distinct from the *money* economy. We all recognize that we live in a money economy, but that does not tell us whether money

[4]Depreciation is treated on the same basis as corporate savings, as an available cash flow for business investment but not for personal consumption. Business interest is treated differently in principle because an interest rate variable is in the investment function.

is important in the sense that it is more than a classical *veil* of facilitating medium that is necessary as a means of exchange. An alternative view is that money is important in the sense that monetary control and banking management determine the level and nature of real economic activity. Money is thought by many economists to have an extraordinarily strong influence on the Japanese economy because there are more than enough opportunities for real investment and a shortage of financial capital for carrying out these investment projects.

The usual way of linking the money and real sectors in models of income determination is to have interest rates influencing real demand decisions for investment and possibly current expenditure, while interest rates get determined, together with other variables, in the money market. In some theories, the general price level may provide a link between the real and monetary sectors. In our model, the interest rate affects investment and gets determined essentially by demand-supply balance in the money market. Interest rate also enters our model as a factor share on the income side of the national income accounts.

In the money market we have four holders of cash (1) Private non-corporate business and households, (2) corporations, (3) banks, (4) government. They hold currency, non-interest-bearing deposits (demand and ordinary deposits), and savings deposits. According to liquidity preference theory we make their cash demand depend on their transactions needs, interest rate, and change in price level. The latter two variables indicate speculative holding for capital gains. The transactions variables are different for each type of holder, and banks have certain reserve restraints that must be met in their demand functions for cash. The procedure followed in our model is to develop overall demand functions for total holdings of currency, demand deposits, and ordinary deposits. Separate equations of currency demand are also estimated, so that deposit demand is computed as a residual. Savings deposits held by personal firms/individual persons and corporations are estimated in separate equations.

The supply side of money is explicitly developed as an endogenous variable in our model. This is in contrast to most theoretical models of the aggregative economy in which the money supply is assumed to be exogenously fixed by the central banking authorities. The supply function of money itself is not defined in our model. Instead, the equations for the loans of private banks and for the determination of interest rate are developed in order to explain the peculiar characteristic of Japanese financial market in post-war years. They are explained in detail in Part II of this chapter.

4. List of Time Series and Symbols

4.1. *Series of production sectors*[5]

(a) Series of sales or value added at current price (hundred billion Yen)

- X_i Sales of the ith industry, where $i = h, t, o$, and M
- X_{ij} Sales of the jth scale group of the ith industry, were $i = h, t$, and o and $j = L$ (large) and S (small)
- X_E Value added of the tertiary sector
- X_A Value added of the agricultural sector
- X_{Aa} Value added of the agricultura! sector in the calendar year

(b) Series of values of material inputs at current prices (hundred billion Yen)

- M_i Value of material inputs of the ith industry where $I = h, t, o$, and M
- M_{ij} Value of material inputs of the jth scale group of the ith industry, where $i = h, t$, and o and $j = L$ and S

(c) Series of employment (million persons)

- N_i Employment by the ith industry, where ith, t, o, M, E, I and A
- N_{ij} Employment by the jth scale group of the ith industry, where $i = h, t$, and o and $j = L$ and S
- N_{Aa} Annual agricultural employment

(d) Series of capital stock and depreciation in 1955 prices (hundred billion Yen)

- K_i Capital stock of the ith industry at the end of the quarter, where $i = h, t, o$, and E
- K_{ij} Capital stock of the jth scale of the ith industry at the end of the quarter, where $i = h, t$, and o and $j = L$ and S
- Δ_{ij} Capital transfer to the jth scale group of the ith industry, where $i = h, t, o$ and $j = L$ and S
- D'_i Capital depreciation of the ith industry, where $i = h, t, o, M, E$, and I
- D'_{ij} Capital depreciation of the jth scale group of the ith industry, where $i = h, t$, and o and $j = L$ and S

---

[5]Production sectors are denoted by the following subscripts: h: (heavy manufacturing and mining), t: (textile manufacturing), o: (other manufacturing), M: (manufacturing and mining), E: (tertiary sector), I: (industry or non-agriculture), and A: (agriculture).

(e) Series of wage bills (hundred billion Yen) and average earnings (hundred Yen) at current prices

W_i Employee compensation paid by the ith industry where $i = h, t, o$ and E

W_{ij} Employee compensation paid by jth scale group of the ith industry, where $i = h, t$, and o and $j = L$ and S

w_i Average quarterly earnings in the ith industry, where $i = h, t, o, M, E$, and I

w_{ij} Average quarterly earnings in the jth scale group of the ith industry, where $i = h, t$, and o and $j = L$ and S

w_A Average quarterly agricultural earnings

σ_{ij} Average labor productivity in the jth scale group of the ith industry, where $i = h, t$, and o and $j = L$ and S (hundred Yen)

(f) Series of profits, depreciation, and business taxes at current p. (¥100 billion)

P Profits of the manufacturing and tertiary sectors

P_i Profits of the ith industry, where $i = h, t, o, M$ and E

P_{ij} Profits of the jth scale group of the ith industry, where $i = h, t$, and o and $j = L$ and S

P_c Corporate profits

D_v Corporate dividend payment

S_C Retained corporate profits

D_i Depreciation allowances of the ith industry, where $i = h, t, o, E$ and A

D_{ij} Depreciation allowances of the jth scale group of the ith industry, where $i = h, t$, and o and $j = L$ and S

T_i Indirect taxes less subsidies of the ith industry, where $i = h, t, o, E$ and A

T_{ij} Indirect taxes less subsidies of the jth scale group of the ith industry, where $i = h, t$, and o and $j = L$ and S

T_C Corporate income taxes

(g) Series of gross fixed investment at current prices (100 billion Yen)

I_i Fixed investment expenditure of the ith industry where $i = h, t, o, E, I$, and A

I_{ij} Fixed investment expenditure of the jth scale group of the ith industry, where $i = h, t$, and o and $j = L$ and S

(h) Series of inventory stock and investment at current prices (100 billion Yen)

H_{fi} Inventory stock of finished products of the ith industry, where $i = h, t$, and o
H_m Manufacturers' inventory stock of raw materials
H_p Manufacturers' inventory stock of goods in process
H_d Dealers' inventory stock of goods
J_{fi} Inventory investment of finished products of the ith industry, where $i = h, t$, and o
J_m Manufacturers' inventory investment of raw materials
J_p Manufacturers' inventory investment of goods in process
J_d Inventory investment of dealers' stock of goods
J_A Inventory investment in agriculture
X_{vm} Constant-price manufacturing output associated with H_m
X_{vd} Constant-price manufacturing output associated with H_d

(i) Series of price-indexes (1955 = 1.00)

p_i Output price index of the ith industry, where $i = h, t, o, M, E$, and A
p_i^m Input price index of the ith industry, where $i = h, t, o$, and M
p_v^m Price index associated with manufacturers' inventory stock of raw materials
p_v^d Price index associated with dealers' inventory stock of goods
p_k Fixed investment goods price index
p_{Aa} Output price index (annual) of the agricultural sector
p_{Aa}^m Index of prices paid by farmers (annual)
p_{Aa}^g Index of government purchase process of farm products (annual)

(j) Series supplementary to the agricultural sector

Z_a Fertilizer inputs (billion Yen)
H_a Damaged area (hundred million cho)

(k) Series of degrees of capacity utilization

ρ_i Degree of capacity utilization in the ith industry, where $i = M$ and E
ρ_{ij} Degree of capacity utilization in the jth scale group of the ith industry, where $i = h, t$, and o and $j = L$ and S

(l) Series of orders and sales in machinery industry (100 billion Yen)

X^u_{h2} Unfilled order in machinery industry
X^n_{h2} New order in machinery industry
X^s_{h2} sales in machinery industry

4.2. *Series of the household sector*

(a) Series of household expenditure at current prices (hundred billion Yen)

C Total private consumption expenditure
C_f Private consumption expenditure on food, beverage and tobacco
C_t Private consumption expenditure on clothing
C_o Private consumption expenditure on other goods and services
I_R Expenditure on residential construction

(b) Series of consumer price-indexes (1995 = 1.00)

p^c General consumer price index
p^c_f Consumer price index of food
p^c_t Consumer price index of clothing
p^c_o Consumer price index of other goods and services
p_R Index of residential building cost
r Index of house rent

(c) Series of housing stock and depreciation (hundred billion Yen)

K_R Stock of residential housing in 1955 prices at the end of the quarter
D'_R Stock depreciation of housing in 1955 prices
D_R Depreciation allowance of housing at current prices

4.3. *Series of external trade*

(a) Series of values of imports (c.i.f.) at current price (hundred billion Yen)

B Total commodity imports
B_{f1} Imports of rice and barley
B_{f2} Imports of other foodstuffs
B_{h2} Imports of machinery and equipment
B_m Imports of other goods

(b) Series of exports (f.o.b.) at current prices (hundred billion Yen)

E Total commodity exports
E_{hl} Exports of ships
$\hat{\hat{E}}_{hl}$ Outstanding orders for ships (export)

$\hat{E}_{hl}$ New orders for ships (export)
E_{h2} Exports of machinery and equipment
E_{h3} Exports of steel and other metal products
E_t^i Exports of textiles to the ith region, where $i = U$ (the United States), E (Europe) and A (the rest of the world)
E_a^i Exports of food to the ith region, where $i = U$ (the United States and Canada), E (Europe) and A (the rest of the world)
E_o^i Exports of other goods to the ith region, where $i = UE$ (the United States, Canada and Europe) and A (the rest of the world)

(c) Series of import price-indexes (1955 = 1.00)

p_{f1}^b Import price index of rice and barley
p_{f2}^b Import price index of other foodstuffs
p_{h2}^b Import price index of machinery and equipment
p_i^{bm} Import price index of raw materials for the ith industry where $i = h, t$, and o
p_m^b Import price index of goods other than foodstuffs and machinery

(d) Series of export price-indexes (1955 = 1.00)

p_{h1}^e Export price index of ships
p_{h2}^e Export price index of machinery and equipment
p_{h3}^e Export price index of steel and other metal products
p_t^e Export price index of textiles
p_a^e Export price index of food
p_o^e Export price index of other goods
p_{hl} Index of contract prices of exported ships
p'_{hl} Moving average of p_{hl}

(e) Miscellaneous external series (all indexes 1955=1.00)

μ Freight tonnage as proportion of merchant tonnage (per cent)
p_i^w World export price index of the ith commodity group, where $i = h_1$, (ships), h_2 (machinery and equipment), h_3 (steel) and o (other goods)
p_t^i Price index of textiles in the ith region, where $i = U$ (US), E (Europe and Canada), and A (the rest of the world)
p_a^i Price index of food in the ith region, where $i = U$ (US and Canada), E (Europe), A (the rest of the world), and w (world average)

- x_i^w World production index, weighted by Japan's exports of the ith commodity group, where $i = h_2$ and h_3
- x_t^A Production index of developing regions, weighted by Japan's exports of textiles
- R_i^A Foreign exchange reserves of Asian countries weighted by exports of the ith commodity group where $i = h_2$ and h_3 (hundred million dollars)
- R^E Foreign exchange reserves of the UK (hundred million dollars)
- A Reparations and loans (million dollars)
- q^U US quota of textile imports from Japan (per cent)
- y^E European personal consumption (hundred billion dollars)
- y^U US personal consumption (hundred billion dollars)
- y^{UE} Personal consumption of US, Canada, and Europe (weighted average, hundred billion dollars)
- y^A Exports of developing regions (hundred billion dollars)

(f) Series relating to the balance of payments accounts (hundred billion dollars)

- E' Exports of goods in the balance of payments
- B' Imports of goods in the balance of payments
- E'_{inv} Invisible exports
- B'_{inv} Invisible imports
- B_k Net capital imports
- R Foreign exchange reserves
- η' Adjustment item for foreign exchange reserves
- η Non-commodity balance in external transactions constant-price value (hundred billion Yen)
- $\frac{\eta}{p_\eta}$ Non-commodity balance in external transactions current-price value (hundred billion Yen)

4.4. *Financial series*

(a) Series of money stock at the end of the quarter (hundred billion Yen)

- L_l Cash currency
- L_l^i Cash currency held by the ith group, where $i = p$ (household and unincorporated business), c (corporate enterprises), b (bands and other financial institutions) and g (government)
- L_2 Deposit currency
- L_3 Time and saving deposits

L_3^i Time and saving deposits held by the ith group, where $i = p$ and c
L^i Cash and deposit currency held by the ith group, where $i = p, c, d$, and g
L^s Total cash and deposit currency

(b) Series of bank loans (hundred billion Yen) and bank rate

V Loans of the Bank of Japan to private banks
V_g Loans of the Bank of Japan to government
i Effective rate of interest on loans & discounts (per cent per annum)

(c) Series of government accounts (hundred billion Yen)

G_n Surplus of the treasury accounts
G_1 Surplus of the Foreign Exchange Fund
G_2 Surplus of the Foodstuff Control Account
G_3 Surplus of other treasury accounts

4.5. *Series related to the government sector (100 billion Yen unless otherwise specified)*

G Government total expenditure on goods & services at current prices
G' Gov. expenditure on goods & services at current prices adjusted
G_I Gov. expenditure on fixed capital formation at current prices
W_G Wages and salaries of government employees
N_G Government employment (million persons)
D_G Depreciation allowances of government enterprises
T Total indirect taxes less subsidies
T_p Personal income tax

4.6. *Series relating to aggregate national accounts (100 billion Yen unless otherwise specified)*

Y_G Gross national product and expenditure at market prices
Y Net national product at factor cost
Y_d Disposable income
d_s Statistical discrepancy
W Total employee compensation
D Total depreciation allowances
I Gross domestic capital formation
I_p Private fixed capital formation
J Private inventory investment
Y_o *Rentier* income

T_R Transfer income and others
ξ Surplus of government enterprise, etc.
π Non-operating profit of corporations
p Implicit GNP deflator, 1955 = 1.00
$-\Delta p_{-1}^{H}$ Inventory valuation adjustment

4.7. *Series of total population and employment*

N Population at the last month of the quarter (ten millions)
N_L Labor force (million persons)
U Unemployment (million persons)

5. A Quarterly Econometric Model of Japan, 1952–1959

The following system of equations and identities is a tentative econometric model of the post-war Japan. The model has been under construction for four years, and is at the final stage of its applications. Many improvements will, however, have to be made in the forms of equations as a result of its applications and the comments that the reader of this article will kindly offer us. Here are published only the estimated structural equations and identities of the model; a detailed discussion of the model and its applications will be published in the book form later.

The entire industry is divided into three sectors: agriculture (including forestry and fishery), manufacturing (including mining), and tertiary. The manufacturing sector is placed in the center of the model and is subdivided into three sub-sectors: heavy manufacturing, textile manufacturing, and other manufacturing. Each of the three manufacturing sectors is further divided into two groups: the large-firm group (corporations with paid-in capital above 50 million Yen) and the small-firm group.

(*a*) *Heavy industry*

(a:1) *Production decision functions*

$$\frac{X_{hL}}{p_h} = \frac{0.53823}{(0.100)} S_{hI} + \frac{1.1487}{(0.311)} S_{hE} + \frac{0.10418}{(0.304)} S_{hJ} + \frac{0.25735}{(0.189)} Q_1 + \frac{0.50647}{(0.215)} Q_2 + \frac{0.46515}{(0.193)} Q_3 - \frac{0.44872}{(0.331)} \qquad \bar{R}^2 = 0.95$$

$$\frac{X_{hS}}{p_h} = \underset{(0.0563)}{0.36409} S_{hI} + \underset{(0.175)}{0.29946} S_{hE} + \underset{(0.171)}{0.27208} S_{hJ} + \underset{(0.106)}{0.11536} Q_1$$

$$+ \underset{(0.121)}{0.25684} Q_2 - \underset{(0.109)}{0.00349} Q_3 + \underset{(0.186)}{0.18765} \qquad \bar{R}^2 = 0.95$$

$(a{:}2)$ *Production functions*

$$\frac{X_{hL}/p_h}{N_{hL}} = \underset{(0.0614)}{0.1514} \frac{\rho_{hL} K_{hL,-1}}{N_{hL}} + \underset{(0.00605)}{0.09516\tau} + \underset{(0.396)}{1.445}$$

$$\bar{R}^2 = 0.96 \quad \delta^2/S^2 = 1.18$$

$$\frac{X_{hS}/p_h}{N_{hS}} = \underset{(0.162)}{0.8536} \frac{\rho_{hS} K_{hs,-1}}{N_{hS}} + \underset{(0.00444)}{0.01980\tau} + \underset{(0.248)}{0.6016}$$

$$\bar{R}^2 = 0.91 \quad \delta^2/S^2 = 0.79$$

$(a{:}3)$ *Wage determination equations*

$$w_{hL} - w_{hL,-4} = \underset{(0.0614)}{0.07572} (\sigma_{hL} - \sigma_{hL,-4}) - \underset{(0.0882)}{0.006870} \frac{1}{4} \sum_{0}^{-3} U$$

$$+ \underset{(0.723)}{0.6176} \qquad \bar{R}^2 = 0.08 \quad \delta^2/S^2 = 0.74$$

$$W_{hS} - W_{hS,-4} = \underset{(0.0650)}{0.5265} (\sigma_{hS} - \sigma_{hS,-4}) - \underset{(0.0835)}{0.1631} \frac{1}{4} \sum_{0}^{-3} U + \underset{(0.680)}{1.185}$$

$$\bar{R}^2 = 0.77 \quad \delta^2/S^2 = 1.73$$

$(a{:}4)$ *Price determination equation*

$$\Delta p_h = \underset{(0.0646)}{0.3983} \Delta p_h^m - \underset{(0.127)}{0.4351} \frac{H_{fh}}{X_h} + \underset{(0.326)}{0.1476} \Delta \frac{W_h}{X_h/p_h} + \underset{(0.0120)}{0.006373} Q_1$$

$$- \underset{(0.00937)}{0.007247} Q_2 - \underset{(0.0104)}{0.002340} Q_3 + \underset{(0.0286)}{0.07527}$$

$$\bar{R}^2 = 0.72 \quad \delta^2/S^2 = 1.12$$

(a:5) *Material input functions*

$$\frac{M_{hL}}{p_h^m} = \underset{(0.0159)}{0.6947} \frac{X_{hL}}{p_h} - \underset{(0.167)}{0.07725} \qquad \begin{array}{r} \bar{R}^2 = 0.99 \\ \delta^2/S^2 = 0.47 \end{array}$$

$$\frac{M_{hS}}{p_h^m} = \underset{(0.0243)}{0.7810} \frac{X_{hS}}{p_h} - \underset{(0.141)}{0.06427} \qquad \begin{array}{r} \bar{R}^2 = 0.97 \\ \delta^2/S^2 = 0.53 \end{array}$$

(a:6) *Material price determination equation*

$$p_h^m = \underset{(0.0146)}{0.06041} w_I + \underset{(0.0613)}{0.07409} p_h^{bm} + \underset{(0.0316)}{0.06832} Q_1 + \underset{(0.0294)}{0.03558} Q_2$$

$$+ \underset{(0.0286)}{0.01525} Q_3 - \underset{(0.121)}{0.04689} \qquad \bar{R}^2 = 0.87 \quad \delta^2/S^2 = 0.76$$

(a:7) *Fixed investment functions*

$$\frac{I_{hL}}{p_k} = \underset{(0.0333)}{0.08578} \left(\frac{X_{hL}}{p_h} - \max \frac{X_{hL}}{p_h} \right) + \underset{(0.0292)}{0.4577} \sum_{-1}^{-2} \frac{(P+D)_{hL}}{p_K}$$

$$- \underset{(0.0814)}{0.1734} \qquad \bar{R}^2 = 0.90 \quad \delta^2/S^2 = 1.16$$

$$\frac{I_{hS}}{p_k} = \underset{(0.0215)}{0.09715} \left(\frac{X_{hS}}{p_h} - \max \frac{X_{hS}}{p_h} \right) + \underset{(0.0358)}{0.1469} \sum_{-1}^{-2} \frac{(P+D)_{hS}}{p_K}$$

$$- \underset{(0.0411)}{0.07806} \qquad \bar{R}^2 = 0.62 \quad \delta^2/S^2 = 1.13$$

(b) **Textile industry**

(b:1) *Production decision functions*

$$\frac{X_{tL}}{p_t} = \underset{(0.0929)}{0.30624} S_{tC} + \underset{(0.0805)}{0.36676} S_{tE} + \underset{(0.00989)}{0.011332} S_{tJ} + \underset{(0.103)}{0.34248} Q_1$$

$$+ \underset{(0.112)}{0.33301} Q_2 + \underset{(0.112)}{0.46946} Q_3 + \underset{(0.186)}{0.020553} \qquad \bar{R}^2 = 0.93$$

$$\frac{X_{tS}}{p_t} = \frac{0.53803}{(0.223)} S_{tC} + \frac{0.78289}{(0.193)} S_{tE} + \frac{0.009068}{(0.0237)} S_{tJ} + \frac{0.65714}{(0.248)} Q_1$$

$$+ \frac{0.56556}{(0.268)} Q_2 + \frac{0.72355}{(0.269)} Q_3 - \frac{0.74301}{(0.445)} \qquad \bar{R}^2 = 0.93$$

(b:2) *Production functions*

$$\frac{K_{tL}/p_t}{N_{tL}} = \frac{0.5493}{(0.0713)} \frac{\rho_{tL} K_{tL,-1}}{N_{tL}} + \frac{0.04671\tau}{(0.00803)} + \frac{0.3569}{(0.295)}$$

$$\bar{R}^2 = 0.99 \quad \delta^2/S^2 = 0.96$$

$$\frac{K_{tS}/p_t}{N_{tS}} = \frac{0.8452}{(0.170)} \frac{\rho_{tS} K_{tS,-1}}{N_{tS}} + \frac{0.06656\tau}{(0.00472)} - \frac{0.5896}{(0.406)}$$

$$\bar{R}^2 = 0.92 \quad \delta^2/S^2 = 1.06$$

(b:3) *Wage determination equations*

$$w_{tL} - w_{tL,-4} = \frac{0.07281}{(0.0364)} (\sigma_{tL} - \sigma_{tL,-4}) - \frac{0.1702}{(0.109)} \frac{1}{4} \sum_{0}^{-3} U + \frac{1.544}{(0.864)}$$

$$\bar{R}^2 = 0.14 \quad \delta^2/S^2 = 1.72$$

$$w_{tS} - w_{tS,-4} = \frac{0.2777}{(0.0530)} (\sigma_{tS} - \sigma_{tS,-4}) - \frac{0.1248}{(0.0631)} \frac{1}{4} \sum_{0}^{-3} U + \frac{0.9796}{(0.509)}$$

$$\bar{R}^2 = 0.52 \quad \delta^2/S^2 = 1.47$$

(b:4) *Price determination equation*

$$p_t = \frac{1.124}{(0.0997)} \Delta p_t^m - \frac{0.1827}{(0.0953)} \frac{H_{ft}}{X_t} + \frac{0.2067}{(0.269)} \Delta \frac{W_t}{X_t/p_t} - \frac{0.02131}{(0.0101)} Q_1$$

$$- \frac{0.004731}{(0.0101)} Q_2 + \frac{0.02117}{(0.0106)} Q_3 + \frac{0.04611}{(0.0264)}$$

$$\bar{R}^2 = 0.92 \quad \delta^2/S^2 = 1.73$$

(*b*:5) *Material input functions*

$$\frac{X_{tL}}{p_t^m} = \underset{(0.0241)}{0.8726}\frac{X_{tL}}{p_t} - \underset{(0.0482)}{0.1281} \quad \bar{R}^2 = 0.98 \quad \delta^2/S^2 = 0.97$$

$$\frac{M_{tS}}{p_t^m} = \underset{(0.0164)}{0.8688}\frac{X_{tS}}{p_t} - \underset{(0.0555)}{0.06829} \quad \bar{R}^2 = 0.99 \quad \delta^2/S^2 = 1.98$$

(*b*:6) *Material price determination equation*

$$p_t^m = \underset{(0.0778)}{0.6905} p_t^{bm} + \underset{(0.0337)}{0.01505} Q_1 + \underset{(0.0336)}{0.007605} Q_2 + \underset{(0.0335)}{0.01392} Q_3 + \underset{(0.0764)}{0.3312} \quad \bar{R}^2 = 0.71 \quad \delta^2/S^2 = 0.76$$

(*b*:7) *Fixed investment functions*

$$\frac{I_{tL}}{p_K} = \underset{(0.0342)}{0.02931}\left(\frac{X_{tL}}{p_t} - \max\frac{X_{tL}}{p_t}\right) - \underset{(0.00766)}{0.01289i} + \underset{(0.0402)}{0.1609} \sum_{-1}^{-2}\frac{(P+D)_{tL}}{p_K} + \underset{(0.0707)}{0.1326} \quad \bar{R}^2 = 0.44 \quad \delta^2/S^2 = 0.68$$

$$\frac{I_{tS}}{p_K} = \underset{(0.0133)}{0.02821}\left(\frac{X_{tS}}{p_t} - \max\frac{X_{tS}}{p_t}\right) - \underset{(0.00256)}{0.02903i} + \underset{(0.0454)}{0.1129} \sum_{-1}^{-2}\frac{(P+D)_{tS}}{p_K} + \underset{(0.0779)}{0.2910} \quad \bar{R}^2 = 0.52 \quad \delta^2/S^2 = 2.16$$

(*c*) ***Other manufacturing industry***

(*c*:1) *Production decision functions*

$$\frac{X_{oL}}{p_o} = \underset{(0.178)}{0.28900} S_{oC} + \underset{(0.192)}{1.7171}(S_{oE} + S_{oI}) + \underset{(0.286)}{0.41330} Q_1 + \underset{(0.404)}{1.0937} Q_2 + \underset{(0.359)}{0.78063} Q_3 - \underset{(0.956)}{1.9462} \quad \bar{R}^2 = 0.96$$

$$\frac{X_{oS}}{p_o} = \underset{(0.134)}{0.011018} S_{oC} + \underset{(0.145)}{1.4180}(S_{oE} + S_{oI}) + \underset{(0.215)}{0.48326} Q_1 - \underset{(0.303)}{0.12569} Q_2 + \underset{(0.270)}{0.43512} Q_3 + \underset{(0.719)}{1.7187} \qquad \bar{R}^2 = 0.96$$

(*c*:2) *Production functions*

$$\frac{X_{oL}/p_o}{N_{oL}} = \underset{(0.0904)}{0.1964} \frac{\rho_{oL} K_{oL,-1}}{N_{oL}} + \underset{(0.0102)}{0.1396\tau} + \underset{(0.911)}{2.894}$$

$$\bar{R}^2 = 0.91 \quad \delta^2/S^2 = 0.40$$

$$\frac{X_{oS}/p_o}{N_{oS}} = \underset{(0.188)}{0.2800} \frac{\rho_{oS} K_{oS,-1}}{N_{oS}} + \underset{(0.00400)}{0.03491\tau} + \underset{(0.352)}{1.161}$$

$$\bar{R}^2 = 0.79 \quad \delta^2/S^2 = 1.05$$

(*c*:3) *Wage determination equations*

$$w_{oL} - w_{oL,-4} = \underset{(0.0402)}{0.1211}(\sigma_{oL} - \sigma_{oL,-4}) - \underset{(0.126)}{0.1593} \frac{1}{4} \sum_0^{-3} U + \underset{(1.03)}{1.526}$$

$$\bar{R}^2 = 0.40 \quad \delta^2/S^2 = 0.96$$

$$w_{oS} - w_{oS,-4} = \underset{(0.0454)}{0.3916}(\sigma_{oS} - \sigma_{oS,-4}) - \underset{(0.0682)}{0.1822} \frac{1}{4} \sum_0^{-3} U + \underset{(0.553)}{1.365}$$

$$\bar{R}^2 = 0.71 \quad \delta^2/S^2 = 1.22$$

(*c*:4) *Price determination equation*

$$\Delta p_o = \underset{(0.0907)}{0.2059} \Delta p_o^m - \underset{(0.0655)}{0.1133} \frac{H_{fo}}{X_o} + \underset{(0.182)}{0.3991} \Delta \frac{W_o}{X_o/p_o} + \underset{(0.00526)}{0.001060} Q_1 - \underset{(0.00451)}{0.008990} Q_2 - \underset{(0.00457)}{0.005950} Q_3 + \underset{(0.0186)}{0.03051}$$

$$\bar{R}^2 = 0.72 \quad \delta^2/S^2 = 1.97$$

(c:5) *Material input functions*

$$\frac{M_{oL}}{p_o^m} = \underset{(0.0107)}{0.6144}\frac{X_{oL}}{p_o} + \underset{(0.123)}{0.3290} \qquad \bar{R}^2 = 0.99 \quad \delta^2/S^2 = 0.56$$

$$\frac{M_{oS}}{p_o^m} = \underset{(0.0182)}{0.6235}\frac{X_{oS}}{p_o} + \underset{(0.167)}{0.5715} \qquad \bar{R}^2 = 0.98 \quad \delta^2/S^2 = 1.26$$

(c:6) *Material price determination equation*

$$P_o^m = \underset{(0.00713)}{0.05385} w_I + \underset{(0.0691)}{0.2631} P_A + \underset{(0.0462)}{0.3172} P_o^{bm} + \underset{(0.0124)}{0.04479} Q_1 + \underset{(0.0115)}{0.02699} Q_2 + \underset{(0.0112)}{0.02573} Q_3 + \underset{(0.115)}{0.1545}$$

$$\bar{R}^2 = 0.75 \quad \delta^2/S^2 = 1.04$$

(c:7) *Fixed investment functions*

$$\frac{I_{oL}}{p_K} = \underset{(0.0516)}{-0.3499i} + \underset{(0.0569)}{0.04383} \sum_{-1}^{-2} \frac{(P+D)_{oL}}{p_K} + \underset{(0.514)}{3.416}$$

$$\bar{R}^2 = 0.89 \quad \delta^2/S^2 = 0.79$$

$$\frac{I_{oS}}{p_K} = \underset{(0.0113)}{0.0283} + \left(\frac{X_{oS}}{p_o} - \max\frac{X_{oS}}{p_o}\right) - \underset{(0.0234)}{-0.1121i} + \underset{(0.0426)}{0.001317} \sum_{-1}^{-2} \frac{(P+D)_{oS}}{p_K} + \underset{(0.234)}{1.136} \qquad \bar{R}^2 = 0.75 \quad \delta^2/S^2 = 1.79$$

(d) ***Agriculture***

(d:1) *Production function*

$$\frac{X_{Aa}/p_{Aa}}{N_{Aa}} = \underset{(5.23)}{17.35} Z_a - \underset{(3.36)}{5.053} Z_d + \underset{(1.89)}{5.771}$$

$$\bar{R}^2 = 0.57 \quad \delta^2/S^2 = 1.18$$

(*d*:2) *Quarterly income equation*

$$\frac{X_A/p_A}{N_A} = \frac{0.2596}{(0.0382)}\frac{X_{Aa}/p_{Aa}}{N_{Aa}} - \frac{0.09256}{(0.0144)}Q_1 - \frac{0.2689}{(0.0144)}Q_2$$

$$-\frac{0.1651}{(0.0144)}Q_3 + \frac{0.1322}{(0.0425)} \quad \bar{R}^2 = 0.93 \quad \delta^2/S^2 = 1.61$$

(*d*:3) *Agricultural employment function*

$$\frac{N_I}{N_A} = \frac{-0.0119}{(0.00429)}\left(\frac{U}{N_I}\right) + \frac{0.8946}{(0.161)}\left(\frac{N_1}{N_A}\right)_{-4} + \frac{0.0097541}{(0.0130)}\frac{1}{4}\sum_{-1}^{-4}\frac{w_M}{w_A}$$

$$+\frac{0.02245}{(0.0116)}Q_1 - \frac{0.01272}{(0.00689)}Q_2 - \frac{0.005604}{(0.00490)}Q_3 + \frac{0.05181}{(0.0335)}$$

$$\bar{R}^2 = 0.96 \quad \delta^2/S^2 = 2.15$$

(*d*:4) *Agricultural price determination equation*

$$p_A = \frac{0.2727}{(0.363)}p_{Aa}^m - \frac{0.2681}{(0.0438)}\left(\frac{X_{Aa}/p_{Aa}}{N_{At}}\right)_{-2} + \frac{0.5556}{(0.104)}p_{Aa}^g$$

$$-\frac{0.01408}{(0.0143)}Q_1 - \frac{0.006706}{(0.0143)}Q_2 + \frac{0.0008750}{(0.0140)}Q_3 + \frac{0.4550}{(0.283)}$$

$$\bar{R}^2 = 0.80 \quad \delta^2/S^2 = 1.44$$

(*d*:5) *Agricultural inventory equation*

$$\frac{J_A}{p_A} = \frac{0.2468}{(0.185)}\frac{1}{4}\sum_{3}^{4}\frac{X_A}{p_A} - \frac{0.1360}{(0.0896)}\frac{C_f}{p_f^c} - \frac{5.482}{(0.126)}Q_1$$

$$-\frac{4.732}{(0.102)}Q_2 - \frac{5.020}{(0.0963)}Q_3 + \frac{3.886}{(0.268)} \quad \bar{R}^2 = 0.99$$

(*e*) ***Tertiary industry***

(*e*:1) *Production decision function*

$$\frac{X_E}{P_E} = \underset{(0.0696)}{0.13373} S_{EC} + \underset{(0.377)}{0.92450} S_{EE} + \underset{(0.435)}{0.43569} S_{EI} + \underset{(0.178)}{0.25698} S_{EJ}$$

$$- \underset{(0.254)}{1.5602} Q_1 - \underset{(0.432)}{0.46702} Q_2 - \underset{(0.355)}{0.85837} Q_3 + \underset{(0.650)}{5.5290} \quad \bar{R}^2 = 0.89$$

(*e*:2) *Production functions*

$$\frac{X_E/p_E}{N_E} = \underset{(0.0280)}{0.1260} \frac{\rho_E K_{E,-1}}{N_E} + \underset{(0.0949)}{0.5267} \quad \bar{R}^2 = 0.42 \quad \delta^2/S^2 = 1.56$$

(*e*:3) *Wage determination equation*

$$w_E - w_{E,-4} = \underset{(0.0763)}{-0.2733} \frac{1}{4} \sum_{0}^{-3} U + \underset{(0.619)}{2.319} \quad \bar{R}^2 = 0.24 \quad \delta^2/S^2 = 0.72$$

(*e*:4) *Price determination equation*

$$p_E = \underset{(0.0116)}{0.06255} W_E \frac{N_E}{X_E/P_E} + \underset{(0.135)}{0.6605} P_u + \underset{(0.0138)}{0.003306} Q_1 + \underset{(0.0130)}{0.02010} Q_2$$

$$+ \underset{(0.0127)}{0.01612} Q_3 + \underset{(0.0876)}{0.03261} \quad \bar{R}^2 = 0.94 \quad \delta^2/S^2 = 0.53$$

(*e*:5) *Fixed investment function*

$$\frac{I_E}{P_K} = \underset{(0.0365)}{0.07910} + \left(\frac{X_E}{P_E} - \max \frac{X_E}{P_E}\right) - \underset{(0.147)}{-0.5860i} + \underset{(0.0501)}{0.1024}$$

$$\sum_{-1}^{-2} \frac{(P+D)_E}{P_K} + \underset{(1.63)}{5.737} \quad \bar{R}^2 = 0.80 \quad \delta^2/S^2 = 1.06$$

(*f*) **Household sector**

(*f*:1) *Consumption functions*

(f:1-f) Food

$$\frac{C_f/p_f^c}{N} = \frac{0.08834}{(0.0258)}\frac{Y_d/p_f^c}{N} - \frac{0.1473}{(0.0897)}\frac{p^{-T}c^{-S}c^{-\pi}}{W + X_A + Y_o}$$

$$+\frac{0.4726}{(0.128)}\sum_{-1}^{-4}\frac{C_f/p_f^c}{4N} - \frac{0.06420}{(0.0182)}Q_1 - \frac{0.03530}{(0.0186)}Q_2$$

$$-\frac{0.04138}{(0.0149)}Q_3 + \frac{0.3328}{(0.0694)} \quad \bar{R}^2 = 0.98 \quad \delta^2/S^2 = 1.03$$

(f:1-t) Textile

$$\frac{C_t/p_t^c}{N} = \frac{0.03064}{(0.00734)}\frac{Y_d/p_t^c}{N} + \frac{0.04722}{(0.0347)}\frac{p^{-T}c^{-S}c^{-\pi}}{W + X_A + Y_o} + \frac{0.4122}{(0.171)}\sum_{-1}^{-4}\frac{C_t/p_t^c}{4N}$$

$$-\frac{0.05706}{(0.00527)}Q_1 - \frac{0.06293}{(0.00572)}Q_2 - \frac{0.06434}{(0.00430)}Q_3 + \frac{0.05999}{(0.0163)}$$

$$\bar{R}^2 = 0.99 \quad \delta^2/S^2 = 2.53$$

(f:1-o) Other

$$\frac{C_o/p_o^c}{N} = \frac{0.1476}{(0.0495)}\frac{Y_d/p_o^c}{N} - \frac{0.03705}{(0.111)}\frac{p^{-T}c^{-S}c^{-\pi}}{W + X_A + Y_o} + \frac{0.7146}{(0.115)}\sum_{-1}^{-4}\frac{C_o/p_o^c}{4N}$$

$$+\frac{0.07213}{(0.0332)}Q_1 + \frac{0.006206}{(0.0315)}Q_2 + \frac{0.00006016}{(0.0250)}Q_3 - \frac{0.06801}{(0.0547)}$$

$$\bar{R}^2 = 0.98 \quad \delta^2/S^2 = 1.45$$

(*f*:2) *Residential investment function*

$$\frac{I_R}{p_R} = \frac{0.01726}{(0.0114)}\frac{Y_d}{p_R} + \frac{0.3253}{(0.113)}\frac{r}{p_R} - \frac{0.0279}{(0.0676)}Q_1 + \frac{0.01353}{(0.0557)}Q_2$$

$$+\frac{0.03737}{(0.0526)}Q_3 - \frac{0.1870}{(0.105)} \quad \bar{R}^2 = 0.92 \quad \delta^2/S^2 = 1.65$$

(*f*:3) *Consumers' price determination equations*

(f:3-f) Food Price

$$p_f^c = \underset{(0.0428)}{0.3873} p_A + \underset{(0.0293)}{0.04490} p_{f2}^b + \underset{(0.00585)}{0.04842} w_{E,-1} - \underset{(0.00784)}{0.02765} Q_1 + \underset{(0.00701)}{0.02467} Q_2 + \underset{(0.00665)}{0.01578} Q_3 + \underset{(0.0670)}{0.3532}$$

$\bar{R}^2 = 0.93 \quad \delta^2/S^2 = 1.75$

(f:3-t) Textile Price

$$p_t^c = \underset{(0.0314)}{0.1412} p_t + \underset{(0.0825)}{0.4763} p_{t,-1}^c - \underset{(0.00705)}{0.01628} Q_1 - \underset{(0.00686)}{0.01028} Q_2 - \underset{(0.00689)}{0.008237} Q_3 + \underset{(0.0669)}{0.3887} \quad \bar{R}^2 = 0.87 \quad \delta^2/S^2 = 1.01$$

(f:3-o) Other Price

$$p_o^c = \underset{(0.0629)}{0.1169} p_E + \underset{(0.0164)}{0.008412} r + \underset{(0.0561)}{0.7903} p_{o,-1}^c - \underset{(0.00321)}{0.001547} Q_1 - \underset{(0.00347)}{0.003693} Q_2 - \underset{(0.00336)}{0.008234} Q_3 + \underset{(0.0364)}{0.09234}$$

$\bar{R}^2 = 0.99 \quad \delta^2/S^2 = 1.69$

(*g*) ***Inventory investment functions***

(*g*:1) *Producers' inventory investment of finished products*

(g:1-h) Heavy Industry

$$\frac{J_{fh}}{p_h} = \underset{(0.00885)}{0.04178} \left(\frac{X_h}{p_h}\right)_{-1} - \underset{(0.0602)}{0.2013} \left(\frac{H_{fh}}{p_h}\right)_{-2} - \underset{(0.383)}{1.062} \Delta p_h + \underset{(0.0329)}{0.004111} Q_1 - \underset{(0.0329)}{0.02567} Q_2 + \underset{(0.0329)}{0.05519} Q_3 - \underset{(0.0778)}{0.04147}$$

$\bar{R}^2 = 0.63 \quad \delta^2/S^2 = 1.99$

(g:1-t) Textile Industry

$$\frac{J_{ft}}{p_t} = \underset{(0.0169)}{0.05881}\left(\frac{X_t}{p_t}\right)_{-1} - \underset{(0.0862)}{0.3113}\left(\frac{H_{ft}}{p_t}\right)_{-2} - \underset{(0.192)}{0.7725}\Delta p_t$$

$$+\underset{(0.0248)}{0.05294}Q_1 + \underset{(0.0247)}{0.1172}Q_2 + \underset{(0.0262)}{0.09795}Q_3 - \underset{(0.0681)}{0.03196}$$

$$\bar{R}^2 = 0.70 \quad \delta^2/S^2 = 2.50$$

(g:1-o) Other Manufacturing Industry

$$\frac{J_{fo}}{p_o} = \underset{(0.0175)}{0.09531}\left(\frac{X_o}{p_o}\right)_{-1} - \underset{(0.0831)}{0.4503}\left(\frac{H_{fo}}{p_o}\right)_{-2} - \underset{(1.42)}{4.913}\Delta p_o$$

$$+\underset{(0.0493)}{0.2736}Q_1 - \underset{(0.0494)}{0.1651}Q_2 + \underset{(0.0491)}{0.2066}Q_3 + \underset{(0.115)}{0.1302}$$

$$\bar{R}^2 = 0.85 \quad \delta^2/S^2 = 2.68$$

(g:2) *Producers' inventory investment of raw materials*

$$\frac{J_m}{p_v^m} = \underset{(0.132)}{0.3760}\frac{B_m}{p_m^b} + \underset{(0.255)}{0.5392}\frac{\Delta X_{h2}^u}{p_h} - \underset{(1.12)}{0.1491}\frac{(H_m/p_v^m)}{x_{vm,-1}} + \underset{(0.180)}{0.1009}Q_1$$

$$+\underset{(0.179)}{0.8666}Q_2 + \underset{(0.171)}{0.2048}Q_3 + 0.6384 \quad \bar{R}^2 = 0.70 \quad \delta^2/S^2 = 1.98$$

(g:3) *Producers' inventory investment of goods in process*

$$\frac{J_p}{p_M} = \underset{(0.0328)}{0.08414}\left(\frac{X_h}{p_h} + \frac{X_t}{p_t} + \frac{X_o}{p_o}\right) - \underset{(0.101)}{0.2441}\left(\frac{H_p}{p_M}\right)_{-1} - \underset{(1.83)}{0.7842}\rho_M$$

$$-\underset{(0.152)}{0.3601}Q_1 - \underset{(0.135)}{0.01222}Q_2 - \underset{(0.135)}{0.2985}Q_3 + \underset{(1.87)}{0.7452}$$

$$\bar{R}^2 = 0.54 \quad \delta^2/S^2 = 1.46$$

(*g*:4) *Dealers' inventory investment*

$$\frac{J_d}{p_v^d} = \frac{-1.401}{(0.475)} \frac{(H_d/p_v^d)_{-2}}{x_{vd,-1}} + \frac{3.565}{(2.08)}(\Delta p_t)_{-1} + \frac{1.028}{(0.293)}Q_1 + \frac{1.390}{(0.293)}Q_2 + \frac{0.9658}{(0.293)}Q_3 + \frac{2.822}{(1.15)}$$

$$\bar{R}^2 = 0.51 \quad \delta^2/S^2 = 2.38$$

(*g*:5) *New order equation*

$$\frac{X_{h2}^n}{P_h} = \frac{0.1830}{(0.0345)}\left(\frac{I_p}{P_K} + \frac{E_h}{P_h^e}\right)_{-2} + \frac{7.717}{(1.33)}(\Delta P_h)_{-2} - \frac{0.1510}{(0.126)}Q_1 - \frac{0.1510}{(0.123)}Q_2 + \frac{0.01849}{(0.124)}Q_3 + \frac{0.2664}{(0.205)}$$

$$\bar{R}^2 = 0.70 \quad \delta^2/S^2 = 1.86$$

(*g*:6) *Machinery sales equation*

$$\frac{X_{h2}^s}{p_h} = \frac{0.1373}{(0.00918)}\frac{X_h}{p_h} - \frac{0.6447}{(0.248)}\rho_h + \frac{0.4890}{(0.247)}$$

$$\bar{R}^2 = 0.90 \quad \delta^2/S^2 = 0.85$$

(*h*) ***Money***

(*h*:1) *Demand for money*

(h:1-p) Private Businesses and Household

$$L^p = 7.8375 + \frac{0.54532}{(0.07521)}L_{-1}^p + \frac{0.41252}{(0.07732)}Y_d - \frac{0.72088}{(0.32982)}i - \frac{1.04780}{(0.61768)}Q_1 - \frac{0.51833}{(0.41086)}Q_2 - \frac{0.63080}{(0.38384)}Q_3$$

$$\bar{R}^2 = 0.993 \quad D - W = 1.641$$

(h:1-c) Corporations

$$L^c = 68.018 + \frac{0.35248}{(0.07660)}Y - \frac{15.295}{(3.2907)}p_M - \frac{5.3794}{(0.8809)}i - \frac{1.1439}{(0.53703)}Q_1$$

$$+\frac{0.60275}{(0.51542)}Q_2 + \frac{0.30666}{(0.47424)}Q_3 \quad \bar{R}^2 = 0.964 \quad D - W = 0.932$$

(h:1-b) Banks

$$L^b - 0.0264L_2 - 0.0054V = 5.7089 - \frac{0.80182}{(0.07086)}i - \frac{-4.8554}{(1.5479)}\Delta p_M$$

$$+\frac{0.1221}{(0.0690)}Q_1 - \frac{0.0566}{(0.0697)}Q_2 + \frac{0.0583}{(0.0638)}Q_3$$

$$\bar{R}^2 = 0.709 \quad D - W = 0.667$$

(h:1-g) Government

$$L^g = -0.2178 + \frac{0.2505}{(0.0181)}G' - \frac{0.02889}{(0.0510)}Q_1 + \frac{0.07016}{(0.1016)}Q_2 + \frac{0.01830}{(0.1017)}Q_3$$

$$\bar{R}^2 = 0.86 \quad D - W = 0.56$$

(*h*:2) *Demand for cash*

(h:2-p) Private Businesses and Persons

$$L_1^p = 3.0169 + \frac{0.13791}{(0.18030)}L_{1,-1}^p + \frac{0.16708}{(0.04003)}Y_d - \frac{0.11479}{(0.22433)}i$$

$$-\frac{0.57228}{(0.4506)}Q_1 - \frac{0.43359}{(0.23028)}Q_2 - \frac{0.75337}{(0.2381)}Q_3$$

$$\bar{R}^2 = 0.954 \quad D - W = 1.565$$

(h:2-c) Corporations

$$L_1^c = 5.3406 + \frac{0.010399}{(0.00422)}Y + \frac{0.63793}{(0.18138)}p_M - \frac{0.43610}{(0.03753)}i$$

$$+\frac{0.00407}{(0.0296)}Q_1 - \frac{0.00760}{(0.0284)}Q_2 - \frac{0.00799}{(0.02614)}Q_3$$

$$\bar{R}^2 = 0.971 \quad D - W = 1.03$$

(h:2-b) Banks

$$L_1^b - 0.0264L_2 = 4.6534 - \underset{(0.05686)}{0.48917}\, i - \underset{(1.24208)}{4.7364}\, \Delta p_M$$
$$+ \underset{(0.05538)}{0.11923}\, Q_1 - \underset{(0.05593)}{0.042091}\, Q_2 + \underset{(0.05518)}{0.085726}\, Q_3$$
$$\bar{R}^2 = 0.721 \quad D - W = 0.599$$

(h:2-g) Government

$$L_1^g = \underset{(0.0266)}{-0.2169} + \underset{(0.00512)}{0.07638}\, G' + \underset{(0.0145)}{0.01333}\, Q_1 + \underset{(0.0144)}{0.01066}\, Q_2$$
$$- \underset{(0.0144)}{0.003045}\, Q_3 \qquad \bar{R}^2 = 0.88 \quad D - W = 1.73$$

(*h*:3) *Demand for time deposit*

(h:3-p) Private Businesses and Persons

$$\Delta L_3^p = 6.3396 + \underset{(0.0351)}{0.0565}\, Y_d - \underset{(0.2517)}{0.58924}\, i - \underset{(1.1043)}{1.0246}\, p^c - \underset{(0.2317)}{0.39357}\, Q_1$$
$$+ \underset{(0.1988)}{0.39794}\, Q_2 + \underset{(0.1892)}{0.17901}\, Q_3 \quad \bar{R}^2 = 0.993 \quad D - W = 3.36$$

(h:3-c) Corporations

$$L_3^c = 23.157 + \underset{(0.07152)}{0.75067}\, L_{3,-1}^c + \underset{(0.06609)}{0.14654}\, Y - \underset{(3.8443)}{16.947}\, P_M$$
$$- \underset{(0.11336)}{0.7012}\, \Delta L_a - \underset{(0.43632)}{0.88471}\, i + \underset{(0.4978)}{2.2176}\, Q_1 + \underset{(0.4319)}{2.0489}\, Q_2$$
$$+ \underset{(0.3482)}{1.4378}\, Q_3 \qquad \bar{R}^2 = 0.998 \quad D - W = 2.01$$

(h:4) *Supply of loans*

(h:4-b) Banks

$$\Delta L_a = 2.8783 - \underset{(0.04646)}{0.22991} L_{a,-1} + \underset{(0.12764)}{0.31604} \Delta V + \underset{(0.323225)}{0.89519} (\Delta i - \Delta i*)$$

$$+ \underset{(0.05697)}{0.27169} (L_2 + L_3) + \underset{(0.9806)}{3.2163} (L^b - 0.0054V - 0.0264L_2)$$

$$- \underset{(0.3609)}{2.3907} Q_1 - \underset{(0.2752)}{1.4967} Q_2 - \underset{(0.2874)}{1.0886} Q_3$$

$\bar{R}^2 = 0.907 \; D - W = 1.87$

(h:4-jo) Bank of Japan to Commercial Banks

$$V = -3.2879 + \underset{(0.14532)}{0.12795} V_{-1} + \underset{(0.05488)}{0.095198} Y_{-1} - \underset{(7.288)}{44.370} \Delta p_m$$

$$+ \underset{(0.08442)}{0.29681} R_{-4} - \underset{(0.38393)}{0.61791} \Delta i * + \underset{(0.10447)}{0.28952} [L_a - 1.112(L_2 + L_3)]$$

$$+ \underset{(0.3196)}{0.18779} Q_1 + \underset{(0.3113)}{0.41718} Q_2 + \underset{(0.3181)}{0.44439} Q_3$$

$\bar{R}^2 = 0.879 \quad D - W = 1.14$

(h:4-g) Loans to Government

$$\Delta V_g = \underset{(0.147)}{0.7934} G_n + \underset{(0.643)}{0.3680} Q_1 - \underset{(0.444)}{1.477} Q_2 - \underset{(0.464)}{0.3695} Q_3 + \underset{(0.647)}{0.3839}$$

$\bar{R}^2 = 0.91 \quad \delta^2/S^2 = 2.92$

(h:4-g$_1$) Balance of Foreign Exchange Funds

$$G_1 = \underset{(0.0824)}{0.04431} \Delta R - \underset{(0.219)}{3.691} Q_1 - \underset{(0.218)}{2.085} Q_2 - \underset{(0.217)}{2.510} Q_3 + \underset{(0.454)}{2.152}$$

$\bar{R}^2 = 0.91 \quad \delta^2/S^2 = 1.85$

(*h*:5) *Determination of interest rate*

$$i = 1.7287 + \underset{(0.0649)}{0.7880} i_{-1} + \underset{(0.0516)}{0.1937} D + \underset{(0.0501)}{0.1061} \Delta i *$$
$$+ \underset{(0.0207)}{0.03663} \left(\frac{I - J_A - S_c}{\Delta L_a} \right)_{-2}$$
$$\bar{R}^2 = 0.963 \quad D - W = 1.08$$

(*i*) ***Imports and exports***

(*i*:1) *Import functions*

(i:1-f-1) Rice and Barley

$$\frac{B_{f1}}{P_{f1}^b} = \underset{(0.0398)}{0.03656} \sum_{-1}^{-4} \frac{C_f/P_f^c}{4} - \underset{(0.0325)}{0.003888} \left(\frac{X_A}{P_A} \right)_{IV,-1} - \underset{(0.489)}{1.199} \sum_{-1}^{-4} \frac{N_I}{N_A}$$
$$+ \underset{(0.0842)}{0.007389} Q_1 + \underset{(0.105)}{0.07046} Q_2 - \underset{(0.0717)}{0.01433} Q_3 + \underset{(0.169)}{0.4580}$$
$$\bar{R}^2 = 0.48 \quad \delta^2/S^2 = 1.33$$

(i:1-f-2) Other Food

$$\frac{B_{f2}}{p_{f2}^b} = \underset{(0.0127)}{0.07179} \sum_{-1}^{-4} \frac{C_f/p_f^c}{4} + \underset{(0.0774)}{0.1200} \frac{p_A}{p_{f2}^b} + \underset{(0.0216)}{0.01677} Q_1$$
$$+ \underset{(0.0215)}{0.02513} Q_2 + \underset{(0.0213)}{0.03280} Q_3 - \underset{(0.0683)}{0.2023}$$
$$\bar{R}^2 = 0.72 \quad \delta^2/S^2 = 2.59$$

(i:1-h-2) Machinery

$$\frac{B_{h2}}{p_{h2}^b} = \underset{(0.00892)}{0.08596} \left(\frac{I_p - B_{h2}}{p_K} \right)_{-2} - \underset{(0.0174)}{0.001980} Q_1$$
$$+ \underset{(0.0174)}{0.009289} Q_2 + \underset{(0.0169)}{0.01096} Q_3 + \underset{(0.0211)}{0.008627}$$
$$\bar{R}^2 = 0.76 \quad \delta^2/S^2 = 1.02$$

(i:1-m) Materials and Others

$$\frac{B_m}{P_m^b} = \frac{0.1366}{(0.0238)}\left(\frac{X_h}{P_h}+\frac{X_t}{P_t}+\frac{X_o}{P_o}\right)_{-1} - \frac{0.1701}{(0.0712)}\left(\frac{H_m}{P_M^m}\right)_{-2}$$

$$+\frac{0.05409}{(0.0317)}\frac{R_{-3}+R_{-4}}{2p_{m-3}^b} + \frac{0.1353}{(0.132)}Q_1 + \frac{0.3020}{(0.131)}Q_2 + \frac{0.02896}{(0.128)}Q_3$$

$$-\frac{0.04246}{(0.345)} \quad \bar{R}^2 = 0.84 \quad \delta^2/S^2 = 0.55$$

(*i*:2) *Export functions of heavy industry's products*

(i:2-1-i) Export of Ships

$$\frac{E_{h1}}{p_{h1}^e} = \frac{0.03592}{(0.0284)} + \frac{0.2086}{(0.0198)}\left(\frac{\hat{\hat{E}}_{h1}}{p'_{h1}}\right)_{-2} \quad \bar{R}^2 = 0.82 \quad \delta^2/S^2 = 2.57$$

(i:2-1-ii) Changes in Outstanding Order for Ships

$$\Delta\frac{\hat{\hat{E}}_{h1}}{p'_{h1}} = \frac{0.9701}{(0.182)}\frac{\hat{E}_{h1}}{p_{h1}} - \frac{0.6008}{(0.147)}\frac{E_{h1}}{p_{h1}^e} \quad \bar{R}^2 = 0.53$$

(i:2-1-iii) New Order for Ships

$$\frac{\hat{E}_{h1}}{p_{h1}} = \frac{0.07762}{(0.0725)}\mu - \frac{0.6486}{(0.218)}\frac{p_{h1}^w}{p_{h1}} - \frac{0.9966}{(0.441)} \quad \bar{R}^2 = 0.65 \quad \delta^2/S^2 = 1.32$$

(i:2-2) Machinery

$$\frac{E_{h2}}{p_{h2}^e} = \frac{0.3169}{(0.149)}\Delta x_{h2}^w + \frac{0.3101}{(0.0865)}\frac{p_{h2}^w}{p_{h2}^e} + \frac{0.02460}{(0.00784)}\frac{R_{h2}^A}{p_{h2}^e}$$

$$+\frac{0.1244}{(0.0137)}\frac{A}{p_{h2}^e} - \frac{0.3521}{(0.107)} \quad \bar{R}^2 = 0.95 \quad \delta^2/S^2 = 1.33$$

(i:2-3) Steel and Other Metal Products

$$\frac{E_{h3}}{p^e_{h3}} = \underset{(0.0743)}{0.07042} x^w_{h3} + \underset{(0.0913)}{0.1747} \frac{p^w_{h3}}{p^e_{h3}} + \underset{(0.00997)}{0.01428} \frac{R^A_{h3}}{p^e_{h3}}$$

$$+ \underset{(0.0169)}{0.01933} \frac{A}{p^e_{h3}} - \underset{(0.108)}{0.1675} \rho_h + \underset{(0.0984)}{0.5898} \left(\frac{E_{h3}}{p^e_{h3}}\right)_{-1}$$

$$- \underset{(0.0168)}{0.07057} Q_1 - \underset{(0.0153)}{0.03823} Q_2 - \underset{(0.0168)}{0.03526} Q_3 - \underset{(0.126)}{0.03403}$$

$$\bar{R}^2 = 0.90 \quad \delta^2/S^2 = 2.92$$

(*i*:3) *Export functions of textile products*

(i:3-U) Textile Exports to the US

$$\frac{E^U_t}{p^e_t} = \underset{(0.269)}{1.397} y^U + \underset{(0.0440)}{0.05057} \frac{p^U_t}{p^e_t} + \underset{(0.148)}{0.4063} \left(\frac{E^U_t}{p^e_t}\right)_{-1} + \underset{(0.0264)}{0.05567} Q^U_t$$

$$- \underset{(0.144)}{0.7465} \qquad \bar{R}^2 = 0.94 \quad \delta^2/S^2 = 1.69$$

(i:3-E) Textile Exports to Europe and Canada

$$\frac{E^E_t}{p^e_t} = 0.2475 y^E + \underset{(0.0366)}{0.008102} \frac{p^E_t}{p^e_t} + \underset{(0.144)}{0.8083} \left(\frac{E^E_t}{p^e_t} - 2.475 y^E\right)_{-1}$$

$$- \underset{(0.00675)}{0.02249} Q_1 - \underset{(0.00667)}{0.006590} Q_2 - \underset{(0.00664)}{0.009659} Q_3 + \underset{(0.0383)}{0.002604}$$

$$\bar{R}^2 = 0.68 \quad \delta^2/S^2 = 2.37$$

(i:3-A) Textile Exports to the Rest of the World

$$\frac{E^A_t}{p^e_t} = \underset{(0.122)}{0.2795} x^A_t + \underset{(0.260)}{0.08732} \frac{p^A_t}{p^e_t} + \underset{(0.186)}{0.440} \left(\frac{E^A_t}{p^e_t}\right)_{-1}$$

$$- \underset{(0.0342)}{0.1295} Q_1 - \underset{(0.0317)}{0.08461} Q_2 - \underset{(0.0316)}{0.09133} Q_3 - \underset{(0.211)}{0.04364}$$

$$\bar{R}^2 = 0.87 \quad \delta^2/S^2 = 2.18$$

(i:3-p) Textile Export-Price Determination

$$p^e_t = \underset{(0.140)}{0.7037} p_t + \underset{(0.504)}{0.4199} p^w_t - \underset{(0.411)}{0.09159} \qquad \bar{R}^2 = 0.72 \quad \delta^2/S^2 = 0.70$$

(i:4) *Export functions of food*

(i:4-U) Food Exports to the US and Canada

$$\frac{E_a^U}{p_e^a} = \underset{(0.125)}{0.06634}(1 - 0.7432)y^U + \underset{(0.0361)}{0.03711}\frac{p_a^U}{p_a^e} + \underset{(0.135)}{0.7432}\left(\frac{E_a^U}{p_a^e}\right)_{-1}$$

$$+ \underset{(0.00546)}{0.0003095}Q_1 + \underset{(0.00540)}{0.004698}Q_2 + \underset{(0.00532)}{0.009850}Q_3 - \underset{(0.0344)}{0.03478}$$

$$\bar{R}^2 = 0.57 \quad \hat{\delta}^2/S^2 = 2.76$$

(i:4-E) Food Exports to Europe

$$\frac{E_a^E}{p_a^e} = 0.1200y^E + \underset{(0.0576)}{0.1250}\frac{p_a^E}{p_a^e} - \underset{(0.127)}{0.4016}\Delta\frac{p_a^E}{p_a^e} + \underset{(0.00107)}{0.003201}\frac{R^E}{p_a^e}$$

$$- \underset{(0.0509)}{0.01930} \qquad \bar{R}^2 = 0.51 \quad \hat{\delta}^2/S^2 = 1.73$$

(i:4-A) Food Exports to the Rest of the World

$$\frac{E_a^A}{p_a^e} = \underset{(0.0204)}{0.04299}y^A + \underset{(0.0268)}{0.03719}\frac{p_a^A}{p_a^e} - \underset{(0.00431)}{0.004575}Q_1 - \underset{(0.00433)}{0.005579}Q_2$$

$$+ \underset{(0.00437)}{0.002126}Q_3 - \underset{(0.0252)}{0.03142} \qquad \bar{R}^2 = 0.28$$

(i:5) *Export functions of other commodities*

(i:5-UE) Other Commodities Exports to the US, Canada and Europe

$$\frac{E_o^{UE}}{p_o^e} = \underset{(0.539)}{1.413}y_o^{UE} + \underset{(0.150)}{0.3202}\frac{p_o^w}{p_o^e} + \underset{(0.165)}{0.6643}\left(\frac{E_o^{UE}}{p_o^e}\right)_{-1}$$

$$+ \underset{(0.0202)}{0.007736}Q_1 - \underset{(0.0205)}{0.02779}Q_2 + \underset{(0.0191)}{0.01441}Q_3 - \underset{(0.329)}{0.9370}$$

$$\bar{R}^2 = 0.94 \quad \hat{\delta}^2/S^2 = 2.39$$

(i:5-A) Other Commodities Exports to the Rest of the World

$$\frac{E_o^A}{p_o^e} = \underset{(0.111)}{0.3452}\frac{Y^A}{p_o^e} + \underset{(0.127)}{0.6181}\left(\frac{E_o^A}{p_o^e}\right)_{-1} - \underset{(0.0113)}{0.04839}Q_1 + \underset{(0.0117)}{0.03469}Q_2 - \underset{(0.0136)}{0.004138}Q_3 - \underset{(0.0537)}{0.1274}$$

$\bar{R}^2 = 0.96 \quad \delta^2/S^2 = 2.28$

(i:5-p) Other Commodities Export-Price Determination

$$p_o^e = \underset{(0.314)}{0.6508}p_o + \underset{(0.127)}{0.4012}p_o^w - \underset{(0.0204)}{0.03161}Q_1 - \underset{(0.0206)}{0.03156}Q_2 - \underset{(0.0202)}{0.003648}Q_3 - \underset{(0.265)}{0.08363} \quad \bar{R}^2 = 0.57 \quad \delta^2/S^2 = 0.99$$

(*j*) ***Miscellaneous equations***

(*j*:1) *Corporate profit determination*

$$p_c = \underset{(0.0762)}{0.4525}p + \underset{(1.12)}{2.365}\rho_M + \underset{(0.00928)}{0.01315}\tau + \underset{(0.101)}{0.3796}Q_1 + \underset{(0.0908)}{0.2132}Q_2 + \underset{(0.0996)}{0.1193}Q_3 - \underset{(1.06)}{3.298} \quad \bar{R}^2 = 0.94 \quad \delta^2/S^2 = 1.27$$

(*j*:2) *Corporate saving function*

$$S_c = \underset{(0.179)}{0.9491}(P_c - T_c) - \underset{(0.0968)}{0.9740}D_{v,-4} + \underset{(0.0323)}{0.03999}Q_1 - \underset{(0.0193)}{0.007404}Q_2 + \underset{(0.0333)}{0.07319}Q_3 - \underset{(0.0492)}{0.005795} \quad \bar{R}^2 = 0.99 \quad \delta^2/S^2 = 2.08$$

(*j*:3) *Rentiers' income equation*

$$Y_o = \underset{(0.00940)}{0.05117}r(K_R)_{-1} + \underset{(0.000715)}{0.001868}(iL_3^p)_{-1} - \underset{(0.0182)}{0.03267}Q_1 - \underset{(0.0181)}{0.05578}Q_2 - \underset{(0.0180)}{0.03156}Q_3 - \underset{(0.0983)}{0.2473}$$

$\bar{R}^2 = 0.99 \quad \delta^2/S^2 = 1.37$

(j:4) *Depreciation allowance equation*

$$\frac{D_1}{p_K} = \underset{(0.0468)}{1.236} D_I' + \underset{(0.262)}{1.835} (q_1 D_1') - \underset{(0.265)}{2.042} q_2$$
$$+ \underset{(0.0222)}{0.07947} Q_1 - \underset{(0.0220)}{0.007840} Q_2 + \underset{(0.0217)}{0.07675} Q_3 - \underset{(0.794)}{0.4847}$$

$\bar{R}^2 = 0.99 \quad \delta^2/S^2 = 2.11$

(j:5) *Commodity-to-Exchange conversion*

(j:5-e) Export

$$E' = \underset{(0.0579)}{2.632} E + \underset{(0.117)}{0.5283} Q_1 + \underset{(0.116)}{0.3784} Q_2 + \underset{(0.115)}{0.2633} Q_3 - \underset{(0.273)}{0.2361}$$

$\bar{R}^2 = 0.99 \quad \delta^2/S^2 = 2.16$

(j:5-b) Import

$$B' = \underset{(0.125)}{2.355} B - \underset{(0.231)}{0.1545} Q_1 - \underset{(0.232)}{0.2434} Q_2 + \underset{(0.230)}{0.1019} Q_3 - \underset{(0.582)}{0.1330}$$

$\bar{R}^2 = 0.93 \quad \delta^2/S^2 = 1.53$

(j:6) *Non-operation profit of corporations*

$$\pi = \underset{(0.0489)}{0.4294} P_c + \underset{(0.0900)}{0.08948} Q_1 - \underset{(0.0894)}{0.05384} Q_2 + \underset{(0.0896)}{0.1299} Q_3 + \underset{(0.211)}{0.06110}$$

$\bar{R}^2 = 0.75 \quad \delta^2/S^2 = 1.02$

(j:7) *Replacement depreciation equation*

(j:7-h) $D'_{hj} = 0.01375(K_{hj} + K_{hj,-1}) \qquad j = L, S$

(j:7-t) $D'_{tj} = 0.01400(K_{tj} + K_{tj,-1}) \qquad j = L, S$

(j:7-o) $D'_{oj} = 0.01490(K_{oj} + K_{oj,-1}) \qquad j = L, S$

(j:7-E) $D'_E = 0.01090(K_E + K_{E,-1})$

(j:7-R) $D'_R = 0.0095(K_R + K_{R,-1})$

(j:8) *Investment deflator*

$$p_k = 0.75 p_h + 0.25 p_R$$

(*k*) ***Identities***

(k:1) $X_i = X_{iL} + X_{iS} \quad i = h, t, o$

(k:2) $p_M = (X_h + X_t + X_o) \Big/ \left(\frac{X_h}{p_h} + \frac{X_t}{p_t} + \frac{X_o}{p_o} \right)$

(k:3) $(P+D)_{ij} = X_{ij} - \frac{1}{10} w_{ij} N_{ij} - M_{ij} - T_{ij} \quad i = h, t, o \quad j = L, S$

(k:4) $(P + D)_E = X_E - \frac{1}{10} w_E N_E$

(k:5) $P = \sum_{i,j} (P + D)_{ij} + (P + D)_E - D_I$

(k:6) $w_M = \sum_{i,j} w_{ij} N_{ij} / \sum_{i,j} N_{ij}$

(k:7) $w_I = \left(\sum_{i,j} w_{ij} N_{ij} + w_E N_E \right) \Big/ \left(\sum_{i,j} N_{ij} + N_E \right)$

(k:8) $N_I = \frac{1}{10} \left(\sum_{i,j} N_{ij} + N_E \right)$

(k:9) $p_M^m = \sum_{i,j} M_{ij} \Big/ \sum_{i,j} \left(\frac{M_{ij}}{p_i^m} \right)$

(k:10) $p^c = (C_f + C_t + C_o) \Big/ \left(\frac{C_f}{p_f^c} + \frac{C_t}{p_t^c} + \frac{C_o}{p_o^c} \right)$

(k:11) $W = \frac{1}{10} \left(\sum_{i,j} w_{ij} N_{ij} + w_E N_E \right) + w_G$

(k:12) $D_v = P_c - S_c - T_c$

(k:13) $D_I' = \sum_{i,j} D_{ij}' + D_E'$

(k:14) $w_A = 10 \frac{X_A}{N_A}$

(k:15) $C = C_f + C_t + C_o$

(k:16) $I_p = \sum_{i,j} I_{ij} + I_E$

(k:17) $E = E_h + E_t + E_A + E_o$

(k:18) $B = B_{f1} + B_{f2} + B_{h2} + B_{m+c}$

(k:19) $K_{ij} = X_{ij,-1} + \dfrac{I_{ij}}{p_K} - D'_{ij} + \Delta_{ij} \qquad i = h, t, o \quad j = L, S$

(k:20) $K_E = K_{E,-1} + \dfrac{I_E}{p_E} - D'_E$

(k:21) $\dfrac{H_{fi}}{p_i} = \left(\dfrac{H_{fi}}{p_i}\right)_{-1} + \dfrac{J_{fi}}{p_i} \qquad i = h, t, o$

(k:22) $\dfrac{H_m}{p_v^m} = \left(\dfrac{H_m}{p_v^m}\right)_{-1} + \dfrac{J_m}{p_v^m}$

(k:23) $\dfrac{H_d}{p_v^d} = \left(\dfrac{H_d}{p_v^d}\right)_{-1} + \dfrac{J_d}{p_v^d}$

(k:24) $\dfrac{H_P}{p_M} = \left(\dfrac{H_P}{p_M}\right)_{-1} + \dfrac{J_P}{p_M}$

(k:25) $J = \sum_i J_{fi} + J_m + J_d + J_p + J_A$

(k:26) $I = I_p + J + I_R + I_A$

(k:27) $Y = W + P + X_A + Y_o - \pi - \xi - \Delta p \cdot H_{-1}$

(k:28) $Y_d = Y - \xi - (T_p - T_R) - T_c - S_c + \Delta p \cdot H_{-1}$

(k:29) $Y_G = C + I + G_I + (G - G_I) + E - B + \eta$

(k:30) $Y_G = Y + T + D + d_s$

(k:31) $G_n = G_1 + G_2 + G_3$

(k:32) $I_P = \sum_{i,j} I_{ij} + I_E$

(k:33) $K_R = K_{R,-1} + \dfrac{I_R}{p_R} - D'_R$

(k:34) $L = L^p + L^c + L_1^b + L^g$

$L_1 = L_1^p + L_1^c + L_1^b + L_1^g$

(k:35) $L_2 = L - L_1 = L^p - L_1^P + L^c - L_1^c + L^g - L_1^g = L_2^P + L_2^c + L_2^g$

$L_3 = L_3^p + L_3^c + L_3^g$

(k:36) $L_1^s = L_1^p + L_1^c + L_1^g + L_1^b$

$L^s = L^p + L^c + L^g + L^b$

(k:37) $\Delta R = E' - B' + E'_{\text{inv}} - R'_{\text{inv}} + B_K + \eta'$

$$\rho_{ij} = \frac{I_{ij}/p_i}{\max(X_{ij}/p_i)} \quad \begin{matrix} i = h, t, o \\ j = L, S \end{matrix}$$

where $\max(X_{ij}/p_i)$ is the maximum of past values of X_{ij}/p_i

(k:39) $\rho_E = \dfrac{I_E/p_E}{\max(X_E/p_E)}$

(k:40) $\rho_M = \dfrac{\sum_{i,j} X_{ij}/p_i}{\max\left(\sum_{i,j} X_{ij}/p_i\right)}$

(k:41) $\rho_h = \dfrac{X_h/p_h}{\max(X_h/p_h)}$

(k:42) $W_{ij} = \dfrac{1}{10} w_{ij} N_{ij}$

(k:43) $W_E = \dfrac{1}{10} w_E N_E$

$$\sigma_{ij} = \frac{X_{ij} - M_{ij}}{p_i N_{ij}} \cdot 10 \quad \begin{matrix} i = h, t, o \\ j = L, S \end{matrix}$$

(k:45) $x_{vm} = 0.545 \dfrac{X_h}{p_h} + 0.990 \dfrac{X_t}{p_t} + 0.128 \dfrac{X_o}{p_o}$

(k:46) $x_{vd} = 0.070 \dfrac{X_h}{p_h} + 1.465 \dfrac{X_t}{p_t} + 0.0237 \dfrac{X_o}{p_o}$

(k:47) $p_v^m = 0.403 p_h^m + 0.416 p_t^m + 0.181 p_o^m$

(k:48) $p_v^d = 0.107 p_h + 0.803 p_t + 0.090 p_o$

(k:49) $X_{h2}^u = X_{h2-1}^u + X_{h2}^n - X_{h2}^s$

(k:50) $U = 10 N_L - \sum_{i,j} N_{ij} - N_E - N_s$

(k:51)

$$p = Y_G \Big/ \left(\frac{C}{p_c} + \sum \frac{I_i}{p_i} + \frac{G_I}{p_i} + \frac{G - G_I}{p_c} + \sum \frac{E_i}{p_i} - \sum \frac{B_i}{p_i} + \frac{\eta}{p_\eta} \right)$$

(k:52) $E_h = E_{hl} + E_{h2} + E_{h3}$

(k:53) $E_t = E_t^U + E_t^E + E_t^A$

(k:54) $E_a = E_a^U + E_a^E + E_a^A$

(k:55) $E_o = E_o^{UE} + E_o^A$

(k:56) $W_h = W_{hl} + W_{hs}$

(k:57) $W_t = W_{tL} + W_{tS}$

(k:58) $W_o = W_{oL} + W_{oS}$

(k:59) $D = D_I + D_R + D_G + D_A$

(k:60) $$\Delta p \cdot H_{-1} = \sum_{i=h,t,o} (p_i - p_{i,-1}) H_{fi,-1} + (p_v^m - p_{v,-1}^m) H_{m,-1} + (p_v^d - p_{v,-1}^d) H_{d,-1} + (p_M - p_{M,-1}) H_{p,-1}$$

(k:61) $$(S_{hI} = 1.5762 \frac{I_p + G_I}{p_K}$$

$$S_{hJ} = 1.6389 \frac{J_{fh}}{p_h} + 0.0805 \left(\frac{J_{ft}}{p_t} + \frac{J_d}{p_d^v} \right) + 0.1042 \frac{J_{fo}}{p_o} + 0.2547 \left(\frac{J_m}{p_m^v} + \frac{J_p}{p_m} \right)$$

(k:62)

$$S_{tC} = 0.0086 \left(\frac{C_f}{p_f^c} - \frac{B_{f1}}{p_{f1}^b} - \frac{B_{f2}}{p_{f2}^b} \right) + 1.6285 \frac{C_t}{p_t^c} + 0.0203 \frac{C_o}{p_o^c} + 0.0365 \frac{G - G_I - W_G}{p^c}$$

$$S_{tE} = 0.0139 \frac{E_h}{P_h^e} + 1.6285 \frac{E_t}{P_t^e} + 0.0193 \frac{E_o}{P_o^e} + 0.0206 \frac{E_{\text{inv}}}{P_{\text{inv}}}$$

$$S_{tJ} = 0.0139 \frac{J_h}{p_h} + 1.6285 \left(\frac{J_{ft}}{p_t} + \frac{J_d}{p_d^v} \right) + 0.0193 \frac{J_{fo}}{p_o} + 0.7610 \left(\frac{J_m}{p_m^v} + \frac{J_p}{p_m} \right)$$

(k:63)

$$S_{oC} = 0.5941\left(\frac{C_f}{P_f^c} - \frac{B_{f1}}{P_{f1}^b} - \frac{B_{f2}}{P_{f2}^b}\right) + 0.4585\frac{C_t}{P_t^c} + 0.3382\frac{C_o}{P_o^c} + 0.3669\left(\frac{G - G_I - W_G}{P^c}\right)$$

$$S_{oE} = 0.3133\frac{E_h}{p_h^e} + 0.4585\frac{E_t}{p_t^e} + 1.3313\frac{E_o}{p_o^e} + 0.2334\frac{E_{\text{inv}}}{p_{\text{inv}}}$$

$$S_{oI} = 0.3160\left(\frac{I_P - G_I}{P_K}\right)$$

$$S_{EC} = 0.1562\left(\frac{C_f}{p_f^e} - \frac{B_{f1}}{p_{f1}^b} - \frac{B_{f2}}{p_{f2}^b}\right) + 0.4189\frac{C_t}{p_t^e} + 1.2737\frac{C_o}{p_o^c} + 1.1987\left(\frac{G - G_I - W_G}{p^c}\right)$$

$$S_{EE} = 0.4295\frac{E_h}{p_h^e} + 0.4189\frac{E_t}{p_t^e} + 0.3499\frac{E_o}{p_o^e} + 1.3978\frac{E_{\text{inv}}}{p_{\text{inv}}}$$

$$S_{EI} = 0.4605\left(\frac{I_b + G_I}{p_K}\right)$$

$$S_{EJ} = 0.4295\frac{J_{fh}}{p_h} + 0.4189\left(\frac{J_{ft}}{p_t} + \frac{J_d}{p_d^v}\right) + 0.3499\frac{J_{fo}}{p_o} + 0.4427\left(\frac{J_m}{p_m^v} + \frac{J_p}{p_M}\right)$$

Chapter 10

Osaka ISER Model

II. Detailed Discussion of the Model

Shinichi Ichimura, Lawrence R. Klein,
Susumu Koizumi and Kazuo Sato

1. Manufacturing Sector[1]

1.1. *Production decision functions*

The Leontief model expresses the output of each sector as a linear function of all final demands, by pre-multiplying the inverted IO coefficient matrix into the final demand vector. A similar relation holds, with a due adjustment of the final demand vector, for the sale of each sector, X_i/P_i, which differs from output by the change of finished inventory in the hands of producers. The total sale of a sector is a function of the final demand for the products of that sector and other sectors. Since the classification of industries does not necessarily coincide with that of final demand, it is not possible to obtain such relations from the IO tables. Moreover, the sale of each manufacturing industry in our model is further divided between groups of large and small firms, but the readily available IO tables do not provide us with this type of classification. A compromise method of finding a linear relation between the sales of each sector and the final demand was sought. The first method attempted was to choose a small number of seemingly most important items of final demands and regress each sector's sale on them. For instance, to explain the heavy industry private fixed investment, we used government fixed investment and exports of heavy industry

[1] Sections 1 to 4 are based on Ichimura, S., L. R. Klein, S. Koizumi, K. Sato and Y. Shinkai (1964). A Quarterly Econometric Model of Japan, 1952–1959. Osaka Economic Papers, 3/1964.

products as relevant and important final demands. The resulting regression equation gave large coefficients for exports and small coefficients for other variables. These results seemed to be due mainly to the collinearity of predetermined variables and exclusion of other relevant, though less important, final demands. Thus, by using IO relations, we expressed these groups of final demand as weighted sums of final demand variables in our model. [See (k:61), (k:62) and (k:63).] The weights 1.5762, 1.6389 etc are derived from the inverse matrix of IO table for 1955.

Then X_{hl}/P_h and X_{hs}/P_h are regressed on S_{hI}, S_{hE} and S_{hJ} so that we estimate the relative shares of large and small enterprises in meeting the final demands for the industry's products. The relative importance of fixed investment, exports and inventory investment can also be obtained from this regression equation.

Table 2.1 shows the elasticities of each sector's sale with respect to each item of final demand. We can tell the relative importance of different final demands for the increase of sales in different sectors. Let us take Heavy Industry as an example; we observe in Table 2.1 that the sales by large firms respond slightly less than the sales by small firms to changes in private and government fixed investment. On the other hand, large firms' sales respond considerably more to the changes in exports.

It is often argued that small businesses in Japan are tied to large corporations as sub-contractors so that the sales of the former are to a large extent regulated by the sales policies of the latter. Large corporations often find it advantageous to stabilize their own sale and production over a cycle by giving the transitory parts above or beyond normally growing sales on a subcontracting basis to small businesses. In this case, we should expect to observe larger changes in small firms' than in large corporations' sales. Since fixed investment, consumption and inventory investment are all variables reflecting the ups and downs of domestic economic activity, the cyclic sensitivities are revealed in higher elasticities for these variables of small business in heavy and textile industries but not in the case of the residual manufacturing industry. In this last group, large and small firms groups produce quite different kinds of products and do not seem to have interrelations as much as in other industrial sectors. The criterion separating the large and small firm groups in our model is fixed at the amount of paid-in capital, 50 million Yen. An increase of average size of firms in terms of paid-in capital may, therefore, increase the share of the large firm group in total sales, even without any changes in individual firms' shares.

Table 2.1. Elasticities of Sector's Sales with Respect to Each Item of Final Demand.

Sector	Final Demands								
	I_p/p_k	G_I/p_k	E_h/p_h^e	E_t/p_t^e	E_o/p_o^e	E_{inv}/p_{inv}	J_{fh}/p_h	J_{ft}/p_t	J_d/p_v^d
X_{hL}/p_h	0.4145	0.2893	0.2817	0.0135	0.0138	0.0087	0.0016	0.00001	0.0005
X_{hs}/p_h	0.4529	0.3161	0.1186	0.0057	0.0058	0.003	0.0067	0.00004	0.0021
X_{tL}/p_t			0.0027	0.3030	0.0028	0.0020	0.00001	0.00007	0.0037
X_{ts}/p_t			0.0045	0.5096	0.0048	0.0033	0.000003	0.000045	0.0024
X_{oL}/p_o	0.2545	0.1776	0.0773	0.1102	0.2527	0.0289			
X_{os}/p_o	0.2014	0.1406	0.0612	0.0872	0.2000	0.0228			
X_E/p_E	0.0564	0.0393	0.0342	0.0325	0.0214	0.0558	0.0006	0.0001	0.0036
	J_{fo}/p_o	J_m/p_v^m	J_p/p_m	C_f/p_f^v	B_{f1}/p_{f1}^b	B_{f2}/p_{f2}^b	C_t/p_t^c	C_o/p_o^c	$\frac{G-G_I-W_G}{p^c}$
X_{hL}/p_h	0.0001	0.0012	0.0013						
X_{hs}/p_h	0.0006	0.0049	0.0055						
X_{tL}/p_t	0.0000	0.0013	0.0015	0.0136	−0.0003	−0.0008	0.0412	0.0232	0.0131
X_{ts}/p_t	0.00001	0.0008	0.0009	0.0188	0.0004	−0.0011	0.5678	0.0322	0.0182
X_{oL}/p_o				0.2447	0.0058	−0.014	0.0301	0.1008	0.0344
X_{os}/p_o				0.0089	0.0002	0.0005	0.0011	0.0037	0.0013
X_E/p_E	0.0007	0.0029	0.0032	0.0178	0.0004	0.0010	0.0076	0.1052	0.0311

Table 2.2. The Number of Firms in Each Sector.

		1952	1959
H	*L*	243	635
	S	21,838	38,455
T	*L*	77	197
	S	10,681	15,781
O	*L*	246	717
	S	55,411	100,293

Table 2.2 shows the number of firms in each group over the sample period. It is observed that the average size of firm seems to have increaseed somewhat in each of three manufacturing sectors. Since this increase in average size of firm accompanied an upward trend of demand variables, it might have contributed to an increase in the computed elasticities for the large firm relative to those for the small firms.

1.2. *Production function*

The relation usually called production function is split into two parts in our model; one is our "production function" which relates sales to the labor and capital inputs, and the other is our "material input function" which relates material inputs to the sales. This treatment is based on the consideration that while substitution between labor and capital is possible, the room for substitution between materials as a whole and other inputs is very limited. This seems to be justified by the empirical observation that in each of the manufacturing industries, material input per unit of output stayed almost constant over the sample period in the face of changing relative factor prices.

In production functions, real sales per unit of labor input are used as the dependent variable, and capital input per unit of labor input and trend are used as explanatory variables. The use of sales as the dependent variable is due to the lack of separate data on production for large and small firm groups. Labor input is measured as the number of workers employed,[2] and capital input is defined as the stock of fixed capital multiplied by the

[2]This includes both the regularly and temporarily employed, but the latter are adjusted for the number of days worked. We regard 75 days of work in a quarter as equivalent to the regular employment of one person.

degree of utilization, which is approximated by the ratio of the current to past maximum sales. This procedure assumes that capacity output can be approximated by the past maximum sales.

The trend variable is included to pick up the effects of technical progress. If a production function is homogeneous of degree one, an increase of labor productivity comes either from an increase in capital intensity or from technical progress. As it stands, the technical progress in our production functions is not neutral but of the *labor-saving* type.

The estimated equations show that the marginal productivity of capital (the coefficient of $\rho K_{-1}/N$) is greater for the small than for the large firm group in each manufacturing industry, and that the productivity improvement due to technical progress is greater for the large than for the small firm group, except for the textile industry.[3]

1.3. *Material input function*

All the inputs other than labor and capital are classified as material inputs. The material inputs, thus defined, are assumed to be, as a whole, non-substitutive for labor and capital and uninfluenced by technical progress. The empirical finding that the constant term in the estimated equation for each sector is statistically very insignificant seems to justify the adequacy of this assumption. In the estimated equations, material input per unit of sales is a bit smaller for the large than for the small firm group in each of three manufacturing industries. This might be interpreted as indicating the existence of economies of scale in production.

Among the three manufacturing industries, material input per unit of sales (in 1955 price) is the largest in the textile industry. No appreciable difference exists between the heavy and other manufacturing industries. This implies a low value added ratio for the textile industry. Since a large part of the materials for the textile industry are imported, this in turn implies a high marginal propensity to import for the income originating in the textile industry. Anticipating the results for the price determination equations (a:4), (b:4) and (c:4) in the next section, this low value-added ratio of the textile industry is reflected in the high sensitivity of textile to material prices.

[3]For another possible interpretation, see Ichimura, S. (1968). Factors for Rapid Economic Growth. In K. Ohkawa and L.R. Klein (ed.), *Economic Growth: Japanese Experiences Since the Meiji Era*. (Homewood, Ill.: Irwin.) It is Chapter 1 in this book.

1.4. *Price determination equations*

The principle of price determination is based on an amalgamation of the mark-up principle and the demand-and-supply principle. We assume that prices of finished products are determined over the long-run by the mark-up principle but over the short-run are subject to changes resulting from variation in demand-and-supply conditions. As the basic factors that determine the cost per unit of output, we choose material price (p^m) and wage cost per unit of output (unit labor cost) $\left(\frac{W}{X/p}\right)$. Thus, our mark-up equation takes the form $p = \alpha p^m + \beta \frac{W}{X/p} + \gamma$. The use of material price rather than material cost per unit of output is based on the consideration that material input per unit of output is very stable, as mentioned above, over time in each industry.

In a dynamic version of the demand-and-supply principle, the time rate of price change is assumed to be an increasing function of excess demand. If the normal inventory sales ratio could be assumed to be fairly stable over time, say equal to k, then the ratio of excess demand to sales would be represented by

$$k - \frac{-H}{X/p}, \quad \text{and we would have } \Delta p = a\left(k - \frac{H}{X/p}\right),$$

where $a =$ speed-of-adjustment coefficient. Combining this and the mark-up equation, we obtain equations like (a:4), (b:4). In order to make the mark-up equation conformable with the dynamic demand-and-supply equation, all variables appearing in the former are expressed in first-differences. Trend-like changes in the mark-up ratio, if any, which will reflect changes in the normal rate of profits, capital output ratio, degree of monopoly etc., are picked up by the constant term.

We observe in the estimated equations that the coefficients of all the explanatory variables have theoretically right signs, although not all of them are statistically significant. The elasticities computed from the sample averages are shown in Table 2.3. Here, the elasticities with respect to material price and unit labor cost are computed as $\alpha \frac{p^m}{p}$ and $\beta \frac{\frac{W/X}{p}}{p}$, respectively, and $a \frac{\frac{H/X}{p}}{\Delta p}$ with respect to inventory-sales ratio. The first two elasticities, therefore, are not comparable with the third. The high elasticity of textile with respect to material price reflects the low value added ratio of textile industry observed above in connection with material input functions. The low elasticities for unit labor costs may be interpreted as reflecting the fact

Table 2.3. Elasticities of Prices with Respect to Different Factors.

	p^m	$W/\frac{X}{P}$	H/X
p_h	0.40	0.026	−6.3
p_t	1.10	0.013	−3.2
p_o	0.21	0.050	−8.5

that a large part of productivity improvement is absorbed by a money wage increase and does not lead to a price decline.

1.5. *Material price determination equations*

A theoretically neat way of formulating the equations of material price determination is to use the information provided by input-output tables. If we denote the input of the ith sector's product per unit of the jth sector's output by a_{ij} and the price of the ith sector's product by p_i, then the material price of the jth sector is given by $p_j^m = \sum_i \frac{a_{ij}}{\sum_i a_{ij}} p_i$. For two reasons, however, we do not adopt this formulation but rely on a looser formulation in which import price of major materials is used as the central explanatory variable. The first reason is theoretical. In order for the IO formulation to produce satisfactory results for an aggregative model, either the proportions in which the products of industries included in an aggregated sector are used as inputs of other sectors must be approximately the same as the proportions which they compose of the output of that sector, or the relative prices of the component industries' products must remain nearly constant over time. In a highly aggregative model like ours, it is very unlikely that these conditions are satisfied. The second reason is statistical. Our material prices are computed not as weighted averages of all the material prices but as weighted averages of prices of a few most important materials. Thus, the import price of metals and primary metal products and the average industrial wage are used as the explanatory variables for heavy industry. The import price of textile materials is used for the textile industry; and the import price of other materials, the price of agricultural products and the average industrial wage are used for the other manufacturing industry. The average industrial wage is introduced in other to account for distribution and partial processing cost of imported materials. The agricultural product price is included in the other manufacturing equation because a part of materials for that sector comes from the agricultural sector. For an economy like

Table 2.4. Elasticities of Material Prices.

	p_h^{bm}	w_I	
p_h^m	0.766	0.250	
	p_t^{bm}		
p_t^m	0.456		
	p_o^{bm}	p_A	w_I
p_o^m	0.321	0.256	0.243

Table 2.5. Wholesale Price Elasticities.

	p^{bm}	w		p_A
P_h	0.306	0.126	−0.026	
P_t	0.502	0.013	−0.013	
P_o	0.067	0.101	−0.050	0.05

Japan whose dependence on imports of raw materials is heavy, this kind of loose formulation may not be too inadequate.

Elasticities computed from the sample averages are shown in Table 2.4. The high elasticities for import prices indicate the heavy reliance of materials on imports. These equations, together with the price determination equations discussed in the preceding section, show that the basic determinants of Japanese wholesale prices, aside from short-run variations, are (1) import prices of materials, (2) money wages and (3) labor productivity in the manufacturing sectors. Substituting the material price determination equations (a:6), (b:6), and (c:6), into the price determination equations (a:4), (b:4), and (c:4), we can express product prices as functions of imported materials, money wages and labor productivity and inventory-sales ratios. From Tables 3.3 and 3.4, we can compute the elasticities of product prices for imported material prices, wage-rate and labor productivity (and agricultural prices for other manufacturing industry), under the assumption that money wage-rates move in the same proportion in all sectors.

The results are given in Table 2.5, which provides rough quantitative information of the way in which wholesale prices will be affected by changes in imported material prices, wage-rates and labor productivity.

1.6. *Wage-rate determination equations*

In the Japanese economy, the wage differentials among different industries or among firms of different sizes are so significant that it is hardly conceivable to make use of the model of perfect competition, which assumes a single wage-rate for homogeneous labor over the entire economy, Thus, in our model, the determination of wage-rate is explained separately for each sector.

Our wage-rate determination equations are essentially dynamic wage adjustment equations of the Phillip type.[4] It should be noted that the dependent variables are not wage-rates in the usual sense, but earnings per worker. This is a result of the lack of statistical data on hourly wage-rates. In each of our equation, in addition to the number of unemployed workers in the entire economy, a productivity change variable is introduced. The equations can be regarded as describing the wage-bargaining process. Under a situation in which the labor market is imperfect and wage rates are determined more or less on an individual firm basis, a productivity improvement is considered to be an important factor for wage-bargaining. Another important factor in the wage-bargaining process is the change of general consumer prices; but a high collinearity between consumer price change and unemployment in the sample period prevents us from including it as a third variable.

The changes of wage-rate and productivity are measured as four-quarter differences, and unemployment enters into the equations as the average of the past for quarters. This formulation is mainly based on the consideration that the change in wage-rate takes place, to a large extent, once a year and not every quarter.

One of the characteristics of the Japanese economy often mentioned is its "dual structure"; the co-existence of efficient modern large-scale firms and inefficient family-enterprise type small-scale firms. This dual structure manifests itself most conspicuously in the wage differentials among firms of different scales. It is generally recognized that behind the wage-differentials exists an imperfect labor market characterized by peculiar institutional set-up having a lifetime employment system and seniority wage system. In terms of our wage-rate determination equations, this phenomenon of wage differentials may be explained as follows. Because of labor immobility, resulting from market imperfection, wage rates are determined more or less on the individual firm basis, and productivity differentials among firms will produce wage-differentials. But the low wage rates in inefficient small firms are made possible by an abundant supply of unorganized labor. Thus when the labor market gets tight and unemployment is reduced, it becomes difficult for small firms to continue the employment of low-wage labor.

---

[4]Phillips (1958, pp. 283–299).

Thus, the wage-differentials will be influenced by the number of the unemployed as well as by productivity differentials, and will be narrowed by a decrease of unemployment. This implies that a change in unemployment affects primarily the wage rates of small firm groups, and the elasticity of wage with respect to unemployment will be larger in the small firm groups than in the large firm groups. This conjecture is supported by the empirical results obtained.

It is observed in the estimated equations that the coefficients for the unemployment variable are not significantly different from zero for all the large firm groups, while they are significant for the small firm groups at the 5% level. Also, as shown in Table 2.6, the elasticities of wages with respect to unemployment are larger for the small firm groups than for the large firm groups.

It should be noted that although the elasticity of wage with respect to labor productivity is also smaller for the large-scale group than for the small-scale group, it does not necessarily imply that the rate of increase of money wage is smaller for the large-scale groups. The result depends also on the relative magnitudes of constant terms in the equations.

The fits of these equations are not very good; especially, those for the heavy industry's large-firm group and the textile industry's large firm group. This may be partly due to the nature of our data: our wage variable is not an hourly wage-rate but quarterly earnings per worker and thus reflects not only changes in hourly wage rate but also changes in the average number of hours worked.

1.7. *Fixed investment functions*

The explanatory variables in our fixed investment functions are (1) profit, (2) interest rate and (3) the amount of excess capacity. The profit variable $(P + D)/p_k$ is defined as net business (corporate and non-corporate)

Table 2.6. Elasticity of Wage with Respect to Labor Productivity and Unemployment.

		$\frac{X/p}{N}$	U
H	L	0.076	−0.072
	S	0.464	−5.145
T	L	0.163	−3.073
	S	0.480	−4.619
O	L	0.340	−1.961
	S	0.710	−16.158

income from *current operation* plus capital depreciation allowances, deflated by the price index of investment goods. The interest rate is a weighed average of interest rates on loans made by commercial banks. For the third variable, a proxy is used. It is defined as the difference between current and the past maximum sales. This is based on the presumption, as in the production functions, that capacity output can be approximated by past maximum sales.

The profit variable is meant to represent both the profitability and the internal funds available for the relevant sector. Here it should be noted that net profit is measured as profit from the current operations and does not include such items as interest paid, and dividends received. We have done this so as to make the variable more accurately represent the profitability of the sector.

In an economy like Japan's in which the capital market is quite imperfect, the interest rate may not be regarded exclusively as the cost of financing capital but should rather be interpreted as an index of the tightness of the capital market. The coefficient of the interest variable should not be interpreted as the investment sensitivity to cost changes but as an indicator of the extent to which investment is affected by the monetary policies of the central bank. The capacity variable is used in order to obtain a variant of the capital stock adjustment mechanism. In the estimated equation, we include only the explanatory variables that showed the theoretically right signs. Thus, the interest rate is dropped from the heavy industry equations and the capacity variable from the equation for the large firm group of the other manufacturing industry.

The interest insensitivity of investment of the heavy industry group may be due to the favorable treatment in borrowing funds for fixed investment given to this industry. Thus, its investment is not much influenced by changes in the tightness of the capital market. It is a common feature of the three manufacturing industries, as observed in Table 2.7, that the

Table 2.7. Elasticities of Investment.

		Profit	Capacity Shortage	Interest
H	*L*	1.443	0.019	
	S	0.491	0.075	
T	*L*	0.729	0.007	−1.832
	S	0.413	0.029	−5.046
O	*L*	0.132		−9.361
	S	0.001	0.012	−7.500

elasticity of investment with respect to profit is greater for the large-firm group than for the small-firm group. The opposite is the case for the elasticity of investment with respect to capacity shortage.

2. Inventory Investment

Ideally, inventory functions should be established for each sector and size class just as fixed investment functions were. In addition, inventory equations are best described by stage of fabrication (materials, goods in process, finished). The stages should be classified by large and small enterprise in each manufacturing group; then inventory investment could be treated with fixed investment and the other separate industry equations. This would cover the manufacturing sectors. Inventory equations must be established for the non-manufacturing sectors.

The ideal is not attainable in the present model, partly because of lack of data. The requirements are great for the kind of detail that is implied by the ideal classification. The inventory process is of crucial importance in a short run model like ours; therefore some compromise formulation that is less than ideal must be used, for inventories have to be explained as best we can.

2.1. *Manufacturing inventories — finished goods*

Of the three stages of fabrication that are significant for inventory investment, most detail is available for finished goods. We have, therefore, three separate equations for investment of inventory in our three branches of manufacturing — heavy, textile, and other manufacturing industry. These three equations all have the same structure. They are stock adjustment relations (flexible accelerator pattern) in which the activity variable is real output of the corresponding manufacturing sector. Each equation also has a price-change variable, where price change is measured at the manufacturing level.

In every case the coefficient of production is a small positive number, less than 0.1, and the coefficient of stock is a negative number, varying between −0.2 and −0.45. These are reasonable values. In all three cases the coefficient of (own) price change is negative. This may, at first glance, seem to be a strange result for inventory *speculation*. Our interpretation, however, is as follows: When prices are rising in the manufacturing sectors, this is evidence of strong demand. Finished goods will be ordered for sale and stocking by dealers. Manufacturers, therefore, will find it difficult to hold finished goods under such conditions of brisk demand, and their inventories will fall, as suggested by our negative coefficients.

All the output, stock and price variables are estimated to have significant coefficients in each of the three equations. It should be noted, though, that inventory investment is a volatile economic process. The overall correlation coefficients are only moderately high (all less than 0.9), while the serial correlation statistics are consistent with the hypotheses of random time variation of errors.

2.2. *Manufacturing inventories — raw materials and goods in process*

The other two parts of the manufacturing inventory process, that *precede* the stage of stocking of finished goods, are treated on a grouped basis for heavy, textile, and other manufacturing industries together. There is one equation for investment in raw material inventories and one for investment in goods in process inventories.

The activity variables in the equation for investment in raw material stocks are real imports of materials and the change in unfilled orders for machinery. The lagged stock term is somewhat different here, compared with the treatment in finished goods inventory; namely, the lagged stock variable is introduced as a ratio to manufacturing output. When the ratio is large, there are plentiful material stocks in relation to output, and this has a depressing effect on further accumulation, the coefficient of this ratio variable is not very significant, from a statistical viewpoint. The activity variables are more significant in this equation.

In the case of goods in process, we use a stock adjustment form for the manufacturing sector as a whole and modify it with a cyclical variable, the degree of capacity utilization in manufacturing. This last variable is not significant, however. These two inventory equations show very moderate degrees of correlation. Possibly disaggregating with introduction of other variables would improve the specifications.

2.3. *Dealers' inventories*

There are no explicit inventory equations for the whole tertiary sector, but the most important part of inventories in this sector are those in dealer's hand. Here we have inventory investment in a stock adjustment form, as a negative function of the lagged stock-production ratio, where production is measured as a weighted sum of manufacturing production over types of manufacturing. We allow for the usual form of price speculation here and introduce a term, with a positive coefficient, represented by the change of textile prices.

2.4. *Orders*

To explain inventory investment in raw materials, we introduced the change in unfilled machinery orders. This would make good sense in this equation. For materials must be made ready to fill orders for production of machinery, as such orders are received.

We have an identity that states that the change in unfilled orders equals new orders *less* sales. We must, therefore, explain new orders and sales of machinery in order to explain the change in unfilled orders. New orders are expressed as a function of total investment and exports from heavy manufacturing industry. We also introduce the price change in heavy industry, and this variable has a significant positive coefficient. Machinery sales are made to depend on heavy industry output and the rate of capacity utilization in heavy industry. The first effect is positive and the second, negative.

2.5. *Agricultural inventory equation*

Inventory investment also occurs in the agricultural sector. Since it consists mainly of rice and other grains, it has a clear seasonal variation due to the new harvest in the third and fourth quarter every year and the gradual consumption over a year. It is explained, therefore, as positively dependent on the sum of those two last quarters' production in the agricultural sector and negatively correlated with the level of consumption of food every quarter. This completes the treatment of inventories and the related orders variables in our model.

3. Tertiary and Agriculture Sectors

3-A. *Tertiary sector*

The structure of equations for this sector is almost the same as that for manufacturing, but the distinction, though important, between large and small firm groups is not made, simply because we have no data necessary for doing so. In fact, this sector is known to consist predominantly of small corporations and private businesses, expect for electric utilities and some construction companies. Another difference is the treatment of output due to the lack of data. Output is defined as real gross value added with no equations of material input or price in this sector.

3-A.1. *Production decision function*

Since the outputs of the sector are used as inputs of almost all sectors, all the final demands are used as explanatory variables. A method similar to the one for manufacturing sectors is used, and four variables S_{Ej} (i = C, E, I and J) are defined corresponding to consumption, exports, fixed investment and inventory investments. The elasticities of tertiary output with respect to the various components of S_{ij} are given in Table 2.1. The results obtained seem to justify this treatment.

3-A.2. *Production function*

The estimated equation differs from the production functions of manufacturing sectors in that the trend variable is missing. The trend variable, if included, does not show a theoretically meaningful sign. This may be interpreted as reflecting the fact that, as we discussed in Part I, the technical progress in this sector was either unimportant or of the labor-using type. The increase in labor productivity came mainly from capital accumulation; i.e. through the increase of capital-labor ratio. The computed elasticity of output with respect to capital input is 0.38.

3-A.3. *Price determination equation*

Since the inventory stock is unimportant for this sector, the price determination equation is essentially based on the mark-up principle. An important price component in this sector, the price of public utilities' output is, however, regulated by the government. We therefore treat this price as an exogenous variable and include it as an explanatory variable. If we exclude public utilities, the main cost item for the remaining part of the tertiary sector is wage cost. Thus, the price of tertiary sector output is assumed to be a function of the price of public utilities output and its unit labor cost. The computed elasticities are 0.64 and 0.32 respectively.

3-A.4. *Wage determination equation*

The specification of the wage equation is the same as that for manufacturing sectors, but, in the estimated equation, the productivity factor is dropped and the wage change is made to depend solely on unemployment. The productivity factor, if included, is neither statistically significant nor of the right sign. In the tertiary sector, where productivity increases have been rather insignificant but the bargaining power of labor unions is strong as in public utilities, wages have increased quite independently of productivity increases, and a cost increase resulting from a wage rise has led to a rise of price.

3-A.5. *Investment function*

The form of the equation is exactly the same as that for manufacturing sectors. The computed elasticities with respect to profit and interest rate are 0.62 and −4.42.

3-B. *Agricultural sector*

3-B.1. *Production function*

The dependent variable in our agricultural production function is the real net value added divided by the number of persons engaged in agricultural production. The latter is adjusted for the number of hours worked. Per capita value added is assumed to be a function of fertilizer input and damaged average. All variables are defined as annual values. In agriculture, production periods are mostly longer than a quarter and vary among different crops. The aggregate production function of agriculture, therefore, cannot be meaningfully formulated on a quarterly basis, but should be formulated on an annual basis.

3-B.2. *Quarterly income equation*

This is a purely empirical relation that converts annual agricultural production (net value added) to quarterly values. It is needed because production in the agricultural sector must be explained on annual basis, while agricultural income must be explained on a quarterly basis in order to link this sector to others. The equation distributes per capita annual real net value added among four quarters by using seasonal variables. This procedure is based on the consideration that most of the variation in agricultural crops, and the income resulting from their sales within a year can be regarded as seasonal variations.

3-B.3. *Agricultural employment function*

This equation explains labor input for agricultural production. It is based on the view that the agricultural sector in the Japanese economy provides a pool of excess labor that gets absorbed in the form of disguised unemployment. Thus, agricultural employment is treated as a kind of residual, and agricultural production is determined by the labor input together with technical and climatic factors. The difference between demand and domestic supply of foods is covered by food import.

In determining the composition of employment, the ratio of the industrial to agricultural employment is chosen as the dependent variable. This is assumed to depend on the ratio of unemployment to total industrial employment and the wage differential between the manufacturing and the agricultural sector. The migration of labor does not adjust the labor distribution instantaneously to changing market conditions but takes place gradually. This justifies the introduction of the lagged industrial-agricultural employment ratio as an additional variable.

3-B.4. *Agricultural price determination equation*

An important part of the price of agricultural output, i.e. the price of rice, is under government control. The government purchase price of rice (p_A^G) is introduced as an explanatory variable in the equation to determine agricultural price. Apart from this, our equation is basically of the mark-up variety. The price of input is represented by the index of prices paid by farmers. To this is added the productivity of labor. Admittedly an important part of agricultural price fluctuations comes from change in demand-and-supply conditions, but the fact that such changes are associated with particular commodities makes it hard to incorporate this aspect in such an aggregative price determination equation.

4. Household Sector

Under the heading of household sector we have three consumption functions, a residential investment function, and three equations that determine consumers' prices. Total consumers' expenditure is disaggregated into three categories: food, textile, and other, and we have three consumers' prices that serve as deflators of the respective expenditures.

4.1. *Consumption functions of food, textile and other*

The three consumption functions are of the ordinary aggregate type, relating consumers' expenditures to their income. We have taken into account the following effects: population size (by expressing the main variables in per capita terms); taxes (by deducting personal taxes from the income data); lags (by introducing a distributed lag formulation); and income distribution. We might also say that we have taken account of relative price effects because we have used three distinct deflators.

Various propensities to consume computed at the point of the sample averages are listed next page. The values of these propensities conform to *a priori* conjecture. The average propensity to consume foods is nearly one-half, but the marginal propensity, both short- and long-run, is small. The propensities to consume textiles are less than 0.1. In the case of *other*, which includes consumers' durables and services, the marginal propensity to consume, especially the long-run propensity, is large.

The long-run propensities are computed on the assumption that population remains unchanged. The effect of a population increase may be approximately evaluated by summing up the constant term and the coefficients of the seasonal variables. The values of constant + 1/4 (the sum of coefficients of Q_1) are computed as: food 0.298, textiles 0.0139, other −0.0484. These figures give the values of increase in consumers' expenditures in hundred billion Yen associated with a ten million increase in population. The overall effect of a population increase on consumers' expenditure is positive, as might be expected. The coefficients of the income distribution variables have expected signs, but none is significantly different from zero.

4.2. *The residential investment function*

Residential investment is made a function of disposable income and the rent index, all variables deflated by the construction cost index. The marginal

Table 2.8. Propensities to Consume.

	Food	Textile	Others
Average*	0.463	0.0741	0.349
Marginal Sort-run	0.0883	0.0306	0.148
Marginal Long-run**	0.168	0.0521	0.517

Note: *Average per capita **with constant population.

propensity to invest is small; so are the elasticities of expenditure on residential construction with respect to income and the rent index. They are, respectively, 0.604 and 0.841. It is to be noted also that in Japan expenditure on residential construction occupies a small fraction of the total GNP, being roughly 2.5% in 1959.

4.3. *Consumers' prices determination equation*

In accordance with the disaggregation of consumers' expenditure, we have three equations to determine three consumers' prices: food price, textile price and the price of other consumer items. Our general procedure is to explain each consumer's price by those wholesale prices that are thought to be relevant on *a priori* grounds. Thus the consumers' price of food is made a function of agricultural price, the price of imported food, and (lagged) wage rate in the tertiary industry. The last variable represents distribution costs, which in the case of food, contribute significantly to the retail price. Actually that may be seen from the elasticity value of 0.213 with respect to the lagged wage rate.

The consumers' prices of textile products and other goods have been subject to less volatile fluctuations than the corresponding producers' prices. They are, therefore, made a function of their respective own price, lagged one period. This formulation amounts to assuming a distributed lag effect of the Koyck type. The independent explanatory variable in the consumers' textile price equation is, naturally, the producers' price of textile. The equation for the consumers' price of other goods has, as explanatory variables, the retail price in the tertiary industry and rent index.

Consumers' expenditure on "others" is an amalgam of such divergent items as housing (including furniture), gas and electricity, consumers' durables, services, etc. It may be suggested, therefore, that the deflator for this expenditure category should take account of variations in producers' price of heavy and "other" industries. An alternative price determination equation for p_o^c will thus be

$$p_o^c = \underset{(0.036)}{0.892}\left[0.834 p_E + 0.166\left(\frac{p_h + p_o}{2}\right)\right] + \underset{(0.116)}{0.182} Q_1 + \underset{(0.115)}{0.184} Q_2 + \underset{(0.115)}{0.126} Q_3 + 0.070 \quad R^2 = 0.94$$

The first variable is a weighted average of the three producers' prices, the weights being the average proportions of the relevant items.

5. The Financial Sector

The model of the monetary sector was constructed as a part of our large econometric model; so it was subject to some limitations as a result of the need for conformity with the rest of the system and the shortage of certain types of statistical data. The first tentative model estimated for 1951–1958 was published in Ichimura (1962) and modified later.[5] After we carried out some experiments in simulating the entire system of equations estimated by the two-stage least squares method within the sample period and for 1960–1961, it was found that a number of equations, including some monetary equations, were particularly responsible for considerable errors in *ex post* predictions of some endogenous variables. Thus, attempts have been made to improve those equations. The model presented here contains the latest version of equations for the monetary sector.

The model does not have an independent supply function of money or a supply function of cash currency but assumes simply that the supply is equated to the demand:

$$L_1^s = L_1^p + L_1^c + L_1^g + L_1^b,$$

$$L^s = L^p + L^c + L^g + L^b.$$

The second equation may well be regarded as determining the amount of money circulating in the economy. Notice that there is no demand function for bank loans corresponding to its supply functions.

5.1. *The demand functions of individuals and private corporations*

The behavior equations of individuals and private corporations cannot be separated in the data of financial statistics. It is not possible to collect similar data from statistics of corporations except for some particular years. The behavior equations consist of L^p, L_1^p and ΔL_3^p. L_2^p is defined as $L_2^p = L^p - L_1^p$. As for L^p and L_1^p, the usual specifications of liquidity preference functions are adopted. They are regarded as a function of $Y_d, i, \Delta i, p^c, \Delta p^c$, Q_1, Q_2, Q_3, but unlike the liquidity preference functions in the US and UK they are assumed to be linear functions, since rates of interest in Japan are still far above liquidity-trap minima. This can easily be observed by drawing a Brown-Tobin diagram of $[L^p - \min(L^p/Y_d),\ Y_d]$ as a function of i.

[5]Ichimura (1962, pp. 10–20). Its modified results: Ichimura (1966).

There is no evidence of concavity toward the origin. The final forms have been chosen by examining the signs and standard errors of all parameters, the multiple correlation coefficient $\bar{R}^2$, and the Durbin-Watson ratios of alternative forms of equations. As for L_3^p, its increment is taken as a part of savings; therefore, we make ΔL_3^p a function of Y_d, i, Δi, p^c, Δp^c, Q_1, Q_2, Q_3. The final form is adopted after the same type of examination that was made for L^p and L_1^p.

	Short-run		Long-run	
	Y_d	I	Y_d	I
L^p	0.412	−0.443	0.905	−0.974
L_1^p	0.528	−0.223	0.612	−0.259

The elasticities of L^p and L_1^p with respect to Y_d and i in the short-run and the long-run are given above. It may be of some interest to notice that the income elasticity is higher for cash than for deposit currency in the short-run but lower in the long run, whereas the interest elasticity is always higher for deposit currency than for cash. Deposit currency appears to be a closer substitute for other forms of financial assets. The elasticity of the increment of time deposit with respect or predetermined variables are:

	Y_d	I	p^c
ΔL_3^p	0.762	−4.891	−1.811

The high elasticity of ΔL_3^p with respect to i is consistent with the fact that time deposits are close substitutes for other financial assets. The income elasticity (0.762) is rather high, indicating that the individuals' saving predominantly take the form of time deposits. The significance of the price effect indicates that the rising of consumers' prices has an important negative effect on time deposits.

5.2. *The demand functions of corporations*

L^c and L_1^c were estimated in various alternative specifications as functions of Y, Y_{-1}, i, Δi, p_M, Δp_M, L_a, ΔL_a, Q_1, Q_2, Q_3 and their own respective preceding values. Here Y is taken as an index of general economic activity. L_a and ΔL_a are included because prevailing practices in Japanese bank

Table 2.9. Elasticity of Corporate Demands for Money.

	Y	I	P_M	L_a
L^c	0.567	−4.494	−1.486	
L_1^c	0.186	−4.057	−0.690	
L_3^c	0.191	−0.601	−1.339	3.449

loans require borrowers to deposit a certain portion of the loaned sum in the lending banks. This raises the effective rates of interest. (This is called "buzumi-ryodate.") The proportion is changed according to the credit standing of borrowers. A very high proportion of L_3^c to L_2^c seems to be due, in Japan, (1.35) to this arrangement. The demand function of L_3^c has been estimated for similar alternative forms. Notice here that it includes ΔL_a so that any change in the expansion of bank loans causes a change in time deposits of corporations. The elasticities of the corporate demands for money are given as follows:

The long-run elasticities can be computed only for L_3^c by multiplying those given above by a factor of 4. L^c and L_1^c seem to respond sufficiently fast within one quarter.

5.3. *The demand functions of the government sector*

	G'
L_1^g	1.250
L_1^g	2.508

L^g and L_1^g may be regarded as the demand for means of payment in the government sector. The appropriate explanatory variable is an index showing the level of current transactions. Since the quarterly series of government expenditure G seem to have random seasonal variations from one year to another, whereas L^g and L_1^g have a steady upward trend, a moving average of G denoted by G', is taken as a regressor. L_3^g is assumed to be exogenous. The elasticities are given in a table above.

5.4. *The behavior equations of the financial sector*

Here all the final intermediaries are taken as one financial sector, and its behavior pattern is analyzed by the demand for cash currency, its deposit in the Bank of Japan and its behavior in making bank loans. As explained earlier, $L^b = L_1^b + L_2^b$. Whenever the Bank of Japan makes loans to private banks (V), they are first credited to L_2^b accounts of private banks. The Bank of Japan could control the supply of money by requiring a certain percentage of V to be in the L_2^b account. The past minimum of the ratio of L_2^b to V is 0.0054. This is taken as the experienced minimum requirement. The amount of L_2^b in excess of 0.0054V *plus* cash holdings must be adjusted as the cash reserve corresponding to the amount of L_2 and L_3. There are neither official nor practical reserve ratios in Japan. The interviews with some bank authorities suggest that they pay little attention to the cash reserve ratios like L^b/L_2 or L^b/L_3. It has been decided, therefore, that the minimum cash reserve ratio maintained in practice by banks is estimated by the minimum of $(L^b - 0.0054V)/L_2$; that is, 0.0264, and the excess of L^b over $0.0054V +$ 0.0264 is taken as the excess reserve. The excess reserve is a function of i, Δi, p_M, Δp_M, Q_1, Q_2, Q_3. Following the same kind of reasoning $L_1^b - 0.0264L_2$ is regressed on the same set of explanatory variables. The final forms are given below.

Bank loans seem to be the crucial variable in the Japanese financial market. In post-war Japan, the textbook type of "reserve-position doctrine" for the supply of money can hardly be justified. The simplified "potential" supply

$$\hat{L}^s = (L_1 + L^b) + L_2 + \frac{(L_1 - L_b)/L_2 + 1}{L^b/L_2 + (L_1 - L^b)/L_2} \cdot L_1,$$

shows the money supply L^s when it is fully adjusted to the given reserve ratios (L^b/L_2) and $(L_1 - L^b)/L_2$ (assumed to be constant) and the given amount of *hith- powered money* L_1, presumably determined by the central bank.[6] Apart from the difference between this potential supply and the

[6]The previous formulation of the supply function of money closely followed this reasoning except for the introduction of V and the loans to the government sector V_g. The estimated equation was:

$$L^s = \underset{(6.25)}{14.50} + \underset{(3.66)}{9.562}(L_1^b - 0.0264L_2) - \underset{(4.26)}{11.16}\frac{L_2}{L_3} + \underset{(0.459)}{2.260}(V_g + V)$$

$$\bar{R}^2 = 0.91, \quad D - W = 1.49.$$

By equating this to the demand equation, we assumed an easy passage of i to equilibrium rate. This hypothesis did not seem to be justified, because the model failed to trace the movement of i over the sample period.

effective supply of money, the Japanese financial market does not seem to fit into this model for two reasons.

First, the Japanese government persistently adopted *the policy of low rate of interest*. The prevailing rate of interest is not the equilibrium rate, but below it. Hence, the demand for the loanable funds seems always to have been above the supply of loanable funds. This makes it almost meaningless to equate L^s or its variant to the demand for money.[7]

Second, the Bank of Japan tried to control the supply of money mainly by the *window control* of V whenever necessary. The commercial banks as a whole hold merely 3% to 4% of total deposit in the form of L^b. The minimum loan-deposit ratio is only 1.35%. They more or less presume that they can get loans from the Bank of Japan within the *reasonable limits based on the credit standing* of individual banks most of the time. Thus it has been thought that the given amount of V may be the most important variable in determining the amount of bank loans to the private sector. There are, however, some factors that must affect ΔL_a. They are the difference between the discount rate of private banks and that of the Bank of Japan $(i - i^*)$, the excess reserve and the amount of deposits. The various alternative forms of specifications have been estimated, and the final form is presented here. The elasticities in each equation with regard to respective predetermined variables are shown below. It is of some importance to notice that the price and interest rate elasticities of L^b and L_1^b are rather large. This indicates that banks adjust the reserve position sensitively to the change in the rate of interest.

	L_2	V	I	P_M
L^b	0.574	0.017	−7.616	−5.365
L_1^b	0.616		−4.982	−5.612

[7]The attempt to explain L_a by relating it to the demand side did not give rise to meaningful behavior equations. One of the relatively interesting equations was:

$$\Delta L_a = \frac{8.0962}{(0.895)}(I - J) - \frac{2.3964}{(0.676)}J + \frac{0.4131}{(2.69)}S_c - \frac{12.4127}{(3.34)}i - \frac{4.9658}{(4.17)}Q_1$$

$$- \frac{3.1582}{(2.57)}Q_2 - \frac{9.0645}{(3.88)}Q_3 + \frac{128.2291}{(31.5)}$$

$$\bar{R}^2 = 0.961,$$

where I = gross private investment, J =inventory investment, S_c = corporate savings. The signs for J and S_c are contrary to what we expect.

5.5. *The determination of the rate of interest*

The rate of interest seems to be influenced by two factors. The first is the policy of the Bank of Japan expressed either in the change in i^* or in the indirect, persuasive pressure on the banks' agreement on "prime rate." The second is the market condition for bank loans. Although the market of loanable funds cannot be regarded as the one that easily reaches temporary equilibrium, it still seems that the increase in demand with given supply raises i, and that the increase in supply with unchanged demand lowers i. The market mechanism at work may be seen in the following diagram. Suppose that the policy of low interest keeps i at the rate i_1, then $D > S$. Since supply is $O\ L_{a1}$, AB is the unrealized excess demand.

If D icreases to D', then the excess demand increases to AC. This wider gap between D and S is likely to cause some rise in the rate of interest even under the general policy of low interest. It may be that i will rise to i_2 and L_a will increase to L_{a2} so as to keep the unrealized excess demand stable relative to the supply of loans. Taking the market of new bank loans and association the supply ΔL_a with the demand factors like fixed capital and inventory investment (I), a new variable $(I - j_A - S_c)/\Delta L_a$ is defined as a proxy variable for the excess demand for new bank loans relative to the supply, where j_A is inventory investment in agricultural commodities and S_c is corporate savings. In the final form, Δ_i is assumed to be a linear function of i_{-1}, Δ_i^*, $(I - j_A - S_c)/\Delta L_{a-2}$ and D. D is a dummy variable to account for the change of data on interest at the second quarter of 1954. The time-lag for the third variable was determined as the most highly correlated case after many regression trials.

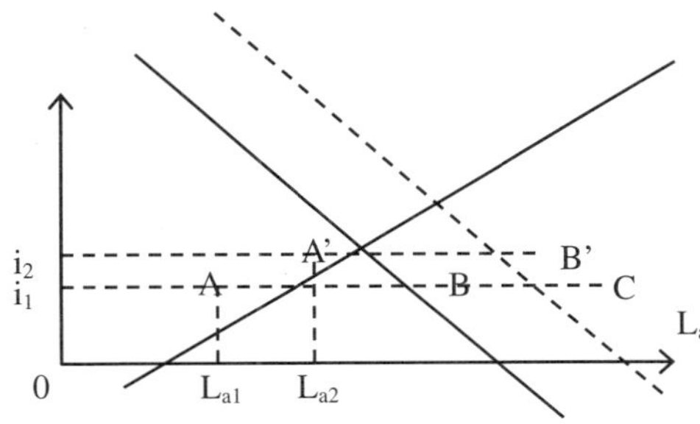

Figure 1. Excess Demand for Loanable Funds and the Interest Rate.

5.6. *The policy equation of the Bank of Japan*

It was debated in Japan whether the BOJ pursued a consistent monetary policy or simply responded to the demand from the private sector, except for some critical periods. The equation shows that V is positively correlated with V_{-1}, Y_{-1}, R_{-4}, $L_a - 1.112(L_2 + L_3)$ but negatively correlated with Δpm and Δ_i^*. Different lags have been tried for Y and R, but Y_{-1} and R_{-4} give the highest $\bar{R}^2$ and the smallest standard errors. The response of V to foreign exchange reserves take one year, and this is a criticism of the policy of the BOJ that it acts too slowly. When prices rise, V seems to have been contracted fairly quickly, *ceteris paribus*. When $\Delta i^* > 0$, this means that monetary policy is tightened. Then the BOJ tries to contract V as well. The larger $L_a - 1.112(L_2 + L_3)$, the more demand for V is forthcoming from banks. V is likely to be expended. It may be noticed that V is not so much influenced by V_{-1}. This is an equation that seems to describe the policy pattern of the BOJ in 1952–1959.

6. The Foreign Trade Sector

6-A. *Import functions*

6-A.1. *Import of food and forage*

The import of food was subdivided into 1. rice and barley and 2. other food and forage, because the two time series show completely opposite movement. The former simply decreases, whereas the latter steadily increases from 1952 to 1961. The import of rice and barley is positively related to food consumption but negatively to the domestic production of food. The term N_1/N_A is also introduced to explain the shift of demand from traditional rice and barley to bread and other flour products in the urban area as urbanization progresses. By comparing different time-lags in regressions it was found that import has one quarter lag in all explanatory variables. The price effect was found to be insignificant. The import of other food was taken as dependent on consumption and relative price. The two import functions together seem to imply that the increase of food consumption induces 10.8% of imports.

	Cons.	X_A/p_A	N_1/N_A	p_A/p_{f2}^b
B_{f1}/p_{f1}^b	1.481	−0.130	−3.277	
B_{f2}/p_{f2}^b	1.18			0.284

The elasticities are shown in the table here. It should be noted that rising consumption induces higher import of food, but urbanization reduces the import of rice and barley. There seems to be an increasing import of other food and forage as the consumption level goes up.

6-A.2. *Import of materials and other*

The imports of raw materials and consumption goods were not distinguished from one another because of the difficulty in commodity classification. This is not too serious up to 1959, because the latter imports were relatively small. The import of raw materials was taken as dependent on the levels of production in manufacturing sector with one quarter time-lag. The relative importance of imported materials in one sector compared with those in another is ignored. Since it is known that the inventory stocks of imported material are important in total materials stocks, it is expected that the current import of materials should be negatively correlated with the inventory stocks H_m / p_M^m. Quantitative restrictions have been imposed on the import of some materials when foreign exchange reserves decrease. Thus $(R_{-3} - R_{-4})/2p_{m,-3}^b$ was introduced as a predetermined variable. The time-lag was determined so as to give the highest $\bar{R}^2$. The elasticities are shown below. Notice here that the elasticity with respect to the production level is greater than unity, implying that as the production increases, the propensity to import is likely to go up.

	X_M / p_M	H_m / p_v^m	F. Ex. Rate
B_m / p_m^b	1.264	−0.415	0.297

6-A.3. *Import of machinery*

The underlying hypothesis is that the amount of imported machines keeps a stable relationship with investment in domestically produced machines. The regression equation shows that proportion is about 8.6%. The elasticity is 0.924.

6-B. *Export functions*

6-B.1. *General remarks*

Classification of sectors requires the separate export functions of heavy, textile, other manufacturing industries' products and food. Since the behaviors of E_{h1}, E_{h2}, E_{h3} within heavy industry's products are considerably different over time, separate equations are set up, respectively. The export functions of textile and other manufacturing industries' products and food gave poor results unless they are disaggregated by destinations. By doing so, we could select more appropriate explanatory variables and obtain plausible values for elasticities.[8]

The export prices were taken as endogenous variables, but except for p_b^e and p_o^e, good equations were not obtained. To obtain similar good results in p_{hi}^e and p_a^e, the breakdowns of heavy industry and agriculture in the other parts of ISER Model, were needed but not made here. It should be emphasized that as the following Table 2.10 shows, the elasticity values are very high, both with respect to the indices of foreign economic activities and relative prices. No wonder that the Japanese exports increased about three times as fast as did world trade.

6-B.2. *Ships*

The gestation period of ship-building is long; most ships take more than a year. Hence, we must distinguish among new orders $\hat{E}_{h1}$, backlog orders

Table 2.10. Elasticities of Each Sector's Sales with Respect to Each Item of Final Demand.

	Elasticity Values for Different Categories of Exports					
	Income or Real Variable	**Relative Price**	**Foreign Exchange Reserve**	**Reparation & Loans**	**Other Variable**	**Multiplier for Long-Run Effect**
Ships	3.99	3.35				
Machinery	1.81*	1.63	0.71	0.42		
Iron & Metal	0.34	0.60	0.32	0.05	−0.63	1.70
Textiles to US	5.72	0.36			−0.12	2.46
Textiles to Europe	2.08**	0.11				1.24
Textiles to Others	0.64	0.18				2.25
Other imports to US & Europe	2.61	1.29				1.51

*The elasticity of E_{h2}/p_{h2}^e with respect to x_{h2}^w alone, while keeping $x_{h2,-1}^w$ unchanged. Notice here that x_{h2}^w is an index of production.

**The elasticity is computed with respect to y^E and p_a^E/p_a^e respectively while keeping its ratio to y_{-1}^E and $(p_a^E/p_a^e)_{-1}$ respectively fixed at the value of ratios of their means.

[8] A serious study was done by Ichimura and Eguchi (1964) with the offer of Eguchi's data.

$\hat{\hat{E}}_{h1}$, and realized exports E_{h1}. Clearly the process is also different, corresponding to them. Thus we used p_{h1}, P'_{h1} and p^e_{h1}, respectively. P'_{h1} was computed as the moving average of p_{h1} over the average period during which backlog orders are held. Monthly data are available for $\hat{E}_{h1}$ and p_{h1} for 55 representative companies.

(i:2-1-ii) should read $\Delta\hat{\hat{E}}_{h1} = \hat{E}_{h1} - E_{h1}$ if data were exact, apart from price index problems. (i:2-1-iii) was adopted after comparing this equation with another which included the freight rate f as an additional explanatory "real" variable. Since, however, f is theoretically a function of μ, we did not use it.

6-B.3. *Machinery*

x^w_{h2} was computed as the weighted average of production indices in four main continents: North America, Latin America, Asia (excluding Japan), Europe. The weights are their average shares in Japanese machinery export over the observed period: 0.639, 0.093, 0.171, and 0.097. Though we computed the equations with x^w_{h2} and Δx^w_{h2}, it is of interest that this equation had a slightly higher $\bar{R}^2$. This seems to mean that machinery exports, being capital goods, are demanded according to the acceleration principle. The elasticity computed as mentioned above is very high. It would mean that the export of machinery is more likely to expand than steel and metal products if world production keeps the same rate of increase.

p^w_{h2} is the weighted average of machinery export prices of US, UK, and Germany; the weights are their shares in Asian countries' imports of machinery (India, Indonesia, Burma, Thailand, Taiwan, Pakistan, Philippines): 0.49682: 0.35404: 0.14910.

The foreign exchange reserves of the above-mentioned Asian countries are weighted by their shares in Japanese machinery exports and taken as a variable to influence the imports of those countries, together with A: government loans (including reparations) to Asian countries. Notice the effect of A is far greater than that of R.

6-B.4. *Steel and other metal products*

x^w_{h3}, R^A_{h3}, p^w_{h3} are constructed similarly to those in b.3. The coefficients of x^w_{h3} and p^w_{h3}/p^e_{h3} are not statistically significant, though their signs are satisfactory. This would probably mean that the export market is not yet well established for ($h3$). ρ_h is introduced to show the effect of the so-called "drive to export" in recessions. If ρ is low, E_{h3} increases. ρ seems to be the best variable to take the effect into account. The coefficient of A is smaller here than in (2). It means that A is more closely tied with the exports of machinery.

x_{h3}^{w} rather than Δx_{h3}^{w} is the explanatory variable in (3). Steel and other metals are mostly the intermediary products used as raw materials to produce finished products, so that they are related to the level of economic activity rather than its rate of change. The lagged value of E_{h3}/p_{h3}^{e} was introduced to express the point that when Japan is cutting in the foreign markets, the short-term effect must be clearly distinguished from the long-term effect. The weights for x_{h3}^{w} are 0.100 (North America): 0.310 (Latin America): 0.497 (Asia): 0.093 (Europe).

6-B.5. *Textiles*

The difficulty confronting Japanese textile exports was the fact that an important part of the export was restricted by quota that was imposed in 1956. To take its effect into account, we introduced a dummy variable D_t which expressed it as follows. The quota is imposed on cotton products. The maximum rate of growth in the export of cotton products for 1952–59 compared to 54–55 was 49.1%. We compare the growth rate of quotas with this value, and define D_t as the growth rate of quota minus 49.1. For example, if the quota is increased by 5%, $D_t = -44.1$. The absolute value of 49.1 is not important in this treatment of quotas, but since D_t is defined in terms of growth rates, D_t decreases year after year unless quotas are increased at the rate of 49.1% a year.

Remember that the income elasticity for Japanese textile exports was very high. Japanese textiles were very much demanded by American consumers. The large multiplier for long-term elasticity would mean that still further penetration into the US markets was possible in time. As for the textile exports to Europe and Canada, y^E is the weighted sum of the OEEC figure of Europe's personal consumption and Canada's personal consumption; the weights being 0.7745 and 0.2255. They are the shares in Japanese exports. The parameter 2.475 was obtained by multiplying the proportion of textile consumption to total consumption by the income elasticity of clothing consumption measured by Houthakker (1957, p. 532.)

Here the distributed lag was assumed for the price effect only. If $D = \alpha y + \beta p + \beta\lambda p_{-1} + \beta\lambda^2 p_{-2} + \cdots$, then $D - \alpha y = \lambda(D - \alpha y)_{-1} + \beta p + \cdots$.

This is the one estimated here, so that the long-term elasticity is meaningful for the price elasticity only. This procedure was adopted, because y in Europe was derived from annual figures so that the quarterly fluctuations of y were averaged out in the near past.

The price elasticity is higher to Europe than to US both in the short and long run. The income elasticity is approximately equal to the original elasticity assumed. (The original was taken from England.) This seems to have kept the income elasticity lower than the true value. Japanese textiles are expanding the market in Europe, so that the value may be expected to be higher. This is partly proved by the high value of the log-term elasticity multiplier.

Textile exports to the rest of the world are related to x_t^B and relative prices. Their dependence on foreign exchange reserves was not significant. x_t^B, rather than Y_t^B, (the sum of exports of Asia, Africa and Latin America) was adopted because E_t^A/p_t^e was explained with better statistical significance by x_t^B than by Y_t^B. Compared with the other areas, both elasticities are lower to this area. This is due to the fact that the competitive capacity of the Japanese textile industry is declining against the rising world industry. p_t^e is highly correlated with domestic price rather than the world price.

6-B.6. *Food*

The coefficients of income variables were computed in the same way as 2.475 for textile exports to Europe and Canada.[9] Here the US and Canada are lumped together. The disaggregation was necessary because we could not obtain plausible coefficients for price variables. The elasticities are low for exports to Europe and Asia but very high to the US.

6-B.7. *Other commodities*

Y^{uE} is the weighted sum of personal consumption in the US, Canada and Europe; the weights being 0.7688, 0.0957 and 0.1354. p_o^{uE} was similarly computed. As for exports to the rest of the world, we could not obtain a suitable equation separating real activity and price variables in it. Y^E is the sum of exports of the rest of the world. This form of equation assumes that we have the same elasticity with respect to income and price. p_o^e is

[9]The original values of elasticities were taken from Stone and Prais and Houthakker. Stone (1954, pp. 315–317) and Prais-Houthakker (1955, pp. 106–107).

more highly correlated with the world price than with the domestic price, contrary to the case of p_o^e.

7. Miscellaneous Equations and Identities

Corporate profits fluctuate more or less in line with total (corporate plus non-corporate) profits. But the share of the former will rise when economic activity is high, in as much as non-corporate profits by and large depend on general consumer expenditures. They follow a more stable time-path than corporate profits, which are sensitive to business conditions. Hence, corporate profits are positively correlated with the capacity utilization ratio of the manufacturing industry. A positive time variable in (j:1) reflects the rising share of corporation among the totality of firms, encouraged partly by our tax policy that favors corporations against un-incorporated firms. The corporate saving equation differs from being an identity $P_c = S_c + T_c + D_v$ only in that the dividend payment is lagged one year, the rationale being that corporations attempt to maintain a stable dividend policy.[10]

Rentier income is made a function of two product terms, representing rents and incomes from liquid assets, respectively. We have thus followed E. Kuh[11] in relating property income to the capital base (housing stock, private time and saving deposits) and to the rates of interest. The result, as seen from (j:3), is satisfactory. Equation (j:4) relates (manufacturing) depreciation in the national income account, D_I, to the sum of replacement depreciation D'_I. As defined by the identities (J:7). This is an empirical relationship, and q_1 and q_2 are 1-0 dummy variables that represent a change in the Ministry of Finance rules for allowable write-off rates.

There are three more empirical relations: two equations that convert exports and imports evaluated at the Custom-House to those appropriate in the Foreign Exchange Account, and one equation that relates (manufacturing) "non-operating profits" to corporate profits.

The replacement depreciation equations, already referred to, are definitional in character, and the *a priori* coefficients attached to the capital stock variables will be explained in data section.[12]

---

[10]Klein and Goldberger (1955, p. 14).

[11]Duesenberry *et al.* (1966, pp. 269–271).

[12]Data section is omitted in this book. See the data secion in Ichimura *et al.* (1977).

Turning to the identities, we note that the majority of the relations listed are simple definitions. Thus $X_i = X_{iL} + X_{iS}$ means that output of the ith industry is the sum of outputs of the large-scale and the small-scale firms in the industry. It will be needless to point out that (k:19) to (k:24) are stock-flow relations. The symbol Δ_{ij} in (k:19) describes the phenomena of small-scale firms becoming large-scale or *vice versa*.

(k:27) through (k:30) define the national income accounts. Here, $p.H_{-1}$ is a term to represent inventory valuation adjustments, and (k:28) implies that capital gains occasioned by price rises are counted as part of the disposable income. η in (k:29) is an adjustment term computed as follows. The foreign account in (k:29), $E - B + \eta$, is taken from the official figures published by the EPA. Our export-input figures, E and B, are those compiled at the Custom-House, and the difference between the two is reflected in. The latter comprise the balance in the invisible trade account, so-called special procurements by the US armed forces, etc.

There are four identities (k:45) through (k:48) that define output and price mixes. p_v^m and p_v^d are, respectively, deflators of producers' inventory of raw materials and of dealers' inventory, and the *a priori* weights in (k:47) and (k:48) are computed from knowledge of the construction of data on inventories. X_{vm} and X_{vd} are weighted sums of industrial outputs, the weights being determined to take account of the industrial differences in the inventory-output ratios and the industrial shares in the inventories.

The identity (k:49) describes the relation: change in unfilled orders is equal to new orders *minus* sales. Our data series on unfilled orders, new orders and sales are such that (k:49) holds with minor errors, because the component series are taken from independent sources.

$$\Delta L_a = \frac{8.0962}{(0.895)}(I - J) - \frac{2.3964}{(0.676)}J + \frac{0.4131}{(2.69)}S_c - \frac{12.4127}{(3.34)}i - \frac{4.9658}{(4.17)}Q_1$$

$$- \frac{3.1582}{(2.57)}Q_2 - \frac{9.0645}{(3.88)}Q_3 + \frac{128.2291}{(31.5)} \quad \bar{R}^2 = 0.961$$

$$L^s = \frac{14.50}{(6.25)} + \frac{9.562}{(3.66)}(L_1^b - 0.0264L_2) - \frac{11.16}{(4.26)}\frac{L_2}{L_3} + \frac{2.260}{(0.459)}(V_g + V)$$

$$\bar{R}^2 = 0.91, \ D - W = 1.49$$

Chapter 10

Osaka ISER Model

III. Dynamic Properties of the Model

Shinichi Ichimura and Lawrence R. Klein

1. Impact Multipliers

Since the Osaka Model was nonlinear in variables (not in parameters), the equations containing nonlinear variables were linearized around the mean values of the variable in 1959. For example, if wN is to be linearized, $wN = (w)N + (N)w - (w)(N)$, where (w) and (N) are the yearly arithmetic means of w and N over four quarters in 1959. Then the linearized model may be written as $Ax = Bz$, where A: a square matrix; B: a rectangular matrix; x: a vector of endogenous variables; and z: a vector of predetermined variables including lagged endogenous variables. The impact multipliers are obtained as $A^{-1}B$. Table 3.1 shows some of its elements.

Notice here that a unitary change of an exogenous variable causes significantly different effects on various sectors of the economy. It is interesting to note that the effects on output are almost always larger for *large scale of enterprises*, but the effects on employment are larger for *small scale of enterprises*. Exports have considerably larger impact multipliers than government expenditure. An interesting characteristic of an open economy is that the changes of import prices have significant effects on national income. Throughout the post-war years the Japanese economy has benefited from falling trend of import prices. Notice also a significant effect of the change of rental price index (p_r) on income. This is a reflection of the shortage of land in Japan.

Table 3.1. Impact Multipliers for Selected Variables.

		G_I	W_g	$G - W_g - G_I$	E_h/P_h^e	E_t/P_t^e	E_o/P_o^e	E_{inv}/P_{inv}	P_h^{bm}	P_t^m	P_r	V	I^*	$\frac{X_A/P_A}{N_A}$
1	X_h/P_h	.866	.003	.013	2.109	.212	.211	.238	−.520	−.002	−.518	0	−.108	.039
2	X_{hs}/P_h	.603	.003	.010	.648	.119	.110	.116	−.453	−.003	−.352	0	−.073	.030
3	X_{tL}/P_t	.012	.014	.014	.027	.613	.028	.034	−.052	−.053	−.013	0	−.001	.172
4	X_{tS}/P_t	019	.025	.024	.046	1.298	.046	.061	−.090	−.077	−.022	0	−.002	.301
5	X_{oL}/P_o	582	.034	.114	.711	.881	2.364	.517	−.341	−.025	−.341	0	−.071	.410
6	X_{oS}/P_o	.468	.003	.011	.564	.710	1.932	.396	−.248	−.009	−.273	0	−.057	.035
7	X_E/P_E	.238	.027	.161	.497	.465	.404	1.365	−.196	−.106	−.142	0	−.029	.322
8	$\sum_1 X/P$	2.808	.104	.347	4.602	4.298	5.095	2.726	−1.900	−.275	−1.661	0	−.341	1.309
9	N_{hL}	.156	.000	.002	.371	.037	.037	.042	−.092	−.004	−.091	0	−.019	.007
10	N_{hS}	.215	.000	.003	.231	.043	.039	.041	−.162	−.011	−.126	0	−.026	.011
11	N_{tL}	002	.003	.002	.005	.110	.005	.006	−.009	−.010	−.002	0	−.000	.031
12	N_{tS}	.007	.010	.009	.018	.509	.018	.024	−.035	−.030	−.008	0	−.001	.118
13	N_{oL}	.060	.004	.012	.074	.091	.245	.054	−.035	−.003	−.035	0	−.007	.042
14	N_{oS}	.195	.001	.005	.236	.297	.807	.165	−.103	−.004	−.114	0	−.024	.014
15	N_E	.233	.026	.158	.487	.456	.397	1.338	−.192	−.104	−.139	0	−.028	.316
16	ΣN		44	.191	1.422	1.543	1.548	1.670	−.628	−.166	−.515	0	−.105	539
17	U	−.964	−.050	−.213	−1.576	−1.711	−1.716	−1.851	.114	.005	.076	0	−.016	−.006

(*Continued*)

Table 3.1. (*Continued*)

		G_I	W_g	$G - W_g - G_I$	E_h/P_h^e	E_t/P_t^e	E_o/P_o^e	E_{inv}/P_{inv}	P_h^{bm}	P_t^m	P_r	V	I^*	$\frac{X_A/P_A}{N_A}$
18	I_{hL}/P_k	076	.000	.001	.181	.018	.018	.020	−.045	−.002	−.044	0	−.009	.003
19	I_{hS}/P_k	.059	.000	.001	.063	.012	.011	.011	−.044	−.003	−.034	0	−.007	.003
20	I_{tL}/P_k	.000	.000	.000	.001	.018	.001	.001	−.002	−.002	−.000	0	−.001	.005
21	I_{tS}/P_k	.001	.001	.001	.001	.037	.001	.002	−.003	−.002	−.001	0	−.003	.008
22	I_{oL}/P_k	.000	.000	.000	.000	.000	.000	.000	.000	.000	.000	0	−.035	.000
23	I_{oS}/P_k	.010	.000	.000	.012	.015	.040	.008	−.005	−.000	−.006	0	−.012	.001
24	I_E/P_k	.019	.002	.013	.039	.037	.032	.108	−.016	−.008	−.001	0	−.061	.025
25	$\Sigma I/P$	.155	.003	.016	.297	.137	.103	.650	−.115	−.017	−.096	0	−.128	.045
26	I_R/P_k	.008	.014	.002	.015	.012	.013	.020	−.029	.006	−.266	0	−.001	−.171
27	Y	1.021	1.047	.221	1.788	1.404	1.723	1.876	−3.346	.973	−.931	0	−.122	12.574
28	Y_d	.549	.942	.152	.991	.764	.890	1.315	1.901	.407	.464	0	.066	11.308
29	C	.139	.263	.038	.249	.202	.224	.333	.388	.164	.097	0	.017	3.158
30	B'	000	.000	.000	.000	.000	.000	.000	.000	.000	.000	0	.000	.000
31	P	502	.021	.092	.877	.617	.880	753	026	.012	.697	0	.059	249
32	W	.663	1.032	145	1.154	.970	1.101	1.245	1.266	.432	.391.	0	.080	379

2. Final Test

The workability of the model as a whole may be tested by calculating the values of x and their errors from actual values by giving the actual observations to exogenous variables. The method and program used in this *final test* of calculation and the following simulations are explained in Ichimura *et al.* (1966). The errors in final test are summarized in Table 3.2.

Table 3.2. Final Test Errors (%).

	Var.	1	2	3	4	5	6	7	8
1	X_{hL}/P_h	−9.0	−16.3	−17.3	−13.1	−20.9	−25.8	−33.0	−30.9
2	X_{hS}/P_h	15.0	−14.3	−9.5	−9.8	8.3	−17.8	−15.5	−20.1
3	N_{hL}	6.0	6.4	13.0	0.8	17.5	17.9	18.5	
4	N_{hS}	14.3	18.3	14.4	1.8	10.7	6.2	5.8	4.1
5	w_{hL}	0.8	0.5	0.2	0.8	4.2	3.7	0.4	2.6
6	w_{hS}	5.3	10.1	14.9	27.8	10.6	16.6	25.7	−43.1
7	P_h	2.51	.21	.43	.24		32.8	4.0	5.0
8	L_{hL}/P_k	8.5	14.0	9.1	11.5	8.8	17.3	14.1	20.3
9	I_{hS}/P_k	19.3	47.4	39.1	12.2	33.8	27.1	43.1	33.4
10	X_{hL}/P_t	10.7	16.2	10.1	10.6	13.7	24.8	18.4	18.2
11	X_{hS}/P_t	18.1	12.3	3.9	9.3	15.2	11.4	1.7	1.
12	N_{tL}	11.6	2.73	.42	2.9	18.7	0.7	14.4	15.6
13	N_{tS}	32.2	34.1	29.9	25.4	45.8	49.5	46.7	39.9
14	w_{tL}	8.5	12.4	12.6	2.9	9.5	14.0	22.0	15.3
15	w_{tS}	30.8	2.6	0.8	2.8	19.3	7.3	9.2	14.2
16	P_t	0.72	.77	.7	5.1	5.0	4.6	9.5	15.5
17	I_{hL}/P_k	32.6	4.4	15.3	4.4	1.2	21.1	26.9	19.3
18	L_{hS}/P_k	15.6	35.4	9.4	25.5	4.8	32.5	70.5	165.6
19	X_{oL}/P_o	2.1	4.3	3.8	0.1	8.6	13.1	22.9	15.0
20	X_{oS}/P_o	14.7	2.9	11.3	4.9	10.5	6.5	0.6	1.0
21	N_{oL}	12.5	8.9	13.3	2.2	13.6	5.7	1.6	8.1
22	N_{oS}	2.7	2.7	0.9	7.5	3.0	12.0	5.0	8.4
23	w_{oL}	2.9	5.5	0.2	3.2	2.5	4.5	16.1	10.2
24	w_{oS}	10.5	2.7	10.7	7.5	2.2	18.1	22.2	32.2
25	P_o	0.2	0.6	1.5	1.0	1.1	1.6	1.7	1.0
26	I_{oL}/P_k	26.2	27.7	37.7	35.2	42.1	47.3	62.5	65.1
27	I_{oS}/P_k	11.1	12.9	2.4	23.4	17.1	14.8	31.2	29.5
28	X_E/P_E	7.5	3.0	1.5	6.1	3.1	4.9	3.8	1.4
29	N_E	15.9	12.6	17.7	4.7	4.3	0.6	5.2	1.6
30	w_E	6.3	10.4	11.2	13.0	20.3	24.5	27.0	26.3
31	P_E	12.0	13.2	14.4	15.7	12.4	12.3	15.1	16.1
32	I_E/P_E	1.5	9.2	4.4	15.0	24.0	23.2	32.2	39.1

(*Continued*)

Table 3.2. **(*Continued*)**

	Var.	1	2	3	4	5	6	7	8
33	N_a	−31.2	−1.4	−4.5	43	−71.5	0.9	2.3	14.0
34	P_k	1.9	0.9	1.0	2.3	3.0	1.9	2.7	3.4
35	C_f/P_f^c	−7.5	−5.3	−8.8	−6.1	−8.0	−8.4	−11.6	−6.7
36	C_t/P_t^c	9.0	1.8	3.7	−4.7	2.0	−1.3	11.4	−10.9
37	C_o/P_o^c	−3.7	−3.3	−3.7	−3.8	−3.9	−3.7	−3.2	−4.2
38	I_R/P_k	9.6	23.8	20.6	1.0	26.5	37.1	34.7	19.5
39	P_t^c	0.4	0.3	0.9	0.3	0.2	1.3	2.5	4.9
40	P_o^c	2.8	3.9	5.0	5.3	6.6	7.9	8.9	9.0
41	L^p	1.6	5.0	5.6	9.1	10.0	12.8	14.3	16.4
42	L^c	17.8	12.0	15.2	19.8	33.7	33.5	33.7	28.9
43	L^b	26.2	14.0	25.3	32.4	38.9	34.3	44.3	59.5
44	i	0.9	1.9	0.9	0.9	2.1	3.1	3.8	2.9
45	L_3^p	0.9	1.6	0.3	0.6	0.3	0.2	1.8	0.8
46	L_3^c	7.0	11.2	18.1	18.9	29.0	31.9	37.6	38.3
47	L_a	2.2	3.4	5.6	7.8	10.7	12.8	15.0	17.1
48	P	15.1	4.3	11.1	13.4	3.4	1.8	3.2	5.4
49	P_c	2.1	16.0	7.3	6.0	18.9	25.9	26.2	13.8
50	S_c	1.9	30.7	15.8	2.0	32.9	59.1	46.8	21.9
51	R	4.1	6.0	7.2	11.6	19.0	40.7	72.4	105.8
52	B'	−7.0	−1.2	−5.6	−10.1	−14.5	−29.3	−29.2	−32.5
53	P_M	1.0	0.3	0.5	1.2	2.0	0.7	1.7	2.8
54	w_I	−1.5	−5.0	−3.9	−10.3	−8.6	−17.9	−21.7	−24.1
55	P_M^m	−1.0	−2.2	−2.6	−1.2	−1.8	−1.7	−0.9	2.7
56	P^c	−0.9	−3.3	−3.0	−4.3	−4.5	−6.8	−6.8	−8.8
57	W	−9.1	−15.7	−17.2	−11.4	−10.9	−19.4	−24.6	−23.4
58	X_A	−31.8	−9.2	−5.1	3.8	−57.8	−5.7	0.1	9.7
59	Y	−7.0	−4.3	−5.7	−1.8	−11.3	−13.8	−13.8	−4.5
60	C	−5.3	−7.0	−8.5	−9.0	−9.6	−12.0	−12.7	−14.9
61	Y_d	5.4	3.8	4.4	1.0	4.3	5.5	7.4	8.0
62	U	52.3	57.3	71.3	0.1	97.1	20.0	16.5	−14.9
63	J_{fh}/P_h	192	122.7	50.0	61.4	590.6	292.5	53.0	92.3
64	J_f/P_t	68.9	116.9	106.5	179.8	117.3	57.8	186.2	129.7
65	J_{fo}/P_t	108.1	291.5	56.6	77.9	41.2	51.3	6.8	144.1
66	J_M/P_M^v	55.0	73.1	34.5	126.5	66.1	45.8	53.1	21.3
67	J_p/P_M	114.3	61.8	78.0	13.4	97.7	68.7	94.6	73.9
68	J_d/P_d^v	63.3	71.4	29.4	89.3	69.3	79.2	85.9	77.9

The results are generally satisfactory for aggregative variables and prices but, needless to say, the model needs further improvements; in particular, the equations of inventory investments. This is by no means easy in limited time. We take this calculated results as a frame of reference — to be called *the control solution* — in order to compare the simulated results with it.

Generally the predictions underestimate the actual observations. There seem to be two major reasons. One is the well-known autocorrelation of error terms in our model. Although the inclusion of lagged endogenous variables among predetermined variables makes the mechanically computed Durbin-Watson ratios larger, this does not give the adequate test for the equations which must be treated the way we described in Part I. (See Ichimura *et al.* (1966) and Moriguchi (1965); Nerlove and Wallis (1966).) The second reason is that the years of 1960 and 61 were exceptionally booming years in Japan. To quote only one figure, the ratio of gross capital formation to GNP was 34%, and 60% of the gross capital formation is private plant and equipment formation. This high ratio has never been experienced before and after then. In fact, this high rate of investment, it is generally agreed, was an over-investment in many sectors which caused the recessions after 1963 to 1965. It is not at all surprising to have considerable underestimation for these two years. The new behavior equations, particularly the investment functions estimated for 1952–1961 instead of 1952–1959 show the marked change in the coefficients.

3. Dynamic Multipliers of Government Expenditure and Exports

The model was used to see how an initial change of a number of exogenous variables or the values of parameters gives rise to a series of changes in endogenous variables by comparing them with the control solution. Tables 3.4 and 3.5 show the various effects of a change in components of government expenditure on endogenous variables. Here for Y, Y_d, P_{ca}, C are shown the ratios of their changes over the control solution to the change of G_I, W_g and $G - G_I - W_g$. For the rest of variables, they are shown as the percentage change.

The initial change in G_I, for example, increases National Income in money value by 1.73 times the initial change after eight quarters. This multiplier may be compared with the similar multiplier in the US economy, computed by M. Evans and L. R. Klein for the Wharton School Model.[1] They are quoted as Tables 3.3 and E.3 through E.10 in the Appendix. Their multipliers are computed for GNP, whereas ours here are for National Income.

[1] As for Evans-Klein multipliers in the US, see Evans and Klein (1968).

Table 3.3. Multipliers for Increase in Government Investment.

	Y	P_c	P_m	Y_d	P_{ca}	U	Ci	I	L_a	w_I
1	1.01	.0	.0	.41	.43	−.7	.12	.00	.00	.00
2	1.33	.0	.0	.99	.20	−1.8	.30	.00	.00	.01
3	1.73	.1	.0	1.42	.14	−2.0	.50	.00	.00	.03
4	1.82	.2	.0	1.63	.03	−3.0	.69	.00	.01	.05
5	1.67	.2	.0	1.43	.01	−1.0	.79	.00	.02	.06
6	1.75	.2	.0	1.62	.06	−2.7	.95	.00	.03	.07
7	1.71	.3	.0	1.69	.14	−1.7	1.07	.00	.04	.07
8	1.73	.3	.0	1.80	.20	−2.0	1.19	.00	.04	.07

*Notations: Y = National Income in current value; P_c = Implicit Consumers' price-index, 1955 = 1.00; P_m = Implicit Manufacturers' price-index, 1955 = 1.00; Y_d = Disposable Income in current value; P_{ca} = Corporate Profit after tax; U = Unemployment, changes in %; C = Consumption in current value; I = Interest Rate, changes in %; L_a = Bank Loans, changes in %; w_I = Average rate of money wages in industry.

Table 3.4. Multipliers for Increase in Government Wage Payment (W_g = 0.7; N_g: .14164).

	Y	P_c	P_m	Y_d	P_{ca}	U	C_i	I	L_a	w_I
1	.92	.00	.00	.86	−.02	−.8	.25	.00	.00	.10
2	.97	.00	.00	.95	−.0	−1.3	.34	.00	.00	.19
3	1.02	.00	.00	1.06	−.10	−1.1	.44	.00	.02	.28
4	1.05	.00	.00	1.14	.15	−1.6	.55	.00	.03	.33
5	.62	.00	.00	.75	−.15	1.6	.54	.00	.03	.39
6	1.02	.00	.00	1.15	−.18	−1.6	.68	.00	.04	.44
7	1.11	.00	.00	1.26	−.19	−.2	.76	.00	.05	.44
8	1.01	.00	.00	1.22	−.22	−1.2	.79	.00	.05	.45

Table 3.5. Multipliers for Increase in Government Consumption ($G - W_g - G_I$: .1).

	Y	P_c	P_m	Y_d	P_{ca}	U	C_i	I	L_a	w_I
1	.22	.00	.00	.13	.06	−.2	.04	.00	.00	.0
2	.25	.00	.00	.18	.05	−.3	.06	.00	.01	.0
3	.39	.00	.00	.36	.00	−.5	.13	.00	.02	.1
4	.40	.00	.00	.41	−.04	−.8	.18	.00	.03	.1
5	.36	.00	.00	.37	−.05	−.3	.21	.00	.03	.2
6	.38	.00	.00	.41	−.07	−.7	.25	.00	.04	.2
7	36	.00	.00	.43	−.09	−.4	.28	.00	.05	.2
8	36	.00	.00	.46	−.10	−.5	.31	−.01	.05	.2

The ratio of GNP to NI in Japan, 1959 is 1.3. Assuming the additional items in GNP change in proportion to NI components, we can obtain the GNP multipliers by multiplying ours by 1.3. The eight period values then become 2.25 for G_I, 1.30 for W_g, 0.47 for $G - W_g - G_I$. Comparing them with the US multipliers, we find the Japanese multipliers smaller.[2]

Since the Japanese economy has the higher propensity to import, the lower propensity to consume and the high rate of growth in National Income, it is not too surprising to find smaller multipliers in this international comparison.[3] To see the effects on other variables, it should be understood that the shift in government expenditure assumed in each case is 10 billion Yen. It seems worth noting that government investment has more significant effects on consumers' price and interest rate than government wage-payment or other types of expenditure.

Exports in ISER Model are not entirely exogenous, but because of the limitation in the best machine available then (IBM 7094), they are treated as exogenous. Hence, the effects of the increase of exports can be computed the same way as we do for government expenditure.

Compare Tables 3.6–3.9 with Evans' Table E.5 in the Appendix. Japanese Exports multipliers range from 2.3 to 3.1 for National Income, which means from 3.0 to 4.0 for GNP. Since the American multipliers in Table E.5 show 3.92, it seems safe to infer that the Japanese multipliers are slightly smaller. The increase in each type of exports is also assumed to be 10 billion Yen. Since, however, the export multipliers are the largest of all the multipliers we have computed, the rapid growth of Japanese exports averaging about 12% during the period, must have contributed a great deal. The usual argument of calling the Japanese Economy an "Export-drifted" growth seems justified in this sense.

---

[2] $(1-\alpha_2)/\{1-\alpha_1-\alpha_2+\beta(1-\alpha_2)\}$, and the smaller α_2 is, the earlier the dynamic multipliers will reach this eventual value. The Japanese Economy has larger β, smaller α_1 and larger α_2 than the US Economy. If, moreover, $C_t = (1-g)C_{t-1}$, then $C_t/Y_t = \alpha_1(1+g)/(1+g-\alpha_2)$, so that the long-run multiplier will be the smaller, the larger the rate of growth g is. All these points seem to imply that *ceteris paribus* the Japanese multipliers tend to be smaller, and that the dynamic multipliers reach the long-run value more gradually than the US multipliers.

[3] Suppose that $Y_t = C_t + E_t - B_t$, $C_t = \alpha Y_t$, $B_t = \beta Y_t$, (B: Imports), which gives the multiplier equal to $1/1 - \alpha + \beta$. If we have $C_t = \alpha_1 Y_t + \alpha_2 C_{t-1}$, the impact multiplier is $1/1 - \alpha_1 + \beta$ and the long-run multiplier is $1/(1 - \alpha_1 - \alpha_2 + \beta)$.

Table 3.6. Multipliers for Increase in Exports of Heavy Industry's Products (E_h/p_h^e).

	Y	P	P_m	Y_d	P_{ca}	U	C	I	L_a	w_I
1	1.77	.0	.2	.76	.72	−1.2	.21	.00	−.01	.3
2	2.29	.0	.2	1.68	.35	−2.8	.51	.00	.01	.4
3	3.05	.0	.3	2.50	.25	−3.4	.88	.00	.04	.7
4	3.22	.0	.4	2.87	.06	−5.0	1.20	.02	.08	.9
5	2.97	.0	.4	2.55	−.02	−1.6	1.38	.04	.10	1.4
6	3.11	.0	.5	2.88	−.11	−4.6	1.66	.06	.11	1.5
7	3.03	.0	.5	2.97	−.23	−2.8	1.87	.07	.12	1.7
8	3.06	.0	.4	3.16	−.33	−3.3	2.07	.07	.12	1.6

Table 3.7. Multipliers for Increase in Exports of Textiles (E_t/p_t^e).

	Y	P	P_m	Y_d	P_{ca}	U	C	I	L_a	w_I
1	1.39	.00	.00	.58	.59	−1.3	.17	.00	.03	.0
2	2.01	.00	.00	1.46	.32	−2.8	.45	.00	.06	.2
3	2.70	.00	.00	2.33	.12	−3.5	.84	−.01	.12	.6
4	2.82	.00	.00	2.80	−.19	−5.8	1.20	.03	.17	.6
5	2.37	.00	.00	2.38	−.31	−1.8	1.36	.07	.21	1.1
6	2.48	.00	.00	2.72	−.46	−5.0	1.65	.08	.23	1.3
7	2.35	.00	.00	2.82	−.60	−3.1	1.87	.09	.24	1.5
8	2.31	.01	.00	3.03	−.74	−3.4	2.08	.08	.24	1.5

Table 3.8. Multipliers for Increase in Exports of Other Manufacturers' Products (E_o/p_o^e).

	Y	P	P_m	Y_d	P_{ca}	U	C	I	L_a	w_I
1	1.71	.0	.1	.65	.77	−1.3	.18	.00	.03	.16
2	2.16	.0	.0	1.54	.37	−2.7	.46	.00	.06	.27
3	2.66	.1	.1	2.21	.19	−3.1	.79	−.02	.12	.56
4	2.72	.2	.1	2.44	.04	−4.3	1.05	.00	.17	.72
5	2.39	.3	.2	2.05	−.06	−1.3	1.17	.00	.21	1.13
6	2.53	.3	.2	2.40	−.16	−3.8	1.42	.00	.25	1.24
7	2.46	.4	.2	2.49	−.25	−2.4	1.59	.00	.28	1.38
8	2.50	.4	.2	2.67	−.34	−2.8	1.76	−.01	.30	1.36

Table 3.9. Multipliers for Increase in Exports of Invisible Trade Items (E_{inv}/p_{inv}).

	Y	P	P_m	Y_d	P_{ca}	U	C	i	L_a	w_I
1	1.86	.0	.1	1.17	.45	−1.4	.31	.00	.03	.23
2	2.10	.0	.0	1.55	.31	−2.6	.49	.00	.07	.38
3	3.25	.1	.1	3.04	−.06	−4.5	1.10	−.01	.13	.83
4	3.33	.3	.1	3.37	−.28	−6.3	1.48	−.02	.21	1.07
5	2.99	.4	.2	3.10	−.41	−2.1	1.72	−.02	.28	1.65
6	3.19	.4	.2	3.49	−.56	−6.2	2.08	−.02	.34	1.85
7	3.00	.6	.2	3.57	−.70	−3.6	2.35	−.03	.39	2.04
8	3.06	.6	.2	3.83	−.82	−4.3	2.60	−.04	.43	2.01

4. Multiplier Effects of the Fall in Impact Prices

In an open economy, the impact of the fall of prices of imported commodities is very far-reaching. Table 3.10 summarizes the intertemporal effects of fall of Import Price-Index of raw materials by 0.1. Since the imports of raw materials occupy about 10% of national income and the price index is approximately 1.00, the direct effect of fall in p_m^b on Y should be 1%. Taking that as a denominator and dividing the computed increment of Y, Y_d, C, P_{ca}, we obtain the multipliers in Table 3.10. They seem to have significant multiplier effects on national income but considerable time-lags. Notice also that domestic prices on the whole are not significantly affected, but interest rate and money wages have rather the inflationary pressure.

Table 3.10. Multipliers for Fall in Import Price of Raw Materials (p_m^b: .1).

	Y	P	P_m	Y_d	P_{ca}	U	C	i	L_a	w_I
1	.05	.0	.0	.04	−.01	.0	−.04	.00	.02	.00
2	.01	.0	.0	.02	−.05	.0	−.01	.00	.01	.00
3	−.02	.0	.0	−.03	−.04	.0	.04	.00	.01	.00
4	.74	.0	.0	.42	.22	−.1	.09	.00	.08	.01
5	1.49	.0	.0	1.29	.04	−.1	.39	.00	.34	.03
6	1.86	.0	.0	1.65	.04	−.4	.62	.01	.50	.04
7	2.10	.0	.0	1.86	.03	−.3	.83	.02	−.23	.06
8	2.16	.0	.0	2.01	−.06	−.4	1.09	.04	.59	.08

*L_a: Increase in current value × 100.

Table 3.11. Multipliers for Rise in Agricultural Productivity ($X_A/p_A\ N_A$: .01).

	Y	P	P_m	Y_d	p_{ca}	U	C	i	L_a	w_I
1	1.01	.0	.0	.90	.02	−.0	.26	.00	.26	.00
2	1.06	.0	.0	.96	.01	−.3	.31	.00	.63	.00
3	1.19	.0	.0	1.10	.00	−.6	.39	−.01	1.08	.07
4	1.25	.1	.0	1.18	−.03	−1.0	.49	−.02	1.58	.12
5	1.29	.1	.1	1.23	−.04	−.5	.59	−.03	2.09	.21
6	1.32	.0	.1	1.28	−.06	−1.3	.67	−.04	2.59	.27
7	1.36	.1	.0	1.36	−.09	−1.0	.76	−.04	3.06	.33
8	1.42	.1	.0	1.43	−.12	−1.4	.84	−.05	3.48	.36

*Multipliers: Change in current value ÷ 0.126 (= 0.01 × N_A).
L_a: Changes in current value ÷ 0.126.

5. Multiplier Effects of Rise in Agricultural Productivity

Table 3.11 summarizes the effects on the same set of variables. The multipliers are computed by dividing the changes in Y etc. by the assumed change in productivity (= 0.01) *times* the average annual number of farmers in 1959 (= 12.6). The computation shows that after eight quarters the national income goes up 1.42 times the original increase in farmers' income due to productivity increase.

The interesting effects on the price side are that money wages tend to go up and interest rates go down. The latter effect is due to the unusual increase of Banks loans indicated by the ninth column of Table 3.11, which shows the multiplier effect on Bank Loans. This is not surprising in the country where the major corps are guaranteed for the government to purchase at a certain fixed price. It is also surprising that this can decrease unemployment by 1.4%. Since it is generally agreed that agricultural productivity has increased throughout post-war years (up to 1964) about 3% a year, we can see how greatly it must have contributed to the rapid Japanese economic growth.

6. Multiplier Effects for Personal Income Tax Reduction

Two types of taxation policies are analyzed here; personal income tax cut and excise taxes cut. Tax equations in the Osaka model are studied by S. Koizumi and estimated by the OLS methods for some recent years only.

They are not yet published but made available here.

$$T_p - T_R = \underset{(0.0210)}{0.087277}(Y_d + T_p - T_R) + \underset{(0.301)}{1.5432}Q_1 + \underset{(0.265)}{0.719}Q_2$$

$$+ \underset{(0.240)}{1.0510}Q_3 - \underset{(0.656)}{1.7192} \quad (\bar{R}^2 = 0.73; \text{ for 59–61}) \quad (6.1)$$

$$T_c = \underset{(0.0214)}{0.34732}P_c - \underset{(0.0658)}{0.22179}Q_1 + \underset{(0.0629)}{0.06927}Q_2 - \underset{(0.0628)}{0.21348}Q_3$$

$$+ \underset{(0.112)}{0.10681} \quad \bar{R}^2 = 0.97; \text{ for 59–61} \quad (6.2)$$

$$T_{hL} = \underset{(0.00032)}{0.014941}X_{hL} + \underset{(0.00401)}{0.0027166} \quad (\bar{R}^2 = 0.994; \text{ for 59–61}) \quad (6.3)$$

$$T_{hS} = \underset{(.000545)}{0.012322}X_{hS} - \underset{(.0338)}{0.017923} \quad (\bar{R}^2 = 0.978; \text{ for 59–61}) \quad (6.4)$$

$$T_{hL} = \underset{(.000951)}{0.0096855}X_{hL} - \underset{(.0182)}{0.0021631} \quad (\bar{R}^2 = 0.90; \text{ for 59–61}) \quad (6.5)$$

$$T_{hS} = \underset{(.00288)}{0.0039467}X_{hS} + \underset{(.0677)}{0.0048753} \quad (\bar{R}^2 = 0.074; \text{ for 59–61}) \quad (6.6)$$

$$T_{oL} = \underset{(.00148)}{0.062219}X_{oL} - \underset{(.164)}{0.082333} \quad (\bar{R}^2 = 0.996; \text{ for 60–61}) \quad (6.7)$$

$$T_{oS} = \underset{(.0251)}{0.033063}X_{oS} - \underset{(.210)}{0.070602}(\bar{R}^2 = 0.094; \text{ for 60–61}) \quad (6.8)$$

$$T_{E+A} = \underset{(0.0208)}{0.14772}(X_E + X_A) + \underset{(2.24)}{10.1587}Q_1 + \underset{(2.13)}{8.600094}Q_2 \quad (6.9)$$

$$+ \underset{(1.80)}{7.370586}Q_3 - \underset{(5.04)}{10.351858} \quad \bar{R}^2 = 0.823; \text{ for 59–61} \quad (6.10)$$

In order to make the effects of personal income tax reduction comparable with the effects of government expenditure increase, which was assumed to increase 10 billion Yen (or 0.1 hundred billion Yen in the units of our computation) every quarter, the changes of parameters in T_p equation were made so that the resulting decrease in T_p for the values of Y_d in *controlled solution* over the years of 60 to 61 (8 quarters) may become 80 billion Yen. The changes are made not only of the marginal propensity to pay personal income tax — 0.087 277 in (6.1) — but also of the other parameters so as to keep the tax-exemption level of Y_d intact. To exemplify the procedure take a simply numerical example of $T_p = 0.1\ Y_d - 10$. The changes of 0.1 and 10 to reduce T_p by 9 for $Y_d = 1000$ can be computed as follows. First to keep the tax exemption point unchanged, the new constant term should be equal to minus the new slope coefficient X 100. Hence, $T_p = \alpha Y_d - 100\alpha = \alpha(Y_d - 100) = 81$, where $Y_d = 1000$. Thus, $\alpha = 0.09$, the constant term $= 9$.

The resulting multiplier effects are very noticeable in their effects on disposable income. They are considerably larger then the American multipliers. This is primarily due to the difference in hypotheses in these two simulations. M. Evans' simulation changed only the slope coefficient. Under this hypothesis the necessary change of the slope to match the assumed change of tax revenue would have been less so that our multipliers would have been smaller. The effects of increased disposable income show up in consumption only after some time lags. Therefore, it seems likely that the long-run multipliers on Y will become considerably larger than those shown in Table 3.12. The upward movement of consumption with very little change in prices seems to decrease unemployment and thereby raise the rate of money wages. The direction and magnitude of the changes look very much like those in the case of increase of $(G - G_I - W_g)$.

Table 3.12. Multipliers for Excise Tax Cut with 100% Shift Hypothesis (T_{ij} : .1).

	Y	P	P_m	Y_d	P_{ca}	U	C	i	L_a	w_I
1	.244	.00	.00	.198	.047	−.04	.01	.00	.88	−.14
2	.273	.00	.00	.068	.204	−.13	.00	.00	1.28	−.12
3	.449	.00	.00	.168	.272	−.24	.02	−.19	1.80	−.10
4	.626	.00	.00	.318	.287	−.51	.06	−.27	2.42	−.07
5	.618	.00	.00	.348	.252	−.25	.10	−.35	3.03	−.04
6	.655	.00	.00	.377	.257	−.63	.12	−.40	3.63	.00
7	.655	.00	.00	.383	.253	−.37	.15	−.43	4.17	.03
8	.751	.00	.00	.421	.311	−.34	.17	−.42	4.25	.05

*The change in the rate of interest ×100.

7. Multiplier Effects of Excise Tax Cut

The next simulation is a purely hypothetical cut of excise tax. We assume that the government cut all the excise taxes so that the resulting reduction of tax revenue from excise taxes is equal to 80 billion Yen over eight quarters. In order to see how much changes of tax rates are implied, we take the above mentioned excise tax equation from (6.3) to (6.8) — we exclude (6.9) — and sum them up. For the given values of X_{ij}'s, we compute the necessary proportional changes in all the slope coefficients and constant terms in these equations.

Since we have no empirical knowledge of the extent of shift of excise taxes in Japan, we simply assume that the 100% of excise taxes reduced will be shifted to the prices. We mean by this that if the 100% shift is made, the industry's profit after excise tax is not changed at all; in other words, the price is fixed in such a way. Since the price indices in the model are only industrial prices, we must assume that, for instance, when $(T_{hL}+T_{hS})$ is changed by $\Delta(T_{hL}+T_{hS})$, p_h is changed by the amount such that for the same X_h/P_h, W_h (wage payments), $(p+D)_h$ may remain unchanged. This can be computed by deciding the assumed change of excise taxes of the industry by the sum of X_h/P_h in control solution.

The next step is to change the parameters in our price determination equations so as to bring about this much price change. The price determination equation in the Osaka model are hybrids of the cost-mark up and demand-supply relations. It would be appropriate, however, to assume that the industry's pricing policy affects only the cost mark-up part. Hence, apart from market conditions, p_h determination equation:

$$\Delta p_h = 0.3983\,\Delta p_h^m + 0.1476\,\Delta\frac{W_h}{X_h/p_h} - 0.4351\frac{H_{fh}}{X_h}$$
$$+0.00637Q_1 - 0.00725\,Q_2 - 0.00234\,Q_3 + 0.07527$$

may be rewritten as

$$p_h = 0.3983\ p_h^m + 0.1476\ \frac{W_h}{X_h/p_h} + \text{a constant},$$

where the constant term is computed to equate the sum of the right-hand side terms to p_h in the first quarter of 1960. To change p_h by the amount corresponding to excise tax cut, we assume that all three parameters in this equation change proportionately. Since the original price determination equation is in the first difference form, the change of the constant term appears only in the first quarter or 1960.

Table 3.13. Multipliers for Personal Income Tax Reduction (T_p: 0.1).

	Y	P	P_m	Y_d	P_{ca}	U	C	i	L_a	w_I
1	.103	00	00	2.03	00	−.09	.54	00	0.23	.01
2	.166	00	00	2.29	00	−.19	.69	00	0.66	.02
3	.277	00	00	2.50	00	−.33	.86	−.05	1.22	.06
4	.378	00	00	3.16	00	−.69	1.18	−.10	1.98	.08
5	.405	00	00	2.49	00	−.32	1.19	−.16	2.44	.14
6	.459	00	00	2.82	00	−.93	1.38	−.24	3.34	.20
7	.482	00	00	2.93	00	−.55	1.53	−.31	4.01	.22
8	.532	00	00	3.61	00	−.70	1.82	−.35	4.72	.30

*i: The change in the rate of interest ×100.

The effects are rather different from those of personal income tax cut. Although price fall is not significant enough to show up in over all aggregative price level, it is noticeable for specific industry prices. As a part of this repercussion wages tend to go down slightly. Profits as well as wage incomes seem to gain due to excise tax cut. Table 3.13 sums up the effects on similar variables as before.

8. Analysis of the Effects of Monetary Policies

Two kinds of monetary policies are taken up here as typical policies in post-war Japan. The first is the change of the BOJ's loans to commercial banks denoted by V, and the second is the reduction of the BOJ's official discount rate. Table 3.14 simply presents the effects of the once-for-all change in V

Table 3.14. Effects of Increase of Central Bank Loans to Commercial Banks (V: 0.01).

	Y	P	P_m	Y_d	P_{ca}	U	C	i	L_a	w_I
1	.00	.000	.000	.00	.00	.00	.00	.000	4.36	.0
2	.00	.000	.000	.00	.00	.00	.00	.000	7.87	.0
3	.12	.000	.001	.07	.01	−.18	.02	−.008	11.17	.9
4	.24	.000	.002	.17	.05	−.38	.05	−.016	14.25	1.6
5	.32	.001	.003	.24	.05	−.22	.08	−.020	16.95	3.1
6	.34	.001	.005	.26	.06	−.59	.11	−.023	19.17	4.6
7	.33	.002	.005	.24	.07	−.30	.12	−.024	20.86	6.1
8	.28	.002	.006	.20	.07	−.20	.12	−.023	21.60	6.7
S		1.63				1.18			.50	

*Price, interest are expressed in terms of index and %. *Wages are ten Yen.

by 10 billion Yen; only the effects on Y, Y_d, P_{ca} and C are multiplied by 10, but others are strictly as computed. The expanded loan to commercial banks must be kept at the banks' account at the Bank of Japan so that not only V is increased but also the banks demand for demand deposit is increased the same amount by shifting the constant term at the same time. This will result in the excess reserve in the Osaka model and cause the expansionary monetary effects.

Table 3.14 shows that the effects take place after significant time lags. The monetary policy should not be expected to exert its significant effects before one year passes by. If the same amount of loans is increased every quarter, then the approximate level of Y increased above that of control solution as a ratio of 10 billion Yen after eight quarters will be given by the sum of eight terms of the first column in Table 3.12, which is 1.63 and corresponds to government investment multiplier in Table 3.3. It is significant that monetary policy causes prices and wages to rise more noticeably than fiscal policy.

The effects of raising the official discount rate by 0.2% are shown in Table 3.15. Its remarkable characteristic is that it causes the fluctuating effects over time on almost all variables. The effect on Y is greater at the beginning and weaker later, just the opposite of the case of increased V. The overall effect over eight quarters is 1.39 so that 2.3% rise of the official rate may be able to change the overall Y in two years by the same amount, but the inter-temporal pattern of change is very different. If the earlier is desirable, the discount policy is more effective, but its effects on other variables are mixed in directions and perhaps rather difficult to evaluate the changes. This quick effect of discount rate policy is different from Evans' results for the US in Table E.9.

Table 3.15. Effects of Raising the BOJ's Official Discount Rate (i^*: 0.2).

	Y	p^c	P_m	Y_d	P_{ca}	U	C	i	L_a	w_I
1	−.0247	−.025	024	−.0104	−.0101	.18	−.002	020	−.29	−.033
2	−.0222	−.044	−.059	−.0170	−.0024	.29	−.005	.016	−.36	−.021
3	−.0306	−.014	−.055	−.0233	−.0034	.33	−.009	.019	−.42	−.058
4	−.0265	−.029	−.026	−.0221	−.0019	.35	−.010	016	−.45	−.072
5	−.0154	−.021	−.004	−.0099	−.0010	−.00	−.008	013	−.46	−.096
6	−.0124	−.046	−.005	−.0102	−.0002	−.06	−.008	.010	−.45	−.084
7	−.0059	−.013	−.015	−.0051	.0006	−.17	−.007	.008	−.42	−.072
8	−.0013	−.016	−.035	−.0028	.0016	−.26	−.006	.005	−.38	−.047

Appendix: M. Evans' Multipliers for the US Economy

Table E.3. Multipliers for Increase in Non-defense Gov. Expenditures.

Quarter	X^a	GNP^b	p^c	DI^b	P^b_{cb}	Un^d	I^a_p
1	1.98	2.33	0.02	1.14	0.50	−0.25	0.00
2	2.35	2.82	−0.03	1.35	0.71	−0.29	0.21
3	2.13	2.69	0.04	1.29	0.67	−0.25	0.25
4	2.03	2.63	0.05	1.27	0.37	−0.23	0.24
5	1.94	2.56	0.05	1.21	0.70	−0.21	0.25
6	1.91	2.55	0.05	1.16	0.73	−0.21	0.27
7	1.95	2.62	0.05	1.20	0.75	−0.22	0.28
8	2.03	2.73	0.05	1.25	0.79	−0.22	0.31
9	2.06	2.81	0.05	1.28	0.81	−0.22	0.33
10	2.06	2.84	0.06	1.29	0.81	−0.2	0.33
11	2.07	2.87	0.06	1.32	0.81	−0.21	0.32
12	2.07	2.92	0.06	1.32	0.82	−0.21	0.32
20	2.13	3.25	0.09	1.54	0.88	−0.20	0.29
40	1.93	3.72	0.13	1.67	1.13	−0.15	0.21

[a]Billions of 1958 dollars; [b]Billions of current dollars; [c]Index, 1958 = 100.0; [d]Percent
*Variables changed: Government purchases + $1.0 Billion, 1958 dollars; Government wage bill + $0.6 Billion, current dollars; Government output originating + $0.5 Billion, 1958 dollars; Government employment + $0.1 Million.

Table E.4. Multipliers for Increase in Defense Government Expenditures.

Quarter	X^a	GNP^b	p^c	DI^b	P^b_{cb}	Un^d	I^a_p
1	2.19	2.60	0.02	1.29	0.63	−0.23	0.00
2	2.96	3.63	0.05	1.70	1.02	−0.31	0.28
3	2.21	2.94	0.06	1.36	0.85	−0.23	0.36
4	2.10	2.82	0.07	1.35	0.83	−0.20	0.30
5	1.71	2.48	0.07	1.12	0.79	−0.16	0.33
6	1.69	2.46	0.08	1.07	0.85	−0.16	0.31
7	1.78	2.58	0.08	1.11	0.89	−0.16	0.35
8	1.88	2.71	0.08	1.17	0.93	−0.17	0.38
9	1.90	2.78	0.08	1.18	0.96	−0.17	0.39
10	1.89	2.79	0.08	1.18	0.98	−0.17	0.39
11	1.90	2.82	0.08	1.21	0.98	−0.17	0.37
12	1.91	2.86	0.08	1.24	0.98	−0.16	0.36
20	2.05	3.21	0.09	1.38	1.11	−0.15	0.33
40	2.02	3.90	0.13	1.57	1.56	−0.12	0.27

Government purchases + $1.0 Billion, 1958 dollars; Government defense purchases + $1.0 Billion, 1958 dollars; Government wage bill + $0.6 Billion, current dollars; Government output originating + $0.5 Billion, 1958 dollars; Government employment + 0.1 million
*Variables changed: [a]Billions of 1958 dollars; [b] Billions of current dollars; [c]Index, 1958 = 100.0; [d] Percent.

Table E.5. Multipliers for Increase in Demand for Export.

Quarter	X^a	GNP^b	p^c	DI^b	P^b_{cb}	Un^d	I^a_p	F^a_e
1	1.75	1.87	0.00	0.87	0.47	−0.20	0.00	1.00
2	2.34	2.60	0.00	1.19	0.72	−0.25	0.17	1.09
3	2.46	2.80	0.00	1.29	0.77	−0.26	0.24	1.20
4	2.69	3.09	0.00	1.44	0.86	−0.27	0.27	1.35
5	2.93	3.40	0.00	1.57	0.97	−0.28	0.31	1.50
6	3.03	3.55	0.01	1.61	1.05	−0.29	0.37	1.55
7	3.17	3.72	0.01	1.69	1.11	−0.30	0.42	1.60
8	3.32	3.92	0.01	1.78	1.16	−0.31	0.47	1.64
9	3.42	4.07	0.01	1.86	1.21	−0.31	0.52	1.67
10	3.48	4.17	0.01	1.88	1.24	−0.31	0.55	1.69
11	3.54	4.25	0.01	1.95	1.25	−0.31	0.57	1.70
12	3.58	4.34	0.01	2.00	1.27	−0.30	0.58	1.72
20	3.70	4.66	0.02	2.19	1.30	−0.28	0.42	1.73
40	3.51	4.92	0.04	2.36	V	−0.20	0.47	1.65

[a]Billions of 1958 dollars; [b]Billions of current dollars; [c]Index, 1958 = 100.0; [d]Percent.
*Variables changed: Shift in export function +$1.0 Billion, 1958 dollars; Long run multiplier per dollars of exports $= \frac{3.51}{1.65} = 2.13$.

Table E.6. Multipliers for Decrease in Personal Income Tax Rates.

Quarter	X^a	GNP^b	p^c	DI^b	P^b_{cb}	Un^d	I^a_p	T^b_p	T^a_p
1	1.19	1.33	0.00	1.69	0.49	−0.06	0.00	−0.97	−0.89
2	1.58	1.88	0.02	1.89	0.73	−0.11	0.25	−0.95	−0.87
3	1.36	1.72	0.02	1.82	0.70	−0.09	0.30	−0.98	−0.91
4	1.35	1.75	0.03	1.85	0.73	−0.08	0.29	−0.99	−0.92
5	1.32	1.77	0.04	1.84	0.78	−0.07	0.32	−1.02	−0.93
6	1.32	1.80	0.04	1.83	0.84	−0.07	0.35	−1.05	−0.95
7	1.40	1.91	0.04	1.89	0.88	−0.07	0.38	−1.06	−0.94
8	1.51	2.06	0.04	1.96	0.95	−0.08	0.42	−1.06	0.95
9	1.56	2.16	0.04	2.00	1.00	−0.08	0.44	−1.07	−0.96
10	1.59	2.22	0.05	2.02	1.04	−0.08	0.46	−1.08	−0.98
11	1.63	2.28	0.05	2.07	1.06	−0.08	0.45	−1.09	−0.99
12	1.67	2.36	0.05	2.12	1.09	−0.08	0.46	−1.11	−0.99
20	2.01	2.92	0.06	2.46	1.33	−0.08	0.47	−1.23	−1.09
40	2.61	4.23	0.09	3.26	1.91	−0.07	0.52	−1.60	−1.35

[a]Billions of 1958 dollars; [b]Billions of current dollars; [c]Index, 1958 = 100.0; [d]Percent.
*Variables changed: Decrease in slope of personal income tax rate of 0.00192, corresponding to a decrease in personal income taxes of $1.0 Billion in constant dollars at 1965. 4 levels of income *Long run multiplier per dollar of tax cut $= \frac{2.61}{1.35} = 1.93$.

Table E.7. Multipliers for Decrease in Corporate Income Tax Rates.

Quarter	X^{a}	GNP^{b}	p^{c}	DI^{b}	P^{b}_{cb}	Un^{d}	I^{a}_{p}	T^{a}_{c}	T^{a}_{c}	D^{b}_{v}
1	0.11	0.14	0.00	0.16	0.05	−0.01	0.00	−1.15	−1.07	0.14
2	0.15	0.20	0.00	0.21	0.08	−0.01	0.02	−1.12	−1.02	0.15
3	0.19	0.24	0.00	0.24	0.09	−0.01	0.04	−1.13	−1.03	0.17
4	0.23	0.30	0.01	0.28	0.12	−0.02	0.06	−1.16	−1.04	0.21
5	0.30	0.38	0.01	0.34	0.15	−0.02	0.09	−1.20	−1.06	0.24
6	0.34	0.43	0.01	0.37	0.18	−0.02	0.12	−1.21	−1.08	0.25
7	0.38	0.50	0.01	0.40	0.21	−0.02	0.14	−1.21	−1.06	0.28
8	0.43	0.56	0.01	0.43	0.24	−0.02	0.17	−1.22	−1.06	0.29
9	0.45	0.60	0.01	0.45	0.26	−0.03	0.19	−1.24	−1.08	0.31
10	0.47	0.62	0.01	0.47	0.28	−0.03	0.20	−1.27	−1.10	0.32
11	0.49	0.64	0.01	0.48	0.29	−0.03	0.20	−1.29	−1.11	0.34
12	0.50	0.67	0.01	0.50	0.30	−0.03	0.21	−1.31	−1.11	0.36
20	0.70	0.92	0.01	0.63	0.39	−0.03	0.24	−1.53	−1.23	0.44
40	1.11	1.57	0.02	0.97	0.62	−0.03	0.29	−2.10	−1.50	0.69

[a]Billions of 1958 dollars; [b]Billions of current dollars; [c]Index, 1958 = 100.0; [d] Percent.
*Variables changed: Decrease in slope of corporate income tax rate of 0.01474, corresponding to a decrease in corporate income taxes of $1.0 Billion in constant dollars at 1965. 4 levels of profits; Long run multiplier per dollar of tax cut = $\frac{1.11}{1.50}$ = 0.74.

Table E.8. Multipliers for Decrease in Excise Tax Rates.

Quarter	X^{a}	GNP^{b}	p^{c}	DI^{b}	P^{b}_{cb}	Un^{d}	I^{a}_{p}	T^{b}_{b}	T^{a}_{b}	D^{a}_{d}
1	1.80	1.17	−0.13	0.91	1.01	−0.10	0.00	−0.98	−0.80	0.91
2	1.99	1.57	−0.11	0.74	1.56	−0.14	0.39	−0.97	−0.79	0.76
3	1.46	1.00	−0.10	0.51	1.38	−0.08	0.38	−1.02	−0.83	0.64
4	1.59	1.16	−0.10	0.58	1.47	−0.09	0.35	−1.03	−0.85	0.62
5	1.75	1.42	−0.10	0.91	1.33	−0.10	0.40	−1.04	−0.85	0.66
6	1.54	1.24	−0.09	0.60	1.56	−0.08	0.49	−1.06	−0.87	0.52
7	1.52	1.18	−0.08	0.63	1.50	−0.06	0.48	−1.08	−0.88	0.53
8	1.62	1.34	−0.08	0.68	1.59	−0.07	0.51	−1.08	−0.88	0.52
9	1.81	1.57	−0.08	0.90	1.54	−0.08	0.53	−1.09	−0.89	0.56
10	1.57	1.31	−0.07	0.54	1.78	−0.07	0.56	−1.11	−0.92	0.43
11	1.55	1.23	−0.08	0.58	1.66	−0.05	0.50	−1.14	−0.94	0.34
12	1.64	1.33	−0.09	0.61	1.75	−0.05	0.50	−1.17	−0.94	0.34
20	1.91	1.60	−0.10	0.72	2.00	−0.06	0.48	−1.32	−1.03	0.33
40	2.34	2.42	−0.06	1.00	2.91	−0.05	0.52	−1.74	−1.31	0.32

[a]Billions of 1958 dollars; [b]Billions of current dollars; [c]Index 1958 = 100.0; [d]Percent.
*Variables changed: Decrease in slope of excise income tax rate of 0.00207, corresponding to a decrease in excise taxes of $1.0 Billion in constant dollars at 1965.4 levels of national income price of consumer durables decreased by 1%; Long run multiplier per dollar of tax cut = $\frac{2.34}{1.31}$ = 1.79.

Table E.9. Multipliers for Decrease in the Discount Rate.

Quarter	X^a	GNP^b	p^c	DI^b	P^b_{cb}	Un^d	I^a_p	I^a_h
1	0.00	0.00	0.00	0.00	0.00	0.00	0.00	0.00
2	0.00	0.00	0.00	0.00	0.00	0.00	0.00	0.00
3	0.36	0.42	0.00	0.19	0.14	−0.02	0.18	0.00
4	3.32	3.97	0.02	1.71	1.29	−0.32	0.55	1.34
5	4.35	5.46	0.06	2.25	1.94	−0.39	1.25	1.24
6	4.65	6.08	0.10	2.43	2.30	−0.37	1.81	1.13
7	4.77	6.47	0.13	2.50	2.63	−0.32	2.28	0.92
8	4.66	6.61	0.17	2.39	2.92	−0.27	2.67	0.69
9	4.52	6.70	0.20	2.22	3.22	−0.22	2.91	0.54
10	4.33	6.70	0.24	2.05	3.43	−0.17	3.04	0.41
11	4.06	6.56	0.25	1.84	3.59	0.12	3.06	0.31
12	3.84	6.46	0.26	1.66	3.73	0.07	3.05	0.23
20	3.23	6.32	0.30	0.75	4.67	+0.12	2.67	-0.02
40	4.27	9.73	0.43	0.64	7.79	+0.15	2.70	-0.10

[a]Billions of 1958 dollars; [b]Billions of current dollars; [c]Index, 1958 = 100.0; [d]Percent.
*Variables changed: Decrease in the discount rate by 1%.

Table E.10. Multipliers for Increase in the Free Reserve Ratio.

Quarter	X^a	GNP^b	p^c	DI^b	P^b_{cb}	Un^d	I^a_p	I^a_h
1	0.00	0.00	0.00	0.00	0.00	0.00	0.00	0.00
2	0.00	0.00	0.00	0.00	0.00	0.00	0.00	0.00
3	0.32	0.37	0.00	0.17	0.13	−0.02	0.16	0.00
4	2.99	3.58	0.02	1.54	1.16	−0.30	0.49	1.20
5	3.92	4.91	0.05	2.02	1.74	−0.35	1.12	1.12
6	4.18	5.47	0.09	2.19	2.07	−0.33	1.63	1.02
7	4.30	5.83	0.12	2.25	2.36	−0.29	2.05	0.83
8	4.20	5.96	0.16	2.16	2.62	−0.25	2.40	0.62
9	4.07	6.04	0.18	2.01	2.89	−0.20	2.62	0.49
10	3.90	3.03	0.21	1.85	3.09	−0.16	2.74	037
11	3.66	5.91	0.23	1.67	3.23	−0.11	2.76	0.28
12	3.46	5.82	0.24	1.50	3.25	−0.06	2.75	0.21
20	2.91	5.69	0.27	0.68	4.20	+0.10	2.41	−0.01
40	3.84	8.75	0.39		7.01	+0.14	2.43	−0.09

[a]Billions of 1958 dollars; [b]Billions of current dollars; [c]Index, 1958 = 100.0; [d]Percent.
*Variables changed: Increase in the ratio of free reserves to required reserves of 10%.

References

Duesenberry, J., G. Fromm, L. R. Klein and E. Kuh (1965). *The Brookings Quarterly Econometric Model of the US Economy*. Chicago: Rand McNally.

Evans, M. K. and L. R. Klein (1968). *The Wharton Econometric Forecasting Model*, 2nd ed. Philadelphia: the Wharton School, Univ. of Pennsylvania.

Ichimura, S., L. R. Klein, S. Koizumi, K. Sato and Y. Shinkai (1964). A Quarterly Econometric Model of Postwar Japanese Economy: 1952–1959. Osaka Economic Papers, March.

Ichimura, S., L. R. Klein, S. Koizumi, K. Sato and Y. Shinkai (1964). A Quarterly Econometric Model of Postwar Japanese Economy, 1952–1959: Data Appendix. Osaka Economic Papers, July.

Ichimura, S., S. Koizumi and Y. Shinkai (1965). Some Further Results of the Osaka Econometric Model. In Baba, M. and Tatemoto, M. (eds.), *Reports of the Rokko Conference on Econometrics*.

Ichimura, S. (1962). The Demand for and Supply of Money. *The Economic Studies Quarterly*, January (Japanese).

Ichimura, S. and H. Eguchi (1964). Japanese Exports Functions. *The Economic Studies Quarterly*, February.

Ichimura, S. (1964). Notes on Identities in the Monetary Sector. *The Economic Studies Quarterly*, February.

Ichimura, S. (1968). Factors for Rapid Economic Growth. In Ohkawa, K. and Klein, L. R. (eds.), *Economic Growth: Japanese Experiences Since the Meiji Era*. Homewood, III: Irwin.

Ichimura, S. (1966). An Econometric Model of the Monetary Sector in Postwar Japan. University of California, Berkeley (Mimeograph).

Ichimura, S., I. Sugiura and H. Tjian (1966). A Simulation System Program for Large Econometric Models. Working Paper No. 198, Center for Research in Management Science, U. of California, Berkeley.

Ichimura, S., L. R. Klein, S. Koizumi and K. Sato (eds.) (1977). *An Econometric Analysis of the Japanese Economy*. The Japanese Society for Asian Studies.

Klein, L. R. and A. S. Goldberger (1955). *An Econometric Model of the United States, 1929–1952*. Amsterdam: North-Holland Publishing Company, p. 14.

Koizumi, S., M. Tatemoto, K. Sato, M. Saito and H. Atsumi (1960). A Quarterly Econometric Model of Postwar Japanese Economy. (Mimeograph) presented at the Annual Convention or the Japanese Association of Theoretical Economics.

Koizumi, S. and M. Saito (1961). Productivity Differentials and Wage Differentials in the Textile Industry. *Handai Keizai-Gaku*, October.

Koizumi, S. (1965). Wages and Prices. *Handai Keizai Gaku*, March.

Moriguchi, C. (1965). A Further Note on the Autocorrelation Bias. *The Economic Studies Quarterly*, November.

Nerlove, M. and K. F. Wallis (1966). Use of the Durbin-Watson Statistic in Inappropriate Situations. *Econometrica*, January.

Orcutt, G. H. *et al.* (1961). *Microanalysis of Socio-Economic Systems: A Simulation Study*. New York: Harper.

Phillips, A. W. (1958). The Relation Between Unemployment and the Rate of Change of Money Wage Rates in UK, 1861–1957. *Economica*, November, 283–299.

Prais, S. J. and H. S. Houthakker (1955). *The Analysis of Family Budgets*. Cambridge Univ. Press, pp. 106–107.

Saito, M. and K. Kuga (1966). Technological Innovations and Japanese Economy. In Inada, K. and Uchida, T. (eds.) *Theory and Measurement of Economic Growth*, Tokyo: Iwanami.

Sato, K. (1966). A Model of Investment Behavior: Fixed Investment and Capacity in Japanese Manufacturing, 1952–1963. *The Economic Studies Quarterly*, June.

Stone, R. (1954). *The Measurement of Consumers' Expenditure and Behavior in the UK 1920–38*, vol. I, Cambridge: Cambridge Univ. Press, pp. 315–317.

Chapter 11

The Japan Model for World Project LINK

Kanemi Ban

1. Introduction

This is the updated Japan model[1] that has been used as a part of the World Project LINK model. Since Project LINK was organized to deal with the worldwide repercussions of the economic activities and policies in any national economy, the Japan model was an indispensable part. Chikashi Moriguchi, among others, was the main architect of the Japan model for many years.[2] I took over his work in 2000.

2. List of Variables in the Ban Model

Table 1. List of Variables.

Variable	Description	Unit
ASEANIM	ASEAN imports	Billions of US$
ASEANPIM	ASEAN imports price index (using Asia)	2000 = 100
BC	Corporate, balance	Billions
BG	Government, balance	Billions
BH	Households, balance	Billions
BPC BOP	Balance of current account	100 millions of yen
BPEX BOP	Trade, exports	100 millions of yen
BPIM BOP	Trade, imports	100 millions of yen
BPINVDA BOP	Investment, direct investment, asset	100 millions of yen

(*Continued*)

[1]The model here is the version updated on September 25, 2008.

[2]He organized a group of business economists in Osaka to use the model for forecasting the economic and business conditions in Japan from 1991 to 2004. Brief reports were made available by the Kansai Institue of Society and Economic Research.

Table 1. (*Continued*)

Variable	Description	Unit
BPINVDL BOP	Investment, direct investment, liability	100 millions of yen
BPINVFA BOP	Stock of financial derivatives, asset	100 millions of yen
BPINVFL BOP	Stock of financial derivatives, liability	100 millions of yen
BPINVOA BOP	Investment, other investment, asset	100 millions of yen
BPINVOL BOP	Investment, other investment, asset	100 millions of yen
BPINVSA BOP	Investment, security investment, asset	100 millions of yen
BPINVSL BOP	Investment, security investment, liability	100 millions of yen
BPKDA BOP	Stock of direct investment. asset	100 millions of yen
BPKDL BOP	Stock of direct investment. liability	100 millions of yen
BPKOA BOP	Stock of other investment, asset	100 millions of yen
BPKOL BOP	Stock of other investment, liability	100 millions of yen
BPKSA BOP	Stock of security investment, asset	100 millions of yen
BPKSL BOP	Stock of security investment, liability	100 millions of yen
BPS BOP	Services, balance	100 millions of yen
BPSCARGPBOP	Services, transport, cargo, debit	100 millions of yen
BPSCARGRBOP	Services, transport, cargo, credit	100 millions of yen
BPSOTHP BOP	Services, other, debit	100 millions of yen
BPSOTHR BOP	Services, others credit	100 millions of yen
BPSP BOP	Services, total, debit	100 millions of yen
BPSPASP BOP	Services, transport, passengers, debit	100 millions of yen
BPSPASR BOP	Services, transport, passengers, credit	100 millions of yen
BPSR BOP	Services, total, credit	100 millions of yen
BPSTRNP BOP	Services, transport, debit	100 millions of yen
BPSTRNR BOP	Services, transport, credit	100 millions of yen
BPSTRVP BOP	Services, travel, debit	100 millions of yen
BPSTRVR BOP	Services, travel, credit	100 millions of yen
BPT BOP	Trade, balance	100 millions of yen
BPTRANS BOP	Transfers	100 millions of yen
BPY BOP	Income, balance	100 millions of yen
BPYD BOP	Income, direct investment, balance	100 millions of yen
BPYDP BOP	Income, direct investment, debit	100 millions of yen
BPYDR BOP	Income, direct investment, credit	100 millions of yen
BPYO BOP	Income, other investment, balance	100 millions of yen
BPYOP BOP	Income, other investment, debit	100 millions of yen
BPYOR BOP	Income, other investment, credit	100 millions of yen
BPYS BOP	Income, security investment, balance	100 millions of yen
BPYSP BOP	Income, security investment, debit	100 millions of yen
BPYSR BOP	Income, decurity investment, credit	100 millions of yen
BPYW BOP	Income, wage, balance	100 millions of yen
BPYWP BOP	Income, wage, debit	100 millions of yen
BPYWR BOP	Income, wage, credit	100 millions of yen
CC	Capital cost	Defined by Eq. (95)

(*Continued*)

Table 1. (***Continued***)

Variable	Description	Unit
CG	Private inventory investment	Billions
CG00	Government consumption	Billions chained 2000¥
CGPID	Price index of corporate goods	2000 = 100
CH	Private consumption of households, total	Billions
CH00	Private consumption of households, total	Billions chained 2000¥
CHINAIM	China, imports	Billions of US dollars
CHINAPIM	China, imports price index (= HongKong)	2000 = 100
CHIR	Private households cons., imputed rent	Billions
CHIR00	Private households cons., imputed rent	Billions chained 2000¥
CHNIR	Private households cons., imputed rent excluded	Billions
CHNIR00	Private households cons. excl. imputed rent	Billions chained 2000¥
CNP	Private consumption of nonprofit org.	Billions
CNP00	Private consumption of nonprofit org.	Billions chained 2000¥
CP	Private consumption, total	Billions
CP00	Private consumption, total	Billions chained 2000¥
CPI	Consumer price index, excluding fresh foods	2005 = 100
CSPI	Price index of corporate services	
D19972	Dummy variable	1 after 1997.2
D19981	Dummy variable	1.0 after 1998.1
DEP	Depreciation	Billions
DEPC	Corporate, depreciation	Billions
DEPG	Government, depreciation	Billions
DEPH	Households, depreciation	Billions
EGS	Exports of goods and services	Billions
EGS00	Exports of goods and services	Billions chained 2000¥
EUGDP00	EU Gross domestic products	Billion of euros
EUPGDP	EU Deflator for GDP	1995 = 1.0
EXASEAN	Exports, to ASEAN	CC base billions of yen
EXCC	Exports, total	CC base billions of yen
EXCHINA	Exports, to China	CC base billions of yen
EXEU	Exports, to EU25	CC base billions of yen
EXNIES	Exports, to NIES	CC base billions of yen
EXO	Exports, to others	CC base billions of yen
EXUSA	Exports, to US	CC base billions of yen
*FXR_*	EURO foreign exchange rate	Dollars per euro
GDP	Gross domestic product	Billions
GDP00	Gross domestic product	Billions chained 2000¥
GNI	Gross national income	Billions
HWCONT	Worked hours, contract	Monthly hours
HWORK	Worked hours, total	Monthly hours
HWOVER	Worked hours, overtime	Monthly hours

(*Continued*)

Table 1. (*Continued*)

Variable	Description	Unit
IFP	Private non-residential investment	Billions
IFP00	Private non-residential investment	Billions chained 2000¥
IG	Government consumption	Billions
IG00	Public investment	Billions chained 2000¥
IHP	Private residential investment	Billions
IHP00	Private residential investment	Billions chained 2000¥
IIG	Public inventory investment	Billions
IIG00	Public inventory investment	Billions chained 2000¥
IIP	Public investment	Billions
IIP00	Private inventory investment	Billions chained 2000¥
IPI	Production index of industry and mining	2000 = 100
JSA	Index of Tokyo stock market	
KBC	Corporate, accumulated balance	Billions
KBG	Government, accumulated balance	Billions
KBH	Households, accumulated balance	Billions
KFDIA	Stock of real foreign direct investment	Billion of 2000¥
KFPOO	Stock of non-residential	Billions chained 2000¥
KFPN	Corporate, non-residential stock	Billions
KGN	Government, net stock	Billions
KHP00	Stock of residential	Billions chained 2000¥
KHPN	Households, net residential stock	Billions
KIP00	Stock of inventory	Billions chained 2000¥
KSH	Households, accumulated savings	Billions
L	Labor, total	Ten thousands
LF	Labor force	Ten thousands
LS	Labor, self employed	Ten thousands
LW	Labor, employed	Ten thousands
LWH	Labor input	Ten thousands
M2CD	Money supply	100 millions
MC	Imports, total	CC base billions of yen
MC01	Imports, foods	CC base billions of yen
MC24	Imports, materials	CC base billions of yen
MC3	Imports, mineral fuels	CC base billions of yen
MC59	Imports, other manufactured	CC base billions of yen
MC7	Imports, machinery	CC base billions of yen
MGS	Imports of goods and services	Billions
MGS00	Imports of goods and services	Billions chained 2000¥
NETF	Net income from abroad	Billions
NIESIM	Korea, Hong Kong, Taiwan imports	Billions of US dollars
NIESPIM	Korea, Hong Kong, Taiwan, Imp. price index	2000 = 100
OEG	Government, other payments	Billions

(*Continued*)

Table 1. (*Continued*)

Variable	Description	Unit
OTHRH	Households, other payments	Billions
PCG	Deflator for CG	2000 = 1.0
PCH	Deflator for CH	2000 = 1.0
PCHIR	Deflator for CHIR	2000 = 1.0
PCHNIR	Deflator for CHNIR	2000 = 1.0
PCNP	Deflator for CNP	2000 = 1.0
PCOALD	Import prices	US$ base US$/ton
PCP	Deflator for CP	2000 = 1.0
PEGS	Deflator for EGS	2000 = 1.0
PEX	Export price index	Total 2000 = 100
PEXASIA	Export price index	To Asia 2000 = 100
PEXCHINA	Export price index	To China 2000 = 100
PEXEU	Export price index	To EU25 2000 = 100
PEXNIES	Export price index	To NIES 2000 = 100
PEXUSA	Export price index	To US 2000 = 100
PGDP	Deflator for GDP	2000 = 1.0
PIFP	Deflator for IFP	2000 = 1.0
PIG	Deflator for IG	2000 = 1.0
PIHP	Deflator for IHP	2000 = 1.0
PIM	Import price index, total	2000 = 100
PIM01	Import price index, foods	2000 = 100
PIM01D	Import price index, foods	US$ base 2000 = 100
PIM24	Import price index, materials	2000 = 100
PIM24D	Import price index, materials	US$ base 2000 = 100
PIM3	Import price index, mineral fuels	2000 = 100
PIM59	Import price index, other manufactured	2000 = 100
PIM59D	Import price index, other manufactured	US$ base 2000 = 100
PIM7	Import price index, machinery	Dollar base 2000 = 100
PIM7D	Import price index, machinery	US$ base 2000 = 100
PLNGD	Import prices	US$ base US$/ton
PMGS	Deflator for MGS	2000 = 1.0
POILD	Import prices	US$ base US$/barrel
POP15	Populations over 15 years old	Ten thousands
POP65	Populations over 65 years old	Ten thousands
Q1	Dummy variable	Q1=0 for the first quarter
Q2	Dummy variable	Q2=1 for the 2nd quarter
Q3	Dummy variable	Q3=1 for the 3rd quarter
RCL	Call rate, overnight	Percent
RCP	Commercial paper rate	Percent
RESID00	Residual	Billions chained 2000¥
REX	Foreign exchange rate	yen per US dollar

(*Continued*)

Table 1. (*Continued*)

Variable	Description	Unit
RLB	Bank loan rate	Percent
RLBOND	Government bond yields	Percent
RLPRM	Long-term prime rate	Percent
RN	Official discount rate	Percent
RTAXH	Rate of households income tax	Billions
RTC	Rate of corporate income tax	Billions
RTCON	Rate of consumption tax	Billions
RU	Unemployment rate	Percent
SAGH	Households, social aids	Billions
SC	Corporate, savings	Billions
SG	Government, savings	Billions
SH	Households, savings	Billions
SSBH	Households, social security benefit	Billions
SSCH	Households, social security contributions	Billions
SUB	Government, subsidy	Billions
SUMG	Government, revenue	Billions
TAXC	Corporate, income tax	Billions
TAXH	Households, income tax	Billions
TAXI	Indirect tax total	Billions
TAXIO	Indirect tax, others	Billions
TAXIV	Indirect tax, value add	Billions
TREND	Time trend	
U	Unemployed	Ten thousands
UCP00	US private consumption	Billions of chained $
UGDP00	US gross domestic product	Billions of chained $
UPCP	US deflator for CP	2000 = 1
UPGDP	US deflator for GDP	2000 = 1
URLG10	US government bond yields	10 years percent
W	Hourly wage	(WAGE/HWORK*100)
WAGE	Wage per employee	(YW*/LW)
WRLDIM	World import	Billions of US dollars
WRLDPIM	World import price index	2000 = 100
YC	Corporate, income	Billions
YDH	Households, disposable income	Billions
YG	Government, corporate income	Billions
YH	Households, total receipts	Billions
YRG	Government, net propriety income	Billions
YRH	Net propriety income	Billions
YS	Income of self employed, total	Billions
YSI	Income of self employed, imputed rent	Billions
YU	Income of self-employed, excl. imputed rent	Billions
YW	Income of employed	Billions

3. The System of Equations

3.1. *Expenditure side equations*

(3.1) *CHNIR00*: Private consumption of households, excluding imputed rent

$$\mathrm{LOG}(CHNIR00) = \underset{(-0.0216)}{-0.06582} + \underset{(1.50)}{0.2867}\,\mathrm{LOG}(YDH/PCHNIR)$$
$$+\underset{(3.34)}{0.1267}\,\mathrm{LOG}(KSH_{-1}/PCHNIR) + \underset{(4.02)}{0.5699}\,\mathrm{LOG}(CHNIR00_{-1})$$

Radj = .763 se = .010 DW = 2.14 Sample: From 1996. 2 to 2005. 1 (No. of obs. = 36)

(3.2) *CHIR00*: Private consumption of households, imputed rent

$$\mathrm{LOG}(CHIR00) = \underset{(15.0)}{+6.376} + \underset{(4.36)}{0.6582}\,\mathrm{LOG}(CPI/CSPI)$$
$$+\underset{(6.34)}{0.5674}\,\mathrm{LOG}(CGPID/CSPI) + \underset{(9.99)}{0.3364}\,\mathrm{LOG}(KHP00_{-1})$$

Radj = .993 se = .005 DW = .86 Sample: From 1996. 2 to 2005. 1 (No. of obs. = 36)

(3.3) *CH00*: Private consumption of households, total IDENT

$$CH00 = CHNIR00 + CHIR00$$

(3.4) *CNP00*: Private consumption of nonprofit organizations

$$\mathrm{DEL}(1,\ \mathrm{LOG}(CNP00)) = \underset{(1.48)}{+0.006018} + \underset{(1.39)}{0.5981}\mathrm{DEL}(1,\ \mathrm{LOG}(CHNIR00))$$
$$\underset{(-2.69)}{-2.955}\,\mathrm{DEL}(1,\ \ \mathrm{LOG}(PCNP/PCHNIR))$$

Radj = .131 se = .024 DW = .67 Sample: From 1996. 2 to 2005. 1 (No. of obs. = 36)

(3.5) *CP00*: Private consumption, total IDENT

$$CP00 = CH00 + CNP00$$

(3.6) *IHP00*: Private residential investment

$$IHP00/4-0.005*KHP00_{-1}=\underset{(-2.54)}{-5844.5}+\underset{(2.70)}{0.02316}\text{PDL}(2,3,1,YDH/PIHP)$$
$$+\underset{(5.84)}{0.6452}(IHP00_{-1}/4-0.005*KHP00_{-2})$$

Radj = .873 se = 117.762 DW = 2.05 Sample: From 1998. 2 to 2005. 1 (No. of obs. = 28)

PDL(2, 3, 1, *YDH/PIHP*) lag coeff. *t*-value: 0).0053, .70 1).0069, 2.70 2).0066, 1.37 3).0043, .99

(3.7) *IFP00*: Private non-residential investment

$$\text{LOG}(IFP00/KFP00_{-1})=\underset{(0.686)}{0.1671}+\underset{(2.23)}{0.06289}\,\text{LOG}(JSA/CC/KFP00_{-1})$$
$$+\underset{(11.6)}{0.8358}\,\text{LOG}(IFP00_{-1}/KFP00_{-2})$$

Radj = .860 se = .029 DW = 2.07 Sample: From 1996. 2 to 2005. 1 (No. of obs. = 36)

(3.8) *IIP00*: Private inventory investment

$$IIP00=\underset{(2.19)}{20735.7}-\underset{(-2.20)}{23.99}\,\text{PDL}(2,4,1,KIP00_{-1}/IPI_{-1})+\underset{(2.86)}{0.4712}IIP00_{-1}$$

Radj = .499 se = 1540.073 DW = 2.10

Sample: From 1996. 2 to 2005. 1 (No. of obs. = 36)

PDL(2, 4, 1, $KIP00_{-1}/IPI_{-1}$)

lag coefficient *t*-value: 0, −12, −2.35 1, −7.1995, −2.83 2, −3.5984, −1.06 3, −1.1981, −.31 4, .0013, .00

(3.9) *CG00*: Government consumption IDENT

$$CG00 = CG/PCG$$

(3.10) *IG00*: Public investment DENT

$$IG00 = IG/PIG$$

(3.11) *EGS00*: Exports of goods and services IDENT

$$EGS00 = EGS/PEGS$$

(3.12) *MGS00*: Imports of goods and services IDENT

$$MGS00 = MGS/PMGS$$

(3.13) *GDP00*: Gross domestic product IDENT

$$GDP00 = CP00 + IHP00 + IFP00 + IIP00 + CG00 + IG00 + IIG00 + EGS00 - MGS00 + RESID00$$

(3.14) *IPI*: Production index of industry and mining

$$\mathrm{LOG}(IPI) = \underset{(-0.669)}{-0.9974} + \underset{(8.40)}{1.013}\,\mathrm{LOG}(GDP00) + \underset{(11.6)}{0.9047}\,\mathrm{LOG}(IPI_{-1}/GDP00_{-1})$$

Radj = .817 se = .017 DW = 1.34 Sample: From 1996. 2 to 2005. 1 (No. of obs. = 36)

(3.15) *KHP00*: Stock of residential IDENT

$$KHP00 = IHP00/4 + 0.995 * KHP00_{-1}$$

(3.16) *KFP00*: Stock of non-residential IDENT

$$KFP00 = IFP00/4 + 0.99 * KFP00_{-1}$$

(3.17) *KIP00*: Stock of inventory IDENT

$$KIP00 = IIP00/4 + KIP00_{-1}$$

(3.18) *CHNIR*: Private consumption of households, imputed rent excluded IDENT

$$CHNIR = CHNIR00 * PCHNIR$$

(3.19) *CHIR*: Private consumption of households, imputed rent IDENT

$$CHIR = CHIR00 * PCHIR$$

(3.20) *CH*: Private consumption of households, totaI IDENT

$$CH = CHNIR + CHIR$$

(3.21) *CNP*: Private consumption of nonprofit Organization IDENT

$$CNP = CNP00 * PCNP$$

(3.22) *CP*: Private consumption, total IDENT

$$CP = CH + CNP$$

(3.23) *IHP*: Private residential investment IDENT

$$IHP = IHP00 * PIHP$$

(3.24) *IFP*: Private non-residential investment IDENT

$$IFP = IFP00 * PIFP$$

(3.25) *IIP*: Private inventory investment

$$\underset{(-0.584)}{IIP = -29.28} + \underset{(44.1)}{1.029} IIP00 * CGPID/100$$

Radj = .982 se = 300.726 DW = 2.77 Sample: From 1996. 2 to 2005. 1 (No. of obs. = 36)

(3.26) *EGS*: Exports of goods and services

$$\mathrm{LOG}(EGS) = \underset{(-1.64)}{-0.2426} + \underset{(38.5)}{0.8474}\,\mathrm{LOG}(BPEX) + \underset{(8.68)}{0.1229}\,\mathrm{LOG}(BPSR)$$
$$+ \underset{(7.95)}{0.02431}\,Q1 + \underset{(10.6)}{0.02645}\,Q2 + \underset{(3.65)}{0.008878}\,Q3$$

Radj = .997 se = .005 DW = 1.62 Sample: From 1996. 2 to 2005. 1 (No. of obs. = 36)

(3.27) *MGS*: Imports of goods and services

$$\mathrm{LOG}(MGS) = \underset{(-3.21)}{-0.3350} + \underset{(122.0)}{0.7439}\,\mathrm{LOG}(BPIM) + \underset{(28.2)}{0.2500}\,\mathrm{LOG}(BPSP)$$
$$+ \underset{(12.9)}{0.02334}\,Q1 + \underset{(14.9)}{0.02713}\,Q2 + \underset{(10.6)}{0.01916}\,Q3$$

Radj = .998 se = .004 DW = 1.57 Sample: From 1996. 2 to 2005. 1 (No. of obs. = 36)

(3.28) *GDP*: Gross domestic product IDENT

$$GDP = CP + IHP + IFP + IIP + CG + IG + IIG + EGS - MGS$$

(3.29) *NETF*: Net income from abroad

$$NETF = \underset{(1.58)}{491.6} + \underset{(24.7)}{0.4396} BPY - \underset{(-14.6)}{2725.7}\,Q1 - \underset{(-6.62)}{996.9}\,Q2 - \underset{(-9.82)}{1554.0}\,Q3$$

Radj = .946 se = 313.877 DW = 2.39
Sample: From 1996. 2 to 2005. 1 (No. of obs. = 36)

(3.30) *GNI*: Gross national income IDENT

$$GNI = GDP + NETF$$

3.2. *Price variables*

(3.31) *CGPID*: Price index of corporate goods

$$\mathrm{DEL}(1,\ \mathrm{LOG}(CGPID/PIM)) = \underset{(-0.949)}{-0.001551} + \underset{(22.4)}{0.9709}\mathrm{DEL}(1,\ \mathrm{LOG}(W/PIM))$$

Radj = .935 se = .010 DW = 2.37 Sample: From 1996. 2 to 2005. 1 (No. of obs. = 36)

(3.32) *CSPI*: Price index of corporate services

$$\mathrm{LOG}(CSPI) = \underset{(-9.22)}{-2.323} + \underset{(7.76)}{0.4871}\ \mathrm{PDL}(2, 4, 1,\ \mathrm{LOG}(W_{-2})) + \underset{(33.5)}{1.135}\ \mathrm{PDL}(2, 3, 1,\ \mathrm{LOG}(CGPID))$$

Radj = .985 se = .004 DW = .93 Sample: From 1996. 2 to 2005. 1

(No. of obs. = 36)

PDL(2, 4, 1, LOG(W_{-2}))lag coefficient t-value : 0).0436, .57

1).1061, 4.96 2).1331, 4.96 3).1244, 3.17 4).0800, 2.60

PDL(2, 3, 1, LOG(*CGPID*))lag coefficient t-value 0).5967, 6.50

1).3406, 33.51 2).1558, 3.25 3).0423, .90

(3.33) *CPI*: Consumer price index, excluding fresh foods

$$\mathrm{LOG}(CPI) = \underset{(13.3)}{2.190} + \underset{(3.51)}{0.2284}\ \mathrm{PDL}(2, 4, 1,\ \mathrm{LOG}(W_{-1})) + \underset{(8.27)}{0.3564}\ \mathrm{PDL}(2, 1, 1,\ \mathrm{LOG}(CGPID))$$

Radj = .920 se = .003 DW = 1.80 Sample: From 1998. 2 to 2005. 1

(No. of obs. = 28)

PDL(2, 4, 1, LOG(W_{-1}))

lag coefficient t-value : 0).0181, .26 1).0493, 2).10

2).0631, 3.05 3).0595, 1.92 4).0384, 1.55

PDL(2, 1, 1, LOG(*CGPID*))

lag coefficient t-value 0).2768, 1.63 1).0796, .43

(3.34) *PCHNIR*: Deflator for CHNIR

$$\mathrm{LOG}(PCHNIR/CPI) = \underset{(-2.80)}{-1.011} + \underset{(2.51)}{0.1618}\,\mathrm{LOG}(W/CPI) + \underset{(2.30)}{0.1702}\,\mathrm{LOG}(CGPID/CPI) + \underset{(9.25)}{0.7408}\,\mathrm{LOG}(PCHNIR_{-1}/CPI_{-1})$$

Radj = .911 se = .004 DW = 2.22 Sample: From 1998. 2 to 2005. 1 (No. of obs. = 28)

(3.35) *PCHIR*: Deflator for *CHIR*

$$\mathrm{DEL}(1,\ \mathrm{LOG}(PCHIR/PIHP)) = \underset{(-0.348)}{-0.0002136} + \underset{(4.86)}{0.5204}\,\mathrm{DEL}(1,\ \mathrm{LOG}(CPI/PIHP))$$

Radj = .456 se = .003 DW = 1.53 Sample: From 1998. 2 to 2005. 1 (No. of obs. = 28)

(3.36) *PCH*: Deflator for *CH* IDENT

$$PCH = CH/CH00$$

(3.37) *PCNP*: Deflator for *CNP*

$$\mathrm{DEL}(1,\ \mathrm{LOG}(PCNP/W)) = \underset{(-1.17)}{-0.0009810} + \underset{(10.6)}{0.8745}\,\mathrm{DEL}(1,\ \mathrm{LOG}(CGPID/W))$$

Radj = .806 se = .004 DW = 1.55 Sample: From 1998. 2 to 2005. 1 (No. of obs. = 28)

(3.38) *PCP*: Deflator for *CP* IDENT

$$PCP = CP/CP00$$

(3.39) *PIHP*: Deflator for *IHP*

$$\mathrm{DEL}(1,\ \mathrm{LOG}(PIHP/W)) = \underset{(0.839)}{0.0005317} + \underset{(16.2)}{1.012}\,\mathrm{DEL}(1,\ \mathrm{LOG}(CGPID/W))$$

Radj = .907 se = .003 DW = 1.84 Sample: From 1998. 2 to 2005. 1
(No. of obs. = 28)

(3.40) *PIFP*: Deflator for *IFP*

$$\begin{aligned} &\mathrm{DEL}(1,\ \mathrm{LOG}(PIFP/PIM)) \\ &\quad = \underset{(-3.82)}{-0.003245} + \underset{(42.1)}{0.9734}\,\mathrm{DEL}(1,\ \mathrm{LOG}(CGPID/PIM)) \end{aligned}$$

Radj = .983 se = .005 DW = 1.58 Sample: From 1997. 2 to 2005. 1
(No. of obs. = 32)

(3.41) *PCG*: Deflator for *CG*

$$\begin{aligned} \mathrm{LOG}(PCG/CPI) &= \underset{(-2.57)}{-1.641} + \underset{(1.58)}{0.2784}\,\mathrm{LOG}(CGPID/CPI) \\ &\quad + \underset{(4.66)}{0.6437}\,\mathrm{LOG}(PCG_{-1}/CPI_{-1}) \end{aligned}$$

Radj = .560 se = .011 DW = 2.32 Sample: From 1998. 2 to 2005. 1
(No. of obs. = 28)

(3.42) *PIG*: Deflator for *IG*

$$\begin{aligned} \mathrm{DEL}(1,\ \mathrm{LOG}(PIG/W)) &= \underset{(1.22)}{0.001214} + \underset{(1.88)}{0.3828}\mathrm{DEL}(1,\ \mathrm{LOG}(PIFP/W)) \\ &\quad + \underset{(3.19)}{0.6627}\,\mathrm{DEL}(1,\ \mathrm{LOG}(CGPID/W)) \end{aligned}$$

Radj = .884 se = .004 DW = 2.50 Sample: From 1998. 2 to 2005. 1
(No. of obs. = 28)

(3.43) *PEGS*: Deflator for *EGS*

$$\begin{aligned} \mathrm{DEL}(1,\ \mathrm{LOG}(PEGS)) &= \underset{(0.00722)}{0.00002854} + \underset{(9.58)}{0.7352}\,\mathrm{DEL}(1,\ \mathrm{LOG}(PEX)) \\ &\quad - \underset{(-3.89)}{0.02335}\,Q1 + \underset{(0.479)}{0.002598}\,Q2 - \underset{(-0.501)}{0.002743}\,Q3 \end{aligned}$$

Radj = .769 se = .010 DW = 1.81 Sample: From 1998. 2 to 2005. 1
(No. of obs. = 28)

(3.44) *PMGS*: Deflator for *MGS*

$$\mathrm{DEL}(1, PMGS) = \underset{(2.09)}{0.009152} + \underset{(11.8)}{0.7144}\,\mathrm{DEL}(1,\ \mathrm{LOG}(PIM)) - \underset{(-3.85)}{0.02476}\,\mathrm{Q1} - \underset{(-0.312)}{0.001834}\,\mathrm{Q2} - \underset{(-1.73)}{0.01035}\,\mathrm{Q3}$$

Radj = .843 se = .011 DW = 2.17 Sample: From 1998. 2 to 2005. 1 (No. of obs. = 28)

(3.45) *PGDP*: Deflator for GDP IDENT

$$PGDP = GDP/GDP00$$

3.3. *Labor and work variables*

(3.46) *HWOVER: Worked hours, overtime*

$$\mathrm{LOG}(HWOVER) = \underset{(-3.08)}{-2.084} + \underset{(5.86)}{1.366}\,\mathrm{PDL}(2, 3, 1,\ \mathrm{LOG}(GDP00/LW)) - \underset{(-3.66)}{1.140}\,\mathrm{PDL}(2, 3, 1,\ \mathrm{LOG}(W/PGDP)) + \underset{(4.82)}{0.4691}\,\mathrm{PDL}(2, 1, 1,\ \mathrm{LOG}(IPI))$$

Radj = .896 se = .012 DW = .59 Sample: From 1997. 2 to 2005. 1 (No. of obs. = 32)

PDL(2, 3, 1, LOG(*GDP00*/*LW*)) lag coefficient *t*-value:
0).2082, .64 1).4100, 5.86 2).4425, 2.91 3).3059, 2.05
PDL(2, 3, 1, LOG(*W*/*PGDP*))
lag coeff. *t*-value : 0) − .7322, −2.81 1) − .3421, −3.67
2) − .0901, −.52 3).0240, .16
PDL(2, 1, 1, LOG(*IPI*)) lag coefficient *t*-value 0).6210, 3.97
1) − .1519, −1.08

(3.47) *HWORK*: Worked hour, total IDENT

$$HWORK = HWCONT + HWOVER$$

(3.48) *LWH*: Labor input

$$\begin{aligned}\mathrm{LOG}(LWH)\\ &= \underset{(2.76)}{4.430} + \underset{(1.68)}{0.08304}\,\mathrm{LOG}(GDP00) - \underset{(-3.83)}{0.3225}\,\mathrm{LOG}(W/PGDP)\\ &\quad + \underset{(7.28)}{0.6772}\,\mathrm{LOG}(LWH_{-1})\end{aligned}$$

Radj = .923 se = .005 DW = 1.74 Sample: From 1996. 2 to 2005. 1 (No. of obs. = 36)

(3.49) *LW*: Labor, employed IDENT

$$LW = LWH/HWORK$$

(3.50) *LS*: Labor, self employed

$$\begin{aligned}\mathrm{LOG}(LS/GDP00) &= \underset{(1.69)}{2.156} - \underset{(-1.71)}{0.6056}\,\mathrm{LOG}(WAGE/PGDP)\\ &\quad + \underset{(28.2)}{0.9656}\,\mathrm{LOG}(LS_{-1}/GDP00_{-1})\end{aligned}$$

Radj = .974 se = .015 DW = 1.72 Sample: From 1996. 2 to 2005. 1 (No. of obs. = 36)

(3.51) *L*: Labor, total IDENT

$$L = LW + LS$$

(3.52) *U*: Unemployed IDENT

$$U = LF - L$$

(3.53) *RU*: Unemployment rate IDENT

$$RU = U/LF * 100$$

(3.54) *W*: Hourly wage (*WAGE*/*HWORK* ∗ 100)

$$\begin{aligned}GR(4, W) &= \underset{(-1.19)}{-2.086} + \underset{(2.53)}{0.9310}\,\mathrm{PDL}(2, 1, 1, GR(4, CPI))\\ &\quad + \underset{(1.15)}{8.774}\,\mathrm{PDL}(2, 1, 1, 1/RU_{-1})\end{aligned}$$

Radj = .442 se = 1.153 DW = 1.04 Sample: From 1996. 2 to 2005. 1 (No. of obs. = 36)

PDL(2, 1, 1, GR(4, CPI))

lag coefficient t-value 0.65901.26 1.2721.55

PDL(2, 1, 1, $1/RU_{-1}$)

lag coefficient t-value 03.0578.10 15.7165.20

(3.55) *WAGE*: Wage per employee ($YW*/LW$) IDENT

$$WAGE = W * HWORK/100$$

(3.56) *YW*: Income of employed IDENT

$$YW = WAGE * LW$$

(3.57) *YRH*: Net propriety income

$$\begin{aligned} &\mathrm{LOG}(YRH/KSH_{-1}) \\ &\quad = \underset{(-2.93)}{-2.269} + \underset{(2.72)}{0.4224}RLB + \underset{(5.76)}{0.6590}\,\mathrm{LOG}(YRH_{-1}/KSH_{-2}) \end{aligned}$$

Radj = .967 se = .065 DW = 2.29 Sample: From 1996. 3 to 2005. 1 (No. of obs. = 35)

(3.58) *YU*: Income of self employed, excluding imputed rent

$$\begin{aligned} &\mathrm{LOG}(YU/LS/GDP00) \\ &\quad = \underset{(-0.358)}{-0.6995} - \underset{(-1.77)}{1.229}\,\mathrm{LOG}(W/PGDP) \\ &\qquad + \underset{(3.33)}{0.5096}\,\mathrm{LOG}(YU_{-1}/LS_{-1}/GDP00_{-1}) \end{aligned}$$

Radj = .468 se = .077 DW = 1.90 Sample: From 1996. 2 to 2005. 1 (No. of obs. = 36)

(3.59) *YSI*: Income of self employed, imputed rent

$$\begin{aligned} &\mathrm{DEL}(1,\ \mathrm{LOG}(YSI)) \\ &\quad = \underset{(4.19)}{0.006240} + \underset{(4.16)}{0.4748}\,\mathrm{DEL}(1,\ \mathrm{LOG}(PIHP * KHP00_{-1})) \end{aligned}$$

Radj = .318 se = .005 DW = 1.77 Sample: From 1996. 2 to 2005. 1 (No. of obs. = 36)

(3.60) *YS*: Income of self employed, total IDENT

$$YS = YU + YSI$$

3.4. *Households sector*

(3.61) *YH*: Households, total receipts IDENT

$$H = YW + YS + YRH + SSBH + SAGH$$

(3.62) *SSBH*: Households, social security benefit

$$\begin{aligned} \text{LOG}(SSBH/POP65) = & -0.7009 + 0.6280\,\text{LOG}(CPI) \\ & (-0.951) \quad (3.14) \\ & + 0.2494\,\text{LOG}(SSBH_{-1}/POP65_{-1}) \\ & \quad (1.59) \end{aligned}$$

Radj = .444 se = .011 DW = 2.42 Sample: From 1996. 2 to 2005. 1 (No. of obs. = 36)

(3.63) *TAXH*: Households, income tax IDENT

$$TAXH = RTAXH/100 * (YH - SSCH)$$

(3.64) *SSCH*: Households, social security contributions

$$\begin{aligned} \text{LOG}(SSCH/L) = & \ 0.1320 + 0.5311\,\text{LOG}(WAGE) \\ & (0.123) \quad (1.76) \\ & + 0.4833\,\text{LOG}(POP65/POP15) \\ & \quad (3.55) \\ & + 0.2877\,\text{LOG}(SSCH_{-1}/L_{-1}) \\ & \quad (1.78) \end{aligned}$$

Radj = .768 se = .019 DW = 2.11 Sample: From 1996. 2 to 2005. 1 (No. of obs. = 36)

(3.65) *YDH*: Households disposable income IDENT

$$YDH = YH - TAXH - SSCH - OTHRH$$

(3.66) *SH*: Households, savings IDENT

$$SH = YDH - CH$$

(3.67) *KSH*: Households, accumulated savings IDENT

$$KSH = SH/4 + KSH_{-1}$$

(3.68) *DEPH*: Households, depreciation

$$DEPH = \underset{(3.00)}{3582.7} + \underset{(3.89)}{0.02401}KHPN_{-1} + \underset{(4.72)}{0.5679}DEPH_{-1}$$

Radj = .984 se = 45.242 DW = .45 Sample: From 1996. 2 to 2005. 1
(No. of obs. = 36)

(3.69) *KHPN*: Households, net residential stock IDENT

$$KHPN = (IHP - DEPH)/4 + KHPN_{-1}$$

(3.70) *BH*: Households, balance IDENT

$$BH = SH + DEPH - IHP$$

(3.71) *KBH*: Households, accumulated balance IDENT

$$KBH = BH/4 + KBH_{-1}$$

(3.72) *YC*: Corporate, income

$$YC = \underset{(0.911)}{10300.7} + \underset{(3.81)}{0.5450}(GNI - DEP - TAXI + SUB - YW - YU)$$
$$\underset{(-2.05)}{-0.07348}RLB * (GNI - DEP - TAXI + SUB - YW - YU)$$

Radj = .278 se = 4855.728 DW = 1.87 Sample: From 1996. 2 to 2005. 1
(No. of obs. = 36)

3.5. *Corporate sector*

(3.73) *TAXC*: Corporate, income tax

$$TAXC = \underset{(0.868)}{2606.1} + \underset{(4.06)}{0.9226}\ \mathrm{PDL}(2, 3, 1, RTC * YC)$$

Radj = .346 se = 1575.168 DW = .74 Sample: From 1997.2 to 2005. 1
(No. of obs. = 32)
PDL(2, 3, 1, $RTC * YC$) lag coefficient t-value:0).0447, .31
1).2768, 4.06 2).3467, 3.81 3).2544, 3.30

(3.74) *SC*: Corporate, savings IDENT

$$SC = YC - TAXC$$

(3.75) *DEPC*: Corporate, depreciation

$$DEPC = -7489.8 + 0.02604\, KFPN_{-1} + 0.8518\, DEPC_{-1}$$
$$(-0.670) \quad (1.19) \qquad\qquad (7.73)$$

Radj = .803 se = 1293.601 DW = 2.15 Sample: From1997. 2 to 2005. 1 (No. of obs. = 32)

(3.76) *KFPN*: Corporate, non-residential stock IDENT

$$KFPN = (IFP - DEPC)/4 + KFPN_{-1}$$

(3.77) *BC*: Corporate, balance IDENT

$$BC = SC + DEPC - IFP - IIP$$

3.6. *Government sector*

(3.78) *TAXIV*: Indirect tax, value add

$$\text{LOG}(TAXIV) = -0.2128 + 0.6658\, \text{LOG}((CP + CG + IHP) * RTCON)$$
$$(-0.220) \quad (9.96)$$

Radj = .760 se = .044 DW = 2.00 Sample: From 1997. 2 to 2005. 1 (No. of obs. = 32)

(3.79) *TAXIO*: Indirect tax, others

$$\text{LOG}(TAXIO) = -4.133 + 0.7654\, \text{LOG}(GDP)$$
$$(-1.16) \quad (2.31)$$
$$+\ 0.4268\, \text{LOG}(TAXIO_{-1})$$
$$(3.00)$$

Radj = .566 se = .020 DW = 2.05 Sample: From 1997. 2 to 2005. 1 (No. of obs. = 32)

(3.80) *TAXI*: Indirect tax total IDENT

$$TAXI = TAXIV + TAXIO$$

(3.81) *YRG*: Government, net propriety income

$$YRG = -3234.7 + 0.001521\, RLBOND_{-1} * KBG_{-1}$$
$$(-2.85) \quad (2.17)$$
$$+\ 0.6240\, YRG_{-1}$$
$$(4.15)$$

Radj = .418 se = 371.903 DW = 2.39 Sample: From 1996. 2 to 2005. 1 (No. of obs. = 36)

(3.82) *SUMG*: Gov. revenue IDENT

$$SUMG = TAXI + TAXH + TAXC + SSCH + YRG + YG$$

(3.83) *SG*: Gov., savings IDENT

$$SG = SUMG - SSBH - SAGH - CG - OEG$$

(3.84) *DEPG*: Government, depreciation

$$\underset{}{DEPG/KGN_{-1}} = \underset{(6.50)}{0.002084} + \underset{(93.9)}{0.9297}\, DEPG_{-1}/KGN_{-2}$$

Radj = .996 se = .000 DW = .45 Sample: From 1996. 3 to 2005. 1 (No. of obs. = 35)

(3.85) *KGN*: Government, nest stock IDENT

$$KGN = (IG - DEPG)/4 + KGN_{-1}$$

(3.86) *BG*: Government, balance IDENT

$$BG = SG + DEPG - IG - IIG$$

(3.87) *KBG*: Government, accumulated balance IDENT

$$KBG = -BG/4 + KBG_{-1}$$

(3.88) *DEP*: Depreciation IDENT

$$DEP = DEPH + DEPC + DEPG$$

3.7. *Financial sector*

(3.89) *M2CD*: Money supply

$$\mathrm{LOG}(M2CD/GDP) = \underset{(3.54)}{0.9467} - \underset{(-3.37)}{0.08750}\, RLB + \underset{(8.30)}{0.7008}\, \mathrm{LOG}(M2CD_{-1}/GDP_{-1})$$

Radj = .991 se = .008 DW = 1.81 Sample: From 1996. 2 to 2005. 1 (No. of obs. = 36)

(3.90) *RCL*: Call rate, overnight

$$RCL = \underset{(2.10)}{0.02863} - \underset{(-2.62)}{0.9037}\, \mathrm{DEL}(4,\ \mathrm{LOG}(M2CD/\mathrm{GDP})) + \underset{(2.46)}{0.5312}\, \mathrm{DEL}(1, RN) + \underset{(23.1)}{0.9454}\, RCL(-1)$$

Radj = .940 se = .045 DW = 1.18 Sample: From 1996. 2 to 2005. 1
(No. of obs. = 36)

(3.91) *RCP*: Commercial paper rate

$$RCP = \underset{(2.39)}{0.05018} + \underset{(6.59)}{1.057}\, RCL + \underset{(1.93)}{0.2192}\, RCP_{-1}$$

Radj = .896 se = .084 DW = 1.64 Sample: From 1996. 2 to 2005. 1
(No. of obs. = 36)

(3.92) *RLB*: Bank loan rate

$$RLB = \underset{(2.91)}{0.1328} - \underset{(-3.37)}{20.01}\, BG/M2CD + \underset{(4.92)}{0.2254}\, RCL + \underset{(36.2)}{0.8567}\, RLB_{-1}$$

Radj = .996 se = .018 DW = 1.58 Sample: From 1996. 2 to 2005. 1
(No. of obs. = 36)

(3.93) *RLPRM*: Long-term prime rate

$$RLPRM = \underset{(1.02)}{0.1587} + \underset{(5.95)}{1.003}\, RLBOND - \underset{(-2.63)}{0.6047}\, RLBOND_{-1}$$
$$+ \underset{(3.52)}{0.5674}\, RLPRM_{-1}$$

Radj = .892 se = .158 DW = 2.00 Sample: From 1996. 2 to 2005. 1
(No. of obs. = 36)

(3.94) *RLBOND*: Government bond yields

$$RLBOND = \underset{(1.33)}{0.4481} - \underset{(-1.86)}{75.87}\, BG_{-1}/M2CD_{-1} + \underset{(2.45)}{0.6909}\, RN$$
$$+ \underset{(3.20)}{0.1609}\, GR(4, CPI) + \underset{(2.43)}{0.4008}\, RLBOND_{-1}$$

Radj = .862 se = .152 DW = 1.64 Sample: From 1997. 2 to 2005. 1
(No. of obs. = 32)

(3.95) *CC*: Capital cost IDENT

$$CC = PIFP * (RLPRM + 8 - GR(4, PIFP))/(1 - RTC)$$

(3.96) *JSA*: Index of Tokyo stock market

$$\begin{aligned}
&\mathrm{LOG}(JSA/KFP00_{-1}/CC)\\
&\quad = \underset{(-2.31)}{-10.00} + \underset{(3.57)}{0.3745}\,\mathrm{LOG}(YC/KFP00_{-1}/CC)\\
&\qquad + \underset{(1.76)}{1.476}\,\mathrm{LOG}(CGPID) + \underset{(3.12)}{0.1325}(URLG10 - RLBOND)\\
&\qquad + \underset{(3.66)}{0.4724}\,\mathrm{LOG}(JSA_{-1}/KFP00_{-2}/CC_{-1})
\end{aligned}$$

Radj = .839 se = .080 DW = .96 Sample: From 1997. 2 to 2005. 1
(No. of obs. = 32)

3.8. *Foreign trade*

(3.97) *PEXUSA*: Export price index, to US

$$\begin{aligned}
&\mathrm{DEL}(1,\ \mathrm{LOG}(PEXUSA))\\
&\quad = \underset{(0.689)}{0.004810} + \underset{(1.67)}{0.9483}\,\mathrm{DEL}(1,\ \mathrm{LOG}(CGPID))\\
&\qquad + \underset{(11.5)}{0.7804}\,\mathrm{DEL}(1,\ \mathrm{LOG}(REX)) + \underset{(2.08)}{0.01913}\,\mathrm{Q1} - \underset{(-0.699)}{0.006506}\,\mathrm{Q2}\\
&\qquad - \underset{(-1.48)}{0.01322}\,\mathrm{Q3}
\end{aligned}$$

Radj = .856 se = .017 DW = 1.67 Sample: From 1997. 2 to 2005. 1
(No. of obs. = 32)

(3.98) *PEXCHINA*: Export price index, to China

$$\begin{aligned}
\mathrm{DEL}(1,\ \mathrm{LOG}(PEXCHINA)) &= \underset{(0.119)}{0.001393} + \underset{(1.48)}{1.409}\mathrm{DEL}(1,\ \mathrm{LOG}(CGPID))\\
&\quad + \underset{(3.47)}{0.3951}\,\mathrm{DEL}(1,\ \mathrm{LOG}(REX)) + \underset{(0.699)}{0.01073}\,\mathrm{Q1}\\
&\quad + \underset{(0.208)}{0.003242}\,\mathrm{Q2} + \underset{(0.725)}{0.01084}\,\mathrm{Q3}
\end{aligned}$$

Radj = .303 se = .028 DW = 1.78 Sample: From 1997. 2 to 2005. 1
(No. of obs. = 32)

(3.99) *PEXNIES*: Export price index, to NIES

$$\begin{aligned}
&\mathrm{DEL}(1,\ \mathrm{LOG}(PEXNIES))\\
&\quad = \underset{(1.21)}{0.008792} + \underset{(3.52)}{2.065}\ \mathrm{DEL}(1,\ \mathrm{LOG}(CGPID))\\
&\qquad + \underset{(5.24)}{0.3671}\ \mathrm{DEL}(1,\ \mathrm{LOG}(REX)) + \underset{(0.413)}{0.003912}\ \mathrm{Q1}\\
&\qquad \underset{(-1.86)}{-0.01795}\ \mathrm{Q2} - \underset{(-0.0989)}{0.0009129}\ \mathrm{Q3}
\end{aligned}$$

Radj = .555 se = .017 DW = 1.62 Sample: From 1997. 2 to 2005. 1
(No. of obs. = 32)

(3.100) *PEXASIA*: Export price index, to Asia

$$\begin{aligned}
&\mathrm{DEL}(1,\ \mathrm{LOG}(PEXASIA))\\
&\quad = \underset{(0.943)}{0.007191} + \underset{(2.54)}{1.575}\ \mathrm{DEL}(1,\ \mathrm{LOG}(CGPID))\\
&\qquad + \underset{(4.90)}{0.3635}\ \mathrm{DEL}(1,\ \mathrm{LOG}(REX)) + \underset{(0.153)}{0.001538}\ \mathrm{Q1} - \underset{(-1.91)}{0.01950}\ \mathrm{Q2}\\
&\qquad + \underset{(0.510)}{0.004986}\ \mathrm{Q3}
\end{aligned}$$

Radj = .492 se = .018 DW = 1.34 Sample: From 1997. 2 to 2005. 1
(No. of obs. = 32)

(3.101) *PEXEU*: Export price index, to EU25

$$\begin{aligned}
\mathrm{LOG}(PEXEU) &= \underset{(3.25)}{1.689} + \underset{(5.36)}{0.3843}\ \mathrm{LOG}(REX) - \underset{(-4.60)}{0.2766}\ \mathrm{LOG}(FXR_\mathrm{EURO})\\
&\quad + \underset{(5.59)}{0.6443}\ \mathrm{LOG}(EUPGDP) + \underset{(1.59)}{0.2298}\ \mathrm{LOG}(PEXEU_{-1})\\
&\quad + \underset{(1.06)}{0.01136}\ \mathrm{Q1} - \underset{(-0.489)}{0.005278}\ \mathrm{Q2} - \underset{(-1.12)}{0.01180}\ \mathrm{Q3}
\end{aligned}$$

Radj = .877 se = .021 DW = 1.65 Sample: From 1997. 2 to 2005. 1
(No. of obs. = 32)

(3.102) *PEX*: Export price index, total

$$
\begin{aligned}
&\mathrm{DEL}(1,\ \mathrm{LOG}(PEX))\\
&\quad = \underset{(2.12)}{0.01172} + \underset{(2.65)}{1.191}\ \mathrm{DEL}(1,\ \mathrm{LOG}(CGPID))\\
&\qquad + \underset{(9.25)}{0.4962}\ \mathrm{DEL}(1,\ \mathrm{LOG}(REX)) + \underset{(0.538)}{0.003899}\ \mathrm{Q1} - \underset{(-3.62)}{0.02662}\ \mathrm{Q2}\\
&\qquad - \underset{(-1.44)}{0.01018}\ \mathrm{Q3}
\end{aligned}
$$

Radj = .777 se = .013 DW = 1.34 Sample: From 1997. 2 to 2005. 1
(No. of obs. = 32)

(3.103) *EXUSA*: Exports, to US, CC base

$$
\begin{aligned}
&\mathrm{LOG}(EXUSA/PEXUSA)\\
&\quad = \underset{(10.5)}{11.53} + \underset{(4.49)}{0.5702}\ \mathrm{SUM}(0,\ 1,\ \mathrm{LOG}(UGDP00))\\
&\qquad - \underset{(-5.37)}{0.7800}\ \mathrm{PDL}(2, 4, 1,\ \mathrm{LOG}(PEXUSA_{-1}/REX_{-1}/UPGDP_{-1}))\\
&\qquad - \underset{(-8.58)}{1.780}\ \mathrm{LOG}(KFDIA_{-1}) - \underset{(-3.76)}{0.05824}\ \mathrm{Q1}\\
&\qquad - \underset{(-3.93)}{0.06181}\ \mathrm{Q2} - \underset{(-1.97)}{0.03073}\ \mathrm{Q3}
\end{aligned}
$$

Radj = .823 se = .033 DW = 1.46 Sample: From 1996. 2 to 2005. 1
(No. of obs. = 36)
PDL(2, 4, 1, LOG($PEXUSA_{-1}/REX_{-1}/UPGDP_{-1}$))
lag coefficient *t*-value : 0) − .2013, −1.23, 1) − .1963, −4.35,
2) − .1736, −2.73, 3) − .1334, −1.47, 4) − .0755, −1.08

(3.104) *EXCHINA*: Exports, to China, CC base

$$
\begin{aligned}
&\mathrm{LOG}(EXCHINA/PEXCHINA)\\
&\quad = \underset{(-2.09)}{-15.49} + \underset{(5.17)}{0.2549}\ \mathrm{SUM}(0,\ 1,\ \mathrm{LOG}(CHINAIM/CHINAPIM))\\
&\qquad + \underset{(2.45)}{1.738}\ \mathrm{LOG}(KFDIA_{-1}) - \underset{(-3.88)}{0.1448}\ \mathrm{Q1} - \underset{(-1.09)}{0.04154}\ \mathrm{Q2} - \underset{(-2.40)}{0.08870}\ \mathrm{Q3}
\end{aligned}
$$

Radj = .964 se = .078 DW = 1.84 Sample: From 1996. 2 to 2005. 1
(No. of obs. = 36)

(3.105) *EXNIES*: Exports, to NIES, CC base

$$\begin{aligned}
&\mathrm{LOG}(EXNIES/PEXNIES)\\
&\quad = \underset{(3.18)}{5.906} + \underset{(9.47)}{1.193}\,\mathrm{LOG}(NIESIM/NIESPIM)\\
&\qquad - \underset{(-2.32)}{0.5943}\,\mathrm{PDL}(2,2,1,\ \mathrm{LOG}(PEXNIES/REX/NIESPIM))\\
&\qquad - \underset{(-2.75)}{0.5559}\,\mathrm{LOG}(KFDIA_{-1}) + \underset{(0.560)}{0.01175}\,\mathrm{Q1} + \underset{(0.199)}{0.003766}\,\mathrm{Q2}\\
&\qquad - \underset{(-0.677)}{0.01228}\,\mathrm{Q3}
\end{aligned}$$

Radj = .943 se = .038 DW = 1.29 Sample: From 1996. 2 to 2005. 1
(No. of obs. = 36)
PDL(2, 2, 1, LOG(*PEXNIES*/*REX*/*NIESPIM*))
lag coefficient t-value :
0) − .2802, −1.27, 1) − .2038, −1.84, 2) − .1104, −.80

(3.106) *EXASEAN*: Exports, to ASEAN, CC base

$$\begin{aligned}
&\mathrm{LOG}(EXASEAN/PEXASIA)\\
&\quad = \underset{(6.63)}{13.05} + \underset{(11.2)}{1.225}\,\mathrm{LOG}(ASEANIM/ASEANPIM)\\
&\qquad - \underset{(-3.51)}{0.8193}\,\mathrm{PDL}(2,2,1,\ \mathrm{LOG}(PEXASIA/REX/ASEANPIM))\\
&\qquad - \underset{(-7.77)}{1.336}\,\mathrm{LOG}(KFDIA_{-1})\\
&\qquad - \underset{(-1.58)}{0.03474}\,\mathrm{Q1} - \underset{(-0.873)}{0.01959}\,\mathrm{Q2} - \underset{(-0.985)}{0.02102}\,\mathrm{Q3}
\end{aligned}$$

Radj = .825 se = .045 DW = .67 Sample: From 1996. 2 to 2005. 1
(No. of obs. = 36)
PDL(2, 2, 1, LOG(*PEXASIA*/*REX*/*ASEANPIM*))
lag coefficient t-value: 0) − .4482, −1.95; 1) − .2603, −2.16;
2) − .1109, −.67

(3.107) *EXEU*: Exports, to EU25 , CC base

$$\begin{aligned}\text{LOG}(EXEU/PEXEU) = & -4.855 + 0.9570\text{SUM}(0, 1, \text{ LOG}(EUGDP95)) \\ & (-1.24) \quad (3.69) \\ & +0.2758 \text{ LOG}(PEXEU/REX/FXR\_EURO/EUPGDP) \\ & \quad (4.24) \\ & -1.908 \text{ LOG}(KFDIA_{-1}) \\ & \quad (-4.78) \\ & -0.02760 \text{ Q1} - 0.03462 \text{ Q2} - 0.05653 \text{ Q3} \\ & \quad (-1.02) \qquad (-1.28) \qquad (-2.10)\end{aligned}$$

Radj = .506 se = .053 DW = .92 Sample: From 1997. 2 to 2005. 1
(No. of obs. = 32)

(3.108) *EXO*: Exports, to others, CC base

$$\begin{aligned}& \text{LOG}(EXO/PEX) \\ & \quad = 0.5384 + 0.7184 \text{ LOG}(WRLDIM/WRLDPIM) \\ & \qquad (0.205) \quad (5.27) \\ & \quad - 2.005 \text{ PDL}(2, 4, 1, \text{ LOG}(PEX_{-1}/REX_{-1}/WRLDPIM_{-1})) \\ & \qquad (-10.1) \\ & \quad - 0.8816 \text{ LOG}(KFDIA_{-1}) + 0.02122 \text{ Q1} - 0.02134 \text{ Q2} \\ & \qquad (-2.94) \qquad\qquad (1.01) \qquad (-1.05) \\ & \quad + 0.05087 \text{ Q3} \\ & \qquad (2.57)\end{aligned}$$

Radj = .834 se = .040 DW = 1.16 Sample: From 1996. 2 to 2005. 1
(No. of obs. = 36)
$\text{PDL}(2, 4, 1, \text{ LOG}(PEX_{-1}/REX_{-1}/WRLDPIM_{-1}))$
lag coefficient t-value : 0) − 1.0261, −4.41, 1) − .6063, −8.31,
2) − .2937, −4.25, 3) − .0885, −.84, 4).0094, .11

(3.109) *EXCC*: Exports, total, CC base IDENT

$$EXCC = EXUSA + EXCHINA + EXNIES + EXASEAN + EXEU + EXO$$

(3.110) *PIM*01: Import price index, foods IDENT

$$PIM01 = PIM01D * REX/107.7675$$

(3.111) *PIM*24: Import price index, materials IDENT

$$PIM24 = PIM24D * REX/107.7675$$

(3.112) *PIM*3: Import price index, mineral fuels

$$\begin{aligned}
&\text{LOG}(PIM3/POILD/REX)\\
&\quad = -3.844 + 0.1142\ \text{LOG}(PCOALD/POILD)\\
&\qquad (-100.3) \quad (14.7)\\
&\qquad + 0.1836\ \text{LOG}(PLNGD/POILD) + 0.008867\ \text{Q1} - 0.001161\ \text{Q2}\\
&\qquad\quad (9.60) \qquad\qquad\qquad\qquad\qquad (1.85) \qquad\qquad (-0.243)\\
&\qquad - 0.007687\ \text{Q3}\\
&\qquad\quad (-1.62)
\end{aligned}$$

Radj = .975 se = .010 DW = 1.28 Sample: From 1996. 2 to 2005. 1 (No. of obs. = 36)

(3.113) *PIM*59: Import price index, other manufactured IDENT

$$PIM59 = PIM59D * REX/107.7675$$

(3.114) *PIM*7: Import price index, machinery, dollar base IDENT

$$PIM7 = PIM7D * REX/107.7675$$

(3.115) *PIM*: Import price index, total

$$\begin{aligned}
&\text{DEL}(1,\ \text{LOG}(PIM))\\
&\quad = 0.0002833 + 0.1352\ \text{DEL}(1,\ \text{LOG}(PIM01))\\
&\qquad (0.329) \qquad (3.57)\\
&\qquad + 0.1532\ \text{DEL}(1,\ \text{LOG}(PIM24)) + 0.1728\ \text{DEL}(1,\ \text{LOG}(PIM3))\\
&\qquad\quad (4.27) \qquad\qquad\qquad\qquad\qquad (16.6)\\
&\qquad + 0.1978\ \text{DEL}(1,\ \text{LOG}(PIM59)) + 0.3271\ \text{DEL}(1,\ \text{LOG}(PIM7))\\
&\qquad\quad (7.44) \qquad\qquad\qquad\qquad\qquad (11.1)
\end{aligned}$$

Radj = .985 se = .005 DW = 2.07 Sample: From 1996. 2 to 2005. 1 (No. of obs. = 36)

(3.116) *MC*01: Imports, foods, CC base

$$\begin{aligned}
&\text{LOG}(MC01/PIM01)\\
&\quad = -0.09379 + 0.3804\ \text{LOG}(CP00)\\
&\qquad (-0.0373) \quad (1.98)\\
&\qquad - 0.4595\ \text{PDL}(2, 3, 1,\ \text{LOG}(PIM01/PCP))\\
&\qquad (-5.77)\\
&\qquad - 0.1130\ \text{Q1} + 0.01372\ \text{Q2} - 0.05099\ \text{Q3}\\
&\qquad (-8.86) \qquad (+1.06) \qquad (-3.99)
\end{aligned}$$

Radj = .817 se = .027 DW = 1.83 Sample: From 1996. 2 to 2005. 1
(No. of obs. = 36)
PDL(2, 3, 1, LOG($PIM01/PCP$))
lag coefficient t-value : 0) − .1181, −1.18; 1) − .1379, −5.78
2) − .1248, −2.23 3) − .0788, −1.49

(3.117) *MC*24: Imports, materials, CC base

$$\begin{aligned}
&\text{LOG}(MC24/PIM24)\\
&\quad = -1.330 + 0.4099\ \text{LOG}(IPI) - 0.1309\text{LOG}(PIM24/CGPID)\\
&\qquad (-1.60) \quad (1.95) \qquad\qquad (-1.90)\\
&\qquad +0.7092\ \text{LOG}(MC24_{-1}/PIM24_{-1})\\
&\qquad (5.85)\\
&\qquad + 0.007780\ \text{Q1} + 0.02659\ \text{Q2} - 0.004302\ \text{Q3}\\
&\qquad (0.475) \qquad (1.61) \qquad (-0.260)
\end{aligned}$$

Radj = .715 se = .034 DW = 1.67 Sample: From 1996. 2 to 2005. 1
(No. of obs. = 36)

(3.118) *MC*3: Imports, mineral fuels, CC base

$$\begin{aligned}
&\text{LOG}(MC3/PIM3/GDP00)\\
&\quad = -9.584 - 0.1098\text{PDL}(2, 6, 1,\ \text{LOG}\ (PIM3_{-2}/PGDP_{-2}))\\
&\qquad (-80.2) \quad (-4.16)\\
&\quad +0.01406\ \text{Q1} - 0.1006\ \text{Q2} - 0.04447\ \text{Q3}\\
&\qquad (0.936) \qquad (-6.70) \qquad (-2.96)
\end{aligned}$$

Radj = .747 se = .028 DW = 1.04 Sample: From 1998. 2 to 2005. 1
(No. of obs. = 28)
PDL(2, 6, 1, LOG($PIM3_{-2}/PGDP_{-2}$))
lag coefficient t-value : 0) − .0262, −1.41, 1) − .0230, −2.67,
2) − .0196, −4.17, 3) − .0161, −2.15, 4) − .0123, −1.31,
5) − .0084, −.94, 6) − .0043, −.74

(3.119) $MC59$: Imports, other manufactured, CC base

$$\begin{aligned}\mathrm{LOG}(MC59/PIM59) &= \underset{(-5.11)}{-35.67} + \underset{(3.35)}{2.204}\,\mathrm{LOG}(GDP00)\\ &\quad \underset{(-11.0)}{-1.408}\mathrm{PDL}\,(2,4,1,\ \mathrm{LOG}(PIM59/CGPID)) + \underset{(4.84)}{0.9853}\,\mathrm{LOG}(KFDIA_{-1})\\ &\quad \underset{(-1.15)}{-0.02500}\,\mathrm{Q1} \underset{(-1.17)}{-0.02696}\,\mathrm{Q2} \underset{(-2.10)}{-0.04735}\,\mathrm{Q3}\end{aligned}$$

Radj = .946 se = .045 DW = 1.25 Sample: From 1996. 2 to 2005. 1
(No. of obs. = 36)
PDL(2, 4, 1, LOG($PIM59/CGPID$))
lag coefficient t-value : 0) − .6234, −5.52, 1) − .4063, −11.34,
2) − .2354, −4.87, 3) − .1107, −1.71, 4) − .0322, −.65

(3.120) $MC7$: Imports, machinery, CC base

$$\begin{aligned}\mathrm{LOG}(MC7/PIM7) &= \underset{(-8.79)}{-49.90} + \underset{(7.13)}{3.608}\,\mathrm{LOG}(GDP00)\\ &\quad \underset{(-5.76)}{-0.6613}\mathrm{PDL}\,(2,2,1,\ \mathrm{LOG}(PIM7/CGPID)) + \underset{(3.97)}{0.5796}\,\mathrm{LOG}(KFDIA_{-1})\\ &\quad \underset{(-3.37)}{-0.05078}\,\mathrm{Q1} \underset{(-1.05)}{-0.01516}\,\mathrm{Q2} + \underset{(1.94)}{0.02807}\,\mathrm{Q3}\end{aligned}$$

Radj = .972 se = .030 DW = 1.08 Sample: From 1996. 2 to 2005. 1
(No. of obs. = 36)
PDL(2, 2, 1, LOG($PIM7/CGPID$))
lag coefficient t-value : 0) − .4178, −2.98,
1) − .1914, −2.60, 2) − .0521, −.48

(3.121) MC: Imports, total, CC base IDENT

$$MC = MC01 + MC24 + MC3 + MC59 + MC7$$

(3.122) *BPEX*: BOP Trade, exports

$$BPEX = \underset{(2.03)}{2501.2} + \underset{(44.0)}{1.000}\,EXCC * 10 - \underset{(-3.29)}{1.147}\,BPSTRNR + \underset{(0.362)}{95.55}\,\mathrm{Q2} + \underset{(1.48)}{411.8}\,\mathrm{Q3}$$

Radj = .997 se = 566.641 DW = .33 Sample: From 1998. 2 to 2005. 1
(No. of obs. = 28)

(3.123) *BPIM*: BOP Trade, imports

$$BPIM = \underset{(1.75)}{+2180.3} + \underset{(74.8)}{0.9661}(MC * 10 - BPSTRNP) + \underset{(0.411)}{149.3}\,\mathrm{Q1} + \underset{(1.39)}{505.8}\,\mathrm{Q3}$$

Radj = .995 se = 783.769 DW = .72 Sample: From 1998. 2 to 2005. 1
(No of obs = 28)

(3.124) *BPT*: BOP Trade, balance IDENT

$$BPT = BPEX - BPIM$$

(3.125) *BPSCARGR*: BOP Services, transport, cargo, credit

$$\begin{aligned}\mathrm{LOG}(BPSCARGR) &= \underset{(-3.86)}{-2.634} + \underset{(3.12)}{0.3406}\,\mathrm{LOG}(BPEX) \\ &\quad + \underset{(2.45)}{0.2001}\,\mathrm{LOG}(BPIM) + \underset{(6.36)}{0.5834}\,\mathrm{LOG}(BPSCARGR_{-1}) \\ &\quad - \underset{(-0.392)}{0.005350}\,\mathrm{Q1} + \underset{(2.90)}{0.04111}\,\mathrm{Q2} + \underset{(2.73)}{0.03710}\,\mathrm{Q3}\end{aligned}$$

Radj = .942 se = .025 DW = 1.87 Sample: From 1998. 2 to 2005. 1
(No. of obs. = 28)

(3.126) *BPSCARGP*: BOP Services, transport, cargo, debit

$$\mathrm{LOG}(BPSCARGP)$$
$$= \underset{(-1.21)}{-1.080} + \underset{(3.57)}{0.3782}\ \mathrm{LOG}(BPIM) + \underset{(5.54)}{0.6364}\ \mathrm{LOG}(BPSCARGP_{-1})$$
$$\underset{(-1.44)}{-0.03671}\ \mathrm{Q1} + \underset{(0.219)}{0.005564}\ \mathrm{Q2} - \underset{(-0.547)}{0.01380}\ \mathrm{Q3}$$

Radj = .833 se = .047 DW = 1.95 Sample: From 1998. 2 to 2005. 1
(No. of obs. = 28)

(3.127) *BPSPASR*: BOP Services, transport, passengers, credit

$$\mathrm{LOG}(BPSPASR/CPI)$$
$$= \underset{(-0.937)}{-0.9034} + \underset{(7.19)}{0.8252}\ \mathrm{LOG}(WRLDIM/WRLDPIM)$$
$$- \underset{(-0.505)}{0.1051}\ \mathrm{LOG}(CPI/WRLDPIM/REX) - \underset{(-0.0192)}{0.0007729}\ \mathrm{Q1}$$
$$- \underset{(-0.494)}{0.02021}\ \mathrm{Q2} + \underset{(5.46)}{0.2217}\ \mathrm{Q3}$$

Radj = .783 se = .073 DW = 1.61 Sample : From 1998.2 to 2005.1
(No. of obs. = 28)

(3.128) *BPSPASP*: BOP Services, transport, passengers, debit

$$\mathrm{LOG}(BPSPASP/UPCP/REX)$$
$$= \underset{(-3.03)}{-38.07} + \underset{(3.80)}{4.026}\ \mathrm{LOG}(CP00)$$
$$- \underset{(-6.38)}{1.988}\ \mathrm{PDL}(2, 1, 3,\ \mathrm{LOG}(UPCP * REX/PCP))$$
$$- \underset{(-1.56)}{0.09888}\ \mathrm{Q1} - \underset{(-0.506)}{0.03222}\ \mathrm{Q2} + \underset{(4.25)}{0.2690}\ \mathrm{Q3}$$

Radj = .667 se = .134 DW = 1.46 Sample: From 1996. 2 to 2005. 1
(No. of obs. = 36)
PDL(2, 1, 3, LOG(*UPCP* ∗ *REX*/*PCP*))lag coefficient *t*-value :
0) − .9942, −6.38, 1) − .9942, −6.38

(3.129) *BPSTRNR*: BOP Services, transport, credit IDENT

$$BPSTRNR = BPSCARGR + BPSPASR$$

(3.130) *BPSTRNP*: BOP Services, transport, debit IDENT

$$BPSTRNP = BPSCARGP + BPSPASP$$

(3.131) *BPSTRVR*: BOP Services, travel, credit

$$\begin{aligned}
&\text{LOG}(BPSTRVR/CPI) \\
&\quad = \underset{(-6.81)}{-23.97} + \underset{(7.97)}{2.019}\,\text{LOG}(WRLDIM/WRLDPIM) \\
&\qquad \underset{(-6.45)}{-4.387}\text{PDL}(2, 3, 1,\ \text{LOG}(CPI/WRLDPIM/REX)) + \underset{(0.568)}{0.06700}\text{Q1} \\
&\qquad + \underset{(0.297)}{0.03621}\ \text{Q2} + \underset{(0.551)}{0.06509}\ \text{Q3}
\end{aligned}$$

Radj = .702 se = .244 DW = .60 Sample: From 1996. 2 to 2005. 1
(No. of obs. = 36)
PDL(2, 3, 1, LOG(*CPI*/*WRLDPIM*/*REX*))lag coefficient *t*-value
0) − 2.0851, −3.02, 1) − 1.3162, −6.45, 2) − .7124, −1.81,
3) − .2737, −.75

(3.132) *BPSTRVP*: BOP Services, travel, debit

$$\begin{aligned}
&\text{LOG}(BPSTRVP/UPCP/REX) \\
&\quad = \underset{(-0.872)}{-10.91} + \underset{(1.74)}{1.842}\ \text{LOG}(CP00) \\
&\qquad \underset{(-5.31)}{-1.650}\,\text{PDL}(2, 1, 3,\ \text{LOG}(UPCP * REX/PCP)) \underset{(-0.725)}{-0.04575}\,\text{Q1} \\
&\qquad \underset{(-1.34)}{-0.08505}\,\text{Q2} + \underset{(1.89)}{0.1193}\,\text{Q3}
\end{aligned}$$

Radj = .509 se = .133 DW = 1.23 Sample: From 1996. 2 to 2005. 1
(No. of obs. = 36)
PDL(2, 1, 3, LOG(*UPCP* ∗ *REX*/*PCP*)) lag coefficient *t*-value:
0) − .8252, −5.32 1) − .8252, −5.32

(3.133) *BPSOTHR*: BOP Services, others credit

$$\begin{aligned}
&\text{LOG}(BPSOTHR/PGDP)\\
&\quad = -5.362 + 0.3716\,\text{LOG}(WRLDIM/WRLDPIM)\\
&\qquad (-3.49) \quad (5.34)\\
&\qquad -1.457\,\text{LOG}(PGDP/WRLDPIM/REX) + 0.1388\,\text{Q1}\\
&\qquad (-8.83) \qquad\qquad\qquad\qquad\qquad\qquad (4.21)\\
&\qquad -0.02534\,\text{Q2} - 0.02083\,\text{Q3}\\
&\qquad\quad (-0.771) \qquad\quad (-0.635)
\end{aligned}$$

Radj = .823 se = .069 DW = .88 Sample: From 1996. 2 to 2005. 1
(No. of obs. = 36)

(3.134) *BPSOTHP*: BOP Services, other, debit

$$\begin{aligned}
&\text{LOG}(BPSOTHP/UPGDP/REX/GDP00)\\
&\quad = -0.4591 - 0.1630\,\text{LOG}(UPGDP * REX/PGDP)\\
&\qquad (-0.830) \quad (-1.38)\\
&\qquad + 0.8383\,\text{LOG}(BPSOTHP_{-1}/UPGDP_{-1}/REX_{-1}/GDP00_{-1})\\
&\qquad\quad (10.0)\\
&\qquad -0.1424\,\text{Q1} - 0.08449\,\text{Q2} - 0.1941\,\text{Q3}\\
&\qquad\quad (-5.35) \qquad (-3.27) \qquad (-7.49)
\end{aligned}$$

Radj = .864 se = .051 DW = 2.45 Sample: From 1996. 2 to 2005. 1
(No. of obs. = 36)

(3.135) *BPSR*: BOP Services, total, credit IDENT

$$BPSR = BPSTRNR + BPSTRVR + BPSOTHR$$

(3.136) *BPSP*: BOP Services, total, debit IDENT

$$BPSP = BPSTRNP + BPSTRVP + BPSOTHP$$

(3.137) *BPS*: BOP Services, balance IDENT

$$BPS = BPSR - BPSP$$

(3.138) *BPYW*: BOP Income, wage, balance IDENT

$$BPYW = BPYWR - BPYWP$$

(3.139) *BPYDR*: BOP Income, direct investment, credit

$$BPYDR/BPKDA_{-1}$$
$$= -0.06208 + 0.007808\,GR(4, REX)$$
$$(-0.726) \quad (5.95)$$
$$+ 0.04076\,URLG10 + 0.07602\,\mathrm{Q1} + 0.05542\,\mathrm{Q2} + 0.03989\,\mathrm{Q3}$$
$$(2.54) \qquad (2.01) \qquad (1.45) \qquad (1.05)$$

Radj = .648 se = .080 DW = 1.14 Sample: From 1996. 2 to 2005. 1
(No. of obs. = 36)

(3.140) *BPYDP*: BOP Income, direct investment, debit

$$BPYDP/BPKDL_{-1} = -0.06664 + 0.09743RLB + 0.06749\,\mathrm{Q1}$$
$$(-0.522) \quad (1.57) \qquad (1.73)$$
$$+ 0.08245\,\mathrm{Q2} + 0.07583\,\mathrm{Q3}$$
$$(2.11) \qquad (1.95)$$

Radj = .130 se = .078 DW = 1.18 Sample: From 1997. 2 to 2005. 1
(No. of obs. = 32)

(3.141) *BPYD*: BOP Income, direct investment, balance IDENT

$$BPYD = BPYDR - BPYDP$$

(3.142) *BPYSR*: BOP Income, decurity investment, credit

$$BPYSR/BPKSA_{-1}$$
$$= 0.004775 + 0.001713\,URLG10$$
$$(0.405) \quad (0.748)$$
$$+ 0.7784\,BPYSR_{-1}/BPKSA_{-2} + 0.03873\,\mathrm{Q1}$$
$$(9.03) \qquad (8.17)$$
$$- 0.0008505\,\mathrm{Q2} + 0.01423\,\mathrm{Q3}$$
$$(-0.176) \qquad (3.11)$$

Radj = .826 se = .009 DW = 2.04 Sample: From 1997. 2 to 2005. 1
(No. of obs. = 32)

(3.143) *BPYSP*: BOP Income, security investment, debit

$$BPYSP/BPKSL_{-1}$$
$$= \underset{(1.06)}{0.006588} + \underset{(1.90)}{0.008410}\, RLBOND$$
$$+ \underset{(8.47)}{0.7421}\, BPYSP_{-1}/BPKSL_{-2} - \underset{(-6.72)}{0.02361}\,\mathrm{Q1} + \underset{(1.38)}{0.004696}\,\mathrm{Q2}$$
$$- \underset{(-7.01)}{0.02590}\,\mathrm{Q3}$$

Radj = .899 se = .007 DW = 2.57 Sample: From 1997. 2 to 2005. 1 (No. of obs. = 32)

(3.144) *BPYS*: BOP Income, security investment, balance IDENT

$$BPYS = BPYSR - BPYSP$$

(3.145) *BPYOR*: BOP Income, other investment, credit

$$BPYOR/BPKOA_{-1}$$
$$= \underset{(-0.996)}{-0.005867} + \underset{(1.12)}{0.002001}\, URLG10$$
$$+ \underset{(9.48)}{0.8508} BPYOR_{-1}/BPKOA_{-2} + \underset{(1.65)}{0.004108}\,\mathrm{Q1}$$
$$+ \underset{(1.40)}{0.003540}\,\mathrm{Q2} + \underset{(1.36)}{0.003363}\,\mathrm{Q3}$$

Radj = .907 se = .005 DW = 2.39 Sample: From 1997. 2 to 2005. 1 (No. of obs. = 32)

(3.146) *BPYOP*: BOP Income, other investment, debit

$$BPYOP/BPKOL_{-1}$$
$$= \underset{(-2.59)}{-0.04372} + \underset{(2.44)}{0.02688}\, RLB + \underset{(5.12)}{0.6555} BPYOP_{-1}/BPKOL_{-2}$$
$$+ \underset{(3.60)}{0.009007}\,\mathrm{Q1} + \underset{(2.06)}{0.005002}\,\mathrm{Q3}$$

Radj = .917 se = .006 DW = 1.89 Sample: From 1997. 2 to 2005. 1 (No. of obs. = 32)

(3.147) *BPYO*: BOP Income, other investment, balance IDENT

$$BPYO = BPYOR - BPYOP$$

(3.148) *BPY*: BOP Income, balance IDENT

$$BPY = BPYW + BPYD + BPYS + BPYO$$

(3.149) *BPC*: BOP balance of current account IDENT

$$BPC = BPT + BPS + BPY + BPTRANS$$

(3.150) *BPKDA*: BOP stock of direct investment. Asset IDENT

$$BPKDA = -BPINVDA/10 + BPKDA_{-1}$$

(3.151) *BPKDL*: BOP stock of direct investment. Liability IDENT

$$BPKDL = BPINVDL/10 + BPKDL_{-1}$$

(3.152) *BPKSA*: BOP stock of security investment, asset IDENT

$$BPKSA = -BPINVSA/10 + BPKSA_{-1}$$

(3.153) *BPKSL*: BOP stock of security investment, liability IDENT

$$BPKSL = BPINVSL/10 + BPKSL_{-1}$$

(3.154) *BPKOA*: BOP stock of other investment, asset IDENT

$$BPKOA = -BPINVOA/10 + BPKOA_{-1}$$

(3.155) *BPKOL*: BOP stock of other investment, liability IDENT

$$BPKOL = BPINVOL/10 + BPKOL_{-1}$$

(3.156) *KFDIA*: Stock of real foreign direct investment IDENT

$$KFDIA = -BPINVDA/10/PIFP + 0.98 * KFDIA_{-1}$$

Chapter 12

The Saito Model of the Japanese Economy

Mitsuo Saito

1. Introduction

This is the summary version of my model[1] with some additional notes to reply L. R. Klein's comments on this work. First, its list of variables and system of equations are given; they are then followed by some notes on the analyses of Japan's long recession in the 90s and the methodology for the model.

2. List of Variables

The number of endogenous variables in the list is 28 and 30 for 1960–1973 and 1974–1993 respectively, equal to the respective numbers of equations in Table 1. The dummy variable for a particular year is denoted by D—, which is 1.0 for year —, and 0 otherwise. For example, D74 means that it is 1.0 for 1974, and 0 otherwise; D923 means that it is 1.0 for 1992 and 93, and 0 otherwise.

3. The System of Equations

All the equations are estimated by the ordinary least squares method. The sample period is in principle 1960–1993. The numbers in parentheses under the coefficients represent the t-ratio, i.e. the estimated values of the coefficients divided by their estimated sampling errors. R^2 is the measure of goodness of fit adjusted for degrees of freedom; D.W. is the Durbin-Watson ratio. The summary of the model structure is presented in Table 2.

[1] Saito, M. (2000). *The Japanese Economy*. WSPC. The model is presented in its Appendix I.

Table 1. List of Variables.

Symbol	Exog.	Definition	Units	Sources
CG	X	General government final consolidated expenditure	Billions of yen in 1985 prices	EPA (1991a) before 1989, (1995) after 1990*.
CP		Private final consumption expenditure	Billions of yen in 1985 prices	**
*D*1	X	Dummy $v. = 1$ for 55–73, and 0 otherwise		
*D*2	X	Dummy $v. = 1$ for 74–93, and 0 otherwise		
DSIG		Difference between savings and investment of general government	Billions of yen in current prices	**
DSIGO	x	Other investment expenditure of general government	Billions of yen in current prices	**
E		Exports of goods and services	Billions of yen in 1985 prices	**
EW		Persons engaged	Thousands of persons	**
*EW**		Desired level of employment	Thousands of persons	Defined by equation (D.1). Tokutsu (1994a).
IG		Gross fixed capital formation, general government	Billions of yen in 1985 prices	**
IHOG	*x*	Gross fixed capital formation, public residential buildings and producers' durables	Billions of yen in 1985 prices	**
IHP		Gross fixed capital formation, private residential buildings	Billions of yen in 1985 prices	**
IOP		Gross fixed capital formation, private producers' durables	Billions of yen in 1985 prices	**
IPUB	*x*	Gross fixed capital formation, public total	Billions of yen in 1985 prices	**
J	*x*	Increase in stocks	Billions of yen in 1985 prices	**

(*Continued*)

Table 1. ***(Continued)***

Symbol	Exog.	Definition	Units	Sources
K		Year-end stock of private producers' durables	Billions of yen in 1985 prices	The series in calendar year in EPA (1991b) for 1955–1970; EPA (1992a) for 1971–1989; extended by *IOP* and a fixed removal ratio for 1989–1993.
K^*		Desired year-end stock of private producers' durables	Billions of yen in private producers' 1985 prices	Defined by equation (E.5). Coefficients: Tokutsu (1994a).
KHP		Year-end stock of residential buildings	Billions of yen in private producers' 1985 prices	Compiled by the formula: KHP_{-1} $(1-0.02)+IHP$. Benchmark in 1970 for *KHP* from Prime Minister's Office (1974).
LF	*x*	Labor force	Thousands of persons	Labor Force Survey, Management and Coordination Agency (1994).
LLBG		Balance of government long-term bonds	Billions of yen in current prices	**
LLBGO	*x*	Increase in the balance of government long-term bonds, excluding *DSIG*	Billions of yen in current prices	Defined by equation (G.4).
LP	*x*	Private year-end balance of Financial assets	Billions of yen in current prices	**#1
M	*x*	Year-end stock of money	Billions of yen in current prices	**#2
MP		Imports of goods and services	Billions of yen in 1985 prices	**
N		Population	Thousands of persons	Labor Force Survey, Management and Coordination Agency (1994).
NETE		Net exports of goods and services	Billions of yen in 1985 constant	Defined by equation (G.6).
PCG		Deflator for *CG*	1985 = 1.0	**
PCP		Deflator for *CP*	1985 = 1.0	**
PEG		Deflator for *E*	1985 = 1.0	**

(Continued)

Table 1. ***(Continued)***

Symbol	Exog.	Definition	Units	Sources
PE		Price of energy	1985 = 1.0	Tokutsu (1994a).
PIG		Deflator for *IG*	1985 = 1.0	**
PIOP		Deflator for *IOP*	1985 = 1.0	**
PMP		Deflator for *MP*	1985 = 1.0	**
PNEG		Price of non-energy materials	1985 = 1.0	Tokutsu (1994a).
PV		Deflator for *V*	1985 = 1.0	**
*PV**		Deflator for *V* demanded by firms	1985 = 1.0	Defined by equation (P.1). Coefficients from Tokutsu (1994a).
PWT	*x*	Price index for *WT*	1985 = 1.0	United Nations (1995b).
RATE	*x*[1]	Exchange rate	yen/dollar	#3
RBOND		Bond yields	Decimal	The average of monthly data. Government bonds 10 years, benchmark, listed on Tokyo Stock Exchange, BOJ (1994).
RDHP	*x*	Removal ratio for *KHP*	Decimal	=0.02. Defined by (removals of housing stock)/KHP_{-1}.
RIOPD	*x*	Discrepancy ratio in private producers' durables between SNA and capital stock series	Decimal	= (private producers'durables in capital stock Series)-I0P/IOP.
RK	*x*	Removals of *K*	Billions of yen in 1985 prices	The same as K.
RUS	*x*	US treasury bill rate	decimal	IMF (1997).
SG		(3 months) saving of general government	Billions of yen in current prices	**
TI	*x*	Time trend	1960 = 1.0	
T2	*x*	Time trend	1974 = 1.0	=0.0 for 1959–1973.
UN		Unemployment rate	%	Labor Force Survey, Management and Coordination Agency (1994).
V		Gross domestic product	Billions of yen, in 1985 prices	**
W		Wage rate	Millions of yen per person	**Defined by (Compens. of employees)/(the number of employees).

(Continued)

Table 1. (*Continued*)

Symbol	Exog.	Definition	Units	Sources
WT	*X*	World trade index	1985 = 1.0	United Nations (1995b).
YDP		Private disposable income	Billions of yen in 1985 prices	**(Disposable income of house-holds and non-profit institute serving house-holds)/PCP.

*EPA means Economic Planning Agency, now it is a part of Cabinet Office.
**means the same source as the one in the first row.
#1 Defined by ((balances of financial assets) − (balances of liabilities)): households and non-profit institutions serving households. #2 Defined by the sum of holdings of currency, demand deposits and other deposits: households, non-profit institutions serving households and non-financial incorporated enterprises. #3 The average of monthly data. Inter-bank rates, spot, on transaction with the largest volume, average of period, Bank of Japan (1995) before 1993, Bank of Japan (1998) after 1994 X' Endogenous for 1974–1993.

Table 2. The Summary of the Model.

Sectors	No. of Equations		
	(1) Stochastic	(2) Definitional	(3) Total
	1. 1960–1973: Sectors 1–4		
1. Expenditure (E.1)–(E.9)	5	4	9
2. Distribution (D.1)–(D.5)	4	1	5
3. Price formation (P.1)–(P.8)	7	1	8
4. Government, banks and external balances (G.1)–(G.6)	2	4	6
Total: Sectors 1–4	18	10	28
	2. 1974–1993: Sectors 1–5		
5. Additions for 1974–1993 (A.1)–(A.2)	2	0	2
Total: Sectors 1–5	20	10	30

Most equations are estimated for the two sub-periods: 1960–1973 and 1974–1993. Since the specification of an equation (e.g. the consumption function) is the same for both periods, the estimated equations in the list are shown by using dummy variables, Dl and 02: Dl (D2) is 1 (0) for the former half of the sample period and 0 (1) for the latter half.

3.1. *The expenditure sector*

(E.1) $V = CP + CG + IHP + IOP + IPUB + J + E - MP$

(E.2) $LOG(CP/N)$

$$= \underset{(-1.63)}{(-0.0480D1} - \underset{(-1.72)}{0.0735D2)} + \underset{(3.23)}{(0.3601Dl} + \underset{(3.18)}{0.4429D2)}\text{LOG}(YDP/N)$$

$$+ \underset{(2.22)}{(0.0486D1} + \underset{(3.18)}{0.1123D2)}\text{LOG}(LP_{-1}/PCP/N) + \underset{(3.80)}{(0.5231D1}$$

$$+ \underset{(2.44)}{0.3025D2)}\text{LOG}(CP_{-1}/N_{-1}) - \underset{(-4.16)}{0.0329D74}$$

$R^2 = 0.999$, $D.W. = 0.91$ for 1956–1993; $R^2 = 0.997$, $D.W. = 1.84$ for 1974–1993.

(E.3) $\text{LOG}(KHP/N)$

$$= \underset{(10.7)}{(0.0804D1} + \underset{(11.4)}{0.0957D2)} + \underset{(14.6)}{(0.1253D1} + \underset{(3.80)}{0.1790D2)}\text{LOG}(YDP/N)_{-1}$$

$$+ \underset{(-1.91)}{(-0.143OD1} - \underset{(-2.14)}{0.1934D2)}RBOND + \underset{(97.5)}{(0.8729D1} + \underset{(28.3)}{0.7895D2)}\text{LOG}(KHP/N)$$

$$+ \underset{(3.09)}{(0.0264D2)}\text{LOG}(LP.llPCPIN) - \underset{(-1.47)}{0.0095D63} - \underset{(-1.48)}{0.0092D85} - \underset{(-1.28)}{0.0060D923}$$

$R^2 = 0.999$, $D.W. = 1.29$ for 1960–1993; $R^2 = 0.999$, $D.W. = 1.69$ for 1971–1993

(E.4) $IHP = KHP - (1.0 - RDHP_{-1})KHP_{-1}$

(E.5) $\text{LOG}(K^*) = \text{LOG}(V) - 0.3021\text{LOG}(PIOP(RBOND + 0.035)/0.098656)$
$+ 0.0962\text{LOG}(W) + 0.0130\text{LOG}(PEG) + 0.1928\text{LOG}(PNEG)$

(E.6) $$\text{LOG}(K) = \underset{(-3.10)}{(-0.2822D1} - \underset{(-0.33)}{0.1210D2)} + \underset{(6.33)}{(0.208801} + \underset{(0.79)}{0.0885D2)}\text{LOG}(K^*)$$

$$+ \underset{(31.6)}{(0.8220D1} + \underset{(11.0)}{0.9279D2)}\text{LOG}(K_{-1}) - \underset{(-0.26)}{(0.0050D92} + \underset{(-0.95)}{0.0182D93)}$$

$R^2 = 0.999$, $D.W. = 1.11$ for 1956–1993; $R^2 = 0.998$, $D.W. = 1.39$ for 1973–1993

(E.7) $IOP_{-1} = (K - (K \cdot 1 - RK)/(1.0 + RIOPD)$

(E.8) $$\text{LOG}(MP) = \underset{(-1.15)}{-0.7609} + \underset{(2.72)}{0.3425}\text{LOG}(Vj + \underset{(7.30)}{0.6631}\text{LOG}(MP_{-1}))$$

$$- \underset{(-3.89)}{0.2267}\text{LOG}(PMP/PV) - \underset{(-2.06)}{0.1269D86} - \underset{(-2.69)}{0.1126D913}$$

$R^2 = 0.993$, $D.W. = 2.52$ for 1960–1993

$$\text{(E.9)}\quad LOG(E) = \underset{(-5.22)}{(-5.2148D1} + \underset{(3.98)}{3.0504D2)} + \underset{(37.7)}{(1.7547D1} + \underset{(27.5)}{1.2757D2)}LOG(WT)$$
$$+ \underset{(0.40)}{(0.2094D1} + \underset{(1.78)}{0.2031D2)}LOG(PWT \cdot RATE/PE) + \underset{(3.48)}{(1.4466D1}$$
$$+ \underset{(10.6)}{0.6244D2)}LOG(PWT \cdot RATE/PE)_{-1} + \underset{(3.50)}{(1.3768D1}$$
$$+ \underset{(8.00)}{0.5561D2)}LOG(PWT \cdot RATE/PE)_{-2} + \underset{(2.53)}{0.1135D85} - \underset{(-2.99)}{0.1170D923}$$

$R^2 = 0.994$, $D.W. = 1.61$ for 1960–1973; $R^2 = 0.986$, $D.W. = 1.75$ for 1974–93

3.2. *The distribution sector*

$$\text{(D.1)}\quad LOG(EW*) = LOG(V) + 0.4114LOG(PV/W) - 0.5886(0.0728T1 - 0.0438T2)$$

$$\text{(D.2)}\quad LOG(EW) = \underset{(5.77)}{0.3989} + \underset{(2.63)}{0.0660}LOG(EW*) + \underset{(35.0)}{0.8967}LOG(EW_{-1})$$
$$- \underset{(-1.76)}{0.0089D72} + \underset{(1.75)}{0.0088D73} - \underset{(-2.52)}{0.0129D74} + \underset{(3.64)}{0.0119D8991}$$

$R^2 = 0.999$, $D.W. = 1.86$ for 1956–1993

$$\text{(D.3)}\quad \Delta W/W_{-1} = \underset{(-3050)}{(-0.8272D1} - \underset{(-2.39)}{1.2601D2)} + \underset{(1.36)}{(0.4036D1}$$
$$+ \underset{(4.48)}{0.4411D2)}(\Delta PCP_{-1}/PCP_{-2} + \underset{(3.81)}{(0.9074D1} + \underset{(2.44)}{1.2561D2)}(EW/LF)$$
$$- \underset{(-1.76)}{0.0170D637} + \underset{(2.98)}{0.0531D73} + \underset{(10.6)}{0.1421D74} - \underset{(-4.07)}{0.0329D923}$$

$R^2 = 0.804$, $D.W. = 0.97$ for 1957–1973; $R^2 = 0.967$, $D.W. = 1.03$ for 1974–1993

$$\text{(D.4)}\quad UN = \underset{(0.98)}{(3.9111D1} + \underset{(1.86)}{17.9319D2)} + \underset{(-0.91)}{(-3.2599D1} - \underset{(-1.80)}{15.9465D2)}(EW/LF)$$
$$+ \underset{(2.73)}{(0.5879D1} + \underset{(1.66)}{0.3758D2)}UN.$$

$R^2 = 0.796$, $D.W. = 1.80$ for 1956–1973; $R^2 = 0.780$, $D.W. = 1.15$ for 1974–1993

$$\text{(D.5)}\quad PCP \cdot YDP = \underset{(2.24)}{(669.2736D1} + \underset{(7.67)}{17861.947D2)} + \underset{(108.8)}{(0.6509D1} + \underset{(86.6)}{0.6366D2)}V \cdot PV$$

$R^2 = 0.998$, $D.W. = 0.75$ for 1955–1973; $R^2 = 0.997$, $D.W. = 0.56$ for 1974–1993

3.3. *The price sector*

(P.1) $\text{LOG}(PV*) = 0.3184(\text{LOG}(W) - 0.5886\{0.0728T1 - 0.0439T2)/0.4114\} + 0.0430\text{LOG}(PEG) + 0.6382\text{LOG}(PENG)$

(P.2)
$$\underset{}{\text{LOG}(PV)} = (\underset{(15.8)}{0.4231D1} + \underset{(2.05)}{0.0643D2}) + (\underset{(13.0)}{0.7280D1} + \underset{(2.00)}{0.3547D2})\text{LOG}(PP) + (\underset{(2.84)}{0.6634D1} + \underset{(23.2)}{0.5635D2})\text{LOG}(PV_{-1}) + \underset{(5.32)}{0.0511D08693}$$

$R^2 = 0.999$, $D.W. = 1.93$ for 1960–1973; $R^2 = 0.991$, $D.W. = 1.52$ for 1974–1993.

(P.3)
$$\text{LOG}(PCP) = (\underset{(5.75)}{0.2830D1} + \underset{(2.67)}{0.0804D2}) + (\underset{(4.12)}{0.4800D1} + \underset{(2.46)}{0.4296D2})\text{LOG}(PV^*) + (\underset{(13.1)}{0.7868D1} + \underset{(6.91)}{0.5925D2})\text{LOG}(PCP_{-1}) + \underset{(2.79)}{0.0477D8693}$$

$R^2 = 0.998$, $D.W. = 1.84$ for 1960–1973; $R^2 = 0.994$, $D.W. = 1.17$ for 1974–1993

(P.4)
$$\text{LOG}(PI0P) = (\underset{(1.04)}{0.0353D1} + \underset{(5.38)}{0.1349D2}) + (\underset{(7.24)}{0.4583D1} + \underset{(5.80)}{0.6760D2})\text{LOG}(PV^*) + (\underset{(5.59)}{0.3919D1} + \underset{(2.13)}{0.1773D2})\text{LOG}(PIOP_{-1}) + \underset{(3.30)}{0.0576D73} - \underset{(-3.16)}{0.0313D923}$$

$R^2 = 0.983$, $D.W. = 1.86$ for 1960–1973; $R^2 = 0.975$, $D.W. = 1.23$ for 1974–1993

(P.5)
$$\text{LOG}(PCG) = \underset{(3.34)}{0.3828D1} + \underset{(0.74)}{0.0310D2} + (\underset{(1.74)}{0.3275D1} + \underset{(0.74)}{0.1603D2})\text{LOG}(PV^*) + (\underset{(19.6)}{0.9719D1} + \underset{(6.37)}{0.6736D2})\text{LOG}(PCG_{-1}) + \underset{(2.60)}{0.0656D8793}$$

$R^2 = 0.998$, $D.W. = 1.40$ for 1956–1973; $R^2 = 0.983$, $D.W. = 1.02$ for 1974–1993

(P.6)
$$\text{LOG}(PIG) = (\underset{(10.4)}{0.3526D1} + \underset{(2.64)}{0.1589D2}) + (\underset{(11.3)}{0.9950D1} + \underset{(2.67)}{0.8083D2})\text{LOG}(PV^*) + (\underset{(4.86)}{0.3237D1} + \underset{(2.11)}{03368D2})\text{LOG}(PIG_{-1}) + \underset{(3.12)}{0.0804D8793}$$

$R^2 = 0.993$, $D.W. = 1.13$ for 1956–1973; $R^2 = 0.967$, $D.W. = 1.40$ for 1974–1993

(P.7)
$$\text{LOG}(PE) = (\underset{(-1.40)}{-0.1166D1} + \underset{(0.85)}{0.0436D2}) + (\underset{(2.21)}{0.1994D1} + \underset{(0.97)}{0.1821D2})\text{LOG}(PV^*) + (\underset{(1.42)}{0.3983D1} + \underset{(2.10)}{0.3157D2})\text{LOG}(PE_{-1}) + \underset{(3.73)}{0.0691D73} - \underset{(-4.77)}{0.1655D8693}$$

$R^2 = 0.927$, $D.W. = 1.42$ for 1960–1973; $R^2 = 0.828$, $D.W. = 0.93$ for 1974–1993

(P.8) $$\mathrm{LOG}(PNEG) = (\underset{(-6.79)}{0.7873D1} - \underset{(-0.19)}{0.0021D2}) + (\underset{(6.06)}{0.7959D1} + \underset{(2.46)}{0.1288D2})\mathrm{LOG}(PMP)$$
$$+ (\underset{(14.5)}{0.8363D1} + \underset{(6.26)}{0.4944D2})\mathrm{LOG}(PNEG_{-1}) + \underset{(2.17)}{0.0535D8693}$$

$R^2 = 0.984$, $D.W. = 1.62$ for 1960–1973; $R^2 = 0.911$, $D.W. = 1.18$ for 1974–1993

3.4. *Government, banks and external balances*

(G.1) $$SG + PCGCG = (\underset{(41.3)}{0.1488D1} + \underset{(19.5)}{0.1977D2})(PV \cdot V) - \underset{(-2.09)}{435.9D1} - \underset{(-4.70)}{15101.1D2}$$

$R^2 = 0.992$, $DW = 0.93$ for 1960–1973; $R^2 = 0.952$, $D.W. = 0.40$ for 1974–1993

(G.2) $DSIG = SG - PIG \cdot IG - DISGO$

(G.3) $IPUB = IG + IHOG$

(G.4) $LLBG = LUG_{-1} + LLBGO - DSIG$

(G.5) $$\mathrm{LOG}(M/PV) = \underset{(-0.17)}{-0.0472} + \underset{(2.43)}{0.1496}\mathrm{LOG}(V) - \underset{(-3.46)}{0.8713RBOND}$$
$$+ \underset{(21.7)}{0.8673}\mathrm{LOG}(MIPV)_{-1} + \underset{(3.63)}{0.0627D61} - \underset{(-3.40)}{0.0660D74} + \underset{(2.50)}{0.0344D923}$$

$R^2 = 0.999$, $D.W. = 2.02$ for 1960–1993

(G.6) $NETE = PE \cdot E - PMP \cdot MP$

3.5. *Additions to the model, 1974–1993*

(A.1) $$\mathrm{LOG}(PMP) = \underset{(-16.6)}{-6.8651} + \underset{(22.3)}{1.3542}\mathrm{LOG}(PWT) + \underset{(8.05)}{0.9274}\mathrm{LOG}(RATE)$$
$$+ \underset{(2.41)}{0.3128}\mathrm{LOG}(RATE_{-1})$$

$R^2 = 0.962$, $D.W. = 1.57$ for 1971–1993.

(A.2) $$\mathrm{LOG}(RATE) = \underset{(2.84)}{1.6087} - \underset{(3.38)}{0.5858}\mathrm{LOG}(E \cdot PE/MP \cdot PMP) - \underset{(-1.75)}{0.0642D8693} \cdot$$
$$(\mathrm{LOG}(RBOND/RUS) + 2.3026) + \underset{(6.98)}{0.7180RATE_{-1}} - \underset{(-3.35)}{0.2667D80} + \underset{(1.11)}{0.0934D85}$$

$R^2 = 0.952$, $D.W. = 1.78$ for 1971–1993

4. Final Test

The explanatory effectiveness of the model as a dynamic system may be examined by the final test: a comparison of a dynamic simulation of the model with actual sample observations.[2] The test was executed for two sub-periods: 1960–1973 and 1974–1993 and summarized in Table 3.

It is seen from the panel for 1960–1973 of the table that the average absolute percentage error is 3.2% for GDP and 2.6% for the GDP deflator. It is of almost the same order for most other variables, but it is higher for private fixed investment, 14.0%, and private residential construction, 11.0%. It can also be observed from the panel for 1974–1993 that the average absolute percentage errors of the real variables are almost comparable with those for 1960–1973, although those of the price variables are higher by about 1–3 points than those for 1960–1973. By and large one can say that the model works tolerably well.

5. D.W. Ratios in the Model

In our system, about 20% of estimated equations have D.W. ratios of less than unity. Many econometricians may consider this too many and re-estimate them by using the de-trended series. It is important, however, not to neglect the information contained in the time-series with trends particularly in the model like mine that deals with the growing economy. In this model whose main objectives are to see the simulation results with some new policies, the final test findings mentioned above are more important than D.W. ratios. They were primarily meant for evaluating the statistical inference for single equation estimators, whereas macroeconometric models are in principle a system of simultaneous equations. For these reasons, we kept some equations, like government sector's with institutional restrictions and technology progress functions with trends, as they are estimated by OLS with original time-series. As a result, they have high D.W. ratios.[3]

[2]See Saito, M. *op. cit.*, pp. 129–130.

[3]Similar ideas to retain the information in the time-series with trends were explored by some econometricians in the late 90s. See the following:

Hatanaka, M. and H. Yamada, (2003). *Co-Trending: A Statistical System Analysis of Economic Trends*, Springer-Verlag; Hendry D. F. and M. Massmann (2007). Co-Breaking: Recent Advances and a Synopsis of Literature, *Journal of Business and Economic Literature*, 25, 33–51.

Table 3. Summary of the Final Test of the Model (Unit: Decimal).

The measure of errors	(1) VGDP	(2) CP Private consumption	(3) IOP Private fixed invest.	(4) IHP Private residen. constr.	(5) E Exports of goods & services	(6) MP Imports of goods & services	(7) PV GDP deflator	(8) PCP Private consoli-dated deflator	(9) PIOP Priv. fixed invest. deflator	(10) W Wage	(11) RBOND Interest rate	(12) EW Persons engaged	(13) RATE Exchange rate
1960–1973													
Error in the average growth rate[a]	0.0007	−0.0019	0.0050	−0.0087	0.0093	−0.0083	−0.0013	−0.0015	−0.0007	−0.0028	—	0.0002	—
Average absolute percent-age error[b]	0.032	0.035	0.140	0.110	0.043	0.050	0.026	0.028	0.014	0.049	0.014[c]	0.004	—
1974–1993													
Error in the average growth rate[a]	0.0023	0.0019	0.0060	0.0143	−0.0037	0.0017	−0.0021	−0.0026	−0.0018	−0.0023	—	−0.0003	0.0006
Average absolute percent-age error[b]	0.031	0.033	0.104	0.142	0.100	0.044	0.036	0.045	0.034	0.076	0.023[c]	0.010	0.086

[a] $G(Y_T) - G(\hat{Y}_T)$, where $G(Y_T)$ and $G(\hat{Y}_T)$ are the average growth rate of actual and computed values of variable Y over T years respectively. T is the number of years of the sample period; i.e. T is 14 for 1960–1973, and 20 for 1974–1993.

[b] $(1/T)\sum_{t=1}^{T} |Y_t - \hat{Y}_t|/|Y_t|$, where Y_t and $\hat{Y}_t$ are the actual and computed values of variable Y in year t respectively.

[c] $(1/T)\sum_{t=1}^{T} |Y_T - \hat{Y}_T|$ (decimal)

6. Changes in the Foreign Exchange Rate and their Effects

In the middle of our sample period, a number of significant changes hit the Japanese economy. We have analyzed those with our model simulations. First, the foreign exchange rate became flexible in the 1970s. The effects of this shift on the performance of the Japanese economy are of great interest and analyzed for the short-term and the long-term.

(i) *Long-term effect* is calculated by the simulation analysis. In summary, the exchange rate between the US dollar and yen rose from ¥280/$ to ¥102/$ between 1973 and 1990, and it brought down the average growth rate of GDP by 1.87%.[4]
(ii) *Short-term effect* is shown. The effect of a 10% weakening of the exchange rate on GDP growth *vis-à-vis* the 1985 control solution is continuously negative for four years and then positive for three years. It is cyclical.[5]

Between 1986 and 1997 the actual values of the foreign exchange rate showed an increase of 10% or more for four years and a decrease of 10% or more for two years, indicating that the effects of business cycles must have been fairly large. I have shown the comparison of the simulation findings on cyclical periods and amplitudes with respect to the actual observations.[6]

This seems to suggest that the J-curve effect is an important reason for elongating the recession period. yen revaluation in 1985 accompanied the favorable current balance — the J-curve effect. Besides, the lag effect makes the adjustment period longer. To estimate the J-curve effects, quarterly models would be more appropriate.

7. Effects of Oil Crisis

Second, two oil crises hit the Japanese economy. Their analysis was done by a comparison between the control solution for 1974–1990 and the hypothetical solution with no oil price hike. It is shown that during the simulation

Hendry and Massmann (2007) deals with the same problems as Hatanaka and Yamada (2003). Since the 1990s, some new methods have been proposed by Christopher Sims, C. Granger, P. Phillips and others to re-estimate the equations with high serial correlations. To my knowledge they have not been used for macroeconometric models yet. I could not make use of those new methods.

[4] See Table 7.5 (column 1, row II) and its exposition on p. 184 of Chap. 7 in Saito (2000).

[5] See Table 8.8, p. 241 in Saito (2000).

[6] On pp. 240–241 and Table 8.2, p. 210 in Saito (2000).

period of 17 years the average GDP growth rate declined by 0.23% due to the oil shock.[7] It indicates that the once-for-all oil shock did not have a significant effect on the average growth rate of GDP, particularly on the recession in the 1990s. Needless to say, the short-term impacts were very large as the figures in 1974 through 1977 demonstrated.

8. An Analysis of the Low Rate of Growth in the 1990s

A very important issue of my study was to clarify quantitatively the factors for rapid growth before the oil crises and those for slow growth afterward through the medium of macroeconometric models. A methodological characteristic of the book was to explain economic growth by exogenous variables as much as possible. One of its conclusions was that the high average growth rate of GDP in 1960–1973 at 9.47% can almost be explained by the contribution of demographic growth: 3.76% and that of the rate of technological progress: 5.56%.[8] In the 1990s, both of these factors decreased dramatically: the former by very low birth rates and the latter by having caught up with the advanced economies and thereby losing the opportunities of learning or obtaining the ready-made advanced technologies. In addition, the effect of yen revaluation in the international economy was also not negligible, as we mentioned above. They are factors that explain the low growth in the lost 1990s.

In concrete terms, the simulation analysis[9] shows that the drop of the GDP growth rate down to 3.9% in 1974–1990 can be attributed to the rise in oil price, yen revaluation, and the decline of technological progress shown by their respective quantitative estimates. In the 1990s a milder yen revaluation took place, and a further decline in the rate of population growth as well as the rate of technological progress also continued, so that it was plausible that 3.9% dropped further by 2.5% to 1.5%.

---

[7]See Table 7.5 on p. 184 in Saito (2000). The figure of column (1), row (1) + 0.23% implies it. The detailed exposition is given in Chap. 7, Sec. 3, pp. 173–176, and the annual figures estimated are given in Table 7.2, p. 176 in Saito (2000).

[8]It is given on pp. 151–152 in Saito (2000).

[9]It is shown in Chap. 7, Sec. 5, Table 7.5, p. 184 in Saito (2000).

Chapter 13

High Frequency Model vs. Consensus Forecast

Yoshihisa Inada

1. Introduction

Macroeconometric models have played an important role in making the economic forecast and evaluating the policy effects for many years. Since around the time of oil crisis, however, their accuracy and reliability have become controversial, and even their methodologies were questioned as the discussions on time series vs. structural models showed. Nevertheless, in practice, more frequent forecasts were demanded not only by the government but also private corporations, as corporate accounting has been shifting from annual to semi-annual or quarterly basis. No alternative methods have been offered to satisfy such practical needs for forecast and policy evaluation. L. R. Klein's High Frequency Model (HF model) gave one answer to this demand for more frequent and accurate forecast.

Since 1993 we have applied his HF model in Japan and continued the forecast on weekly basis to improve the accuracy of our previous quarterly forecasts. Our records at Kansai Institute of Social Economic Research (KISER) since fiscal year 2005 confirm improvement in the forecast accuracy. This chapter purports to report the forecast accuracy of HF model in comparison with the semi-official *consensus forecast*. Next, Section 2 explains and examines first the *consensus forecast*. Section 3 explains the features of HF model in detail. Section 4 compares the features of the forecasts by the two methods and examines their performances in the most recent financial crisis. Lastly, Section 5 gives some concluding remarks.

2. Consensus Forecast

The so-called *consensus forecast* is a survey of professional forecasters and has a long tradition in the US but relatively recent in Japan for forecasting quarterly the growth rates of real GDP and its main components. According to the research that uses the data of the US,[1] up to now the *consensus forecast* has shown an excellent performance in comparison with an individual economist's. It is not just the average of the forecasts of individual economists. Given appropriate weights in combining the individual forecasts, it performs not only unexpectedly well but better. In Japan, the announcement of *consensus forecast* is more recent, so that its content and performance are examined below.

2.1. *ESP forecast survey*

The Economic Planning Association affiliated with Cabinet Office investigates and releases the private economists' macro forecasts every month. It is called the "Economy Society Policy Forecast survey" (ESPF). The *consensus forecast* is announced at the same time as the mean value of the individual economists' forecasts in ESPF (*http://www.epa.or.jp/esp/fcst/fcst.html*). 37 private economists participate in this ESPF in strict anonymity. It was started, after a trial in April 2004, in full scale in May 2004 and has continued until now. The Economic Planning Association questions each private economist on the investigation items of annual forecast (corresponding fiscal year and next year) and the quarterly forecast (until the final quarter of next year). It questions also on the real GDP growth rate for fiscal year. The seasonally-adjusted real GDP growth rate (annualized), the CPI inflation rate, and the unemployment rate are questioned on quarterly basis. In ESPF, the time limit for participating forecasters to supply the forecast every month is set around the fifth, and the result is announced around the tenth. Thus, they can factor in the information of economic indicators announced before the end of last month or at the beginning of this month, to update their forecasts every month.

In this section, however, our examination of the forecast accuracy of quarterly real GDP growth rates is limited to the current quarter concerned, not until the final quarter of the next year, because in the next section the HF model forecast deals with economic growth in the current and the next quarter so as to avoid complex and lengthy comparisons.

2.2. *Forecast errors*

The errors of the *consensus forecast* for the real GDP growth rate from April–June 2004 to January–March 2008 are shown in Figure 1. If we

[1] Diebold and Lopez (1996), Armstrong (2001), and Timmermann (2006).

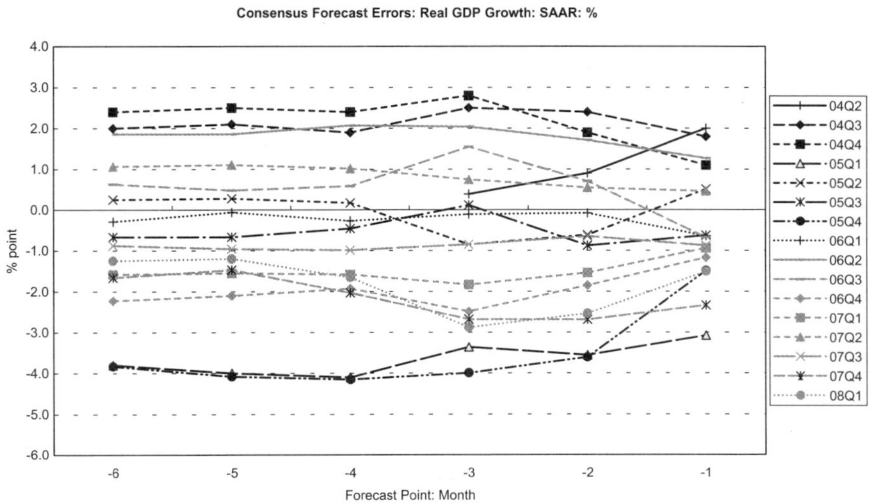

Figure 1. Errors of Consensus Forecast.

denote the ith economist's forecast value of the seasonally adjusted annualized rate of growth in quarterly real GDP at the time point j of the tth quarter by f_{ijt}, and the realized value by y_t, the prediction error is expressed: $e_{ijt} = y_t - f_{ijt}$ The *consensus forecast* is the average of each f_{ijt}, so that if we define $f_{cjt} \equiv \sum_i f_{ijt}/N$ where N is the number of economists engaged, it is $e_{cjt} = y_t - f_{cjt}$.

Since in Japan, quarterly GDP is revised five times after the first preliminary QE is announced, we adopt as the realized value the first "preliminary estimates of GDP" (QE). In the present system, it is unveiled about one month *plus* ten days after the current quarter ends. The second preliminary QE will be released after another month. The revised value is announced during the first ten days in December next year, and also the definite value is released during the first ten days in December two years later. In addition, the base year is revised every five years. It should be noted that seasonal adjustment is conducted retroactively whenever QE is announced, so that the seasonally adjusted value changes every time.

In Figure 1, the vertical axis shows the percentage errors of the *consensus forecast*, while the horizontal axis shows the time point of forecast to be executed (j-t) months before the first QE is announced. Take as an example the January–March quarter 2008. Its first QE is announced on May 16. Figure 1 shows the error percentage point of the real GDP growth rate forecast and the realized value in the January–March. Here, ESPF announcement in May corresponds to the time point of −1 and goes back one by one for six months each. More concretely, forecast of GDP for the quarter started in December 2007 and ended in May 2008 when the basic monthly data to estimate GDP in the period of January through March were not available in first three months (December, January, and February). The monthly data of the January–March become available one by one for the latter three months (March, April, and May), and a more accurate business condition can be grasped. Naturally, the forecast error is expected to change smaller as time advances.

2.3. *Accuracy of consensus forecast*

Kawagoe (2007) evaluated the *consensus forecast* accuracy by using individual data of ESPF in fiscal year 2004 and 2005 in terms of Root Mean Square of the average forecast errors. As for the ranking of its accuracy in forecasting the growth rate of quarterly real GDP, it roughly ranked the 10th, far higher than a median of 37 individuals' forecasts ranked the 19th in both fiscal years. He concluded that the *consensus forecast* performed not about an average of individual forecasts but unexpectedly far better. The reasons may be that first a combination of individuals' different forecasts cancels the factors missed by each forecast each other. It is the same as the idea of the diversified investment in portfolio theory. Second, individuals' extreme errors tend to cancel each other.

Conversely, it is relatively easy for an individual economist's forecast in some year to win against the *consensus forecast*. Judging from its good performance, however, individual economists cannot keep winning. According to Kawagoe (2007), about 85% of the participants won against the *consensus forecast* at least once, but among eight games in fiscal 2004 and 2005, individual economists won 2.4 times on the average. Only 20% of them won seven times, but none kept winning seven times or more.

Similarly, Inada (2008) compared the HF model forecast with the *consensus forecast* for 2004 through 2007 and showed that among 17 games the HF model got 7 victories, 7 defeats, and 2 ties. Thus, the forecast performance of HF model is better than individual participants in ESPF, but surprisingly, the *consensus forecast* performs very well anyway.

The accuracy of the real GDP growth rate by the two methods must be more carefully examined. Clearly, the *consensus forecast* is conducted monthly, whereas the HF forecast is compiled weekly, so that devices are needed to make them comparable. We compare the former with the latter in

Table 1. Real GDP Growth Rate and Forecast Win-Loss Table.

		Forecast Errors: % Point		Win and Loss	
	Official Figure	High Frequency Forecast	Consensus Forecast	High Frequency Forecast	Consensus Forecast
04Q2	1.7	0.3	2.0	○	×
04Q3	0.3	1.5	1.8	○	×
04Q4	−0.5	1.3	1.1	×	○
05Q1	5.3	−0.1	−3.1	○	×
05Q2	1.1	2.5	0.5	×	○
05Q3	1.7	−1.3	−0.6	×	○
05Q4	5.5	−1.5	−1.5	△	△
06Q1	1.9	−1.4	−0.6	×	○
06Q2	0.8	0.5	1.3	○	×
06Q3	2.0	−3.1	−0.7	×	○
06Q4	4.8	0.6	−1.2	○	×
07Q1	3.3	−0.9	−0.9	△	△
07Q2	0.5	0.9	0.5	×	○
07Q3	2.6	−2.4	−0.9	×	○
07Q4	3.7	0.4	−2.3	○	×
08Q1	3.3	−0.4	−1.5	○	×

the first week of every month for the periods of 16 quarters from April–June 2004 to January–March 2008. A brief explanation of the HF model and its forecast method is now in order before comparison.

3. High Frequency Model Forecast

3.1. *Use of monthly or weekly data in HF model*

The HF model uses the data available more frequently than quarterly. For example, the most-watched data are industrial production, jobless rate, household consumption, new housing starts, private machinery orders, consumer price index, corporate goods price index, trade data, and quarterly GDP etc. The HF model makes the best use of the news flash of those monthly data, adjusts the forecast frequently so as to reflect the most recent changes in the forecast of quarterly GDP.[2] For this purpose it is important

[2]L. R. Klein showed the basic idea in the late 1980s, and some models were built in the 1990s (Klein and Sojo, 1989; Klein and Park, 1993, 1995). It is applied particularly in the US and Japan but also in many other economies like China, South Korea, Hong Kong, Thailand, India, Mexico, Russia, and France. Models of some countries are reported in the website of Project LINK. (http://www.chass.utoronto.ca/link/cqm.htm).

(1) to have an accurate, stable model and (2) to ascertain the accurate initial conditions. Since the model is nonlinear, the latter conditions are especially important.

The statistical relations between monthly data and the main entries of quarterly GDP and their components are technical in the HF model so that no personal data adjustment enters the process. Every week current and next quarter forecasts are revised on a forward rolling basis. This method may be called "Current Quarter Model Forecast" (CQM Forecast).

Preliminary GDP statistics are estimated from basic monthly data. QE is estimated according to a manual by the staff of national accounts calculation unit of the Economic and Social Research Institute (ESRI) in Cabinet Office. Following their method, we can reproduce QE from the basic monthly data. The HF model contains this process in modeling and its forecast. In this sense, it is an *accurate, stable model* mentioned above.

3.2. *Forecasting weekly GDP by ARIMA model*

A device to *set accurate initial conditions* is to estimate the basic monthly data of GDP components by Auto-Regressive Moving Average model (ARIMA). Thus, when monthly data are announced, the new information is provided in the following week, and the new, accurate initial conditions are always provided. Incorporating this information of new monthly data announced every week, the HF model forecasts GDP weekly. An example of HF model forecast for the expenditure side is concretely explained. The forecast takes the following four steps.[3]

(1) *Preprocessing of monthly data*

First, the data for the model are selected, and the unit root test is given to them. Next, regular data filtering procedure such as taking the first difference to secure stationary condition is taken. Actually, the monthly data used for the Japanese HF model (expenditure side model) are about 50 variables.[4]

---

[3]For the methodology of the HF model, see Klein and Ozumucur (2007).

[4]For the basic monthly data used to estimate QE, refer to Department of National Accounts, ESRI, Cabinet Office, *The Estimation Method of Quarterly GDP (QE)*, 5th ed. (2006) (Japanese). Only typical, indispensable data are used in the CQM, though a great number of data are used for estimating actual GDP.

(2) *Use of ARIMA model to set the accurate initial conditions*

First, the auto-regressive moving average model is estimated for each variable (y_t) of data that explains GDP components after filtering mentioned above.

$$y_t = \alpha_1 y_{t-1} + \alpha_2 y_{t-2} + \cdots + \varepsilon_t \quad (\varepsilon_t\text{: error terms})$$

Next, the best model (or degree of the variable) is selected, and it forecasts six months ahead. Their forecast performance has been found very well. The forecast values of the basic data for six months ahead are converted to two quarters.

(3) *Estimation of the bridge equations to estimate GDP components from those quarterly values*

As an example, the case of residential investment (*JP_IFR*) is explained. It is regressed on the construction works expense for dwelling (*ICVDW*) deflated by construction cost deflator (*PCDWELL*). Both data are in quarterly basis. Note that *ICVDW* is originally monthly data but converted to quarterly. This regression is called a bridge equation. If the number of basic monthly data that estimate the GDP component is one, the coefficient of the explanatory variable becomes near almost one usually. The variable takes the first difference (DIFF).

QUARTERLY DATA FOR 57 PERIODS FROM 1994Q2 TO 2008Q2

DIFF (*JP_IFR*)

$$= 0.75277^{*}\ \text{DIFF}\ (MOVAVG\ (2,\ (ICVDW)/PCDWEL) - 40.6730$$
$$(12.3470) \qquad\qquad\qquad\qquad\qquad\qquad (0.68478)$$

SUM SQ: 1E+07 STD ERR: 443.156 LHS MEAN: -152.80

R SQ: 0.7349 R BAR SQ: 0.7301 F: 1, 55 152.448

DW(1): 1.8813 DW(4): 1.3785,

where *JP_IFR*: real residential investment, *MOVAVG*: moving average, *ICVDW*: construction work expense for dwelling, *PCDWELL*: construction cost deflator.

Another example of bridge equation is exports of goods and services (*JP_EXM*). It is regressed on the goods (*EXCC&Y*) and services (*BPSVTRSR* + *BPSVTRVR* + *BPSVOSR*) deflated by corresponding price deflators (*EPIY and CPIF001*) respectively.

QUARTERLY DATA FOR 57 PERIODS FROM 1994Q2 TO 2008Q2

$$\begin{aligned}
&\mathrm{DIFF}\,(JP_EXM)\\
&\quad = \underset{(23.6149)}{0.94019}{}^{*}\mathrm{DIFF}\,(REX^{*}EXCC\&Y/EPIY) + \underset{(6.58136)}{0.75356}\\
&\quad {}^{*}\mathrm{DIFF}((BOPSVTRSR + BOPSVTRVR + BOPSVOSR)/CPIF001)\\
&\quad\ \ \underset{(0.60731)}{+38.9335}
\end{aligned}$$

SUM SQ: 8745066 STD ERR: 402.425 LHS MEAN: 911.275
R SQ: 0.9203 R BAR SQ: 0.9174 F: 2, 54 311.847
DW(1): 2.8624, DW (4): 0.6384

where notations are as follows. *REX* denotes balance of payment/custom clearance factor, *EXCC&Y*: goods exports in custom clearance basis, *BPSVTRSR*: transportation receipt in BOP basis, *BPSVTRVR*: travel receipt in BOP basis, *BPSVOSR*: other services receipt in BOP basis, *EPIY*: export price index in yen basis, *CPIF001*: overall CPI.

Such bridge equations are estimated for all GDP components. The monthly variables used for them are shown in Table 2.

(4) *The CQM forecast by the bridge equations two quarters ahead*

Substituting the two quarters estimates obtained in step (2) into the bridge equations for GDP components generates the forecast of each item of GDP and total GDP two quarters ahead. Steps (2) through (4) are repeated every week, though the step (1) is done quarterly. Thus, the information of new monthly data can be woven into weekly update of GDP forecast on a forward rolling base. The accuracy of GDP forecast improves, as the fresh data are acquired. This process is repeated until the following first preliminary QE is released.

Notice that the forecast value of GDP changes not quarterly but weekly. Appropriate judgment can be exercised accordingly with the information of the super short-term economic changes. The HF model forecast gives valuable information to the market, economists and the government alike for their decision-making.

Table 2. Data used in Bridge Equations.

GDP Exponent	Corresponding Monthly Data
Private Consumption	Household Consumption, Household Number, Retail Sales, New Car Sales, New Housing Starts, Floor Space
(Deflator)	CPI (Goods, Services), CPI (Auto, Imputed Rental, Overall)
Govemment Consumption	Activity Index for Public Sector
(Deflator)	CPI (Services)
Residential Investment	Dwelling Construction Works Expense
(Deflator)	Constructbn Cost Deflator (Dwelling)
Nonresidentia l Investment	Sales of Information Services, Private Machinery Orders, Non-dwelling Construction Works Expense, Capital Goods Shipment
(Deflator)	Corporate Service Price Index (Software), Input/Output Price Index (Electro machinery), CGPI (Capital Goods)
Public Investment	Public Works Construction
(Deflator)	Constructbn Cost Deflator (Public Works)
Change in Private Inventory	Inventory Index (Overall, Final Goods)
(Deflator)	Domestic CGPI
Change in Public Inventory	Food Stuff Control
(Deflator)	Domestic CGPI
Exports of Goods & Services	Customs Clearance (Goods Export), Balance of Payment (Receipt of Transportation, Tourism, and Other Services)
(Deflator)	Export Price Index, CPI (Overall)
Factor Income: Receipt	Balance of Payments (Income Receipt)
(Deflator)	Domestic CGPI, CPI (Overall), Export Price Index
Imports of Goods & Services	Customs Clearance (Goods Import), Balance of Payment (Payment of Transportation, Tourism, and Other Services)
(Deflator)	Import Price lidex, CPI (Overall)
Factor Income: Payment	Balance of Payments (Income Payment)
(Deflator)	Domestic CGPI, CPI (Overall), Import Price Index
Compensation of Employee	Total Cash Earnings, Employment Number

4. Prediction Errors: Consensus vs. HF Model Forecast

4.1. *Timing of data announcement and forecast errors*

Figure 1 showed the relations between the forecast time points and the prediction errors of the *consensus forecast*. Information on basic monthly data to estimate the current quarterly GDP is not available for the first half of the entire six months period. The basic data all present themselves one by one during the three months in the second half.

If the economists participating in *consensus forecast* adopt as a method of "go by the numbers" the statistical relations between monthly index and GDP, then the prediction error will decrease rapidly in the latter half of the forecast period. Figure 1 shows, however, that the pace is extremely gradual, though the more closely it approaches to the time of GDP release, the more certainly the prediction errors become smaller.

Figure 2 shows the relations of the HF model between the forecast time points and the prediction errors for the same period. Its prediction errors appear to decrease rapidly three or four months before the first preliminary QE is released. That is, the forecast performance rapidly improves as monthly data related to GDP estimate become available.

4.2. *Features of prediction errors in both forecasts*

Figures 3.1 and 3.2 show both the simple average of the error and that of the absolute error at the time of forecast for both *consensus forecast* and HF model forecast. As for the forecast, if the average forecast error of both (Figure 3.1) is seen, it is always understood that it has a bias to the overestimate for the period of the April–June 2004 and the January–March 2008.

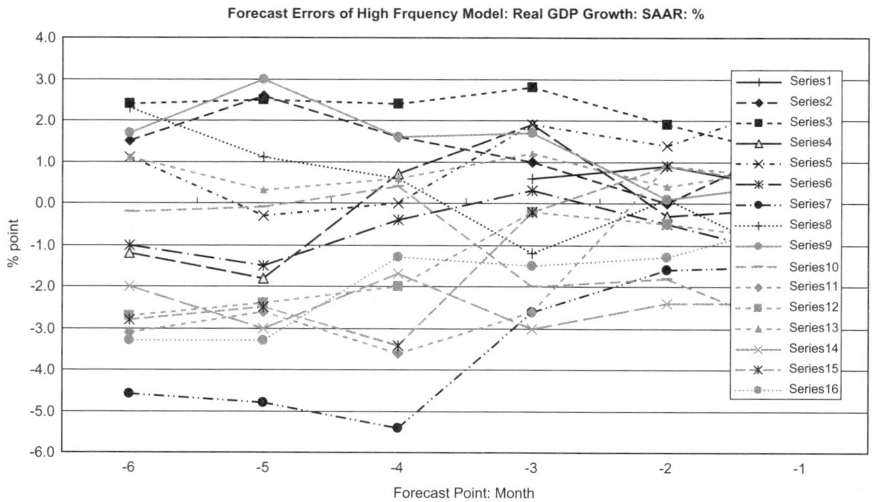

Figure 2. Dynamics of the High Frequency Model Forecast.

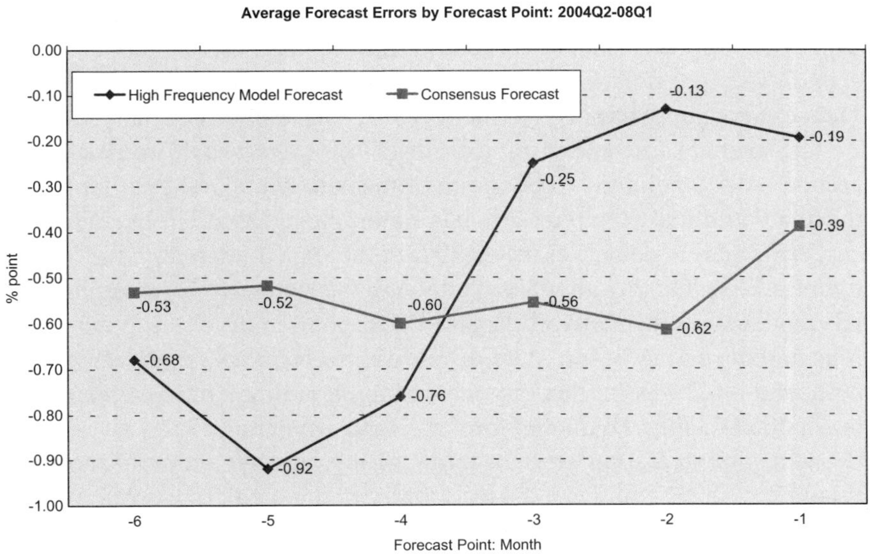

Figure 3.1. Comparison of Forecast Errors by Forecasting Point: Simple Average.

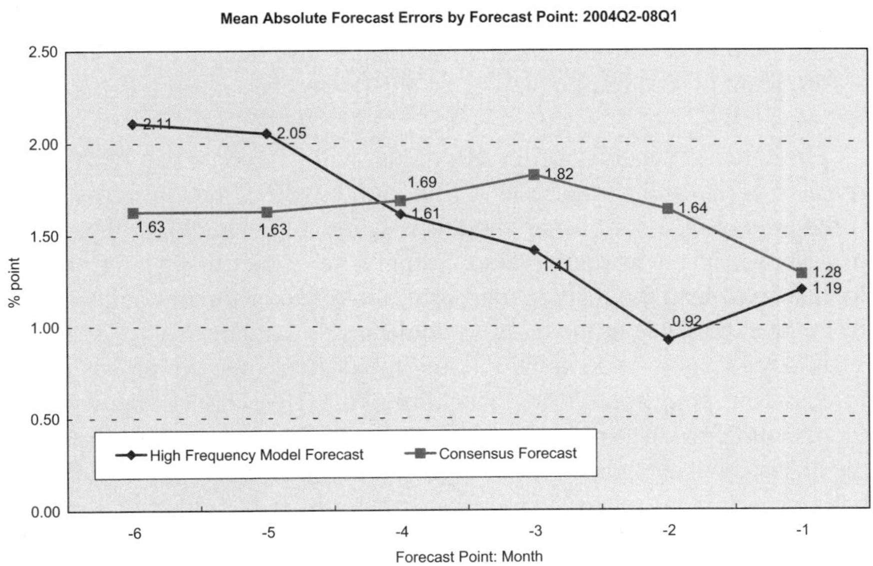

Figure 3.2. Comparisons of Forecast Errors by Forecasting Point: Mean Absolute Errors

On average, there were a lot of periods when the economic recovery expectation (forecast) had exceeded results because the magnitude of the economic expansion was small and the pace was very gradual though Japanese economy has been in the recovery phase since February, 2002.

The average forecast error margin of the *consensus forecast* hovers around −0.5% point to −0.6% point from six to two months earlier before the first preliminary QE release and is almost changeless. The average forecast error margin decreases to −0.39% point one month before the official figure release. On the other hand, although the average error margin of the HF model stays at relatively large −0.7% point and −0.9% point six to four months earlier before the QE release, it decreases rapidly to −0.1% point and −0.2% point three to one month before the official release. It is understood that the HF model forecast is very dynamic.

Next, the prediction error in terms of the absolute value is shown in Figure 3.2. In case of the *consensus forecast*, the prediction error expands from 1.63% point six months before to 1.82% point three months before the QE release. The prediction error is 1.64% point one month earlier and falls to minimum 1.28% point in the last month forecast. On the other hand, in case of the HF model, the mean absolute forecast error decreases monotonously from 2.11% point at the time point 6 months ago to 0.92% point at the time point two months before the release, and the forecast accuracy improves as time goes. However, the error margin is slightly up to 1.19% point in the last month forecast and the forecast accuracy somewhat worsens.

The forecast accuracy of the HF model will overcome that of the *consensus forecast* at the time point of four months before the QE release even if the prediction error of both models is seen on the simple average or on the average of the absolute value. Though we expect that the HF model forecast will lead the market consensus about two to three months earlier from the experience of the past, we could say so statistically.

It can be easily understood that the forecast accuracy improves as the forecast time point approaches to the time of the QE release, because the HF model combines the time series model and the bridge equation. However, the accuracy of the *consensus forecast* hardly improves until two months before the official release. The improvement of 0.4% point (in terms of the mean absolute error) was only seen in the last month forecast. Only in the last month when almost all monthly data for the current quarter are available, economists joining ESPF appear to forecast from the relation between the basic monthly data and the GDP components. At the time

Table 3. Standard Deviation of Forecast Errors.

	Standard Deviation	
Forecast Point	**Hiqh Frequency Forecast**	**Consensus Forecast**
−6	1.15	1.11
−5	1.29	1.21
−4	1.48	1.22
−3	0.89	1.18
−2	0.73	1.11
−1	0.86	0.73

when almost all monthly data are available for the quarter, the newspapers carry special feature article on the economic forecast. This might influence the forecast pattern of the economists. Many economists take the different approach once in six forecasts.

4.3. *Forecast time-point and the prediction errors*

It is Table 3 that shows the variation of the forecast error by the forecast time point (standard deviation of the average of absolute error margin). The standard deviation of the *consensus forecast* error is the same 1.11 both six months and two months before the QE release. Standard deviation hits maximum 1.22 four months before the release. It decreases rapidly to 0.73 one month before. This suggests that the forecast method one month before it might be different from other five months.

For the HF model, the standard deviation of the forecast error exceeds one for six through four months before the QE release but turns to fall below one, staying at 0.7 to 0.8 three to one month before it. As for the HF model forecast, it is understood that the variation of the forecast becomes stable rapidly as the basic monthly data of the current quarter become available.

4.4. *Dynamic forecast process — recent experiences*

Two episodes may be mentioned to reinforce the conclusion in the preceding Section and close this section. Figures 4.1 and 4.2 show the recent movement of the HF model forecasts and the *consensus forecast*s and express well the features of both forecasts. Figure 4.1 is the tracking record of the movement of HF model forecasts on weekly basis and the same of *consensus forecast*s on monthly basis for real GDP growth rate during the period of October–December 2007.

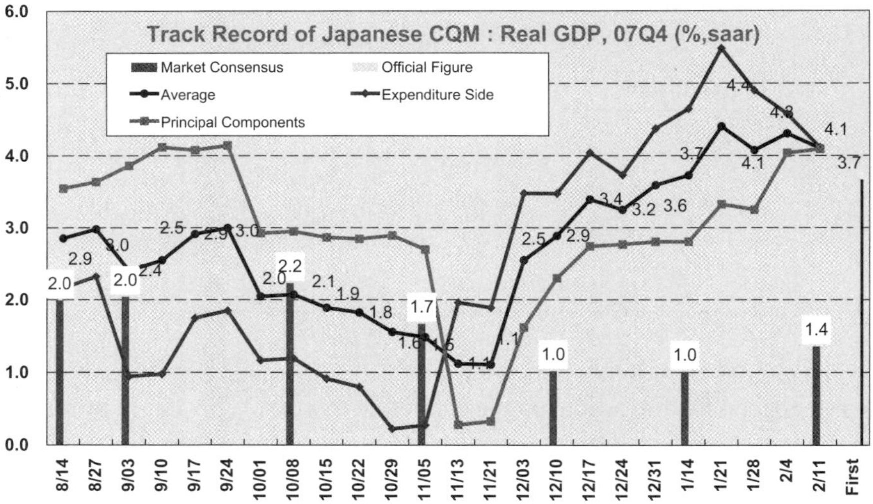

Figure 4.1. Forecast Dynamics of High Frequency Model Forecast: 2007Q4.

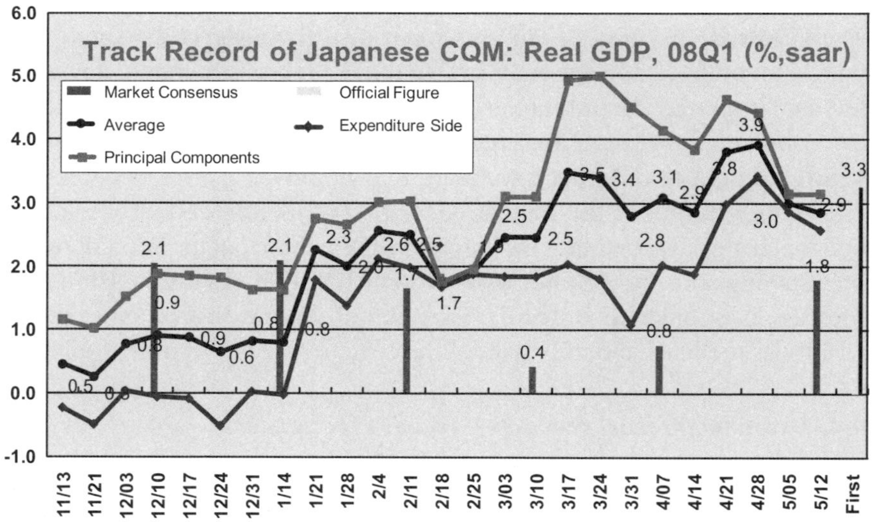

Figure 4.2. Forecast Dynamics of High Frequency Model Forecast: 2008 Q1.

The HF model forecast for October–December has started since the middle of August when the first QE of the April–June quarter was announced. Although "subprime loan" problem came to light in August and the turmoil in the financial markets started, the optimistic view prevailed at first. Therefore, the *consensus forecast* of the real GDP growth in August through November stayed around 2%. The HF model (the mean forecast value of the expenditure side model and the principal component analysis model) showed an almost similar forecast pattern.

The *consensus forecast* is revised downward from 1.7% in November to 1.0% in December. On the other hand, the HF model forecast jumps from 1% level to 2–3% level. The *consensus forecast* has stayed to the last minute at a low forecast of 1% level, though the HF model keeps forecasting the growth of 3–4% level until February 14 when the first preliminary figure (+3.7%) for the October–December is announced.

Behind the downward revision of the *consensus forecast* from 1.7% in November to 1.0% in December was the deepening financial market turmoil in the US and the EU. In December, five central banks including ECB and Fed injected money in large scale to the financial market. More attention was paid to the subprime loan problem again. The *consensus forecast* was very much influenced by the financial market debacle. On the other hand, the HF model forecast's shift to 3–4% growth reflected the result of strong trade data in October and November. The *consensus forecast* continued to predict 1% growth even in the prior month before the QE release. The HF model forecast is the one that is not affected by the mood of the market. It is quite natural because it judges the economy from the technique of "Go by the Numbers" that treats economic statistics always objectively. Similar observations can be made on the forecast formation in January–March 2008 (see Figure 4.2). The forecast of the real GDP growth rate for that quarter started from the latter half of November 2007 and ended one week before the first QE release on May 16, 2008. When we entered in March, both forecasts show large divergence. The *consensus forecast* posted 1.7% growth in June but was revised down to 0.4% in March and 0.8% in April. It greatly fell below the first QE (+3.3%) though it was revised up indeed to 1.8% in May.

Japanese stock prices plunged below 13,000 Yen in early March. J. P. Morgan and Chase declared the relief to US brokerage firm Bear Sterns crisis on March 16, and Fed also declared the capital support. Market factored in this event and stock prices fell below 12,000 Yen level temporarily, and the Yen exceeded 100 Yen. Such a background influenced the *consensus forecast*. On the other hand, the HF model forecast was revised up from 1.9% at the end of February to 3.5% in the middle of March. The HF model forecast can grasp the turning point of business cycles more clearly as these two examples show.

5. Concluding Remarks

The provisional conclusions obtained from the examination here are:

1. As for the *consensus forecast*, it is not just an average of an individual forecast but its forecast accuracy is unexpectedly high. Actually, there is no inferiority compared with the performance of the HF model forecast.
2. The *consensus forecast* is very stable and lacks the change, when the forecast dynamics is seen by the time point of forecast. That is, it is not understood well where a turning point of business cycle is.
3. The HF model forecast is dynamic and its accuracy rises further as the basic monthly data of current quarter GDP become available. It has been understood that the HF model forecast can lead the market consensus for two to three months and offer an accurate forecast.
4. Moreover, the *consensus forecast* has been influenced from the mood of the market though it is stable as some examples show.
5. The HF forecast model that deals with economic statistics objectively and judges by the way of "Go by the Numbers" is an effective method.

References

Armstrong, J. S. (2001). Combining Forecasts. In J. S. Armstrong (ed.), *Principle of Forecasting: A Handbook for Researchers and Practitioners*. Kluwer, pp. 417–439.

Department of National Accounts, ESRI, Cabinet Office (2006). *The Estimation Method of Quarterly GDP (QE)*, 5th ed. (Japanese).

Diebold, F. X. and J. A. Lopez (1996). Forecasting Evaluation and Combination. In G. S. Maddala and C. R. Rao (eds.), *Handbook of Statistics*, vol. 4. North-Holland, pp. 241–268.

Inada, Y. (2008). High Frequency Forecasting Model and Its Application to the Japanese Economy. In L. R. Klein (ed.), *The Making of National Economic Forecasts*. Edward Elgar Pub. pp. 172–197.

Inada, Y. (2007). Konan University Current Quarter Model Forecast for the Japanese Economy. Project LINK web-site, http://www.chass.utoronto.ca/LINK.

Klein, L. R. and E. Sojo (1989). Combination of High and Low Frequency Data in Macroeconometric Models. In Klein and Marquez (eds.), *Economics in Theory and Practice: An Electric Approach*. Kluwer, pp. 3–16.

Klein, L. R. and J. Y. Park (1993). Economic Forecasting at High-Frequency Intervals. *Journal of Forecasting*, 12, 301–319.

Klein, L. R. and J. Y. Park (1995). The University of Pennsylvania Model for High-Frequency Economic Forecasting. *Economic and Financial Modeling*, autumn, 95–146.

Klein, L. R. and S. Ozmucur (2007). The University of Pennsylvania Models for High-Frequency Macroeconomic Modeling. Project LINK website, (http://www.chass.utoronto.ca/link/cqm.htm).

Kawagoe, M. (2007). Is the Consensus Forecast Just the Average? — Re-examining an Evaluation of the ESP Forecast. ESRI Discussion Paper Series No. 180 (J).

Timmermann, A. (2006). Forecast Combinations. In Elliot G., W. J. Granger, and A. Timmermann, (eds.), *Handbook of Economic Forecasting*. North-Holland, pp. 135–196.

Chapter 14

Policy Alternatives for Japan Toward 2020

Shuntaro Shishido, Akira Kawakami
and Kiyoshi Tamashiro

1. Introduction

Since the early 1990s, the Japanese economy has experienced a long recession which is still persisting. This chapter applies our model called DEMIOS to the analysis of the recession and the search for alternative policies to realize Japan's growth potential. First, an overview of the basic structure of DEMIOS is presented. It was originally designed for multiple purposes.[1] Then, the properties of the model are explained in terms of various dynamic multipliers. Third, it is applied to examine if the stagnation from 1992 to 2005 was unavoidable. Lastly, to achieve higher rates of growth up to 2020 policy alternatives are sought for by simulating the model.

---

[1]The project was initiated in the late 1980s with a grant from National Institute of Research Advancement (NIRA) to promote the Japan-US economic co-operation. A Japanese team was organized jointly at the U. of Tsukuba and International U. of Japan primarily to construct the annual input-output database since 1973 and estimate an econometric model with 64 sectors. A US counterpart team headed by L. R. Klein and F. G. Adams was organized at the U. of Pennsylvania. They used the long term annual model with about 80 sectors, and the bilateral US-Japan trade linkage was studied by Byron Gangnes. (Adams *et al.*, 1993) This bilateral model was integrated with the Project Link System and produced various policy scenarios. (Adams and Shishido, 1988 and Adams *op. cit.*) In the late 1990s the Japanese NIRA-LINK model (G2) increased 64 sectors to 81 and was linked with North East Asian models to analyze some international issues, in collaboration with ERINA (Economic Research Institute for Northeast Asia) and NIRA. (Shishido *et al.*, 2007a).

2. The Structure of Model DEMIOS

2.1. *Features of the model*

It is a typical Leontief-Keynesian model with 81 sectors for output, exports, imports, investment, capital stock, employment, output prices, input prices, wage rates, and capital costs, and value added. Its macroeconomic block includes all fiscal and monetary variables, such as various tax revenues, fiscal expenditures and balances, transfers between central and local governments, and social security system. Monetary block includes money supply, short- and long-term interest rates, stock prices and exchange rates as strategic policy variables. It is basically demand-oriented but considers some supply-side variables like output capacity, labor supply, financial constraints etc. as Figure 1 shows. It was designed for medium- and long-term projection and policy simulations from the very beginning.

Hence, it has several features. The first is to contain a demographic block with some variables like the rates of fertility, mortality and migration and distinguishes the three age groups: young population less than 15, productive age population, and old population over 65. The second feature is its emphasis on the role of technical changes, explicitly treating both neutral and biased technical progress on sectoral basis. The blocks of IO and PX etc. shown above analyze total factor productivity in the system of V-RAS, as will be discussed below. The third feature is that its macroeconomic block is integrated with an IO model and a demographic block. The three blocks are interrelated in the medium and long runs. Each block is explained in detail below.

2.2. *Demographic block*

The present version includes three age groups: (a) *POP0* (population under 15, (b)*POP15* (between 16 and 64, (c) *POP65* (over 65). Total population (*POPT*), the most important in this block, is defined as

$$POPT = POPT(-1) + POPB - POPD + POPSO, \qquad (2.1)$$

where POPB = births, POPD = deaths, POPSO = net migrants.

To analyze population dynamics, three demographic variables were regressed on related socio-economic variables as follows, where $(-i)$

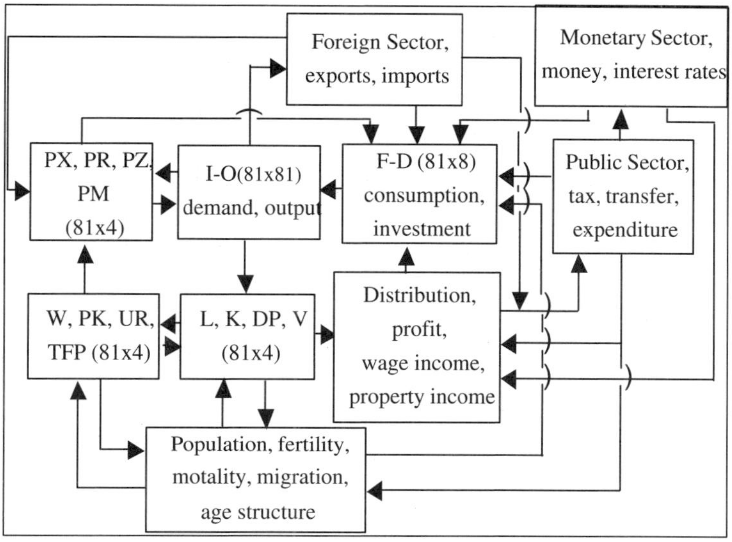

Note:
F-D = final demand
L = employment
V = value added
UR = unemployment rate
PX = output price
I-O = input-output matrix
K = capital stock
W = wage rate
TFP = total factor productivity
PR = input price of intermediate Input
DP = depreciation
PK = capital cost
PZ = total input price

Figure 1. Flow Chart of DEMIOS.

denotes time lag and (+) or (−) indicates a sign of parameter. The estimated equations are shown in the Appendix at the end.

$$POPB/POPT = [\underset{(+)}{POP15(-i)/POP15(i-1)},\ \underset{(+)}{KH(-i)},\ \underset{(-)}{URATE(-i)},\ \underset{(+)}{CG(-i)/GDP(-i)}] \quad (2.2)$$

$$POPD/POPT = [\underset{(+)}{POP65/POPT},\ \underset{(-)}{CP(-i)/CP(-i-1)},\ \underset{(-)}{TRH(-i)/GNP\_N(-i)},\ \underset{(-)}{CG/GDP}] \quad (2.3)$$

$$POPSO = [\underset{(+)}{(IP(-1)+IG(-1))/GDP(-1)},\ \underset{(-)}{TRH(-1)/GNP},\ (-1),\ \underset{(+)}{EXR}] \quad (2.4)$$

$$POP0/POP = [\underset{(+)}{POP15(-i)/POP15(i-1)},\ \underset{(+)}{KH(-i)},\ \underset{(-)}{URATE(-i)},\ \underset{(+)}{CG(-i)/GD(-i)}] \quad (2.5)$$

$$POP65/POPT = [\underset{(+)}{POP15(-i)/POPT(-i)},\ \underset{(+)}{POPT(-i)/POPT(-i-1)},\ \underset{(+)}{TRH(-i)/GNPN(-i)},\ \underset{(+)}{CG(-i)/GDP(-i)}] \quad (2.6)$$

where *KH* = housing stock, *URATE* = unemployment rate, *CG* = government consumption (real), *GDP* = GDP (real), *CP* = private consumption (real), *TRH* = transfer from government, *GNP_N* = GNP (nominal), *IP* = business investment (real), *IG* = government investment(real), *EXR* = exchange rate (¥/$).

Our findings show that demographic variables are highly sensitive to cyclical factors such as the unemployment rate, housing stock, business investment etc, if time lags are properly considered. They are also responsive to the government's, especially local governments' expenditures for social benefits and medical care. It is noteworthy that the age component like *POP65/POPT* significantly depends on government financial support in our model. Both *POPB* and *POP0* are similarly specified in the above equations, but different time lags are used, depending upon different economic and policy variables. Interestingly, these findings are different from the official view by the Research Institute of Demographic and Social Affairs. Their forecast is based on a cohort-type model which disregards economic and policy variables, whereas ours takes into consideration the social policies and obtains flexible scenarios for demographic variables.

2.3. *Input-output block*

The benchmark IO table becomes available every five years. Our project, started in 1987, has succeeded in building up an annual time series of IO tables in more aggregated level of 64 to 81 sectors since 1973, including employment, distinguishing employees and non-employees, fixed investment and capital stocks for both private and public. All of them are available in terms of three consistent series; i.e. real, nominal, and deflators now and for the same period. They enables us to perform productivity analysis on a consistent sectoral basis. (For multi-sectoral models in Japan, see Shishido, 2002a, b).

In our model Leontief's IO coefficient matrix is transformed to flexible IO coefficients in the framework of what we call V-RAS (Shishido, 1991 and 1992). Its feature is to integrate IO coefficients, including primary factors, in a rectangular matrix, as shown below, and analyze both individual coefficients and TFP in each column, while at the same time tracing the output price repercussions in each row from the upper to the lower stream. The system is summarized below. Unlike the ordinary IO matrix, the V-RAS matrix is rectangular with more rows than columns, as it covers primary factors such as labor services, capital, and land, etc.

$$a^*_{kj} = \begin{bmatrix} a_{11} & \cdots & a_{1n} \\ \vdots & \ddots & \\ a_{n1} & \cdots & a_{nm} \\ v_{11} & \cdots & v_{1n} \\ \vdots & & \vdots \\ v_{m1} & \cdots & v_{mn} \end{bmatrix} \tag{2.7}$$

$$\tau_j = \frac{1}{\sum_k a^*_{kj}} \quad \begin{matrix} (k = 1, 2, \ldots, n+m) \\ (j = 1, 2, \ldots, n) \end{matrix} \tag{2.8}$$

All values are shown in terms of constant prices of the base year, implying $\boldsymbol{\tau}_j = 1$. The V-RAS formula and parameters for inter-factor substitution $\boldsymbol{r}$, total savings $\boldsymbol{s}$, and cost-price relations are specified below in equations (2.3) to (2.10).

$$a^*_{kj} = r_k \hat{a}_{kj} s_j \tag{2.9}$$

$$S_j = f\left(\frac{1}{\tau_j}, \cdots\right) \tag{2.10}$$

$$r_k = [r_i; r_s]_{(I=1,\ldots,n)(s=1,\ldots,m)} \tag{2.11}$$

$$r_i = f(\hat{p}_i, \cdots) \tag{2.12}$$

$$\hat{p}_i = \frac{(p_i/\bar{p}_i)}{(\tilde{p}_i/\bar{\tilde{p}}_i)} \tag{2.13}$$

$$p_i = (1 - \mu_i)p_{x,i} + \mu_i p_{m,i} \tag{2.14}$$

$$p_{x,j} = \sum_i a_{ij} p_i + p_{v,j} \tag{2.15}$$

$$p_{v,j} = \sum_s v_{k,j} p_{f,s} + \pi_j \tag{2.16}$$

where a^*_{kj} = the IO coefficient of a rectangular matrix including primary factors (v) for the base year, $\hat{a}_{kj}$ = the base year IO coefficient, τ_j = the total factor productivity of the jth sector, r_k = the substitution parameter of the kth sector, s_m = the efficiency parameter of the jth sector, p_x = the output price, p_m = the input price, p = the average of p_x and p_m, μ = import dependency, $\hat{p}$ = the average import price, and $\bar{p}$ = the base year price.

While equations (2.9) to (2.11) are related to total input, including primary inputs, equations (2.12) and (2.13) are related only to intermediate inputs. S_i and r_i are derived from the annual IO table in constant prices and calculated by using equations (2.10) and (2.12) by ordinary least squares method, where $\boldsymbol{\tau}_i$ and $\hat{p}_i$ play significant roles respectively. The r_s substitution parameters for primary inputs are also derived from the V-RAS formula and used as important indicators for the demand functions of primary inputs. A direct sectoral approach to primary factor demand, however, was taken by using conventional methods for factor demand functions on a sectional basis, as described later. In the present version of DEMIOS, this V-RAS method has been slightly modified temporarily by simplifying the procedure of estimating sectoral intermediate demand on the same idea of price-sensitive technology of the original V-RAS.[2]

[2]In view of growing importance of information technology (IT), as L. R. Klein group emphasized (Klein *et al.*, *op. cit.*), the strengthening of V-RAS is now under way for database and sub-modeling. This system is also highlighted due to the growing importance of inter-fuel substitution, waste disposal, and especially environmental issues.

The production side is derived as a dual price-cost relationship, and the following system is formulated *a la* conventional Leontief model.

$$U_i = \sum a_{ij} \cdot X_j \tag{2.17}$$

$$D_i = U_i + F_i + E_i \tag{2.18}$$

$$X_i = D_i - M_i \tag{2.19}$$

$$M_i = f[D_i, p_{mi}/p_n] \tag{2.20}$$

$$U_{ri} = \sum_i a_{ij} X_j \tag{2.21}$$

$$Z_j = U_{rj} + \bar{\omega}_j \cdot L_j + \bar{p}_{kj} \cdot K_j + \bar{p}_{aj} \cdot A_j \tag{2.22}$$

$$\tau_j = X_j / Z_j \tag{2.23}$$

where U_i = intermediate demand, U_r = intermediate input, D_i = demand total, F_i = final demand, E_i = exports, M_i = imports, K_i = capital, A_i = land, and Z_j = total input.

All the equations related to supply and demand variables are price sensitive, thus being affected by sectonal changes in TFP and foreign prices as well as market conditions. Unlike conventional specifications for business investment, one of the features of the present model is government investment in social overheads which is significant, with a two or three year time-lag, for important private sectors such as agriculture, basic manufacturing, and public utilities, etc. Private housing investment partly depends on government investment such as highway access, and renewal of urban facilities, etc. Thus, the present model explicitly considers the forward IO linkage effects of the public sector to the external economy. The typical private investment equations are shown in the Appendix.

The household consumption function has improved by considering demographic changes such as the increasing share of elderly people and their growing demand for medical care. A two stage approach was adopted, firstly 12 major categories for consumption which are highly price-sensitive to own-price and cross-price as in the Rotterdam School model, while in the second stage a consumption converter matrix (81 × 12) was used, supplemented by related price changes.

The log-linear labor demand functions are inherited from the preceding model along with output and relative wage rates as explanatory variables.

These factor demand equations are summarized as follows.

$$L_j = f[X_j,\ W_j/PX_j,\ L_{j-1}] \tag{2.24}$$

$$KP_j = IP_j - DP_j + KP_{j-1} \tag{2.25}$$

$$IP_j = f[X_j,\ KP_{j-1},\ INTGB_{-1},\ PX_j/PZ_j,\ IG\_i] \tag{2.26}$$

where L_j = employment, W_j = wage rate, PX_j = producer price, PZ_j = input price, KP_j = capital stock, IP_j = business investment, DP_j = depreciation, $INTGB$ = long-term interest rate, and IG = government investment by type.

Finally, producer prices are determined by the total input price, a proxy rate of capacity utilization, the unemployment rate, and exchange rates, etc.

$$\begin{aligned} l_nPX_j = f[&l_nPZ_j,\ l_n(KP_{j-1}/X_{j-1}),\ l_nURATE, \\ &l_nEXR_{-1},\ l_nPX_{j-1}] \end{aligned} \tag{2.27}$$

where PX_j = producer price, PZ_j = input price of all factors, $URATE$ = unemployment rate, and EXR = exchange rate (¥/$).

At an aggregate level, the potential GDP^C was estimated in order to evaluate the rate of operation, i.e., ζ (= GDP/GDP^C). The aggregate production function, which includes a scale effect and technical progress represented by TFP, was estimated. The Cobb-Douglas function was calculated by using private fixed-capital stock, labor inputs, the unemployment rate, and time trends. The result was normalized in terms of working hours and the unemployment rate to obtain the value of capacity of GDP.[3]

2.4. *Macroeconomic block*

The basic structure of final demand remains the same, except for the public sector. While business investment and exports in this block are only the summation of the results of 79 sectoral equations in the IO block, other major behavioral equations such as private consumption, residential investment, and private inventory investment are independently estimated. Government consumption, changes in government inventories and fixed investment, including its sectoral components are all treated as exogenous variables. The important equations in this block are explained below.

[3]An explicit inclusion of the impact of IT revolution and quality improvement of labor is under study in the context of V-RAS. For the analysis of sectoral and aggregate productive capacity, see Shishido (2004).

As for private consumption, the ordinary specification is adopted.

$$
\begin{aligned}
CP = & -14264.36 + 0.70927^{*}YDP/PC^{*}100 \\
& \quad (-0.30) \qquad (19.72) \\
& - 51083.64^{*}PC(-1)/PC(-2) - 758.472^{*}INTGB(-2) \\
& \quad (-2.99) \qquad\qquad\qquad (-1.32) \\
& + 422343.7^{*}POP65(-2)/POPT(-1) + 0.54967POPT(-1) \\
& \quad (7.61) \qquad\qquad\qquad (1.43) \\
& \quad R^2 = 0.998 \quad SE = 2361.6 \quad DW = 1.493 \qquad (2.28)
\end{aligned}
$$

where YDP = disposable income, PC = consumer's price, $INTGB$ = long-term interest rate.

As is shown here, private consumption is explained by five variables. Real disposable income indicates the largest impact. Total population and its age group over 65 comes next. Inflationary expectation and financial constraints show expected negative sign.

Residential investment which recently accounts for less than 4% of the GDP is dependent on the following factors.

$$
\begin{aligned}
IH = & \ 36612.87 + 0.135704YDP()(-1)/PC(-1)^{*}100 \\
& \quad (4.11) \qquad (4.21) \\
& - 0.099867KH\_NEW(-3) \\
& \quad (-6.04) \\
& - 18771.74^{*}PIH(-1)/PC(-1) + 1.329341^{*}STOCKPR(-1) \\
& \quad (-2.51) \qquad\qquad\qquad (1.90) \\
& - 451.1625INTGB(-1) - 34.31515^{*}EXR(-1) \\
& \quad (-2.06) \qquad\qquad (-2.74) \\
& \quad R^2 = 0.866 \quad SE = 1.19E+3 \quad DW = 1.899 \qquad (2.29)
\end{aligned}
$$

where KH_NEW = housing stock, PIH = deflator of residential investment, $STOCKPR$ = stock market price index (TOPIX), EXR = exchange rate (¥/$).

The main explanatory variables in residential investment are disposable income and residential capital stock. Others are price and financial factors such as deflator for residential investment, long-term interest rate and exchange rate. Stock price is added as an important proxy variable for asset effect. A negative sign of exchange rate signifies the competitiveness of imported construction materials.

Inventory investment at macro-level is estimated as follows.

$$\begin{aligned} JP = {} & \underset{(4.10)}{7298.727} + \underset{(4.11)}{0.03619}{}^{*}GDP - \underset{(-3.56)}{0.313964}{}^{*}KJP(-1) \\ & - \underset{(-3.17)}{73500.29}{}^{*}EXC(-2)/GDP(-2) - \underset{(-0.34)}{39.79237}INTORA(-1) \\ & R^2 = 0.556 \quad SE = 931.2 \quad DW = 1.739 \end{aligned} \tag{2.30}$$

where KJP = inventory stock, EXC = exports of goods, $INTORA$ = policy rate of BOJ.

The major explanatory variables are GDP and inventory stock which are explained in terms of a stock adjustment formula. Additionally, a share of commodity exports in the GDP is included as a negative factor because of higher efficiency of inventory management in export-oriented industries. A financial variable is added as a negative factor, but it happens to be weak as shown in the Appendix. With regard to sectoral break down of inventory investment at the 80-sector level, we simply used fixed component ratios in the base year, since we are more concerned about medium-term movement of sectoral output.

In this block improvements were made for the fiscal and monetary subblocks. The public sector is divided into central government, local government and social insurance. Financial assets and liabilities, various types of expenditure, taxes and transfer payments are specified and endogenized. Although ordinary tax functions in macro-model are more or less institutional and disregard various cyclical factors such as interest rates, stock prices, unemployment rate, etc. the tax revenue functions in our model fully take account of them to allow for much more flexibility in government revenues and fiscal balances.

As an example, corporate income tax function is given here.

$$\begin{aligned} TC = {} & \underset{(-2.46)}{18681.55} + \underset{(6.78)}{0.401085}YC + \underset{(1.73)}{112.8159}{}^{*}ROUSP(-4) \\ & + \underset{(6.80)}{1585.172}{}^{*}INTGB(-1) + \underset{(4.60)}{3.956991}{}^{*}STOCKPR(-1) \end{aligned}$$

$$- 27.53178^{*}EXR(-1) + 0.157569^{*}DIRIV$$
$$(3.80) \qquad (2.18)$$
$$R^2 = 0.977 \quad SE = 8.16 + E2 \quad DW = 2.462 \qquad (2.31)$$

where *TC* = corporate income tax, *YC* = corporate income, *ROUSP* = the rate of GDP capacity utilization, *DIRIV* = foreign direct investment.

Corporate income tax is highly sensitive to cyclical factors, as is shown above in the rate of GDP capacity utilization and stock prices. Besides, the growing investment overseas makes the corporate income tax depend positively on the profit from FDI.

In the monetary block, the stock price index and exchange rates are endogenized so that the fiscal and monetary blocks become much more interrelated with the BOJ's monetary policy and the government's management of national debt. For instance, the long-term interest rate of national bond is specified as (see Appendix).

$$INTGB = 2.275253 + 0.817206^{*}INTORA(-1) + 20.98911^{*}ISGAPR$$
$$(6.14) \qquad (5.73) \qquad (-1.32)$$
$$+ 22.59056^{*}(P - P(-1))/(P(-1)) - 1.2355^{*}(STOCKPR(-5)$$
$$(1.69) \qquad (-1.18)$$
$$- STOCKPR(-6))/STOCKPR(-6)$$
$$R^2 = 0.886 \quad SE = 0.9 \quad DW = 1.156 \qquad (2.32)$$

where *INTORA* = policy rate, *ISGAPR* = excess saving over (investment plus current surplus), *P* = GDP deflator, *STOCKPR* = Stock Price Index of Tokyo Stock Market.

As the flow chart showed, three blocks, i.e. demographic, IO, and macroeconomic blocks, are mutually interdependent with various different time lags. The total number of endogenous variables in our model is about four thousand, and to solve this system the Gaus-Seidel method was used similarly to many other econometric models.

3. Dynamic Multipliers

DEMIOS is featured by (a) demographic flexibility and (b) the impact of public investment on private investment through the external economy induced by improved overhead capital. Hence, it shows a little higher impact on the economy than most other Japanese macroeconometric models. The dynamic simulations are shown in Table 1 in terms of fiscal monetary policies: (a) government investment, (b) personal income tax, (c) interest rate, (d) corporate tax cut on accelerated depreciation, (e) government consumption on medical care, and (f) consumption tax.

Compared with the other models in Japan, its features are:

(1) The labor supply is rather flexible, because of endogenized demographic factors, allowing for a milder wage rate adjustment and price reaction;
(2) Business and housing investments are more sensitive to aggregate demand and supply side changes, especially to public investment, as in the case of the investment by the car industry stimulated by highway network expansion which tends to be disregarded in the short-term macro- models. Similarly, communication and IT sectors are also quite sensitive to the government investment in infra-structure of IT network;
(3) The response of private consumption is rather slow in all multipliers but gradually keeps on growing, as in the case of personal income tax cut. In the long run the effect of income tax reduction exceeds the multiplier of government investment in terms of private consumption;
(4) Demographic factors are especially noticeable in the case of government consumption for medical care. While GDP tends to respond very slowly in the first half of our observation period, the multiplier tends to exceed considerably that of government investment during the second half in response to population growth in particular of the elderly population and birth rate recovery;
(5) As for fiscal issues, the high responses of tax revenues in all the cases of multipliers are noteworthy. The tax functions in our model explicitly take into accout cyclical factors to reflect Japan's fiscal experiences suffering from low tax revenues after the bubble burst in 1991. During the chronic recession years the serious fiscal deficits continued in all public sectors, including central, local, and social security funds. The model is constructed to reflect a fairly flexible dynamic property of government revenues.

4. Japan's Stagnation During 1992–2005 was Avoidable

The causes of Japan's stagnation after the bubble burst in 1991 have been hotly debated for the past 15 years. "Supply-siders" have argued that the

Table 1. Multiplies (% Deviation from Baseline).*

	2007	2008	2009	2010	2011	2012	2013	2014	2015	2016	2017	2018	2019	2020
A. Government Investment, 5 Billion Yen Up														
GDP (GDP, real)	1.26	1.70	2.01	2.20	2.37	2.38	2.57	2.49	2.44	2.33	2.20	2.20	2.07	2.00
GDP, nominal (GDP_N)	0.49	0.89	1.20	1.55	2.09	2.57	3.07	3.40	3.66	3.85	3.84	3.89	3.81	3.67
Private consumption (CP82)	−0.06	0.05	0.19	0.40	0.63	0.88	1.14	1.37	1.50	1.71	1.80	1.84	1.95	1.93
Business investment (IPXSUM)	2.86	4.20	5.50	5.97	6.72	6.46	6.25	5.96	5.50	4.85	4.52	4.38	4.14	4.18
Housing investment (IH)	0.00	3.29	2.53	2.77	2.83	2.80	2.47	2.70	2.28	1.99	1.68	1.46	1.41	1.17
Exports (E82)	−0.08	0.21	0.41	0.56	0.51	0.51	0.60	0.38	0.44	0.40	0.27	0.33	0.25	0.17
Imports (M82)	1.01	1.05	1.14	1.06	1.30	1.33	0.65	1.29	1.24	1.52	1.88	1.64	2.20	2.27
Disposable income (YDP)	0.26	0.52	0.81	1.09	1.57	1.89	2.33	2.60	2.76	2.90	2.93	2.88	2.87	2.76
Total employment (L82)	0.54	0.95	1.28	1.44	1.49	1.41	1.35	1.18	1.03	0.85	0.68	0.59	0.49	0.43
Unemployment rate (URATE)	0.00	0.11	0.15	0.19	0.21	0.22	0.21	0.21	0.19	0.17	0.14	0.12	0.11	0.09
Wage rate (W)	0.63	0.65	0.60	0.34	0.17	0.77	1.25	1.77	2.19	2.55	2.72	2.78	2.82	2.73
Long-term interest rate (INTGB)	−0.08	0.10	0.12	0.12	0.17	0.05	0.10	0.14	0.04	0.02	0.01	0.09	0.02	0.05
Consumer's price(PC_SUB)	0.0	−0.4	−0.4	−0.3	−0.2	0.1	0.5	0.9	1.1	1.4	1.6	1.7	1.8	1.8
Exchange rate Yen/$ (EXR)	0.04	1.85	2.24	2.61	1.57	2.08	2.83	0.48	2.15	1.53	0.61	1.89	0.72	0.43

(Continued)

Table 1. *(Continued)*

	2007	2008	2009	2010	2011	2012	2013	2014	2015	2016	2017	2018	2019	2020
Total population (POPT)	0.00	0.01	0.04	0.05	0.07	0.08	0.09	0.10	0.11	0.12	0.12	0.13	0.14	0.14
Stock price index (STOCKPR)	8.68	4.85	2.45	3.45	2.86	2.61	6.95	5.06	7.07	8.26	7.02	9.34	8.76	7.72
Tax and other rev. (TSUM_SUB)	0.57	1.59	1.74	2.47	2.93	3.60	4.33	4.84	5.73	5.89	5.78	6.20	6.20	5.98
Potential GDP (GDPCSPFF)	0.00	0.00	0.00	0.12	0.27	0.46	0.63	0.81	0.95	1.06	1.14	1.20	1.23	1.24
B. Personal Income Tax Cut, 5 Billion Yen Down														
GDP (GDP, real)	0.09	0.61	1.15	1.52	1.80	1.95	2.14	2.28	2.37	2.45	2.36	2.37	2.38	2.24
GDP, nominal (GDP_N)	0.03	0.25	0.57	0.87	1.30	1.71	2.11	2.50	2.82	3.10	3.29	3.44	3.55	3.55
Private consumption (CP82)	0.14	0.38	0.75	1.06	1.38	1.71	1.93	2.15	2.38	2.55	2.72	2.80	2.87	2.86
Business investment (IPXSUM)	0.05	0.40	0.81	1.31	1.72	1.87	2.02	2.05	2.13	2.23	2.07	2.05	2.10	2.08
Housing investment (IH)	0.00	3.30	4.75	5.74	5.98	5.79	5.55	5.44	4.97	4.52	4.32	3.72	3.45	3.36
Exports (E82)	0.01	0.48	0.83	0.89	0.98	0.91	0.88	0.90	0.88	0.86	0.75	0.78	0.74	0.61
Imports (M82)	0.04	0.72	1.35	1.39	1.60	1.41	1.78	1.89	1.57	1.43	0.94	0.94	0.92	0.48
Disposable income (YDP)	1.63	2.28	2.59	2.80	3.09	3.39	3.63	3.89	4.06	4.18	4.31	4.34	4.37	4.40
Total employment (L82)	0.03	0.27	0.58	0.85	1.05	1.13	1.17	1.16	1.11	1.07	0.96	0.87	0.80	0.69
Unemployment rate (URATE)	0.00	0.01	0.05	0.10	0.14	0.17	1.19	0.20	0.21	0.21	0.21	0.20	0.20	0.19
Wage rate (W)	0.04	0.29	0.48	0.51	0.29	0.09	0.42	0.80	1.14	1.44	1.77	1.97	2.12	2.27

(Continued)

Table 1. (*Continued*)

	2007	2008	2009	2010	2011	2012	2013	2014	2015	2016	2017	2018	2019	2020
Long-term interest rate (INTGB)	0.11	0.08	0.07	0.12	0.14	0.14	0.10	0.11	0.12	0.07	0.09	0.03	0.00	0.05
Consumer's price (PC_SUB)	0.00	0.03	0.05	0.17	0.24	0.08	0.13	0.34	0.60	0.80	1.00	1.19	1.36	1.44
Exchange rate; Yen/$ (EXR)	0.04	3.23	3.79	2.88	3.32	2.63	2.74	3.06	2.83	2.87	2.22	3.17	2.85	1.94
Total population (POPT)	0.00	0.00	0.01	0.02	0.04	0.05	0.06	0.08	0.09	0.11	0.13	0.14	0.15	0.17
Stock price index (STOCKPR)	0.61	3.46	4.10	2.34	2.47	2.46	4.05	4.85	5.10	7.26	6.13	7.09	8.63	6.87
Tax and other rev (TSUM_SUB)	0.05	0.32	0.85	1.20	2.16	2.83	3.27	3.87	4.39	5.05	5.42	5.59	5.96	6.01
Potential GDP (GDPCSPFF)	0.00	0.00	0.00	0.00	0.02	0.05	0.10	0.16	0.21	0.26	0.31	0.35	0.39	0.42
C. Long-term Interest Rate, 1% Point Up														
GDP (GDP, real)	0.01	−0.18	−0.66	−1.22	−1.55	−1.68	−1.99	−2.00	−2.23	−2.32	−2.14	−2.28	−2.15	−1.95
GDP nominal (GDPN)	0.00	−0.07	−0.29	−0.61	−1.01	−1.30	−1.79	−2.11	−2.53	−2.92	−3.05	−3.31	−3.42	−3.32
Private consumption (CP82)	0.06	0.12	0.06	0.00	−0.27	−0.46	−0.68	−0.95	−1.08	−1.32	−1.53	−1.55	−1.78	−1.74
Business investment (IPXSUM)	−0.08	−0.18	−2.22	−4.09	−4.74	−4.95	−5.21	−4.90	−4.98	−4.75	−4.57	−4.43	−3.97	−3.87
Housing investment (IH)	0.00	−0.30	−1.12	−2.16	−4.02	−4.51	−4.17	−4.35	−3.95	−3.76	−3.57	−2.86	−2.71	−2.32
Exports (E82)	0.00	−0.45	−0.54	−0.94	−0.88	−0.94	−1.13	−0.98	−1.14	−1.18	−0.81	−1.10	−0.88	−0.66
Imports (M82)	0.01	0.88	0.86	1.37	1.21	1.31	2.15	1.73	2.49	2.31	1.26	2.19	1.40	0.90

(*Continued*)

Table 1. (*Continued*)

	2007	2008	2009	2010	2011	2012	2013	2014	2015	2016	2017	2018	2019	2020
Disposable income (YDP)	0.77	0.57	0.36	−0.01	−0.38	−0.67	−0.93	−1.34	−1.54	−1.83	−2.06	−2.10	−2.24	−2.25
Total employment (L82)	0.02	−0.04	−0.24	−0.56	−0.79	−0.93	−1.04	−1.01	−1.01	−0.96	−0.80	−0.74	−0.59	−0.43
Unemployment rate (URATE)	0.00	0.00	0.01	0.06	0.11	0.14	0.15	0.18	0.17	0.18	0.17	0.15	0.15	0.13
Wage rate (W)	−0.01	0.09	0.31	0.50	0.39	0.15	−0.17	−0.60	−0.93	−1.34	−1.74	−1.93	−2.21	−2.32
Long-term interest rate (INTGB)	0.94	1.00	0.94	1.01	0.90	0.86	1.00	0.86	1.03	0.97	0.85	1.07	0.95	0.95
Consumer's price (PC_SUB)	0.0	0.0	−0.1	0.1	0.2	0.2	0.0	−0.2	−0.4	−0.7	−1.0	−1.1	−1.4	−1.5
Exchange rate;Yen/$ (EXR)	0.00	−2.82	−1.77	−4.26	−2.14	−3.23	−4.34	−2.33	−4.32	−4.00	−0.77	−5.45	−2.02	−1.33
Total population(POPT)	0.00	0.00	−0.01	−0.02	−0.03	−0.05	−0.06	−0.07	−0.09	−0.10	−0.11	−0.13	−0.13	−0.15
Stock price index (STOCKPR)	0.07	−6.26	−6.83	−15.82	−15.31	−13.32	−17.45	−14.08	−14.54	−18.44	−13.04	−17.37	−16.75	−12.98
Tax and other rev. (TSUM_SUB)	0.11	−0.08	−0.61	−4.26	−5.51	−5.65	−6.48	−6.70	−7.14	−8.26	−8.23	−9.01	−9.10	−8.64
Potential GDP (GDPCSPFF)	0.00	0.00	0.00	0.00	−0.01	−0.10	−0.24	−0.39	−0.52	−0.64	−0.74	−0.82	−0.88	−0.93
D. Government Medical Care, 5 Billion Yen Up														
GDP (GDP, real)	0.93	1.15	1.29	1.50	1.64	1.74	2.02	2.46	2.68	3.05	3.22	3.33	3.45	3.30
GDP nominal (GDPN)	0.35	0.63	0.80	1.01	1.33	1.64	2.03	2.48	2.88	3.36	3.84	4.16	4.53	4.72
Private consumption (CP82)	−0.17	−0.09	0.01	0.33	0.62	0.85	1.17	1.47	1.85	2.27	2.68	2.99	3.26	3.38

(*Continued*)

Table 1. *(Continued)*

	2007	2008	2009	2010	2011	2012	2013	2014	2015	2016	2017	2018	2019	2020
Business investment (IPXSUM)	0.44	0.50	0.82	0.93	0.99	1.19	1.35	1.83	2.01	2.37	2.70	2.84	2.87	2.83
Housing investment (IH)	−0.14	2.77	1.51	1.39	1.68	1.67	1.66	2.06	2.40	2.75	2.43	2.58	2.51	2.51
Exports (E82)	0.00	0.31	0.44	0.49	0.44	0.41	0.57	0.87	0.79	0.93	0.88	0.82	0.83	0.66
Imports (M82)	0.33	−0.09	−0.30	−0.43	−0.27	−0.13	−0.48	−1.24	−0.89	−1.18	−0.96	−0.64	−0.64	−0.03
Disposable income (YDP)	0.16	0.32	0.43	0.51	0.79	1.01	1.39	1.59	1.87	1.92	2.33	2.47	2.73	2.93
Total employment (L82)	0.36	0.60	0.77	0.89	0.95	0.96	1.02	1.15	1.23	1.35	1.40	1.41	1.40	1.30
Unemployment rate (URATE)	0.00	−0.03	−0.07	−0.10	−0.13	−0.15	−0.17	−0.19	−0.22	−0.24	−0.27	−0.28	−0.29	−0.30
Wage rate (W)	−0.47	−0.42	−0.34	−0.29	−0.05	0.25	0.46	0.60	0.86	1.08	1.48	1.79	2.13	2.54
Long-term interest rate (INTGB)	−0.05	0.09	0.13	0.05	0.10	0.04	0.18	0.10	0.12	0.10	0.12	0.05	0.05	0.05
Consumer's price (PC_SUB)	0.0	−0.3	−0.2	−0.2	−0.2	0.0	0.2	0.4	0.5	0.6	0.8	1.0	1.2	1.5
Exchange rate; Yen/$ (EXR)	−0.35	1.76	1.78	1.79	1.13	1.30	2.72	4.66	2.52	4.28	3.46	3.16	3.76	2.19
Total population (POPT)	0.00	0.12	0.14	0.14	0.15	0.15	0.16	0.17	0.18	0.20	0.21	0.23	0.24	0.25
Stock price index (STOCKPR)	6.08	3.10	0.96	2.61	2.17	1.65	5.93	7.19	6.91	8.09	7.62	7.58	9.68	7.34
Tax and other revenues (TSUM_SUB)	0.33	1.26	1.23	1.72	2.04	2.39	3.24	3.81	4.81	5.34	6.39	6.90	7.63	7.97
Potential GDP (GDPCSPFF)	0.00	0.01	0.02	0.05	0.08	0.11	0.15	0.18	0.21	0.25	0.30	0.35	0.40	0.46

(Continued)

Table 1. (*Continued*)

	2007	2008	2009	2010	2011	2012	2013	2014	2015	2016	2017	2018	2019	2020
E. Consumption Tax, 3% Up														
GDP (GDP, real)	0.03	−2.37	−3.28	−3.67	−4.89	−4.89	−5.91	−7.19	−6.96	−8.36	−7.89	−8.23	−9.32	−7.70
GDP, nominal (GDP_N)	3.01	2.05	1.24	0.70	−1.07	−1.94	−3.04	−4.71	−5.41	−6.80	−7.65	−8.12	−9.37	−9.13
Private consumption (CP82)	0.04	−0.74	−1.27	−1.60	−2.54	−3.27	−4.27	−5.24	−5.78	−6.52	−7.35	−7.90	−8.79	−9.14
Business investment (IPXSUM)	0.04	−1.20	−2.37	−3.91	−5.13	−5.11	−5.84	−7.07	−7.63	−8.83	−7.99	−8.48	−9.29	−8.18
Housing investment (IH)	0.00	1.70	−1.10	−2.57	−2.20	−3.80	−3.71	−5.70	−7.37	−6.21	−8.72	−6.68	−7.05	−9.24
Exports (E82)	0.00	−4.34	−4.25	−3.73	−4.93	−3.93	−4.51	−5.08	−3.90	−5.10	−3.92	−3.98	−4.46	−2.74
Imports (M82)	0.08	7.99	7.94	6.93	10.39	7.87	9.24	10.49	6.44	10.10	6.63	7.15	9.40	2.53
Disposable income (YDP)	−0.27	−0.16	−0.55	−1.01	−2.02	−2.92	−3.51	−4.46	−5.39	−5.80	−6.82	−7.16	−7.55	−8.47
Total employment (L82)	0.11	−0.81	−1.40	−1.83	−2.38	−2.41	−2.68	−3.10	−3.07	−3.53	−3.33	−3.32	−3.53	−2.91
Unemployment rate (URATE)	0.00	−0.01	0.21	0.28	0.34	0.46	0.47	0.57	0.68	0.64	0.76	0.69	0.72	0.79
Wage rate (W)	−0.02	1.23	1.32	1.10	0.35	−0.85	−1.30	−2.01	−3.24	−3.60	−5.14	−5.58	−5.99	−7.39
Long-term interest rate (INTGB)	−0.67	−0.04	−0.29	−0.56	−0.35	−0.64	−0.21	−0.25	−0.74	0.10	−0.61	−0.18	0.35	−1.13
Consumer's price (PC_SUB)	0.00	−0.01	−0.14	0.46	0.46	−0.37	−0.74	−1.29	−1.79	−2.17	−2.93	−3.45	−3.98	−4.41
Exchange rate; Yen/$ (EXR)	−0.01	−20.33	−10.36	−8.01	−15.70	−7.09	−13.38	−15.01	−5.68	−18.20	−6.93	−12.83	−16.81	0.52
Total population (POPT)	0.00	−0.01	−0.03	−0.10	−0.13	−0.16	−0.21	−0.23	−0.27	−0.33	−0.35	−0.41	−0.44	−0.48

(*Continued*)

Table 1. (*Continued*)

	2007	2008	2009	2010	2011	2012	2013	2014	2015	2016	2017	2018	2019	2020
Stock price index (STOCKPR)	5.36	−10.89	−6.09	4.38		−2.55	−12.26	−24.80	−9.48	−31.42	−20.04	−19.69	−46.19	−14.77
Tax and other rev. (TSUM_SUB)	9.93	9.34	6.90	6.91	2.12	1.08	0.43	−2.93	−3.89	−6.54	−8.52	−7.64	11.59	10.71
Potential GDP (GDPCSPFF)	0.00	0.00	0.00	0.00	−0.06	−0.15	−0.30	−0.46	−0.61	−0.76	−0.93	−1.10	−1.29	−1.41
F. Accelerated Depreciation, by 10%														
GDP (GDP, real)	0.67	1.13	1.38	1.65	1.79	1.88	2.08	2.12	2.27	2.42	2.46	2.71	2.78	2.73
GDP nominal(GDPN)	0.26	0.56	0.80	1.06	1.40	1.71	2.09	2.37	2.67	3.02	3.24	3.53	3.75	3.84
Private consumption (CP82)	−0.12	0.18	0.45	0.78	1.12	1.37	1.61	1.77	1.98	2.26	2.50	2.75	2.93	3.05
Business investment (IPXSUM)	4.72	5.27	5.87	6.27	6.49	6.81	7.04	7.29	7.46	7.61	7.83	8.22	8.54	8.72
Housing investment (IH)	0.00	1.99	1.81	1.79	2.01	1.99	1.94	2.11	1.99	2.09	2.22	2.11	2.47	2.49
Exports (E82)	−0.04	0.12	0.16	0.28	0.23	0.19	0.34	0.26	0.32	0.34	0.23	0.37	0.32	0.24
Imports (M82)	1.02	0.95	1.13	1.02	1.43	1.72	1.40	1.87	1.75	1.81	2.30	1.91	2.24	2.67
Disposable income (YDP)	0.10	0.23	0.39	0.53	0.78	1.00	1.27	1.52	1.68	1.89	2.07	2.20	2.36	2.50
Total employment (L82)	0.24	0.51	0.69	0.84	0.90	0.93	0.97	0.94	0.94	0.94	0.92	0.97	0.98	0.96
Unemployment rate (URATE)	0.00	−1.45	−2.42	−3.08	−3.91	−4.44	−4.93	−5.30	−5.27	−5.39	−5.43	−5.43	−5.70	−5.65

(*Continued*)

Table 1. ***(Continued)***

	2007	2008	2009	2010	2011	2012	2013	2014	2015	2016	2017	2018	2019	2020
Wage rate (W)	−0.34	−0.46	−0.43	−0.38	−0.11	0.18	0.45	0.78	1.03	1.30	1.54	1.66	1.85	2.03
Long-term interest rate (INTGB)	−2.59	0.43	5.75	1.89	4.23	2.71	2.76	7.81	2.89	1.71	3.32	−0.66	0.88	1.97
Consumer's price (PC_SUB)	0.00	−0.24	−0.29	−0.29	−0.23	−0.10	0.10	0.33	0.49	0.69	0.86	0.98	1.13	1.20
Exchange rate Yen/$(EXR)	−0.28	0.82	0.55	1.37	0.42	0.47	1.87	0.53	1.58	1.40	0.50	2.42	1.21	0.78
Total population (POPT)	0.00	0.01	0.02	0.03	0.04	0.05	0.05	0.06	0.07	0.08	0.09	0.11	0.12	0.13
Stock price index (STOCKPR)	4.59	4.53	2.16	2.95	2.82	2.25	5.71	5.08	6.39	9.08	7.03	10.62	11.96	9.20
Tax and other revenue (TSUM_SUB)	0.30	0.88	1.07	1.59	2.13	2.45	3.16	3.58	4.26	4.91	5.14	5.83	6.38	6.56
Potential GDP (GDPCSPFF)	0.00	0.00	0.00	−0.10	−0.16	−0.19	−0.21	−0.21	−0.21	−0.21	−0.21	−0.20	−0.20	−0.19

*URATE & INTGB = Deviation, others = % Deviation.

postwar period of high economic growth was over and serious institutional and structural problems hindered continuous growth, including the deceleration of demographic growth and aging population. They estimated the growth rate of potential capacity output was only around 1–2% and further acceleration of growth would worsen inflationary pressure. Some economists ponted out also that the impact of fiscal policy was weakening in terms of Keynesian multiplier effects, citing the results of several short-term models. They were mostly estimated for the stagnant period.

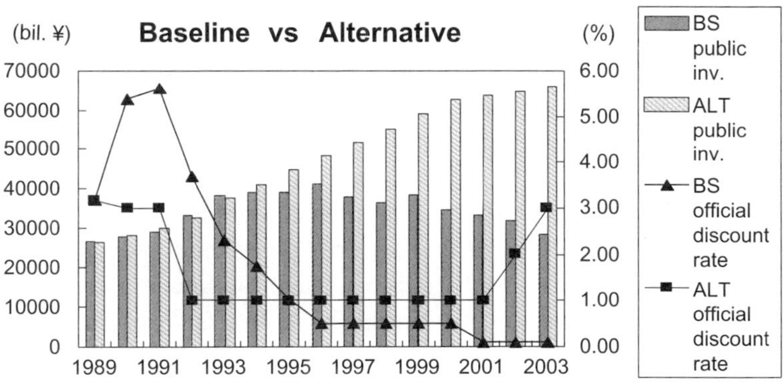

Figure 2. Expost Simulation: Baseline vs Alternative Policy.

	Public Investment (Bil.)		Official Discount Rate (%)	
	Baseline	Alternative	Baseline	Alternative
1989	26462	26462	3.17	3.17
1990	27931	28226	5.39	3.00
1991	28945	29990	5.62	3.00
1992	33185	32636	3.69	1.00
1993	38166	37583	2.31	1.00
1994	39027	40996	1.75	1.00
1995	39045	44686	1.02	1.00
1996	40987	48261	0.50	1.00
1997	37929	51639	0.50	1.00
1998	36328	55254	0.50	1.00
1999	38380	59122	0.50	1.00
2000	34396	62669	0.50	1.00
2001	33374	63743	0.10	1.00
2002	31778	64817	0.10	2.00
2003	28445	65890	0.10	3.00

"Demand-siders" claimed that the institutional issues were related to long-run factors which could not occur suddenly after 1991–1992, and that excessive demand restrictions under tight monetary-fiscal policies were main factors for lasting stagnation. It is true that some stimulating policies were attempted several times but they were weak and short-lived. These two views are examined here by means of model simulation against the following real course of policies undertaken.

In 1990, the Kaifu Cabinet of Japan decided after consulting with the US governments to adopt an ambitious plan of public investment of 430 trillion Yen over nine years to promote domestic demand. It implemented the program for the first three years, but the following Cabinets abandoned the plan thereafter, because of growing burden on the fiscal budget.

Monetary policy, on the other hand, was tightened in view of a growing inflationary pressure on stocks and land prices, and the Bank of Japan suddenly raised its official discount rate from 2.5% in 1988 to 5.39% in 1990. In 1993, as our Table 2 shows, the discount rate was lowered to 2.31%, and in 1996 the BOJ further lowered the rate down to a historically all time low of 0.50%. This was to compensate the disincentive fiscal policy. Public investment came down to the level of 28.4 trillion Yen, as low as 5.5% of GDP in 2003. Yet optimism was prevailing that the reduction of public investment has little negative effect on the macro-economy because of a falling Keynesian multiplier.

Our experiment is to explore an alternative macroeconomic policy-mix, i.e. an earlier and modest discount rate adjustment with an aggressive fiscal policy, as originally planned by the government in 1989. The annual time schedule is indicated in the above table. Particularly noteworthy outcome is the return of the discount rate to the normal level of 3% and the complete spending of 430 trillion for nine years during 1991 to 2001. A resulting alternative growth path is shown in Table 2 and its figures. Average economic growth was around 3–4% and the unemployment rate was around 3.0–3.6%, though slightly interrupted by the Asian financial crisis in 1997 and 1998, much lower than actual 3.5–4.5%. The growth rate of potential GDP was 3.5%, much higher than the baseline, indicating that the capacity level in 2003 is 51.2% higher than in 1990 due to the active expansion of both government and private fixed capital stock.

This alternative simulation indicates that Japan's long-running stagnation was avoidable if an active aggregate demand policy had been conducted with the appropriate "supply side" support by a sound monetary policy without falling into a *liquidity trap*, as at the present time. One worry might be what would happen especially to the fiscal debt.[4] As Table 1 shows, fiscal debt position of the government, defined as the ratio of general government net financial liabilities to GDP improves in 2003 by about 18%, i.e. from 59–41% as a result of relatively higher tax increases than GDP.[5] Thus, we could support the demand siders.

5. Alternative Scenarios on Economic Growth for 2020

The following are some alternative growth strategies by our DEMIOS for the period of 2007 to 2020. All the parameters estimated in the model are, in principle, estimated from the long period of 34 years from 1970 to 2004. This implies that the model experienced several business cycles, unlike many short-run macro-models in Japan which are based on a much shorter period recently which is dominated by recession years, thus indicating multipliers with weak and rigid responses from exogenous impacts and forecasting relatively pessimistic scenarios. A tendency of productive-age

Table 2. Assumptions for Baseline and Policy Scenario.

Assumptions	Baseline Scenario	Policy Scenario
1. World trade, real	5.5%	5.5%
2. Sector-level import prices and foreign export prices		common in two scenarios
3. Policy rate of Bank of Japan	0.5%	0.5%
4. Government consump., real	2%	2.5%+special addition of medical care of 5 trillion Yen
5. Government investment, real	0%	15% — 2007–2009, 13–10% — 2010–2015, 3% — 2016–2020
6. Government transfers	2%	2.5%
7. Private housing investment	—	5 trillion Yen 2007–2020
8. Business investment	—	tax credit with accelerated depreciation of 10% — 2007–2020

[4]Another point to be stressed in our simulation is the increase in population, amounting to 413 thousand up by 0.33% in 2003 as compared with the baseline.

[5]In order to obtain a more precise response pattern of government expenditure and tax revenues, a quarterly model is needed. To smoothen the quarterly pattern of expenditure amounts and revenues is important, but our annual model cannot handle this matter. Instead, it can indicate the long-run impacts of public investment including demographic elements.

population to decline and the image of aging society and growing fiscal deficits of the government all help to contribute to many pessimistic forecasts which affect policy makers and mass-media.

In contrast to the pessimists, there are others, such as L.R. Klein's group and some Japanese economists who suggest higher growth potentials in view of past growth records before and after World War II with empirical simulations of econometric models (Klein, *et al.*, *op. cit.*; Shishido, 2007b). Our model DEMIOS has shown a wider range of policy alternatives above, and now attempts below first to present the most likely growth pattern under the present government as Baseline and then an alternative aggressive policy scenario as Policy Scenario.

5.1. *Baseline scenario*

This scenario is not a forecast but broadly follows the basic stance of the present government. i.e. restoring the primary balance of the fiscal budget of central and local governments, no consumption tax increases, continuation of present low policy rate of the Bank of Japan, etc. Our result in Table 3.1 and its graph indicates a continued stagnant economy, especially under the high unemployment rate of over 4%. The GDP grows at 1–2% until 2012 followed by a slight slow down, and finally recovers to around a 2% level.

Particularly noteworthy under the high rate of unemployment is the expected continuation of the income disparities among income groups and different regions. There is no clear indication of improvement in fiscal deficits, reflecting a stagnant and deflationary trend of the Japanese economy. This implies that the Japanese growth is likely to depend heavily on foreign demand and weakly on domestic demand despite strong potentials such as industrial technology and huge domestic savings. The Yen/$ exchange rate seems to indicate an appreciating tendency, around 75–80 Yen per dollar between 2015 and 2020, reflecting huge current account surplus and deflation trend.

5.2. *Policy scenario*

Our policy scenario is an experiment among various policy alternatives. This option requires a basic change in the present policy stance, especially in terms of fiscal policy with which the government has exerted much effort for the reduction of fiscal deficits, albeit under the present deflationary economy. In contrast to this direction, our policy scenario assumes more

Table 3.1. Baseline Scenario (Billion Yen).

	2007	2008	2009	2010	2011	2012	2013	2014	2015	2016	2017	2018	2019	2020
GDP (GDP, real)	569723	580992	595757	608051	621631	639245	644343	650252	655098	657621	669822	676000	683071	701973
%		1.98	2.54	2.06	2.23	2.83	0.80	0.92	0.75	0.39	1.86	0.92	1.05	2.77
GDP, nominal (GDP_N)	542754	562140	590405	617831	639970	664698	684520	701630	719677	730565	744401	755747	765740	784079
%		3.57	5.03	4.65	3.58	3.86	2.98	2.50	2.57	1.51	1.89	1.52	1.32	2.39
Private consump. (CP82)	299226	305014	311189	318736	326798	336129	341569	346203	351040	356820	363685	371389	379933	391889
%		1.93	2.02	2.42	2.53	2.86	1.62	1.36	1.40	1.65	1.92	2.12	2.30	3.15
Housing investment (IH)	16273	19141	23998	25317	25564	25575	25669	25272	25453	25895	25708	26638	26774	26978
%		17.62	25.38	5.50	0.98	0.04	0.36	−1.54	0.72	1.73	−0.72	3.62	0.51	0.76
Business investment (IPXSUM)	91025	91775	90844	90161	90914	90764	89876	89689	89786	89274	90082	91139	90801	92440
%		0.82	−1.01	−0.75	0.83	−0.17	−0.98	−0.21	0.11	−0.57	0.90	1.17	−0.37	1.81
Exports (E82)	79990	84376	93015	100936	105963	112474	116778	121977	127810	134112	142916	150258	158691	169378
%		5.48	10.24	8.52	4.98	6.14	3.83	4.45	4.78	4.93	6.56	5.14	5.61	6.73
Imports (M82)	64753	70123	71665	73035	74028	75443	82381	87976	93022	97532	96884	101857	104704	102664
%		8.29	2.20	1.91	1.36	1.91	9.20	6.79	5.74	4.85	−0.66	5.13	2.80	−1.95

(Continued)

Table 3.1. (*Continued*)

	2007	**2008**	**2009**	**2010**	**2011**	**2012**	**2013**	**2014**	**2015**	**2016**	**2017**	**2018**	**2019**	**2020**
Long-term interest rate (INTGB)	1.79	2.32	1.30	2.30	2.16	1.68	2.33	1.64	1.82	2.40	2.49	3.41	3.41	3.03
%		29.68	−43.98	77.38	−6.13	−22.12	38.12	−29.72	11.13	31.89	3.81	36.95	0.19	−11.36
Consumer's price (PC)	96.2	97.6	100.6	103.3	104.4	105.5	108.1	110.2	112.8	114.3	114.5	115.5	116.1	115.9
%		1.42	3.04	2.70	1.08	1.02	2.50	1.95	2.39	1.31	0.20	0.82	0.53	−0.21
Wage rate, 1000 Yen (W)	4931	5067	5252	5460	5607	5727	5902	6049	6209	6328	6375	6444	6493	6511
%		2.76	3.66	3.97	2.68	2.14	3.06	2.49	2.64	1.91	0.74	1.09	0.76	0.27
Unempolyment rate (URATE)	4.22	4.10	4.17	4.16	4.21	4.24	4.19	4.33	4.46	4.62	4.80	4.85	4.99	5.10
%		−2.82	1.83	−0.18	1.08	0.64	−1.06	3.34	3.01	3.47	4.00	1.11	2.77	2.16
Exchange rate Yen/$ (EXR)	125.4	101.2	100.8	98.3	94.2	98.8	82.2	79.8	76.8	74.4	82.1	73.0	73.5	81.6
%		−19.27	−0.40	−2.44	−4.21	4.91	−16.78	−3.01	−3.78	−3.13	10.40	−11.03	0.64	11.01
Tax and other rev. (TSUM_SUB)	164189	167267	181834	193111	196411	212811	215916	222866	232721	230743	237947	241760	240423	243752
%		1.87	8.71	6.20	1.71	8.35	1.46	3.22	4.42	−0.85	3.12	1.60	−0.55	1.38

(*Continued*)

Table 3.1. (*Continued*)

	2007	2008	2009	2010	2011	2012	2013	2014	2015	2016	2017	2018	2019	2020
Net Finan. Ass of Gen. Gov. (GGFDN)	306745	286077	268418	278518	279796	279306	290388	282501	297255	315934	324915	344973	349729	354612
%		−6.74	−6.17	3.76	0.46	−0.18	3.97	−2.72	5.22	6.28	2.84	6.17	1.38	1.40
do.% of GDPN (GGFDN/GDPN)	0.565	0.509	0.455	0.451	0.437	0.420	0.424	0.403	0.413	0.432	0.436	0.456	0.457	0.452
%		−9.95	−10.66	−0.84	−3.02	−3.89	0.96	−5.09	2.58	4.70	0.93	4.58	0.06	−0.98
Current a/c Surplus, % of GDPN	0.032	0.033	0.038	0.051	0.056	0.061	0.062	0.061	0.064	0.068	0.076	0.080	0.083	0.092
%		3.11	16.25	33.78	9.11	7.73	1.85	−1.52	5.02	6.46	11.67	5.73	4.19	10.76
Capital Stock of Gen. Gov.	320103	318639	317278	316015	314841	313751	312738	311798	310925	310113	309360	308660	308010	307406
%		−0.46	−0.43	−0.40	−0.37	−0.35	−0.32	−0.30	−0.28	−0.26	−0.24	−0.23	−0.21	−0.20
Total population, (POPT) 1000	128111	128302	128444	128529	128646	128764	128848	128944	129014	129090	129157	129214	129290	129335
%		0.15	0.11	0.07	0.09	0.09	0.06	0.07	0.05	0.06	0.05	0.04	0.06	0.03

aggressive fiscal policy including government investment, and consumption for medical care, tax reform for accelerated depreciation, etc.

First, government investment is assumed to play a role for *pumping up* the economy, especially business investment, at the first stage of our forecast. This policy instrument has not been used ever since 2000, resulting in zero growth or even falling trend of infra-structure, as the baseline scenario shows. In the alternative scenario the government investment may be concentrated in such new areas as environment, alternative energy, IT network, science and technology, education, medical care and social services as well as traditional investment like airport, highway, anti-calamity measures, urban planning, etc. They are all the more important in global competition.

Regarding government consumption, the medical care needs to be particularly strengthened in the aging society, so that the additional medical care amounting to 5 trillion Yen is assumed. As Table 2 shows, its expected multiplier effects will be significant on economic and demographic factors. Tax policy plays an important role in our policy scenario. As L. R. Klein's group suggested, investment tax credit with accelerated depreciation is highly effective in Japan as well as in the US for stimulating business investment. This policy becomes especially important at a time of the "liquidity trap" that Japan has suffered since 1996. We assume the period for depreciation to be cut by 10% for all industry, regardless of size and sector, as shown in Table 2. A strong and lasting impact is expected as a result of induced demand for renewal investment and cash flow effect from corporate tax cut.

Finally, housing investment is also assumed to be increased by 5 billion Yen in view of policy consideration to stimulate aggregative demand from the financial sector. The results are presented in Table 3.2 and its graph, giving a remarkable contrast to the baseline scenario. The real GDP growth rate is accelerated to around 4% for the entire period between 2008 and 2020, as compared with 1–2% for the baseline scenarios. The rate of unemployment falls to the level of 2% in 2020, the same level in 1990. The rate of capacity operation is around 100% during 2015 and 2020, implying that the economy is running under its full capacity. Consumer's price is modestly rising at around 2% during the first half of our period, but slightly leveling off to 1–2% during the second half. There is no sign of over-heating.

Business investment also indicates a sound growth trend around 5% during the first half, followed by around 4% in the latter half due to strong

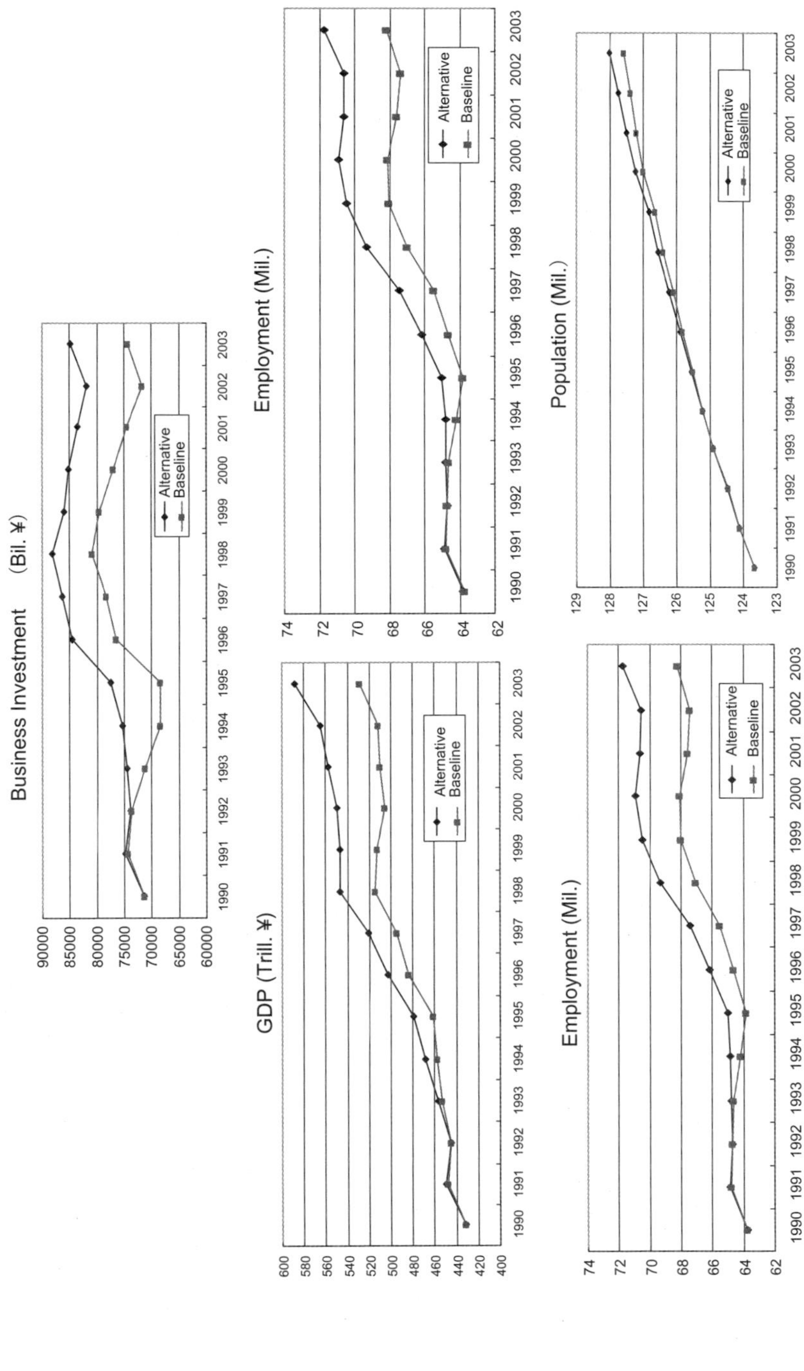

Figure 3. Expost Simulation: Baseline vs Alternative Policy — For Major Variables.

Table 3.2. Policy Scenario (Billion Yen).

	2007	2008	2009	2010	2011	2012	2013	2014	2015	2016	2017	2018	2019	2020
GDP	585373	609939	639995	671212	705597	743948	774205	804294	836815	867087	903364	940071	978283	1026526
%		4.20	4.93	4.88	5.12	5.44	4.07	3.89	4.04	3.62	4.18	4.06	4.06	4.93
GDP_N	548616	575939	614388	656280	698083	747565	800398	856023	920292	985667	1055769	1131075	1210803	1301198
%		4.98	6.68	6.82	6.37	7.09	7.07	6.95	7.51	7.10	7.11	7.13	7.05	7.47
CP82	297822	304779	312482	324449	339514	357551	373345	389584	408397	432577	459648	490763	525338	567027
%		2.34	2.53	3.83	4.64	5.31	4.42	4.35	4.83	5.92	6.26	6.77	7.05	7.94
IH	16273	23216	31281	33543	34486	35284	35744	35882	36601	37768	38099	39450	40523	41846
%		42.67	34.74	7.23	2.81	2.31	1.30	0.39	2.01	3.19	0.88	3.55	2.72	3.26
IPXSUM	97926	102668	107202	113561	121901	128573	134412	141197	148126	153406	160358	168646	175972	186040
%		4.84	4.42	5.93	7.34	5.47	4.54	5.05	4.91	3.56	4.53	5.17	4.34	5.72
E82	79850	84119	93008	101762	107344	113927	119491	125105	131696	139055	147521	155824	164661	174639
%		5.35	10.57	9.41	5.49	6.13	4.88	4.70	5.27	5.59	6.09	5.63	5.67	6.06
M82	66353	73334	76321	78360	81291	85608	93729	103089	111039	117394	121961	129585	136807	142155
%		10.52	4.07	2.67	3.74	5.31	9.49	9.99	7.71	5.72	3.89	6.25	5.57	3.91
INTGB	1.47	1.43	0.64	1.71	1.68	1.26	2.10	1.63	1.82	2.29	2.72	3.23	3.17	2.92
%		−2.92	−55.34	167.71	−1.70	−24.81	66.49	−22.30	11.96	25.60	18.78	18.52	−1.89	−7.61
PC	94.2	94.3	95.9	97.2	97.6	98.7	101.5	104.4	108.0	111.6	114.7	118.1	121.5	124.4
%		0.06	1.74	1.39	0.35	1.15	2.79	2.90	3.45	3.31	2.76	2.99	2.92	2.36
W	4865	4968	5127	5319	5488	5677	5950	6251	6600	6973	7325	7698	8080	8450
%		2.13	3.19	3.75	3.17	3.46	4.80	5.06	5.57	5.66	5.05	5.08	4.97	4.57

(Continued)

Table 3.2. *(Continued)*

	2007	2008	2009	2010	2011	2012	2013	2014	2015	2016	2017	2018	2019	2020
URATE	4.22	3.86	3.76	3.53	3.31	3.05	2.75	2.60	2.50	2.40	2.34	2.24	2.16	2.06
%		−8.33	−2.73	−6.08	−6.33	−7.69	−9.87	−5.42	−4.03	−4.06	−2.21	−4.30	−3.85	−4.26
EXR	124.0	100.0	102.0	105.0	101.1	104.7	94.8	90.1	90.5	91.7	96.1	92.9	93.2	98.4
%		−19.37	2.03	2.98	−3.77	3.58	−9.44	−5.01	0.48	1.32	4.77	−3.31	0.31	5.58
TSUM_SUB	166137	173810	192739	212740	230080	260324	279933	307384	344445	371485	412823	456741	500353	548885
%		4.62	10.89	10.38	8.15	13.15	7.53	9.81	12.06	7.85	11.13	10.64	9.55	9.70
GGFDN	307655	286644	251501	246281	230965	213059	199686	171321	163875	161716	149999	148740	140027	128650
%		−6.83	−12.26	−2.08	−6.22	−7.75	−6.28	−14.21	−4.35	−1.32	−7.25	−0.84	−5.86	−8.12
GGFDN/ GDPN	0.5608	0.4977	0.4094	0.3753	0.3309	0.2850	0.2495	0.2001	0.1781	0.1641	0.1421	0.1315	0.1156	0.0989
%		−11.25	−17.75	−8.33	−11.83	−13.86	−12.46	−19.78	−11.03	−7.86	−13.40	−7.44	−12.06	−14.51
BLCRAT	0.0245	0.0186	0.0176	0.0236	0.0221	0.0178	0.0156	0.0099	0.0069	0.0065	0.0071	0.0072	0.0059	0.0047
%		−24.29	−5.34	34.11	−6.11	−19.67	−11.94	−36.70	−30.40	−5.08	7.80	1.42	−17.34	−20.30
KGGSNA	323484	329046	338684	352091	369192	389413	412967	440093	471061	506177	545780	590248	640004	695518
%		1.72	2.93	3.96	4.86	5.48	6.05	6.57	7.04	7.45	7.82	8.15	8.43	8.67
POPT	128110	128345	128594	128780	129019	129273	129503	129779	130074	130381	130692	130999	131317	131630
%		0.18	0.19	0.14	0.19	0.20	0.18	0.21	0.23	0.24	0.24	0.23	0.24	0.24

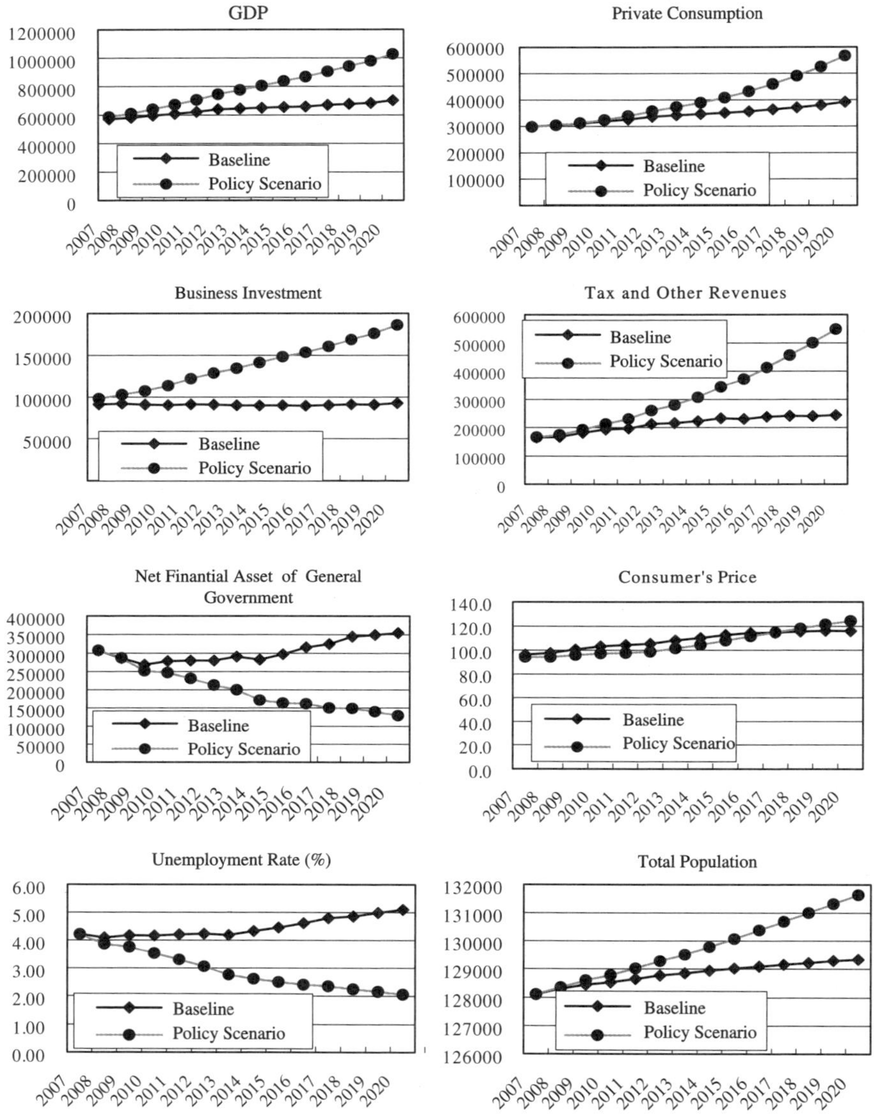

Figure 4. Policy Simulation 2007 to 2020 for Major Variables.

government investment during the first half and tax policy of accelerated depreciation for the entire period. An increase in private consumption is noticeable, growing slowly for the first three years around 2–3%. But later it remarkably accelerates from 5–7%, mainly due to the multiplier effect of government medical care expenditure and other positive demographic factors such as an increase in the elder population with the higher propensity to consume.

Finally, in contrast to most demographers' forecast, total population in policy scenario indicates the increase of 2.8%, while that of the baseline scenario shows the increase of 1.0%. These results can be compared with the government's Research Institute of Demographic Problems, whose estimate is −2.8%. This significant difference is, as noted earlier, because the Institute's method disregards economic and policy factors. The difference is particularly notable in forecasting the elderly population, pop65, for which DEMIOS estimates 8.9% and 21.3% in policy and baseline scenarios, respectively. The Institute forecasts 36.2% for this age group, since it simply forecasts on the basis of recent trend of its cohort type model. Particular attention is needed as regards the difference in forecasts of the elderly population by DEMIOS, where faster population growth accompanies the increase in the share of the younger generation which tends to check the increase in the share of the elderly population.

5.3. *Sector-level production*

Regarding sectoral production, notice that there is a marked contrast between the two scenarios. Table 4 shows that in the baseline scenario, public utilities and manufacturing sectors achieve the highest record and are followed by finance and other services among major categories. In general, however, production activities are weak, except for other electrical machinery, automobiles, communication, and social services for the aging society.

The policy scenario, on the other hand, indicates much vibrant activities. In general, during the first half of the period, production activities are a little stronger than in the second half for all major categories. Particularly noteworthy is the construction sector which is strongly affected by government investment during the first half of the period. A similar impact is also observed for the cement industry as shown in the table. In terms of major categories, however, a weakening sign is observed for agriculture, etc., due to growing agricultural imports from Asia. In a sharp contrast in specific sector levels, the highest growth is observed for other social services in the baseline scenario. For manufacturing, automobiles and various IT-related machinery industries show a higher record. The communications sector

Table 4. Sectoral Production (%: Rate of Change).

	I 2008–2013; II 2014–2020			
	Baseline Sc.		Polcy Sc.	
	I	II	I	II
1. Production in Major Categories (2000 price)				
Agriculture, etc	0.46%	−1.09%	3.14%	1.80%
Manufacturing	2.47%	1.98%	4.83%	3.54%
Construction	1.91%	0.50%	8.46%	3.91%
Public utility	2.83%	1.13%	4.99%	3.52%
Trade, communication	2.21%	0.99%	4.44%	3.91%
Finance, other services	2.34%	1.29%	4.88%	4.59%
Total	2.30%	1.38%	5.00%	3.98%
2. Production, Specific Sectors				
Final chemicals	2.37%	1.90%	3.55%	3.09%
Cement	0.31%	−0.29%	4.67%	2.58%
Steel	0.89%	1.00%	2.46%	−0.20%
Other industry Machineries	1.86%	1.83%	5.73%	4.27%
Other electr. Machineries	3.33%	3.75%	5.27%	4.39%
Automobiles	4.82%	4.13%	6.91%	5.49%
Waste disposal	3.93%	1.72%	6.45%	4.86%
Air transport	2.56%	2.85%	4.22%	4.28%
Communication	5.19%	2.89%	6.41%	8.72%
Information services	2.58%	1.41%	6.93%	5.37%
Education	1.23%	0.88%	2.34%	2.25%
Medical cares	1.31%	1.27%	3.98%	2.16%
Other social services	4.51%	2.62%	8.35%	7.24%
Aggregative Productive Capacity or Potential GDP and the Rate of Utilization				

also shows a higher record, especially in the second half of the period. The education sector, although twice as high as that in baseline, remains relatively weak as compared with other sectors in the policy scenario. In view of the growing importance of IT-related society amid global competition, more resources appear to be necessary, as suggested by L. R. Klein group in the Japanese study. (Klein *et al.*, *op. cit.*) In order to evaluate macro-economic policy performance, potential GDP was estimated as a reference indicator by using a long time series since 1973. The result of our estimation of a modified Cobb-Douglas type production function is given in the Appendix.

As described earlier, the GDP is explained by capital stock of private and public enterprise, total employment, average hours worked, the rate of unemployment, capital stock of general government (infrastructure), and time trend. The result indicates a slight margin of scale effect of 0.08, and a total factor productivity of 1.8%, and business capital stock elasticity of 0.26, employment elasticity of 0.82, general government capital stock elasticity of 0.12, as measured in terms of the ratio of change over the previous year. The unemployment rate elasticity is −0.12. In normalizing for maximum capacity, the unemployment is set at 2.1% and the hours worked at 170 hours in 1990, when the economy is assumed to be running at near full-capacity. A remarkable difference is observed in Table 5 and its figure, showing a falling trend in the rate of operation in the baseline scenario and worsening business condition, despite a weak recovery in 2020, while a gradual acceleration in terms of capacity and a rising tendency of the rate of operation is observed in the policy scenario. The total factor productivity increase by 1.8% is encouraging for the long-term growth of the Japanese economy, although our method must be improved for sectorial analysis.

6. Concluding Remarks and Future Research

This study on policy alternative is only one experiment, but now various other policy alternatives are under study, such as income tax reduction, reduction of working hours to stimulate private consumption, specific tax incentives for environment like carbon tax and for promotion of IT in specific sectors, etc. It is commonly thought that the Japanese economy is still not only in a *liquidity trap* but also in a *fiscal debt trap,* meaning the fiscal stimulus limited by large fiscal debt. This *double-trap* may force the increase in the tax burden such as consumption tax, and hinder the economic recovery. One policy scenario presented above clearly indicates, however, that fiscal policy can stimulate the economy and reduce the fiscal debts through "natural tax increase" under the accelerated economic growth with no new tax rate hike. It implies that automatic stability mechanism can work quite well. More flexible idea on fiscal policy would be desirable.

Our model itself needs further improvements particularly in handling technological progress. The V-RAS system is being improved with special emphasis on IT, new environmental technology, improvements in agricultural technology and management and so on. We are planning to take up these various challenges with the new models.

Table 5. Growth of Potential GDP and the Rate of Utilization.

	2007	2008	2009	2010	2011	2012	2013	2014	2015	2016	2017	2018	2019	2020
Potential GDP														
Baseline Sc	Na	2.4%	2.4%	2.4%	2.4%	2.4%	2.3%	2.4%	2.3%	2.3%	2.2%	2.2%	2.2%	2.2%
Policy Sc	Na	2.6%	2.6%	2.5%	2.7%	2.9%	3.1%	3.3%	3.3%	3.3%	3.4%	3.4%	3.3%	3.3%
Rate of utilization														
Baseline Sc	85.8	85.4	85.5	85.2	85.1	85.5	84.2	83.0	81.7	80.2	79.9	78.9	78.1	78.5%
Policy Sc	88.1	89.5	91.5	93.6	95.8	98.2	99.1	99.7	100.4	100.7	101.5	102.1	102.9	104.4

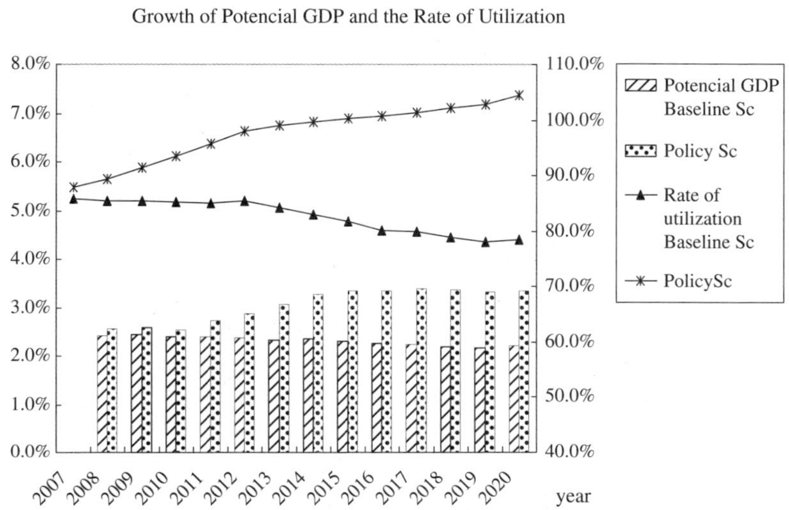

Figure 5. Growth Rate of Potential GDP and the Rate of Utilization.

Appendix

1. Demographic Equations Births (POPBI)								
	Method: Least Squares			Date: 04/20/07 Time: 22:00				
Depend Variable: *POPB1/POPT*	Sample(adj) 1977–05			Included observations: 29 after adjustments				
Variable	Coeff.	St. Err.	t-Stat.	Prob.	*R*-squared	0.9752	SD Dep. var.	0.002
(*POP15*(−1)-*POP15*(−2))/*POP15*(−2)	0.0912	0.0164	5.6048	0	Adj. R^2	0.9711	Akaike in. crit.	−12.934
(*KH*(−5)-*KH*(−6))/*KH*(−6)	0.0325	0.0024	13.42	0	S.E. of regres	0.0003	Schwarz crit.	−12.698
URATE(−7)	−0.0007	0.0002	−3.7317	0.001	Sumsq. resid	2.90E-06	F-statistic	235.93
CG(−3)/*GDP*(−3)	0.0473	0.0094	5.0076	0	Log likelih.	192.54	Prob(F-stati)	0
C	0.003	0.0014	2.1026	0.0462	DW stat	1.949		
					Mean dep. Var.	0.011		
Deaths (POPDE)	Method: Least Square			Date: 01/29/07 Time: 19:02				
Dependent Variable: *POPDE/POPT*	Sample (adj)1976–04			Included observations: 29 after adj.				
Variable	Coeff.	St. Err	t-Stati.	Prob.	R-squared	0.9808	Mean dep. Var.	0.0068
POP65/POPT	0.0245	0.0019	13.014	0	Adj R^2	0.9777	S.D. dep. var.	0.0007
(*CP*(−1)-*CP*(−3))/*CP*(−6)	−0.0016	0.0009	−1.8457	0.0773	S.E. of regres	0.0001	Akaike in-Crit	−15.407
(*TRH1*+*TRH2*)/*GNP_N*	−0.0134	0.0044	−3.0191	0.0059	Sum sq. res.	2.45E-07	Schwarz crit	−15.172
CG(−2)/*GDP*(−3)	−0.0024	0.0036	−0.6719	0.5081	Log likelih.	228.41	*F*-statistic	307.24
C	0.0055	0.0004	14.343	0	DW	2.2744	Prob. (F-stat)	0

(*Continued*)

Appendix (*Continued*)

Net Immigrants	Method: Least Sq			Date: 02/26/07Time: 14:21				
Depen Variable: *POPSO/POPT*	Sample (adj): 1972-05			Included observ. 34 after adjustments				
Variable	Coeff.	Std. Err.	t-Stat.	Prob.	*R*-squared	0.2001	Mean dep. var.	−1.81E-05
(IP(−1)+*IG*(−1))/*GDP*(−1)	0.0113	0.0052	2.1747	0.0377	Adj *R*-sq.	0.1201	S.D. dep. var.	0.0003
(*TRH1*(−1) + *TRH2*(−1))/ *GNP_N*(−1)	0.0136	0.005	2.6977	0.0113	S.E. of regres	0.0003	Akaike InCrit	−13.405
EXR	4.66E-06	1.94E-06	2.4037	0.0226	Sum sq. resi.	2.37E-06	Schwar z crit.	−13.225
C	−0.0046	0.0018	−2.5353	0.0167	Log Likelih.	231.88	F-statistic	2.5016
					DW	2.2996	Prob. (F-stati)	0.0783
Population under 15	Method: Least Squares			Date: 01/29/07 Time: 19:01				
Dependent Variable: *POP0_BI*	Sample (adj.): 1981 2004			Included observations: 24 after adj.				
Variable	Coeff.	Std. Error	t-Statistic	Prob.	R-squared	0.934012	Mean depend var.	0.170332
((*POP*15(−7) + *POP*15(−8) + *POP*15(−9)) − (*POP*15(−8) + *POP*15(−9) + *POP*15(−10)))/(*POP*15(−8) + *POP*15(−9) + *POP*15(−10))	8.354324	1.545002	5.407321	0	Adj. *R*-squared	0.92012	SD. Depend var.	0.027795
(*KH*(−5) − *KH*(−6))/*KH*(−6)	0.426233	0.141974	3.002177	0.0073	SE of regres	0.007856	Akaike in crit.	−6.67213
URATE(−8) + *URATE*(−9)	−0.01112	0.002714	−4.09697	0.0006	Sum sq. resid	0.001172	Schwarz crit.	−6.4267
CG(−3)/*GDP*(−3)	3.195846	0.512937	6.230481	0	Log likelihood	85.06556	F-statistic	67.23262
C	−0.3488	0.088191	−3.955	0.0008	DW	1.017713	Prob. (F-stat)	0

(*Continued*)

Appendix (*Continued*)

Population over 65	Method: Least Squares			Date: 12/17/07 Time: 08:24				
Dependent Variable: *POP65/POPT*	Sample (adj): 1980 2004			Included observ.: 25 after adj.				
Variable	Coeff.	Std. Err.	t-Stat.	Prob.	*R*-squared	0.998548	Mean dep. var.	0.1345
(*TRH1*(−7) + *TRH2*(−7))/*GNP_N*(−7)	0.353773	0.084725	4.175541	0.0005	Adj. *R*-sq.	0.998166	SD. Dep. var.	0.033793
CG(−4)/*GDP*(−4)	0.956022	0.046016	20.77596	0	SE of regres.	0.001447	Akaike in crit.	−10.033
(*POP15*(−7) + *POP15*(−8) + *POP15*(−9))/ (*POPT*(−7) + *POPT*(−8) + *POPT*(−9))	1.994605	0.084367	23.64198	0	Sum sq resid.	3.98E-05	Schwarz crit.	−9.74044
(*POPTNA*(−4) − *POPTNA*(−5))/ *POPTNA*(−5)	−3.70461	0.765644	−4.83855	0.0001	Log likelihood	131.4122	F-statistic	2613.828
DUM9700	−0.00749	0.001028	−7.28335	0	DW	2.300972	Prob (F-stat)	0
C	−1.38423	0.066658	−20.7661	0				

2. GDP & Business Investment : Examples

GDP	Method: Least Squares			Date 01/18/07Time: 12:39				
Dependent Variable: LOG(*GDPX*)	Sample (adj): 1973 2004			Included observations: 32 after adjustments				
Variable	Coeff.	St. Err.	t-Stat.	Prob.	*R*-squared	0.999019	Mean dep. var.	12.85672
C	−3.86935	1.347111	−2.87233	0.008	Adj. *R*-sq.	0.99883	SD dep. var.	0.269658
LOG(*KPG82*(−3))	0.264386	0.034859	7.584472	0	S.E. of regrdx	0.009223	Akaike in crit.	−6.3668
LOG(*L***LHRTL*)	0.817434	0.10347	7.900228	0	Sum sq. resid.	0.002212	Schwarz crit.	−6.09197
LOG(*URATE*)	−0.15392	0.01969	−7.81702	0	Log likelihood	107.8688	F-statistic	5294.371
LOG(*KGGSNA/KGGSNA*(−1))	0.120499	0.091872	1.311593	0.2011	DW	1.847756	Prob. (F-stati)	0
@TREND	0.018457	0.001299	14.20538	0				

(*Continued*)

Appendix (*Continued*)

47. Automobile	Method: Least Squares			Date 06/27/08Time11:38				
Dependent Variable: *IP_47*	Sample (adj.): 1974–2003			Included observations: 30 after adjustments				
Variable	Coeff.	St. Err.	*t*-Stat.	Prob.	*R*-sq.	0.949913	Mean dep. var.	1992.875
C	−137.064	787.6692	−0.17401	0.8633	Adj. *R*-sq.	0.939478	SD dep. var.	866.5829
X47(−1)	0.000131	1.63E-05	8.041942	0	SE of regres.	213.1893	Akaike in crit.	13.73909
KP_47(−3)	−0.21412	0.043765	−4.8924	0.0001	Sum sq. resid.	1090792	Schwarz crit.	14.01933
INTGB(−2)	−217.137	45.1758	−4.80649	0.0001	Log likelihood	−200.086	F-statistic	91.03355
EXR(−1)	4.819227	2.153183	2.238188	0.0348	DW	1.794739	Prob. (F-stat)	0
IGXSUM(−2)	9.41E-05	3.14E-05	2.995513	0.0063				
70. Finance	Method: Least Squares			D. 06/27/08Time 11:43				
Dependent Variable: *IP_70*	Sample (adj.): 1975–2003			Included observations: 29 after adjustments				
Variable	Coeffi.	St. Err.	*t*-Stat.	Prob.	*R*-squared	0.940094	Mean dep. var.	1632.761
C	−107.124	572.1503	−0.18723	0.8531	Adj *R*-sq.	0.927071	SD dep. var.	796.4739
X70(−2)	4.27E-05	1.89E-05	2.26654	0.0331	SE of regress.	215.0913	Akaike in crit.	13.76199
KP_70(−5)	−0.28336	0.059737	−4.74351	0.0001	Sum sq. resid.	1064079	Schwarz crit.	14.04488
INTGB(−2)	−169.939	51.39212	−3.30671	0.0031	Log likelihood	−193.549	F-statistic	72.18656
CP(−1)	0.014016	0.003407	4.113618	0.0004	DW	1.107607	Prob. (F-stati)	0
IGXSUM(−4)	6.36E-05	3.73E-05	1.704785	0.1017				

(*Continued*)

Appendix (*Continued*)

71. Real estate	Method: Least Squares			Date 06/27/08 Time: 11:43				
Dependent Variable: *IP_71*	Sample (adjusted): 1976–2003			Included observations: 28 after adjustments				
Variable	Coefficient	Std. Error	*t*-Statistic	Prob.	R-squared	0.800338	Mean dependent var	1772.824
C	792.9262	1721.193	0.460684	0.6495	Adjusted R-squared	0.75496	S.D. dependent var	819.678
X71	0.000105	4.14E-05	2.534901	0.0189	S.E. of regression	405.7531	Akaike info criterion	15.03678
KP_71(−5)	−0.254153	0.06786	−3.745235	0.0011	Sum squared resid	3621982	Schwarz criterion	15.32225
PX71(−3)/*PZ71*(−3)	−980.6333	1473.98	−0.665296	0.5128	Log likelihood	−204.5149	F-statistic	17.63721
INTGB(−3)	−373.8321	106.098	−3.523461	0.0019	Durbin-Watson stat	0.846515	Prob(F-statistic)	0
IGX71	0.003753	0.001158	3.24033	0.0038				
72. Information service	Method: Least Squares			Date 06/27/08 Time: 11:44				
Dependent Variable: *IP_72*	Sample (adjusted): 1973–2003			Included observations: 31 after adjustments				
Variable	Coefficient	Std. Error	*t*-Statistic	Prob.	R-squared	0.933201	Mean dependent var	592.2935
C	149.6961	363.7565	0.411528	0.6842	Adjusted R-squared	0.919841	S.D. dependent var	503.1192
X72	6.70E-05	1.99E-05	3.371364	0.0024	S.E. of regression	142.4447	Akaike info criterion	12.92777
KP_72(−3)	−0.038376	0.034003	-1.12861	0.2698	Sum squared resid	507262.2	Schwarz criterion	13.20532
PX72/*PZ72*	295.6524	168.7088	1.752443	0.092	Log likelihood	−194.3804	F-statistic	69.85151
INTGB(−3)	−93.65543	33.94929	-2.758686	0.0107	Durbin-Watson stat	1.007582	Prob(F-statistic)	0
IGXSUM	1.70E-05	8.25E-06	2.065413	0.0494				

(*Continued*)

References

Adams, F. G. and S. Shishido (1988). Structure of Trade and Industry in the US-Japan Economy. NIRA Output NRS-85-1, February.

Adams, F. G., B. Gangnes and S. Shishido (1993). *Economic Activity, Trade and Industry in the US-Japan-World Economy*. Praeger Publishers.

Klein, L. R., F. G. Adams, Y. Kumasaka and A. Shinozaki (2007). *Accelerating Japan's Economic Growth: Resolving Japan's Growth Controversy*. Routledge.

Shishido, S., K. Harada and Y. Matsumura (1991). Technical Progress in an Input-Output Framework with Special Reference to Japan's High Technology Industries. In Peterson, W. (ed.), *Advances in Input-Output Analysis: Technology, Development, and Planning*. Proceedings of Eighth International Conference on Input-Output Techniques. Oxford University Press.

Shishido, S. and O. Nakamura (1992). Induced Technical Progress and Structural Adjustment: A Multi-Sectoral Model Approach to Japan's Growth Alternatives. *Journal of Applied Input-Output Analysis*, 1, 1–23.

Shishido, S. *et al.* (2002a). *A Study on Methods for Multi-Sector Dynamic Econometric Models of Japanese Economy*. Research Institute of Economy, Trade and Industry (Japanese).

Shishido, S. *et al.* (2002b). *A Study on Multi-Sector Dynamic Econometric Models for Medium- and Long-Term Economic Forecasting*, Research Institute of Economy, Trade and Industry (Japanese).

Shishido, S. (2004). Japan's Economic Growth and Policy-Making in the Context of Input-Output Models. In Dietzenbacher, E. and Lahr, M. L. (eds.), *Wassily Leontief and Input-Output Economics*. Oxford: Cambridge University Press.

Shishido, S., A. Kawakami, M. Kurokawa, A. Movshuk and K. Tamashiro (2007a). Policy Simulations with an Integrated Model for Japan and Northeast Asia. The *Journal of Econometric Study of Northeast Asia (JESNA)*, 6(1), 1–27.

Shishido, S. (2007b). Japan Can Grow at 4%, Once Her Fiscal Policy is Started. *ECONOMIST*, July 10, Mainichi (Japanese).

Author Index

Subject Index